Footprint Scotland
Highlands & Islands

Alan Murphy
2nd edition

*"The sky was draped with the weightless trails of evening clouds.
They were the colours of the prayer flags which Buddhists leave on
mountain passes and their brightness had been bleached by wind
and sun. Below them, in the stillness of the evening, every inch of the
horizon was rimmed with distant sunlit mountains".*

Adam Nicolson, The Sea Room (2001)

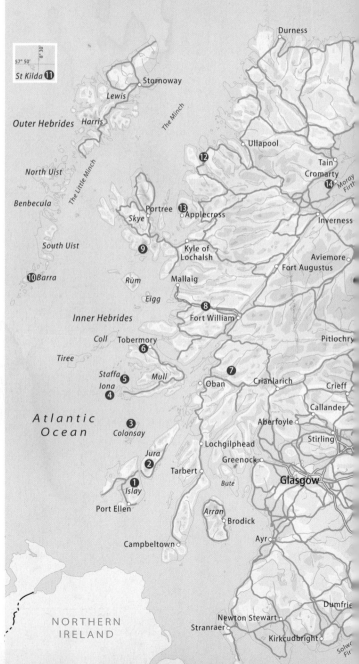

Scotland Highlands & Islands Highlights

See colour maps at back of book

1 Islay distillery
Savour the delights of an Islay malt on a tour of one of the island's distilleries

2 Jura
Take a ferry to Jura, where George Orwell wrote *1984*, and trek to the legendary Corryvreckan, the second largest whirlpool in the world

3 Kiloran Bay
Witness the finest beach in the Hebrides

4 Iona
Hire a bike and explore this divine little island

5 Fingal's Cave
Spectacular cave on Staffa which echoes to the rhythm of Mendelssohn's romantic overture

6 Tobermory
What's the story in Tobermory? Take a whale-watching cruise from Mull's capital and find out

7 Loch Etive
Take a cruise on this hidden watery jewel

8 West Highland railway
Climb aboard for one of the world's great train rides

9 Loch Coruisk
Sail into the gaping maw of this loch for a close up view of the mighty Cuillins

10 Barra
Fly to Barra and land on the world's only beach runway

Durness

St Kilda **11**
57° 50'

Stornoway
Lewis
The Minch
Outer Hebrides
Harris
Ullapool
12
Tain
Cromarty
14
Moray Firth
North Uist
Benbecula
The Little Minch
Portree **13**
Skye
Applecross
Inverness
South Uist
9
Kyle of Lochalsh
Aviemore
Fort Augustus
10 Barra
Rùm
Mallaig
Eigg
8
Fort William
Inner Hebrides
Coll
Tobermory
6
Pitlochry
Tiree
Staffa **5**
Iona
4
Mull
7
Crianlarich
Oban
Crieff
Atlantic Ocean
3
Colonsay
Callander
Aberfoyle
Lochgilphead
Stirling
2
Jura
Tarbert
Greenock
Glasgow
1
Islay
Bute
Port Ellen
Arran
Brodick
Ayr
Campbeltown
Dumfrie
NORTHERN IRELAND
Newton Stewart
Stranraer
Kirkcudbright
Solwa Fir

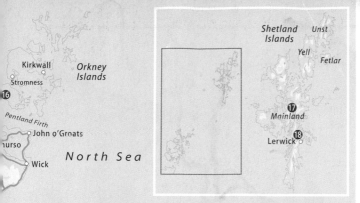

Kirkwall
Stromness
Orkney Islands
16
Pentland Firth
John o'Groats
urso
Wick

Shetland Islands
Unst
Yell
Fetlar
Mainland **17**
Lerwick **18**

North Sea

Elgin
Huntly
Peterhead
Aberdeen
Montrose

Dundee
rth
St Andrews
Anstruther
nfermline *Firth of Forth*
EDINBURGH

Peebles
Selkirk
Kelso
Jedburgh
Hawick

ENGLAND

N

0 km   40
0 miles   40

Voyag
perilous
these myst
haunted island
for the ultimate
adventure

12 Inverewe
Enjoy someone
else's garden:
over 50 acres
of horticultural
heaven

13 Applecross
A stunning
approach and a
great seafront
pub serving super-
fresh seafood and
great ales. In a
word: perfect

14 Cromarty
Timeless village
where you can see
the resident
dolphins at play
from the shore

15 Lairig Ghru
Explore the heart
of the mighty
Cairngorm
mountains on
this classic hike

**16 Old Man
of Hoy**
Spectacular clifftop
walk to one of
Orkney's most
distinctive
landmarks

**17 Northern
Lights**
Travel to Shetland
between
November and
February to see
(and hear) the
Northern Lights

18 Up Helly-Aa
Take part in
Shetland's fire
festival, when over
800 flaming torches
are carried through
darkened streets

ntents

Glen Etive runs south from Glen Coe, carving its way through prime Highland scenery and providing some great opportunities for wild camping.

North & Northwest Highlands

Skye & the Small Isles

Outer Hebrides

Orkney & Shetland

Background

Footnotes

Stoned love
The ancient standing stones at Calanais on Lewis are not only older than Stonehenge but also in a more beautiful setting and can be hugged to your heart's content.

A foot in the door

The Highlands and Islands of Scotland are Europe's last great wilderness: one of the few places in this increasingly cluttered continent where you can really get away from it all. Forget nightclubs or multi-screen cinemas, people come here for peace and quiet and an unequalled variety and quality of landscape: white beaches, turquoise seas, heather-clad mountains, magical glens, towering waterfalls and deep, mysterious lochs. When the rain stops falling and the mist clears, there is no more beautiful place on Earth. If there is a heaven, then it must look like the Scottish Highlands, but let's hope the petrol's cheaper.

About the only thing Scotland doesn't have going for it is a dependable climate. As the nation's most famous stand-up, Billy Connolly, once quipped: "Scotland has two seasons; June and winter". That's a bit of an exaggeration, but you get the idea. If you want to lie on a beach all day soaking up rays then you really ought to try somewhere else. Another perennial problem has been the clichéd image of bagpipes, haggis and shortbread; the dreadfully twee tartan tat and Celtic kitsch that, sadly, still exists in the 21st century, and is too often passed off as a genuine Highland experience. The Scottish Tourist Board has been trying to change people's perceptions, and, thankfully, has largely succeeded, promoting the country as the perfect destination for a romantic break. It makes perfect sense – if the weather's rubbish then you'll have more time to stay in bed. It scandalized the more puritanical elements of the Scottish establishment as well as giving a whole new meaning to the term Highland fling. Heaven forfend that Scotland should become a sexy destination.

Gaelic symbol

Like many beautiful parts of the world, the landscape has a tragic and painful story to tell. The Highlands and Islands of Scotland are synoymous with the Clearances of the 19th century; those years of state-sponsored genocide that followed in the wake of two successive failed Jacobite rebellions in the 18th century and which sealed the fate of the traditional Highland way of life. However, after two centuries of decline, Gaelic, the ancient language of the Highlands and Islands, has been making a comeback, thanks to financial help from government agencies and the European Union. There has also been a resurgence of confidence in Gaelic culture, spurred on by the commercial success of Gaelic-language bands such as Runrig and Capercaillie. Not forgetting the crucial role of the Free Church of Scotland, a bastion of tradition in the Outer Herbides, where religion still plays a vitally important role in the islanders' lives.

Peak and choose
Buachaille Etive Mór, one of Scotland's most recognizable mountains, stands guard at the southern entrance to Glen Coe.

Highland grievances

Life in the Highlands and Islands has changed dramatically for many people following the new Scottish Parliament's most radical and far-reaching legislation, the Land Reform (Scotland) Act of 2003, which, among other things, gives crofters – small tenant farmers – the right to collectively purchase the land on which they live and work, whether or not the landowner wants to sell. It also grants them fishing and mineral rights on and contiguous with the land. The act has not gone down too well with Scotland's big estate owners, many of whom are apoplectic with rage, describing it as a brand of Marxism and comparing the move to the seizure of white-owned land by Zimbabwe's President, Robert Mugabe. Their anger may be understandable, but few tears will be shed for Scotland's 343 landowners who, between them, own half of all private land in the country. Meanwhile, those with longer memories may see this simply as a some form of compensation for the iniquities of the Highland Clearances.

School's out
The low lying islands of Orkney, breaching the storm-lashed North Atlantic like a school of passing whales, are a world away from the Scottish mainland in terms of culture and heritage.

1 *The loveable puffin, an ever-present sight on the Scottish islands in the summer, is still eaten as a delicacy by islanders.* ▸▸ *See page 60.*

2 *Flight times on the island of Barra, where incoming planes land on the beach, are determined by the tides.* ▸▸ *See page 302.*

3 *Castle Tioram, on the Ardnamurchan peninsula, is one of the most delightful castle ruins in the country.* ▸▸ *See page 202.*

4 *Scapa Flow on Orkney is one of the world's best wreck diving sites.* ▸▸ *See page 324.*

5 *The remarkable chapel on Orkney, built by Italian POWs, is fittingly known as 'The Miracle of Camp 60'.* ▸▸ *See page 323.*

6 *The 5,000-year-old site of Skara Brae is the best preserved Stone Age village in northern Europe.* ▸▸ *See page 319.*

7 *Scotland's malt whiskies are known and loved the world over and the island of Islay has seven distilleries alone.* ▸▸ *See page 47.*

8 *The red squirrel may have disappeared from many parts of southern Britain but it's alive and being as cute as ever in the Scottish Highlands.* ▸▸ *See page 385.*

9 *The town of Oban is the main ferry port for the southern Hebridean islands.* ▸▸ *See page 109.*

10 *Impromptu folk jamming sessions are an integral part of Orkney life.* ▸▸ *See page 333.*

11 *The tiny island of Iona, once the most sacred religious site in Europe, still draws pilgrims in their thousands to visit its beautiful 13th-century abbey.* ▸▸ *See page 142.*

12 *Dolphins are a feature of much of the coastline of the Highlands and Islands but the Moray Firth is one of the best viewing spots.* ▸▸ *See page 59.*

14 Northern exposure

The Scottish mainland is surrounded by hundreds of islands, each one with its own distinct history and culture. Crossing to these islands doesn't just feel like entering a different country but stepping into another time zone. Where else could you find a police station using gerbils as paper shredders, people living by the the the old Julian calendar, or the swings in children's playgrounds being padlocked to ensure strict observance of the Sabbath?

Lying off the west coast are the Hebrides, home of the Gaelic culture, where the road signs include English spellings almost as an afterthought and local people speak Gaelic as their native tongue. Lying off the northern tip of the mainland is Orkney, an archipelago of 70 islands, which has spawned some of Scotland's greatest writers. Not surprising perhaps, given that Orkney has such a fascinating history and eventful history. The islands were ruled by the Vikings for 650 years until the 15th century and despite its remote location played a dramatic role at the end of the First World War when the German fleet was scuttled in Scapa Flow. But if you think Orkney seems remote, you ain't seen nothing yet. The Shetland Isles are so far north they can only be included on maps as an inset and the nearest mainland town is Bergen, in Norway. Unbelievable as it may seem, even Shetland is made to look like the hub of civilization by St Kilda, the most remote community in Europe until evacuation of its entire population in 1930. The white-knuckle boat trip across perilous Atlantic seas, must surely be the ultimate romantic voyage.

The magnificent golden eagle, king of the skies, can be seen in many parts of the Scottish Highlands, particularly on the Isle of Rùm.

The dark winter nights on Shetland are illuminated in January during Up Helly-Aa, a spectacular fire festival celebrating the islands' Viking heritage.

Going to extremes

Scotland has never been a place for softies. Its challenging weather and dramatic scenery really do convey a sense of being in the great outdoors. There are mountains galore to climb, lochs to fish and wildlife to watch, or you can just sit back and take in all that stunning scenery. There are countless opportunities to leave civilization a long way behind. You could explore Scotland's long-distance footpaths, such as the West Highland Way, which snake through some of the country's finest scenery. The more adventurous can try their hand (or feet) at 'Munro Bagging', which is not some dubious public school practice but the name given to the popular pursuit of climbing Scotland's 284 mountains higher than 3,000 feet. This offers the chance to explore wild areas of unparalleled beauty such as Glen Coe, Torridon, Kintail or the Cairngorms. If even that is too tame for you, then don't worry, Scotland is fast becoming the extreme sports capital of the Northern Hemisphere, with some of the best diving, surfing and mountain biking in the world, as well as new pursuits like canyoning, funyakking and the positively terrifying Tyrolean Traverse.

Scotland's wide, open spaces are also home to a rich and diverse wildlife. On land, you can see pine martens, red squirrels, wildcats, even reindeer, while golden eagles, ospreys and rare sea eagles rule the skies. In the lochs and seas that punctuate much of the northwest highlands live otters, dolphins, porpoises, whales and, according to some, even the occasional prehistoric monster.

Sound of the sea
The massive, cathedral-like interior of Fingal's Cave, on the island of Staffa, is an experience not to be missed.

Essentials

Footprint features

Planning your trip

Where to go

Scotland is a small country but there's a lot to see and trying to cram everything into a first visit can be very frustrating. There are many, many places of great natural beauty and the country's long, turbulent history has left a rich heritage of medieval castles, cathedrals, palaces, abbeys, neolithic stone circles, Bronze Age brochs and even a 5,000-year-old village. Which parts of the Scottish Highlands and Islands you choose will be determined by your own particular interests, as well as by the length of your stay and the size of your wallet. It goes without saying (but we'll say it anyway), that a longer trip will alow you to visit the wild and remote parts of the country and get much more out of your visit. For details of all transport options, see page 37.

One week

If you only have a week or two, you can head straight for the hills from Glasgow and Edinburgh. A short distance north of Glasgow is Loch Lomond, gateway to the Western Highlands and a beautiful introduction to the spectacular sights which lie in wait farther north. From Loch Lomond you should head north through Glencoe, one of the main highlights of a visit to Scotland, to Fort William, the main tourist centre for the Western Highlands. From Fort William there are two routes to another of Scotland's most popular attractions, the Isle of Skye. The quickest route is by road and bridge, via Kyle of Lochalsh, but by far the most romantic and scenic route is by train from Fort William to Mallaig, and by ferry from there to Armadale. You should then leave at least three days to explore the island, or more if you plan to do any walking.

Alternatively, it's only a short drive north from Edinburgh to Perthshire. Though not as dramatic as the northwest, the mountains, rivers, lochs and glens of the Perthshire Highlands are very beautiful and easily accessed from the town of Perth. Perthshire leads seamlessly into the visual delights of the Trossachs, a thick wedge of lochs, forests and mountains forever associated with Sir Walter Scott, tucked in between Stirling and Loch Lomond.

Two weeks

An alternative to Fort William and Skye, or in addition if you have more time, would be to head to Oban, the main ferry port of the west coast, and make the short trip to the beguiling Isle of Mull, which tends to be attract fewer visitors than Skye in the summer months, and from where you can pop across to its divine neighbour, Iona, or explore the inspirational Fingal's Cave on Staffa. Or you could head south from Oban, through Argyll, with its many prehistoric sites, and take a ferry to the little-visited islands of Islay, famous for its malt whiskies, and Jura. Both are great places for walking holidays. Also within reach of Argyll, or Ayrshire, is the island of Arran, described as 'Scotland in miniature' and ideal for walking or cycling.

Three to four weeks

If you have three or four weeks at your disposal then you can follow the long and winding road north from Kyle of Lochalsh, as it twists and turns along the coast to Ullapool. Most visitors don't make it north of Ullapool but those who do are rewarded with the starkly beautiful, almost primeval landscapes of the far northwest. You can sail from Ullapool across to the Outer Hebrides, a long, narrow archipelago stretching from Lewis and Harris in the north to Barra in the south. Alternatively, you could include a trip to the Orkney Islands, littered with important Stone Age ruins and also one of the world's best dive sites. If time and money really are no object, then head for the culturally-distinct Shetland Isles, home to Viking festivals and millions of seabirds, so far north of the mainland that they can only be included on maps as an inset.

When to go

The high season is from May to September, and this is when Scotland receives the vast majority of visitors. Though the weather tends to be better during the summer months, prices for accommodation are higher in the high season and hotels and guesthouses in the most popular places need to be booked in advance. It's also a good idea to make reservations at this time on ferries to the islands, especially to Skye and Mull. A major advantage to visiting in the summer months is the long hours of daylight, especially in the far north, where the sun doesn't set till around 2300 or later in June and July.

During the low season, from October to Easter, many tourist sights are closed, and travelling around the Highlands and Islands can be difficult as public transport services are limited. Many of the smaller tourist offices are also closed during the low season. Though some hotels and guesthouses close during the low season, the majority are now open all year round, as are most restaurants. Taking everything into consideration, May and September are probably the best months to visit the Scottish Highlands and Islands.

Climate

The Scottish climate is notoriously unpredictable, especially on the west coast, where a bright, sunny morning can turn into a downpour in the time it takes to butter your toast. Predicting the weather is not an exact science and tables of statistics are most likely a waste of time. There's an old saying in Scotland that if you don't like the weather, then wait 20 minutes, and this just about sums it up. The west coast receives far more rain than the rest of the country and the east coast gets more sunshine. The west coast is also milder in the winter due to the relatively warm waters of the Gulf Stream. Winters in the north can be very harsh, especially in the mountains and glens, making hiking conditions treacherous. Winter storms also make it difficult to travel around the islands as ferry services are often cancelled. Generally speaking, May to September are the warmest months, with an average summer high of around 18-19°C and, though they are often the driest months, you can expect rain at any time of the year, even in high summer. So, you'll need to come prepared, and remember the old hikers' adage that there's no such thing as bad weather, only inadequate clothing.

The MET office Weather Call service provide weather forecasts. Call T09014 722 plus the following three digits: Central Scotland 071; Borders 072; East Highlands 074; West Highlands and Islands 075; Orkney and Shetland 076. (60p per minute)

Tour operators

There are many companies offering general interest or special interest tours of Scotland. Travel agents will have details, or you can check the small advertisements in the travel sections of newspapers, or contact the British Tourist Authority or Scottish Tourist Board for a list of operators.

⁝ Bus hop

A great cheap way to get around Scotland is on one of the jump-on-jump-off backpacker bus tours. These leave from Edinburgh daily, except Sunday, and stop off at independent hostels in Perth, Pitlochry, Inverness, Loch Ness, the Isle of Skye, Fort William, Glencoe, Oban and Glasgow. You can hop on and off whenever you please, and you don't need to stay at any of the hostels. Prices start at around £69. The same companies also run excellent-value Highland tours, leaving from Edinburgh. Prices start at around £79 for three days, up to around £139 for six days. Prices do not include accommodation or food. See Tour operators below for details of companies offering these tours.

In the UK

Assynt Guided Holidays, Birchbank, Knockan, Elphin, Sutherland, T/F01854-666215. Specialize in walking tours of this rugged corner of the northwest.
Avalon Trekking Scotland, Bowerswell Lane, Kinnoull, Perth, PH2 TDL, T/F01738-624194. Good all-round hillwalking tours.
Bespoke Highland Tours, T/F0141-342 4576, www.highland-tours.co.uk. Specialize in personalized walking, cycling and long distance trekking holidays.
Classique Tours, Glasgow, T0141-8894050, www.classiquetours.co.uk. For those who prefer something a wee bit different, tartan-free tours of the 'real Scotland' in a vintage bus. 5-day tours start at £275 and their 7-day Grand Hebridean Tour is £485.
Cndo Scotland, 32 Stirling Enterprise Park, Stirling, T01786-445703, www.cndoscotland.co.uk. Walking holidays in NW and islands, from £420 per week including accommodation and ferries.
Explore NW Scotland, 65 Cradlehall Park, Westhill, Inverness, T077489-75638 (mob), www.explorenwscotland.co.uk. Highly recommended walking and sailing holiday company run by Richard Knotts. Offer a variety of 6-day packages for groups of up to 5, with accommodation in tents, bothies, bunkhouses or guesthouses. Prices range from £395 up to £535 for single travellers, less for 2 or more.
Gael Connexions, T01855-841219, T0776-99 22463 (mob), www.gaelconnexions.co.uk. Fort William-based company organizing genealogy tours for foreigners wishing to trace their ancestors. Their guide and researcher will point you in the right direction or plan your entire journey. Free consultation offered.
Go Blue Banana, Edinburgh, T0131-5562000, www.gobluebanana.com. Backpacker bus tour operators, see box.
Haggis Backpackers, 11 Blackfriars St, Edinburgh, EH1 1NB, T0131-5579393, www.haggis-backpackers.com. Backpacker bus tour operators, see box.
Heart of Scotland Tours, T0131-558 8855, www.heartofscotlandtours.co.uk. Runs 1- and 2-day coach tours, £27-57, departing from Edinburgh Backpackers Hostel.
Lomond Walking Holidays, 34c James St, Riverside, Stirling, FK8 1UG, T/F01786-447752, www.biggar-net.co.uk/lomond. Offer a variety of walking packages.
Macbackpackers, Edinburgh, T0131-5589900, www.macbackpackers.com. Backpacker bus tour operators, see box.
North-West Frontiers, 18A Braes, Ullapool, IV26 2BZ, T/F01854-612628, www.nwfront iers.com. Walking tours for small groups. A bit more hardcore than the rest.
Ossian Guides, Sanna, Newtonmore, Inverness, PH20 1DG, T/F01540-673402. Reliable walking guide company.
Rabbie's Trail Burners, 207 High St, Edinburgh, T0131-226 3133, www.rabbies.com. Run 1-5 day coach tours of the Highlands, from £22 up to £159 per person.
Saga Holidays, Saga Building, Middelburg Sq, Folkestone, Kent CT20 1AZ, T0800-300 500. Sightseeing tours for the silver traveller.
Scottish Cycling Holidays, 87 Perth St, Blairgowrie, Perthshire, PH10 6DT, T01250-876100, www.scotcycle.co.uk. Various 2-wheeled packages.

Timberbush Tours, 555 Castlehill, Edinburgh, T0131-226 6066, www.timberbush-tours.co.uk. Run a variety of 1-3 day guided coach tours around the country, £22-£90.

Walkabout Scotland, 2 Rossie Place, Edinburgh, T0131-661 7168, www.walk aboutscotland.com. Walking tours around Edinburgh and the Highlands.

Wild in Scotland, 9 South St Andrew St, Edinburgh, T0131-478 6500, www.wild -in-scotland.com. Run various coach tours from 3 days (£65) to 6 days (£119).

In North America

Abercrombie & Kent, T1-800-3237308, www.abercrombiekent.com. General sightseeing tours.

Above the Clouds Trekking, T800-2334499, www.gorp.com/abvclds.htm. Walking tours.

British Coastal Trails, T800-4731210, www.bctwalk.com. Walking tours.

Cross-Culture, 52 High Point Dr, Amherst MA01002-1224, T800-4911148, www.cross cultureinc.com. General sightseeing tours.

Golf International Inc, T1-800-8331389, golfing tours from the USA offered.

Jerry Quinlan's Celtic Golf, T1-800-5356148, www.jqcelticgolf.com, organizes golfing packages from the USA.

Prestige Tours, T1-800-8907375. General sightseeing tours.

Saga, 222 Berkeley St, Boston, MA 02116, USA. General sightseeing tours.

Sterling Tours, T1-800-7274359, www.sterl ingtours.com. General sightseeing tours.

In Australia and New Zealand

Adventure Specialists, 69 Liverpool St, Sydney, T02-92612927. Adventure tours.

Adventure Travel Company, 164 Parnell Rd, Parnell, East Auckland, T09-3799755. New Zealand agents for **Peregrine Adventures**. Offers a range of activity tours.

Peregrine Adventures, 258 Lonsdale St, Melbourne, T03-96638611, www.peregrine. net.au; also branches in Brisbane, Sydney, Adelaide and Perth. Offers a wide range of activity tours throughout Scotland.

Saga, Level 1, 10-14 Paul St, Milsons Point, Sydney 2061. General sightseeing tours.

Finding out more

The best way of finding out more information for your trip to Scotland is to contact the British Tourist Authority (BTA), who represent the Scottish Tourist Board abroad. Their website, www.bta.org.uk, is very useful as a first stop directory for accommodation. Alternatively, you can write (or email) direct to the head office of the Scottish Tourist Board (STB). Both organizations can provide a wealth of free literature and information such as maps, city guides, events calendars and accommodation brochures. Travellers with special needs should also contact their nearest BTA office. If you want more detailed information on a particular area, contact the area tourist boards.

BTA offices

Australia, Level 16, The Gateway, 1 Macquarie Pl, Circular Quay, Sydney NSW 2000, T02-93774400, F93774499.

Belgium and Luxembourg, 306 Av Louise, 1050 Brussels, T2-6463510, F6463986.

Canada, 111 Avenue Rd, Suite 450, Toronto, Ontario MR5 3J8, T416-9256326, F9612175.

Denmark, Montergade 3, 1116 Copenhagen K, T33-339188, F140136.

France, Maison de la Grande-Bretagne, 19 Rue des Mathurins, 75009 Paris, T1-44515620, F44515621.

Germany, Austria and Switzerland, Taunustrasse 52-60, 60329 Frankfurt, T69-2380711.

Ireland, 18/19 College Green, Dublin 2, T1-6708000, F6708244.

Italy, Corso Vittorio Emanuele II No 337, 00186 Rome, T6-68806821, F6879095.

Netherlands, Stadhouderskade 2 (5e), 1054 ES Amsterdam, T20-6855051, F6186868.

New Zealand, 17th floor, Fay Richwhite Building, 151 Queen St, Auckland 1, T09-3031446, F3776965.

South Africa, Lancaster Gate, Hyde Park Lane, Hyde Park 2196, Johannesburg, T011-3250342.

USA, 7th floor, 551 Fifth Av, New York, NY 10176-0799, T212-986-2200/ 1-800-GO-2-BRITAIN. 10880 Wiltshire Blvd, Suite 570, Los Angeles, CA 90024, T310-4702782.

Scottish Tourist Boards

Scottish Tourist Board Central Information Department, 23 Ravelston Terr, Edinburgh, EH4 3EU, T0131-3322433, www.visitscotland.com; and 19 Cockspur St, London SW1 5BL, T020-7930 2812.
Aberdeen & Grampian Tourist Board 27 Albyn Pl, Aberdeen, AB10 1YL, T01224-632727, www.agtb.org.
Argyll, the Isles, Loch Lomond, Stirling & Trossachs Tourist Board, 7 Alexandra Par, Dunoon, Argyll, PA23 8AB, T01369-701000, www.visitscottish heartlands.com.
Ayrshire & Arran Tourist Board, Burns House, Burns Statue Sq, Ayr, KA7 1UP, T01292-288688, www.ayrshire-arran.com.
The Highlands of Scotland Tourist Board Peffery House, Strathpeffer, IV14 9HA, T01479-810363, UK T0870-5143070, www.visithighlands.com.
Orkney Tourist Board, 6 Broad St, Kirkwall, Orkney, KW15 1NX, T01856-872856, www.visitorkney.com.
Perthshire Tourist Board, Lower City Mills, West Mill St, Perth, PH1 5QP, T01738-627958, www.perthshire.co.uk.
Shetland Islands Tourism, Market Cross, Lerwick, Shetland, ZE1 0LU, T01595-693434, www.visitshetland.com.
Western Isles Tourist Board, 26 Cromwell St, Stornoway, Isle of Lewis, HS1 2DD, T01851-703088, www.visit hebrides.com.

Useful websites

The official Scottish Tourist Board site and the various area tourist board sites have information on accommodation, transport and tourist sights as well as outdoor activities such as walking, skiing, fishing etc.

Travel and leisure
www.britannia.com A huge UK travel site. Click on 'Scotland guide' for a massive selection of subjects plus links to various sites including newspapers.

www.bbc.co.uk The UK's most popular site with an excellent what's on guide.
www.whatsonwhen.com Has a huge range of upcoming events around the world.
www.scotland.net Scotland online with good information on golf, walking and climbing and also features.
www.travelscotland.co.uk Run in conjunction with the Scottish Tourist Board, with magazine-style features and reviews.
www.scotland-info.co.uk Good for local information on hotels, shops and restaurants.
www.aboutscotland.co.uk Useful for information on accommodation.
www.uktrail.com Provides comprehensive information on transport and hostels.
www.hebrides.com Comprehensive site.

Outdoors
www.walkscotland.com Suggested walks, contacts and practical information for hikers and climbers.
www.walkingworld.com Perhaps the best directory of British walks though you have to pay to download their detailed maps.
www.golfscotland.co.uk Everything you need to know on golf in Scotland.
www.skiscotland.net Information on ski conditions at all centres, updated daily.
www.born2ski.com and **www.ifyouski.com** Both have Scotland pages with useful ratings.
www.sustrans.org.uk Official site of the charity that co-ordinates the National Cycle Network. The clickable map lets you zoom in on sections of the route.
www.visitscotland.com/cycling Excellent site; even shows how steep the climbs are.
www.goodbeachguide.co.uk How to check your kids won't be bathing in sewage. Lists facilities and activities for over 400 recommended UK beaches.

History, politics and culture
www.electricscotland.com Massive directory with lots of information on clans, travel etc. In-depth history pages.
www.ceolas.org Celtic music site with lots of information and sounds.
www.scotchwhisky.net Everything you ever wanted to know about the 'water of life'.
www.scotland.gov.uk Updates on government affairs in Scotland.
www.scottish.parliament.uk Easy to use guide to the Scottish Parliament.

Language

Though the vast majority of Scots speak English, to the untutored ear the Scottish dialect can be hard to understand, as many words and expressions are derived not from English but from Lowland Scots, or lallans, which is now recognized as a separate language as opposed to simply a regional dialect. In the Highlands and Islands, however, the accent is very clear and easy to understand.

Scotland's oldest surviving language is Scottish Gaelic (*Gaidhlig*, pronounced 'Gallic'), spoken by only about 2% of the population. This is in the Gaidhealtachd, the Gaelic-speaking areas of the Outer Hebrides, parts of Skye, and a few of the smaller Hebridean islands, where road signs are predominantly in in Gaelic. Those wishing to teach themselves Gaelic could start with the BBC *CanSeo* cassette and book. A good phrasebook is *Everyday Gaelic* by Morag MacNeill (Gairm). Also, the Celtic Heritage Centre, based on Arran, has a great store of Gaelic and Celtic information and documents; they publish a quarterly newsletter. *Macbain's Etymological Dictionary of the Gaelic language* contains a wealth of words and information. For more on the history of Gaelic, see page 379, and for a glossary of Gaelic words, see page 390.

Disabled travellers

For travellers with disabilities, visiting Scotland independently can be a difficult business. While most theatres, cinemas and modern tourist attractions are accessible to wheelchairs, accommodation is more problematic. Many large, new hotels do have disabled suites, but will charge more, and most B&Bs, guest houses and smaller hotels are not designed to cater for people with disabilities. Public transport is just as bad, though newer buses have lower steps for easier access and some ScotRail intercity services now accommodate wheelchair-users in comfort. Taxis, as opposed to minicabs, all carry wheelchair ramps, and if a driver says he or she can't take a wheelchair, it's because they're too lazy to fetch the ramp.

Wheelchair users, and blind or partially sighted people are automatically given 30-50 per cent discount on train fares, and those with other disabilities are eligible for the Disabled Person's Railcard, which costs £14 per year and gives a third off most tickets. There are no reductions on buses however.

If you are disabled you should contact the travel officer of your national support organization. They can provide literature or put you in touch with travel agents specializing in tours for the disabled. The **Scottish Tourist Board** produces a guide, *Accessible Scotland*, for disabled travellers, and many local tourist offices can provide accessibility details for their area. A useful website is www.atlholidays.com which specializes in organizing holidays for disabled travellers, recommends hotels with good facilities and can also arrange rental cars and taxis.

Useful organizations include: **Disability Scotland**, Princes House, 5 Shandwick Place, Edinburgh EH2 4RG, T0131-229 8632; **The Royal Association for Disability and Rehabilitation (RADAR)**, Unit 12, City Forum, 250 City Road, London, EC1V 8AF, T020-7250 3222, www.radar.org.uk, is a good source of advice and information, and produces an annual guide on travelling in the UK (£7.50 including P&P); and **The Holiday Care Service**, second floor, Imperial Building, Victoria Road, Horley, Surrey RH6 7PZ, T01293-774 535, provides free lists of accessible accommodation and travel in the UK.

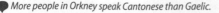 *More people in Orkney speak Cantonese than Gaelic.*

Gay and lesbian travellers

Don't assume that because men are wearing skirts in the Highlands that people take a relaxed attitude to homosexuality. The same prejudices apply as elsewhere in rural parts of the UK. Though Scotland is generally tolerant of homosexuality, overt displays of affection are not advised. Gay couples may also come up against subtle forms of discrimination, such as B&Bs spontaneously 'losing' bookings for a double room and being left with the option of taking two singles. The magazine, *Gay Scotland*, is a good source of information, as is the **Gay Switchboard**, T0131-556 4049, or the **Lesbian Line**, T0131-557 0751. For a good selection of gay events and venues, check out www.whatson when.com. Other good sites include: www.gaybritain.co.uk and www.gaytravel.co.uk.

Student travellers

Discount passes

There are various official youth/student ID cards available. The most useful is the **International Student ID Card (ISIC)**. For a mere £6 the ISIC card gains you access to the exclusive world of student travel with a series of discounts, including most forms of local transport, up to 30 per cent off international airfares, cheap or free admission to museums, theatres and other attractions, and cheap meals in some restaurants. There's also free or discounted internet access, and a website, www.usitworld.com, where you can check the latest student travel deals. You'll also receive the ISIC handbook, which ensures you get the most out of services available. ISIC cards are available at student travel centres, see page 30. US and Canadian citizens are also entitled to emergency medical coverage, and there's a 24-hour hotline to call in the event of medical, legal or financial emergencies.

If you're aged under 26 but not a student, you can apply for a **Federation of International Youth Travel Organisations (FIYTO)** card, or a **Euro 26 Card**, which give you much the same discounts. If you're 25 or younger you can qualify for a **Go-25 Card**, which gives you the same benefits as an ISIC card. These discount cards are issued by student travel agencies and hostelling organizations, see page 43.

Studying in Scotland

If you want to study in Scotland you must first prove you can support and accommodate yourself without working and without recourse to public support. Your studies should take up at least 15 hours a week for a minimum of six months. Once you are studying, you are allowed to do 20 hours of casual work per week in the term time and you can work full-time during the holidays. In North America full-time students can obtain temporary work or study permits through the **Council of International Education Exchange (CIEE)**, 205 E 42nd Street, New York, NY 10017, T212-822 2600, www.ciee.org. For more details, contact your nearest British embassy, consulate or high commission, or the **Foreign and Commonwealth Office** in London, T020-7270 1500.

Travelling with children

Visiting the Scottish Highlands with kids is no different from other parts of the UK, though you may find that the locals are just that little bit more tolerant and helpful. If you're near a beach, toddlers will be in rock pool heaven, rooting around to their little heart's content as you sit nearby, shivering in the rain. Even teenagers should have no reason to moan as there are all manner of thrill-a-minute adventure sports to try, see Activities and sports on page 52 for more details.

If you're travelling with babies and/or toddlers you may find eating out a frustrating experience in some establishments, though the days of families being banished to some grubby room at the back, well out of the way of other diners, are, thankfully, a thing of the past in most places. The attitude to breastfeeding, while some way behind the likes of Scandinavia, is more relaxed than the US and becoming ever more civilized and progressive. In major towns and cities, Italian restaurants are generally more child-friendly. The child may not be quite be king here, but at least they are allowed to be seen and heard.

If you are flying, inform the airline in advance that you're travelling with a baby or toddler, and check out the facilities when booking as these vary with each aircraft. British Airways now has a special seat for under 2s; check which aircraft have been fitted with them when booking. Pushchairs can be taken on as hand luggage or stored in the hold. Skycots are available on long-haul flights. Take snacks and toys for in-flight entertainment, and remember that swallowing food or drinks during take-off and landing will help prevent ear problems.

A recommended website is www.babygoes2.com, while www.mumsnet.com/bigissues/travel.html, is useful for parents with older kids.

Women travellers

Travelling in Scotland is neither easier nor more difficult for women than travelling in other parts of the UK. Generally speaking, Scots are friendly and courteous and even lone women travellers should experience nothing unpleasant, however, common sense dictates that single women would do well to avoid hitching on their own in the middle of nowhere. In the main cities and larger towns, the usual precautions need to be taken and you should avoid walking in quiet, unlit streets and parks at night.

Working in Scotland

Citizens of European Union (EU) countries can live and work in Britain freely without a visa, but non-EU residents need a permit to work legally. This can be difficult to obtain without the backing of an established company or employer in the UK. Also, visitors from Commonwealth countries who are aged between 17 and 27 may apply for a working holiday-maker's visa which permits them to stay in the UK for up to two years and work on a casual basis (ie non-career oriented). These certificates are only available from British embassies and consulates abroad, see page 27, and you must have proof of a valid return or onward ticket, as well as means of support during your stay. Commonwealth citizens with a parent

⁂ *Pick up a copy of* What Scotland, *a free guide for independent travellers living and working in Scotland;* T020-/384 9330.

or grandparent born in the UK can apply for a Certificate of Entitlement to the Right of Abode, allowing them to work in Britain.

An option for citizens of some non-Commonwealth countries is to visit on an au pair placement to learn English by living with an English-speaking family for a maximum of two years. Au pairs must be aged between 17 and 27, and come from one of the following countries: Andorra, Bosnia-Herzegovina, Croatia, Cyprus, the Czech Republic, The Faroe Islands, Greenland, Hungary, Macedonia, Malta, Monaco, San Marino, the Slovak Republic, Slovenia, Switzerland or Turkey. This can be a good way to learn English, but check out the precise conditions of your placement before taking it up.

Those wishing to devote their time helping the environment, or simply gain some valuable experience can begin their search with the following organizations: **The British Trust for Conservation Volunteers**, 33 St Mary's Street, Wallingford, Oxon, OX10 OEU, T01491-821600, www.btcv.org, get fit in the 'green gym', planting hedges, creating wildlife gardens or improving footpaths; **Earthwatch,** 57 Woodstock Road, Oxford, OX2 6HJ, T01865-318 838, team up with scientists studying our furry friends; **Jubilee Sailing Trust,** Hazel Road, Southampton, T023-8044 9108, www.jst.org.uk, work on deck on an adventure holiday; and **Waterway Recovery Group,** PO Box 114, Rickmansworth, WD3 1ZY, T01923-711 114, www.wrg.org.uk, help restore a derelict canal.

Also check out the organizations listed on page 60, as well as the Scottish Youth Hostel Association (SYHA), see page 43.

Before you travel

Getting in

Visas

Visa regulations are subject to change, so it is essential to check with your local British embassy, high commission or consulate before leaving home. Citizens of all European countries – except Albania, Bosnia Herzegovina, Bulgaria, Macedonia, Romania, Slovakia, Yugoslavia and all former Soviet republics (other than the Baltic states) – require only a passport to enter Britain and can generally stay for up to three months. Citizens of Australia, Canada, New Zealand, South Africa or the USA can stay for up to six months, providing they have a return ticket and sufficient funds to cover their stay. Citizens of most other countries require a visa from the commission or consular office in the country of application.

The **Foreign Office's** excellent website, www.fco.gov.uk, provides details of British immigration and visa requirements. Also the **Immigration Advisory Service (IAS)**, County House, 190 Great Dover Street, London SE1 4YB, T020-7357 6917, www.vois.org.uk, offers free and confidential advice to anyone applying for entry clearance into the UK.

For visa extensions contact the **Home Office, Immigration and Nationality Department,** Lunar House, Wellesley Road, Croydon, London CR9, T020-8686 0688, before your existing visa expires. Citizens of Australia, Canada, New Zealand, South Africa or the USA wishing to stay longer than six months will need an Entry Clearance Certificate from the British High Commission in their country. For more details, contact your nearest British embassy, consulate or high commission, or the Foreign and Commonwealth Office in London, T020-7270 1500.

Customs

Visitors from EU countries do not have to make a declaration to customs on entry into the UK. The limits for duty-paid goods from within the EU are 800 cigarettes, or 1 kg of tobacco, 10 litres of spirits, 20 litres of fortified wine, 90 litres of wine and 110 litres of beer. There is no longer any duty-free shopping. Visitors from non-EU countries are allowed to import 200 cigarettes, or 250 grams of tobacco, two litres of wine, and two litres of fortified wine or one litre of spirits. There are various import restrictions, most of which should not affect the average tourist. There are tight quarantine restrictions which apply to animals brought from overseas (except for Ireland). For more information on British import regulations, contact **HM Customs and Excise** ① *Dorset House, Stamford Street, London SE1 9PJ, T020-7928 3344, www.hmce.gov.uk.*

Many goods in Britain are subject to a Value Added Tax (VAT) of 17.5 per cent, with the major exception of books and food. Visitors from non-EU countries can save money through the Retail Export Scheme, which allows a refund of VAT on goods to be taken out of the country. Note that not all shops are participants in the scheme and that VAT cannot be reclaimed on hotel bills or other services.

British embassies

Austria, Jauresgasse 10, A-1030 Vienna, T71613-5151, www.britishembassy.at.
Australia, High Commission: Commonwealth Av, Yarralumla, Canberra, ACT 2600, T02-62706666, www.uk.emb.gov.au.
Belgium, Rue d'Arlon 85 Aarlenstraat 1040 Brussels, T2-287 6211, info@britain.be.
Canada, High Commission: 80 Elgin St, Ottowa, K1P 5K7, T613-2371530, www.bis-canada.org.
Denmark, Kastelsvej 36-40, DK-2100 Copenhagen, T35 44 52 00, www.britishembassy.dk.
France, 9 Av Hoche, 8e, Paris, 01-42663810.
Germany, Friedrich-Ebert-Allee 77, 53113, Bonn, T0228-234061.
Ireland, 29 Merrion Rd, Ballsbridge, Dublin 4, T01-2053700.
Israel, 192 Hayarkon St, Tel Aviv, T3-7251222, www.britemb.org.il.

Italy, Via XX Settembre 80, I-00187 ROMA RM, T06 4220 0001, www.britishembassy.gov.uk.
Japan, 1 Ichiban-cho, Chiyoda-ku, Tokyo 102-8381, T(3) 5211 1100.
Netherlands, Koningslaan 44, 1075AE Amsterdam, T20-6764343.
New Zealand, High Commission: 44 Hill St, Wellington, T04-4726049, www.brithighcomm.org.nz.
Norway, Thomas Heftyesgate 8, 0244 Oslo, T23 13 27 00, www.britain.no.
South Africa, 91 Parliament St, Cape Town 8001, T21-4617220.
Spain, C/Fernando el Santo 16, 28010 Madrid, T91-7008200.
Sweden, Skarpögatan 6-8, Stockholm, T8 671 3000, www.britishembassy.se.
Switzerland, Thunstrasse 50, 3005 Berne, T31-359 7700, www.britishembassy.gov.uk.
USA, 3100 Massachusetts Av NW, Washington DC 20008, T202-4621340, www.britain-info.org.

Essentials Before you travel

What to take

You'll be able to find everything you could possibly need for your trip in Scottish cities, so if you wish you can pack light and buy stuff as you go along. Given the climate, you will more than likely need warm and waterproof clothing, whatever the time of year. Also bring light clothes in the summer, preferably long-sleeved to protect you from the midges, see page 63. If you're planning on doing some hillwalking you should come properly prepared, as the weather can change rapidly in the mountains, see also page 53. It's worth treating your boots with a waterproofing agent as some of the trails cross boggy ground.

If you are backpacking, a sleeping bag is useful in hostels, and a sleeping sheet with a pillow cover is needed if staying in Scottish Youth Hostel Association (SYHA) hostels (or you can hire one there). A padlock can also be handy for locking your bag if it has to be stored in a hostel for any length of time. Other useful items include an alarm clock (for those early ferry departures), an adaptor plug for electrical appliances, an elastic clothes line and, if you're hillwalking or camping, a Swiss Army knife, torch (flashlight) and compass are essential.

Insurance

It's a good idea to take out some form of travel insurance, wherever you're travelling from. This should cover you for theft or loss of possessions and money, the cost of all medical and dental treatment, cancellation of flights, delays in travel arrangements, accidents, missed departures, lost baggage, lost passport, and personal liability and legal expenses. There are a variety of policies to choose from, so it's best to shop around to get the best price. Your travel agent can also advise you on the best deals available. **STA Travel**, www.statravel.co.uk, with branches nationwide, and other reputable student travel organizations often offer good-value travel policies. Another company worth calling for a quote is **Columbus Direct**, T020-7375 0011. Older travellers should note that some companies won't cover people over 65 years old, or may charge high premiums. The best policies for older travellers are offered by **Age Concern**, T01883-346 964. Travellers from North America can try the **International Student Insurance Service (ISIS)**, which is available through **STA Travel**, T1-800-777 0112, www.sta-travel.com. Some other recommended travel insurance companies in North America include **Travel Guard**, T1-800-826 1300, www.noelgroup. com; **Access America**, T1-800-284 8300; **Travel Insurance Services**, T1-800-937 1387; and **Travel Assistance International**, T1-800-821 2828.

Points to note: you should always read the small print carefully. Some policies exclude 'dangerous activities' such as scuba diving, skiing, horse riding or even trekking. Not all policies cover ambulance, helicopter rescue or emergency flights home. Find out if your policy pays medical expenses direct to the hospital or doctor, or if you have to pay and then claim the money back later. If the latter applies, make sure you keep all records. Whatever your policy, if you are unfortunate enough to have something stolen, make sure you get a copy of the police report, as you will need this to substantiate your claim. See page 62 for details of medical insurance.

Money

The British currency is the pound sterling (£), divided into 100 pence (p). Coins come in denominations of 1p, 2p, 5p, 10p, 20p, 50p, £1 and £2. Bank of England banknotes are legal tender in Scotland, in addition to those issued by the Bank of Scotland, Royal Bank of Scotland and Clydesdale Bank. These Scottish banknotes (bills) come in denominations of £5, £10, £20, £50 and £100 and are legal tender in the rest of Britain, though some less intelligent shopkeepers south of the border may be reluctant to accept them.

Banks

The larger towns and villages have a branch of at least one of the big four high street banks – **Bank of Scotland, Royal Bank of Scotland, Clydesdale** and **TSB Scotland**. Bank opening hours are Monday to Friday from 0930 to between 1600 and 1700. Some larger branches may also be open later on Thursdays and on Saturday mornings. Banks are usually the best places to change money and cheques. You can withdraw cash from selected banks and ATMs (or cashpoints as they are called in Britain) with your cash card. In more remote parts, and especially on the islands, ATMs are few and far between and it is important to keep a ready supply of cash on you at all times. Outside the ferry ports on most of the smaller islands, you won't find an ATM. Your bank will give you a list of locations where you can use your card. **Bank of Scotland** and **Royal Bank** take **Lloyds** and **Barclays** cash cards; **Clydesdale** takes **HSBC** and **National Westminster** cards. **Bank of Scotland, Clydesdale** and most building society cashpoints are part of the Link network and accept all affiliated cards. See also Credit cards below. In addition to ATMs, bureaux de change can be used outside banking hours. These can be found in most city centres and also at the main airports and train stations. Note that some charge high commissions for changing cheques. Those at international airports, however, often charge less than banks and will change pound sterling cheques for free. Avoid changing money or cheques in hotels, as the rates are usually very poor.

In small and remote places, and on some islands, there may only be a mobile bank which runs to a set timetable. This timetable will be available from the local post office.

Credit cards

Most hotels, shops and restaurants accept the major credit cards such as MasterCard and Visa and, less frequently, Amex, though some places may charge for using them. They may be less useful in more remote rural areas and smaller establishments such as B&Bs which will often only accept cash or cheques.

Visa card holders can use the **Bank of Scotland, Clydesdale Bank, Royal Bank of Scotland** and **TSB** ATMs; Access/MasterCard holders can use the Royal Bank and Clydesdale; Amex card holders can use the Bank of Scotland.

Travellers' cheques

The safest way to carry money is in travellers' cheques. These are available for a small commission from all major banks. **American Express (Amex), Visa** and **Thomas Cook** cheques are widely accepted and are the most commonly issued by banks. You'll normally have to pay commission again when you cash each cheque. This will usually be one percent, or a flat rate. No commission is payable on Amex cheques cashed at Amex offices. Make sure to keep a record of the cheque numbers and the cheques you've cashed separate from the cheques themselves, so that you can get a full refund of all uncashed cheques should you lose them. It's best to bring sterling cheques to avoid changing currencies twice. Also note that in Britain travellers' cheques are rarely accepted outside banks, so you'll need to cash them in advance and keep a good supply of ready cash.

Money transfers

If you need money urgently, the quickest way to have it sent to you is to have it wired to the nearest bank via **Western Union**, T0800-833 833, or **Moneygram**, T0800-894 887. Charges are on a sliding scale; ie it will cost proportionately less to wire out more money. Money can also be wired by **Thomas Cook** or **American Express**, though this may take a day or two, or transferred via a bank draft, but this can take up to a week.

Cost of travelling

The Highlands and Islands of Scotland can be an expensive place to visit, and prices are higher in more remote parts, but there is plenty of budget accommodation available and backpackers will be able to keep their costs down. Petrol in particular is very expensive in the Highlands and Islands, where it can cost up to 10p per litre more than in central and southern parts of Scotland. Accommodation and restaurant prices also tend to be higher in more popular destinations and during the busy summer months.

The minimum daily budget required, if you're staying in hostels or cheap B&Bs, cycling or hitching, and cooking your own meals, will be around £25-30 per person per day. If you start using public transport and eating out occasionally that will rise to around £35-40. Those staying in slightly more upmarket B&Bs or guesthouses, eating out every evening at pubs or modest restaurants and visiting tourist attractions, such as castles or museums, can expect to pay around £45-60 per day. If you also want to hire a car and use ferries to visit the islands, and eat well, then costs will rise considerably and you'll be looking at least £75 per person per day. Single travellers will have to pay more than half the cost of a double room in most places, and should budget on spending around 60 per cent of what a couple would spend.

Though using a credit/debit card is by far the easiest way of keeping in funds, you must check with your bank what the total charges will be; this can be as high as 4-5 per cent in some cases.

Getting there

Air

Generally speaking, the cheapest and quickest way to travel to Scotland from outside the UK is by air. There are good links to Edinburgh and Glasgow, with direct flights from many European cities, and direct flights from North America to Glasgow. There are also flights from a few European cities to Aberdeen and Inverness. There are no direct flights from North America to Edinburgh; these are usually routed via London or Dublin. There are also daily flights from Ireland and regular flights to most Scottish airports from other parts of the UK. There are no direct flights to Scotland from Australia, New Zealand, South Africa or Japan. You will have to get a connection from London. Those wishing to visit England as well should note that it is generally cheaper to fly to Scotland from the rest of Britain if you use an Airpass bought in your own country. This is offered by British Airways and British Midland. Airpasses are valid only with an international scheduled flight ticket.

Buying your ticket

There is a mind-boggling number of outlets for buying your plane ticket, and finding the best deal can be a confusing business. Fares will depend on the season. Ticket prices to Scotland are highest from around early June to mid-September, which is the tourist high season. Fares drop in the months either side of the peak season – mid-September to early November and mid-April to early June. They are cheapest in the low season, from November to April, when very few visitors are willing to brave the Scottish winter. The exception is during Christmas and New Year when seats are at a premium and prices rise sharply. It's also worth noting that flying at the weekend is normally more expensive. It is always worth spending a bit of time researching the various options available and starting early, as some of the cheapest tickets have to be bought months in advance and the most popular flights sell out quickly. One of the best ways of finding a good deal is to use the internet. The following **websites** are worth trying: www.expedia.co.uk, www.lastminute.com, www.cheapflights.co.uk, www.travelocity.com, wwww.ebookers.com and www.opodo.com.

Also try **STA**, 27 Forrest Road, Edinburgh, T0131-226 7747; 86 Old Brompton Road, London, SW7 3LH, T020-7361 6161, www.statravel.co.uk, or **Trailfinders**, 194 Kensington High Street, London W8 6FT, T020-7938 3939. Both are specialists in low-cost student/youth flights and tours, also good for student IDs and insurance. **STA** have other branches in London, as well as in Brighton, Bristol, Cambridge, Leeds, Manchester, Newcastle-upon-Tyne and Oxford and on many university campuses.

From the UK and Ireland

There are direct flights to Scotland's three main airports – Glasgow, Edinburgh and Aberdeen – almost hourly from London Heathrow, Gatwick, Stansted and Luton airports. There are also daily flights from provincial UK airports and from Dublin. To fly on to the smaller airports, you'll need to change planes, see page 37 for domestic flights. The cheapest flights leave from London Luton or Stansted, plus a few provincial airports, with **Ryanair** and **easyJet**. If you book on-line, fares can be as little as £5 one-way during promotions, but usually you can expect to fly for under £50 return. These tickets are often subject to rigid restrictions, but the savings can make the extra effort worthwhile. Cheaper tickets usually have to be bought at least a week in advance, apply to only a few midweek flights, and must include a Saturday night stayover. They are also non-refundable, or only partly refundable, and non-transferable. A standard flexible and refundable fare from London to Glasgow or Edinburgh will cost at least £150-200 return. London to Glasgow and Edinburgh is roughly one hour.

To Glasgow International British Airways fly from Gatwick, Heathrow, Bristol, Southampton, Birmingham, Manchester, Cork and the Isle of Man. BMI from Manchester, Heathrow, Leeds/Bradford. easyJet from Bristol, Belfast, Luton, Stansted. BMI baby from East Midlands.

To Edinburgh Aer Arran fly from Cork. Aer Lingus from Dublin. BMI from East Midlands, Leeds/Bradford and Manchester. British Airways from Belfast City and International, Birmingham, Bristol, Cardiff, Gatwick, Heathrow, Jersey, Manchester, Southampton. British European from Birmingham, Guernsey and Jersey. easyJet from Bristol, Gatwick, Luton and Stansted. Eastern Airways from Humberside and Norwich. Euromanx from the Isle of Man. Ryanair from Dublin. ScotAirways from London City.

To Glasgow Prestwick Ryanair from Stansted and Bournemouth, BMI from Cardiff.

To Aberdeen British Airways from Heathrow and Gatwick, Belfast International, Birmingham, Leeds/Bradford, Manchester and Newcastle. British European from London City. British Midland from Manchester. Eastern Airways from East Midlands, Humberside, Norwich and Teeside. easyJet from Luton. KLMUK from London City.

To Inverness British Airways from Gatwick. easyJet from Luton.

To Wick Eastern Airways from Newcastle.

From the rest of Europe

To Glasgow International BMI fly from Copenhagen, easyJet from Amsterdam and KLM from Amsterdam. Ryanair fly from Paris Beauvais, Dublin, Frankfurt Hahn, Stockholm, Brussels, Milan, Oslo, Barcelona.

To Edinburgh Air France fly from Paris (CDG). British Airways from Paris (CDG) and Zurich. KLMUK from Amsterdam. BMI from Brussels and Copenhagen. Lufthansa from Frankfurt.

To Glasgow Prestwick Ryanair fly from Paris Beauvais, Dublin, Franfurt Hahn, Stockholm, Brussels, Milan, Oslo, Barcelona.

To Aberdeen Direct flights from Amsterdam, Copenhagen and Stavanger.

To Inverness Direct flights from Amsterdam and Zurich.

From North America

Because of the much larger number of flights to London, it is generally cheaper to fly there first and get an onward flight, see above for the best deals. For low season Apex fares expect to pay around US$400-600 from New York and other East Coast cities, and around US$500-700 from the West Coast. Prices rise to around US$700-900 from New York, and up to US$1,000 from the West Coast in the summer months. Low season Apex fares from Toronto and Montreal cost around CAN$600-700, and from Vancouver around CAN$800-900, rising to CAN$750-950 and CAN$950-1150 respectively during the summer. East Coast USA to Glasgow takes around six to seven hours direct. To London it takes seven hours. From the West Coast it takes an additional four hours.

To Glasgow International Continental Airlines fly from New York, American Airlines fly from Chicago and Air Canada from Toronto.

Airline contact details

Aer Arran, T0800-587 2324, www.skyroad.com.

Aer Lingus, T08450-844 444, www.aerlingus.com.

Air Canada, T1-800-776 3000, www.aircanada.ca.

Air France, T08450-845 444, www.airfrance.com.

American Airlines, T1-800-433 7300, www.americanair.com.

BMI, T0870-607 0555, www.flybmi.com.

British Airways, T0870-850 9850, www.britishairways.com.

British European, T0870-567 6676,
www.flybe.com.
Continental, T1-800-231 0856,
www.flycontinental.com.
Eastern Airways, T01652-680 600,
www.easternairways.com.
easyJet, T0870-600 000,
www.easyjet.com.
Emirates, T0870 243 2222,
www.emirates.com/uk.

Euromanx, T0870-166 0102,
www.euromanx.com.
Icelandair, T08457-581 111,
www.icelandair.com.
KLMUK, T0870-507 4047, www.klm.com.
Lufthansa, T08457-737 747,
www.lufthansa.com.
Ryanair, T0871-246 0016, www.ryanair.com.
ScotAirways, T0870-606 0707,
www.scotairways.com.

Rail

There are fast and frequent rail services from London and other main towns and cities in England to Glasgow, Edinburgh, Aberdeen and Inverness. Journey time from London is about 4½ hours to Edinburgh, five hours to Glasgow, seven hours to Aberdeen and eight hours to Inverness. Two companies operate direct services from London to Scotland: **GNER** trains leave from Kings' Cross and run up the east coast to Edinburgh, Aberdeen and Inverness; and **Virgin** trains leave from Euston and run up the west coast to Glasgow. **Scotrail** operate the *Caledonian Sleeper* service if you wish to travel overnight from London Euston to Aberdeen, Edinburgh, Glasgow, Inverness and Fort William. This runs nightly from Sunday to Friday.

    Eurostar, T08705-186 186, www.eurostar.com, operates high-speed trains through the Channel Tunnel to London Waterloo from Paris (three hours), Brussels (two hours 40 minutes) and Lille (two hours). You then have to change trains, and stations, for the onward journey north to Scotland. If you're driving from continental Europe you could take *Le Shuttle*, which runs 24 hours a day, 365 days a year, and takes you and your car from Calais to Folkestone in 35-45 minutes. Fares range from £84 to £165 per carload, depending on how far in advance you book or when you travel, T08705-353 535 for bookings.

Enquiries and booking

National Rail Enquiries, T08457-484 950, are quick and courteous with information on rail services and fares but not always accurate, so double check. They can't book tickets but will provide you with the relevant telephone number, see also below. The website **www.qjump.co.uk** is a bit hit-and-miss but generally fast and efficient and shows you all the various options on any selected journey, while **www.thetrain line.co.uk** also has its idiosyncrasies but shows prices clearly. For advance credit/ debit card bookings, T08457-550 033. **GNER**, T08457-225 225, www.gner.co.uk; **Virgin**, T08457-222 333; and **ScotRail**, T08457-550 033, www.scotrail.co.uk.

Fares

To describe the system of rail ticket pricing as complicated is a huge understatement and impossible to explain here. There are many and various discounted fares, but restrictions are often prohibitive, which explains the long queues and delays at ticket counters in railway stations. The cheapest ticket is a Super Apex, which must be booked at least two weeks in advance, though this is not available on all journeys. Next cheapest is an Apex ticket which has to be booked at least seven days before travelling, and again tickets are restricted in number. Other discount tickets include a Saver return, which can be used on all trains, and a Super Saver, which costs slightly less but cannot be used on a Friday or during peak times. For example, a GNER London-Edinburgh Saver return costs £82.50, while an Apex is £51. A standard return with Scotrail on this route is £65. All discount tickets should be booked as quickly as

possible as they are often sold out weeks, or even months, in advance, especially 33
Apex and Super Apex tickets. The latter tickets guarantee seat reservations, but Saver
and Super Saver tickets do not. These can be secured by paying an extra £1. A
Caledonian Sleeper Apex return ticket from London to Edinburgh or Glasgow costs
£89, while an open return is £125.

Railcards

There are a variety of railcards which give discounts on fares for certain groups. Cards
are valid for one year and most are available from main stations. You need two
passport photos and proof of age or status.

Young Person's Railcard For those aged 16-25 or full-time students in the UK. Costs
£18 and gives 33 per cent discount on most train tickets and some ferry services.

Senior Citizen's Railcard For those aged over 60. Same price and discount as above.

Disabled Person's Railcard Costs £14 and gives 33 per cent discount to a disabled
person and one other. Pick up application form from stations and send it to Disabled
Person's Railcard Office, PO Box 1YT, Newcastle-upon-Tyne, NE99 1YT. It may take up
to 21 days to process, so apply in advance.

Family Railcard Costs £20 and gives 33 per cent discount on most tickets (20 per
cent on others) for up to four adults travelling together, and 60 per cent discount for
up to four children.

Road

Bus/coach

Road links to Scotland are excellent, and a number of companies offer express coach
services day and night. This is the cheapest form of travel to Scotland. The main
operator between England and Scotland is **National Express**, T08705-808080,
www.nationalexpress.com. There are direct buses from most British cities to
Edinburgh, Glasgow, Aberdeen and Inverness. Tickets can be bought at bus stations
or from a huge number of agents throughout the country. Fares from London to
Glasgow and Edinburgh with **National Express** start at around £28 return for an
economy advance return. Fares to Aberdeen and Inverness are a little higher. The
London to Glasgow/Edinburgh journey takes around eight hours, while it takes
around 11-12 hours for the trip to Aberdeen and Inverness. From Manchester to
Glasgow takes around 6½ hours and costs from £23.

Car

There are two main routes to Scotland from the south. In the east the A1 runs to
Edinburgh and in the west the M6 and A74(M) runs to Glasgow. The journey north
from London to either city takes around eight to 10 hours. The A74(M) route to
Glasgow is dual carriageway all the way. A slower and more scenic route is to head off
the A1 and take the A68 through the Borders to Edinburgh. There's an Autoshuttle
Express service to transport your car overnight between England and Scotland and
vice versa while you travel by rail or air. For further information T08705-133714;
reservations T08705-502 309. See also Getting around page 39.

Sea

There are direct routes to Scotland from Europe on the **Smyril Line** (Aberdeen,
T01224-572 615; Lerwick, T01595-690 845, www.smyril-line.com) service to Lerwick
(Shetland) from Norway (Bergen), Iceland (Seydisfjordur) and the Faroe Islands
(Torshavn). It sails from mid-May to early September only once a week and takes 12

hours. A sleeping berth one way from Norway and Faroe Islands costs from £68 in high season. You then have to get from Lerwick to Aberdeen. **Northlink Ferries**, www.northlinkferries.co.uk, sail from Lerwick to Aberdeen, see page 352.

P&O Irish Sea, T0870-242 4777, www.poirishsea.com, has several crossings daily from Larne to Cairnryan (one hour) fares from £60 single for car and driver, and from Belfast to Troon (2½ hours) fares from £70 singles for car and driver). **Stena Line**, T0870-707 070, www.stenaline.co.uk, run numerous ferries (three hours) and high-speed catamarans (1½ hours) from Belfast to Stranraer, fares from £90 single for car and driver. **Seacat Scotland** run daily services from Belfast to Troon (2½ hours; £250 for two adults and a car), T0870-552 3523, www.seacat.co.uk.

Touching down

Airport information

Glasgow International, T0141-887 1111, is eight miles west of the city, at junction 28 on the M8. It handles domestic and international flights. Terminal facilities include car hire, bank ATMs, currency exchange, left luggage, tourist information, T0141-848 4440, and shops, restaurants and bars. There's also a Travel Centre, T0141-848 4330, in the UK Arrivals concourse (open daily 0800-2200 in summer and till 1800 in winter), and a First Options Hotel and Travel Reservations desk in the International Arrivals concourse, T0141-848 4731. **Glasgow Prestwick**, T01292-511 000, www.gpia.co.uk, is 30 miles southwest of the city. **Edinburgh airport**, T0131-333 1000, has all facilities, including a tourist information desk, currency exchange, ATMs, restaurants and bars (first floor), shops (ground floor and first floor) and car hire desks in the terminal in the main UK arrivals area. Among Scotland's other main airports are **Aberdeen**, T01224-722 331, **Inverness**, T01463-232 471 and **Wick**, T01955-602 215.

Tourist information

Tourist Information Centres

Tourist offices – called tourist information centres (TICs) – can be found in most Scottish towns. Their addresses, phone numbers and opening hours are listed in the relevant sections of this book. Opening hours vary depending on the time of year, and many of the smaller offices are closed during the winter months. All tourist offices provide information on accommodation, public transport, local attractions and restaurants, as well as selling books, local guides, maps and souvenirs. Many also have free street plans and leaflets describing local walks. They can also book accommodation for you, see page 41, for a small fee. Addresses of the main office of the Scottish Tourist Board and the Area Tourist Boards are given on page 21.

Museums, galleries and historic houses

Most of Scotland's tourist attractions, apart from the large museums and art galleries in the main cities, are open only from Easter to October. Full details of opening hours and admission charges are given in the relevant sections of this guide.

Over 100 of the country's most prestigious sights, and 185,000 acres of beautiful countryside, are cared for by the **National Trust for Scotland (NTS)**, 26-31 Charlotte Square, Edinburgh EH2 4ET, T0131-2439300, www.nts.org.uk. National Trust properties are indicated in this guide as 'NTS', and entry charges and opening hours are given for each property. If you're going to be visiting several sights during your

⦂ Touching down

Business hours 0900-1700.
Electricity The current in Britain is 240V AC. Plugs have three square pins and adapters are widely available.
Emergencies For police, fire brigade, ambulance and, in certain areas, mountain rescue or coastguard, dial 999.
Laundry Most towns have coin-operated launderettes. The average cost for a wash and tumble dry is about £3. A service wash, where someone will do your washing for you, costs around £4-5. In more remote areas, you'll have to rely on hostel and campsite facilities.
Time Greenwich Mean Time (GMT) is used from late October to late March, after which time the clocks go forward an hour to British Summer Time (BST). GMT is five hours ahead of US Eastern Standard Time and 10 hours behind Australian Eastern Standard Time.

Telephone To call Scotland from overseas, dial 011 from USA and Canada, 0011 from Australia and 00 from New Zealand, followed by 44, then the area code, minus the first zero, then the number.
Useful numbers: operator T100; international operator T155; directory enquiries T192; overseas directory enquiries T153.
Toilets Public toilets are found at all train and bus stations and motorway service stations. They may charge 20p, but are generally clean, with disabled and baby-changing facilities. Those in town centres are often pretty grim.
Weights and measures Imperial and metric systems are both in use. Distances on roads are measured in miles and yards, drinks poured in pints and gills, but generally, the metric system is used elsewhere.

Essentials Touching down

stay, then it's worth taking annual membership. This costs £33, £12 for 25 years and under, and a family ticket £54. There are also touring passes for three, seven and 14 days: a 14-day pass costs £22 for an adult. YHA and HI members and student-card holders get 50 per cent discount on NTS admission charges.

Historic Scotland (HS), Longmore House, Salisbury Place, Edinburgh EH9 1SH, T0131-668 8800, www.historic-scotland.gov.uk, manages more than 330 of Scotland's most important castles, monuments and other historic sites. Historic Scotland properties are indicated as 'HS', and admission charges and opening hours are also given in this guide. **Historic Scotland** offer an Explorer Ticket which allows free entry to 70 of their properties including Edinburgh and Stirling castles. A three-day pass (can be used over five consecutive days) costs £16 adult, £12 concession, family £32, seven-day pass (valid for 14 days) £22/16.50/44, 10-day pass (valid for 30 days) £25/19/50. It can save a lot of money, especially in Orkney, where most of the monuments are managed by Historic Scotland.

Many other historic buildings are owned by local authorities, and admission is cheap, or in many cases free. Most fee-paying attractions give a discount or concession for senior citizens, the unemployed, full-time students and children under 16 (those under five are admitted free everywhere). Proof of age or status must be shown. Many of Scotland's stately homes are still owned and occupied by the landed gentry, and admission charges are usually between £4 and £6.

The Countryside Code

1 Drive carefully and behave courteously to other motorists and cyclists on narrow, winding island roads. Park vehicles where they will not be a hazard or disruption to other motorists, residents or businesses.

2 Keep to public paths through farmland to minimise crop damage, and avoid 'short-cuts' on steep terrain to prevent soil erosion and damage to natural vegetation.

3 Litter is an eye-sore, harmful to farm animals, wildlife and the water supply – leave no waste and take all your rubbish home.

4 Protect wildlife, plants and trees.

5 Respect ancient monuments, buildings and sites of religious importance – do not vandalize or cause graffiti.

6 Many of the abandoned crofts are derelict and dangerous – keep out for your own safety.

7 Avoid damaging crops, walls, fences and farm equipment; fasten all gates.

8 Do not collect wildflowers, seabird eggs or historical artefacts.

9 Avoid pollution of water supplies – there are few toilets outside of villages so when walking in the countryside bury human waste and toilet paper in the ground and at least 30 metres from water courses.

10 Guard against risk of fire from matches, cigarettes, stoves and campfires.

11 Keep dogs under careful control, especially when near to sheep at lambing-time and seabird nesting sites at cliff edges, and avoid dog-fouling in public places.

12 Respect the peace, solitude and tranquillity of the islands for others to enjoy – keep noise to a minimum.

13 The landscape can be spectacular but dangerous – take particular care along precipitous cliff edges, hilltops and slippery coastal rocks.

14 Stay away from working areas on the moors and hills during grouse-shooting, lambing season, deer culling and heather burning, and respect other locally or nationally imposed access restrictions.

15 Report any damage or environmental concerns to the landowner or the Scottish Environment Protection Agency (SEPA), T01851-706 477.

16 Be adequately prepared when you walk in the hills – check the weather forecast, carry warm, waterproof clothing and adequate food and water supplies, and know how to use a map and compass.

Local customs and laws

Visitors will generally find their Scottish hosts to be friendly and obliging. In fact, the level of hospitality should be a significant part of the enjoyment of your trip. Those visiting the Outer Hebrides need to be aware of the strict observance of the Sabbath on those islands.

Tipping

Believe it or not, people in Scotland do leave tips. In a restaurant you should leave a tip of 10-15 per cent if you are satisfied with the service. If the bill already includes a service charge, you needn't add a further tip. Tipping is not normal in pubs or bars.

Taxi drivers will expect a tip for longer journeys, usually of around 10 per cent; and most hairdressers will also expect a tip. As in most other countries, porters, bellboys and waiters in more upmarket hotels rely on tips to supplement their meagre wages.

Responsible tourism

The Highlands and Islands of Scotland are beautiful, dramatic and wild, but also a living, working landscape and a fragile and vulnerable place. By adhering to the Countryside Code (see box opposite) , you can help to minimize your impact and protect the natural and cultural heritage of this unique island environment so that it can continue to be appreciated by other visitors.

> ● *Offset your flight's carbon emissions by paying to have the appropriate number of trees planted in sustainable forests through Future Forests, www.futureforests.com.*

For further information on what action is being taken either in Scotland, throughout UK or across the world to control against the negative aspects of tourism on the natural environment and traditional cultures, contact Tourism Concern, T020-7753 3330, or the Tourism and Environment Forum, www.greentourism.org.uk.

Safety

Incidences of serious crime in Highlands and Islands tend to be the exception rather than the rule. Even in relatively sizeable communities such as Tobermory on Mull, people don't lock their doors at night. The major safety issue when visiting the Highlands and more remote parts relates to the unpredictable weather conditions. Everyone should be aware of the need for caution and proper preparation when walking or climbing in the mountains. For more information on mountain safety, see page 56.

Getting around

It is easy to visit the main towns and tourist sights by bus or train, but getting off the beaten track without your own transport requires careful planning and an intimate knowledge of rural bus timetables. Public transport can also be expensive, though there's a whole raft of discount passes and tickets which can save you a lot of money. Hiring a car can work out as a more economical, and certainly more flexible, option, especially for more than two people travelling together. It will also enable you to get off the beaten track and see more of the country. Even if you're driving, however, getting around the remote Highlands and Islands can be a time-consuming business as much of the region is accessed only by a sparse network of tortuous, twisting single-track roads. Be sure to allow plenty of time for getting around and book ferries in advance during the busy summer season.

Air

As well as the main airports of Glasgow, Edinburgh, Aberdeen and Inverness, there are also numerous small airports, many of them on islands (one of them, on Barra, uses the beach as an airstrip). Internal flights are expensive, however, and not really necessary in such a small country, unless you are short of time. For example a return flight from Edinburgh or Glasgow to Shetland costs over £250. There are discounted tickets available, such as Apex fares, which must be booked at least 14 days in advance, and

Essentials Getting around

special offers on some services. BA's **Highland Rover** costs £189 and allows you to take any five flights within seven days (except inter-island flights within Orkney or Shetland). There is no departure tax on flights form Highlands and Islands airports.

The majority of flights are operated by **British Airways/Loganair**, To870-850 9850, www.british-airways.com. For inter-island flights in Shetland, you should book direct through **Loganair**, To1595-840 246. For information on flight schedules, call the airports listed on page 34, or **British Airways**. The British Airports Authority (BAA) publishes a free Scheduled Flight Guide.

Rail

The rail network in Scotland is limited and train travel is comparatively expensive, but trains are a fast and effective way to get around and also provide some beautifully scenic journeys. The West Highland line to Fort William and Mallaig and the journey from Inverness to Kyle of Lochalsh are amongst the most beautiful rail journeys in the world and well worth doing. Services between Glasgow, Edinburgh, Stirling, Perth, Dundee and Aberdeen are fast and frequent, and there are frequent trains to and from Inverness.

ScotRail operates most train services. You can buy train tickets at the stations, from major travel agents, or over the phone with a credit/debit card. For information and advance credit/debit card bookings call To845-755 0033, or visit www.sco trail.co.uk. Details of services are given throughout the guide. For busy long-distance routes it's best to reserve a seat. Seat reservations to Edinburgh, Glasgow, Aberdeen or Inverness are included in the price of the ticket when you book in advance. If the ticket office is closed, there's usually a machine on the platform. If this isn't working, you can buy a ticket on the train. Cyclists should note that though train companies have a more relaxed attitude to taking bikes on trains, reservations for bikes (£3.50) are still required on some services.

Eurorail passes are not recognized in Britain, but **ScotRail** offers a couple of worthwhile travel passes. The most flexible is the **Freedom of Scotland Travelpass**, which gives unlimited rail travel within Scotland. It is also valid on all **CalMac** ferries on the west coast, many **Citylink** bus services in the Highlands, some regional buses, and Glasgow Underground. It also gives 33 per cent discount on **P&O Ferries** from Scrabster to Orkney and 20 per cent discount on **Northlink Ferries** from Aberdeen to Orkney and Shetland. It costs £89 for four days' travel out of eight consecutive days, £119 for eight in 15. The **Highland Rover** is more limited. It allows unlimited rail travel in the Highlands region, plus the West Highland line from Glasgow, and travel between Aberdeen and Aviemore. It also allows free travel on **Citylink** buses between Oban, Fort William and Inverness. It costs £59 for any four out of eight consecutive days.

Road

Bus and coach

Travelling around Scotland by bus takes longer than the train but is much cheaper. There are numerous local bus companies, but the main operator is **Scottish Citylink**, To8705-505 050, www.citylink.co.uk. Bus services between towns and cities are good, but far less frequent in more remote rural areas. Note that long-distance express buses are called coaches. There are a number of discount and flexible tickets available and details of these are given on the **Citylink** website which is fast and easy to use.

The **Tourist Trail Pass** offers unlimited travel on all **Scottish Citylink** and **National Express** services throughout Britain. Passes cost from £49 for two days' travel out of three, up to £190 for 14 days' travel out of 30. They can be bought from

Scottish towns and cities. **National Express Explorer Pass** offers unlimited travel within a specified period on **Scottish Citylink** buses. It is available to overseas visitors but must be bought outside Britain. **Smart Card** and **Discount Coach Card** holders can get a 30 per cent discount on these prices. In North America these passes are available from **British Travel International**, T1-800-327 6097, www.britishtravel.com, or from **US National Express**, T502-298 1395. The SYHA sells its own **Explore Scotland bus pass**, which allows free travel on **Citylink** services. It costs £155 for five days and £250 for eight days, and the price includes seven nights' hostel accommodation, free **SYHA** membership and free entry to many of Historic Scotland's properties. They also sell a **Scottish Wayfarer ticket** which is similar but also includes rail travel and **CalMac** ferries.

> ❀ *Various companies offer backpacker bus tours operating on a jump-on-jump-off basis. They are an affordable option for those on a modest budget, see page 20.*

Many parts of the Highlands and Islands can only be reached by Royal Mail **postbuses**. These are minibuses that follow postal delivery routes and carry up to 14 fare-paying passengers. They set off early in the morning from the main post office and follow a circuitous route as they deliver and collect mail in the most far-flung places. They are often very slow on the outward morning routes but quicker on the return routes in the afternoons. It can be a slow method of getting around, but you get to see some of the country's most spectacular scenery, and it is useful for walkers and those trying to reach remote hostels or B&Bs. There's a restricted service on Saturdays and none on Sundays. A free booklet of routes and timetables is usually available from local tourist information centres, or visit www.postbus.royalmail.com/RouteFinder.asp for a comprehensive route-planning service.

Car

Travelling with your own private transport is the ideal way to explore the country. This allows you to cover a lot of ground in a short space of time and to reach remote places. The main disadvantages are traffic congestion and parking, but this is only a problem in the main cities and on the motorways in the central belt. Roads in the Highlands and Islands are a lot less busy than those in England, and driving is relatively stress-free, especially on the B-roads and minor roads. In more remote parts of the country, on the islands in particular, many roads are single track, with passing places indicated by a diamond-shaped signpost. These should also be used to allow traffic behind you to overtake. Remember that you may want to take your time to enjoy the stupendous views all around you, but the driver behind may be a local doctor in a hurry. Don't park in passing places. A major driving hazard on single track roads are the huge numbers of sheep wandering around, blissfully unaware of your presence. When confronted by a flock of sheep, slow down and gently edge your way past. Be particularly careful at night, as many of them sleep by the side of the road (counting cars perhaps).

To drive in Scotland you must have a current **driving licence**. Foreign nationals also need an international **driving permit**, available from state and national motoring organizations for a small fee. Those importing their own vehicle should also have their vehicle registration or ownership document. Make sure you're adequately **insured**. In all of the UK you drive on the left. **Speed limits** are 30 miles per hour (mph) in built-up areas, 70 mph on motorways and dual carriageways, and 60 mph on most other roads.

It's advisable to join one of the main UK motoring organizations during your visit for their 24-hour breakdown assistance. The two main ones in Britain are the **Automobile Association (AA)**, T0800-448866, www.theaa.co.uk, and the **Royal Automobile Club (RAC)**, T0800-550550, www.rac.co.uk. One year's membership of the AA starts at £46 and £39 for the RAC. They also provide many other services, including a reciprocal agreement for free assistance with many overseas motoring organizations. Check to see if your organization is included. Both companies can also extend their cover to include Europe. Their emergency numbers are: AA To800-887 766; RAC To800-828 282. You can call these numbers even if you're not a member, but you'll have to a pay a large fee. In remote areas you may have to wait a long time for assistance. Also note that in the Highlands and Islands you may be stranded for ages waiting for spare parts to arrive.

Car hire can be expensive in Scotland and you may be better off making arrangements in your home country for a fly/drive deal through one of the main multi-national companies. The minimum you can expect to pay is around £150-180 per week for a small car. Local hire companies often offer better deals than the larger multi-nationals, though **easycar** can offer the best rates, at around £10 per day, if you book in advance and don't push up the charges with high mileage. They are based at Glasgow airport and there are plans to open a branch in Edinburgh. Some companies such as **Melvilles** offer the flexibility of picking up in Glasgow and leaving in Edinburgh, and vice versa. Most companies prefer payment with a credit card, otherwise you'll have to leave a large deposit (£100 or more). You'll need a full driver's licence (one or two years) and be aged over 21 (23 in some cases).

> ‡ Note that petrol in the Highlands and Islands is a lot more expensive than in other parts of the UK, and that petrol stations and garages are few and far between.

Car hire companies

Arnold Clark, T0131-228 4747 (Edinburgh); T0141-339 9886 (Glasgow), www.arnold clark.co.uk.
Avis, T08705-900 500, www.avis.co.uk, in the US T800-331 1084.
Budget, T0800-181 181, www.budget rentacar.co.uk, in the US T800-527 0700.
Discount Car Hire Scotland, T0870-243 0733, www.discount-car-hire- scotland.co.uk.
easycar, T0906-333 333 (60p per min) www.easycar.com.

Europcar, T08457-222 525.
Hertz, T08705-996 699, www.hertz.co.uk, in the US T800-654 3001.
Holiday Autos, T8705-300 400, www.holidayautos.co.uk, in the US T800-422 7737, www.holiday/colauto.com.
National Car Rental, T08705-365 365, in the US T800-CAR-RENT, www.nationalcar.com.
Thrifty, T0131-337 1319 (Edinburgh), T0141-445 4440 (Glasgow), in the US T800-367 2277, www.thrifty.com.

Hitching

As in the rest of the UK, hitching is never entirely safe, and is certainly not advised for anyone travelling alone, particularly women travellers. Those prepared to take the risk should not find it too difficult to get a lift in the Highlands and Islands, where people are far more willing to stop for you. Bear in mind, though, that you will probably have to wait a while even to see a vehicle in some parts.

Sea

There are around 60 or so inhabited islands off the coast of Scotland, and nearly 50 of them can be reached by a scheduled ferry service. Most ferries carry vehicles and can be booked in advance. If you're travelling to the islands by car, it's a good idea to book ferries in advance whatever the time of year, particularly to the more popular islands.

The majority of ferry services on the west coast are operated by **Caledonian MacBrayne**, To8705-650 000, www.calmac.co.uk, or **CalMac** as they're more commonly known. They sail from Oban, Mallaig and Ullapool to over 20 islands in the Inner and Outer Hebrides. They also run services on the Firth of Clyde. Fares are expensive, especially with a car, but if you're planning on using ferries a lot, you can save a lot of money with an **Island Hopscotch ticket**, which offers reduced fares on 17 set routes. The ticket is valid for one month and you need to follow your set itinerary, though this can be changed en route without too much fuss. For more details and some sample fares, see under the relevant destination. A more flexible option is the **Island Rover,** which offers unlimited travel on **CalMac** ferries for a set period, though you still need to make reservations. An eight-day pass costs £47.50 per passenger and £228 for a car, and a 15-day pass costs £69 per passenger and £341 for a car. **CalMac** schedules are complicated, but details of sailings are given under each relevant destination in this guide. **Western Ferries,** T0141-332 9766, runs services between Gourock and Dunoon and Islay and Jura.

    Northlink Ferries, T01856-851 144, www.northlinkferries.co.uk, run car ferries to Orkney and Shetland. Ferries to Orkney depart from Aberdeen or from Scrabster, near Thurso. There's also a passenger ferry from John O'Groats to Orkney which sails daily during the summer only (May-September) and is run by **John O' Groats Ferries,** T01955-611 353. Ferries to Shetland sail from Aberdeen.

    The Orkney islands are linked by services run by **Orkney Ferries,** T01856-872 044, while Shetland's inter-island ferries are run by **Shetland Islands Council,** T01595-744 866, www.shetland.gov.uk. There are also numerous small operators offering day-trips to various islands. Details of these are given in the relevant chapters.

Maps

You'll find a good selection of maps of Scotland in many bookshops and at the main tourist offices. Road atlases can be bought at most service stations. The best of these are the large-format ones produced by the AA, Collins and Ordnance Survey which cover all of Britain at a scale of around three miles to one inch and include plans of the major towns and cities. The Michelin and Bartholomew fold-out maps are also excellent, as are the official regional tourist maps published by Estate Publications, which are ideal for driving and are available from most tourist offices.

    The best detailed maps for walking are the Ordnance Survey maps, which are unsurpassed for accuracy and clarity. These are available at different scales. The Landranger series at 1:50,000 (1¼ inches to a mile) covers the whole of Britain and is good for most walkers. The new Explorer and Outdoor Leisure series are 1:25,000 and offer better value for walkers and cyclists. An excellent source of maps is **Stanfords** at 12-14 Longacre, London WC2E 9LP. There are branches of Stanfords in Bristol and Manchester too.

Sleeping

Staying in the Highlands and Islands of Scotland can mean anything from being pampered to within an inch of your life in a baronial mansion to roughing it in a tiny island bothy with no electricity. If you have the money, then the sky is very much the limit in terms of sheer splendour and excess. We have listed many of the top class establishments in this book, with a bias towards those that offer that little bit extra in terms of character. Those spending less may have to forego the four-posters and Egyptian cotton sheets but there are still many good value small hotels and guesthouses with that essential wow factor – especially when it comes to the views. At the bottom end of the scale, there are also some excellent hostels in some pretty special locations.

    We have tried to give as broad a selection as possible to cater for all tastes and budgets but if you can't find what you're after, or if someone else has beaten you to the draw, then the tourist information centres (TICs) will help find accommodation for you. They can recommend a place within your particular budget and give you the

Hotel price codes explained

Accommodation prices in this book are graded with the letters below and are based on the cost per person for two people sharing a double room with en suite bathroom during the high season. Cheaper rooms with shared bathrooms are available in many hotels, guest houses and B&Bs. Many places, particularly larger hotels, offer substantial discounts during the low season and at weekends. All places listed are recommended as providing good quality and value within their respective price category. Note that price codes for youth hostels are not given in the accommodation listings, as they all cost under £15 per person per night.

L   £80 plus
A   £66-80
B   £46-65
C   £36-45
D   £26-35
E   £16-25
F   £15 and under

charge a small fee (usually £1) for booking a room, while others ask you to pay a deposit of 10 per cent which is deducted from your first night's bill. Most tourist offices also offer a Book-a-Bed-Ahead service, which reserves accommodation for you at your next destination. This costs £3 per booking and is particularly useful in July and August, or if you'll be arriving in a town late. Details of town and city TICs are given throughout the guide. There are also several websites that you can browse and book accommodation. Amongst the best are www.aboutscotland.com and www.s-h-systems.co.uk/shs.html.

Accommodation in Scotland will be your greatest expense, particularly if you are travelling on your own. Single rooms are in short supply and many places are reluctant to let a double room to one person, even when they're not busy. Single rooms are usually more than the cost per person for a double room and in some cases cost the same as two people sharing a double room.

Hotels, guesthouses and B&Bs

Area tourist boards publish accommodation lists which include campsites, hostels, self-catering accommodation and STB-approved hotels, guest houses and Bed and breakfasts (B&Bs). Places participating in the STB system will have a plaque displayed outside which shows their grading, determined by a number of stars ranging from one to five. These reflect the level of facilities, as well as the quality of hospitality and service. However, do not assume that a B&B, guesthouse or hotel is no good because it is not listed by the tourist board. They simply don't want to pay to be included in the system, and some of them may offer better value.

Hotels

At the top end of the scale, there are some fabulously luxurious hotels, often in spectacular locations. Many of them are converted baronial mansions or castles and offer a chance to enjoy a taste of aristocratic grandeur and style. At the lower end of the scale, there is often little to choose between cheaper hotels and guesthouses or B&Bs. The latter often offer higher standards of comfort and a more personal service, but many smaller hotels are really just guesthouses, and are often family-run and every bit as friendly. Note that some hotels, especially in town centres or in fishing ports, may also be

If you'd like to stay in a Scottish castle as a paying guest of the owner, contact Scotts Castle Holidays, T0131-229 7111, www.scottscastles.com.

rather noisy, as the bar can often be the social hub. Rooms in most mid-range to expensive hotels almost always have bathrooms en suite. Many upmarket hotels offer excellent room-only deals in the low season. An efficient last-minute hotel booking service is www.laterooms.com, which specializes in weekend breaks. Also note that many hotels offer cheaper rates for online booking through agencies such as www.lastminute.com.

Guesthouses

Guesthouses are often large, converted family homes with up to five or six rooms. They tend to be slightly more expensive than B&Bs, charging between £25 and £35 per person per night, and though they are often less personal, usually provide better facilities, such as en suite bathroom, colour TV in each room and private parking. In many instances they are more like small budget hotels. Many guest houses offer evening meals, though this may have to be requested in advance.

Bed and breakfasts (B&Bs)

B&Bs provide the cheapest private accommodation. At the bottom end of the scale you can get a bedroom in a private house, a shared bathroom and a huge cooked breakfast for around £17-20 per person per night. Small B&Bs may only have one or two rooms to let, so it's important to book in advance during the summer season and on the islands where accommodation options are more limited. More upmarket B&Bs have en suite bathrooms and TVs in each room and usually charge from £21-26 per person per night. In general, B&Bs are more hospitable, informal, friendlier and offer better value than hotels. Many B&B owners are also a great source of local knowledge and can even provide OS maps for local walks. B&Bs in the Outer Hebrides also offer dinner, bed and breakfast, which is useful as eating options are limited, especially on a Sunday.

Some places, especially in ferry ports, charge room-only rates, which are slightly cheaper and allow you to get up in time to catch an early morning ferry. However, this means that you miss out on a huge cooked breakfast. If you're travelling on a tight budget, you can eat as much as you can at breakfast time and save on lunch as you won't need to eat again until evening. This is particularly useful if you're heading into the hills, as you won't have to carry so much food. Many B&B owners will even make up a packed lunch for you at a small extra cost.

Hostels

For those travelling on a tight budget, there is a large network of hostels offering cheap accommodation. These are also popular centres for backpackers and provide a great opportunity for meeting fellow travellers. Hostels have kitchen facilities for self-catering, and some include a continental breakfast in the price or provide cheap breakfasts and evening meals. Advance booking is recommended at all times, and particularly from May to September and on public holidays, and a credit card is often useful.

Scottish Youth Hostel Association (SYHA)

The **Scottish Youth Hostel Association (SYHA)** ① *7 Glebe Crescent, Stirling FK8 2JA, T01786-451 181, www.syha.org.uk*, is separate from the YHA in England and Wales. It has a network of over 60 hostels, which are often better and cheaper than those in other countries. They offer bunk-bed accommodation in single-sex dormitories or smaller rooms, kitchen and laundry facilities. The average cost is £9-12 per person per night. Though some rural hostels are still strict on discipline and impose a 2300 curfew, those in larger towns and cities tend to be more relaxed and doors are closed as late as 0200. Some larger hostels provide breakfasts for around £2.50 and

⁝ Room at the inn?

There are plenty of B&Bs and guest houses scattered throughout the islands, many of which offer better value than the hotels. Most don't have private bathrooms, but they're comfortable, very welcoming and will offer evening meals. There are numerous self-catering style cottages across the islands, many of which are advertised in the Western Isles brochure published annually by the Western Isles Tourist Board. Also consult the websites listed on page 22. There are several official youth hostels in converted crofts scattered around the islands in isolated locations. Some are difficult to get to without your own transport, but you can always hitchhike. They are run by the SYHA or the Gatliff Hebridean Hostels Trust, see page 283.

three-course evening meals for £4-5. For Scottish residents, adult membership costs £6, and can be obtained at the SYHA National Office, or at the first SYHA hostel you stay at. SYHA membership gives automatic membership of Hostelling International (HI). The SYHA produces a handbook (free with membership) giving details of all their youth hostels, including transport links. This can be useful as some hostels are difficult to get to without your own transport. You should always phone ahead, as many hostels are closed during the day. Phone numbers are listed in this guide. Many hostels are closed during the winter. Details are given in the SYHA Handbook. Youth hostel members are entitled to half-price entry to all National Trust for Scotland properties. The SYHA also offers an **Explore Scotland** and **Scottish Wayfarer** ticket, which can save a lot of money on transport and accommodation, especially if you're not a student, see page 38.

Independent hostels

The Independent Backpackers Hostels of Scotland is an association of nearly 100 independent hostels/bunkhouses throughout Scotland. They charge between £6 and £15 per person per night, though the average is around £8-10. They tend to be more laid-back, with fewer rules and no curfew, and no membership is required. They all have dormitories, hot showers and self-catering kitchens. Some include continental breakfast, or provide cheap breakfasts. All these hostels are listed in the *Blue Hostel Guide*, which is available from tourist offices, or send an A5 SAE to: Pete Thomas, Croft Bunkhouse & Bothies, Portnalong, Isle of Skye, IV47 8SL. They also have a website, www.hostel-scotland.co.uk.

Campsites and self-catering

Campsites

There are hundreds of campsites around Scotland. They are mostly geared to caravans, and vary greatly in quality and level of facilities. The most expensive sites, which charge up to £10 to pitch a tent, are usually well-equipped. Sites are usually only open from April to October. If you plan to do a lot of camping, you should buy *Scotland: Camping & Caravan Parks* (£3.95), available from most tourist offices. It lists around 150 camping and caravan parks graded by the STB.

North Americans planning on camping should invest in an international camping carnet, which is available from home motoring organizations, or from Family Campers and RVers (FCRV), 4804 Transit Road, Building 2, Depew, NY 14043, T1-800-245 9755. It gives you discounts at member sites.

One of the most cost-effective ways to holiday in the Highlands and Islands is to hire a cottage with a group of friends. There are lots of different types of accommodation to choose from, to suit all budgets, ranging from luxury lodges, castles and lighthouses to basic bothies with no electricity.

The minimum stay is usually one week in the summer peak season, though many offer shorter stays of two, three or four nights, especially outside the peak season. Expect to pay at least £150-200 per week for a two-bedroom cottage in the winter, rising to £300-500 in the high season, or more if it's a particularly nice place. A good source of self-catering accommodation is the STB's guide (£5.95), which lists over 1,200 properties and is available to buy from any tourist office, but there are also dozens of excellent websites to browse. Amongst the best of many websites are the following: www.cottages-and-castles.co.uk; www.scottish-country-cottages.co.uk; www.cottages 4you.co.uk; and www.ruralretreats.co.uk. If you want to tickle a trout or feed a pet lamb, www.farmstay.co.uk offer over a thousand good value rural places to stay around the UK, all clearly listed on a clickable map. **Highland Hideaways** has a range of more individual self-catering properties, mainly in the Highlands and Islands. For a free brochure write to them at 5-7 Stafford Street, Oban, Argyll PA34 5NJ, T01631-526 056.

The National Trust for Scotland owns many historic properties which are available for self-catering holidays. Prices start at around £250 per week in high season rising to £1000 for the top of the range lodges. Contact them at 5 Charlotte Square, Edinburgh EH2 4DU, T0131-226 5922, www.nts.org.uk.

Eating

While Scotland's national drink is loved the world over, Scottish cooking hasn't exactly had a good press over the years. This is perhaps not too surprising, as the national dish, haggis, consists of a stomach stuffed with diced innards and served with mashed *tatties* (potatoes) and *neeps* (turnips). Not a great start. And things got even worse when the Scots discovered the notorious deep-fried Mars bar.

But Scottish cuisine has undergone a dramatic transformation in recent years and Scotland now boasts some of the most talented chefs, creating some of the best food in Britain. The heart of Scottish cooking is local produce, which includes the finest fish, shellfish, game, lamb, beef and vegetables, and a vast selection of traditionally-made cheeses. What makes Scottish cooking so special is ready access to these foods. What could be better than enjoying an aperitif whilst watching your dinner being delivered by a local fisherman, knowing that an hour later you'll be enjoying the most delicious seafood?

Modern Scottish cuisine is now a feature of many of the top restaurants in the country. This generally means the use of local ingredients with foreign-influenced culinary styles, in particular French. International cuisine is also now a major feature on menus all over the country, influenced by the rise of Indian and Chinese restaurants in recent decades. In fact, so prevalent are exotic Asian and Oriental flavours that curry has now replaced fish and chips (fish supper) as the nation's favourite food. In Scotland, proper fish and chips use only haddock – cod is for Sassenachs and cats.

Food

Fish, meat and game form the base of many of the country's finest dishes. Scottish beef, particularly Aberdeen Angus, is the most famous in the world. This will, or

Restaurant price codes explained

The price ranges in this book are based on a two-course meal (main course plus starter or dessert) without drinks. We have tried to include an equal number of choices in each category, though this is not always possible. All places listed are recommended as offering relatively good value, quality and standards of service within their respective price category.

£££ over £20 a head
££ £10-20 a head
£ under £10 a head

should, usually be hung for at least four weeks and sliced thick. Game is also a regular feature of Scottish menus, though it can be expensive (dear), especially venison (deer), but delicious and low in cholesterol. Pheasant and hare are also tasty, but grouse is, quite frankly, overrated.

Fish and seafood are fresh and plentiful, and if you're travelling around the northwest coast you must not miss the chance to savour local mussels, prawns, oysters, scallops, langoustines (called prawns here), lobster or crab. Salmon is, of course, the most famous of Scottish fish, but you're more likely to be served the fish-farmed variety than 'wild' salmon, which has a more delicate flavour. Trout is also farmed extensively, but the standard of both remains high. Kippers are also a favourite delicacy, the best of which come from Loch Fyne or the Achiltibuie smokery, see page 224.

Haggis has made something of a comeback, and small portions are often served as starters in fashionable restaurants. Haggis is traditionally eaten on Burns Night (25 January) in celebration of the great poet's birthday, when it is piped to the table and then slashed open with a sword at the end of a recital of Robert Burns' 'Address to the Haggis'. Other national favourites feature names to relish: **cock-a-leekie** is a soup made from chicken, leeks and prunes; **cullen skink** is a delicious concoction of smoked haddock and potatoes; while at the other end of the scale of appeal is **hugga-muggie**, a Shetland dish using fish's stomach. There's also the delightfully named **crappit heids** (haddock heads stuffed with lobster) and **partan bree** (a soup made form giant crab's claws, cooked with rice). Rather more mundane is the ubiquitous **Scotch broth**, made with mutton stock, vegetables, barley, lentils and split peas, and **stovies**, which is a mash of potato, onion and minced beef.

Waist-expanding puddings or desserts are a very important part of Scottish cooking and often smothered in butterscotch sauce or syrup in order to satisfy a sweet-toothed nation. There is a huge variety, including **cranachan**, a mouth-watering mix of toasted oatmeal steeped in whisky, cream and fresh raspberries, and **Atholl Brose**, a similar confection of oatmeal, whisky and cream.

Eaten before pudding, in the French style, or afterwards, are Scotland's many home-produced cheeses, which have made a successful comeback in the face of mass-produced varieties. Many of the finest cheeses are produced on the islands, especially Arran, Mull, Islay and Orkney. **Caboc** is a creamy soft cheese rolled in oatmeal and is made in the Highlands.

Anyone staying at a hotel, guesthouse or B&B will experience the hearty **Scottish breakfast**, which includes bacon, egg, sausage and black pudding (a type of sausage made with blood), all washed down with copious quantities of tea, Scotland's staple drink. Although coffee is readily available everywhere, do not expect cappuccinos and café lattes: filter coffee is the staple 'tea-substitute' in most hotels and B&Bs. You may also be served kippers (smoked herring) or porridge, an erstwhile Scottish staple, which is now eaten by few people. Made with oatmeal and has the consistency of Italian polenta, it is traditionally eaten with salt, though heretics are offered sugar instead. Oatcakes (oatmeal biscuits) may also be on offer, as well as potato scones, baps (bread rolls) or bannocks (a sort of large oatcake). After such a huge cooked breakfast you probably won't feel like eating again until dinner, or tea, taken between 1700 and 1800, and a national institution consisting of a cooked main course (usually fish and chips) and a smorgasbord of scones and cakes, washed down with more pots of tea.

Drink

Beer

Beer is the staple alcoholic drink in Scotland. The most popular type of beer is lager, which is generally brewed in the UK even when it bears the name of an overseas brand and is almost always weaker than in both strength and character than the lagers in mainland Europe. However, examples of the older and usually darker type of beers, known as ales, are still widely available, and connoisseurs should try some of these as they are far more rewarding. Indeed, the best of them rival Scotland's whiskies as gourmet treats.

Traditionally, Scottish ales were graded by the shilling, an old unit of currency written as /-, according to strength. This system is still widely used by the older established breweries, though many of the newer independents and 'micros' have departed from it. 70/- beers at around 3.5% ABV (alcohol by volume), known as 'heavy', and 80/- beers (4.5 per cent sometimes known as 'export', are the most popular, while 60/-, 'light' (3-3.5 per cent) is harder to find. Very strong 90/- beers (6.5 per cent + ABV), known as 'wee heavies', are also brewed, mainly for bottling.

The market is dominated by the giant international brewers: Scottish Courage with its McEwans and Youngers brands; Interbrew with Calders and Carslberg; and Tetley with Tennents lagers. Tennents, the first British brewery to produce a continental-style lager commercially back in the 19th century, is today best known for its bland but very strong canned lagers popular with winos and those who like to get drunk very quickly and cheaply.

Much better are the ales from smaller independent breweries. Edinburgh's Caledonian is a world-class brewer producing many excellent beers, including a popular 80/- and a renowned golden hoppy ale, Deuchars IPA. Belhaven, an old, established family brewery in Dunbar, has some superb traditional beers including a malty 80/-, once marketed as the Burgundy of Scotland. Broughton, a micro-brewery in the Borders, produces the fruity Greenmantle and an oatmeal stout. Another micro, Harvieston of Clackmannanshire (once an important brewing country) offers a wide and adventurous range of specialities, including Ptarmigan 80/- and a naturally brewed cask lager, Schiehallion. The Heather Ale Company, near Glasgow, has the spicy and unusual Fraoch (pronounced 'Frooch') which is flavoured with real heather as well as hops.

Draught beer in pubs and bars is served in pints, or half pints, and you'll pay between £1.50 and £2.50 for a pint. In many pubs the basic ales are chilled under gas pressure like lagers, but the best ales, such as those from the independents, are 'real ales', still fermenting in the cask and served cool but not chilled (around 12°C) under natural pressure from a handpump, electric pump or air pressure fount. All Scottish beers are traditionally served with a full, creamy head.

Whisky

No visit to the Scottish Highlands would be complete without availing oneself of a 'wee dram'. There is no greater pleasure on an inclement evening than enjoying a malt whisky in front of a roaring log fire whilst watching the rain outside pelt down relentlessly. The roots of Scotland's national drink (*uisge beatha*, or 'water of life' in

Turn water into whisky

Malt whisky is made by first soaking dry barley in tanks of local water for two to three days. Then the barley is spread out on a concrete floor or placed in cylindrical drums and allowed to germinate for between eight and 12 days, after which it is dried in a kiln, heated by a peat fire. Next, the dried malt is ground and mixed with hot water in a huge circular vat called a 'mash tun'. A sugary liquid called 'wort' is then drawn from the porridge-like result and piped into huge containers where living yeast is stirred into the mix in order to convert the sugar in the wort into alcohol. After about 48 hours the 'wash' is transferred to copper pot stills and heated till the alcohol vaporizes and is then condensed by a cooling plant into distilled alcohol which is passed through a second still. Once distilled, the liquid is poured into oak casks and left to age for a minimum of three years, though a good malt will stay casked for at least eight years.

Gaelic) go back to the late 15th century, but it wasn't until the invention of a patent still in the early 19th century that distilling began to develop from small family-run operations to the large manufacturing business it has become today. Now more than 700 million bottles a year are exported, mainly to the United States, France, Japan and Spain.

There are two types of whisky: single malt, made only from malted barley; and grain, which is made from malted barley together with unmalted barley, maize or other cereals, and is faster and cheaper to produce. Most of the popular brands are blends of both types of whisky – usually 60-70 per cent grain to 30-40 per cent malt. These blended whiskies account for over 90 per cent of all sales worldwide, and most of the production of single malts is used to add flavour to a blended whisky. Amongst the best-known brands of blended whisky are *Johnnie Walker*, *Bells*, *Teachers* and *Famous Grouse*. There's not much between them in terms of flavour and they are usually drunk with a mixer, such as water or soda.

Single malts are a different matter altogether. Each is distinctive and should be drunk neat to appreciate fully its subtle flavours, though some believe that the addition of water helps free the flavours. Single malts vary enormously. Their distinctive flavours and aromas are derived from the peat used for drying, the water used for mashing, the type of oak cask used and the location of the distillery. Single malts fall into four groups: Highland, Lowland, Campbeltown and Islay. There are over 40 distilleries to choose from, most offering guided tours. The majority are located around Speyside, in the northeast. The region's many distilleries include that perennial favourite, *Glenfiddich*, which is sold in 185 countries. A recommended alternative is the produce of the beautiful and peaceful Isle of Islay, whose malts are lovingly described in terms of their peaty quality. Scots tend to favour the 10 year-old *Glenmorangie*, while the most popular in the USA is *The Macallan*.

Eating out

There are places to suit every taste and budget. In the large towns and cities you'll find a vast selection of eating places, including Indian, Chinese, Italian and French restaurants, as well as Thai, Japanese, Mexican, Spanish and, of course Scottish, but beyond the main cities, choice is much more limited. More and more restaurants are moving away from national culinary boundaries and offering a wide

☷ Which whisky?

Opinions vary as to what are the best single malts and as to when you should drink them. As a rough guide, we would recommend a Speyside malt such as Glenmorangie or Glenlivet before dinner and one of the Islay malts – Ardbeg, Bowmore, Bunnahabhain (pronounced 'bun-a-haven'), Lagavulin, or the very wonderful Laphroaig (pronounced 'la-froig') – after dinner.

If the Islays are not to your taste, then you could try instead the versatile Highland Park from Orkney or perhaps Tamdhu or Aberlour from Speyside. Those eternal favourites, Glenfiddich and The Macallan, can be enjoyed at any time.

range of international dishes and flavours, so you'll often find Latin American, Oriental and Pacific Rim dishes all on the same menu. This is particularly the case in the many continental-style bistros, brasseries and café-bars, which now offer a more informal alternative to traditional restaurants. Vegetarians are increasingly well catered for, especially in the large cities, where exclusively vegetarian/vegan restaurants and cafés are often the cheapest places to eat. Outside the cities, vegetarian restaurants are thin on the ground, though better-quality eating places will normally offer a reasonable vegetarian selection.

For a cheap meal, your best bet is a pub, hotel bar or café, where you can have a one-course meal for around £5-7 or less, though don't expect gourmet food. The best value is often at lunchtime, when many restaurants offer three-course set lunches or business lunches for less than £10. You'll need a pretty huge appetite to feel like eating a three-course lunch after your gigantic cooked breakfast, however. Also good value are the pre-theatre dinners offered by many restaurants in the larger towns and cities (you don't need to have a theatre ticket to take advantage). These are usually available from around 1730-1800 till 1900-1930, so you could get away with just a sandwich for lunch. At the other end of the price scale are many excellent restaurants where you can enjoy the finest of Scottish cuisine, often with a continental influence, and these are often found in hotels. You can expect to pay from around £25 a head up to £40 or £50 in the very top establishments.

The biggest problem with eating out in Scotland, as in the rest of the UK, is the ludicrously limited serving hours in most pubs and hotels. These places only serve food between 1230 and 1400 and 1700 and 1900, seemingly ignorant of the eating habits of foreign visitors, or those who would prefer a bit more flexibility during their holiday. In small places especially it can be difficult finding food outside these strictly enforced times. Places which serve food all day till 2100 or later are restaurants, fast-food outlets and the many chic bistros and café-bars, which can be found not only in the main cities but increasingly in smaller towns. The latter often offer very good value and above-average quality.

Entertainment

Bars and clubs

As in the rest of Britain, pubs are the main focus of social life and entertainment for most Scots. These vary greatly, from traditional old inns full of character (and often full of characters) to chic and trendy bars where you can order focaccia bread with sundried tomatoes washed down with your bottle of continental lager. Many pubs in large towns are owned by the large breweries and only serve their own particular beers, while in more remote parts the local hotel bar is often the only watering hole for miles around. Pubs generally are open from 1100 till 2300 Monday-Saturday and Sunday from 1100-1200 till 2230, though many close for a couple of hours between 1400 and 1600, which can be very annoying on a wet afternoon. In towns and cities many pubs are open till 2400 or 0100 on Friday and Saturday nights.

Cinema

Scotland, like the rest of the UK, has succumbed to the rise of home entertainment and many of the finest cinemas have long gone, replaced by bingo halls and out-of-town leisure and entertainment complexes showing a vast array of Hollywood blockbusters and little else. That's not to say that independent cinema is dead. Inverness, Perth and Oban all have independent cinemas showing the occasional arthouse film.

Dance

One of the most vibrant expressions of Celtic culture is the ceilidh (pronounced 'kay-lee') an evening of Scottish music and dance, the music provided by a ceilidh band, which normally consists of a fiddler, an accordionist, a drummer and a singer. Here you can spend the evening sampling the delights of Gay Gordons or Dashing White Sergeants. In case you're wondering, these aren't people who frequent these events – they are actually Scottish country dances which, along with eightsome reels, figure prominently in the ceilidh dance-band repertoire. Beware the well-meaning local lad or lassie bearing gifts of whisky, however – an excellent evening enjoying the music can often lead to a spectacular hangover the following morning. The local TIC, or newspaper, will have details of what's on where.

Music

Folk music clubs still thrive in Scotland although, sadly, seem to be restricted to an 'early-in-the-week' slot of a Monday or Tuesday evening in bars, as landlords attempt to bring in customers on what are generally quieter nights for business. Even the Scots, with their fearsome (and well-earned) reputation for partying, can't do it every night of the week. Look out for boards outside pubs which proclaim 'Live Music Tonight' or 'Folk Music Session – All Welcome', when the normally funereal atmosphere of the local pub is transformed into something resembling one of those Hollywood film scenes featuring Julia Roberts or Andie McDowell in an Aran jumper.

Theatre

The main focal points of Scottish theatre are, not surprisingly, the cities of Edinburgh and Glasgow. The latter in particular stages some of the UK's most exciting and innovative drama in its Citizens' and Tramway Theatres. Outside the big two, Perth, Pitlochry and Inverness all have thriving summer programmes.

Festivals and events

There is a huge range of organized events held throughout Scotland every year, ranging in size and spectacle from the Edinburgh Festival, the largest arts festival in the world, to more obscure traditional events featuring ancient customs dating back many centuries. The Scottish Tourist Board publishes a comprehensive list, *Events in Scotland*, twice a year. It's free and is available from the main tourist offices. The most popular tourist events are the **Highland Games (or Gatherings)**, a series of competitions involving lots of kilts, bagpipes and caber-tossing, which are held across the Highlands and Islands, the northeast and Argyll from June to September.

The best known is the **Braemar Gathering**, see page 88, which is attended by various members of the Royal Family. Those at Oban and Dunoon are large events, but smaller gatherings are often more enjoyable and 'authentic'. Details of Highland Gatherings are listed throughout the guide.

Folk festivals take place all over the country, from Arran to Shetland, and are great fun. Musicians from all over Scotland gather to play the tunes, sing the songs and maybe, just maybe, drink the odd beer or two. Among the best of the folk festivals is the **Shetland Folk Festival**, held over a long weekend in mid-April. Also recommended are those held in in Inverness in July and August, Killin at the end of June, Islay during the last two weeks in May, Arran in early June, Skye at the end of July and Kirriemuir on the first weekend in September.

> ❖ *Details of local festivals are given in the listings sections of individual towns and cities; also visit www.whatsonwhen.com.*

Details of these festivals, and many others, are available from the Scottish Area Tourist Boards, see page 34.

Festivals

Jan New Year's Day A variety of ancient local celebrations take place, including the Kirkwall Ba' Game, a mixture of football and mud wrestling.

Up Helly-Aa Re-enactment of the ancient Viking fire festival held on Shetland on the last Tue in Jan, see p339.

Burns Night Burns suppers held on 25 Jan all over the country to celebrate the poet's birthday. Lots of haggis, whisky and poetry recitals.

May Spirit of Speyside Whisky Festival Held on Speyside in May.

The Highland Festival Held over 2 weeks from late May till early Jun at venues throughout the Highland region. For details, T01463-719000, www.highlandfestival.org.uk.

Sep Braemar Highland Gathering Attended by the Royal Family in Sep.

Oct National Mod Competitive Gaelic music festival held at various locations.

Tour of Mull Rally The highlight of the Scottish rally season, run over the island's public roads (no wonder they're in such appalling condition) in Oct.

Dec-Jan Hogmanay Old year's night, and the most important national celebration. Possible derivations of the word include Holag Monath, Anglo Saxon for 'holy month', and Hoog min dag, which is Dutch for 'great love day' Edinburgh's huge street party Is the largest in the northern hemisphere.

Bank holidays

New Year's Day and **2 Jan**, **Good Friday** and **Easter Monday**, **May Day** (the first Mon in May), **Victoria Day** (the last Mon in May), **25 and 26 Dec** (Christmas Day, Boxing Day). There are also local public holidays in spring and autumn. Dates vary from place to place. Banks are closed during these holidays, and sights and shops may be affected to varying degrees. Contact the relevant Area Tourist Board for more details.

Shopping

Scottish textiles, especially the **tartan** variety, are popular and worth buying. You can get hold of everything from a travelling rug to your own kilt outfit. Shops up and down the country, and especially in Inverness, can tell which clan your family belongs to and make you a kilt in that particular tartan. For the full outfit, including kilt, sporran, jacket, shoes and *skeann dhu* dagger, expect to pay in the region of £600, or more if you want more elaborate accessories. **Harris Tweed** is also a good buy and you can watch your cloth being woven on the Hebridean islands of Harris and Lewis (see box on page 293).

Knitwear is also good value and sold throughout Scotland. Shetland is a good place to find high-quality wool products. Note that Aran jumpers are not from the island of Arran, but from Aran (with one 'r') in Ireland. **Jewellery** is another popular souvenir and there are many excellent craft shops throughout the Highlands and Islands making beautiful jewellery with Celtic designs. **Glassware** is also popular, particularly Edinburgh crystal and Caithness glass, as well as pottery.

Food is another good souvenir and not just the ubiquitous shortbread sold in tartan tins. If you haven't far to travel home, smoked salmon, or any other smoked product, is good value. One of the best places for food products is the island of Arran, where you can buy their delicious local mustards and preserves, smoked fish and game, and cheeses. And, of course, there's **whisky**. Most distilleries will refund the cost of their guided tour in the form of a discount voucher on a bottle of their brand whisky.

Shop hours in Scotland are generally Monday to Saturday from 0900-1730 or 1800. In larger towns and cities, many shops also open on Sundays and late at night, usually on a Thursday and Friday. Large supermarkets and retail complexes found outside large towns are open till 2000 or later Monday to Saturday and till 1600 on Sunday. In the Highlands and Islands, few shops are open on Sunday, most notably in the Outer Hebrides where nothing is open on a Sunday. Also note that in many rural areas there is an early-closing day when shops close at 1300. This varies from region to region, but the most common day is Wednesday.

Sport and activities

Scotland has never been a place for softies. Its challenging weather and dramatic scenery really give you a sense of being in the great outdoors. Many visitors come specifically to enjoy the magnificent scenery as they walk in the hills, cycle through forests, ski down mountains or head off in search of rare wildlife. The coastline, lochs and rivers are ideal for fishing and offer plenty of opportunities for a whole range of watersports, including windsurfing, sailing and scuba diving. Aside from the more traditional outdoor pursuits, however, Scotland's rivers, mountains and coast are fast making it a centre for extreme activities. So before you head off to the other side of the world for a spot of whitewater rafting, check out Scotland to see what's on offer. At the end of this section is a list of organizations that are able to provide further information on sports and activities in Scotland, see page 60.

Canoeing, kayaking and rafting

Scotland's rivers, lochs and deeply indented coastline offer great opportunities canoeing, kayaking and the highlands has also gained a reputation for being one of the most exciting locations for whitewater rafting. Rapids are ranked from grade one (paddling pool standard) to grade six (stupidly scary). **Monster Activities**, 25 miles from Fort William, run trips on a dam-released river, which ensures that flows are kept even in the summer months, with grade three rapids, which are serious but safe enough for children aged 10 and over. Scotland's other main rafting centre is Perthshire, where companies offer fun yakking, which is like whitewater rafting but in boats for two people without a guide. See page 60 for details organizations and companies offering information, courses and trips.

Canyoning

Head downriver in a gorge, dropping several hundred feet by swimming, jumping into plunge pools, sliding down log flumes and abseiling. In Perthshire you can also go cliff-jumping from heights of up to 60 ft into rock pools combined with headfirst descents of waterfalls. If that's too tame then try the Tyrolean Traverse, which involves crossing a gorge at a height of 300 ft. See page 60 for companies offering canyoning trips.

Climbing

Scotland is a great place to try rock climbing and its arduous winter cousin, ice climbing. The Cairngorms and Cuillins offer the most challenging climbing, as do Glencoe and Torridon. Most mountaineering clubs have regular weekend meets in the hills as well as social gatherings closer to home. Some useful websites are: www.winternetscotland.co.uk, www.scotclimb.org.uk and www.nae-limits.com.

Cycling

The bicycle was invented in Scotland, so it seems appropriate that travelling by bike is one of the best ways to explore the country. Most towns, however, are not particularly cycle-friendly. Very few have proper cycle routes, and there's the added problem of security. It's best to stick to rural backroads, especially unclassified roads and country lanes, which are not numbered but are signposted and marked on OS maps. There are also forest trails and dedicated routes along canal towpaths and disused railway tracks. The main problem in rural areas, though, is the availability of spare parts.

The wild and remote Highlands are popular with cyclists, but this is also walking country, and cyclists should stick to tracks where a right to cycle exists and be considerate towards walkers. The Forestry Commission has 1,150 miles of excellent off-road routes up and down the country. These are detailed in a series of *Cycling in the Forest leaflets*, which are available from Forestry Enterprise offices and from most tourist offices.

You can cut down on the amount of pedalling you have to do by transporting your bike by train. Bikes can be taken free on most local rail services on a first come, first served basis (call ScotRail bookings, T08457-550033). On long-distance routes you'll have to make a reservation and pay a small charge (£3.50). Space is limited on trains so it's a good idea to book as far in advance as possible. Bus and coach companies will not carry bikes, unless they are dismantled and boxed. Ferries transport bikes for a small fee and airlines will often accept them as part of your baggage allowance. Check with the ferry company or airline about any restrictions.

Bike rental is available at cycle shops in most large towns and tourist centres. Expect to pay from around £6 to £15 per day, or from £50 a week, plus a refundable deposit. There's also the option of a cycling holiday package, which includes transport of your luggage, prebooked accommodation, route instructions and food and backup support. A list of specialists is given above.

The STB publishes a free booklet, *Cycling in Scotland*, which is useful and suggests routes in various parts of the country, as well as accommodation and repair shops. Many area tourist boards also provide cycling guides for their own areas. For a list of useful cycle guides and books, see page 387. The website www.spokes.org.uk is useful.

There is also some extreme cycling to be done. Scotland is one of the hottest **mountain-bike** destinations in the world. According to who? According to the

Colorado-based **International Mountain Biking Association**, that's who. Further evidence is that the 2002 World Cup Downhill was held on the bottom ski slopes of the Nevis Range near Fort William. This black run is Britain's biggest downhill and is open May to September. Hook your bike up to the gondola and climb up to 2,050 ft before beginning the 1.6 mile steep and rough course. The lift operates 1045-1445 and a single run costs £9.75 (day access £17.50). Bike hire from **Off Beat Bikes** in Fort William, www.offbeatbikes.co.uk. ▶▶ *See also Books, page 387, for cycling guidebooks.*

Diving

Scotland may not have the Great Barrier Reef but it does have some of the finest diving locations in the world, featuring shipwrecks, reefs, sheer underwater cliffs, soft corals and abundant sea life. The West Coast offers the best diving, as the water is warmed by the effects of the Gulf Stream and is not cold, even without a dry suit. Among the best sites are the west coast of **Harris**, the **Summer Isles** and the remote island of **St Kilda**. There are lots of wrecks in the **Sound of Mull**, and the chance to find a Spanish Galleon off **Tobermory**. **Scapa Flow** in Orkney is world-renowned as the burial site of the German World War I fleet. For a list of organizations, see page 60.

Fishing

Scotland's rivers, streams, lochs and estuaries are among the cleanest waters in Europe and are filled with salmon, trout (sea, brown and rainbow) and pike. Not surprisingly, then, fishing (coarse, game and sea) is hugely popular in Scotland.

There is no close season for coarse fishing or sea angling. For wild brown trout the close season is early October to mid-March. The close season for salmon and sea trout varies from area to area and between net and rod fishing. It is generally from late August to early February for net fishing, and from early November to early February for rod fishing. No licence is required to fish in Scotland, but most of the land and rivers are privately owned so you must obtain a permit from the owners or their agents. These are often readily available at the local fishing tackle shop and usually cost from around £15, though some rivers can be far more expensive.

The STB's booklet *Fish Scotland* is a good introduction and a source of all kinds of information. It is available free from tourist offices, or by post, see page 21. For a list of organizations, see page 60.

Golf

Scotland has over 400 golf courses, with more being built all the time, and therefore has more courses per head of population than any other country in the world. Any decent-sized town in Scotland will have a golf course nearby and most, if not all, are available for play. There are many public courses, which tend to be both cheap and extremely busy, often have excellent layouts. The majority of private clubs allow visitors, although many have restrictions as to what days these visitors can play. Weekends are usually reserved for club competitions for the members so it is best to try to play on a weekday. All private clubs have a dress code and it is inadvisable to turn up for a round in a t-shirt and jeans. These minor caveats aside, you are more than likely to receive a warm and courteous welcome. To arrange golfing holidays visit www.scotland-golf-tours.co.uk.

Many clubs offer a daily or weekly ticket. A Golf Pass Scotland costs between £46 and £70 for five days (Monday to Friday), depending on the area. *Golf in Scotland* is a

free brochure listing 400 courses and clubs with accommodation details. Contact the
Scottish Tourist Board for a copy. The British Tourist Authority (BTA) has a very useful
Golfing Holidays booklet which provides details of golfing holidays and major golf
tournaments in Britain. BTA and STB addresses are given on page 21. For a list of
recommended golf books, see page 387. For a list of organizations, see page 60.

Health and beauty

Nothing can be more relaxing after a hard day's walking or sightseeing than spending
an hour or two being preened and pampered in a spa. One hotel that really know how
to do it style is the **Gleneagles Hotel Spa**, see page 76.

Hillwalking

Scotland is a walker's paradise. Throughout the country there are numerous marked
trails, ranging from short walks to long-distance treks from one side of the country to
the other. Whatever your taste or level of fitness and experience, you'll find plenty of
opportunities to get off the beaten track and explore the countryside.

The best time for hiking in the mountains is usually from May
to September, though in the more low-lying parts, April to October *Walking routes, ranging*
should be safe. Winter walking in the Highlands requires technical *from a coastal stroll to an*
equipment such as ice axes and crampons and a lot of *arduous mountain trek,*
experience. July and August are the busiest times, though only the *are denoted throughout*
most popular routes, such as Ben Nevis, get really crowded. *the guide by* ▲
Another problem during these months are midges, see page 63. May to mid-June is
probably the most pleasant time overall, as the weather can often be fine and the
midges have yet to appear. September is also a good time, though it can be a lot colder.
For a list of helpful organizations, see page 60.

Access

Scotland has a long tradition of generally free responsible access to mountain and
moorland. This free access, of course, relies on walkers behaving responsibly and
recognizing that the countryside is a place of work as well as recreation. Most land in
Scotland is privately owned and at certain times of the year, such as the main shooting
seasons, walkers may be asked to respect certain restrictions on access. The main deer
stalking season runs from mid-August to 20 October and the grouse shooting season is
between 12 August (referred to as the 'Glorious Twelfth') and 10 December. For more
information on this, see *Heading for the Scottish Hills* which is published by the
Mountaineering Council of Scotland, see page 53, and the Scottish Landowners
Federation and gives estate maps and telephone numbers to call for local advice. There
may also be restricted access during the lambing season from March to May.

It is not an offence to walk over someone's land in Scotland but, especially during
the stalking and shooting seasons, you may be asked to take a different route, though
this rarely happens. Scotland's first national parks opened in recent years: Loch
Lomond and the Trossachs National Park (www.lochlomond-trossachs.org) in 2002
and Cairngorms National Park (www.cairngorms.co.uk), in 2003. There is free access at
all times of the year to areas owned by the National Trust for Scotland. These areas
include Torridon and Glencoe. There is also free access to most land owned by the
Forestry Commission, and there is good public access to land owned by the John Muir
Trust, Scottish Natural Heritage, the Royal Society for the Protection of Birds and the
Woodland Trust, though these areas are not marked on Ordnance Survey (OS) maps.
Also not shown on OS maps are Rights of Way, which are signposted by the Scottish

Mountain safety

Visitors to Scotland should be aware of the need for caution and safety preparations when walking or climbing in the mountains. The nature of Scottish weather is such that a fine sunny day can turn into driving rain or snow in a matter of minutes. Remember that a blizzard can be raging on the summit when the car park at the foot of the mountain is bathed in sunshine. It is essential to get an up to date weather forecast before setting off on any walk or climb. Whatever the time of year, or conditions when you set off, you should always carry or wear essential items of clothing. A basic list for summer conditions would be: boots with a good tread and ankle support and a thick pair of socks; waterproof jacket and trousers, even on a sunny day; hat and gloves are important if the weather turns bad; warm trousers should be worn or carried, tracksuit bottoms are okay if you also have waterproof trousers; spare woolly jumper or fleece jacket will provide an extra layer; map and compass are essential to carry and to know how to use. Other essentials are food and drink, a simple first aid kit, a whistle and a torch. A small 25-30 litre rucksack should be adequate for carrying the above items. Also remember to leave details of your route and expected time of return with someone, and remember to inform them on your return.

In the winter extra warm clothing is needed, as well as an ice axe and crampons, and the ability to use them. The skills required for moving over ice or snow should be practised with an experienced and qualified mountain guide/instructor.

Rights of Way Society's green metal signs. The society publishes maps of rights of way, many of which follow ancient 'drove roads' through the hills.

Information and advice

The Scottish Tourist Board is a useful source of information for walkers and local tourist information centres have details of interesting local walks. Many walk descriptions and maps are given in this guidebook, but these should ideally be used in conjunction with a good map, such as the Ordnance Survey (OS) Landranger series. The relevant map numbers have been listed, where possible, with the route description. OS maps can be found at tourist information centres and also at outdoor shops, which are usually staffed by experienced climbers and walkers who can give good advice about the right equipment. The best-equipped shops are **Tiso**, www.tiso.co.uk, who have branches in the main towns and cities; and **Nevisport** in Fort William. For a list of recommended walking guidebooks and maps, see page 387.

Long-distance walks

There is a network of long walking trails across Scotland which are carefully prepared to provide ideal walking conditions together with sufficient places for accommodation and supplies en route. These walks can be attempted in full, or sampled in part by less experienced walkers. Area tourist boards and local tourist offices can provide information and advice for their own particular sections. One of the main trails, the **Speyside Way**, see page 97, is covered in the relevant section of this guide.

The best-known, and busiest, long-distance trail is the **West Highland Way**, which runs for 95 miles from Milngavie (pronounced 'mull-guy'), just north of Glasgow, to Fort William. The route progresses steadily from the Lowlands, along the

⦂ Munros, Corbetts and Grahams

There are 284 mountains over 3,000 ft (914 m) in Scotland, known as 'Munros', after Sir Hugh Munro, first president of the Scottish Mountaineering Club (SMC), who published the first comprehensive list of these mountains in 1891. In the 1920s a further list was published, of the 221 summits between 2,500-3,000 ft, by J Rooke Corbett, and these became known as 'Corbetts'. A third list, of summits between 2,000-2,500 ft was compiled by Fiona Graham and published in 1992. This list was subsequently revised and corrected and now all peaks that are between 2,000-2,500 ft are called 'Grahams'.

This is where the term Munro-bagging comes from – one of Scotland's favourite pastimes – climbing as many peaks over 3,000 ft as possible

eastern shore of Loch Lomond and the traverse of the western edge of Rannoch Moor, to enter Glencoe at White Corries. It continues over the Devil's Staircase, past Kinlochleven, and through Glen Nevis to Fort William. Many walkers finish off with an ascent of Ben Nevis (4,406ft), the highest mountain in Britain, see page 187. Further information, including a trail leaflet with accommodation and facilities guide, is available from **West Highland Way Ranger Service**, Balloch Castle, Balloch G53 8LX, To1389-758216.

Short walks

Many of the most popular short walks, including the ascent of Ben Nevis, are described in this guidebook. These range from gentle strolls through forest glades to strenuous hikes, steep hills and mountains, and also include some beautiful coastal trails. One of the most popular pastimes in Scotland is Munro-bagging, see also box above, which involves climbing as many peaks over 3,000 ft as possible. The best area for this is the Highlands, which provide many challenging peaks, and it's possible to climb several in a day. Many of these hills are straightforward climbs, but many also require a high level of fitness and experience, and all require proper clothing, see next page 56. You should never attempt walks beyond your abilities.

Other good areas for walking include the Isles of Arran, Mull, Islay and Skye, and Perthshire and the Trossachs. The mighty Cairngorms are better known as a winter ski area, but provide excellent year-round hillwalking and climbing. This is extremely wild terrain, however, and suitable only for experienced walkers. There are many opportunities for less experienced walkers in Rothiemurchus Estate and Glenmore Forest Park around Aviemore. Other areas which are best left to serious climbers are Torridon, Kintail and Glencoe, though the latter also offers a few more straightforward walks through spectacular scenery, see page 193.

Kite surfing

The newest adrenaline sport is kite surfing, which involves whizzing over the sea with your surfboard attached to a giant kite at speeds of up to 50mph. One of the best places in the country is the windy Hebridean island of Tiree. See page 60 for details of companies offering courses.

Paragliding

If you fancy getting high during your visit, you can try your hand at the exciting sport of paragliding. The Isle of Arran offers some of the best sites in the UK for both beginners and experts, while Nevis Range, near Fort William, is a spectacular alternative. See pages 60 for details of companies offering flights.

Pony trekking and horse riding

Pony trekking is a long-established activity in Scotland and miles of beautiful coastline, lochsides, and moorland are accessible on horseback. There are numerous equestrian centres around the country catering to all levels of riders. The Scottish Tourist Board produces a *Trekking & Riding* brochure listing riding centres around the country, all of them approved by the **Trekking and Riding Society of Scotland (TRSS)** or the **British Horse Society (BHS)**. Centres offer pony trekking (leisurely strolls at walking pace for novices), hacks (short rides at a fast pace for experienced riders) and trail riding (long distance rides at no more than a canter). For general information contact the TRSS. For a list of organizations, see page 60.

Skiing

Conditions in Scotland are not as good or reliable as anywhere in the Alps, but on a clear, sunny day, and with good snow, you can enjoy some decent skiing. However, at weekends, in conditions like these, expect the slopes to be very busy. Scotland offers both alpine (downhill) and nordic (cross-country) skiing, as well as the increasingly popular snowboarding. The high season is from January to April, but it is possible to ski from as early as November to as late as May. Ski packages are available, but it's easy to arrange everything yourself and there's plentiful accommodation and facilities in and around the ski centres.

Ski centres

There are five ski centres in Scotland. The largest are **Glenshee**, which has the most extensive network of lifts and selection of runs, as well as snow machines, and

‡ *Check out www.born 2ski.com for everything from snow reports to après ski ratings.*

Cairngorm, which has almost 30 runs spread over an extensive area. **Glencoe** is the oldest of the ski resorts, and the **Nevis Range**, at Aonach Mor near Fort William, has the highest ski runs and only gondola in Scotland, as well as a dry slope. **The Lecht** is the most remote centre, and is good for beginners and families and for nordic skiing. Access to all five centres is easiest by car. Each resort has a ski patrol and facilities for snowboarding.

Costs

Ski equipment and clothing can be hired at all resorts, but lessons should be booked in advance. Prices vary from centre to centre, but on average expect to pay around £13 per day for hire of skis, sticks and boots, and around £12 per day for ski clothes. Snowboard hire is around £16-17 per day for board and boots. Lift passes cost around £18-20 per day, or £68-80 for five days. Ski lessons are around £18 for four hours. Packages including ski hire, tuition and lift pass cost from around £125 to £155 for five days. These prices are for adults; prices for juniors are less.

Information

Details for each of the five resorts, including phone numbers, are given in the appropriate place in the main text. For further general information contact the **Scottish Tourist Board** for its Ski Scotland brochure and accommodation list, or visit their website, www.ski.scotland.net, which is updated daily. Or you can contact the **Scottish National Ski Council**.

The Ski hotline weather-report service gives the latest snow and weather conditions plus a five-day forecast: T0891-654 followed by 655 for Cairngorm; 656 for Glenshee; 657 for The Lecht; 658 for Glencoe; 660 for Nevis Range; and 659 for cross country skiing.

Surfing

Scotland has some of the best surfing beaches in Europe. But this is no Hawaii, with its sunbleached hair and bronzed bodies: surfing in Scotland is strictly for the hardy, with water temperatures rarely above 15°C and often as low as 7°C. A good wetsuit is therefore essential. The waves, though, make up for the freezing waters and compare with those in Hawaii and Australia. The main season is September to December.

The best beaches on the West Coast are to be found at the northern tip of the Isle of Lewis and at Machrihanish, down near the Mull of Kintyre. On the north coast the top spot is Thurso, especially at Dunnet Head to the east of town. Another recommended place is Strathy Bay, near Bettyhill, halfway between Thurso and Tongue. There is a bi-monthly surf magazine, *Surf*, which is a good source of information. Also try the surf shops, which sell equipment and provide information on the best breaks. Useful websites, www.sas.org.uk and www.hebrideansurf.co.uk.

Wildlife watching

Almost anywhere around the northern coasts of Scotland there is a chance to see bottlenose dolphins, white-beaked dolphins, Risso's dolphins, common dolphins, white-sided dolphins, pilot whales, minke whales, porpoises, seals and, occasionally Orcas (killer whales). The best places to see **dolphins** (bottlenose) are at Cromarty and Chanonry Point, both on the Moray Firth. Other good places to catch glimpses of bottlenose and other dolphins, as well as porpoises and minke whales, are the westerly tip of Ardnamurchan (page 201), Neist Point on Skye (page 259), Gairloch and Rubha Reidh lighthouse (page 215), Stoer Head (page 225), Handa island (page 226), Cape Wrath (page 232), Strathy Point (page 233), Dunnet Head (page 234), Duncansby Head (page 235), Lybster (page 244), Brora and Golspie (page 243) and Tarbat Ness (page 292). The Dolphin Centre at North Kessock, near Inverness (see page 237) has more information on where to see dolphins and seals locally. Generally speaking, the best time to see the various species of marine mammals (cetaceans) is late summer, from late July to early September. The Hebridean Whale and Dolphin Trust promotes a greater understanding of marine mammals off the west coast of Scotland, see page 146 for details, or contact the Sea Watch Foundation, www.seawatchfoundation.org.uk. Also contact the local Ranger Services: Caithness T01847-821531; Sutherland T01571-844654; Wester Ross T01854-633350; Skye and Lochalsh T01471-822905; Lochaber T01397-705922; Inverness and Nairn T01463-724260.

Seals can be seen in abundance. They can often be observed lolling about on sandbanks when the tide is out, and there are plenty of seal-spotting boat trips on offer from spring to autumn. **Otters** are more elusive. They tend to live on undisturbed remote stretches of the seashore or quiet areas of a river. If you are determined to spot the creatures, contact **Skye Environmental Centre,** home to the International **Otter Survival Fund,** T01471-822487 for further information.

Scotland is great for **birdwatching**. Over 450 species have been recorded, including vast colonies of seabirds, birds of prey and many rare species. Among the best places in Scotland to see birds are Handa Island off the coast of Sutherland, and the Treshnish Islands, off Mull, where you'll see colonies of shags, razorbills, guillemots and puffins. Details of how to get there are given in the relevant sections. Another excellent place for birdwatching is Loch Garten by Boat of Garten, where you can see ospreys. Many of the Hebridean islands, such as Islay and Mull, are home to a rich variety of seabirds and you can also see golden eagles. Orkney and Shetland are famous for their rich variety of birdlife and are home to large colonies of seabirds and migratory birds. There are puffins, kittiwakes, fulmars, shags, razorbills, guillemots and even auks.

Useful organizations

Birdwatching **Royal Society for the Protection of Birds**, 17 Regent Terr, Edinburgh EH7 5BT, T0131-5573136.
Scottish Ornithologists Club, 21 Regent Terr, Edinburgh EH7 5BT, T0131- 5566042.
Scottish Wildlife Trust, Cramond House, Cramond Glebe Rd, Edinburgh EH4 6NS, T0131-3127765, which owns and runs over 100 nature reserves.
Canoeing **Scottish Canoe Association**, Caledonia House, South Gyle, Edinburgh EH12 9DQ, T0131-3177314, www.scot-canoe.org. Organizes tours including introductory ones.
Splash Rafting, Aberfeldy, splashraft@ compuserve.com.
Canyoning **Nae Limits**, T0771-8918275, www.nae-limits.com, in Blairgowrie, Perthshire has half-day canyoning for £35 and the Tyrolean Traverse for £25.
Vertical Descents, T01855-821593, www.activities-scotland.com, 8 miles south of Fort William has 2 hrs canyoning for £30.
Climbing **Mountaineering Council of Scotland**, The Old Granary, West Mill St, Perth, T01738-638227, www.mountaineer ing-scotland.org.uk.
Cycling **Cyclists' Touring Club (CTC)**, Cotterell House, 69 Meadrow, Godalming, Surrey GU7 3HS, T01483-417217, www.ctc.org.uk, is the largest cycling organization in the UK, providing a wide range of services and information on transport, cycle hire and routes including day rides and longer tours.
Scottish Cyclists' Union (SCU), The Velodrome, Meadowbank Stadium, London Rd, Edinburgh EH7 6AY, T0131-6520187, www.btinternet.com/~scottish.cycling,

produces an annual handbook and calendar of events for road racing, time trialling and mountain biking.
SUSTRANS, 53 Cochrane St, Glasgow G1 1HL, T0141-5720234, www.sustrans.co.uk, provides information on new cycle trails.
Diving **The Puffin Dive Centre**, see p115, is the UK's most comprehensive diving facility and runs intensive PADI courses.
Scottish Sub Aqua Club, 40 Bogmoor Pl, Glasgow, G51 47Q, T0141-4251021.
Fishing **Scottish Federation of Sea Anglers**, Brian Burn, Flat 2, 16 Bellevue Rd, Ayr, KA7 2SA, T01292-264735.
Scottish National Anglers Association, David Wilkie, Administration Office, Caledonia House, South Gyle, Edinburgh EH12 9DQ, T0131-3398808.
General **Forestry Commission**, 231 Corstorphine Rd, Edinburgh EH12 7AT, T0131-3340303.
Forestry Enterprise, 21 Church St, Inverness, IV1 1EL, T01463-232811, will provide information on Scotland's extensive network of forest trails for walking or cycling.
John Muir Trust, 41 Commercial St, Edinburgh EH6 6JD, T0131-5540114.
National Trust for Scotland (NTS), 26-31 Charlotte Sq, Edinburgh EH2 4ET, T0131-2439300, www.nts.org.uk.
Scottish Natural Heritage, 12 Hope Terr, Edinburgh EH9 2AS, T0131-4474784, www.snh.org.uk.
Scottish Rights of Way Society www.scotways.com.
Scottish Tourist Board Central Information Department, 23 Ravelston Terr, Edinburgh EH4 3EU, T0131-3322433, www.visitscotland.com; and 19 Cockspur St, London SW1 5BL, T020-7930 2812.

Woodland Trust, Glenruthven Mill, Abbey Rd, Auchterarder, Perthshire PH3 1DP.

Horse riding British Horse Society Scotland, Woodburn Farm, Crieff, T01764-656334.

Trekking and Riding Society of Scotland (TRRS), Horse Trials Office, Blair Atholl, Perthshire, T01796-481543.

Kitesurfing Wild Diamond, T01879-220399, www.tireewindsurfing.com, offers a 2-day introductory course costing £120, which includes equipment, insurance and transfers to and from the island. Accommodation is extra.

The Wind Wizard, Glasgow, T0141-332 8407, www.windspells.com, runs courses.

Paragliding Flying Fever, Isle of Arran, www.flyingfever.net, offers a tandem flight for £45, or elementary pilot's course for £295 for 4-5 days. Chief instructor Zabdi Keen was a former Scotland female champion.

Skiing Scottish National Ski Council, T0131-3177280, www.snsc.demon.co.uk. They produce the useful *Snowsport Scotland Handbook*.

Surfing British Surfing Association, Champions Yard, Causewayhead, Penzance, Cornwall, T01736-360250.

Scottish Surfing Federation is being re-vamped, in the meantime, contact Andrew Bain of Surf Thurso, T01847-841300. Good shops include:

Boardwise, 1146 Argyle St, Glasgow, T0141-3345559;

Clan Surf, 45 Hyndland St, Partick, Glasgow, T0141-3396523;

Granite Reef, 45 Justice St, Aberdeen, T01224-621193; and

Momentum, 22 Bruntsfield Pl, Edinburgh, T0131-2296665.

Whitewater rafting Monster **Activities**, T01809-501340, www.monsteractivities. com, run trips on a dam-released river near Fort William.

Freespirits, the Riverside Inn, Grandtully, by Pitlochry, T01887-840400, www.freespirits.co.uk, daily 0930-1630, prices range from £25-35 for a half-day trip.

Spectator sports

Football

Football (soccer) is Scotland's most popular spectator sport. The Scottish Football League, established in 1874, is the main competition, with three divisions of 10 teams and one of 12. Scottish football is dominated, and always has been, by the two main Glasgow teams, **Rangers** and **Celtic**, known collectively as the 'Old Firm', who regularly attract crowds of over 50,000. For a brief period in the 1980s this stranglehold was broken by **Aberdeen** and **Dundee United**, but events since have proved this an aberration rather than a trend. Money is the main reason for this and the Old Firm have seemingly endless pots of the stuff, which is why they have been able to fill their team with expensive foreign imports and win most of the domestic competitions. Though neither side has fared too well in European competition in recent years, Celtic were the first British side to win the **European Cup**, in 1967.

Scotland's top 12 teams make up the **Premier League**, which has become a battle between the big two for the championship. Teams in the lower divisions mostly exist on a shoestring budget, though the other major competition, the **Scottish FA Cup**, still throws up occasional upsets, such as Celtic's defeat at the hands of Inverness Caledonian Thistle in 1999. The domestic football season runs from early August to mid-May. Most matches are played on Saturdays at 1500, and there are often games through the week, on Tuesday and Wednesday evenings at 1930. There is usually a match on a Sunday afternoon, which is broadcast live on satellite TV. Tickets range from £10 up to £20 for big games.

The national team play at the recently renovated Hampden Park in Glasgow. Their passionate supporters, known as the 'Tartan Army', have gained something of an international reputation for their fun-loving attitude and self-deprecating humour in the face of defeat. This has stood them in good stead over the years for, despite qualifying for most **World Cup Finals** since 1974, Scotland have never managed to reach the second round, failing against such footballing giants as Iran and Costa Rica along the way. The patience of the Tartan Army has been severely tested, however, in recent times as the national side have struggled to a 2-2 with the Faroe Islands and, most recently, a dire 1-1 draw with Moldova (yes, it's a real country). This latter debacle led to the resignation of boss, Bertie Vogts.

Rugby Union

Rugby is one of the major sports of the country but lags a long, long way behind football in terms of popularity. The national team plays at Murrayfield in Edinburgh, and during match weekends there's always a great atmosphere in the city. Every year, in February and March, Scotland takes part in the **Six Nations Championship**, along with the other home teams, plus France and Italy. The most important game, though, is the clash with the 'Auld enemy', England. Tickets for games are hard to come by, but you can contact the **Scottish Rugby Union (SRU)**, T0131-3465000, for details of upcoming home fixtures and where to find tickets.

The game in Scotland has been in a state of disarray ever since the advent of professionalism and the national side's performances in the 2004 Six Nations championship were nothing short of a joke. Things can only get better. The club rugby season runs from September to May.

Shinty

Shinty (or *camanachd* in Gaelic) is an amateur sport similar to Ireland's hurling. It's a physical game played at a fast and furious pace, and is a bit like hockey, but with more blood. The game is played mostly in the Highlands, and the highlight of the season is the **Camanachd Cup Final**, which attracts a large crowd and is televised on STV.

Health

No vaccinations are required for entry into Britain. Citizens of EU countries are entitled to free medical treatment at National Health Service hospitals on production of an E111 form. Note that from 2005 all E111 forms will be issued on an individual not family basis and that old E111 forms are only valid until 31 December 2004 and need to be replaced. During 2005, the UK will be adopting the European Health Insurance Card, issued to those who apply for the new E111 form. See also the Department of Health website, www.dh.gov.uk/travellers. Also, Australia, New Zealand and several other non-EU European countries have reciprocal health-care arrangements with Britain.

Medical emergency: dial T999 or T112 (both free) for an ambulance.

Citizens of other countries will have to pay for all medical services, except accident and emergency care given at Accident and Emergency (A&E) Units at most (but not all) National Health hospitals. Health insurance is therefore strongly advised for citizens of non-EU countries.

Pharmacists can dispense only a limited range of drugs without a doctor's prescription. Most are open for normal shop hours, though some are open late, especially in larger towns. Local newspapers will carry lists of which are open late. Doctors' surgeries are usually open from around 0830-0900 till 1730-1800, though times vary. Outside surgery hours you can go to the casualty department of the local hospital for any complaint requiring urgent attention. For the address of the nearest hospital or doctors' surgery, T0800-665544. See also individual town and city directories throughout the book for details local medical services.

You should encounter no major problems or irritations during your visit to Scotland. The only exceptions are the risk of hypothermia if you're walking in the mountains in difficult conditions, see page 56, and the dreaded midge, see box page 63.

Small but effective

The major problem facing visitors to the Highlands and Islands of Scotland during the summer months is *Culicoides Impunctatus* – or the midge, as It's more commonly known. These tiny flying creatures are savage and merciless in the extreme and hunt in huge packs. No sooner have you left your B&B for a pleasant evening stroll, than a cloud of these bloodthirsty little devils will descend, getting into your eyes, ears, nose and mouth – and a few places you forgot you even had. The only way to avoid them is to take refuge indoors, or to hide in the nearest loch.

Midges are at their worst in the evening and in damp, shaded or overcast conditions, and between late May and September, but they don't like direct sunlight, heavy rain, smoke and wind. Make sure you're well covered up and wear light-coloured clothing (they're attracted to dark colours). Most effective is a midge net, if you don't mind everyone pointing and laughing at you. Insect repellents have some effect, particularly those with DEET, but herbal remedies such as bog myrtle, lavender, citronella or eucalyptus are considered equally effective. Once you've been attacked the best treatments are antihistamine creams or dock leaves – and don't scratch the bites!

Keeping in touch

Communications

Internet

It is now de rigeur amongst travellers to get an email address you can access through the internet, such as hotmail or yahoo. Even in the Highlands of Scotland, internet access is extensive. Every major town now has at least one internet café, with more springing up daily. Email works out much, much cheaper than phoning home and is also useful for booking hotels and tours and for checking out information on the web. Many hotels now have internet and many hostels also offer internet access to their guests. Websites and email addresses are listed where appropriate in this guide. The Scottish Tourist Board and area tourist boards have their own websites and these are given on page 22. Cybercafés are also listed under each relevant section. In the absence of any cybercafés listed under a particular town try the public library for internet access or ask at the tourist office.

Post

Most post offices are open Monday-Friday 0900 to 1730 and Saturday 0900 to 1230 or 1300. Smaller sub-post offices are closed for an hour at lunch (1300-1400) and many of them operate out of a shop. Post offices keep the same half-day closing times as shops.

Stamps can be bought at post offices, but also from vending machines outside, and also at many newsagents. A first-class letter to anywhere in the UK costs 27p and should arrive the following day, while second-class letters cost 19p and take between two to four days. Airmail letters of less than 20g cost 37p to Europe. To the USA and Australia costs 45p for 10g and 65p for 20g. For more information about Royal Mail postal services, call To8457-740740 or www.royalmail.com.

Most public payphones are operated by British Telecom (BT) and are fairly widespread in towns and cities, though less so in rural areas. BT payphones take either coins (20p, 50p and £1) or phonecards, which are available at newsagents and post offices displaying the BT logo. These cards come in denominations of £2, £3, £5 and £10. Some payphones also accept credit cards.

⁑ Useful numbers include: operator T100, international operator T155; directory enquiries T192; overseas directory enquiries T153.

For most countries (including Europe, USA and Canada) calls are cheapest between 1800 and 0800 Monday-Friday and all day Saturday and Sunday. For Australia and New Zealand it's cheapest to call from 1430 to 1930 and from midnight to 0700 every day. Area codes are not needed if calling from within the same area. Any number prefixed by 0800 or 0500 is free to the caller; 08457 numbers are charged at local rates and 08705 numbers at the national rate. To call Scotland from overseas, dial 011 from USA and Canada, 0011 from Australia and 00 from New Zealand, followed by 44, then the area code, minus the first zero, then the number. To call overseas from Scotland dial 00 followed by the country code. Country codes include: Australia 61; Ireland 353; New Zealand 64; South Africa 27; USA and Canada 1.

Media

Newspapers and magazines

The main British daily and Sunday newspapers are widely available in Scotland and some of them publish special Scottish editions, among them the *Scottish Daily Mail*, *Scottish Daily Express* and Rupert Murdoch's notorious scandal sheet, *The Sun*.

The Scottish press produces two main 'quality' newspapers, *The Scotsman*, published in Edinburgh, and *The Herald*, published in Glasgow, which is the oldest daily newspaper in the English-speaking world, dating from 1783. The biggest-selling daily is the *Daily Record*, a tabloid paper (or red top as they are known). The Sunday equivalents of the dailies are *Scotland on Sunday* from the Scotsman stable, the *Sunday Herald* and the *Sunday Mail*, published by the Daily Record. *The Sunday Post*, published by DC Thomson's in Dundee, is also widely read. Provincial newspapers are widely read in Scotland. The main Highlands varieties are the weekly *Oban Times* and the radical, crusading *West Highland Free Press* published on Skye.

TV and radio

There are five main television channels in Scotland; the publicly funded BBC 1 and 2, and the independent commercial stations, Channel 4, Channel 5 and ITV. The ITV network in Scotland is formed by STV, which serves central Scotland and parts of the West Highlands, as well as the Aberdeen-based Grampian TV which produces a lot of Gaelic programmes.

The BBC network also broadcasts several radio channels, most of which are based in London. These include: Radio 1 aimed at a young audience; Radio 2 targeting a more mature audience; Radio 3 which plays mostly classical music; Radio 4 which is talk-based and features arts, drama and current affairs; and Radio 5 Live which is a mix of sport and news. Radio Scotland (92-95FM, 810MW) provides a Scottish-based diet of news, sport, current affairs, travel and music. It also provides a Gaelic network in the northwest, and local programmes in Orkney and Shetland. There are also a large number of local commercial radio stations, stretching from Shetland in the north to the Borders.

Central Highlands

⁞ Footprint features

Introduction

The vast swathe of Central Highlands is not a distinct region but rather the sum of disparate parts of other regions, including Perthshire, the Trossachs, Angus Glens, Deeside, Don Valley, the Grampians, Speyside, Strathspey and Loch Lomond .

The historically important regions of Perthshire and Stirling straddle the Highland Boundary Fault, the dividing line between the heavily-populated Central Lowlands and the wild and empty Highlands. Just across this 'border' is the Trossachs, a picture-postcard area of mountains, forests and lochs that stretches west from Callander to the eastern shore of Loch Lomond, and the glens of Perthshire, whose atmospheric lochs and mountains are rich in history.

The spectacular and varied landscape ranges from the gentle pleasures of Loch Tay to the rugged peaks of the Grampian Mountains, where there are Munros aplenty for the bagging and decent winter skiing. On the eastern shores of Loch Lomond, is the West Highland Way, Scotland's most popular long-distance hike. In the northeast, in the Spey Valley, are the tasty staples of a Highland tourist diet – whisky and salmon – while, nearby stand many of Scotland's most notable castles, one of which is the holiday home of the most famous family in the UK.

★ Don't Miss...

1 **Glen Lyon** Take a picnic to this glorious glen and try, if you can, to imagine a more perfect place, page 75.

2 **Duke's Pass** Travel the road from Aberfoyle to Callander, and capture the special appeal of the Trossachs, page 81.

3 **Monachyle Mhor Hotel** Perfect peace, perfect views and food to dine for, page 84.

4 **Drover's Inn** Spend an evening in the archetypal Highland watering hole sampling the finest single malts, page 85.

5 **Boat of Garten** Catch a glimpse of the elusive ospreys, Britain's most famous bird of prey, page 100.

Perthshire

*Perth is the main gateway to the eastern side of the Highlands and the A9, the road
north, is a gentle introduction to the wild northern reaches of Scotland. The Perthshire
Highlands may lack the sheer magisterial grandeur of the northwest but they have
their own serene beauty. Numerous remnants from the highland's troubled past are
scattered around the glens of Perthshire, including Blair Castle and Scone Palace.*
▸▸ *For Sleeping, Eating and all other listings, see pages 76-79.*

Ins and outs

Getting there Perth is accessible from almost anywhere in the country. It's only
1½ hours from Edinburgh or Glasgow, and half an hour from Dundee by road, and is
on the main train lines to these cities, as well as on the main lines north to Aberdeen
and Inverness. ▸▸ *For further details, see Transport page 78.*

Getting around Though the more remote northerly parts of Perthshire are difficult
to reach by public transport, much of the region is easily accessible. The main road
north to Inverness, the A9, runs through the heart of the region. Dunkeld and Pitlochry
are on the Perth-Inverness rail line and there are several daily trains to Perth. Strathtay
Scottish, T01382-228054, run hourly buses (less frequently on Sunday) from Perth to
Blairgowrie and Glenshee on the A93.

Tourist information The region, from Kinross in the south to Blair Atholl in the north
and from Glenshee in the east to Rannoch Moor in the west, is covered by the
Perthshire Tourist Board ① *www.perthshire.co.uk*, with tourist offices in Aberfeldy,
Auchterarder, Blairgowrie, Crieff, Dunkeld, Kinross, Perth and Pitlochry.

Perth and around → *Phone code: 01738. Colour map 4, grid B-C3. Population: 48,000.*

'The Fair City' of Perth is aptly named. Situated on the banks of Scotland's longest
river, the Tay, Perth and its surrounding area boasts some of the most beautiful
scenery in the country. Perth was once the capital of Scotland, and there are many
interesting sights to visit. The jewel in Perth's crown, though, is undoubtedly Scone
(pronounced 'scoon') Palace, on the outskirts of town. Scone was the home of the
Stone of Destiny for nearly 500 years, and the site where every Scottish king was
crowned. The city is also well-placed for other outdoor activities such as walking,
cycling and skiing. ▸▸ *For Sleeping, Eating and other listings, see pages 76-79.*

Ins and outs

Getting around The train and bus stations are almost opposite each other at the
west end of town, where Leonard Street meets Kings Place. The town centre is very
compact and it's easy to get around on foot, but Scone Palace and many of the B&Bs
are on the eastern bank of the river, so you may wish to take a bus. Local buses are
run by **Stagecoach**, T01738-629339. An enjoyable way to see the sights is to use the
Guide Friday bus tour of Perth. Tour tickets are valid all day, so you can get on and off
as often as you please and you can join the tour at various locations throughout the
city. For more details, T0131-5562244, or contact the tourist office.

Tourist information **Perth TIC** ① *Lower City Mills, West Mill St, T01738-450600.
Apr-Jun, Sep and Oct Mon-Sat 0900-1730, Sun 1100-1600, Jul and Aug Mon-Sat
0900-1830, Sun 1100-1700, Nov-Mar Mon-Sat 0900-1600.*

A few minutes' walk north of the High Street, on North Port, is the **Fair Maid's House**, the fictional home of Sir Walter Scott's virginal heroine in his novel, *The Fair Maid of Perth*. Close by, at the corner of Charlotte Street and George Street, is the **Museum and Art Gallery** ① *T01738-632488, Mon-Sat 1000-1700, free*, with displays on local history, art, archaeology, natural history and whisky.

In the 18th century the world-famous Black Watch regiment was raised in Perth, and the **Black Watch Museum** ① *T0131-3108530, May-Sep Mon-Sat 1000-1630, closed last Sat in Jun, Oct-Apr Mon-Fri 1000-1530, free*, housed in the 15th-century Balhousie Castle, is well worth a visit even to the most un-military minded. The museum is on Hay Street, on the edge of the North Inch, to the north of the town centre. Back in the town centre, in West Mill Street is Lower City Mills (also home to the tourist office), a restored and working 19th-century oatmeal mill powered by a huge water wheel (closed to visitors at the time of writing). Perth's other museum contains the excellent **Fergusson Gallery** ① *T01738-441944, Mon-Sat 1000-1700,*

Perth

Sleeping 🛏
Achnacarry Guest House 2
Kinnaird Guest House 1
Quality Station 3

Sunbank House 5
SYHA Youth Hostal 4

Eating 🍴
Let's Eat Again 4

Let's Eat Bistro 5
No 63 6
Seafood Restaurant 8

free, a display of works by the renowned Scottish colourist, John Duncan Fergusson. The gallery is found at the south end of Tay Street, near South Inch, in a splendid neo-classical building which was once Perth's waterworks.

For those with more horticultural leanings, **Branklyn Garden** ① *116 Dundee Rd, T01738-625535 (NTS), Mar-Oct daily 0930-sunset, £5, £3.75 concession*, has been described as "the finest two acres of private garden in the country". With an impressive collection of rare and unusual plants, it includes superb examples of Himalayan poppies. Well worth a visit at any time of year, many of the plants grown there are on sale in the shop.

Kinnoull Hill Woodland Park is a beautiful wooded area on the outskirts of the city. The trip to the top of Kinnoull Hill (783 ft) itself affords an astounding view across Perth, down to the Tay estuary and through Fife to the Lomond hills. To the north, the views stretch from Ben More in the west to Lochnagar in the northeast. There are four walks through the Woodland Park – Nature Walk, Tower Walk, Jubilee Walk and Squirrel Walk – and each of these is graded according to how difficult it is and what type of conditions the walker can expect. However, none of the walks are extremely strenuous, though the Squirrel Walk is most suitable for the less able. If you're feeling particularly energetic, cycling and horse riding take place in specific zones in the park, principally in the Deuchny Wood area. There is a Countryside Ranger Service in the park and they will be happy to answer any questions you may have about their work or the park itself. Also ask at the tourist office in town for details.

Huntingtower Castle ① *T01738-627231 (HS) Apr-Sep daily 0930-1830, Oct- Mar Mon-Wed and Sat 0930-1630, Thu 0930-1200, Sun 1400-1630, closed Fri, £2.50, £1.90 concession*, three miles west of Perth on the A85 to Crieff, is also worth a visit. It consists of two complete towers dating from the 15th and 16th centuries, linked by a 17th-century range, and features some fine 16th-century painted ceilings. The castle, once owned by the Ruthven family, has some interesting history of its own. Prior to the building of the range, a daughter of the house once leapt between the two towers to avoid being caught in her lover's bedroom.

Scone Palace

① *T01738-552300, www.scone-palace.net, 1 Apr-31 Oct 0930-1730 (last admission 1645), £6.75, £5.70 concession, £3.80 children, grounds only £3.40/£2.80/£2.*

A few miles outside Perth on the A93 Braemar Road, is the unmissable Scone Palace, one of the most historically important places in the country. The home of the Earls of Mansfield, Scone has a long and fascinating history. It was the capital of the Pictish Kingdom in the sixth century and home of the Celtic church. Here, Kenneth MacAlpin united Scotland, and in AD 838, placed the stone of Scone (or 'Stone of Destiny') on Moot Hill, opposite the palace entrance. This became the ancient crowning place of Scottish kings, including Macbeth and Robert the Bruce. The Royal City of Scone became the seat of government, and the kings of Scotland resided at the Palace of Scone before their coronations. The coronation stone was removed to Westminster by that most hated foe, Edward I, in 1296, and only recently returned to Scotland in a desperate, but failed, Conservative attempt to win back support north of the border. The famed stone currently resides in Edinburgh Castle. In 1651, the last coronation in Scotland took place when King Charles II was crowned by the Scots on the Moot Hill. The ceremony was attended by Lord Stormont, forefather of the present occupier, Lord Mansfield. Part of the church where this took place still remains.

❋ *Though historically important, much of the present palace building only dates from the 19th century.*

Aside from its impressive history, the palace also houses beautiful collections of porcelain, needlework, royal furniture, clocks, ivories and many other absorbing artefacts. You could also spend a few hours walking in the magnificent 100-acre gardens, filled with bluebells, rhododendrons, roses and rare trees, with strutting

peacocks and Highland cattle roaming around. There's also a maze, picnic park and   71
children's adventure playground, plus a gift shop and coffee shop with delicious
home baking.

Dunkeld and Birnam

Twelve miles north of Perth is the attractive village of **Dunkeld**, standing right on the
Highland line. It's definitely worth making a stop here, if only to admire the **cathedral**
ⓘ *Apr-Sep 0930-1830, free*, in the most idyllic situation on the banks of the
fast-flowing, silvery Tay. Half of it is still in use as a church and the other half is in
ruins. The oldest part of the cathedral is the 14th-century choir, which now forms the
parish church, while the 15th-century nave and tower are also still standing. Much of
the original was damaged during the orgy of ecclesiastical destruction that
accompanied the Reformation. It was damaged again in the Battle of Dunkeld in
1689, fought between supporters of the protestant William of Orange and the Stuart
monarch James VII. Dunkeld offers excellent walking opportunities, details of which
are available from the TIC at The Cross ⓘ *T01350-727688*.

Across the bridge from Dunkeld is **Birnam**, made famous in Shakespeare's
Macbeth. Birnam was the inspiration for another famous literary figure, **Beatrix
Potter**, who spent her childhood summers here. Visitors can explore the origins of the
Peter Rabbit stories at the **Beatrix Potter Exhibition** ⓘ *daily 1000-1700, free*.

▲▲ A short distance north of Dunkeld on the A9 is the turning to **The Hermitage**.
A marked woodland walk starts from the car park and follows the river Braan to the
Black Linn Falls, overlooked by Ossian's Hall, an 18th-century folly built by the Duke of
Atholl. It's a lovely spot, which has inspired the likes of Wordsworth and
Mendelssohn. Further on is Ossian's Cave. Buses to Pitlochry stop at the turning for
The Hermitage.

A few miles northeast of Dunkeld, off the A923 to Blairgowrie, is the **Loch of the
Lowes Visitor Centre** ⓘ *Apr-Sep daily 1000-1700, free but donation advised*,
managed by the Scottish Wildlife Trust. There's a hide with binoculars for viewing a
pair of ospreys which breed here and which can be seen on the loch from early April
to early September.

Pitlochry and around → *Phone code: 01796. Colour map 4, grid B2-3.*

Despite being one of the busiest Highland tourist towns in the summer, Pitlochry's
setting on the shores of the River Tummel, overlooked by Ben y Vrackie, makes it a
pleasant enough base for exploring the area, especially out of season. The town also
has a few attractions of its own. ▶▶ *For Sleeping, Eating and other listings, see pages 76-79.*

Sights

Pitlochry's main attraction is the **fish ladder**, part of the power station and dam which
formed man-made **Loch Faskally** when it was constructed on the River Tummel. The
ladder allows salmon to swim up to their spawning grounds and you can watch them
leaping spectacularly in the spring and summer. The best months are May and June.
The fish ladder is across the river, a short distance from the **Pitlochry Festival Theatre**,
see Entertainment page 78.

Also here is **Scottish Plant Collector's Gardens** ⓘ *T01796-484626, www.scottish
plantcollectorsgardens.com, Apr-Oct Mon-Sat 1000-1700, Sun 1100-1700, £3, £2.50
concession, £1 child*. Scotland's newest public garden features a programme of visual
arts, sculpture, music and drama throughout the summer.

There are two excellent whisky distilleries to visit. The larger of the two is Bell's
Blair Atholl Distillery ⓘ *T01796-482003, www.malts.com, Easter-Sep Mon-Sat
0930-1700, Sun 1200-1700, Oct Mon-Fri 1000-1600, Nov-Easter Mon-Fri 1300-1600,*

tours every 20 mins, £4, redeemable in shop, at the southern end of town, heading towards the A9 to Perth. A couple of miles east of town, on the A924, is the **Edradour Distillery** ① *T01796-T472095, www.edradour.com, Jan and Feb Mon-Sat 1000-1600, Sun 1200-1600, Mar-Oct Mon-Sat 0930-1800, Sun 1130-1700, Nov and Dec Mon-Sat 0930-1700, Sun 1200-1700, free*, the smallest in Scotland, which can be a blessing or a curse, depending on how busy it is.

▲ The tourist office sells a useful leaflet *Pitlochry Walks* which describes four long local walks, and there are many other fine walks in the surrounding area. The greatest walking attraction is **Ben y Vrackie** (2,758 ft), a steep six-mile walk (there and back) from the tiny hamlet of Moulin, a mile north of Pitlochry on the A924 (turn left at the **Moulin Inn**). The path is well trodden and the going is relatively easy, across bleak moorland, until the steep final ascent on scree. On a clear day the views from the summit of the Trossachs are wonderful, and it's best not to attempt this on a cloudy day. In spite of its proximity to Pitlochry, you need to be properly equipped and take the usual safety precautions, see page 56.

OS Landranger maps Nos 43 and 52 cover all the walks, and the OS Explorer map No 21 (Pitlochry and Loch Tummel) covers them in greater detail.

Another excellent walk from Pitlochry, described in the tourist office leaflet, leaves town on the north road and turns left past the boat station. It then crosses the Cluanie footbridge and follows the road to Loch Faskally and up the River Garry to Garry Bridge over the Pass of Killiecrankie, see below. The path returns to Pitlochry along the west bank of the River Garry, before turning west up the River Tummel, passing close by the Linn of Tummel, then crossing the Tummel and following the west shore of Loch Faskally to the dam and fish ladder.

Pass of Killiecrankie

Four miles north of Pitlochry the A9 cuts through the Pass of Killiecrankie, a spectacular wooded gorge which was the dramatic setting for the Battle of Killiecrankie in 1689, when a Jacobite army led by Graham of Claverhouse, Viscount 'Bonnie Dundee', defeated the government forces under General Hugh Mackay. One government soldier allegedly evaded capture by making a jump of Olympic gold medal-winning proportions across the River Garry at **Soldier's Leap**. The NTS visitor centre ① *T01796-473233, Apr-Oct daily 1000-1730, free (honesty box £1 donation advised)*, has displays on the battle and the local natural history.

▲ A three-mile waymarked trail around the **RSPB Killiecrankie Nature Reserve** starts from the Balrobbie Farm car park. Follow the signs for the reserve from Killiecrankie village, take the minor road over the River Garry, then take the left fork up a steep hill. Turn right at the sharp bend into the farm car park. Access to the reserve is free, but there's a cairn for donations and a parking charge.

Head down the driveway, then turn right along the road which climbs uphill below wooded crags. Turn right through as gate, opposite a cottage and follow a grassy track to a gate in a stone wall. Through the gate, the path climbs diagonally under the crags to an iron gate beside a bench. Go through the gate and the path zigzags steeply up to an area of open marsh. The path curves right and continues to climb across a heather moor and past a ruin.

At the crest of the hill, from where there are wonderful views down to Blair Atholl, go downhill, over a stile and enter woodland. Beyond the trees is another bench, then the trail turns to the right. After another two stiles the path heads left downhill, then zigzags down a rocky slope, before heading diagonally downhill to the right to an iron gate. Pick up the path again by a stone wall and follow it back to the car park.

Blair Castle

① T01796-481207, Apr-Oct 1000-1800 (0930 in Jul and Aug), house and grounds £6.25, grounds only £2.

Seven miles from Pitlochry, and a mile from the village of Blair Atholl, is Blair Castle, the traditional seat of the Earls and Dukes of Atholl. This whitewashed, turreted castle dates from 1269 and presents an impressive picture on first sight. This is the headquarters of Britain's only private army, the Atholl Highlanders, and one of them usually pipes in new arrivals. Thirty-two rooms in the castle are open for public viewing and are packed full of paintings, furniture, armour, porcelain and much else besides, presenting a startling picture of aristocratic Highland life in previous centuries. The surrounding landscaped grounds are home to peacocks and Highland cattle, and there are woodland walks and a walled Japanese water garden to enjoy.

▲▲ Falls of Bruar

Eight miles from Blair Atholl, just off the A9, are the Falls of Bruar. A well-maintained path leads from the lower falls along the gorge of the Bruar River to the upper falls and back down the other side. It's a 1½-mile round trip.

From the House of Bruar, turn right by the adventure playground, then left up the river bank. The path passes under a railway arch and through a kissing gate. It then heads through open forest to a rocky outcrop, from where you can see the lower falls. A series of wooden steps leads down from the outcrop, then a ricky path climbs up till it forks. Go right, then cross the bridge, from where there's a good view of the lower falls. From here a clear path leads up the far side till it reaches a deer fence. Climb up to the gate, go through it and continue uphill through trees till the path levels out high above the gorge. Further on there's a picnic area, then the path curves left down to the upper bridge, which is a great vantage point from which to admire the stunning view. The path heads left through more trees. It then crosses a stream before descending to the lower bridge and then back to the car park.

By the car park is the excellent **House of Bruar**, a huge shopping emporium designed like a Victorian hunting lodge where you can buy just about any kind of souvenir and enjoy some very fine Scottish cooking.

From Blair Atholl to Kinloch Rannoch

The B8019 turns off the B8079 road from Pitlochry to Blair Atholl and runs west along the shores of beautiful lochs Tummel and Rannoch, best seen in the autumn when the trees change their colours. At the eastern end of Loch Tummel is **Queen's View**, a spectacular viewpoint which looks down the loch and across to Schiehallion. There's a **visitor centre** ① T01796-473123, Apr-Oct daily 1000-1730, free, £1 parking charge, with displays and audio-visual programmes about the area.

▲▲ **Schiehallion** (3,547 ft) is one of Scotland's best-loved mountains, whose distinctive conical peak made it ideal for use in early experiments in 1774 to judge the weight of the earth. These were not an unqualified success, but led to the invention of contour lines as an aid to surveying the mountain. The walk to the summit is fairly straightforward, except for the very rocky final stretch. You'll need to be properly clothed and equipped and take a map and compass. The route to the summit starts at the car park on the B846 Kinloch Rannoch to Aberfeldy road, near Braes of Foss. OS sheet No 51 covers the route.

Beyond Loch Tummel is the village of **Kinloch Rannoch**, where hikers can stock up on supplies before heading into the hills. Sixteen miles west of the village the road ends at Rannoch station, for trains north to Fort William or south to Glasgow.

▲▲ Blair Atholl to Glen Fincastle walk

A lovely three-mile linear walk leads from Blair Atholl village to Glen Fincastle, passing through woodland and across moorland and pasture. Starting in the village, head

66 99 On a summer's day there can be few lovelier places on earth, as the River Lyon tumbles through corries and gorges and through flowering meadows, with high mountain peaks on either side and eagles soaring overhead...

down past the watermill and stay on the road unti it ends at the river. Then follow a path left till it takes you to a footbridge over the River Garry. Cross the footbridge and then over two stiles till you reach the main A9. Cross the road, taking care as it's usually busy, to another stile, then continue through trees to a gate with a footprint sign. On the otherside of the gate, the path zigzags up through a wood which thins out as you reach the top of the hill.

Here, the path fords a stream then continues across open moorland to the other side of the hilltop, where there's a gate. Go through the gate and follow the grassy track down to Tomanraid cottage. From here you can see down into Glen Fincastle. Before the cottage go left over a stile and then down to a gate. Through the gate, head straight along the track till you reach a junction. Go through the gate ahead and down a grassy lane to another gate. Then the path curves diagonally to the left down to a metal gate at the end of a public road. To return to Blair Atholl simply retrace your steps.

Aberfeldy and Loch Tay → *Phone code: 01887. Colour map 4, grid B2.*

The little town of Aberfeldy stands on the banks of the River Tay, on the A827 which runs between the A9 and Loch Tay. It's well placed geographically for exploring the northern part of Perthshire, though Pitlochry has better tourist facilities. The 14-mile-long Loch Tay is surrounded by some of the loveliest scenery in Perthshire and is well worth exploring. ►► *For Sleeping, Eating and other listings, see pages 76-79.*

Aberfeldy

The River Tay is spanned by Wade's Bridge, built by General Wade in 1773 during his campaign to pacify the Highlands. Also in the town, building is underway on the new Aberfeldy Watermill development, which will comprise a bookshop, art gallery, music and coffee shop, planned for opening in Spring 2005.

Dewar's World of Whisky ① *T01887-822010, www.dewars.com/worldofwhisky, Apr-end Oct Mon-Sat 1000-1800, Sun 1200-1600, Nov-Mar Mon-Fri 1000-1600, £5, concession £3, children £2.50,* just outside Aberfeldy, is one of a new breed of distillery visitor centres. The tour is always interesting, though the hard sell may not be to everyone's taste.

A mile west of Aberfeldy, across the Tay at Weem, is **Castle Menzies** ① *T01887-820982, Apr-mid Oct Mon-Sat 1030-1700, Sun 1400-1700, £3.50, £3 concession,* an impressive, restored 16th-century 'Z-plan' fortified tower house, the former seat of the chief of Clan Menzies.

▲▲ A popular local walk is to the **Falls of Moness**, through the famous **Birks of Aberfeldy**, forever associated with the poet Robert Burns who was inspired by the *birks* (birch trees) to write his eponymous song. It's a fairly easy walk along a marked trail up to the impressive falls, and the views of Strathtay and the surrounding hills on the descent also make it worthwhile. It's about four miles there and back.

At the northeast end of Loch Tay is **Kenmore,** a neat little village of whitewashed cottages dominated by a huge archway which stands at the gateway to Taymouth Castle, built by the Campbells of Glenorchy in the early 19th century and now a very fine **golf course** ① *To1887-830228*. Near the village, on the southern bank of the loch, is the excellent **Scottish Crannog Centre** ① *To1887-830583, Mar and Nov daily 1000-1600, Apr to mid-Oct 1000-1730, £4.25, concession £3.85*, an authentic reconstruction of a *crannog*, an artificial Bronze-Age island-house built for the purpose of defence.

> ‡ *Loch Tay is a major watersports centre, see Activities and tours page 78, for details.*

For those with their own transport, two of the least-known and loveliest routes in the country are at hand. The first is the spectacular road which winds its way south from Kenmore high up into the mountains, across a bleak and barren plateau and down the other side to the tiny hamlet of **Amulree**. This road is often closed in the winter and there are gates at either end. From Amulree you can continue south to Crieff (see below), through the gentler, but equally stunning scenery of the **Sma' Glen**. Alternatively, you could head north to Aberfeldy and then complete the circuit back to Kenmore.

A few miles west of Kenmore a minor road turns off the A827, which runs along the north bank of the loch, and heads to **Fortingall**, a tiny village of classic beauty which features on many a calendar. It's little more than a row of thatched cottages which wouldn't even get a mention were it not for two amazing claims. The 3,000-year-old yew tree in the churchyard is claimed to be the oldest living thing in Europe. More astonishing is the claim that this is the birthplace of **Pontius Pilate**, said to be the son of a Roman officer who was stationed here. Furthermore, it is believed that Pilate returned here to be buried, and a gravestone in the churchyard bears the initials 'PP'. If you have your own transport, make a detour up **Glen Lyon**, one of the most beautiful of all Scottish glens. On a summer's day there can be few lovelier places on earth, as the River Lyon tumbles through corries and gorges and through flowering meadows, with high mountain peaks on either side and eagles soaring overhead. It's no surprise that Wordsworth and Tennyson waxed lyrical over its qualities. The road from Fortingall runs all the way to the head of the glen, at Loch Lyon. This is walking and fishing paradise. There are several Munros to 'bag' and fishing permits are available at the **Fortingall Hotel**, see Sleeping page 76.

▲ Ben Lawers → *OS sheet No 51 covers the area.*

The highest mountain in Perthshire, Ben Lawers (3,987 ft), dominates the north side of Loch Tay. Its massif of seven summits includes six Munros which are linked by an eight-mile ridge which can be walked in one day by fit and experienced hillwalkers. The best access to the ridge is from Glen Lyon. The trek to the main summit starts from the NTS Visitor Centre, two miles along a track which turns off the main A827 about halfway between Kenmore and Killin. This track continues over a wild pass to Bridge of Balgie in Glen Lyon. Leaflets describing the climb are available from the visitor centre. It's a seven-mile walk there and back, and though the route is straightforward and easy to follow, it's a very steep, tough climb of 2,700 ft from the centre to the summit. Allow five to six hours. You should be fit, properly clothed, see page 56, and have some previous hillwalking experience, but the views from the top on a clear day are amazing, across to the North Sea in the east and the Atlantic Ocean in the west. There's also a much easier one-mile nature trail, and an accompanying booklet describing the rare Alpine flora is available at the centre.

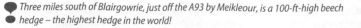
● *Three miles south of Blairgowrie, just off the A93 by Meikleour, is a 100-ft-high beech hedge – the highest hedge in the world!*

Central Scotland Perthshire

Blairgowrie and Glenshee → *Phone code: 01250. Colour map 4, grid B3.*

The other major road running north from Perth is the A93, soon reaching the respectable town of **Blairgowrie**, or Blairgowrie and Rattray to give it its full title. It lies amidst the raspberry fields of Strathmore and is conveniently placed to serve as an accommodation centre for **Glenshee Ski Centre**, see Activities and tours page 78. The **TIC** ① *26 Wellmeadow, T01250-872960, Apr-Oct daily, Nov-Easter Mon-Sat.* There's little of real interest to detain passing tourists, but **Keathbank Mill** ① *Apr to early Oct daily 1030-1700, £4.25*, off the A93 to Braemar, is worth a look. This huge 19th-century jute mill has a steam turbine dating from 1862 driven by the largest water wheel in Scotland. There's also a heraldry museum, model railway and woodcarving workshops.

The A9s continues north passing the Glenshee ski resort on its way to Braemar and then heads east through Deeside to Aberdeen.

● Sleeping

Perth and around *p68, map p69*
L Hilton Dunkeld, Dunkeld, T01796-727771, www.dunkeld.hilton.com. Luxurious former home of the Duke of Atholl, now with full leisure and outdoor activity facilities.
L Kinnaird House, Dalguise, about 8 miles north of Dunkeld via the A9 and the B898, T01796-482440. The top hotel in the area. The setting, the style, the service and the restaurant are all excellent.
A Ballathie House Hotel, Kinclaven, near Stanley, 2 miles north of Perth, just off the A9, T01250-883268, www.ballathiehouse hotel.com. 43 rooms. Pick of the bunch. This elegant, award-winning 19th-century former hunting lodge has a reputation for superb Scottish cuisine (**£££**).
B Huntingtower Hotel, T01738-583771, F583777, www.huntingtowerhotel.co.uk, 1 mile west of Perth off the A85 to Crieff, 34 rooms. Another excellent option. Elegant country house hotel in its own landscaped gardens, good food in the dining room (**££**) and bar meals in the conservatory (**£**).
B Quality Station Hotel, next to the train station, Leonard St, Perth, T01738-624141, admin@gb628-u-net.com. 70 rooms. A grand old Victorian edifice close to the town centre.
C Sunbank House Hotel, 50 Dundee Rd, Perth, T01738-624882, F442515. 9 rooms. A lovely little hotel overlooking the Tay and close to Branklyn Garden and Kinnoull Hill, great value.

D The Bridge B&B, 10 Bridge St, Dunkeld, T01796-727068, www.visitscotland.com/thebridge.
D The Pend, 5 Brae St, Dunkeld, T01796-727586, www.thepend.com, one of several B&Bs in Dunkeld.
E Achnacarry Guest House, 3 Pitcullen Cres, on the A94 Coupar Angus road, T01738-621421. Good choice on a road full of B&Bs.
E Kinnaird Guest House, 5 Marshall Pl, overlooking the South Inch, Perth, T01738-6280121, www.kinnaird-guesthouse.co.uk.
F SYHA Youth hostel, 107 Glasgow Rd, T01738-623658, open Mar-Oct, about half a mile west of the town centre (take bus No 7).
F Western Caputh Independent Hostel at Caputh, 5 miles east of Dunkeld, on the A984 to Coupar Angus, T01738-710617. It has 18 beds and is open all year.

Camping
Cleeve Caravan Park, on Glasgow Rd, near the ring road, about 2 miles from town, T01738-639521, open Apr-Oct.
Scone Palace Camping & Caravan Club Site, T01738-552308, open Apr-Oct.

Pitlochry and around *p71*
There are numerous guest houses and B&Bs in Pitlochry, far too many to list here. The tourist office will provide a full list.
B Killiecrankie Hotel, a few miles north of Pitlochry, in the village of Killiecrankie, T01796-473220, www.killiecrankiehotel.

● *For an explanation of sleeping and eating price codes used in this guide, see inside the*
● *front cover. Other relevant information is found in Essentials, see pages 41-49.*

co.uk. Open Mar-Dec. 10 rooms. It's a quiet, cosy country house hotel which offers quite possibly the very finest food in the area.

B Pine Trees Hotel, Strathview Terr, Pitlochry, T01796-472121, wwwpinetreeshotel.co.uk. The best hotel in town is this superb Victorian country house set in 10 acres of gardens away from the tourist bustle. Its **Garden Restaurant** has a fine reputation.

C Atholl Arms Hotel, near the train station in Blair Atholl village, T481205, does B&B and serves bar meals.

C Dunfallandy Country House Hotel & Restaurant, T01796-472648, dunfalhse@aol.com. A mile out of Pitlochry on the road to Logierait. 8 rooms. Top-class hotel. Georgian mansion offering great views, peace and quiet and superb cuisine, no smoking, excellent value.

D Craigroyston House, 2 Lower Oakfield, T1796-472053. Recommended guest house.

E Arrandale House, Knockfarrie Rd, Pitlochry, T1796-472987. Comfortable.

E Bunrannoch House, Kinloch Rannoch, T01882-632407, www.bunrannoch.co.uk, a former Victorian shooting lodge which offers good cooking.

E Craigatin House & Courtyard, 165 Atholl Rd, Pitlochry, T1796-472478. Good value.

F SYHA Youth Hostel, T1796-472308, on Knockard Rd overlooking the town centre of Pitlochry, open all year.

Aberfeldy and Loch Tay *p74*

L-A Farleyer House Hotel, Weem, a mile west from Aberfeldy, T01887-820332, 100127.222@compuserve.com. Best of the hotels around town. Magnificent 15th-century building.

B Guinach House, Aberfeldy, T01887-820251. Family-run country house in a lovely setting by the Birks, with a superb restaurant (**£££**).

C Ailean Chraggan, Weem, a mile or so west from Aberfeldy, T01887-820346. Serves very good food in the bar (**££**).

C Kenmore Hotel, Kenmore, T01887-830205. Claims to be Scotland's oldest coaching inn, dating from 1572. Whether or not this is true, there's no denying that it's full of character and very comfortable. Excellent food is to be had in the lovely bar (**££**).

C Weem Hotel T01887-820381, in Weem, about a mile west of Aberfeldy on the B846 to Strathtummel. Very friendly welcome.

D Fortingall Hotel, next to the churchyard in Fortingall, T01887-830367, hotel@fortingall.com. Wonderful and very popular.

E Tigh'N'Eilean Guest House, Taybridge Dr, Aberfeldy, T01887-820109. Recommended.

🍴 Eating

Perth and around *p68, map p69*

££ Let's Eat Bistro, Kinnoull St, T01738-643377. Tue-Sat 1200-1400, 1830-2130. Very classy establishment which provides a modern Scottish menu with Mediterranean influences, all meals cooked fresh to order. Sister restaurant, **Let's Eat Again**, 33 George St, is open till 2145.

££ No. 63, 63 Tay St, T01738-441451. Tue-Sat 1200-1400, 1830-2100. Swish restaurant down by the river. Serves contemporary Scottish food.

££ The Seafood Restaurant, 168 South St, T01738-449777. Specializes in fish and game.

Pitlochry and around *p71*

£££ East Haugh Country House Hotel & Restaurant, a couple of miles south of Pitlochry on the old A9 road, T01796-473121, www.easthaugh.com. A 17th century country house with excellent and elegant dining and great bar lunches.

£££ Killiecrankie Hotel, see Sleeping, is expensive but the best place to eat. The bar is less formal and cheaper than the restaurant.

£££ Loft, Golf Course Rd, Blair Atholl, T01796-481377, www.theloftrestaurant.co.uk. The best food hereabouts. Superior Modern Scottish/Mediterranean food.

££ Port-na-Craig Inn & Restaurant, T01796-472777, just below the Festival Theatre on the banks of the River Tummel. It offers great Scottish cooking with a bistro ambience.

£ Moulin Inn, a few miles north of Pitlochry, at Moulin on the A924, T01796-472196, www.moulin.u-net.com. Food daily till 2130. Serves good, cheap pub food and fine real ales (try their 'Braveheart') with a great atmosphere.

☻ Entertainment

Perth and around *p68, map p69*
Perth Theatre, 185 High St, Perth,
T01738-621031, is a beautiful Victorian-era
theatre with an excellent reputation for
high-class productions.
Playhouse, 6 Murray St, Perth, T01738-
623126, offers a dose of escapism on the
big screen.

Pitlochry and around *p71*
Pitlochry Festival Theatre, T01796-
484626, is across the river from the
town centre. It stages a different play
every night 6 nights a week from
May to Oct.

❀ Festivals and events

Perth and around *p68, map p69*
Aug Perth Highland Games are held on the
second Sun in Aug, on the same weekend
as the **Perth Show**, which takes place on
South Inch.

▲ Activities and tours

Perth and around *p68, map p69*
Fishing Sandyknowes fly-fishery at
Bridge of Earn, T01738-813033, a few
miles southeast of Perth. Located between
the rivers Earn and Tay, there are facilities
for the novice, right up to the most
experienced angler with great fishing in
a beautiful landscape. The season runs
from Mar-Dec and currently costs £10 per
day. Details of all the Perthshire fisheries
are available from the TIC.
Horse racing Perth Racecourse, near
Scone Palace, T01738-551597, has regular
jump racing events during the summer.
Leisure centres Bell's Sports Centre,
Hay St, T01738-622301, daily 0900-2200,
covers virtually every sport and leisure
activity imaginable.
Dewar's Rinks, next door to the pool,
T01738-624188, where the visitor can curl,
ice skate or bowl.
Perth Leisure Pool, T01738-492410,
open daily 1000-2200, west of the town
centre on the Glasgow Rd, claims to have
the best leisure swimming pool in Scotland.

Pitlochry and around *p71*
Cycling Atholl Mountain Bikes, Blair
Atholl, 01796-T473553, have a leaflet listing
various cycle routes, including the Glen Tilt
route above.
Escape Route, 8 West Moulin Rd, Pitlochry,
T/F01796-473859. Touring and off-road
bikes for £14 per day.

Aberfeldy and Loch Tay *p74*
Croft-Na-Caber, near the Crannog Centre,
Kenmore, T01887-830588, Scotland's best
watersports and activities centre, where you
can try water-skiing, windsurfing, sailing,
rafting, jet biking, river sledging, fishing,
parascending, clay-pigeon shooting, walking
and Nordic skiing.
Loch Tay Boating Centre, Kenmore,
T01887-830291, open Apr-Oct, hires
speedboats, fishing boats and canoes, as
well as bicycles.

Blairgowrie and Glenshee *p76*
Glenshee ski centre, T01339-741320,
www.ski.scotland.net, is at the crest of the
Cairnwell Pass (2,199 ft), the highest main
road pass in Britain. It is the most extensive
skiing area in Scotland, with 38 pistes, as well
as Nordic skiing. Ski rental is £13 per day (£12
for snowboards) and lessons £18 for 4 hrs. A
1-day lift pass costs £18, or £72 for 5 days,
including tuition and hire. For the latest
weather conditions, call the **Ski Hotline**
T0900-1-654656.

☻ Transport

Perth and around *p68, map p69*
Stagecoach run local buses to **Dunkeld**,
Pitlochry, **Aberfeldy** and **Crieff**; and
Strathtay Scottish (T01382-228054) buses
serve **Blairgowrie** (via Dunkeld), **Alyth** and
Dundee. Citylink buses between Perth and
Inverness stop at the train station by **Birnam**
several times daily in either direction.
Scottish Citylink buses, T08705-505050, run
frequently to **Glasgow** (1 hr 25 mins),
Edinburgh (1½ hrs), **Dundee** (35 mins),
Aberdeen (2½ hrs) and **Inverness** (2½ hrs).
Arnold Clark, St Leonard's Bank, Perth,
T01738-442202, hires cars.
There are also hourly trains to **Stirling** (30
mins), **Dundee** (25 mins) and **Aberdeen**
(1 hr 40 mins), and several daily to **Inverness**

via **Pitlochry** (30 mins) and **Aviemore**. There's an hourly train service (Mon-Sat; 2-hourly on Sun) to **Glasgow Queen St** (1 hr); and frequent trains to **Edinburgh** (1 hr 20 mins).

Pitlochry and around *p71*
From Pitlochry not all trains stop at Blair Atholl. Elizabeth Yule Transport, T01796-472290, runs a service between Pitlochry and **Blair Atholl**, via Killiecrankie, a few times daily, except Sun. See also section above.

Blairgowrie and Glenshee *p76*
The only public transport to the ski resort is a daily postbus service (Mon-Sat only) from **Blairgowrie** to **Spittal of Glenshee**, or from **Braemar** and **Ballater**.

The Trossachs and Loch Lomond

Strictly speaking, the Trossachs is the narrow wooded glen between Loch Katrine and Loch Achray, but the name is now used to describe a much larger area between Argyll and Perthshire, stretching north from the Campsies and west from Callander to the eastern shore of Loch Lomond. It's a very beautiful and diverse area of sparkling lochs, craggy mountains and deep, forested glens, and for this reason is often called the 'Highlands in miniature', best visited in the autumn when the hills are purple and the trees are a thousand luminous hues, from lustrous gold to flaming scarlet and blazing orange. The Trossachs was one of the country's first holiday regions, and remains a major tourist destination. Its enduring appeal is due in no small measure to Sir Walter Scott, who eulogized its great natural beauty in his epic poem, Lady of the Lake, *and whose historical novel,* Rob Roy, *brought to public attention the region's other great attraction, Rob Roy MacGregor, one of the great romantic Highland figures.*

West of the Trossachs is Loch Lomond, Britain's largest inland waterway, measuring 22 miles long and at certain points up to five miles wide. Its once 'bonnie' banks are now one of the busiest parts of the Highlands, due to their proximity to Glasgow (only 20 miles south along the congested A82). During the summer the western shore in particular becomes a playground for day-trippers who tear up and down the loch in speedboats and on jet skis, obliterating any notion visitors may have of a little peace and quiet. The eastern shores are altogether less hectic and form part of the new Loch Lomond National Park, the first to be established in the country. ▶ *For Sleeping, Eating and other listings, see pages 83-86.*

Ins and outs

Getting there There are regular buses from Stirling to Aberfoyle and Callander, T0870-6082608. There are also daily services to Aberfoyle from Glasgow, via Balfron. There's a Scottish Citylink service once daily in summer between Edinburgh and Fort William which stops in Callander. There's a postbus service, T01752-494527, www.royalmail.com/postbus, from Aberfoyle to Inversnaid on Loch Lomond. A postbus leaves Callander daily, except Sunday, at 0915 to Trossachs Pier and connects with cruises on Loch Katrine, see page 81. There's also a postbus during the week in the afternoons between Callander and Aberfoyle, via Port of Menteith. ▶ *For further details, see Transport page 85.*

Getting around The Trossachs Trundler is a bus which makes a circuit of the Trossachs, linking Stirling, Callander, Aberfoyle and Port of Menteith, and stopping off at various scenic places en route. It also connects with departures of the *SS Sir Walter Scott* on Loch Katrine. It runs from June to September except Wednesdays and costs £8 for a day ticket. Contact the local TIC for details, see below.

Central Scotland The Trossachs and Loch Lomond

Tourist information **Aberfoyle TIC** ① *on the main st, To1877-382352, Apr-Jun, Sep and Oct daily 1000-1700, Jul and Aug 0930-1900, weekends only Nov-Mar.* **Callander TIC** ① *Ancaster Sq, To1877-330342, Mar-May and Oct-Dec daily 1000-1700, Jun 0930-1800, Jul and Aug 0900-2000, Sep 1000-1800, Jan and Feb weekends only 1000-1600*, shares the same building as the Rob Roy and Trossachs Visitor Centre. **Loch Lomond Shores** ① *To1389-721500*, is a large visitor centre and orientation centre as you come into town, which operates as the gateway to the National Park. At the 100-acre site you can see a film celebrating the area in addition to shops, restaurants and the restored steamer *Maid of the Loch*. **Tarbet TIC** ① *To1301-702260, Apr-Oct.*

The Trossachs → *Phone code: 01877. Colour map 4, grid C1-2.*

▲▲ Walking in the Trossachs → *OS Landranger maps 56 and 57 covers these routes.*

The Trossachs is superb walking country. The two most challenging peaks are Ben Venue and Ben A'an around Loch Katrine and Loch Achray, about 10 miles west of Callander. **Ben Venue** (2,385 ft) is the more difficult climb. It starts from behind the **Loch Achray Hotel** and is waymarked, but it's a strenuous climb which requires hillwalking experience, proper clothing and all the usual safety precautions. Allow about five hours for the return trip. **Ben A'an** (1,520 ft) isn't a giant of a hill, but it's a steep climb from the start, from the car park of the former **Trossachs Hotel** (now a timeshare development) on the north bank of Loch Achray, and there's a bit of scrambling involved near the summit. It takes about 1½ hours to the top. The views from both hills are stupendous on clear days, but remember that the weather is as unpredictable in the Trossach mountains as anywhere else in the Highlands. A useful guide is Collins' *Walk Loch Lomond and the Trossachs*.

Both these mountains lie within the **Queen Elizabeth Forest Park**. This vast and spectacular wilderness of 75,000 acres borders Loch Lomond to the west and incorporates Loch Ard, Loch Achray and Loch Lubnaig, as well as Ben Venue, Ben A'An and **Ben Ledi**, which overlooks Callander. The park is run by the Forestry Commission and is criss-crossed by a network of less difficult waymarked trails and paths which start from the **Queen Elizabeth Park Visitor Centre** ① *To1877-382258, Mar-Oct daily 1000-1800, Oct-Dec 1100-1600 (parking £1)*, about half a mile north of Aberfoyle on the A821. Available at the centre are audio-visual displays on the park's flora and fauna and information on the numerous walks and cycle routes around the park. Full details of the park are available from the Forest Enterprise in Aberfoyle.

Aberfoyle

The sleepy village of Aberfoyle suddenly bursts into life in the summer with the arrival of hordes of tourists. It lies on the edge of the Queen Elizabeth Forest Park and, along with Callander to the east, is one of the main tourist centres for the Trossachs. It makes an ideal base for walking and cycling in the surrounding hills. There's plentiful accommodation, though you'll have to book during the busy summer season.

Three miles east of Aberfoyle is the **Lake of Menteith**, the only lake in Scotland (as opposed to loch). On **Inchmahome Island** in the middle of the lake are the beautiful and substantial ruins of **Inchmahome Priory** ① *To1877-385294 (HS), Apr-Sep Mon-Sun 0930-1830, £3.30, £2.60 concession*, the 13th-century Augustinian priory where the four-year-old Mary, Queen of Scots was sent in 1547, safe from the clutches of Henry VIII. A ferry takes visitors over to the island from **Port of Menteith**.

To the north of Aberfoyle is Doon Hill, better known as the **Fairy Knowe**. The tree at the top is said to be the home of the 'People of Quietness', and in 1692 a local minister was less than discreet in telling the world of their secrets. As punishment he was taken away to fairyland, and his spirit has languished there ever since. If you go

Better red than dead

As the tourist board never tires of reminding us, the Trossachs is Rob Roy country. Rob Roy ('Red Robert' in Gaelic) was one of Scotland's most notorious outlaws or one of the bravest Highland heroes, depending on your point of view. It is true that he was a freebooter, but he was also defending Highland clan culture and more specifically fighting for the very survival of his own clan against proscription and persecution by the government and its supporters.

Rob Roy MacGregor (1671-1734) was born in Glengyle, to the northwest of Loch Katrine. The MacGregors' lands included those previously owned by the rival Campbells but bestowed on the MacGregors for services rendered to Alexander II in his conquest of Argyll. For a long time the clan kept possession of their lands by right of the sword, but the constant attempts by neighbouring clans to displace them led to retaliation by the MacGregors and earned them a reputation for being aggressive. Rob Roy did little to change this image, and his bitter feud with the powerful Duke of Montrose led to his being outlawed and eventually captured and sentenced to transportation. He was pardoned and returned to Balquhidder, where he stayed for the rest of his life. He now lies buried in the churchyard.

The Rob Roy story was first popularized by Sir Walter Scott's eponymous 19th-century novel, and his life continues to be romanticized, most recently in the 1995 film starring Liam Neeson and Tim Roth. Like Robin Hood before him, his courage in refusing to bow to the forces of authority seems to strike a chord with people.

round the tree seven times, your wish will be granted, but go round it backwards and... well, we won't be held responsible. It's about an hour and a half up and back. Follow the road across the bridge south of the car park by the Visitor Centre, then follow the road till it forks – take the left fork, a waymarked path, to the hilltop.

Aberfoyle to Callander

The A821 route north from Aberfoyle, through the spectacular **Duke's Pass**, and then east past Loch Achray and Loch Vennachar, is one of the most beautiful routes in the country and not to be missed. There are a couple of worthwhile diversions along the way. About five miles north of Aberfoyle, a track branches to the right and runs through Achray Forest and along the shores of **Loch Drunkie**, before rejoining the A821 further north. A few miles further on, a road turns left to **Trossachs Pier** on the eastern shore of **Loch Katrine**. This is the departure point for cruises on the *SS Sir Walter Scott*, see Activities and tours page 85. In the mornings (daily except Wednesday) it sails to the remote settlement of **Stronachlachar** on the far western shores of the loch and back. In the afternoons it only sails around the loch for an hour. There's a road and cycle path around the loch as far as Stronachlachar, and you could take the morning cruise there and then cycle back to the pier. For cycle hire, see page 85.

Callander and around

Callander sits at the eastern end of the Trossachs, 14 miles northwest of Stirling, its main street totally and unashamedly devoted to tourism and lined with tearooms, restaurants and craft shops. The town is a good base for exploring the Trossachs. The overworked tourist information centre shares the same building as the **Rob Roy and Trossachs Visitor Centre** ① *Mar-May and Oct-Dec daily 1000-1700, Jun 0930-1800,*

Jul and Aug 0900-2000, Sep 1000-1800, Jan and Feb weekends only 1000-1600, £3.25, which gives an entertaining account of the life of Rob Roy MacGregor.

▲▲ A recommended local walk is to Bracklinn Falls, reached by a woodland trail which leads from Bracklinn Road. It's about 30 minutes each way. Another trail from Bracklinn Road leads up to Callander Crags, from where there are great views of the surrounding area. Allow 1½ hours there and back. The most challenging walk in the area is to the summit of Ben Ledi (2,857 ft), but it's a tough climb and you'll need to be fit, experienced and prepared

Two miles north of Callander, on the A84 route to the Highlands, are the **Falls of Leny**, in the narrow and dramatic Pass of Leny. The falls are accessible from the car park by the roadside or via the **Callander to Strathyre Cycleway**, which follows the old train line to Oban, from Callander north along the west bank of **Loch Lubnaig**. This forms part of the **Glasgow to Killin Cycleway**, which runs from the centre of Glasgow, via Balloch, Aberfoyle, Callander, Balquhidder and Lochearnhead, to Killin. This is the best way to see the Trossachs.

The A84 heads north from Callander along the east bank of Loch Lubnaig, and beyond towards **Loch Earn**. A few miles further north, a side road branches left to the tiny village of **Balquhidder**, famous as the burial place of Rob Roy. His grave in the churchyard, by his wife and two of his sons, is thankfully understated.

North of Callander to Lochearnhead and Killin

A few miles north of the turning to Balquhidder, where the A84 meets the A85 from Crieff to Crianlarich, is **Lochearnhead**, at the western tip of Loch Earn. The loch is a highly popular watersports centre, see Activities and tours page 85. Lochearnhead is also a good base for walking in the surrounding hills. In the far northwestern corner of Stirling region, just to the west of Loch Tay, is **Killin**, a pleasant little village which makes a good base for walkers wishing to explore the wild mountains and glens of the ancient district of **Breadalbane** (pronounced *Bread-albinn*). Killin's picture-postcard setting, with the beautiful **Falls of Dochart** tumbling through the centre of the village, makes it a popular destination for tourists. The **TIC** overlooks the falls ① *Mar-Oct daily*.

Twelve miles west of Killin is **Crianlarich**, at the crossroads of the A82 Glasgow-Fort William road and the A85 to Perth, and at the junction of the Glasgow to Fort William and Oban rail lines. It is a staging post on the **West Highland Way**. Six miles further north is tiny **Tyndrum**, which shot to prominence a few years ago after the discovery of gold in the surrounding hills. There's a seasonal TIC ① *Main Rd, T01838-400246, Apr-Nov daily*.

Callander

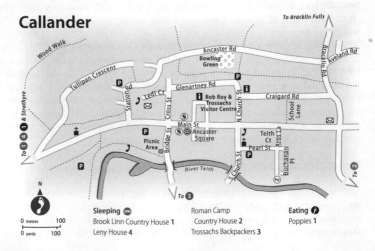

Sleeping
Brook Linn Country House 1
Leny House 4

Roman Camp
Country House 2
Trossachs Backpackers 3

Eating
Poppies 1

Loch Lomond → *Colour map 4, grid C1.*

Britain's largest inland waterway, measuring 22 miles in length and at certain points up to five miles wide, is one of Scotland's most famous lochs, thanks to the Jacobite ballad about its 'bonnie banks'. These same banks are now one of the busiest parts of the Highlands, due to their proximity to Glasgow (only 20 miles south along the congested A82). During the summer the loch becomes a playground for day-trippers who tear up and down the loch in speedboats and on jet skis, obliterating any notion visitors may have of a little peace and quiet.

At the southern end of the loch is the resort town of **Balloch**, packed full of hotels, B&Bs, caravan parks and any number of operators offering boat trips around the loch's overcrowded waters. At the northern end of the town is **Loch Lomond Shores** ① *T01389-722199, daily year round*, a huge visitor centre-cum-shopping mall, which includes the TIC and National Park Gateway Centre , as well as shops, restaurants, bars and cafés. Here you can pick up all the information you need on the national park, as well as book a loch cruise, hire bikes, kayaks or sailing dinghies, or simply enjoy the views from the Drumkinnon Tower. See Activities and tours page 85 for further information.

The west bank of the loch, from Balloch north to Tarbet, is one long, almost uninterrupted development of marinas, holiday homes, caravan parks and exclusive golf clubs. The most picturesque village here is **Luss**, though it is more of theme park than a real village. It is to the genuine Highland experience what Ozzy Osbourne is to philosophical debate. One and a half hour boat trips leave from Luss pier. Further north, things begin to quiten down a bit. At **Inverbeg**, you can take a pedestrian ferry across the loch to Rowardennan (T01360-870273 for times). North of Tarbet, at the narrow northern end of the loch, things quieten down a great deal more and the road to **Ardlui**, at its northern tip, is very beautiful and peaceful. The A82 continues north of Ardlui, past Inverarnan, to meet the A85 at **Crianlarich**.

▲▲ The tranquil east bank of Loch Lomond is a great place for walking. The **West Highland Way** follows the east bank all the way from **Drymen**, through **Balmaha**, **Rowardennan** and **Inversnaid**. Beyond Rowardennan this is the only access to the loch's east bank, except for the road to Inversnaid from the Trossachs. From Rowardennan you can climb **Ben Lomond** (3,192 ft), the most southerly of the Munros. It's not too difficult and the views from the top, in good weather, are

> ❣ *Finish off the walk to Conic Hill with a pint and a meal at the Oak Tree Inn (see Eating, page 85).*

astounding. An easier climb is **Conic Hill**, on the Highland fault line and very close to Glasgow. The route starts from the Loch Lomond Visitor Centre car park at Balmaha. It takes about 1½ hours to reach the top, from where the views of the loch are stunning.

◗ Sleeping

The Trossachs *p80*
A Lake Hotel, in Port of Menteith, on the lakeshore overlooking Inchmahome, T01877-385258, www.lake-of-menteith -hotel.com. The best place to stay in the area. It's stylish, comfortable, very romantic and boasts a fine restaurant (lunch ££; dinner £££).

A MacDonald Forest Hills Hotel, Loch Ard, on the B829 from Aberfoyle, T01877-387277, www.macdonald-hotels.co.uk. 54 rooms. Graceful 19th century country house converted into resort/hotel offering multitudinous facilities and activities such as indoor pool with sauna, steam room and fully-equipped gym, sailing courses, pony

● Loch Lomond, along with a large chunk of the Cowal Peninsula, the Campsies and the
● Trossachs, are all part of the Loch Lomond and the Trossachs National Park, which become Scotland's first National Park, as late as 2002.

Central Scotland The Trossachs and Loch Lomond *Listings*

trekking, kayaking, canoeing, windsurfing, quad biking, fly fishing, clay pigeon shooting and curling on their indoor rink. The Garden Restaurant features an unfussy menu which focuses on local produce and the staff are attentive and welcoming. Family friendly, weekend deals available off season.

A Monachyle Mhor Hotel, Balquhidder, on the road to Inverlochlarig, T01877-384622, www.monachylemhor.com. It offers great views of the loch, peace and quiet and fabulous Modern Scottish cuisine (see Eating below). Price includes dinner but you'd be crazy not to dine here anyway.

A Roman Camp Country House Hotel, Callander, T01877-330003, www.roman-camp-hotel.co.uk. An exquisite 16th-century hunting lodge set in extensive grounds by the river, away from the hoi polloi. Queen Victoria was quite taken with the place. Also serves superb Scottish cuisine (£££).

B The Four Seasons, in the village of St Fillans, a few miles east of Lochearnhead, T01764-685333, www.thefourseasonshotel.co.uk. Spectacular setting on the shores of Loch Earn, this 19th-century house, surrounded by wooded hills, also delivers on the food and service fronts.

B Leny House, Callander, T01877-331078, www.lenyestate.com. Open Apr-Oct. A 5-star B&B in the parkland of the Leny Estate.

C Creagan House, at the northern end of Loch Lubnaig, in Strathyre, T01877-384638, a family run 17th-century farmhouse offering excellent food (£££-££) and comfortable accommodation. Open Mar-Jan.

D Brook Linn Country House, Callander, T01877-330103, open Easter-Oct, a fine Victorian house overlooking the town.

D Creag-Ard House, in Milton, 2 miles west of Aberfoyle overlooking Loch Ard, T01877-382297. Lovely place with fishing and boat hire available.

D Dall Lodge Country House Hotel, Killin, T01567-820217, www.dalllodgehotel.co.uk, open Mar-Oct. The best place to stay in the village, offers idiosyncratic style and very good food.

F Trossachs Backpackers, a couple of miles out of Callander, along the Invertrossachs Rd which turns off the A81, T01877-331200, trosstel@aol.com. 30 beds, with dorms and family rooms. Relaxed and peaceful independent hostel which also rents bikes.

Camping

Cobeland Campsite, T01877-382392, open Apr-Oct, 2 miles south of Aberfoyle on the edge of the Queen Elizabeth Forest Park.
Trossachs Holiday Park, T01877-382614, open Mar-Oct. An excellent site set in 40 acres with mountain bike hire.

Loch Lomond p83

C Rowardennan Hotel, Rowardennan, T01360-870273, comfortable choice, serves bar meals.
D Inversnaid Hotel, on the northeast shore, and only accessible by road via the B829 from Aberfoyle, T01877-386223. Splendidly isolated.
F Loch Lomond SYHA Youth Hostel, Arden, T01389-850226, www.syha.org.uk Grand 19th-century turreted mansion complete with the obligatory ghost.

Camping

There's a good campsite at **Lomond Woods Holiday Park** at Tullichewan T01389-755000, on the Old Luss Rd, where you can hire mountain bikes.

● Eating

The Trossachs p80

£££ Roman Camp Hotel, Callander, see Sleeping. The best place to eat by far, simply superb.
£££ Monachyle Mhor Hotel, see Sleeping. This renowned restaurant makes stylish and imaginative use of the superb local ingredients on offer. One of the very best places to eat in the country. Lunch (££) is more affordable.
££ Braeval Old Mill, T01877-382711, a few miles east on the A873 to Port of Menteith. The best place to eat, excellent and very popular.
££ Brig O' Turk Tearoom, Brig O' Turk, Callander. Look out for the shabby green hut with peeling paint and tired-looking hanging baskets outside. Inside it's like a scout hut with higgledy-piggledy chairs and mismatching crockery and table-cloths. Wonderfully informal and very good food.
££ Byre Inn, just before Brig o' Turk, on the A821 from Aberfoyle direction, T01877-376292. A cosy bar serving good ales and hearty food, ideally placed for walkers and

cyclists. Open 1200-1430 and 1800-2300. Also has 3 rooms for B&B.

££ Poppies, Leny Rd, Callander, T01877-330329. Small, unassuming restaurant that surprises with the depth and quality of the dishes on offer, all using local ingredients.

Loch Lomond *p83*
££ Coach House Coffee Shop, Luss, T01436-860341. Huge portions of good, wholesome food and home baked goodies served to the ever-present hordes of tourists. A tad overpriced and overrated perhaps, but worth stopping for.
££ Inverbeg Inn, a few miles north of Luss, at Inverbeg, T01436-860678. Good, no-nonsense food.
££ Oak Tree Inn, Balmaha, T01360-870357. On the east side of the loch. Excellent pub food served with a touch of finesse. Try the very rare arctic char from Orkney, followed by the quite superb clootie dumpling. Has double rooms for B&B (**D**), should lunch become dinner.

⊙ Bars and clubs

Loch Lomond *p83*
Drover's Inn, Inverarnan, T01301-704234. The famous Highland watering hole, with smoke-blackened walls, low ceilings, bare floors, open fires, a hall filled with stuffed animals, barman in kilt and a great selection of single malts. The perfect place for a wild night of drinking in the wilderness. It simply doesn't get any better than this.

▲ Activities and tours

The Trossachs *p80*
Lochearnhead Watersports, T01567-830330, has water-skiing, canoeing and kayaking on the loch.
SS Sir Walter Scott, T01877-376316, www.incallander.co.uk/steam.htm, £6.80 return, concession £4.80, children under 5 free. Cruises leave from Loch Katrine daily, except Wed, Apr-Oct, at 1100, 1345 and 1515. Bikes can be taken on the 1100 cruise (book in advance), allowing you to return along the private North Shore Road. For bike hire see Transport below.

Can You Experience, T01389-602576, www.canyouexperience.com. Offers guided walks around Loch Lomond, £18 for 3 hrs, and bike rides. Canoe, kayak and pedalo hire, £10 for 30 mins, £15 for 1 hr, also available as well as guided canoe trips.
Cruise Loch Lomond, Tarbet, T01301-702356, www.cruiselochlomond ltd.com, sail from the north end of the loch at 0930, stopping on the eastern shore where you can walk part of the West Highland Way, visit a bird sanctuary or see the dramatic Arklet Falls, £6 per person.
Lomond Adventure, T01360-870218, Balmaha House, Balmaha. Canoe/kayak hire c. £20 per day, sailing in dinghys/catamarans from £35 a day, waterskiing £45 for 1hr.
Lomond Shores National Park Gateway, T08707-200631, open daily is the centre for all activities on Loch Lomond. See p83.
Sweeney's Cruises, T01389-722406, www. sweeney.uk.co, are based at **Lomond Shores** and offer a wide range of trips, starting at around £4-5 for an hour. A daily 2½-hr cruise from Balloch to Luss leaves at 1430 (£7).
Walk Wild Loch Lomond, T01360-870476, www.walkwildlochlomond.co.uk. Offer day guided walks in the National Park, pick up from Balloch or Drymen. £29 per person including lunch and possible boat trip.

⊙ Transport

The Trossachs *p80*
There are buses to **Killin** from Stirling via **Callander** (1¾ hrs). There's a postbus from **Callander** once daily Mon-Fri (1 hr), which continues to **Crianlarich** and **Tyndrum**. There's also a postbus service from **Aberfeldy**. Scottish Citylink buses, between **Glasgow** and **Oban** and **Fort William** stop in both villages. There's also a postbus service between **Crianlarich** and **Tyndrum** and **Killin** (Mon-Sat).

There are 2 train stations at **Tyndrum** and **Crianlarich**. One serves the **Glasgow** to **Oban** line and the other the **Glasgow** to **Fort William** line.

Cycle hire from **Wheels**, Invertrossachs Rd, Callander, T01887-331100. **Trossachs Cycle Hire**, at Loch Katrine, T01877-376316, Apr-Oct daily 0900-1700, £8 per ½ day, tandems and trailers available.

Central Scotland The Trossachs & Loch Lomond Listings

Scottish Citylink buses run regularly from Glasgow to **Balloch** (45 mins), and on to **Luss** and **Tarbet** (1 hr 10 mins). Some buses go to **Ardlui** (1 hr 20 mins) and on to **Crianlarich**.

There's a passenger ferry service across the loch between **Inverbeg** and **Rowardennan**, T01360-870273, 3 times daily (Apr-Sep).

There are 2 rail lines from Glasgow to **Loch Lomond**. One runs to **Balloch** every 30 mins (35 mins) the other is the West Highland line to **Fort William** and **Mallaig**, with a branch line to Oban. It reaches Loch Lomond at **Tarbet** and there's another station further north at **Ardlui**.

❶ Directory

The Trossachs *p80*
Internet DOT Computers, Main St, Callander, Mon-Sat 1000-2100, Sun 1300-2100.

Deeside → *Colour map 4, grid A4-6.*

The River Dee rises in the Cairngorms and flows down through the surrounding hills, eastwards to the sea at Aberdeen. The valley of the Dee is known as Deeside, or rather Royal Deeside, for its connections with the royal family, who have holidayed here, at Balmoral, since Queen Victoria first arrived in 1848. Originally, Queen Victoria and Prince Albert were looking for an estate further west, but were advised that the Deeside climate would be better for Albert's delicate constitution. The queen fell in love with this area and its people, and following Albert's death she sought out the company of straight-talking northerners, preferring their down-to-earth honesty to the two-faced toadies she endured at court.

Today, Deeside's royal associations have made it the tourist honeypot of the northeast, but the royal presence has also saved it from mass development. There's an air of understated affluence and refinement in the villages strung out along the A93 that runs along the north bank of the Dee and, as well as the obvious attraction of Balmoral, there are many other fine examples of baronial castles. Deeside is also a great area for various outdoor activities, such as hiking in the surrounding mountains, mountain biking, canoeing and skiing. ▶▶ *For Sleeping, Eating and other listings, see pages 90-92.*

Ins and outs

Getting there
Aberdeen airport is seven miles northwest of the city centre, at Dyce, off the A96 to Inverness. There are regular domestic flights to Scottish and UK destinations, including Orkney and Shetland, as well as international flights to several European destinations. For airport information, T01224-722331. There's car hire and currency exchange at the airport. Buses 27 run at peak times to and from the city centre (35 minutes, £1.35 single). For more information, T01224-650065. Alternatively, take a train to Dyce station and a bus or taxi from there. A taxi from the airport to Dyce railway station costs around £5, and £14 to the city centre. ▶▶ *For transport details, see page 92.*

Aberdeen is linked to Lerwick in Shetland and Kirkwall in Orkney by Northlink ferries, T0845-6000449, www.northlinkferries.co.uk. There are regular sailings from the passenger terminal in the harbour, a short walk east of the train and bus stations.

Tourist information
For details of the Castle Trail, Victorian Heritage Trail and Deeside Tourist Route, contact the TIC in Aberdeen, or in any of the towns along the way. **Banchory TIC** is in the local museum ① *Bridge St, behind the High St, Apr-late Oct,* can provide information on walking and fishing in the area. **Ballater TIC** ① *T01339-755306,*

ballater@agtb.org, daily Jan-end May 1000-1700, end May-end Sep 0900-1800, end Sep-end Dec 1000-1700, is housed in the Old Royal Station. **Braemar TIC** ① *Balmoral Mews, on Mar Rd, T01339-741600, braemar@agtb.org, daily all year, 1000-1800 end May-end Sep, closes earlier and for lunch rest of year, Sun afternoons only end Sep-end May.*

Sights

Aberdeen to Banchory → *Colour map 4, grid A5-6.*

The first sight of interest heading west from Aberdeen is **Drum Castle** ① *T01330-811204, www.drum-castle.org.uk, Apr-31 May and 1-30 Sep daily 1230-1730, 1 Jun-31 Aug daily 1000-1730, gardens same dates daily 1000-1800, grounds all year daily 0930 till dusk, castle, gardens and grounds £7, £5.25 concession, car park £2, garden and grounds only £2.50, £1.90 concession, three miles west of Peterculter (pronounced 'Petercooter').* It's a combination of a 13th-century square tower, Jacobean mansion house and later Victorian additions. It was given to one William de Irvine by Robert the Bruce for service rendered at Bannockburn and was in the family's hands for over 650 years, until it was taken over by the National Trust for Scotland in 1976. There's a beautiful walled garden and a trail through the 100-acre ancient Wood of Drum which forms part of the castle grounds.

A few miles southeast of Peterculter is its sister village, Maryculter (pronounced 'Marycooter'), where you'll find **Storybook Glen** ① *T01224-732491, www.storybook glen.aberdeen.co.uk, Mar-Oct 1000-1800, Nov-Feb 1000-1600, £3.95, children £2.95,* the northeast's answer to Disneyland. This very attractive and tasteful 'theme park' is a great place to take the kids and features giant tableaux and lifesize characters from many childhood fairy tales and nursery rhymes.

Fifteen miles west of Aberdeen, where the A93 meets the A957 from Stonehaven, is **Crathes Castle** ① *T01330-844525, castle 1 Apr-30 Sep 1030-1730, 1-31 Oct 1030-1630 (last admission to castle 45 mins before closing); licensed restaurant 1 Apr-31 Oct 1030-1730, less often rest of year; grounds and garden open all year daily 0900-dusk; gardens only £4.50, concession £3; castle and grounds combined £7, concession £5,* a perfect 'fairytale' castle built over 40 years in the mid-16th century. The turreted tower house is still furnished with many period pieces and wall hangings, and is notable for its superb painted ceilings. There are narrow spiral staircases leading to tiny rooms, one of which is said to be inhabited by an obligatory ghost. The castle is well worth exploring but is almost overshadowed by the exceptional gardens, which shouldn't be missed. There are no fewer than eight of them, so take your time. There's also a visitor centre, restaurant and shop.

Banchory to Alford → *Phone code: 01330. Colour map 4, grid A5.*

Banchory makes a very pleasant base for exploring the area, with the River Dee burbling through, but there's not a great deal to do here, apart from salmon fishing, which is popular in these parts. You can watch salmon leaping spectacularly at the Bridge of Feugh, to the south of town. There is a sad tale, though, of a lady-in-waiting who was staying at Balmoral when the royal family were in residence some years ago. She was standing fishing in the river, in quite deep water, and wearing chest-height waders, when the sovereign rode by. Seeing the king, she curtsied, whereupon the water flowed quickly into her waders and she sank beneath the water and drowned.

From Banchory head northwest on the A980 to Alford, in the Don Valley, see page 92. Roughly halfway is the village of **Lumphanan**, thought to be the burial place of Macbeth, the Scottish king so misrepresented by Shakespeare (he is actually buried on Iona). Macbeth's Cairn is instead a prehistoric cairn. Just to the south of the village is the **Peel Ring**, a 12th-century Motte, and one of Scotland's earliest medieval sites.

The attractive little village of Aboyne is 30 miles west of Banchory on the A93. A few miles further on is Dinnet. In the Muir of Dinnet National Nature Reserve you can explore the Burn o' Vat, a sheltered valley which attracts many butterflies and dragonflies. During the walk, you'll come to a huge circular stone chamber and, in nearby Loch Kinord, there are crannogs, which are ancient man-made islands.

Ballater and Balmoral → *Colour map 4, grid A4.*

The neat little town of Ballater is proud of its royal connections. You can buy meat from the butcher with his 'By Royal Appointment' sign, or clothes from royal outfitters. This is where Lizzie and Phil pop down to the shops for a pint of milk or perhaps to choose a DVD for a quiet night in. Ever since Queen Victoria first arrived by train from Aberdeen in 1848, the royal family have been spending their holidays here in their summer residence, Balmoral. She was not amused at the prospect of having an unsightly rail station on her doorstep, so the line ended eight miles east, at Ballater. The line has been closed for some time, but you can still visit the old train station, which now houses an elegant tea room.

The royals are not the only famous summer visitors. The poet **Byron** (who attended Aberdeen Grammar School) spent many childhood summer holidays at **Ballaterach**, a few miles east of Ballater. He had a narrow escape when he slipped and nearly fell into the fast flowing stream at the Linn of Dee, beyond Braemar. He was rescued just in time and went on to wax poetic about the beautiful hills which are Ballater's other great attraction. The town makes the ideal base for **hiking** (see below) as well as a number of other outdoor activities. Many of the walks set off from **Loch Muick** (pronounced 'Mick'), nine miles southwest of Ballater, at the head of Glen Muick. There's a visitor centre and car park at Spittal of Glenmuick. From here a track leads along the west shore of the loch to the lodge where Queen Victoria met John Brown. For guides and equipment for canoeing, climbing, mountain biking and skiing, contact **Adventure Scotland** in Banchory, see page 91.

Balmoral Castle → *Colour map 4, grid A4.*

ⓘ *T01339-742334, Apr to end Jul, 1000-1700, £5, concession £4, children £1.*

Eight miles west of Ballater is the area's main attraction, Balmoral Castle. The 16th-century tower house, formerly owned by the local Gordon family, was bought for Queen Victoria by Prince Albert in 1852 and converted into today's baronial mansion. It has been the royal family's summer retreat ever since. Only the ballroom and the grounds are open to the likes of you and me, and only for three months of the year. Pony trekking and pony cart rides are available around the estate grounds and are favourite ways of enjoying the wonderful scenery. Opposite the castle gates is **Crathie Church**, which is used by the family when they're in residence. There's a small souvenir shop next to the main gates and a visitor centre which gives a lot of information on the castle and its owners.

Braemar → *Colour map 4, grid A3.*

Nine miles west of Balmoral, is Braemar, the final town on Deeside, lying at the foot of the awesome, brooding **Cairngorm massif,** which dominates the Eastern Highlands. Even at the height of summer you can see a dab of snow still lying in a hollow in the surrounding mountains, and Braemar is an excellent base for hiking, see below, and winter skiing at Glenshee, see page 76. It's an attractive little place, much loved by Queen Victoria and much visited during its annual **Braemar Gathering** (or games), which attracts tens of thousands of visitors each year, amongst them members of the royal family. **Braemar Highland Heritage Centre** ⓘ *Balmoral Mews by the tourist office, T01339-741944, Apr-Sep 0900-1800 (Jul-Aug till 2000), Oct-Mar 1000-1700, free,* includes informative talks (in several languages) on the area, an exhibition and shops.

Just north of the village, and well signposted, is **Braemar Castle**① T01339-741219, *Mid-Apr to end Oct Sat-Thu 1000-1800, £3.50, concession £3, children £1,* dating from 1628. This impressive fortress was used by Hanoverian troops after the Jacobite Rising of 1745. It is L-shaped, with a star-shaped defensive wall and a central round tower with a spiral stair. There are barrel-vaulted ceilings and an underground prison. The world's largest cairngorm – a semi-precious stone, a variety of quartz, which is yellow, grey or brown in colour – weighing 52 lbs is on display in the morning room. There's also a piece of tartan worn by Prince Charles Edward, Bonnie Prince Charlie.

A very scenic side trip from Braemar is to the **Linn of Dee**, six miles west of the village, at the end of the road. Here, the river thunders through a narrow gorge to spectacular effect. There are numerous walks from here along the river, or for the more adventurous, the famous **Lairig Ghru**, which runs through the Cairngorms to Aviemore, see page 98. Between the Linn of Dee and the tiny settlement of **Inverey**, a mile to the east, there's a very basic youth hostel (open mid-May to early October), which has no phone, so book through **Braemar youth hostel**, see page 90. A postbus runs in the afternoon (Monday to Saturday) from Braemar to the Linn of Dee, via the hostel.

▲ Walks in Deeside

Ballater and Braemar are ideal bases for walking in the surrounding Grampian Mountains, and if you feel like 'bagging a Munro' (ie climbing a mountain over 3,000 ft), there are some close at hand. All of this area is included in the new Cairngorms National Park, which opened in 2003. This is the largest national park in Britain, covering a vast 4,500 sq km, from Aboyne in the east to Dalwhinnie in the west, and from Blair Atholl north to Grantown-on-Spey.

Lochnagar → *OS Landranger No 44.*
The best walk in the area is to the summit of Lochnagar (3,786 ft), made famous by Prince Charles in the book he wrote for his brothers when young, *The Old Man of Lochnagar.* The noble and mysterious mountain dominates the Royal Forest of Balmoral and takes its name from a small loch at its foot (it's also known as the White Mounth). This fine granite mass is approached from the car park by the Rangers' Visitor Centre at Spittal of Glen Muick. The path to the top is well trodden and well marked, though steep as you near the summit. It's 10 miles there and back, so allow a full day for the climb. You'll need to be properly equipped and take a map.

Cambus o' May and Morrone → *OS Landranger No 43.*
An easier walk is to Cambus o' May, on the river, about four miles east of Ballater. It's a great spot for a picnic, or to swim in the river, or to enjoy a stroll along the riverbank. A good walk from Braemar is to the summit of Morrone (2,818 ft), the mountain to the southwest. The walk takes about four hours in total.

Glen Tanar to Glen Esk → *OS Landranger No 44.*
Another good climb is the route up **Mount Keen** (3,077 ft), the most easterly Munro, which lies between Deeside and Glen Esk, the loveliest of the Angus glens. Again, you should allow a whole day for this expedition. It can be approached from the visitor centre in Glen Tanar, at the end of the little road that runs southwest off the B976, across the river from Aboyne. You can climb to the summit and return by the same route but, if your party has two cars, it is well worth walking over to Glen Esk, 14 miles away. Drive around to the Invermark car park at the head of Glen Esk and park one car there. From Glen Tanar follow the old drove road which at times runs with the Mounth road. Skirting the **Home Farm** with its Arboretum and its dammed lake, the fairly flat track winds along Glen Tanar through the forest for about four miles. Then comes the Halfway

⁝ We are most certainly amused

There has been a gathering of some sort at Braemar for 900 years, ever since Malcolm Canmore set contests for the local clans so that he could pick the strongest and bravest of men for his army. These events take place up and down the country throughout the summer, but none is as famous, or well attended, as Braemar's. Queen Victoria attended in 1848 and the Gathering is still patronized by the royal family. Crowds come from all over the world to proclaim the monarch as Chieftain of the Braemar Gathering.

At the gathering the visitor will see contests in traditional Scottish events, such as tossing the caber, Highland dancing and bagpipe competitions and displays. There is an inter-services tug o' war championship, a medley relay race and a hill race up Morrone. The sounds of the massed pipes echoing around the encircling heather-clad hills and a plethora of tartan also help to make this a real tourist highlight. The royal connection (and the crowds) apart, many other local communities hold similar games.

Hut, used for rest by former shooting parties. You pass shooting butts en route. The next stretch is through open country with the **Clachan Yell** (626 ft) on the left.

The walk proper then begins to take shape. Cross the stone bridge of **Etnach**, and then the path begins to lead up to the **Shiel of Glentanar**. The second bridge forks left and the track heads for the summit. The rough path continues along a ridge, the shoulder of Mount Keen. From the summit with its stone marker, **Dinnet**, see page 88, and its two lakes is visible to the north, and the River Esk glints its way down the valley to the south. Watch out for adders around here. On the descent, you'll pass the **Queen's Well**, used by Queen Victoria when she and her party went down to Fettercairn posing as a wedding party. The well is decorated with a graceful granite crown which was erected in 1861. The royal party covered much of the climb on hill ponies. The stone arch at Fettercairn commemorates this visit.

◉ Sleeping

Banchory p87
There are some very fine places to stay in and around Banchory.
B Banchory Lodge Hotel, T01330-822625. An excellent choice is this sporting lodge-type hotel superbly situated on the banks of the river near the town centre. It's also a great place to stop and have a bite to eat for lunch. The river runs past the lawn and you can watch the salmon leap as you perhaps enjoy the fruits of their labour.
B Raemoir House Hotel, T01330-824884, www.raemoir.com. Three miles north of town on the A980 is this wonderful country mansion set in 3,500 acres of woods and parkland with 20 rooms.
B Tor-na-Coille Hotel, T01330-822242, www.tornacoille.com, outside town on the Inchmarlo Rd. This tastefully furnished

Victorian country house hotel is set in lovely grounds and boasts a considerable reputation for its modern Scottish cooking (£££-££).
E Towerbank House, at 93 High St, T01330-824798, diane@dawps.fsnet.co.uk.
E June Little, 73 High St, T01330-824666, an excellent choice.

Camping
Silver Ladies Caravan Park, T01330-822800, at Strachan, just outside Banchory.

Ballater and Balmoral p88
There's plenty of accommodation in Ballater, from expensive hotels to reasonable B&Bs.
A Balgonie Country House Hotel, T/F01339-755482, on the western outskirts of town, off the A93. 9 rooms, open Feb-Dec.

Friendly and comfortable country house hotel, excellent food (£££).

A-B Hilton Craigendarroch, Braemar Rd, T01339-755858, www.hilton.com. 45 rooms. Victorian country house converted into a modern resort hotel with full leisure and sports facilities, 2 good restaurants.

B Darroch Learg Hotel, T01339-755443, darroch.learg@exoams.wk.com, half a mile from town, off the A93 heading west to Braemar. 18 rooms, open Feb-Dec. Pick of the bunch. Friendly country house hotel with fine views and a reputation for superb food (£££), good value.

C Deeside Hotel, set back from the A93 heading out of town towards Braemar, T01339-755420, www.deesidehotel.co.uk. Friendly, good value and good food (££).

C Glen Lui Hotel, Invercauld Rd, T01339-755402, www.glen-lui-hotel.co.uk. 19 rooms. Comfortable hotel with fine food (££-£).

C Inverdeen House, 11 Bridge Sq, T01339-755759, www.inverdeen.com. Amoung the many B&Bs, this one is recommended. French, German and Polish spoken, great breakfasts, no smoking.

D Moorside House, T/F01339-755492, on the Braemar Rd. This B&B is also good.

Camping
Anderson Road Caravan Park, T01339-755727, open Apr-Oct.

Braemar *p88*
Accommodation is hard to find before and during the Braemar Gathering, but at other times of the year there's plenty to choose from including many B&Bs and guest houses.

A-C Braemar Lodge Hotel, T01339-741627, www.braemarlodge.co.uk, on the outskirts of the village on the road south to Glenshee and Blairgowrie. This is the best choice in the area.

C Callater Lodge Hotel, Glenshee Rd, T01339-741275, www.hotel-braemar.co.uk. Small and comfortable.

C Invercauld Arms Hotel, T01339-741605. 68 rooms. Large Victorian landmark on the edge of the village.

D Clunie Lodge, T01339-741330, on Cluniebank Rd. 5 rooms, 3 en suite. Good value guesthouse with good views.

D Schiehallion House, T01339-741679, open Jan-Oct on Glenshee Rd. 6 rooms, 5 en suite. Traditional Highland welcome in this friendly house.

F Rucksacks, 15 Mar Rd, T01339-741517, a cheap and friendly bunkhouse that's popular with hikers and rents out mountain bikes.

F SYHA Youth Hostel, T01339-741659, open all year, at Corrie Feragie on Glenshee Rd.

Camping
Invercauld Caravan Site, T01339-741373, open Dec-Oct, on Glenshee Rd.

🍴 Eating

Banchory *p87*
££ Burnett Arms Hotel, High St, T01330-824944. Aside from the hotels listed above, this is the best place to eat.
££ Le Bistroquet, has a varied menu.
££ The Milton Restaurant, opposite the gates of Drum Castle, T01330-844566, serves excellent food daily till 2100 (lunch only on Sun and Mon).
£ The Shieling, a good café and gift shop.

Ballatar and Balmoral *p88*
See also Sleeping.
£££ The Green Inn, on the green in the town centre, T/F01339-755701. It boasts a well-deserved reputation as one of the very best restaurants in the region, classic Scottish cooking with an imaginative and health-conscious twist, also has 3 rooms upstairs (**C** full board).
££ La Mangiatoia, on Bridge Sq, T/F01339-755999. Serves tasty fare in its family-friendly restaurant.
££ Inver, Crathie, T01339-742345, an 18th-century inn which serves good, honest food (best to book).

Braemar *p88*
The only decent places to eat are the bars of the larger hotels, which are a bit on the expensive side.
££ Braemar Lodge serves meals 1200-1400 and 1800-2100.

⛰ Activities and tours

Deeside *p92*
Adventure Scotland, T01330-850332, dlatham@netcomuk.co.uk, is a Banchory-based company offering a wide range of

adventure activities, including white-water rafting, mountain biking, skiing and hiking. For ski rental, try the **The Braemar Ski School Hire**, in Victoria Hall on Glenshee Rd.
Glen Tanar Equestrian Centre, south of Aboyne, in Glen Tanar (see Walks), T01339-886448, offers riding in the forests and hills.

⊛ Festivals and events

Deeside *p92*
Sep Braemar games are held on the first Sat in Sep. Booking is essential and tickets can be bought in advance from the Booking Secretary, BRHS, Coilacreich, Ballater, AB35 5UH, T01339-755377, info@braemargathering.org.

⊙ Transport

Deeside *p92*
All the main tourist attractions on Deeside can be reached by bus from Aberdeen. To reach **Balmoral** by bus from Aberdeen catch the one destined for **Braemar**. Contact **Bluebird Northern**, T01224-212266, or Traveline, T0870-6082608, for information.

If you wish to explore Deeside along a less popular route (though even in the summer, crowds are never great) take the B976 along the south bank of the River Dee.

The Don Valley → *Colour map 4, grid A4-5.*

North of Royal Deeside is the lesser-known valley of the Don, Aberdeen's second river. This relatively little-visited corner of the northeast is an historian's and archaeologist's dream, littered with medieval castles, Pictish stone circles and Iron-Age hillforts. A quarter of all Britain's stone circles can be found here (if you look hard enough). Local tourist offices have free leaflets on the region's archaeological sites, with background information and details of how to find them. The main sites are included in the tourist board's 'Stone Circle Trail'. There's also a well-signposted 'Castle Trail', which includes the area's main castles. One of these castles, Corgarff, stands at the southern end of the notorious Lecht Road, which runs from Cock Bridge to Tomintoul. This area, known as The Lecht, is one of Scotland's main ski centres.
▸▸ *For Sleeping, Eating and other listings, see pages 94-95.*

Inverurie and around → *Colour map 4, grid A5.*
The solid farming town of Inverurie is 17 miles northwest of Aberdeen on the A96 to Inverness. It makes a useful base for visiting the numerous castles and ancient relics dotted around the area. The **Thainstone Mart**, south of town just off the A96, is one of the largest livestock markets in the country, and interesting if you like that sort of thing. It's held Monday, Wednesday and Friday around 1000. There's a **TIC** ① *18 High St, T01467-625800, inverurie@agtb.org, Apr-Sep.*

About six miles southwest of Inverurie, off the B993 (turn first left after the village of Kemnay), is the magnificent **Castle Fraser** ① *T01330-833463, castle Apr-end June and 1-30 Sep Fri-Tue 1200-1730, 1 Jul-31 Aug daily 1100-1730; garden and grounds all year daily 0800 till dusk, castle, garden and grounds £7 concession £5.25*, built in 1575 by the 6th Earl of Mar and similar in style to Crathes and Craigievar. The interior was remodelled in 1838 and many of the furnishings date from that period. There's a walled garden, tea room and trails through the estate.

▲ Close by, and signed off the B993, is the 4,000 year-old **Easter Aquhorthies Stone Circle**. This archaeological site is overshadowed by Bennachie (1,732 ft), by far the best hill in the area and thought to be the site of Mons Graupius, in 83 AD, when the Romans defeated the Picts. It's a straightforward two-hour walk to the summit and the views from the top are great. There are various trails, though the most commonly-used route starts from the **Bennachie Centre** ① *a mile beyond Chapel of Garioch,*

*signposted off the A96 at Pitcaple, 5 miles northwest of Inverurie, T01467-681470,
Apr-Oct Tue-Sun 1000-1700, Nov-Mar Wed-Sun 1000-1700.* Near here is the **Maiden
Stone**, a 10-ft high Pictish gravestone with relief carvings showing what looks like an
elephant, along with other creatures not normally found around these parts.

A few miles west of the turn-off to Chapel of Garioch, the B9002 heads west off the
A96 to the village of Oyne, site of the **Archaeolink Prehistory Park** ① *T01464-851500,
www.archaeolink.co.uk, Apr-Oct daily 1000-1700, £4.25, children £3.* This
state-of-the-art interpretative centre takes you on a journey back in time. It's a great
introduction to the numerous ancient sites in the area and explains why the stone
circles were built and what the various carved symbols mean. The 40-acre park
includes various interesting features such as a reconstructed Iron Age farm, Stone-Age
settlement and Roman camp, as well as a hilltop Iron-Age fort. The Archeodrome
features audio-visual presentations which bring to life the ancient history of the area.

Near the village of Daviot, north of the A96 off the B9001 from Inverurie, or via the
A920 west of Oldmeldrum, is the **Loanhead of Daviot Stone Circle**. This impressive
6,000 year-old site is 500 yards from the village and consists of two stone circles, the
smaller of which encloses a cremation cemetery dating from 1500 BC. Thirteen miles
north of Inverurie is **Fyvie Castle**, off the A947 between Oldmeldrum and Turriff.

Alford → *Colour map 4, grid A5.*

The main tourist centre on Donside is the little country town of Alford (pronounced
'Ah-ford'), 25 miles west of Aberdeen. The principal point of interest in town is the
Grampian Transport Museum ① *T01975-562292, end Mar to end Oct daily, 1000-
1700, £4, £3.10 concession, £1.60 child*, which features a comprehensive and
fascinating display of transport history, with collections of cars, buses, trams,
steam engines and some more unusual exhibits. Almost next door is the terminus
for the **Alford Valley Railway** ① *T01975-562811, steam engine runs 1st Sun of
month, diesel engine runs Apr-May and Sep Sat-Sun 1300-1700, Jun-Aug daily
1300-1700, £2, £1 child*, a narrow-gauge passenger steam railway that runs for
about a mile to Murray Park and back again (total journey time one hour). The
railway station is also where you'll find the tourist information centre
① *T01975-562052, daily Apr-Sep.* Also in town is the **Alford Heritage Centre** ① *Mart
Rd, T01975-562906, Apr-Oct Mon-Sat 1000-1700, Sun 1300-1700, £3, concession
£0.50*, which has a large display of agricultural and domestic items. Alford is close
to Lecht ski centre, see page 97, but you can ski here year round on the local dry ski
slope, **Alford Ski Centre** ① *Greystone Rd, T01975-563024.* There's also
snowboarding, instruction and equipment hire.

Craigievar Castle

① *T01339-883280, castle open mid-Apr-30 Sep Fri-Tue 1200-1730 (last admission
1645); grounds open all year daily 0930-dusk, £9, £5.25 concession.*
Six miles south of Alford is one of the northeast's most gorgeous castles, the classic
tower house of Craigievar, with its impressive turrets, balustrades and cupolas. The
castle remains much as it was when it was built in 1626 by wealthy local merchant,
William Forbes. Unfortunately, though, its popularity led to its deterioration and the
NTS now restricts entry to only a small number of visitors at a time to prevent further
damage. The castle stands in well-tended grounds.

Kildrummy Castle → *Phone code: 01975.*

① *T01975-571331. Apr-Sep daily 0930-1830. £2.20, £1.60 concession, £0.75 child.*
Six miles west of Alford, the A944 meets the A97 which heads north towards the town
of Huntly on Speyside, see page 96. A few miles south of the junction stand the
extensive and impressive ruins of Kildrummy Castle, Scotland's most complete
13th-century castle. Amongst the most infamous events in the castle's long and

bloody history was the treacherous betrayal of Robert the Bruce's family to the English during the Wars of Independence. It was the seat of the Earls of Mar and used as an HQ for the Jacobite rebellion of 1715, after which the 6th Earl of Mar ('Bobbing John') fled to exile in France and the castle fell into ruin.

Strathdon and Corgarff Castle

The tiny village of Strathdon, 10 miles southwest of Kidrummy, is famous for the **Lonach Highland Gathering**. Held on the third Saturday in August, it has a healthy blast of authenticity in comparison to the more glitzy affair in Braemar on Deeside.

Five miles west of Strathdon the A944 meets the A939 Ballater-Tomintoul road. A few miles beyond the junction is the austere **Corgarff Castle**, a 16th-century tower house, later turned into a garrison post, with an eventful and gruesome history. Here Margaret Forbes and her family were burned alive by the Gordons in 1571 during the bitter feud between the two families. In the wake of the ill-fated 1745 rebellion the government remodelled the castle, building a star-shaped defensive wall, and garrisoned 60 men to maintain order and communications in this part of the Highlands. Corgarff continued in use into the 19th century when English Redcoats were stationed here in order to prevent whisky smuggling.

Tomintoul → *Colour map 4, grid A4. Altitude: 1,600 ft.*

Beside Corgarff is the hamlet of **Cock Bridge**, standing at the end of one the most beautiful and notorious stretches of road in the country. In winter, the Tomintoul to Cock Bridge road is almost always the first road in Scotland to be blocked by snow (you have been warned!). From Cock Bridge the A939 rises steeply to the Lecht Pass (2,089 ft) before dropping dramatically to Tomintoul, the highest village in the Highlands. Tomintoul is well-placed for both the Whisky and Castle Trails. It is also the nearest settlement of any size to The Lecht, one of Scotland's top five ski resorts (see below), and it marks the end of the long-distance Speyside Way (see page 97), so is popular with walkers and skiers. The **TIC** ① *T01807-580285, tomintoul@agtb.org, Apr-end Oct*, is on the village square, as is the **Museum and Visitor Centre** ① *T01807-673701, Jun-Sep Mon-Sat 1000-1600, Oct-May Mon-Fri 1000-1600, free*, which has a display of local history, wildlife, landscape and outdoor activities. Ten miles north of Tomintoul on the B9008 is the **Glenlivet Crown Estate** ① *T01807-580283, www.crownestate.co.uk/ glenlivet*, with an extensive network of hiking paths and cycle trails, as well as lots of wildlife, including reindeer.

● Sleeping

Inverurie and around *p92*
A-B Pittodrie House Hotel, near Chapel of Garioch, T01467-681444, www.macdonald. hotels.co.uk. 27 rooms. This is best place to stay around Inverurie. A magnificent baronial mansion, it originally belonged to the Earls of Mar. The 2,000-acre estate was granted to them by Robert the Bruce for their loyalty at the Battle of Bannockburn. The opulent surroundings are matched by superb cuisine.
B Thainstone House Hotel, to the south of Inverurie off the A96, T01467-621643, is a luxurious country mansion offering excellent cuisine and leisure facilities.
D Breaslann Guest House, Old Chapel Rd, T01467-621608. One of a decent selection.

Alford *p93*
B-C Frog Marsh, Mossat, Alford, T01975-571355, www.frogmarshcafe.com. Good.
D Bydand, 18 Balfour Rd, T01975-563613. One of a selection of good B&Bs.
D Forbes Arms Hotel, a mile west, Bridge of Alford, T01975-562108, decent bar fod (**££-£**).

Kildrummy Castle *p93*
L Kildrummy Castle Hotel, T01975-571288, www.kildrummycastelhotel.co.uk. A baronial country mansion spectacularly sited set in beautiful grounds across the river from the castle ruins. One of the very best hotels in the northeast. It also has an excellent restaurant.

Corgarff Castle *p94*
F Jenny's Bothy, T01975-651449,
open all year. Just before the castle,
an old military road leads for about
a mile to this basic but wonderfully
remote bunkhouse.

Tomintoul *p94*
C Glenavon Hotel, T01807-580218.
There are a few hotels around the
main square, the nicest of which is
this option. It is also the best place for
a drink, and popular with après-skiers,
tired walkers and locals.
D Livet House, Main St, T01807-580205.
A pleasant B&B.
F SYHA Hostel, on Main St, T0870-0041152.

⊖ Transport

The Don Valley *p92*
Travelling around the Don Valley without your
own transport is not easy. There are regular
trains and buses to **Inverurie** from **Aberdeen**
and **Inverness**. Bluebird Northern, T01224-
212266, No 220 runs regularly every day from
Aberdeen to **Alford** (1¼ hrs). Bus No 219 runs
from **Alford** to **Strathdon** (Mon -Sat), but
there are few services beyond Strathdon.
There are buses to **Tomintoul** from **Keith** via
Dufftown (Tue and Sat only), from **Elgin** (Thu
) and from **Aberlour** (on schooldays, with
connection to Elgin). Call **Roberts of
Rothiemay**, T01466-711213.

Speyside → *Colour map 2, grid C3-4.*

*The River Spey is Scotland's second longest river, rising in the hills above Loch Laggan
and making its way northeast to where it debouches at Spey Bay, on the Moray Coast.
Speyside is one of Scotland's loveliest valleys and is synonymous with two of
Scotland's greatest products, salmon and whisky. The upper part, Strathspey, is
equally famous for its hiking, skiing and watersports. It is covered in the Highlands
chapter (see page 247). This section covers the lower part of the valley and comprises
the famous Malt Whisky Trail. There are more malt whisky distilleries in this small area
than in any other part of the country, including some famous brands such as Glenlivet
and Glenfiddich. However, it's not all whisky in these parts: there's also some fine
walking along the Speyside Way which runs from Spey Bay south to Tomintoul. ₩ For
Sleeping, Eating and other listings, see pages 97-98.*

Dufftown and around → *Colour map 2, grid C4.*
A good place to start your whisky tour is Dufftown, founded in 1817 by James Duff, the
fourth Earl of Fife, and the self-proclaimed 'Malt Whisky Capital of the World'. There's
more than a grain of truth in that assertion, for there are no fewer than seven working
distilleries here. This is indeed the town that was built on seven stills.

Just outside of town, on the A941 to Craigellachie, is the **Glenfiddich Distillery**, the
town's most famous distillery and one of the best known of all malt whiskies, see box,
page 100. Behind the distillery are the 13th-century ruins of **Balvenie Castle** ① *T01340-
820121, Apr-Sep daily 0930-1830, £1.80, £1.30 concession, £0.50 child*, built by
Alexander 'Black' Comyn, then added to in the 15th and 16th centuries, and visited by
Mary, Queen of Scots in 1562. Four miles north of Dufftown, at the junction of the A941
and A95, is the little village of Craigellachie, site of the Speyside Cooperage, see box,
page 100, and where you can see Thomas Telford's beautiful bridge over the River Spey.

At nearby village of **Aberlour** is the home of **Walkers Shortbread** ① *T01340-
871555*. Also here is the expensive but superb **Aberlour Distillery** ① *T01340-881249,
www.aberlour.com, tours at 1030 and 1400 Apr-Nov Mon-Sat, and 1130 and 1500 on
Sun, £7.50*. Close by is the exclusive **Macallan Distillery** ① *T01340-872280, www.the
macallan.com, tours every hour Mar-Oct Mon-Sat 0900-1530, Nov-Easter Mon-Fri,
booking essential, free (incredibly)*.

Central Scotland Speyside

About eight miles southwest of Craigellachie, on the A95 to Grantown-on-Spey, is beautiful **Ballindalloch Castle** ① *T01807-500206, Easter-Sep Sun-Fri 1030-1700. £5 entry, £4 concessions, child £2*, a mile west of the village of **Marypark**. The castle is one of the loveliest in the northeast and has been lived in continuously by its original family, the Macpherson-Grants, since 1546. It houses a fine collection of Spanish paintings and the extensive grounds are home to the famous Aberdeen-Angus herd of cattle, which have been bred here since 1860. Also in Ballindalloch is the **Glenfarclas Distillery** ① *T01807-500257, www.glenfarclas .co.uk, tours Apr-Sep Mon-Fri 1000-1700, Jun-Sep also Sat 1000-1700, Oct-Mar Mon-Fri 1000-1600, £3.50, children free*, which despite the relatively high entrance fee is a worthwhile experience.

Dufftown's Tourist Information Centre ① *clock tower, centre of the main square, T01340-820501, Apr-Oct*, has maps and information on the whisky trail.

Huntly and around → *Colour map 2, grid C5.*

Ten miles east of Dufftown is the pleasant and prosperous-looking little town of Huntly. Close to the Whisky Trail and on the main Aberdeen to Inverness train route, it makes a convenient base from which to explore this area. The town also boasts a lovely little castle all of its own. The 16th-century **Huntly Castle** ① *T01466-793191, Apr-Sep daily 0930-1830, Oct-Mar Mon-Wed and Sat 0930-1630, Thu 0930-1200, Fri and Sun 1400-1630, £3, £2.30 concession, children £1*, stands in a beautiful setting on the banks of the River Deveron, on the northern edge of town. It was built by the powerful Gordon family and is notable for its fine heraldic sculpture and inscribed stone friezes, particularly over the main door. Near the castle is the **Nordic Ski Centre** ① *T01466-794428*, the only year-round cross-country ski centre in the UK. The centre also hires out ski equipment and mountain bikes. **Huntly TIC** ① *T01466-792255, huntly@agtb.org, Apr-Oct*.

Seven miles south of town, near the village of Kennethmont, is **Leith Hall** ① *T01464-831216, Easter 1200-1700, and 1 May-30 Sep Fri-Tue 1200-1700, garden and grounds open all year daily 0930-dusk, £7, £5.25 concession, £1.90 child*, an unprepossessing mid-17th-century mansion house. The house contains the personal possessions of successive Leith lairds, most of whom saw military service overseas, but more interesting are the extensive grounds which include a six-acre garden, 18th-century stables and ice house, two ponds, a bird observation hide and countryside walks.

▲ The Tap o' Noth walk

→ *Colour map 4, grid A5. OS Landranger No 37.*

Eight miles south of Huntly on the A97 is the village of Rhynie, where you turn off for one of the best walks in the northeast. The Tap o' Noth (1,851 ft) dominates this part of rural Aberdeenshire and the panoramic views from the top make it a worthwhile climb. It's also a fairly easy walk to the conical summit, where there's a vitrified fort. The total distance is of this walk is three miles. Allow at least two hours there and back.

Start the walk from the car park at Scurdargue, a few miles west of Rhynie, off the A941. Leave the car park and head straight up the track to a gate. Go through the gate and cross some rough pasture into woodland. At the northwest corner of the wood, go through another gate and turn left onto a track. Follow this grassy track uphill beside a fence until you see another area of forestry ahead, with rough pastureland on the right. Follow the faint track across the pasture to the broad track which then climbs up

It's believed that the name, Tap o' Noth, derives from the Gaelic *taip a'nochd*, which translates as look-out top. But there's also a local legend that the hill's giant, Jack o'Noth, stole the sweetheart of his neighbour, Jack o'Bennachie. In retaliation, the cuckolded neighbour hurled a huge boulder and flattened Jack on his own hilltop.

the Tap's western slopes. Follow this all the way to the top, up the tight zigzag on the southern flank and through the eastern entry to the hillfort, into a large enclosure. On the way back down look out for a subsidiary path under the fort's western ramparts. This path descends steeply to the left, south of the main track. It then joins the main track and you can retrace your steps back to the car park.

▲ The Speyside Way

The Speyside Way follows the River Spey from its mouth at Spey Bay inland as far as Ballindalloch, then crosses high moorland to Tomintoul. The 45-mile route takes three to five days to complete. Much of it is on an old railway line and passes close to several small villages, meaning that it can easily be broken down into shorter walks. It also passes several distilleries along the way. There are plans to extend the route in the next few years, from Buckie, on the Moray coast, to Aviemore.

There is no guidebook to the Speyside Way, but OS Landranger maps Nos 28 & 36 cover the entire route. Further information and route leaflets are available from the **Moray Council Ranger Service** ① *Boat of Fiddich, Craigellachie, T01340-881266, www.moray.org/area.speyway/webpages/swhome.htm, open Easter-Oct 0900-1700.*

The Lecht → *Colour map 4, grid A5.*

① *Day ticket £15 adults, £8 for children; half-day ticket £12. There's a ski school and equipment hire at the base station, T01975-651440, thelecht@sol.co.uk. For latest snow and weather conditions call the base station, or the Ski Hotline, T09001-654657.*
The Lecht is a ski resort for all seasons. It offers dry-slope skiing throughout the year and its snowmaking facilities mean that the winter season can be extended beyond January and February. The Lecht's gentler slopes make it ideal for beginners and intermediates and the emphasis is on family skiing. There's a snowboard fun park with half pipe, log slide, gap jump and table top. However, there are also more difficult runs for the more experienced skier, and extensive off piste skiing. There's also a summer activity area with quad bikes, a tubing slope and funkarts.

● Sleeping

Dufftown and around *p95*
A Craigellachie Hotel, Craigellachie, T01340-881204, www.craigellachie.com. 25 en suite rooms. Superb country hotel offering style and comfort in spades. Best place to stay around here. Also good food.
A Minmore House Hotel, 10 miles southwest of Dufftown, in the village of Glenlivet, T01807-590378, www.minmore househotel.com, open May-end Jan. Right beside the distillery and is the former home of the owner. Recommended.
C Highlander Inn, on Victoria St, Craigellachie, T/F01340-881446. Popular and serves decent bar meals.
D Gowanbrae Guest House, Dufftown, T01340-820461, www.gowanbrae-duff town.co.uk. A good B&B.
D Tannoch Brae, Dufftown, T01340-820541, www.tannochbrae.co.uk. 6 en suite rooms. Very comfortable guest house with a reputation for fine food (**££**).

Huntly and around *p96*
C The Castle Hotel, T01466-792696, castlehot@enterprise.net. The most impressive place to stay is this former home of the Duke of Gordon, approached through the castle entrance and then over the river.
D Greenmount Guesthouse, 43 Gordon St, T01340-792482; **D New Marnoch**, 48 King St, T01340-792018; and **D Strathlene**, on MacDonald St, T01340-792664, decent B&Bs.

❶ Eating

Dufftown and around *p95*
££ A Taste of Speyside, Balvenie St, Dufftown, T01340-820860, is good choice.
££ La Faisandarie, Dufftown, T01340-821273, has a good reputation, book first.
£ The Mash Tun, 7 Broomfield Sq, Aberlour, T01340-881771. Best known for its superb real ales, but also serves pretty fine pub grub (1200-1430 and 1800-2100). Sitting on the

banks of the Spey with playground to keep the saucepan lids entertained.

Huntly and around *p96*
Auld Pit is a good pub.
Borve Brew House, Ruthven, a few miles off the A96 to Keith, good food and fine real ale.

☻ Entertainment

Dufftown and around *p95*
Commercial Hotel, T01340-820313, Church St, has ceilidhs second Thu during summer.

☻ Festivals and events

Speyside *p95*
May Spirit of Speyside Whisky Festival a celebration of 'the water of life' with various whisky-related events taking place throughout the region. For details visit www.spiritofspeyside.com.

☻ Transport

Speyside *p95*
A restored old train powered by a diesel engine runs from Dufftown to Drummuir (5 miles) and on to Keith (10 miles) on Sat and Sun, at 1330 and 1500, £6, T01340-821181.
   Bluebird Buses, T01224-212266, run a daily service from **Elgin** (No 336). There's also a service (Nos 360 & 361) which connects **Dufftown** with **Keith** and **Aberlour** (Mon-Fri). For details call WW Smith, T01542-882113.

Strathspey and the Cairngorms

One of Scotland's busiest tourist areas is Strathspey, the broad valley of the River Spey, Scotland's second longest river, which rises high in the hills above Loch Laggan and flows northeast to its mouth on the Moray Firth. The lower reaches are famous for salmon fishing and whisky and are covered in the Speyside section of this guide (see page 95), while the upper reaches attract outdoor sports enthusiasts in droves. Hemmed in between the mighty Monadhliath Mountains to the north and the magnificent Cairngorms, Britain's second highest range, to the south, this is an area which offers excellent hiking, watersports, mountain biking and above all, winter skiing. The Cairngorms were officially declared a national park in September 2003, the largest in Britain. ▸▸ *For Sleeping, Eating and other listings, see pages 102-104.*

Ins and outs

Getting there and around This part of the Highland region is easily accessible by public transport as Aviemore is one of the main hubs, with regular buses and trains to and from Inverness, Perth, Edinburgh and Glasgow. ▸▸ *For further details, see page 104.*
Tourist information **Aviemore TIC** ① *Grampian Rd, about 400 yards south of the train station, T01479-810363, Apr-Oct Mon-Fri 0900-1800, Sat 1000-1700, Sun 1000-1600, Nov-Mar Mon-Fri 0900-1700, Sat 1000-1700*, will book accommodation as well as provide free maps and leaflets on local attractions and change foreign currency. The train station, banks, restaurants and pretty much everything else are all found along Grampian Road. Buses stop here too.

Aviemore and around → *Phone code: 01479. Colour map 4, grid A3. Population: 2,500.*
The main focus of the area is the tourist resort of Aviemore, a name synonymous with winter sports. In the 1960s Aviemore was transformed from a sleepy Highland village into the jumble of concrete buildings, tacky gift shops and sprawling coach parks that it is today. The extent of the tourist tat here is so awful it makes Fort William seem charmingly understated by comparison, however it is working hard at turning itself around and was recently described as 'most improved' resort. It is certainly more pleasant than it used to be and the range of accommodation is steadily improving.

There's little of real interest in Aviemore (aside from the Strathspey Railway, see page 104). The real enjoyment lies in the surrounding mountains and forests, though there are a few interesting places close at hand. A great place for kids is the **Cairngorm Reindeer Centre** ① *Glen More Forest Park, on the road from Coylumbridge, 7 miles from Aviemore, T01479-861228, £6, children £3*, where there are guided walks to see the herd and feed them daily at 1100, and at 1430 during the summer.

Aviemore is surrounded by towering peaks, lochs, rivers and forests of native Caledonian pine which are home to rare wildlife such as pine martens, wildcats, red squirrels, ospreys and capercaillie, and Britain's only herd of wild reindeer. Most of upper Strathspey is privately owned by the Glen More Forest Park and Rothiemurchus Estate which has been in the possession of the Grant family since the 16th century, but both owners allow free access to their lands and provide generous outdoor facilities.

▲▲ An easy circular walk of about four hours around Loch an Eilean in Rothiemurchus Estate starts from the end of the side road which turns east off the B970 two miles south of Aviemore. From the car park at the end of the road head for the lochside. The route around the loch is clearly marked and it's difficult to lose your way as it follows the loch shore. It's a very pleasant walk through woodland with views of a 14th-century castle ruin on an island in the middle of the loch. You can extend the walk by around a mile by including the circuit around Loch Gamhna. The paths around Loch an Eilein are also connected with the massive network of trails around Rothiemurchus. OS Sheet 36 covers the route.

Cairngorm National Park

The area around Aviemore is only a small part of the Cairngorms National Park, whose boundaries extend from Grantown on Spey to the heads of the Angus Glens, and from Ballatar on Deeside to Loch Laggan. Scotland's second national park is also the UK's largest at 1400 sq miles. It is home to 25% of Scotland's native woodland and is a refuge for many rare plants and animals, including 25% of the Uk's threatened species. Probably the most famous of the park's wild residents is the osprey, but you'll also see golden eagles, ptarmigan, the extremely rare crossbill, red deer, red squirrel and pine marten. As well as the park's natural attractions, there are also countless outdoor activities on offer. The Cairngorms is one the UK's prime climbing and hiking areas, and there's also excellent mountain biking, watersports and winter sports such as skiing and snowboarding at three centres – Cairngorm (see page 103), the Lecht (see page 97) and Glenshee (see page 78).

▲▲ Lairig Ghru

The famous Lairig Ghru is an ancient route through the Cairngorms which passes between Ben Macdui and Braeriach. It is a very strenuous walk and only for fit and experienced hikers. An easier proposition is a 12-mile loop which leads to the start of the Lairig Ghru pass, starting from Loch Morlich.

To reach Loch Morlich take the B970 east from the southern end of Aviemore, beyond Coylumbridge. The route starts at the western end of Loch Morlich where a forestry track runs south from the road. It leads to a bridge over the River Luineag. Cross the bridge and continue along the track, keeping straight on where another track heads off left. About a mile further on, another track heads off to the right, but keep to the left fork, signposted for Rothiemurchus Lodge.

The track climbs up towards the lodge. Just before it, turn right on to a clear track which leads up to a reservoir. Soon another track heads off to the right signposted for the Lairig Ghru. Follow this path through heather moorland. The path then heads left, climbing up through open moorland to the lip of the glen. The entrance to the Lairig Ghru is straight ahead.

After about a mile, as the hills begin to encroach on either side, a rough path almost doubles back to the left. Follow this path up the slope to the gap between Creag

Whisky-a-go-go

Speyside is Scotland's most prolific whisky-producing region and the Malt Whisky Trail is a well-signposted 70-mile tour around seven of the most famous distilleries, plus the Speyside Cooperage. Most of the distilleries offer guided tours, and most (with the exception of Glenfiddich) charge an entry fee, which can then be discounted, in full or in part, from the cost of a bottle of whisky in the distillery shop. Tours also include a free dram. Those listed below are the most interesting. See also www.maltwhiskytrail.com.

Strathisla, *Keith, T01542-783044. Open Apr to Nov Mon-Sat 0930-1600, Sun 1230-1600. £4 (includes £2 discount voucher)*, is the oldest working distillery in the Highlands (1786) and perhaps the most atmospheric, in a beautiful setting on the River Isla. This is a relatively rare malt, which is also used in the better-known Chivas Regal blend.

Speyside Cooperage, *T01340-871108, all year Mon-Fri 0900-1600, £3.10, concessions £2.50, children £1.80*, is near Craigellachie, four miles north of Dufftown. You can watch the oak casks for whisky being made.

Cardhu, *T01340-872555, Jan-Mar Mon-Fri 1100-1500, Apr-Jun 1000-1700, Jul-Sep Mon-Sat 1000-1700, Sun 1200-1600, Oct Mon-Fri 1100-1600,* *Nov/Dec Mon-Fri 1100-1500, tours every 30 mins, £4*, is seven miles west of Craigellachie, at Knockando on the B9102. This lovely little distillery is now owned by United Distillers, and their fine malt is one of many used in the famous Johnnie Walker blend.

Glen Grant, *T01542-783318, Apr-Oct Mon-Sat 1000-1600, Sun 1230-1600, free*, is in Rothes, on the A941 to Elgin. This distillery tour has the added attraction of a Victorian garden and orchard, woodland walks by the burn and the rebuilt 'Dram Pavilion'.

Glenfiddich, *T01340-820373, www. glenfiddich.com, Apr to mid-Oct Mon-Sat 0930-1630 and Sun 1200-1630, mid-Oct to Mar Mon-Fri only, free*, is just north of Dufftown, on the A941. Probably the best known of all the malts and the most professionally run operation. It's the only distillery where you can see the whisky being bottled on the premises, and the only major distillery that's free, including the obligatory dram.

Glenlivet, *T01542-783220, www.the glenlivet.com, Apr-Oct, free*, is 10 miles north of Tomintoul on the B9008. This was an illicit whisky until it was licensed in 1824. The distillery was later founded in 1858 and this malt has gone on to become one of the world's favourites. It was then taken over in 1978 by Seagram's.

a' Chalamain and Creag an Leith- choin. The deep gully, the Chalamain Gap, is filled with huge boulders and requires great care when clambering through it. Beyond the gully a path leads through heather and pine saplings, dropping down to the side of a burn, then climbing up on the other side of the burn. Continue on this path, which then drops steeply down to the side of the burn. Cross the footbridge and climb the slope beyond to reach the main road. Turn left along the road to return to the start of the route.

Boat of Garten → *Phone code: 01479. Colour map 4, grid A3.*

Eight miles northeast of Aviemore is the tiny village of Boat of Garten which suddenly shot to fame when a pair of ospreys, which had disappeared from these shores, reappeared on nearby Loch Garten, two miles east of the village. Now these beautiful birds of prey have established themselves here and elsewhere and there are thought be well over 100 pairs throughout the Highlands. **Abernethy Forest RSPB Reserve** ① *T01479-821409, daily in season 1000-1800, £2.50 for non-members, on the shore* *of Loch Garten*, is best visited during the nesting season, between late April and August, when the RSPB opens an observation centre. This is the only place in the world to see Scottish crossbills. You can also see ospreys at the Rothiemurchus trout loch at Inverdruie, and maybe even on Loch Morlich and Loch Insh. The reserve is also home to several other rare species such as capercaillie, whooper swans and red squirrels. 'Caperwatch' takes place from April-mid May 0530-0800.

Carrbridge → *Phone code: 01479. Colour map 4, grid A3.*

At Carrbridge, a pleasant little village seven miles north of Aviemore, is the **Landmark Forest Heritage Park** ① *T01479-841613, Apr to mid-Jul daily 0930-1800, mid-Jul to Aug 0930-1900, Sep and Oct 0930-1800, Nov-Mar 1000-1700, £7.95, children £5.95*, a woodland theme park which combines entertainment, education and shopping. There's a raised Treetop Trail for viewing wildlife, a fire tower, maze and various nature trails and fun rides. It manages to avoid being tacky and is good fun for kids. In the village itself is the decidedly fragile-looking 18th-century **Bridge of Carr**, which is not for vertigo sufferers.

Kingussie → *Phone code: 01540. Colour map 4, grid A2. Population: 1,500.*

The quiet village of Kingussie (pronounced *King-yoosie*) lies 12 miles southwest of Aviemore and makes a pleasant alternative as a place to stay. The main attraction here is the excellent **Highland Folk Museum** ① *T01540-661307, May-Aug Mon-Fri 0930-1730, Sat and Sun 1300-1700; Apr, Sep and Oct guided tours only Mon-Fri 1030-1630, £4, concession and children £2.40*, which contains a fascinating collection of traditional highland artefacts, as well as a farming museum, an old smokehouse, a water mill and traditional Hebridean 'blackhouse'. During the summer there are also demonstrations of spinning, woodcarving and peat- fire baking.

Another worthwhile attraction is **Ruthven Barracks**, standing on a hillock across the river. This former barracks was built by the English Redcoats as part of their campaign to tame the Highlands after the first Jacobite rising in 1715. It was destroyed by the Jacobites in the wake of defeat at Culloden to prevent it from falling into enemy hands, and it was from here that Bonnie Prince Charlie sent his final order which signalled the end of his doomed cause. Access is free and the ruins are particularly attractive at night when floodlit.

At nearby Kincraig village, between Kingussie and Aviemore, is the **Highland Wildlife Park** ① *T01540-651270, Apr, May, Sep and Oct daily 1000-1800, Jun-Aug till 1900, Nov-Mar 1000-1600, park tours £7.50, concession £6, children £5*, which has a captive collection of rare native animals. Those who mourn the loss of the hit TV show, *One Man and His Dog*, will be excited at the prospect of visiting the **Working Sheepdogs Show** ① *T01540-651310, Apr-end Oct, £4, at the nearby Leault Farm*, where you can see demonstrations of dogs rounding up a flock of sheep.

The **TIC** ① *T01540-661297*, is housed in the Folk Museum and has the same opening hours.

Grantown-on-Spey → *Phone code: 01479. Colour map 4, grid A3. Population: 3,250.*

This genteel Georgian holiday town is 15 miles northeast of Aviemore and attracts the more mature tourist by the coach-load. Everything here is geared towards fishing, and anyone wishing to get kitted out in proper style should get themselves down to either **Mortimers** or **Ritchies** on the High Street. The tourist information centre ① *T01479-872773, Apr to Oct 0900-1800*, is also here.

● *Much of this area is better known to many as* Monarch of the Glen *country, where the*
● *successful BBC TV series is filmed. The fictional Glenbogle is actually Ardverikie, near Loch Laggan, but many places like Aviemore, Grantown-on-Spey, Newtonmore and Kingussie have featured in the series.*

● Sleeping

Aviemore p98

D Vermont Guest House, T01479-810470;
D Ravenscraig Guest House, T01479-810278, www.aviemoreonline.com, B&Bs both on Grampian Rd.
F Aviemore Independent Bunkhouse & Backpackers Hostel, T01479-811137, Dalfaber Rd.
F SYHA hostel, T01479-810345, Grampian Rd, near the tourist office and open all year.

Around Aviemore p98

A Corrour House Hotel, Inverdruie, 2 miles southeast of Aviemore, T01479- 810220, www.corrourhouse.co.uk, open Dec-Oct. This Victorian country house oozes charm, enjoys wonderful views and offers superb cuisine. The best choice in the area.
C Rowan Tree Restaurant & Guest House, Loch Alvie, 1½ miles south of Aviemore on the B9152, T01479-810207, enquiries@ rowantreehotel.com, open Jan-Dec. This is one of the oldest hotels in the area and offers excellent food (lunch **£**, dinner **££**).
C Lynwilg House, T01479-811685, 1 mile south of Aviemore at Lynwilg, marge@lyn wilg.co.uk. Set in a beautiful house, this charming and friendly guest house also has a reputation for good food.
C Old Minister's House, Rothiemurchus, T01479-812181, www.theoldministers house.co.uk, set in its own grounds.

Camping

Forest Enterprise site, Glenmore, T01479-861271.
Rothiemurchus Camping & Caravan Park, Coylumbridge, T01479-812800.

Boat of Garten p100

B-C Boat Hotel, T01479-831258, www.boat hotel.co.uk, offers cheap and tasty meals.
C Heathbank - The Victorian House, T01479-831234, www.heathbankhotel.co.uk, is a must for art nouveau lovers. Good food.
C Glenavon House, T01479-831213, is a lovely guest house on Kinchurdy Rd.
C Moorfield House, Deshar Rd, T01479- 8316 46, www.moorfieldhouse.com, a good choice.

Camping

Boat of Garten Caravan and Camping Park, T01479-831652.

Carrbridge p101

A-B Dalrachney Lodge Hotel, T01479-841252, www.dalrachney.co.uk. Top of the range is this stylish hotel. A former Victorian hunting lodge with a good restaurant.
D Cairn Hotel, T01479-841212, cairn.carrbrid ge@lineone.net. A comfortable option serving good-value bar meals.
F Carrbridge Bunkhouse Hostel, T01479-841250, Dalrachney House, half a mile north.

Kingussie p101

C Arden House, Newtonmore Rd, T01540-661369, www.arden-house.info. A good guest house. *= 29th = 2nd Aug*
C The Osprey Hotel, Ruthven Rd, T01540-661510, www.ospreyhotel.co.uk, is a comfortable little hotel with a very good restaurant (**£££**).
C Scot House Hotel, Newtonmore Rd, T01540-661351, www.scothouse.com, is another good choice and also offers great food (lunch **£**; dinner **££-£££**).
D Avondale House, Newtonmore Rd, T01540-661731, avondalehouse@talk21. com. Comfortable guest house.
D Glengarry, East Terrace, T01540-661386, www.scot89.freeserve.co.uk. A B&B.
D Greystones, on Acres Rd, T01540-661052, greystones@ lineone.net. Comfortable B&B.
D Homewood Lodge, Newtonmore Rd, T01540-661507, www.homewood-lodge -inkgussie.co.uk. Friendly and good value.
F Bothan Airigh Bunkhouse, T01540-661051, is at Insh, a few miles east of Ruthven Barracks on the B970.
F Kirkbeag Hostel, T01540-651298, is in Kincraig, between Kingussie and Aviemore.
F The Laird's Bothy, T01540-661334, High St, next to **Tipsy Laird** pub. A decent hostel.

Grantown-on-Spey p101

As you'd expect in such a respectable place, there's a wide range of upmarket accommo- dation and a number of very good places to eat. The best places in town are all on Woodland Terr.
L Culdearn House, Woodlands Terr, T01479-872106, www.culdearn.com. Best place to stay, offering wonderful food.
A-B Muckrach Lodge Hotel & Restaurant, a few miles southwest of town at Dulnain

Bridge, T01479-851257, www.muckrach. co.uk, is this handsome hotel, with a well-regarded restaurant.
C Ardconnell House, Woodlands Terr, T01479-872104, info@ardconnel.com. Another great choice offering excellent food.
C Auchendean Lodge Hotel, a few miles southwest of town, T01479-851347, www. auchendean.com. An elegant hotel at Dulnain Bridge with a superb restaurant.
F Speyside Backpackers, T01479-873514, an independent hostel, also known as **The Stop-Over**, at 16 The Square. Great value.

🍴 Eating

Aviemore p98
££ Old Bridge Inn, T01479-811137, on Dalfaber Rd. Apart from the hotels and guest houses listed in Sleeping, this is the best place to eat in Aviemore. A lovely old pub, it serves excellent-value food and hosts ceilidhs and Highland dinner dances in the summer months.
££ Cairngorm Hotel, T01479-810233, also has a good reputation for food locally.

Around Aviemore p98
££ Loch Insh Watersports Centre, at Kincraig, between Aviemore and Kingussie, a good lochside restaurant which doubles as a café during the day.

Kingussie p101
£££ The Cross, T01540-661166, on Tweed Mill Brae, a private drive leading off Ardbroilach Rd. This is an outstanding place to eat. Award-winning, it is expensive but it is worth it. They also have rooms (**A** for dinner, **B&B**). Open from Feb to just before Christmas, Tue-Sat.
££ Osprey Hotel and **££ Scot House Hotel** both have very good restaurants.
£ La Cafetière is a nice café.
£ Tipsy Laird pub serves good meals and real ales.

⛰ Activities and tours

Strathspey & the Cairngorms p98
Fishing
Fishing is a major pursuit in the area. You can fish for trout and salmon on the River Spey, and the Rothiemurchus Estate has trout

fishing on its stocked loch at Inverdruie, where you can hire rods. Fishing permits cost around £10-15 per day for the stocked lochs and £20-30 per day for the River Spey. They are sold at local shops such as **Speyside Sports** in Aviemore, and at **Monster Activities** which also hires out rods and tackle. **Alvie Estate**, T01540-651255, near Kingussie also hires rods.

Horse riding
Horse riding and pony trekking are on offer at various places throughout Strathspey.
Alvie Stables, Alvie, near Kincraig, T01540-651409, T0831-495397 (mob).
Carrbridge Trekking Centre, Station Rd, Carrbridge, T01479-841602.
Strathspey Highland Pony Centre, Rowanlea, Faebuie, Grantown-on-Spey, T01479-873073.

Mountain biking
Rothiemurchus and Glen More estates are great areas for this, with lots of great trails.
Bothy Bikes, Unit 7, Grampian Rd, Aviemore, T01479-810111, daily 0900-1800. Bike hire and good advice on routes is available here.
Rothiemurchus Visitor Centre (see below) at Inverdruie has maps and you can hire bikes.

Skiing
Cairngorm is Scotland's longest-established ski resort and remains Scotland's largest ski area, with 28 runs and over 20 miles of pistes. When the sun shines, the snowfall is good and the crowds are thin, it can be a very satisfying experience. The season normally runs from Jan until the snow disappears, which can be as late as Apr.
Cairngorm Ski Area, 9 miles southeast of Aviemore, above Loch Morlich in Glen More Forest Park, is reached by a frequent bus service. You can rent skis etc (£13 per day, and snowboard hire is £16) and buy a lift pass (£21 per day) from the **Day Lodge**, T01479-861261, at the foot of the ski area.
Cairngorm Mountain Railway, T01479-861261, www.cairngorm mountain.com, is a funicular railway that runs to the top of Cairn Gorm from May-Oct, 1000-1630, on demand in winter, £8.00 adult, concessions available. For more information, T01479-873535, www.cairngorms.co.uk.
Loch Morlich and Rothiemurchus Estate and around provide good cross-country

skiing if there's enough snow, though in recent years snowfall has been below average. For more information, see p58. TIC provides a free *Cairngorm Piste Map & Ride Guide* leaflet and a *Ski Scotland* brochure which lists ski schools and rental facilities.

Walking

The walks around Strathspey are covered by OS Landranger map No 36 (1:50,000 scale) or OS Outdoor Leisure Map No 3 (1:25,000 scale).

The Cairngorms provide some of Scotland's most challenging walking, with no fewer than 49 Munros and half of Britain's eight mountains over 4,000 ft (Ben MacDrui, Braeriach, Cairn Toul and Cairn Gorm). These mountains come into their own in winter, providing experienced climbers with a wide range of classic ice climbs. They should not be taken lightly. They require a high degree of fitness, experience and preparation (see p56).

The summit of **Cairn Gorm** (4,084 ft) is readily accessible as you take the mountain railway up to the **Ptarmigan Restaurant**. However the railway cannot be used to access the high mountain plateau beyond the ski area and mountain walkers may not use the railway for their return journey.

There are 50 miles of footpaths through this area, including some lovely walks through the forests. There are also ranger-led guided walks. You can find out more at the **Rothiemurchus Estate Visitor Centre**, T01479-810858, which is a mile from Aviemore along the Ski Rd. It's open daily 0900-1700 and can provide a free *Visitor Guide and Footpath Map*.

Another good area for walking is around **Glen More Forest Park**. The visitor centre, T01479-861220, near Loch Morlich, has a **Glen More Forest Guide Map** which details of local walks.

The best known of the long-distance trails is the **Lairig Ghru**, a 25-mile hike from Aviemore over the Lairig Ghru Pass to Braemar. The trail is well marked but can take at least 8 hrs and is very tough in parts, so you'll need to be properly equipped and prepared. See p99.

Watersports

In summer, the main activities are watersports, and there are 2 centres which offer sailing, canoeing and windsurfing tuition and equipment hire.

Loch Morlich Watersports Centre, T01479-861221, lochmorlichw-s@sol.co.uk, open Apr-Oct, is 3 miles east of Aviemore. **Loch Insh Watersports Centre**, T01479-651272, user@lochinsh.dial.netmedia.co.uk, open Apr-Oct, offers the same facilities, plus fishing, mountain bike hire and ski instruction on a dry ski slope.

⊖ Transport

Aviemore *p98*
There are **Scottish Citylink** buses, T0990-505050, between Aviemore and **Inverness** (45 mins), **Kingussie** (20 mins), **Pitlochry** (1¼ hrs), **Perth** (2 hrs), **Glasgow** (3½ hrs) and **Edinburgh** (3½ hrs). For **Aberdeen**, change at Inverness.

Car hire from **MacDonald's Self Drive**, 13 Muirton, T01479-811444.

There are direct trains to and from **Glasgow** and **Edinburgh** (3 hrs) and **Inverness** (40 mins). Strathspey Steam Railway, T01479-810725, www.strathspey railway.co.uk, runs between **Aviemore**, **Boat of Garten** and **Broomhill**. The station is just to the east of the main train station.

Boat of Garten *p100*
The best way to get to Boat of Garten is on the **Strathspey Steam Railway** which runs at least 5 times daily from **Aviemore**, T01479-810725. **Loch Garten** is not easy to reach without your own transport, check with TICs for tours.

Carrbridge *p101*
There are several buses daily (except Sun) to **Carrbridge** from **Inverness** and **Grantown-on-Spey** with Highland Country Buses, T01463-233371.

Kingussie *p101*
Kingussie is on the main **Inverness** to **Perth/Glasgow/Edinburgh** routes. All Perth-Inverness trains stop here and most **Citylink** buses. There's also an infrequent school bus service run by Highland Country Buses between **Kingussie**, **Aviemore**, **Newtonmore** and **Dalwhinnie**.

Grantown-on-Spey *p101*
There are several buses (Mon-Sat) between Grantown and **Aviemore** (35 mins); 2-3 buses daily (Mon-Sat) to/from **Inverness** (1¼ hrs).

Argyll & Inner Hebrides

🔹 Footprint features

Introduction

Stretching north from the Mull of Kintyre almost to Glencoe and east to the shores of Loch Lomond, the region of Argyll marks the transition from Lowland to Highland. Argyll may be Highlands-lite to some – less starkly dramatic and more lush – but it has its own special beauty. It's a region of great variety, with all the ingredients of the classic Scottish holiday: peaceful wooded glens, heather-clad mountains full of deer, lovely wee fishing ports, romantic castles and beautiful lochs. Despite its proximity to the massive Glasgow conurbation, Argyll is sparsely populated. The main tourist centre and second largest town, Oban, has only 8,000 inhabitants. Oban is also the main ferry port for Argyll's Hebridean islands.

The Inner Hebrides comprise the great swathe of islands lying off the western coast of Argyll, each with its own distinct appeal. The most accessible, and most popular, is Mull, a short ferry ride from Oban. The variety of scenery on offer is astounding and its capital, Tobermory, is the most attractive port in western Scotland. A stone's throw from Mull is tiny Iona, one of the most important religious sites in Europe, with some divine beaches. Boat trips can be made to the dramatic island of Staffa, looming out of the sea like a great cathedral and the inspiration for Mendelssohn's Hebrides Overture. Further west, windswept Coll and Tiree offer miles of unspoilt beaches and great windsurfing and, to the south, Colonsay is a stress-free zone that makes Mull seem hectic. Those who enjoy a good malt whisky should head for Islay, famed for its distilleries, while neighbouring Jura is a wild and beautiful place, perfect for some off-the-beaten-track hiking. If you're after some peace and quiet on Jura then you're in good company, for this is where George Orwell came to write 1984.

★ Don't miss...

❶ Loch Etive Take a cruise on this hidden treasure, inaccessible except by boat, page 116.

❷ Inverawe Fisheries and Smokery Sample the finest of piscine cuisine, preferably to take away for a picnic, page 118.

❸ Kilmartin Glen Explore the archaeological wonders of Argyll's very own pre-history park, page 119.

❹ Tighnabruaich Best seen at the end of a drive down the southwest coast of Cowal, with wonderful views across the Kyles of Bute, page 125.

❺ Mount Stuart Take a look around this magnificent Gothic fantasy, page 126.

❻ Staffa Take a boat to this spectacular island and witness the cathedral-like Fingal's Cave, which inspired Mendelssohn, page 139.

❼ Iona Hire a bike and explore the most spiritual, and one of the loveliest, of Hebridean islands, page 142.

❽ Jura Follow in the footsteps of George Orwell on one of Scotland's most remote islands, page 155.

Argyll & Inner Hebrides

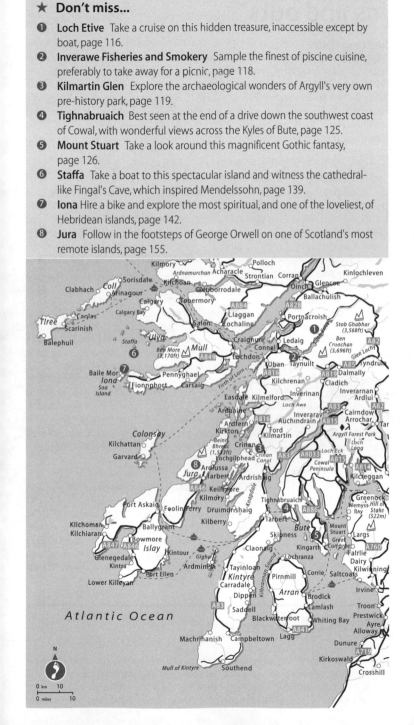

Ins and outs

Getting there

There are plenty of buses and trains from Glasgow and Fort William to Oban. For full details of bus connections contact **Scottish Citylink**, T08705-505050, or contact the TIC in Oban, T01631-563122. Bus, train and ferry times can be found in Argyll & Bute Council's free *Area Transport Guides to Lorn, Mull and Islay & Jura*, available at most tourist offices. There are flights from Glasgow to Port Ellen (Islay) and to Tiree. For full details of flight times and prices call **British Airways Express**, T08457-733377, the local TICs, or **Port Ellen airport**, T01496-302022, and Tiree airport, T01879-220309.

CalMac car and passenger ferries sail to and from Mull, Islay, Coll, Tiree, Colonsay and Gigha, and passenger-only ferries sail to Iona (and to the Small Isles, see page 270). The departure point for ferries to Mull, Coll, Tiree and Colonsay is Oban. Ferry times change according to the day of the week and time of the year. Services listed in the Transport sections for each separate island are for the summer period (2 April-16 October). For full details see the *CalMac Ferry Guide* or call **CalMac** ① *T01475-650100, www.calmac.co.uk (general enquiries)*. The departure point for ferries to Islay (and on to Jura), and some ferries to Colonsay, is Kennacraig.
▸▸ *For further details, see the relevant Transport sections: Mull, page 147; Coll, page 149; Tiree, page 149; Colonsay, page 150; Islay, page 156; Jura, page 156.*

Getting around

Most ferries to the islands and remote peninsulas are run by **CalMac**, see above for contact details. If you're planning on taking more than a couple of ferries, especially with a car, it may be more economical to buy an Island Hopscotch ticket. They can be used on a variety of route combinations and are valid for a month. They require advance planning but are better value than buying single tickets. Contact CalMac for details. During the peak summer months it's essential to book ferry tickets in advance.

Public transport is limited in much of Argyll, though the main towns are served by buses. The main bus operators are **Scottish Citylink**, T0990-505050, and **Oban & District Buses**, T01631-562856. The Oban to Glasgow rail line passes through the northern part of the region. Times of local buses and trains can be checked at local tourist offices. ▸▸ *For further details, see the relevant Transport sections, pages 115, 129, 135, 146, 149 and 156.*

Tourist information

There are TICs in Oban, Craignure and Tobermory (Mull) and Bowmore (Islay). Oban tourist office has information on all the islands covered in this chapter. Most of this chapter is covered by the **Argyll, the Isles, Loch Lomond, Stirling & Trossachs Tourist Board** ① *T01369-706085, www.scottish.heart lands.org*. The main offices, which are open all year round, are in Oban, Inveraray, Dunoon, Rothesay and Campbeltown. There are smaller seasonal offices in Lochgilphead, Tarbert, Ardgarten and Helensburgh. The island of Arran is covered by the **Ayrshire & Arran Tourist Board** ① *T01292-262555, www.ayrshire-arran.com*.

Oban and around

Oban is a busy little place: not only is it the largest port in northwest Scotland and the main departure point for ferries to the Hebrides, it is also the main tourist centre in Argyll. Not surprisingly, it gets very crowded in summer, with passing traffic and people using it as a base for exploring the region. Oban manages to avoid being

overly kitsch thanks it being a no-nonsense working port as a well as a tourist hub. It has a wide range of hotels, guest houses, B&Bs, restaurants and shops, and a number of tourist attractions, which is useful to know if you're stuck here in bad weather. The town lies in the beautiful setting of a wide, crescent-shaped bay backed by steep hills, with the island of Kerrera, just offshore, providing a natural shelter. Oban lies at the centre of the northerly part of Argyll, known as Lorn, which comprises several relatively peaceful islands including Lismore, Kerrera, Seil and Luing.
▸▸ *For Sleeping, Eating and other listings, see pages 113-116.*

Ins and outs

Getting there and around Oban is reasonably well served by buses and trains from Glasgow, Fort William and Inverness, and there are a number of west coast local bus services to and from Lochgilphead, Dalmally and Kilmartin. There are regular local buses around town and around Lorn, including to Clachan Seil, North Cuan, Isle of Luing, North Connel, Dalavich, Bonawe, and Ganavan Sands. These are mostly operated by **Oban & District Buses or Royal Mail Postbuses** ⓘ *T01463-256200.*
▸▸ *For further details, see Transport page 115.*
Tourist information Oban Tourist Information Centre ⓘ *Argyll Sq, T01631-563122, open daily all year round, hours subject to variation*, has internet access.

Oban → *Phone code: 01631. Colour map 3, grid B5.*

The town's great landmark is **McCaig's Tower**, an incongruous structure that resembles Rome's Coliseum and which dominates the skyline. The tower was built by local banker John Stuart McCaig in the late 19th century, as a means of providing work for unemployed stonemasons. Unfortunately, McCaig died before the project was complete, and to this day no one is quite sure of his intentions. There's not much to see, apart from the exterior walls, but the views of the town and bay are quite magnificent and well worth the climb up. There are various routes on foot, but the most direct is to go up Argyll Street and on the left beside the church climb the set of steps known as Jacob's Ladder, which lead to Ardonnel Terrace. Turn left here and the tower soon comes into view and is well signposted.

‡ *Don't leave town without a visit to Sweeties, a glorious, old-fashioned sweet shop with over 350 varieties to choose from, most of them hand-made in Scotland.*

Another good walk is to the ruins of **Dunollie Castle**, north of town on the Corran Esplanade towards Ganavan, from where there are also wonderful views. The castle was built on the site of an ancient stronghold of the King of Scots, and was then taken over in the 13th century by the MacDougalls, Lords of Lorn. Continue round the corner to **Ganavan Sands**, a long, safe sandy beach about 1½ miles north of the town, for a romantic west coast sunset.

If the weather's bad you can take a tour round the excellent **Oban Distillery** ⓘ *Stafford St, opposite the North Pier, T01631-572004, Easter to Jun Mon-Fri 0930-1700, Sat 0930-1700, Jul-Sep Mon-Fri 0930-1930, Sat 0930-1900, Sun 1200-1700, Oct Mon-Sat 0930-1700, Oct-Nov Mon-Fri 0930-1700, Dec-Mar Mon-Fri 1230-1700, £4.* The **War and Peace Museum** ⓘ *Mon-Sat 1000-1600, 1900-2100, free,* is also worth a look. It tells the story of Oban's role in the Second World War through a number of old photos and memorabilia and is staffed by enthusiastic volunteers.

Dunstaffnage Castle ⓘ *T01631-562465, Apr-Sep daily 0930-1830, Oct-Mar daily Sat-Wed 0930- 1630, castle grounds open all year round, £2.50, concession £1.90, children £0.75,* three miles north of Oban, off the A85, is this 13th-century fort built on an impressive site, and much of the curtain wall remains intact. The ruins of the little chapel nearby are worth a look. The castle served as a temporary prison for Flora MacDonald, see page 256.

Two miles east of Oban along the Glencruitten Road is the **Rare Breeds Farm Park** ① *T01631-770608, late Mar to late Oct daily 1000-1730 (mid-Jun to end of Aug till 1930), £6, concession/children £3.75.* It's a fun place for kids, with lots of strange-looking, yet familiar animals native to these shores. Three buses daily, during the week, leave from Oban train station to the farm.

Around Oban

Isle of Kerrera → *Phone code: 01631. Colour map 3, grid B-C5.*
A good place to get away from the crowds and enjoy some peace and quiet and some fine walking is the island of Kerrera, which protects Oban Bay. It's only five

Oban

To Connel, Glasgow & Fort William (A85)

To Dunollie Castle & Ganavan Sands

St Columba's Cathedral

Oban Bay

North Pier

War & Peace Museum

Oban Cycles

Highland Theatre

Atlantis Leisure

McCaig's Folly

Stafford St Oban Distillery

Jacob's Ladder

Gordon Grant Tours & Terus Mara

Bowman's Tours

Railway Pier

Laundrette

CalMac Ferry Terminal

Station Sq

Bus Stops

Argyll Sq

South Pier

To Kerrera Ferry & ⑨ ⑩

Gallanach Rd

Villa Rd

To ⑬

To Glasgow

Co-op

Tesco Supermarket

To Lochgilphead & Campbeltown (A816)

To Rare Breeds Park, Glen Lonan & Taynuilt

N

0 metres   200
0 yards   200

Sleeping 🛏
Alexandra **13**
Barriemore **1**
Caledonian **2**
Dungallan House **10**
Glenbervie Guest
  House **3**
Glenburnie House **4**
Jeremy Inglis Hostel **5**

Manor House **6**
Oban Backpackers
  Hostel **7**
Oban Caravan &
  Camping Park **9**
Oban Divers
  Caravan Park **11**
SYHA Youth Hostel **8**
Thornloe Guest House **12**

Eating 🍴
Ee'usk **2**
The Lorne **1**
The Reservation **6**
The Studio **7**
The Waterfront **3**

Bars & clubs 🍷
Oban Inn **5**

miles by two, so can be explored easily on foot or by bike. The highest point on the island is 600 ft, from where there are great views across to Mull, the Slate Islands, Lismore and Jura. Otherwise, there's a good trail down to the ruins of **Gylen Castle**, built by the MacDougall's in 1582, which is perched on a cliff-top on the south coast. A mile northwest of the ferry jetty is **Slatrach Bay**, a nice sandy beach and a great place for a picnic.

Connel to Barcaldine Castle → *Phone code: 01631. Colour map 3, grid B5.*

Five miles north of Oban an impressive steel cantilever bridge carries the A828 across the mouth of Loch Etive at Connel. It's worth stopping here to see the **Falls of Lora**, a wild tide-race created by the narrow mouth of the sea loch and the reef that spans most of it, thus restricting the flow of water. The result is the impressive rapids, which are best seen from the shore in the village or from halfway across the bridge.

Continue on this road to reach **Barcaldine Castle** ① *T01631-720598, Jul-Aug Tue-Sun 1200-1700, £3.60*, built by the Campbells in the late 16th century. The tower house is still occupied by Campbells, having been sold in the mid-19th century and then bought back as a ruin 50 years later. It's now open to the public and, though there are no real treasures, there are interesting stories to be told, a dungeon (with obligatory ghost) and a tearoom where you can try Mrs Campbell's home baking.

Near Barcaldine Castle, on the main A828, is the **Oban Sealife Centre** ① *T01631-720386, daily 0900-1800 (1000-1700 in the winter months), £6.95, children £5, buses to from Oban to Fort William pass by the Sealife Centre (see page 115)*, on the shore of Loch Creran. It's enormous fun and also environmentally friendly as they rescue seals and other aquatic life and then release them back into the wild at the end of the season. You can see lots of strange underwater creatures at close quarters and even touch some of them.

Appin → *Phone code: 01631. Colour map 3, grid B5.*

The road runs around Loch Creran and enters the district of Appin, made famous in Robert Louis Stevenson's *Kidnapped*, which was based on the 'Appin Murder' of 1752. A road turns southwest off the main Fort William road to **Port Appin**, on the western tip of the peninsula, the departure point for the passenger ferry to Lismore. To the north of Port Appin is the irresistibly photogenic **Castle Stalker**. Standing on its own tiny island with a background of islands and hills, it's probably second only to the famous Eilean Donan in its portrayal of Scotland's romantic image. It was built in the 16th century by the Stewarts of Appin before falling into Campbell hands after the ill-fated 1745 rebellion. The current owners open it to the public for a limited period in July and August. Check opening times at the tourist office in Oban.

Isle of Lismore → *Phone code: 01631. Colour map 3, grid B5.*

The island of Lismore lies only a few miles off the mainland, in Loch Linnhe, yet feels a world away. It makes an ideal day trip and offers great opportunities for walking and cycling, as well as wonderful views across to the mountains of Morvern and Mull, the Paps of Jura to the south and Ben Nevis to the north. It's a fertile little island (the name *leis mór* is Gaelic for the big garden) and once supported a population of 1,400, though the present population is about a tenth of that. Lismore has a long and interesting history. It was the ecclesiastical capital of Argyll for several centuries and the **Cathedral of St Moluag** was founded here in the 12th century, just north of Clachan. All that remains is the choir, which is now used as the parish church. The cathedral occupies the site of a church founded by the Irish saint, who established a religious community on the island about the same time as St Columba was busy at work in Iona. Legend has it that the two saints were racing to the island, in an attempt to be the first to land and found a monastery. Such was Moluag's religious zeal that he cut off his finger and threw it on to the shore, thus claiming possession. This sort of behaviour is, of course, frowned upon in Olympic rowing events. Not far from the church, is the 2,000-year-old **Broch of Tirefour**, one of the best-preserved prehistoric monuments in Argyll, with surviving circular walls up to 16-ft high. Other interesting sights include **Castle Coeffin**, a 13th-century fortress built by the MacDougalls of Lorn, on the west coast, and in the southwest of the island the 13th-century Achadun Castle, built for the Bishops of Argyll. It's a short walk from here to **Bernera Island**, which can be reached at low tide (but don't get stranded).

South Lorn and the Slate Islands → *Phone code: 01852. Colour map 3, grid C4-5.*

Eight miles south of Oban the B884 turns west off the A816 and wriggles its way round glassy lochs and knobbly, green hills studded with copper-coloured cattle to the tiny Slate Islands, so called because in the mid-19th century, the island's slate quarries exported millions of roofing slates every year. The quarrying industry has long since gone, leaving behind dilapidated old buildings as well as pretty little villages of whitewashed cottages built for the slate workers.

The most northerly of the Slate Islands is **Seil** (or Clachan Seil), which is reached from the mainland across the seriously humpbacked Clachan Bridge, better known as the 'Bridge over the Atlantic', built in 1792, with its elegant, high arch to allow ships

> **!** *Seil is well worth a visit, for its walks and fascinating island history. It is also the departure point for exciting wildlife cruises, see page 115.*

to pass beneath. Beside the bridge is an old inn, **Tigh an Truish**, or 'House of the Trousers', where islanders would have to swap kilt for trousers in order to conform to the post-1745 ban on the wearing of Highland dress. There's also a petrol pump and souvenir shop here. Two miles south, at **Balvicar**, the road turns right and climbs up and over to the main village of **Ellanbeich**, an attractive wee place with rows of white cottages around the harbour. This was once a tiny island itself until the intensive slate quarrying succeeded in silting up the narrow sea channel. The village is also, rather confusingly, known by the same name as the nearby island of Easdale, so renowned was the latter for its slate deposits. Another road runs south from Balvicar to **North Cuan**, from where the car ferry sails across the treacherous Cuan Sound to **Luing**, see below.

Endearingly tiny **Easdale** is separated from Seil by a 500-yd-wide channel which has to be dredged to keep it open. The island, only 800 yards by 700 yards, was the centre of the slate industry. There was once a population of over 450 here, but the quarries were flooded during a great storm in 1881 and the industry collapsed. The fascinating history of the island is explained at the **folk museum** ① *T01852-300370, Apr-Oct daily 1030-1730, £2.25, children £0.50*, a few minutes' walk from the ferry pier. The whitewashed former slate workers' cottages have been refurbished and now house a burgeoning local population as well as a number of holiday homes and self-catering cottages. The island's lively social life revolves around the community hall and neighbouring **Puffer Bar**. The old quarries can still be seen, now filled with water and venue for the world stone-skimming championships, see Festivals and events page 114. For more information on the island, visit www.easdale.org.

The long, thin island of **Luing** (pronounced 'Ling') once had a population of around 600 which was drastically reduced during the Clearances to make way for cattle. The island is still well known for its beef, and is the home of a successful new breed named after it. The island is small, six miles by two, and mostly flat, making it ideal for exploring by bike. Bikes can be hired in the pretty little village of **Cullipool**, a mile or so southwest of the ferry, see Transport page 115. The only other village is Toberonochy, three miles from Cullipool on the east coast. It's another village of attractive white cottages built for slate workers and nested below a ruined church.

South of the turn-off to the Slate Islands is **Arduaine Gardens** ① *T01852-200366, daily all year 0930 till sunset, £5, concession £4*, a beautiful place and an absolute must for all gardening enthusiasts. The 20-acre garden, now owned by the National Trust for Scotland, is best visited in May and June when you can enjoy the spectacular rhododendrons, but there are also beautiful herbaceous borders, ponds filled with water lilies, woodland and sweeping lawns to admire, as well as great views across to Jura and the Slate Islands.

This is boating country, and just south of Arduaine, on the northern coast of the Craignish Peninsula, is surreal **Craobh Haven**, a yachting marina built in the style of a reproduction 18th-century fishing village. South of Craobh Haven is another yachting marina at **Ardfern**, where there's a hotel and B&Bs, a popular pub, restaurant and delicatessen. You can arrange boat trips from Ardfern around Loch Craignish and to the offshore islands, see Activities and tours page 115.

● Sleeping

Oban *p108, map p110*
Oban is the main ferry port for the islands and gets busy in the summer with traffic. It's often an idea to get the tourist office to find a place, which costs more, but saves time and effort.
L Caledonian Hotel, Station Sq, T0871-2223415, www.go2oban.com. Huge landmark building overlooking the ferry pier. For a touch of luxury try one of the Captain's rooms, with prime views across the bay and all the requisite pampering facilities.
A Alexandra Hotel, Corran Esplanade, T01631-562381. Large hotel with well-equipped rooms and good facilities including pool, steam room and beauty salon.
A Manor House Hotel, Gallanach Rd, T01631-562087, F563053. 11 rooms, open Feb-Dec. Overlooking the bay on the road south out of town towards the Kerrera ferry. Offers comfort, style and superb cuisine.
C Dungallan House Hotel, Gallanach Rd, T01631-563799, www.dungallanhotel-oban.co.uk. 13 rooms, open Jan, Mar-Oct and Dec. A Victorian house set in 5 acres of woodland, offering great views, hospitality and fine food.
D Barriemore Hotel, Corran Esplanade, T/F01631-566356. 13 rooms, open Mar-Nov. More of a guest house, and a superior one at that. Great views and a friendly atmosphere.
D Glenburnie House, Corran Esplanade, T/F01631-562089. 15 rooms, open Apr-Oct. Another very good guest house along the seafront, which is lined with more upmarket guest houses and hotels.
D Thornloe Guest House, Albert Rd, T/F01631-562879, www.thornloeoban.co.uk. 7 rooms. Quiet and centrally located guest house run by Alan and Valerie Bichener. Friendly and welcoming, good-sized en suite rooms and limited off-street parking. Continental breakfast available.
E Glenbervie Guest House, Dalriach Rd,

T01631-564770, F566723. 8 rooms. Lovely house high above the town on a street full of good accommodation, good value.
F Jeremy Inglis Hostel, T01631-565065, at 21 Airds Cres, opposite the TIC. Cheaper and with breakfast included, smaller and quirkier.
F Oban Backpackers, T01631-562107, on Breadalbane St. Mar-Oct and 21 Dec-14 Jan.
F SYHA Youth Hostel, T01631-562025, open all year from Mar, is on Corran Esplanade, just beyond St Columba's Cathedral.

Camping
Oban Caravan & Camping Park, T01631-562425, F566624, Apr to mid-Oct, Gallanach Rd, 2 miles south of town near the Kerrera ferry.
Oban Divers Caravan Park, T/F01631-562755, open Mar-Nov, on the Glenshellach Rd, 1½ miles south of the ferry terminal.

Around Oban *p110*
L Airds Hotel, Port Appin, T01631-730236, F730535. 12 rooms. This classy little roadside hotel boasts one of the very best restaurants in the whole country.
A Loch Melfort Hotel, Arduaine, T01852-200233, www.loch-melfort.co.uk. 26 rooms. Open all year. It enjoys great views and a reputation for the finest seafood.
A Willowburn Hotel, Seil, T01852-300276, www.willowburn.co.uk. Open Mar-Nov. 7 rooms. Great little hotel overlooking the Sound of Seil. As well as the peace and quiet you can also enjoy the superb food on offer.
C Pierhouse Hotel, Port Appin, T01631-730302, F730400. Sitting right by the tiny pier, this cosy little hotel has a deserved reputation for excellent, moderately priced local seafood.
E Wendy Baldock, Easdale island, T01852-300438. 2 rooms. Friendly B&B in refurbished

quarry workers' cottage. Evening meals also available (££).

F Kerrera Bunkhouse, Isle of Kerrera, T01631-570223. Open Apr-Sep. 6 beds. Can arrange transport to and from ferry pier.

● Eating

Oban *p108, map p110*
£££ Ee'usk, North Pier, T01631-565666. Glass-fronted fish restaurant which has the edge over its competitors in style, though the jury is still out on whether its food is the best in town. Superb fish and seafood. Open daily 1100-1600 and 1800-2130.

£££ The Waterfront, Ferry Pier, T01631-563110. Contender for the best seafood restaurant in town, with mouth-watering dishes such as sea bass fillets with ginger and coriander noodles. Open daily 1130-1400 and 1800-late.

££ The Reservation, 108 George St, T01631-563542. Very popular though the name refers to its North American theme. Mostly burgers, fajitas and other meat-based dishes. Open daily 1100-2200.

££ The Studio, Craigard Rd, T01631-562030. Good-value 3-course set dinner and good à la carte menu, popular with locals, so you'll need to book. Wide-ranging menu featuring fish, seafood and steaks. Open daily 1800-2200 (cheap 'early bird special' served 1800-1830).

£ John Ogden has his world-famous green shed by the ferry terminal. For a cheap snack look no further here. His prawn sandwiches are widely held to be the best on the planet (£2.50). Open 0930-1800.

£ The Lorne, Stevenson St, T01631-570021. Busy local pub with beer garden and a good selection of bar meals, including burgers and fish dishes. Food served all day. Fine value.

Around Oban *p110*
££ The Barn, Cologin, Lerags, T01631-564618. Good, wholesome pub grub served with a smile. Open daily Mar-Nov.

££ Seafood and Oyster Bar, Ellenabeich pier, Seil, T01852-300121. Wide range of fish

and seafood dishes, from half-a-dozen oysters for £7.50 to scallops and lobster. Great fish and chips to take away and eat on the harbour wall.

££ The Wide-mouthed Frog, Dunstaffnage Marina, Connel, T01631-567005. Popular with the boating fraternity. Lots of fresh fish and seafood dishes, plus meat and game. Kids meals and cheap snacks too. Outdoor seating. Rooms available.

● Bars and clubs

Oban *p108, map p110*
Not exactly the party capital of Scotland, so don't expect much in the way of late-night diversion.
Oban Inn, by the north pier, is the nicest pub in town and serves bar food.

Around Oban *p110*
In Ardfern is a popular pub, and in Easdale, **Puffer bar**, serves as a focal point of the community.

● Entertainment

Oban *p108, map p110*
The Highland Theatre, at the north end of George St, T01631-562444, is confusingly the local cinema. It shows most of the popular current releases.

● Festivals and events

Oban and around *p108, map p110*
Apr Highlands & Islands Music & Dance Festival is held at the end of Apr/beginning of May.
Aug Argyllshire Gathering (Oban Games) is held at the end of Aug in Mossfield Park.
Sep World stone-skimming championships are held on Easdale on the last Sun. Lots of drinking and merriment, there's even talk of a mariachi band circumnavigating the tiny island. For the lowdown on what's on, or the chance to defeat the Aussies, visit www.stoneskimming.com.

For an explanation of sleeping and eating price codes used in this guide, see inside the front cover. Other relevant information is found in Essentials, see pages 41-49.

▲ Activities and tours

Oban *p108, map p110*
Boat trips Boat trips can be made from Oban to Mull, Iona, Staffa and The Treshnish Islands with a variety of companies.
Bowman's Tours, Queens Park Pl, T01631-566809, bowmanstours@supanet.com.
Gordon Grant Tours, T01631-562842; and **Turus Mara**, T01631-566999, www.turus mara.com, both on Railway Pier, all offer offer a variety of island and wildlife cruises, ranging in price from £30-40.
Borro Boats, Dungallan Parks, Gallanach Rd, T01631-563292. Boats for rent.
Diving Puffin Dive Centre, Gallanach Port, Gallanach Rd, T01631-566088, or booking office at George St, T01631-571190. Diver training centre and facilities (open 0800-2000).
Swimming Atlantis Leisure, Dalriach Rd, T01631-566800, www.atlantisleisure.co.uk. Sports and leisure centre with pool.

Around Oban *p110*
Boat trips Craignish Cruises,
T01852-500540, www.craignishcruises.co.uk, runs private charters and fishing trips from Ardfern Yacht Centre to the Sound of Jura, Corryvreckan and Firth of Lorne.
Kerrera Sea Adventures, T07786-963279, runs 1-hr trips around Kerrera on an rigid inflatable boats (RIB).
Seafari Adventures, T01852- 300003, www.seafari.co.uk, offers excitement from the harbour at Ellenabeigh on Seil (but can be booked in advance at Oban TIC). They use 300hp RIBS (rigid inflatable boats) to take you on a thrilling ride across the Corryvreckan (see p155). They also stop to check out the local wildlife; seals, porpoises and lots of seabirds, perhaps even a golden eagle. Trips cost £22 per person.
Horse riding Ardfern Riding Centre, **Craobh Haven**, T01852-500632, appaloosa holidays@talk21.com. Offers a variety of trails and pub rides, from £15 for 1 hr.
Watersports Linnhe Marine Watersports Centre, Lettershuna, just beyond Port Appin, T01631-730227, where you can hire motor boats, sailing dinghies or windsurfing boards, take sailing or windsurfing lessons, or try water-skiing, pony trekking or even clay pigeon shooting. May-Sep 0900-1800.

◉ Transport

Oban *p108, map p110*
There are regular daily buses to and from **Fort William**, via **Benderloch** and **Appin** (1¾ hrs) with **West Coast Motors**, T01586-552319, **Highland Country Buses**, T01463-233371, and **Oban & District Buses**, T01631-562856. There's a regular daily service to and from Glasgow (3 hrs) with **Scottish Citylink Coaches**, T08705-505050, and to **Inverness** (1¼ hrs). There are regular daily buses to and from **Dalmally**, via **Cruachan Power Station**, **Lochawe** and **Taynuilt Hotel**, operated by **Oban & District**, Scottish Citylink, Awe Service Station, T01866-822612, and LF Stewart, T01866-833342. There's a service to **Lochgilphead**, via **Kilmartin**, a couple of times a day (Mon-Sat) from **Oban & District**, Scottish Citylink and West Coast Motors.
Oban is the main ferry port for many of the Hebridean islands. **CalMac** ferry terminal, T01631-566688, is on Railway Pier, to the south of the town centre. See the island's Transport sections for details.
Only 100 yds away is the train station which is next to the bus terminal. There are 3 trains daily to **Glasgow**, via **Crianlarich**, where the Oban train connects with the Mallaig/Fort William-Glasgow train.
Car hire from **Flit Van & Car Hire**, Glencruitten Rd, T/F01631-566553. From £33.50 per day. **Practical Car & Van Rental**, Robertson's Motor Repairs, Lochavullin Industrial Estate, T01631-570900. From £36 per day. **Hazelbank Motors**, Lynn Rd, T01631-566476, F566783. From £35 per day. You can rent bikes from **Oban Cycles**, 9 Craigard Rd, T01631-566966. For details of cycle routes through the forests of Argyll, see the Forest Enterprise leaflet, *Cycling in the Forest*, available at the tourist office.

Around Oban *p110*
The departure point for ferries to **Kerrera** is 1½ miles along the Gallanach Rd. They leave several times daily between 0845 and 1800 (between 1030 and 1700 on Sun).
A passenger ferry leaves from **Port Appin** pier to the north point of **Lismore** island (daily every 1-2 hrs, 10 mins, £2.10 return). For times T01631-562125. A tiny passenger ferry sails from **Ellanbeich** on Seil to

Easdale, making the 5-min trip at regular intervals between 0745 and 2100 Mon-Sat (between 0930 and 1500 on Sun), partly to schedule, partly on request. Ring the bell in the shelter on the pier. A car ferry to **Luing** (South Cuan) sails from South Cuan on Seil (5 mins), Mon-Sat every 15-30 mins from 0745 to 1815 (later in summer) and on Sun every 30 mins from 1100 to 1800. Return fare is £1.20 per passenger and £4.90 per car. Check times at Oban tourist office.

Cycle hire from **Isle of Luing Bike Hire**, Isle of Luing, T01852-314256. £10 per day.

❶ Directory

Oban and around *p108, map p110*
Banks All the major banks have branches with ATMs in the centre and you can change foreign currency at the TIC. **Internet** Oban Backpackers charge £1.50 for 15 mins. Also at **Fancy That**, George St, T01631-562996. Daily 0900-2200. £1.50 per 15 mins.

Mid-Argyll, Kintyre, Cowal and Bute

Further south from Oban the long finger of Mid-Argyll and Kintyre points south into the wild Atlantic Ocean, sheltering the Isle of Arran on the leeward side and Islay and Jura on its starboard. This is a very attractive, slightly out-of-the-way region of sea lochs, rolling hills, huge forests and, in Kilmartin Glen, one of the most important prehistoric sites in Europe. The Mull of Kintyre is the tip, barely a stone's throw from Northern Ireland, and one of the loneliest spots in the country. On the other side of Loch Fyne is the giant claw of the Cowal Peninsula, looking like it's about to crush in its grasp the aptly-named Isle of Bute, home to one of Scotland's most fantastical stately homes.
▸▸ *For Sleeping, Eating and other listings, see pages 127-130.*

Ins and outs

Cowal's main **TIC** is in Dunoon ① *Alexandra Parade, T01369-703785, Apr-Oct;* **Helensburgh TIC** ① *clock tower on the waterfront, T01436-672642, Apr-Oct;* **Bute TIC** ① *Promenade, Rothesay, T01700-502151;* **Inveraray TIC** ① *Front St, T01499-302063;* **Lochgilphead TIC** ① *Lochnell St, T01546-602344, Apr-Oct;* **Tarbert TIC,** ① *Harbour St, T01880-820429;* and **Campbeltown TIC** ① *Old Quay, T01586-552056.*

Loch Awe and Loch Etive → *Colour map 3, C5, grid B5-6.*

Loch Awe is the longest freshwater loch in Scotland and, further north, is the beautiful Loch Etive. There's enough here to justify a couple of days' exploration, particularly the little-visited west shore of Loch Awe, and there are plenty of other places to visit around Inveraray to the south.

At the northeastern tip of Loch Awe, between the villages of of **Dalmally** and **Lochawe**, is the romantic ruin of **Kilchurn Castle**, on a promontory jutting out into the loch. It can be visited by boat from the pier in Lochawe village. Also worth a look around here is the lovely, and rather bizarre, **St Conan's Church** ① *free, donation requested,* just off the A85 by Lochawe village. Built in the late 19th century but not used until 1930, the church's interior is well worth seeing. Inside is an effigy of Robert the Bruce, with one of his bones buried underneath. The exterior, especially the south side overlooking the loch, is a riot of eccentric detail. Look out for the rabbit head drainpipes.

A few miles west of Lochawe, and almost a mile inside Ben Cruachan (3,695 ft) is the underground **Cruachan Power Station** ① *Apr-Nov 0930-1700, Jul-Aug 0930-1800, £3.50, children £1.50,* or "Hollow Mountain". From the visitor centre on the shores of Loch Awe, a bus trip takes you into the heart of the mountain through tunnels until you reach the generating room. The whole effect is somewhere between a Gerry Anderson production or an evil villain's lair in an early Bond movie.

Further west, and 12 miles east of Oban, is the tiny village of **Taynuilt**, near the shore of Loch Etive. Just before the village, at Bridge of Awe, is a sign for **Inverawe Fisheries Country Park** ① T01866-822777, www.smokedsalmon.co.uk, daily 0800-1800, where you can take fishing lessons, learn about traditional smoking techniques, or wander along a series of nature trails. If the weather's fine, you can buy some of their delicious smoked products and have a picnic, see box, page 118. If you fancy more of the same delivered to you at home, make sure you sign up for their mailing list.

North of the village on the shores of Loch Etive is **Bonawe Iron Furnace** ① T01866-822432, Apr-Sep, daily 0930-1830, £2.80, concession £2, children £1. Founded in 1753 by a group of Cumbrian ironmasters, Bonawe used the used the abundant woodlands of Argyll to make charcoal to fire its massive furnace. At its height, it produced 600-700 tons of pig-iron a year. This was then shipped out to the forges of England and Wales. Iron production ceased at Bonawe in 1876 and it has now been restored as an industrial heritage site, with displays explaining the whole production process. Beyond Bonawe is the pier from which Loch Etive Cruises depart. The loch is inaccessible except by boat, and the three-hour cruise of one of Scotland's great hidden treasures is definitely worth it, see Activities and tours page 129.

Running south from the village is the very lovely and very quiet Glen Lonan. About four miles along the Glen Lonan road is **Barguillean's Angus Garden** ① T01866-822333, daily 0900-1800, free, one of Argyll's youngest and smallest gardens, but also one of the most peaceful and evocative, set around the shores of little Loch Angus. It was created in 1957, in memory of Angus MacDonald, a journalist and writer killed in Cyprus in 1956.

▲▲ A single-track road runs southwest of Kilchrenan along the shores of Loch Awe to the tiny villages of **Dalavich** and **Ford**, through the very beautiful Inverinan Forest, a Forestry Commission property which has a series of undemanding marked trails running through the hills overlooking the loch. The first walk starts out from the little hamlet of **Inverinan**. Red waymarkers lead you from the car park into the woods surrounding the gorge of the River Inan. Part of the route follows the old drove road along which cattle were driven from the Highlands down to the markets in south and central Scotland. The walk is three miles long and should take around an hour and a half. Further along the road, half a mile north of Dalavich, is a car park at **Barnaline Lodge**, the starting point for a nine-mile bike route, a waymarked walk through the Caledonian Forest Reserve, and a couple of other woodland walks. The longest of the walks is the five-mile route that leads along the River Avich, then along the shores of Loch Avich before returning to the lodge. Two and a half miles south of Dalavich is a car park, which marks the starting point for a blue waymarked walk along the shores of Loch Awe. The route passes through Mackenzie's Grove, a sheltered gorge containing some of the largest conifers on the west coast. The route then runs along the shores of the loch, from where you can see the remains of a crannog, one of over 40 of these Iron-Age settlements on Loch Awe. The route then heads back to the car park; about three miles in total. These routes are all outlined, with accompanying maps, in the Forestry Commission leaflet, 'A Guide to Forest Walks and Trails in North Argyll', available at tourist offices.

● Between Loch Awe and Loch Etive runs the River Awe, which squeezes through the dark and ominous Pass of Brander, so steep and narrow that legend has it that it was once held against an entire army by an old woman brandishing a scythe.

Piscine cuisine

The whole philosophy of smoking fish varies greatly from one producer to another.

At **Inverawe Fisheries and Smokery**, see above, they buy smaller farmed salmon because they believe the lower fat content makes them tastier than larger ones. Traditional methods prevail here. The fish are dry salted, washed, smoked over oak logs for anything from 16 to 24 hours, depending on conditions, and then hand-sliced. The result is a rich and freshly oaky taste in a huge range of formats from a 112 g sliced pack (£5.95) to a whole side (£20.65), as well as gravadlax, smoked trout, eel and halibut, plus a whole range of

pre-packed hampers.

Knipoch Smokehouse, in South Lorn near Oban, T01852-316251, www.knipochsmokehouse.co.uk, on the other hand, believes that large salmon, weighing 6-7 kg, produce the best quality. Its approach involves a dry salt cure strengthened with sugar, whisky, juniper and rowan berries, plus a lengthy two to three day smoke. The fish comes out so black it has to be washed and trimmed to look presentable, and the taste is a rather unusual one: strong, sweet, sharp and almondy. A whole side costs £45, but it can be cut to any size: sliced at £17.60 per 500 grams, unsliced at £15.95.

Inveraray and around

Inveraray → *Phone code: 01499. Colour map 3, grid C6.*

Inveraray is the classic 18th-century planned town (don't call it a village), with its straight, wide streets and dignified Georgian houses, and enjoys the most stunning of settings, on the shores of Loch Fyne. It was rebuilt by the third Duke of Argyll, head of the Campbell clan, at the same time as he restored the nearby family home, which now attracts hordes of summer visitors. As well as its natural beauty and elegance, and fine castle, Inveraray has several other notable attractions in and around the town and you could quite happily spend a few days here, whatever the weather.

One of Argyll's most famous castles, **Inveraray Castle** ① *T01499-302203, Apr-Jun, Sep-Oct Mon-Thu and Sat 1000-1300 and 1400-1745, Sun 1300-1745, Jul-Aug Mon-Sat 1000-1745, Sun 1300-1745, £5.50, concession £4.50, children £3.50*, has been the clan seat of the Campbells for centuries and is still the family home of the Duke of Argyll. The present neo-Gothic structure dates from 1745, and its main feature is the magnificent armoury hall, whose displays of weaponry were supplied to the Campbells by the British government to quell the Jacobite rebellion. The elaborately furnished rooms are also on display, as is the fascinating and troubled family history in the Clan room. There are extensive grounds with fine walks, particularly up to the hill-top folly. has been the clan seat of the Campbells for centuries and is still the family home of the Duke of Argyll.

Inveraray Jail ① *T01499-302381, Apr-Oct daily, 0930-1800, Nov-Mar daily 1000-1700, £5.75, concession £3.75, children £2.80, family £15.70*, the Georgian prison and courthouse in the centre of the village has been brilliantly restored as a fascinating museum that gives a vivid insight into life behind bars from medieval times up till the 19th century. You can sit in on an 1820 courtroom trial, then visit the cells below and learn all about some of the delightful prison pursuits, such as branding with a hot iron, ear nailing and public whipping. The whole experience is further enhanced by the guides, who are dressed as warders and prisoners. Makes you want to stay on the right side of the law, though, thankfully conditions have improved – as you will see for yourself.

Another worthwhile diversion, especially if you've got kids in tow, the **Inveraray Maritime Museum** ① *T01499-302213, Apr-Sep daily 1000-1800, Oct-Mar daily 1000-1700, £3.60, concession £2.60, children £2*, housed in the *Arctic Penguin*, one of the world's last iron sailing ships, which is moored at the loch-side pier. Below decks are lots of interesting displays on Clyde shipbuilding and the Highland Clearances, as well as various 'hands-on' activities.

A few miles southwest of town, on the A83 to Lochgilphead, **Argyll Wildlife Park** ① *T01499-T302264, daily 1000-1700, £4, concession £3, children £2*, is another great place for kids. Amongst the native wildlife wandering around the forest-clad hills are pine martens, badgers, foxes, deer, wildcats, wild goats, a variety of wildfowl and birds of prey, racoons and wallabies, though the more informed of you will have noted that the last two are not native to Scotland. There's also the obligatory tearoom and shop.

Three miles beyond Argyll Wildlife Park is **Auchindrain Township** ① *T01499-500235, 1 Apr-30 Sep daily 1000-1700, £3.80, concession £3, children £1.80*, a complete reconstruction of an original West Highland village. The thatched cottages, barn and blacksmith have all been perfectly restored, and are all furnished and equipped to give a real insight into what rural life must have been like in the Highlands before the Clearances. There's also an informative visitor centre, with a bookshop and tearoom.

Four miles further down the A83 is **Crarae Gardens** ① *T01546-886614, Mar-Oct 0900-1800, from dawn till dusk in winter, £5, concession £4*, one of Scotland's very best public gardens, dramatically set in a deep wooded glen on the shores of Loch Fyne. There are marked woodland walks winding their way through a spectacular array of rhododendrons, azaleas and numerous other exotic plants towards the tumbling waterfalls of the 'Himalayan Gorge'. May is a good time to see the gardens in full bloom, as is autumn for the vast variety of deciduous trees, but any time of year is worth it.

Kilmartin and around → *Phone code: 01546. Colour map 3, grid C5.*

Much of this region was once part of the ancient Kingdom of Dalriada, established by the Irish Celts (known as the *Scotti*, hence Scotland) who settled here in the fifth century. North of Lochgilphead, on the A816 to Oban, is **Kilmartin Glen**, an area of Neolithic and Bronze-Age chambered and round cairns, stone circles, rock carvings, Iron-Age forts and duns, Early-christian sculptured stones and medieval castles. Before exploring this fascinating area, it's a good idea to stop off at **Kilmartin House** ① *T01546-510278, daily all year 1000-1730, £3.90, concession £3.10, children £1.20*. This multi award-winning interpretive centre is housed in the old manse next to the parish church in the tiny village of **Kilmartin**. Imaginative and interesting, it helps to explain the bewildering array of prehistoric sites lying all around, and includes artefacts from the various sites and prehistoric music. The café/restaurant does not disappoint either, and serves cheap snacks and meals, using local produce, and excellent coffee from 1230 till 1700. Next door in the church graveyard are the **Kilmartin crosses**, dating from as far back as the ninth and 10th centuries. Also within the graveyard is one of the largest collections of medieval grave slabs in the West Highlands.

Two miles north of Kilmartin, sitting high above the A816, is **Carnasserie Castle**, an imposing 16th-century tower house built by John Carswell, Bishop of the Isles, who translated *The Book of the Common Order* in 1567, the first book to be printed in Gaelic. Entry to the castle is free, but it's a little way from the car park.

Most notable of all is the **linear cemetery**, a line of burial cairns that stretch southward from Kilmartin village for over two miles. The largest and oldest of the group is the Neolithic cairn, Nether Largie South, which is over 5,000 years old and big enough to enter. The other cairns, Nether Largie North, Mid Nether Largie and Ri Cruin, are Bronze Age and the huge stone coffins show carvings on the grave slabs. Nearby are the Temple Wood Stone Circles, where burials took place from Neolithic times to the Bronze Age.

On the other side of the A816, and visible from the road, is a group of monuments which can all be reached from Dunchraigaig Cairn. This is a huge Bronze-Age cairn with some of the covering stones removed to reveal three stone coffins. From here a path is signed to **Ballymeanoch Standing Stones**, the tallest of which is 12-ft high. Two of the stones are decorated with cup marks, prehistoric rock carvings that can be found at numerous locations throughout the Kilmartin area. There's also a henge monument in the same field. These were generally round or oval platforms with an internal ditch, and it's thought they were used for ceremonial purposes. The best example of rock carvings is at Achnabreck, near Cairnbaan village, the largest collection anywhere in Britain. The purpose and significance of these cup- and ring-marked rocks is still a matter of debate.

A few miles south of Kilmartin village is the Iron-Age hill fort of **Dunadd**, which stands atop a rocky outcrop and dominates the surrounding flat expanse of **Moine Mhór** (Great Moss), one of the few remaining peat bogs in the country and now a nature reserve. Dunadd Fort became the capital of the ancient kingdom of Dalriada around AD 500 and is one of the most important Celtic sites in Scotland. The views from the top are wonderful and worth the visit alone, but you can also see carved out of the exposed rock, a basin and footprint, thought to have been used in the inauguration ceremonies of the ancient kings of Dalriada. There's also an inscription in *ogham* (a form of early writing from Ireland) and the faint outline of a boar, possibly of Pictish origin.

Crinan Canal → *Colour map 3, grid C5.*

Kilmartin Glen is bordered to the south by the Crinan Canal, a nine-mile stretch of waterway linking Loch Fyne at Ardrishaig with the Sound of Jura. It was designed and built by Sir John Rennie in 1801, with the assistance of the ubiquitous Thomas Telford, to allow shipping to avoid the long and often hazardous journey round the Mull of Kintyre and to help stimulate trade in the islands. These days you're more likely to see pleasure yachts and cruisers sailing on the canal than the cargo vessels which once transported coal and other goods to the islands and returned with livestock. You don't need to come in a boat to appreciate the canal. You can walk or cycle along the towpath that runs the entire length of the canal, from Ardrishaig to Crinan, and watch boats of all shapes and sizes negotiating a total of 15 locks. The best place to view the canal traffic is at **Crinan**, a pretty little fishing port on Loch Crinan at the western end of the canal, see Activities and tours page 129.

▲ Knapdale

Running south from the Crinan Canal down to Kintyre is Knapdale, a forested, hilly area that gets its name from its Gaelic description, *cnap* (hill) and *dall* (field). It's an area worth exploring, for there are many walking trails and superb views from the west coast across to the Paps of Jura. Immediately south of the canal is Knapdale Forest, which stretches from coast to coast over hills dotted with tiny lochs. The Forestry Commission has marked out several lovely trails. Three fairly easy circular trails start from the B8025 which runs south from **Bellanoch**, just east of Crinan.

One sets out from the car park at the Barnluasgan Interpretation Centre and runs up to a point beyond **Loch Barnluasgan**, with great views over the forest and the many lochs. It's a mile in total. A second trail, also a mile long, starts from a car park a little further along the B8025 and heads through the forest to the deserted township of **Arichonan**. The third trail starts out from the car park between the starting points for the first and second trails. It runs right around **Loch Coille-Bharr** and is three miles long. A more strenuous walk starts from a car park about 100 yards into the forest, off the B841, about half a mile west of Cairnbaan, and climbs up to the peak of **Dunardy** (702 ft).

At the Barnluasgan Interpretation Centre a little side road turns south down the eastern shore of beautiful Loch Sween, past the village of Achnamara, to the 12th-century **Castle Sween**. First impressions of the castle, situated on the shores of the lovely loch with the forested hills all around, are completely ruined by the criminally distasteful caravan park nearby. Unfortunately, the caravans were not there when Robert the Bruce attacked the castle, otherwise he might have done us all a favour by razing them. Three miles south is the ruined 13th-century **Kilmory Knap Chapel**. A new glass roof protects the carved stones inside. The most notable of these is the 8-ft high, 15th-century **MacMillan's Cross**, which shows the Crucifixion on one side and a hunting scene on the other.

Lochgilphead → *Colour map 3, grid C5.*

The main town in the area of Mid-Argyll, and administrative centre for the entire Argyll and Bute region, is Lochgilphead, a sleepy little place at the head of Loch Gilp, an arm of Loch Fyne. Lochgilphead started life as a planned town, but the industries came and went, leaving it with the customary grid plan of wide streets but little else. Today it serves as a useful base for exploring the area, with a decent range of accommodation, a bank and supermarket. There's a nice easy walk from the car park at Kilmory Castle Gardens, about a mile east of town, up to Kilmory Loch. It takes about an hour there and back and is well marked. The gardens also make a pleasant stroll and there are other marked walks, including up to Dun Mór (360 ft).

Kintyre → *Phone code: 01880. Colour map 3, grid A-B2.*

The long peninsula of Kintyre is probably best known as the inspiration for Paul McCartney's phenomenally successful 1970s dirge, *Mull of Kintyre*, but don't let that put you off. Kintyre has all the usual Highland ingredients, such as great scenery, wildlife, bags of history, golf and whisky, but also has the added attraction of being one of Scotland's least explored spots. The peninsula would be an island, were it not for the mile-long isthmus between West and East Loch Tarbert, a fact not lost on King Magnus Barefoot of Norway. In the 11th century he signed a treaty with the Scottish king, Malcolm Canmore, giving him all the land he could sail round, and promptly had his men drag his longboat across the narrow isthmus, thus adding Kintyre to his kingdom. ▸▸ *For Sleeping, Eating and other listings, see pages 127-130.*

Ins and outs

Getting around Kintyre without your own transport requires time and patience. There's a bus service running up and down the west coast, and also a limited service from Campbeltown to places around the peninsula. There are buses from Tarbert to Kennacraig (for ferries to Islay) several times daily except Sunday. Also from Tarbert to Claonaig (for ferries to Lochranza on Arran) and Skipness (two to three daily Monday to Saturday). Details from **Argyll & Bute Council**, T01546-604695, or the TIC. ▸▸ *For further details, see Transport page 129.*

Tarbert

The fishing village of Tarbert sits at the head of East Loch Tarbert, in a sheltered bay backed by forested hills, and is one the most attractive ports on the west coast. Tarbert (the name derives from the Gaelic *An Tairbeart* meaning 'isthmus') has a long tradition of fishing, and in the 18th and 19th centuries was a major herring port. Today, prawns and other shellfish are the main catch and though there is still a sizeable fleet, fishing has declined in importance to the local economy. Tourism, meanwhile, is a growing source of income, and Tarbert attracts its fair share of yachties, particularly in May when the village hosts the second largest racing series in the UK after Cowes attracting hundreds of boats and thousands of visitors. **TIC** ① *Harbour St, T01880-820429, Apr-Sep.*

Overlooking the harbour is the dramatically sited ruin of **Robert the Bruce's** 14th-century castle. There's not much left to see, other than the five-storey 15th-century keep. It's unsafe to investigate the ruins too closely, but the view alone is worth the walk. There are steps leading up to the castle, next to the Loch Fyne Gallery on Harbour Street. Behind the castle there are several marked trails leading up into the hills, with great views over Loch Fyne and the islands. Less strenuous is the short walk at the end of Garvel Road, on the north side of the harbour, which leads to the beach. At the end of East Pier road, beyond the Cowal Ferry, is another good walk, to the **Shell Beaches**. You can also explore the lovely gardens at **Stonefield Castle Hotel**, see Sleeping page 127.

Gigha

The small island of Gigha (pronounced *Gee-a* with a hard 'g') translates from Norse as 'God's Island'. A grand claim, perhaps, but there's no question that this most accessible of islands is also one of the loveliest (and pretty much midge-free!). It's only a 20-minute ferry ride away, and only six miles by one mile, so it can be visited easily in a day, which is just about enough time to appreciate why the Vikings loved it so much. Like so many of the Hebridean islands, Gigha has had a long list of owners, including various branches of the MacNeils and, more recently, in 1944, Sir James Horlick, he of bedtime drink fame. Now, though, the islanders are the proud owners of their own little piece of paradise, thanks to a successful buy-out in 2001.

It was Horlick who created the island's single greatest attraction is the wonderful **Achamore Gardens** ⓘ *To1583-505254, daily all year 0900 till dusk, £2,* one mile south of the ferry terminal. Thanks to Gigha's mild climate, the 50-acre woodland garden has an amazing variety of tropical plants, including rhododendrons, azaleas, camellias as well as other, more exotic, species. The sight of albino peacocks strutting among the palm trees will have you doubting that this an island off the coast of Scotland. There are two marked walks through the gardens, which start out from the walled garden. The gardens are best seen in early summer, when the rhodies are in full bloom.

The island's other delights include some good walks, white sandy beaches and fantastic views across to Jura on one side and Kintyre on the other. One of the best walks is to take the path left after the nine-hole golf course, signed Ardaily, past Mill Loch to the Mill on the west shore. The views from here are just magnificent. Another good idea is to walk, or cycle (see Transport page 129) to the peninsula of Eilean Garbh at the north of the island. About half a mile beyond Kinererach Farm a path leads left to the peninsula where two crescent-shaped beaches are separated by a thin spit of land. And if the weather's good enough for a picnic, make sure you try some of the island's famously distinctive cheese.

Campbeltown and around

At the southern end of the Kintyre Peninsula is **Campbeltown**. This may be the largest town by far in this part of Argyll, but it has a real end-of-the-line feel, due in part to its geographical isolation, but also because the town has long since lost its raison d'être – whisky. Six miles from Campbeltown, on the west coast of Kintyre, is **Machrihanish**, site of Campbeltown's airport and a magnificent beach – five miles of glorious unspoiled sand backed by dunes and washed by gigantic Atlantic breakers. Not surprisingly, this is a cracking place for windsurfing and surfing – one of the very best in the country, in fact. It also boasts a dramatic 18-hole championship golf course. The beach can be approached either by walking north from the village, or south from the car park on the main A83 to Tayinloan and Tarbert, where it leaves the coast.

If the weather's good, it's worth taking a walk up to **Beinn Ghulean**, which overlooks the town and loch. Follow the signs for the A83 to Machrihanish until you reach Witchburn Road. After passing the creamery on your left, turn left into Tomaig Road and continue till you come to a wooden gate. Cross over the stile and follow the track through the fields, crossing two more stiles, before you reach the Forest Enterprise sign which marks the start of the walk. It's about four miles there and back from the end of Tomaig Road.

One of the most popular day trips is to the uninhabited **Davaar Island**, connected to the peninsula by a tidal breakwater. Here you can see the cave painting of the Crucifixion, completed in secret by a local artist in 1877. The island can be visited at low tide from Kildalloig Point, a couple of miles east of town. Check tide times at the tourist office before setting out.

It's only a short drive south from Campbeltown to the tip of the peninsula, the Mull of Kintyre, eulogized by one-time resident Paul McCartney in the irritating eponymous hit single. There's nothing much to see in this bleak, storm-battered place, apart from the coast of Ireland, a mere 12 miles away and clearly visible on a good day. The road out to the lighthouse, built in 1788 and remodelled by Robert Stevenson, grandfather of Robert Louis, is pretty hairy, to put it mildly. It's possible to walk from here up to Machrihanish (about 10 miles), past the ruined township of **Balmavicar** and the **Largiebaan Bird Reserve**. The views are great and there's a chance of seeing golden eagles.

The southernmost village on Kintyre is **Southend**, a bleak, windswept place with a wide sandy beach. At the east end of the beach, jutting out on a rocky promontory, are the scant remains of **Dunaverty Castle**, once a MacDonald stronghold, where 300 Royalists were brutally massacred in 1647 by the Covenanting army of the Earl of Argyll, despite having already surrendered. To the west of Southend, below the cliffs, is the ruined 13th-century **Keil Chapel**, which is said to mark the spot where St Columba first set foot on Scottish soil, before heading north to Iona. Close by is a pair of footprints carved into the rock, known as Columba's footprints.

The slow and winding single track B842 meanders up the east coast from Campbeltown to Skipness and **Claonaig**, departure point for the ferry to Arran, see page 130. The scenery en route is gentle and pleasant, with nice views of Arran, and there are some worthwhile places to stop, but public transport is somewhat limited.

Ten miles up the coast are the idyllic ruins of **Saddell Abbey**, a Cistercian establishment founded by Somerled in 1160. The abbey fell into ruin in the early 16th century and much of the stone was used in the building of Saddell Castle for the Bishop of Argyll. Though little remains, there are some impressive medieval grave slabs, depicting knights, monks, ships, animals and other images.

▲ A few miles further north is the village of **Carradale**, the only place of any size on the east coast, nestling in the sandy sweep of beautiful Carradale Bay. There are several pleasant marked walks through the woods between the B842 and the shore. The shortest of these walks (with green waymarkers) starts from the Network Centre (see below) and is a mile long. There's a three-mile walk with red waymarkers which starts at the Port Na Storm car park and follows the forest road to the left. After 150 yards the route turns left again at the road junction. A mile further on, you turn right off the road and follow the track up to the summit of Cnoc-nan Gabhor, from where there are great views of Kintyre and across to Arran. A third walk (six miles; blue waymarkers) also starts from the Port Na Storm car park. This time the route heads right at the junction 150 yards beyond the car park and then runs north along the shore, with a chance of seeing dolphins and basking shark. The path then swings west towards the road, then turns south with views of Carradale Glen.

Twelve miles north of Carradale the B842 ends at **Claonaig**, which is actually nothing more than a slipway for the ferry to Arran, see below. From here the B8001 heads west to meet the A83 near the Kennacraig ferry pier. A dead-end road runs north for a few miles to the tiny village of **Skipness**, where you can visit the substantial ruins of the 13th-century Skipness Castle and nearby chapel.

Cowal Peninsula and the Clyde Coast

→ *Colour map 3, grid C5-6.*

The Cowal Peninsula reaches out into the Firth of Clyde, framed by Loch Fyne and Loch Long. This is the most visited part of Argyll due to its proximity to Glasgow, but, despite the summer hordes, much of it is undisturbed. Most people head straight for Dunoon, the main ferry port and one of the major Clyde seaside resorts, leaving more adventurous souls to enjoy the forests and mountains of Argyll Forest Park in the north or the peace and tranquillity of the southwest coastline. ►► *For Sleeping, Eating and other listings, see pages 127-130.*

Argyll Forest Park

The northern part of the peninsula is largely covered by the sprawling Argyll Forest Park which extends from Loch Lomond south to Holy Loch. This area contains the most stunning scenery in Cowal, and includes the **Arrochar Alps**, a range of rugged peaks north of Glen Croe which offer some of the best climbing in Argyll. The most famous of these is Ben Arthur (2,891 ft), better known as **The Cobbler**. Rather less imposing are the hills south of Glen Croe, between Loch Goil and Loch Long, in an area known as Argyll's Bowling Green (not because it's flat, but an English corruption of the Gaelic *Baile na Greine*, meaning 'Sunny Hamlet'). There are also numerous footpaths and cycle tracks threading their way through the park, and details of these can be found in the Forestry Commission leaflets available at the tourist office in Ardgarten.

Arrochar to Dunoon

The gateway to Cowal, Arrochar, sits at the head of Loch Long on the main A83, only a few miles west of Tarbet and the shores of Loch Lomond. It's a small, unremarkable place but the setting is dramatic, with The Cobbler towering overhead. A few miles beyond Arrochar, on the shores of Loch Long, is **Ardgarten**, where there's a tourist office and visitor centre ① *To1863-702342, daily Apr-Oct 1000-1700, till 1800 in Jul and Aug*, and provides useful advice and information on hillwalking and wildlife, as well as organizing various activities. From Ardgarten the A83 climbs steeply up Glen Croe to reach one of Scotland's classic viewpoints at the top of the pass, the **Rest and be Thankful**. The hordes of like-minded tourists, eager for that memorable photograph, cannot detract from the majestic views of the surrounding craggy peaks. Here the road forks. The A83 continues towards **Inveraray**, see page 118, and the single-track B828 heads southwest to meet the B839, which runs down to the village of Lochgoilhead, in a beautiful setting on Loch Goil. There are several hotels and B&Bs as well as an unsightly village of self-catering holiday chalets next door. At the end of the road, several miles down the west side of Loch Goil, are the ruins of 15th-century **Carrick Castle**.

The A83 meanwhile runs down through **Glen Kinglas** to reach the village of **Cairndow**, at the head of Loch Fyne. A mile or so further on towards Inveraray, at **Clachan**, beside Loch Fyne, is the highly acclaimed **Loch Fyne Oyster Bar**, see page 128. At the southern end of Loch Eck, at Benmore, is the **Younger Botanic Garden** ① *To1369-706261, 1 Mar-31 Oct daily 0930-1800, £3, concession £2.50, children £1*, a lovely woodland garden and offshoot of the Royal Botanic Garden in Edinburgh. Its 140 acres are laid out with over 250 species of rhododendrons and feature an avenue of Giant Redwoods.

Dunoon

The largest town in Cowal, with around 8,000 inhabitants, is Dunoon, one-time favourite holiday destination for Glaswegians, who came in their hordes on board the many paddle steamers that sailed "doon the watter" from Glasgow. Dunoon still

attracts visitors, albeit in much smaller numbers, but the town has fallen on 125
desperately hard times with the recent closure of the US nuclear submarine base on
nearby Holy Loch, which was the town's lifeblood. Nevertheless, the town still comes
to life during the **Cowal Highland Gathering**, see page 129. There's not much to detain
you here, though the **Castle House Museum** ① *Easter-Oct Mon-Sat 1030-1630, Sun
1400-1630, £1.50, concession £1, child free*, on Castle Hill overlooking the town,
allows you to bone up on Cowal's often grisly past.

The southwest

One of the most beautiful parts of Argyll is the southwest of Cowal, particularly the route
down to the little village of **Tighnabruaich**. The A8003 runs down the west side of Loch
Riddon and there are few lovelier sights than the view from this road across the **Kyles of
Bute**, the narrow straits that separate Cowal from the island of Bute. Tighnabruaich gets
busy in the summer with visitors who come here to enjoy the best sailing on the west
coast. A few miles southwest of Kames, is **Portavadie**, on the west coast of Cowal. A
CalMac car and passenger ferry sails from here to Tarbert, on the Kintyre Peninsula,
saving a lot of time if you're heading for the islands of Islay, Jura or Colonsay.

Helensburgh

Overlooking the Clyde is the town of Helensburgh, its wide, grid-plan streets lined
with elegant Georgian houses. The town is most famously known for its connection
with the great Glasgow architect, **Charles Rennie Mackintosh**. In the upper part of the
town is **Hill House** ① *Upper Colquhoun St, T01436-673900, Apr-Oct daily 1330-1730,
£8, concession £6, tearoom open 1330-1630*, trains from Glasgow Queen Street
station to Helensburgh Central, one of the best examples of Mackintosh's work. The
house was designed for Glasgow publisher Walter Blackie in 1902-1904, and is now
owned by the National Trust for Scotland. The house is a masterpiece of balanced
perfection and artistry and there's much to admire. The attention to detail, the use of
natural light, the symbolism of the floral patterns and use of light and dark –
hallmarks of his personal art nouveau style – are all very much in evidence. After
exploring the house, you can visit the kitchen, which has been tastefully converted
into a tearoom.

Isle of Bute

Barely a stone's throw off the south coast of Cowal is the island of Bute, another
favourite holiday destination for people from Glasgow and Ayrshire, who come here in
droves during the busy summer months. But though the island is small (15 miles long
by five miles wide), it's deceptively easy to escape the hordes, who tend to
congregate around the east coast resort of Rothesay, leaving the delights of the
sparsely populated west coast free for those who enjoy a bit of peace and quiet. ►► *For
Sleeping, Eating and other listings, see pages 127-130.*

Rothesay

The sole town on Bute is Rothesay, with its handsome period mansions lining the
broad sweep of bay, its elegant promenade lined with palm trees and the distinctive
1920s **Winter Gardens**, now refurbished and housing a cinema and restaurant, as
well as the TIC. **Rothesay Castle** ① *Apr-Sep Mon-Sat 0930-1830, Sun 1400-1830,
Oct-Mar Mon-Sat 0930-1630, Sun 1400-1630 closed Oct-Dec Thu and Fri, Jan-Mar Thu
afternoons, Fri and Sun morning, £2.50, concession £1.90, children £0.75*. One thing
you must do before leaving Rothesay is spend a penny in the palatial **Victorian public
toilets** ① *Easter-Sep, 0800-2100, Oct-Mar 0900-1700, £0.15*. Rather more than that
(£300,000 to be exact) has already been spent on restoring this architectural gem to
its former glory. Gents get the best deal but the ladies can also take a peek.

ⓘ *To1700-503877, www.mountstuart.com, Easter weekend and May-Sep/Oct daily except Tue and Thu, gardens 1000-1800, house 1100-1700, hours vary every year so check in advance, house/gardens £7, children £3.*

One of Bute's main attractions is Mount Stuart, a unique Victorian Gothic house set in 300 acres of lush woodland gardens, three miles south of Rothesay. This magnificent architectural fantasy reflects the Third Marquess of Bute's passion for astrology, astronomy, mysticism and religion, and the sheer scale and grandeur of the place almost beggars belief. This is truly one of the great country houses of Scotland and displays breathtaking craftsmanship in marble and stained glass, as well as a fine collection of family portraits and Italian antiques. Much of the existing house dates from 1877, and was built following a terrible fire which destroyed the original, built in 1719 by the Second Earl of Bute. Equally impressive are the landscaped gardens and woodlands, established by the Third Earl of Bute (1713-1792), who advised on the foundation of Kew Gardens in London, and the stunning new visitor centre. The present owner is Johnny Dumfries (only the Daily Mail calls him the 7th Marquis of Bute), former racing driver who won Le Mans in 1988 and who, famously, gave up his house for the headline-grabbing wedding of Stella McCartney, daughter of Paul, in 2003. It's worth spending a whole day here in order to take in the amazing splendour of the house and to explore the beautiful gardens. And if the weather's fine, why not bring a picnic and enjoy the wonderful sea views.

Other sights around the island

Just before Mount Stuart is the tidy little village of **Kerrycroy**, designed by the wife of the Second Marquess of Bute and featuring an interesting mix of building styles. South of Mount Stuart and the village of Kingarth is **Kilchattan Bay**, an attractive bay of pink sands and the start of a fine walk down to Glencallum Bay, in the southeastern corner of the island.

Southwest of Kilchattan Bay is **St Blane's Chapel**, a 12th-century ruin in a beautifully peaceful spot near the southern tip of the island. The medieval church stands on the site of an earlier monastery, established in the sixth century by St Blane, nephew of St Catan, after whom Kilchattan is named. The ruin can be reached by road from Rothesay, or as part of the walk from Kilchattan Bay (see above). Four miles north of St Blane's, on the west coast, is **Scalpsie Bay**, the nicest beach on the island and a good place for seal-spotting. A little further north is **St Ninian's Point**, looking across to the island of **Inchmarnock**. At the end of the beach are the ruins of a sixth-century chapel, dedicated to St Ninian.

The Highland-Lowland dividing line passes through the middle of Bute at Loch Fad, which separates the hilly and uninhabited northern half of the island and the rolling farmland of the south. The highest point on the island is **Windy Hill** (913 ft) in the north, from where there are great views across the island. A less strenuous walk is up **Canada Hill**, a few miles southwest of Rothesay, above Loch

Bute

Fad. Walk along Craigmore promenade and turn off at the old pier to **Ardencraig**
Gardens. Then continue uphill along the golf course to the top of the hill for great views of the Firth of Clyde.

▲▲ Kilchattan Bay to Glencallum Bay walk

A longer walk is the circular route from Kilchattan Bay south to Glencallum Bay and back, via St Blane's chapel. The walk is five miles in total. Allow about three hours. There are buses to and from Rothesay. The route is waymarked, but if you want to take a map, it's OS Landranger sheet 63.

Follow the signpost for 'Kelspoke Path' beside Kiln Villas and take the track which climbs steadily before turning sharply back on itself. Go through a gate and shortly before the next gate turn right. Follow the rough track, which swings right, then left over open ground to the ruins of Kelspoke Castle.

Continue along the grassy path, past a reservoir on your right, then cross the stile and go down and across a small burn. Turn left and follow the burn, before heading right to join the shore path and follow this past the lighthouse on your left and around the headland to Glencallum Bay. Continue round the shoreline and at the far end of the bay follow the waymarks as the path climbs to cross the headland. The path then levels out and from here there are great views across to the mountains of Arran.

The path then reaches the col above Loch na Leighe. Drop down to the loch and follow the waymarks south over open ground. Before reaching a farm called 'The Plan', go right over two footbridges, then left below a low ridge. Keep to the right of the buildings, following the waymarks across open ground to the stile that crosses to the ruins of St Blane's Chapel (see above). Leave the chapel by the gap in the boundary wall and go through a gate, turning left on a clear track which climbs steadily to a stile. Cross the stile and turn right, following the edge of the field down to a gate. Walk uphill on the left side of the field to Suidhe Hill. At the top of the field, cross the fence and keep going, turning right at the corner of the fence. Go through a gate at the next corner and look for a waymark about 100 m downhill. Follow the path steeply downhill, passing through a kissing gate and staying close to the wall. You then reach a drying green at the foot of the hill; turn left and follow a path around the buildings and back onto the road at Kilchattan.

● Sleeping

Loch Awe and Loch Etive *p116*
L Ardanaiseig Hotel, T01499-833333, www.ardanaiseig-hotel.com. 3 miles east of Kilchrenan village on an unclassified road. Open Feb-Dec. The most luxurious place to stay, and the best place to eat.
B Taychreggan Hotel, T01499-833211. Not as grand as the **Ardanaiseig Hotel**, but with equally wonderful views and superb cuisine.
C Blarcreen Farm, Archattan, T01631-750272, www.blarcreenfarm.com. A mile past Archattan Priory on the road from Oban to Bonawe. Elegant Victorian farmhouse standing on its own surrounded by lovely countryside. Beautiful rooms and superb cuisine. Recommended.

Inveraray and around *p118*
L Crinan Hotel, T01546-830261, www.crinan hotel.com. One of the most beautifully located hotels in the country, at the end of the Crinan canal with views across to Jura. Pampering at its most decadent and a sensational restaurant make it worth the expense.
A Fernpoint Hotel, T01499-302170, fernpoint.hotel@virgin.net. Lovely Georgian house overlooking the loch. Specializes in vegetarian food.
B Cairnbaan Hotel, T01546-603668, F606045. Lovely 18th-century coaching inn overlooking the Crinan Canal in the village of Cairnbaan, just north of Lochgilphead. Very good food in the restaurant.

 For an explanation of sleeping and eating price codes used in this guide, see inside the front cover. Other relevant information is found in Essentials, see pages 41-49.

B George Hotel, Main St, T01499-302111. 18th-century building with tasteful, spacious and comfortable rooms, a cosy bar and excellent food. Recommended.
D Bellanoch House, Bellanoch Bay,on the B841 near Crinan, T01546-830149, house@bellanoch.free-online.co.uk. Italian-owned Gothic mansion overlooking the canal basin. Great location. Dinner served on request.
D Kilmartin Hotel, opposite the church in Kilmartin village, T01546-510250, F606370. Comfortable and serves meals all day.
D Tigh-na-Glaic, Crinan, T01546-830245. On a hill behind the Crinan Hotel. Great views at a fraction of the cost. Friendly and comfortable.

Kintyre *p121*
L-A Stonefield Castle Hotel, 3 miles north of Tarbert, on the A82 to Lochgilphead, T01880-820836, F820929. Price includes dinner. A Baronial Victorian mansion set in acres of woodland garden, with great views across the loch.
B Columba Hotel, on Pier Rd, Tarbert, T/F018 80-820808, www.columbahotel.com. 10 rooms on the waterfront with restaurant and bar.
C Gigha Hotel, Ardminish on Gigha, T01583-505254, www.isle-of-gigha.co.uk/hotel.shtml. 13 rooms. Open Mar-Oct. Offers comfort, great views and good, solid bar food.
C Kilberry Inn, west of Tarbert on the B8024, T01880-770223, www.kilberry inn.com. 3 rooms, open Easter-Oct. Offers superb food and perfect peace.
C Tayinloan Inn, at the ferry port of Tayinloan, 01583-T441233, a small and cosy 18th-century coaching inn.
E Post Office House, T01583-505251, a short walk from the ferry. The McSporrans also run the post office and general store, provide good home cooking and even rent out bikes.

Cowal Peninsula and the Clyde Coast *p124*
B Ardfillayne House, a mile south of Dunoon on the Innellan Rd, T01369-702267, www.argyll-business.directory.com. Atmospheric Victorian country house surrounded by 16 acres of woodland gardens and offering fine Scottish/French cooking (booking required).

C Kames Hotel, Kames, T01700-811489, tcandrew@aol.com. Great views and live music in the bar.
C The Royal Hotel, Tighnabruaich, T01700-811239, royalhotel@btinternet.com, on the waterfront, with a multi-gym and sauna, and restaurant.
F SYHA youth hostel, T01700-811622, open Apr-Sep, sits high above the village with great views across the Kyles and is often full.

Isle of Bute *p125*
A Balmory Hall, 3 miles south of Rothesay, at Ascog, T/F01700-500669, www.balmory hall.com. Superior guest house, with elegant and sumptuous rooms. The 7-course breakfast is an event in itself.
B Cannon House Hotel, Battery Pl, Rothesay, T01700-502819, F505725. A comfortable Georgian townhouse. Convenient for the ferry.
E Ascog Farm, 3 miles south of town, at Ascog, T01700-503372. Feng shui farmhouse offering excellent-value. Very friendly.
E Kingarth Hotel, Kingarth in the south of the island, T01700-831662, simon@kingarth hotel.com. Quiet, unassuming little hotel not far from the beach. Does good bar meals (**££**). Great value. Stella McCartney's hubby-to-be had his stag night here, attended by Macca himself and his rock-star chums.

● Eating

Inveraray and around *p118*
££ Loch Fyne Oyster Bar, T01499-600264. About 9 miles east of Inveraray on the A83 near Clachan. This restaurant, shop and smokehouse is the best for miles and popular with many local celebs who travel all the way from Glasgow to sample their classy crustacea. Open Nov-Mar daily 0900-1800, from mid-Mar onwards 0900-2100 (booking essential at weekends).

Cowal Peninsula and the Clyde Coast *p124*
££ Chatters, 58 John St, Dunoon, T01369-706402. Aside from the hotels in town the best food can be found at this informal and outstanding little restaurant offering French-style Scottish cuisine. Mon-Sat.

Isle of Bute p125

££ **The Bistro**, Discovery Centre, Winter Gardens, T01700-505500. Handily placed for the ferry, this modern-style bistro serves up contemporary Scottish cooking in a relaxed atmosphere.

£ **West End Café**, 1-3 Gallowgate, Rothesay, T01700-503596. It is a must while you are on Bute to sample the fish and chips at this award-winning chippie. It's open all year round except Mon.

⊛ Festivals and events

May The **Isle of Bute Jazz Festival** is held during the May Bank Holiday weekend.
Jul There's also the **Isle of Bute International Folk Festival** and **World Ceilidh Band Championships**, a massive festival of music and dance held over the third weekend in Jul.
Aug If you're around Campbeltown at the end of Aug, don't miss the **Mull of Kintyre Music Festival**, 3 days of the best in traditional Celtic music, held throughout the town. **Dunoon Highland Games**, held on the last weekend of the month, are the world's largest and culminate in a spectacular march of massed pipes and drums through the streets.
Sep Tarbert hosts an excellent **folk music festival**, over a weekend at the end of the month. For details, call T01880-820343.

▲ Activities and tours

Loch Awe and Loch Etive p116
Boat trips Loch Etive Cruises, T01866-822430, cruises depart at 1000 and 1200 (1½-hr cruise) and 1400 (3 hr cruise), Easter-Oct Sun-Fri, Apr and Oct at 1400 only. 1 ½ hr cruise £5, children £3; 3-hr cruise £9, children £5. No booking necessary but arrive in plenty of time. The departure point is beyond the Bonawe Heritage Site. The 3-hr cruise is very highly recommended.
Fishing Lochawe Boats, The Boat House, Ardbrecknish, by Dalmally, T01866-833256. From £15 per day for a rowing boat up to £45 for a motor boat with cabin. Canoes for hire.

Inverary and around p118
Boat trips Gemini Cruises, based at Crinan harbour, T/F01546-830238,

www.gemini-crinan.co.uk, take out boat trip offerering 2-hr wildlife spotting cruises round Loch Craignish or longer trips out to the Gulf of Corrievreckan. The trips cost £11 (2-hrs), children £7.50; £18/11 (4-hrs).
Vic 32, the last functioning Clyde 'puffer' on the west coast, are available through Rachel and Nick Walker, The Change House, Crinan Ferry, Lochgilphead, T01546-510232, www.highlandsteamboats.com. They run 5-day summer cruises on the west coast on board this 85-ft vessel. Prices is £475 pp and includes all meals and bed linen.
Horse riding Argyll Riding, Dalchenna Farm, 2 miles south of Inveraray on A83, T01499-302611, www.horserides.co.uk. Riding school, trekking and hacking tours.
Argyll Trail Riding, Brenfield Farm, Ardrishaig, T01546-603274, www.brenfield. co.uk. Riding trails, pub trails and beach gallops, week-long stays and lessons. Also clay-pigeon shooting.
Walking tour Tales on the Hoof, www.ansgeulaiche.co.uk. Storytelling tours of Kilmartin Glen, £5, children £2.50. Book through the TIC in Oban or Lochgiphead.

⊖ Transport

Inverary and around p118
There are buses from **Lochgilphead** to **Cairnbaan**, **Crinan**, **Achnamara** and **Tayvallich** several times daily Mon-Sat. There are buses and taxis to **Oban** via **Kilmartin** (Mon-Sat) and a postbus to **Inveraray** (Mon-Sat). There's a service to and from **Ardrishaig**. See also Kintyre below for buses from Glasgow.
  Crinan Cycles, 34 Argyll St, Lochgilphead, T01546-603511. Bikes for rent from £12 per day, also parts and repairs and will advise on routes and provide maps. Mon-Sat 0930-1730.
  Mid Argyll Taxis, 4 Slockavullin, Kilmartin, T01546-510318, for taxi hire.

Kintyre p121
There are 2 flights daily (35 mins), all year round from Glasgow to **Machrihanish** airport. For times and reservations, contact **British Airways Express**, T08457-733377.
  There are several daily buses from Glasgow to **Campbeltown** (4½ hrs) (via **Inveraray**, **Lochgilphead**, **Kennacraig** and **Tarbert**). There are buses from Campbel-

town to **Machrihanish** (hourly Mon-Sat, 3 on Sun; 15 mins), to **Carradale** (45 mins) and **Saddell** (4 daily Mon-Sat, 2 on Sun; 25 mins), to **Southend** (several daily; 25 mins).

There is a car and passenger ferry from Portavadie on the Cowal peninsula to **Tarbert** (25 mins, £3 per passenger, £13.70 per car), which leaves daily every hour in summer, less frequently in winter. There are ferries from **Lochranza** on Arran from **Claonaig** on the west coast of Kintyre, south of Kennacraig (see p) several times daily (30 mins, £4.35 per passenger, £19.45 per car). Ferries leave from **Kennacraig**, 5 miles south of Tarbert, to **Islay** (see p156) and to **Colonsay** (see p148). A small car and passenger ferry leaves from Tayinloan to the ferry pier at Ardminish on Gigha, daily all year round (hourly 0800-1800 Mon-Sat, 1100-1700 Sun), 20 mins, £5.15 per passenger, £19.30 per car.

Cowal Peninsula and
the Clyde Coast *p124*
To Dunoon there are CalMac ferries every hr (0620-2020) from **Gourock**, with train connections to and from Gourock to **Glasgow Central**, 25 mins, £3 one way per person, £7.45 per car. There is also a ferry service from McInroy's Point, 2 miles from

Gourock, with **Western Ferries**, www.western-ferries.co.uk. It leaves every 15-20 mins during peak times, less frequently in the evenings, £3.10 per passenger, £8.70 per car.

Isle of Bute *p125*
The service provided by **Western Buses** is fairly good, though limited on Sun. The best way to see Bute is by bike; the island is fairly flat, the roads are quiet and in good condition.

Bute is easily accessible from **Glasgow**. Take a train from Glasgow Central to the ferry terminal at **Wemyss Bay** (1 hr 10 mins), and from there it's a 35-min crossing to Rothesay. They leave every 45 mins from 0715 till 1945 (later on Fri, Sat and Sun), 35 mins, £3.55 one way per passenger, £14.20 per car. For times, T01700-502707.

There are also buses to Rothesay from **Tighnabruaich** in southwest Cowal once or twice a day Mon-Thu (1 hr). For times, contact **Western Buses**, T01631-502076. A car/passenger ferry makes the 5-min crossing from **Colintraive** to **Rhubodach**, at the northern end of Bute, daily every half hour or hour; from 0530-1955 Mon-Sat and 0900-1955 Sun in the summer (21 Apr-27 Aug). It costs £1.15 one way per person and £7.15 per car.

Isle of Arran → *Phone code: 01770. Colour map 5, grid A-B3.*

In the wedge of sea between Ayrshire and Kintyre lies the oval-shaped and very beautiful island of Arran. It manages to combine the classic features of the Northwest Highlands with the more sedate pleasures of the Southern Lowlands, thus earning the sobriquet, 'Scotland in Miniature'. This obvious appeal, coupled with its easy accessibility, makes Arran a very popular destination, but it remains unspoiled, and at 25 miles long is big enough never to feel crowded. ▶▶ *For Sleeping, Eating and other listings, see pages 134-135.*

Ins and outs
Getting there The main ferry route to Arran is from the distinctly unappealing Ayrshire town of Ardrossan to the island's main town, Brodick. There are train connections from Glasgow and bus connections from Edinburgh to Ardrossan. The other ferry route is from Claonaig, near Skipness, to Lochranza in the north of the island. ▶▶ *For further details, see Transport page 135.*

Getting around It's possible to explore the island using public transport, as there are regular bus and postbus services.

Tourist information Brodick Tourist Information Centre ⓘ *beside the pier and bus terminal, T01770-302140, www.ayrshire-arran.com, Mar-Sep Mon-Sat 0900-1930, Sun 0900-1700, also open daily in winter, all hours vary so check beforehand.*

Brodick

The largest and busiest settlement on Arran, and main ferry port, is Brodick, lying in a wide bay (hence its Norse name *breidr vik*, meaning 'broad bay') backed by a range of steep crags. It's not the most attractive village on the island, and consists of little more than one long street that sweeps round the bay, but you'll find a wide range of tourist facilities and services here.

A few miles north of town is the impressive **Brodick Castle** ① *T01770-302202, castle and restaurant 1 Apr-30 Jun and 1 Sep-31 Oct, daily 1100-1630, 1 Jul-31 Aug, daily 1100-1700, garden and country park all year, daily 0930-1700 (park till sunset), castle, garden and country park £8, £6 concession, garden and country park only £3,* one of the island's top sights and a flagship NTS property. Until recently this was the family seat of the Dukes of Hamilton, erstwhile owners of the island. The oldest part of the castle dates from the 13th century, with extensions added in the 16th, 17th and 19th centuries. The hour-long tour of the sumptuously furnished rooms and kitchens is interesting and can be rounded off with a visit to the castle restaurant, where you can enjoy home-cooked meals or light snacks. On a good day you can sit outside on the castle terrace and have lunch whilst admiring the views. The walled garden is worth a look, and the surrounding country park includes 11 miles of way-marked trails.

Arran

Halfway between the village and the castle is the **Arran Heritage Museum** ⓘ *T01770-302636, www.arranmuseum.co.uk, Apr-Oct daily 1000-1630, £2.25, £1 children*, an interesting diversion which explains the island's archaeology, geology and social history. There's also a very good café.

South Arran

The south of Arran is a fertile landscape of rolling hills and pretty little seaside villages, where you'll find the bulk of the island's population and tourists. A few miles south of Brodick is **Lamlash**, a quiet and attractive place set in a wide, sheltered bay but with an unappealing mud beach.

Lying just offshore is the humpbacked **Holy Island**, which is owned by a group of Scottish Buddhists who have retired here for peace and meditation. A ferry runs to and from the island several times daily from 1 May to 4 September (limited service 5 September to 30 October). The first ferry departs Lamlash at 1000 and the last one returns at 1715, leaving you just enough time to climb up to the highest point, **Mullach Mór** (1,030 ft).

The little fishing village of **Blackwaterfoot** is set round a bay with a tiny harbour. Two miles north along the coast are the **King's Caves**, where, according to legend, Robert the Bruce watched a spider try, try and try again and was thus inspired to secure his own and Scotland's destiny. It's a 45-minute walk from where you leave the car to the cathedral-like main cave, which has an iron gate to keep out wandering sheep.

Four miles north of Blackwaterfoot, off the main coast road, is **Machrie Moor**, site of the most impressive of Arran's Bronze-Age **stone circles**. Park by the Historic Scotland sign and then walk for one and a half miles along the farm track to reach an area boasting no fewer than six stone circles. Many of them are barely visible above the ground, but the tallest is over 18 ft high. A few miles further on, just south of the turn-off to Machrie village, is another Historic Scotland sign, this time for **Moss Farm Road Stone Circle**, which lies about a half mile walk along the farm track.

North Arran

The north half of Arran contrasts sharply with the southern part. It looks and feels more like the Scottish Highlands – desolate, unspoiled and much of it accessible only to the serious hillwalker. But though the north is scenically more spectacular, it attracts few visitors. Six miles north of Brodick is Arran's loveliest village, **Corrie**. Corrie has a couple of hotels and B&Bs, a good pub, and makes an attractive alternative to Brodick as a starting point for the ascent of Goatfell. The main coastal road continues north from Corrie to **Sannox**, with its sandy beach, then it cuts inland and climbs northwest towards Lochranza. It's worth taking your time to admire the view and on the other side of the pass, in **Glen Chalmadale**, you can see red deer heading down to the shore at dusk.

The most spectacular introduction to Arran is to arrive at **Lochranza**, the most northerly village and second ferry port. This charming village is guarded by its ruined 13th-century castle and backed by looming mountains. **Lochranza Castle** can be visited free of charge (the key is available from the **Lochranza Stores**). Lochranza is also the site of Scotland's newest distillery, **Isle of Arran Distillers** ⓘ *T01770-830264, www.arranwhisky.com, Apr-Oct daily 1000-1800, £3.50, £2.50 concessions*, which opened in 1995 and is the first legal whisky distillery on the island for over 150 years. There are guided tours of the distillery, followed by the obligatory dram, and also an excellent restaurant, see Eating page 135.

▲ Walks on Arran → *OS map No 69 covers these walks.*

Arran is a hill walker's paradise. The north part of the island boasts ten peaks of over 2,000 ft and dozens of ridge walks while the gentler south features a variety of less strenuous forest walks. Note that you should only attempt these routes in good weather and avoid climbing any rockfaces. Some ridge walks – A'Chir, Witches Step, Suidhe Fherghas and Cioch Na Oighe – involve quite a lot of scrambling and can be dangerous. They should only be attempted by fit and experienced climbers. Ropes and good OS maps should also be taken. Ask local advice during the deer stalking season (late August to late October).

The **Glenashdale Falls and Giants' Graves walk** is one of the most popular on the island. It's a steady, easy climb through woodland with the considerable incentive of a beautiful waterfall at the end of it. Both walks can be done together and should take around two to three hours in total, though you should allow some time to enjoy the falls. If you want to take a picnic, pop into the Village Shop which has a wide range of deli-type foods and local cheeses. The trail starts by the bridge over Glenashdale Burn, next to the Youth Hostel. There's a map board here showing the route. Walk up the track alongside the burn till you see the sign for the path leading to the left up to the Giants' Graves. It's about 40 to 45 minutes up to the graves and back to this point, but it's a stiff climb up a steep staircase of 265 steps. At the top continue left along a path through the trees, which then curves right till you reach a clearing and the graves, which are chambered tombs, believed to be around 5,000 years old. Depending on the light, this can be a very eerie, but almost magical place. Return back down the steps, and head left along the main path as it climbs steadily above the burn, past smaller falls, till you reach the main falls. The setting is stunning and the falls are spectacular as they plummet 140 ft into the pools below. You can rest and have a picnic at the top of the falls, or follow the paths down to the pools below which you can swim. The path back down to Whiting Bay passes the scant remains of an Iron-Age fort, then turns back uphill to reach a broad track. Turn right, cross a small burn by stepping stones, then follow the track downhill all the way to the main road, a short way along from the car park.

Arran's most popular peak, **Goatfell**, is also its highest, at 2,866 ft. There's a path leading up from Corrie, but most people begin the walk from the car park at Cladach sawmill, near Brodick Castle. The path is well marked, easy to follow and, apart from the final section, relatively easy. It runs initially through the Brodick Country Park, then follows the Cnocan burn as it rises steadily through woodland before crossing the Mill burn. Beyond the burn is a deer fence which runs across the entire island to keep the deer from the north away from the farming in the south. Above the deer fence the landscape changes to heather moorland and the path begins to climb the flanks

Glenashdale Falls & Giants' Graves walk

of the mountain. The final 650 ft up to the top is steep and rocky and the path is not always clear. The last section requires some scrambling on loose scree but the views that greet you at the top on a clear day are magnificent, stretching right across from Ireland to Mull. The walk to the summit and back should take about five hours. Though it's considered a fairly straightforward ascent, remember that this should be treated with the same caution and respect as any Scottish mountain. You should be dressed and equipped appropriately and be prepared for any sudden change in the weather. There are also numerous ridge walks around Goatfell as well as other high peaks to climb.

Many of the walks start from Glen Rosa Farm. One of these takes in the three Beinns; **Beinn Nuis**, **Beinn Tarsuinn** (2,681 ft) and **Beinn A'Chliabhain**. Start at Glen Rosa Farm and go up the Wood Road to the High Deer Gate, then to Torr Breac and the 'Y' junction at the top of the Garbhalt and on to the path which runs round the Three Beinns. This is a full day's walk.

Another excellent walk is from Glen Rosa to the head of the Glen; then take the path up into the Coire Buidhe and on to the ridge between **Cir Mhor** (2,617 ft) and

❖ Ordnance Survey map no 69 covers these walks on Arran.

A'Chir (known as the Ceems Ridge). Then follow the path around the west side of A'Chir. This is not easy to find, but takes you around the back of A'Chir to Bowman's Pass and the north end of Beinn Tarsuinn. From here take the path to Beinn A'Chliabhan and down to the foot of Garbhalt Ridge and back down to Glen Rosa.

Cir Mhor can also be climbed from Glen Rosa. Before going over into Glen Sannox take the steep path straight up. On the way back down, head into Coire Buidhe and back down the glen. You can also continue from the top of Cir Mhor and take the path around the west side of A'Chir to the north end of the Bowman's Pass up on to Beinn Tarsuinn and along the ridge to Beinn Nuis, then down the path to the Garbhalt Bridge.

Finally, you can also climb **Caisteal Abhail** (2,818 ft) from Glen Rosa. Go straight up into Coire Buidge on to the Ceems Ridge. Then take the path round the west side of the A'Chir through the Bowman's Pass and on to Beinn A'Chliabhain down the side of the Garbhalt to Glen Rosa.

There are also several walks in and around **Glen Sannox**. It's a pleasant walk just to make your way up the head of the Glen and return the same way. You can walk up the Glen to beyond the old mine then make your way up towards the Devil's Punchbowl until you reach the main path and follow that down into the Coire. Take the main path back down into Glen Sannox instead of trying to climb out of the Devil's Punchbowl. You can also walk from Glen Sannox to Glen Rosa, which takes around four hours.

● Sleeping

Brodick *p131*

A Kilmichael Country House Hotel,
T01770-302219, www.kilmichael.com.
7 rooms. Take the road north towards the castle, turn left at the golf course and follow the signs for about a mile. Enjoy refined elegance in the island's oldest house. Their award-winning restaurant is the best on the island. Booking is essential for non-residents. No children under 12.

A Auchrannie Country House Hotel, just beyond the turning to Kilmichael, T01770-302234, www.auchrannie.co.uk. 28 rooms (also self-catering and time-share lodges).

May lack the charm of Kilmichael but makes up for it with superb facilities and leisure complex. It also has a 36-bedroom spa resort. Their **Garden Restaurant** is also highly rated and the **Brambles Bistro** offers less expensive bar meals.

C Glen Cloy Farmhouse, Glen Cloy Rd, T01770-302351. A B&B a cut above the rest.

Camping

Glen Rosa, T01770-302380, open Apr-Oct, 2 miles from town on the road to Black-waterfoot, is the nearest campsite.

South Arran p132

A Argentine House Hotel, Whiting Bay, T01770-700662, www.argentinearran.co.uk. 5 rooms, on the seafront and recognizable by the flags flying outside. Excellent cooking.
A-B Burlington Hotel, T01770-700255, www.mllford.co.uk/go/burlingtonarran. html. 9 rooms, open Easter-Oct. Comfortable rooms and a reputation for superb seafood; moderately priced set 3-course dinner in dining room or à la carte in bistro.

North Arran p132

B Apple Lodge, Lochranza, T/F01770-830229. A lovely country house with 4 double rooms, offering home cooking for residents.
B Corrie Hotel, Corrie, T01770-810273. Friendly and good value with a lively bar.
C Castlekirk, Lochranza, T01770-830202, a converted church opposite the castle.

Camping

There's a campsite next to the golf course in Lochranza, with facilities, T01770-820273, office@lochgolf.demon.co.uk, Apr-Oct.

● Eating

Brodick p131

£££-££ Creelers Seafood Restaurant, at the Home Farm, a mile or so north of town on the road to the castle, T01770- 302810. Some of the best seafood in the whole country.
££-£ Brodick Bar, behind Wooley's bakery and opposite the post office. Superior pub grub served in the bar or in the restaurant next door.

North Arran p132

££ Harold's Restaurant, T01770-830264, arranvc@aol.com, in the distillery visitor centre. Here you can enjoy innovative Scottish/Caribbean cuisine. Open till 2100.

● Transport

Arran p130

Local There are regular daily buses from **Brodick** to **Blackwaterfoot** (30 mins) via

'The String'; to **Lamlash** (10 mins) and **Whiting Bay** (25 mins) and on to **Blackwaterfoot** (1 hr, 10 mins); to **Corrie** (20 mins), **Sannox** (25 mins), **Lochranza** (45 mins), **Catacol** (50 mins), **Pirnmill** (1 hr), **Machrie** (1 hr, 10 mins) and **Blackwaterfoot** (1 hr, 20 mins). There's also a postbus service from **Brodick** to **Corrie, Sannox, Lochranza, Catacol, Pirnmill, Machrie, Blackwaterfoot** and back to Brodick; and from Brodick to **Lamlash, 'The Ross', Kildonan, Whiting Bay** and back to Brodick. For details of bus services to Claonaig, T01546-604695.

Arran is best appreciated on a bike, however. **Whiting Bay Hires**, on the jetty in Brodick, T01770-700382, hires out bikes. **Whiting Bay Garage**, T/F01770-700345, for car hire, taxis, or island tours.

Long distance The main ferry route is from **Ardrossan** to **Brodick**. CalMac car/passenger ferry makes the 55-min journey 5-6 times daily Mon-Sat, 4 times on Sun, 55 mins, £4.80 one-way per passenger, £35 per car. There's a regular train connection between Ardrossan and **Glasgow Central**. There's also a bus connection to and from **Edinburgh**. By car, from the south the main route to Arran is from the M74 motorway, on to the A71 via Kilmarnock, to Irvine and Ardrossan. For more ferry information, contact Ardrossan ferry office, T01294-463470, or Brodick, T01770-302166. The other ferry route to Arran is from **Claonaig**, near **Skipness**, to **Lochranza** in the north of the island. The non-bookable car/passenger ferry makes the 30-min trip 7 to 9 times daily during the summer (Apr-Oct), less frequently in winter, £4.35 per passenger, £19.45 per car. For ferry times, T08705 650000, www.calmac. co.uk; for reservations on sailings to Lochranza, T01880-730253.

● Directory

Brodick p131

Banks Brodick has banks with ATMs but these are the only ones on the island. **Post** The post office is just off the seafront, opposite the petrol station and pharmacy.

Mull and Iona → *Colour map 3, grid B3-4, C3-4.*

The island of Mull, a short hop from Oban, is the third largest of the Hebridean islands and, after Skye, the most popular. Everyone has their own favourite island, but Mull has enough going for it to appeal to most tastes: spectacular mountain scenery, 300 miles of wild coastline, castles, wildlife, a narrow-gauge railway, some of the best fishing in Scotland, and some of the prettiest little villages, all in an area roughly 24 miles from north to south and 26 miles from east to west. It's worth spending time on Mull to fully appreciate its pleasures and take the time to make a pilgrimage to tiny Iona, the most spiritual of places and one of the loveliest. ▶▶ *For Sleeping, Eating and other listings, see pages 144-147.*

Ins and outs

Getting there and around Mull is served by regular car/passenger ferry services, mostly from Oban but also from Kilchoan on the Ardnamurchan Peninsula and Lochaline on the Morvern Peninsula. Once on the island you can get to most parts of the island by bus. Services given in the Transport section are for April to October. Winter services are less frequent. There are regular five-minute sailings to and from Iona. ▶▶ *For further details, see Transport page 146.*

Tourist information Craignure TIC ① *opposite the pier in the same building as the CalMac office, T01680-812377, Easter-end Oct.* **Tobermory TIC** ① *at the far end of Main St, T01688-302182, Apr-Sep,* is also in the same building as the CalMac office.

Mull

Mull

Craignure to Tobermory

The arrival point for visitors is the village of Craignure. One and a half miles south of here is **Torosay Castle** ① *To1680-812421, easter-mid Oct daily 1030-1730, gardens open all year daily 0900-1900, £5*, more of a baronial family home than a full-blown castle. The best way to arrive at the castle is by the **Mull and West Highland Railway** ① *To1680-812494, Easter-mid Oct, £3.75 return*.

A couple of miles east of Torosay is **Duart Castle** ① *To1680-812309, May-mid Oct daily 1030-1800, £4*, the 13th-century ancestral seat of the Clan Maclean stands imperiously at the end of a promontory, commanding impressive views over Loch Linnhe and the Sound of Mull. The castle's main feature is the tower house, built in the late 14th century when it became the main residence of the Macleans of Duart. Today it's a fascinating place to visit, with many relics and artefacts on display. There's also an excellent tearoom serving delicious home-baked scones.

Midway between Craignure and Tobermory on the main A849 is the pretty village of **Salen**. It stands on the east coast at the narrowest point on the island, and is only three miles from the west coast, making it a good base from which to explore the island. There are a couple of interesting sights around Salen. Just to the north, overlooking the bay, is the ruin of **Aros Castle**, built in the 14th century and one of the strongholds of the Lords of the Isles. Tradition holds that the treasure of the Spanish galleon sunk in Tobermory Bay in 1588, see page 139, was recovered by the Macleans and still lies buried beneath the ruins of Aros Castle.

Four miles southwest of Salen, near Gruline and Loch Ba, is the **MacQuarrie Mausoleum**, which houses the remains of Major-General Lachlan MacQuarrie (1761-1824). He took over as Governer-General of New South Wales from the unpopular William Bligh, formerly of the *Bounty*, and became known as the 'Father of Australia'. The mausoleum is maintained by the NTS, on behalf of the National Trust of Australia.

Tobermory

There is no prettier port in the west of Scotland than Tobermory, Mull's main village. The brightly painted houses that line the harbour front date from the late 18th century when the British Fisheries Society built Tobermory as a planned herring port. It never really took off as a fishing port, however, and nowadays you're more likely to see pleasure yachts anchored in the protected waters of the natural harbour. Lying at the bottom of the harbour is a galleon of the Spanish Armada, which sank in mysterious circumstances, along with its treasure of gold doubloons, see box page 139. Not only is Tobermory the only Highland town to have a Womble named after it, it is also the setting for the BBC's hugely popular children's TV show, *Balamory*.

The harbour front – known as Main Street – is where you'll find most of what you want: hotels, guest houses, restaurants, pubs and shops and the tourist office. Mercifully, though, it's free from the tartan tat that blights so many other tourist hot-spots. Here you'll find the **Mull Museum** ① *To1688-302493, Easter-end Oct Mon-Fri 1030-1630, Sat 1030-1330, £1*, housed in an old bakery. It's worth visiting on a rainy day and you'll learn all about the island's history. At the foot of the main road down to the harbour is the tiny **Tobermory Distillery** ① *To1688-302645, www.burnstewartdistillers.com, Easter to end-Oct Mon-Fri 1000-1700, Oct-Easter by appointment, £2.50, concession £1, children 18 free*, which offers a guided tour rounded off with a sampling of the island's single malt. At the top of Back Brae, on Argyll Terrace, is **An Tobar** ① *To1688-302211, www.antobar.co.uk, Mon-Sat all year 1000-1800, free*, an excellent arts centre housed in an old schoolhouse and featuring a varied programme of exhibitions, music and workshops. Or you can just have a coffee and admire the view.

Mull's west coast is where you'll find some of the island's most stunning scenery. The B8073 winds its way anti-clockwise from Tobermory in a series of twists and turns as it follows the contours of the coastline. The road climbs west from Tobermory then makes a dramatic descent, with hairpin bends, to Dervaig.

Dervaig is a lovely village of whitewashed cottages, beautifully situated at the head of Loch Cuin. It has two very notable features. One is **Kilmore Church**, which has an unusual pencil-shaped spire. Dervaig's claim to fame, though, is the **Mull Little Theatre** ① *T01688-400245, May-Sep*, the smallest professional theatre in Britain, with only 43 seats. It puts on an impressive programme of plays in the summer. One mile beyond Dervaig take the turn-off to Torloisk to reach the **Old Byre Heritage Centre** ① *T01688-400229, Easter to end-Oct daily 1030-1830, £3, concession £2, children £1.50*, which stands out as one of the few genuinely interesting examples of these places. It also features a video of Mull's history and a tearoom, see Eating, page 145.

Tobermory

Sleeping 🛏
Baliscate Guest House **1**
Failte Guest House **3**

Mishnish **5**
SYHA Youth Hostel **6**
Western Isles **8**

⁑ Shiver me timbers

The history of 16th-century Europe is littered with the remains of carefully forged and hastily broken political alliances between the various superpowers. One such deal between England and Spain was broken in 1588, prompting Philip II of Spain to send the Spanish Armada, a massive force of 130 ships, to take on the English navy. Originating in Cadiz, the Spanish force moved north and left Lisbon on 20 May. They met Queen Elizabeth's ships in the English Channel, where they were duly routed.

A number of Spanish ships fled up the east coast, chased by the British fleet as far as the Firth of Forth. Denied entry into the estuary by further British naval forces, the tattered remnants of these great Spanish galleons were no longer considered to pose a threat and were left to their own fate. Many continued up the east coast of Scotland, only to be wrecked in the perilous North Sea. Not all the crews drowned, however, and several integrated into local communites, where their descendants still live to this day. Most of their offspring were distinctively black haired and there is strong facial resemblance even today between some on the northeast coast of Scotland and the residents of Cadiz, from where the Armada originally sailed.

Some Spanish ships headed for the west coast, but were lost in a violent storm in the Hebrides. One galleon, the Florida, was lost in Tobermory harbour, reputedly carrying £300,000 worth of gold bullion. However, during recent dives all that was found on the seabed were rotted timbers, a sailor's bangle and a silver spoon.

Five miles west of Dervaig is **Calgary Bay**, Mull's most beautiful beach ringed by steep wooded slopes with views across to Coll and Tiree. Calgary in Alberta, Canada was named after the former township. Many emigrants were forcibly shipped to Canada from here during the Clearances. There are some wonderful paths through Calgary Wood, just past **Calgary Farmhouse Hotel**, including a half hour circular walk.

Isle of Ulva

If you have the time and need to escape the hectic bustle of Mull, then take a day out on idyllic Ulva (meaning 'wolf island' in Norse), just off the west coast. You won't see any wolves around, but you're almost guaranteed to spot deer, golden eagles, buzzards and seals offshore. There are several woodland and coastal trails across the island, including one to the southwest where there are basalt columns similar to those on Staffa, or you can follow the trail to the top of the hill for views across to the Cuillins on Skye (on a clear day), or cross to Ulva's even smaller neighbour **Gometra** by a causeway. For more information on the island walks and on its history, visit the **Boathouse Heritage Centre** ① *T01688-500241, ulva@mull.com, Easter-Oct Mon-Fri 0900-1700 and Sun Jun-Aug only, entry is included in the ferry fare (see Transport)*, close to the ferry slip on Ulva. There's also a tearoom where you can try the local oysters with Guinness.

Staffa

The tiny uninhabited island of Staffa, five miles off the west coast of Mull, is one of the most spectacular sights not just in Scotland but anywhere in the world. It consists of immense hexagonal, basalt pillars which loom up out of the sea like a giant pipe organ. Staffa was formed 60 million years ago by the slow cooling of Tertiary basalt

Things to do on Mull when it's wet

It rains a lot on Mull, but luckily there's a fairly large number of indoor options to keep you nice and dry until the weather changes. If you've just arrived off the ferry from Oban and it's chucking it down, then head straight for **Torosay Castle**, just to the south of Craignure. And if the weather changes whilst exploring the interior, don't miss the gardens. Just beyond the castle is **Wings Over Mull**, a bird of prey conservation centre which offers indoor hawk-handling and a chance to learn about the island's incredible bird life. Nearby is Mull's greatest fortification, **Duart Castle**, which is also worth a peek. If all that history gets too much then you could do worse than hole up in the bar of the **Craignure Inn** and relax in front of their roaring log fire.

In the north of the island, the most appealing option by far is the **Old Byre Heritage Centre**, not far from the picturesque village of Dervaig. When in Tobermory do as the locals do, and get yourself down to the **bar of the Mish**, though you shouldn't really need the excuse of inclement weather. Meanwhile, over in Fionnphort, the departure point for the pilgrimage to Iona, you can seek spiritual assistance with a wee dram in the cosy **Keel Row Bar**.

lavas. These have been carved by the pounding sea into huge cathedral-like caverns such as the mightily impressive **Fingal's Cave**. The sound of the sea crashing against the black crystalline columns made such an impression on Felix Mendelssohn in 1829 that he immortalized the island in his *Hebrides Overture*. The composer was obviously aware of its original name in Gaelic, which means 'The Melodious Cave'. You can land on the island – if the weather is good enough – and walk into the cave via the causeway; an experience not be missed. But even if the seas are too rough, it's worth making the 90-minute boat trip just to witness the columns and cave.

South Mull

From Ulva Ferry the B8073 heads east along the north shore of **Loch na Keal** then enters a wide flat valley, where the road forks east to Salen and west along the south shore of Loch na Keal. This part of Mull is dominated by **Ben More** (3,170 ft), the island's highest mountain. All around is a spectacular region of high jutting mountains and deep glens, extending west to the **Ardmeanach Peninsula**. The peninsula may look impenetrable, but with the proper walking gear can be explored on foot. On the north coast, about a mile from the road, is the massive entrance to **MacKinnon's Cave**, which runs for about 100 yards back under the cliffs. Make sure to visit only at low tide. The area around the headland, now owned by the National Trust for Scotland, is known as **The Wilderness**. Near the headland is **MacCulloch's Tree**, a remarkable fossilized tree 40 ft high and thought to be 50 million years old, which was discovered in 1819. The tree is only accessible by a seven-mile footpath which begins at Burg Farm. You should have a map of the area and also time your arrival with low tide.

Mull's southernmost peninsula stretches west for 20 miles from the head of Loch Scridain as far as Iona. Most visitors use it merely as a route to Iona but there are a couple of interesting little detours along the way. A twisting side road leads south from Pennyghael over the hills and down to **Carsaig Bay**, from where you can head east or west along the shore for some dramatic coastal scenery. Two roads lead south from Bunessan. One leads to **Scoor**, near where is a great beach at Kilveockan. The other road splits near the coast: the left branch leads to **Uisken Bay**,

where there's a nice beach; the righthand branch leads to **Ardlanish Bay**, which also
has a good beach.

The road ends at **Fionnphort**, the departure point for the small passenger-only ferry to Iona, just a mile across the Sound of Iona. The village is little more than a car park, a row of houses, a pub and a shop, but there are several inexpensive B&Bs for those arriving too late to make the crossing. Even if you're not staying, it's worth stopping off in the village to visit the **Columba Centre** ① *mid-May to end-Sep Mon-Sat 1000-1800, Sun 1100-1800, £2, children £1*, a museum which relates the saint's life story.

A road runs south from Fionnphort to **Knockvologan**, opposite **Erraid Island**, which is accessible at low tide. The island has literary connections, for it was here that Robert Louis Stevenson is believed to have written *Kidnapped*. **Balfour Bay** on the south of the island is named after the novel's hero who was shipwrecked here.

▲ Walks on Mull → *OS Landranger maps 47, 48 and 49 cover the entire island.*
Mull presents numerous walking opportunities, ranging from gentle forest trails to wild and dramatic coastal routes, or even a spot of Munro-bagging for the more intrepid. With the exception of the Cuillins on Skye, Mull's highest peak, Ben More (3,170 ft) is the only Munro not on the mainland.

The trail starts at a lay-by on the B8035, at Dishig, and is fairly clear, though it can be tricky near the top. Return the same way, or more experienced climbers could continue down the narrow ridge to the eastern summit, **A'Chioch**, then descend the eastern face to the road that skirts **Loch Ba**. The views from the top are magnificent, across the other Hebridean islands and even as far as Ireland. If it's a cloudy day, it's worth postponing the ascent until there's clear weather. Allow around six hours for the round trip.

There are a couple of excellent coastal walks which start out from Carsaig Bay. A good path heads west along the shore to **Carsaig Arches** at Malcom's Point. The path runs below the cliffs out to the headland and then around it, and after about a mile reaches **Nun's Cave**, a wide and shallow cave where the nuns of Iona took refuge after being expelled during the Reformation. The path continues for another mile or so, but becomes a bit exposed in places and traverses a steep slope above a sheer drop into the sea. The famous arches are columnar basalts worn into fantastic shapes. One is a free-standing rock stack and another is a huge cave with two entrances. You'll need to allow about four hours in total plus some time at the arches.

Heading east from Carsaig Bay is a spectacular 4½-mile walk to **Lochbuie**, past **Adnunan stack**. It starts out through woodland, then follows the shore below the steep cliffs, with waterfalls plunging straight into the sea. It's easy at first but then gets very muddy in places and there's quite a bit of wading through boggy marsh, so make sure you've got good walking boots. Allow about five to six hours in total.

A shorter walk takes you to the Bronze-Age **Lochbuie Stone Circle** at the foot of **Ben Buie**. Leave your car at the stone bridge before you reach the village. Look for the green sign on the gate to your left and follow the white marker stones across the field. The stone circle is hidden behind a wall of rhododendrons, so follow the marker stones across the plank bridge until you see it. It takes about 30 minutes.

There are a few marked trails through Forestry Commission land on Mull. The first walk is to **Aros Park**, on the south side of Tobermory Bay. Start out from the car park near the distillery in Tobermory and follow the shoreline for about a mile to Lochan a'Ghurrabain, which is good for trout fishing. From here there is also a marked path around the loch (one mile). A longer walk is to **Ardmore Bay**, three miles north of Tobermory. The trail/cycle path starts at the car park by the road that runs northwest from Tobermory. From here, it runs out almost to Ardmore point and back again, passing a couple of ruined villages on the way. There's a good chance of seeing seals and lots of sea birds in Ardmore Bay. The trail is four miles in total.

Four miles north of Craignure is the car park and picnic site at **Garmony Point**, where a two-mile trail leads to the ferry terminal at **Fishnish**, hugging the shore all the way. Another trail (four miles) runs out to Fishnish Point and back through the forest to the car park by the old harbour.

Iona → *Phone code: 01681. Colour map 3, grid C3. Population: 130.*

Iona is a small island – barely three miles long and a little over a mile wide – but its importance to Christianity is out of all proportion to its size. Iona's place in religious history was guaranteed when St Columba arrived with his 12 disciples and founded a monastery there in AD 563. The Irish monk then set about converting a large part of pagan Scotland and much of northern England. Iona went on to become the most sacred religious site in Europe and has been a place of pilgrimage for several centuries. Today that pilgrimage has turned into more of an invasion, with daytrippers making the five-minute ferry trip from Mull to visit the abbey. Few, however, venture beyond the main village, **Baile Mór**, and it's easy to find a quiet spot, particularly on the west coast with its sparkling silver beaches washed by turquoise sea. It's worth spending a day or two here to soak up the island's unique spiritual peace so well conveyed in the words of Dr Johnson: "that man is little to be envied whose...piety would not grow warmer among the ruins of Iona".

Background

Iona is known as the 'Cradle of Christianity in Scotland', and was a centre of the arts. The monks produced elaborate carvings, manuscripts, ornate gravestones and Celtic crosses. Their greatest work was the beautiful *Book of Kells*, which dates from AD 800, and which is now on display in Dublin's Trinity College. This proved to be the high point of the church's history. Shortly after came the first of the Viking raids, in AD 806, when many monks were slaughtered at Martyrs' Bay, followed by another in AD 986 which destroyed the work of many years. The relentless pressure from the established church ended with the suppression of the Celtic Church by King David in 1144.

In 1203 Iona became part of the mainstream church with the establishment of a nunnery for the Order of the Black Nuns, as well as a Benedictine Abbey by Reginald of the MacDonalds of the Isles. Iona became overshadowed by the royal city of Dunfermline, and its final demise came with the Reformation when buildings were demolished and all but three of the 360 carved crosses destroyed.

The abbey lay in ruins until in 1899 the island's owner, the eighth Duke of Argyll, donated the buildings to the Church of Scotland on condition that the abbey church was restored for worship. Then in 1938 the Reverand George Macleod founded the Iona Community as an evangelical Church of Scotland 'brotherhood', with the abbey buildings as its headquarters, and by 1965 had succeeded in rebuilding the remainder of the monastic buildings. Now the abbey complex has been completely restored and the island of Iona, apart from the abbey buildings, is owned by the National Trust for Scotland.

The abbey

ⓘ *Open all year and at all times, free but a donation at the entrance is appreciated.*
The present abbey dates from around 1200, though it has been rebuilt over the centuries and completely restored in the 20th century. The oldest part is the restored **St Oran's Chapel**, to the south of the abbey on the right, which is plain and unadorned save for its splendid 11th-century Norman doorway. It is said that Columba was prevented from completing the building of the original chapel until a living person had been buried in the foundations. His friend Oran volunteered and was duly buried.

⁝ The story of St Columba

St Columba (*Colum Cille* in Gaelic), a prince of Ireland and grandson of the Irish King, Niall of the Nine Hostages, came to Scotland not as a missionary, but as an act of self-imposed penance for his actions. He stubbornly refused to hand over his copy of the Gospels, illegally copied from St Finian's original, which led to a bitter dispute with the king. This ended in a pitched battle in which Columba's supporters prevailed, but he was so overcome with remorse at the bloodshed he had caused that he fled Ireland, finally settling on Iona as it was the first place he found from where he couldn't see his homeland. Columba, however, was not retiring into obscurity. His missionary zeal drove him to begin work on building the abbey. He also banished women and cows from the island, declaring that "where there is a cow there is a woman, and where there is a woman there is mischief". Workers at the abbey had to leave their womenfolk on nearby Eilean nam Ban (Women's Island). Not content with that, he also banished frogs and snakes from Iona, though there are plenty on Mull. He is even said to have pacified the Loch Ness Monster during a visit to Inverness. He went on to found the Celtic Church, or the Church of the Culdees, with centres through-out Scotland, which differed in many ways from the Church of Rome.

Columba later asked for the face to be uncovered so that he could bid a final farewell to his friend, but Oran was found to be alive and claimed he had seen Heaven and Hell, describing them in such blasphemous terms that Columba ordered he be covered up immediately!

Surrounding the chapel is the **Reilig Odhrain**, the sacred burial ground, which is said to contain the graves of 48 Scottish kings, including Macbeth's victim, Duncan, as well as four Irish and eight Norwegian kings. The stones you see today are not the graves of kings but of various important people from around the West Highlands and Islands. The most notable is that of John Smith, leader of the British Labour Party from 1992 until his untimely death in 1994.

Beside the Road of the Dead, which leads from the abbey church to St Oran's Chapel, stands the eighth-century **St Martin's Cross**. This is the finest of Iona's Celtic high crosses and is remarkably complete, with the Pictish serpent-and-boss decoration on one side and holy figures on the other. Standing in front of the abbey entrance is a replica of **St John's Cross**, the other great eighth-century monument. The restored original is in the **Infirmary Museum**, at the rear of the abbey, along with a fine collection of medieval gravestones.

No part of St Columba's original buildings survives, but to the left of the main entrance is **St Columba's Shrine**, the small, steep-roofed chamber which almost certainly marks the site of the saint's tomb. This is **Torr an Aba**, where Columba's cell is said to have been. The **Abbey** itself has been carefully restored to its original beautiful simplicity and inside, in a side chapel, are marble effigies of the eighth Duke of Argyll and his third wife, Duchess Ina.

⁝ *You get a good view of the whole complex from the top of the small grassy knoll opposite the abbey entrance.*

Baile Mór

The passenger ferry from Fionnphort on Mull lands at Baile Mór, Iona's main village, which is little more than a row of cottages facing the sea. There are over a dozen places to stay but, as demand far exceeds supply during the busy summer season, it's best to book in advance at one of the tourist offices on Mull, or in Oban. There's also a post office, a very good craft shop and general store in the village. Just outside the village, on the way to the abbey, are the ruins of the **Augustinian nunnery**. Just to the north, housed in the parish church manse, built by Thomas Telford, is the **Iona Heritage Centre** ① *Apr-Oct Mon-Sat 1030-1630, £1.50*, which features displays on the island's social history. Nearby stands the intricately carved 15th-century **Maclean's Cross**.

Around the island

On the west coast are some lovely beaches of white sand and colourful pebbles. The best of the lot is the **Bay at the Back of the Ocean**, beside the golf course, and only a mile and a half walk from the ferry. This was one of John Smith's favourite places and it's easy to see why. At the southern tip of the island is another sandy beach at **St Columba's Bay**, believed to be the spot where the saint first landed. Another good walk is to the top of **Dun I**, the only real hill, which rises to a height of 300 ft.To get there, continue on the road north from the abbey, past MacDougal's Cross, then go through a gate to the right of Bishop's Walk Farm and follow the fence up to where you join a footpath up to the top. It's only about half an hour up and down and there are great views from the top of the entire island and the coastline of Mull.

● Sleeping

Mull *p136*

L Western Isles Hotel, Tobermory, T01688-302012, F302297. 23 rooms. Open all year, the biggest and grandest hotel on the island, set high above the harbour with great views from the comfortable rooms, has 3 excellent restaurants, including the lovely conservatory bar.

A Druimard Country House Hotel, Dervaig, T01688-400291, www.druimard.co.uk. 6 rooms, open end Mar-Oct. This Victorian country house is right beside the Mull Little Theatre; the room rate includes dinner in their excellent restaurant.

A Highland Cottage, Breadalbane St, Tobermory, T01688-302030, www.highlandcottage.co.uk. 6 rooms. Open Mar to mid-Oct. Cosy little hotel that's best known for its quite superb restaurant. The high standard of Scottish cooking means it's a very popular dining choice for islanders and often fully booked.

D Calgary Farmhouse Hotel, Calgary Bay, T01688-400256. 9 rooms, open Apr-Oct. This farmhouse is one of Mull's gems, and the adjoining **Dovecote Restaurant** serves excellent food (££). There's also a tearoom, The Carthouse, which offers light lunches and home baking.

D Craignure Inn, Craignure, T01680-812305, www.craignure-inn.co.uk. 3 rooms, open all year. Its cosy bar serves decent food (££-£) and is a good place to seek refuge on a wet day.

D Mishnish Hotel, Main St, Tobermory, T01688-302009, www.mishnish.co.uk. Open all year, 10 rooms. Its bar is the live music focus of the town and social hub (see below).

D Old Mill Guest House & Restaurant, 3 miles south of Craignure, at Lochdon, T/F01680-812442. 3 rooms. Their cosy little restaurant has a deserved reputation for fine cuisine, so you'll need to book in advance.

D Pennyghael Hotel, Pennyghael, overlooking the loch, T01681-704288, F704205, which is open from Easter to Oct and has an excellent restaurant.

E Achaban House, just before Fionnphort, T01681-700205, www.achabanhouse.co.uk. 7 rooms. This former manse is comfortable and well-furnished, and also offers dinner.

E Baliscate Guest House, a short walk from Tobermory, T01688-302048, F302666. 3 en suite rooms. They also organize fishing and wildlife trips, see Activities and tours p146.

E Failte Guest House, Main St, Tobermory, T/F01688-302495. Open Mar-Oct, 7 rooms. Best of the guest houses, excellent.

E Uisken Croft, Uisken Bay, T01681-700307, open Apr-Oct. Idyllic.

Iona *p142*

B Argyll Hotel, T01681-700334, www.argyllhoteliona.co.uk. 17 rooms, open Apr-Oct. This is the better of the island's 2 upmarket hotels, and its good restaurant serves lunches 4-course dinners.

F Iona Hostel, T01681-700642. An

exceptional hostel with views to the Treshnish Islands about a mile from the ferry along the path past the abbey. It's best to book ahead in summer.

🍴 Eating

Mull *p136*
See also Sleeping above for some of the best eating options on the island.
£££-£ Western Isles Hotel, Tobermory, see Sleeping, offers the best eating in town. Here you can choose between 3 restaurants. A 3-course à la carte in the dining room or the oriental **Spices Bistro** (expensive to mid-range), while cheap bar meals are served in the **Conservatory Bar**.
£££ Mediterranea, Salen, T01680-300200, www.mullonthemed.com. Apr-Oct and Dec 1800-2300, Jan-Mar Thu-Sun only. Excellent Italian restaurant run by Giovani and Francesca, serves up classic dishes with a Sicilian twist. 4 course set menu is great value at £20. No licence but BYO for a small corkage fee.
££ Mishnish hotel, see Sleeping above. The 'Mish' serves gargantuan platefuls of pleasing grub to locals and visitors alike. Their monster fish and chips will fill even the emptiest of tummies.
££ Dovecote Restaurant, adjoining **Calgary Farmhouse Hotel**, Calgary Bay, see Sleeping, serves excellent food. There can be no better way to end the day than dinner here followed by a stroll along the beach at sunset. There's also a tearoom, **The Carthouse**, which offers light lunches and home baking.
£ Old Byre Heritage Centre, Dervaig, see Sights above. Open Apr to end-Oct. Simple, home-made delights offered all day. Not a huge menu but a worthwhile lunch stop.

🎭 Entertainment

Mull *p136*
Mishnish Hotel, Main St, Tobermory. An absolute must when in town is a night in the 'Mish'. After one of their pub meals and several pints of ale, bending over the pool table is an effort, not to mention jigging along to some good live folk music.

For the sake of choice, other pubs and live music venues are available, namely **MacGochan's**, at the other end of the harbour, near the distillery. There are also music events at **An Tobar**, Tobermory, see Sights p137.

🎉 Festivals and events

Mull *p136*
Apr Mull Music Festival, known as the **Whisky Olympics**, is held on the last weekend of the month. It is a great time to be on Mull when you can enjoy a feast of Gaelic folk music and, of course, whisky. The focus of the festival is the bar of the **Mishnish Hotel**, Tobermory. For details T01688-302383.
Jul Mendelssohn on Mull Festival, held over 10 days in early Jul, this is another great festival. It is held to commemorate the famous composer's visit here in 1829.
Jul Tobermory Highland Games, annually on the 3rd Thu in Jul.
Sep The Sound of Mull, a day long celebration of local rock and pop acts, takes place at the end of Sep.
Oct Tour of Mull Rally, held in early Oct, should not be missed by rally enthusiasts.

🛍 Shopping

Mull *p136*
Despite its popularity, Tobermory hasn't succumbed to the dreaded tartan disease that afflicts so many other tourist hot-spots. You're more likely to find shops selling fishing tackle or diving gear than tacky souvenirs, and the ones that do cater for the tourist market are tastefully done.
Isle of Mull Cheese, on the edge of town, 500 yds off the Dervaig Rd, at Sgriob-Ruadh Farm, T01688-302235. Here you can savour their award-winning traditionally made cheese and their wonderful glass barn. Open Apr to end-Sep Mon-Fri 1000-1600.
Mull Pottery, T01688-302057, tasteful pots in different shapes and sizes.
Mull Silver Company, T01688-302345, open 0900-1730, are tastefully done and enjoyable places to browse in on a wet afternoon.
Tobermory Chocolate Company, at the

foot of Back Brae, which leads steeply up from the harbour to the upper part of the village, T01688-302526, open May-Oct Mon-Sat 0930-1730. Here you can try out their speciality – chocolate made with the local whisky.

▲ Activities and tours

Mull *p136*
Boat trips
Alternative Boat Hire, T01681-700537, offer trips around the coastline and handline fishing on a traditional wooden boat. You can hire by the hour or for an afternoon, May-Oct, from Fionnphort and Iona.
Edge of the World, T01688-302808, www. edge-of-the-world.co.uk, operate powerboat trips from Tobermory around Mull and as far as Ardnamurchan. One-hour trips cost £12, 2-hr trips £20. Seals, porpoises, basking sharks and even minke whales can be seen.
Turus Mara, www.turusmara.com. Trips to Staffa and the Treshnish Isles leave from Oban, Dervaig, Ulva Ferry, Iona or Fionnphort, weather permitting. A full-day cruise including Staffa and the Treshnish Isles costs £33 per person (£17 for children); a cruise to Staffa only costs around £15.

Diving
Seamore Diving offer diving trips and courses. Book through **Seafare Chandlery & Diving Service**, Main St, Tobermory, T/F01688-302277.

Fishing
Amidas Sea Fishing & Wildlife Trips, based at Baliscate House, see Sleeping, or book at Tackle & Books, T01688-302336, offers fishing trips. They cost around £15 for 3 hrs, or £30 for a full day.
A Brown & Son, 21 Main St, Tobermory, T01688-302020, F302454. Permits for trout fishing are available from here.
For more details pick up the *Tobermory Angling Association* leaflet from the tourist office.

Wildlife tours
Island Encounter Wildlife Safaris,
Arla-Beag, Aros, T01680-300441. These can be made from Aros, just to the north of Salen, with Richard Atkinson. A full-day wildlife safari with a local guide costs £25 including lunch. You'll see golden eagles, white-tailed sea eagles, hen harriers, divers, merlins, peregrine falcons, seals and porpoises, to name but a few.
Sea Life Surveys, T01688-302787. Whale- and dolphin-watching trips can be made from Tobermory with this outfit. A full-day tour costs £45 (£48 in Jul/Aug), and there's a maximum of 12 people per trip. You can find out more at the **Hebridean Whale and Dolphin Trust**, 28 Main St, Tobermory, T01688-302620, www.hwdt.org, Apr-Oct daily 1000-1700, Nov-Mar Mon-Fri 1100-1700, a charity which aims to protect the marine environment through education, and at **Isle of Mull Landrover Wildlife Expeditions**, Ulva House Hotel, T01688-302044, David Woodhouse.

❂ Transport

Mull *p136*
Bicycle There are many places to rent bikes. In Tobermory there's **Tom-a' Mhuillin**, the Salen Rd, T01688-302164, **Brown's Hardware** shop on Main St, T01688-302020, or try the **youth hostel** in Tobermory. In Salen there's **On Yer Bike**, T01680-300501, which also has a shop by the ferry terminal in Craignure, T01680-812487.

Bus There's a bus from Tobermory post office to **Dervaig** and **Calgary**, 5 times a day Mon-Fri and twice on Sat (operated by RN Carmichael, T01688-302220). The **Craignure** to Tobermory via **Salen** service runs 5 times a day Mon-Fri, 8 times on Sat and 3 times on Sun (operated by Bowman's Coaches, T01680-812313, and Highlands & Islands Coaches, T01680-812510). There's a bus from **Craignure** to **Fionnphort** (for Iona) 6 times a day Mon-Fri, 4 times on Sat and 1 on Sun (Bowman's and Highlands & Islands). There's also a postbus service from **Salen** to **Burg** (Kilninian) via the Ulva Ferry twice a day Mon-Sat (Royal Mail, T01463-256200). For bus times, contact the operators or pick up the *Mull Area Transport Guide* at the tourist office in Oban, Tobermory or Craignure. This also includes ferry times.

Car Tobermory is a 30- to 40-min drive north from the ferry pier at **Craignure**. There are daily buses from Craignure which coincide with ferry arrivals. A small bicycle/passenger- only ferry makes the 2-min crossing on demand from Ulva Ferry, Apr-Oct Mon-Fri 0900-1700, and on Sun Jun-Aug. This includes entry to the **Boathouse Heritage Centre, Sheila's Cottage** (a musuem of island life) and access to all walks. At other times call to make arrangements, T01688-500226.

Ferry From **Oban** to **Craignure** (45 mins) 5-7 times daily Mon-Sat and 5 times daily on Sun, £3.85 one way per passenger, £34.50 per car, 5-day return £6.60 and £46.50. **CalMac** offices: Oban, T01631-566688, and Craignure, T01680-812343. **Lochaline** on the Morvern Peninsula (see p199) to **Fishnish** (15 mins, £2.40 per passenger, £10.45 per car) hourly 0700-1830 Mon-Sat and 4 times on Sun. Some ferries from **Oban** to **Coll** and **Tiree**

(see below) call in at **Tobermory**. There are also ferries from **Kilchoan** on the Ardnamurchan Peninsula (see p199) to **Tobermory** 7 times daily Mon-Sat and 5 times daily on Sun (Jun-Aug).

Iona *p142*
To Iona, a passenger-only ferry leaves from Fionnphort on Mull (5 mins) frequently 0845-1815 Mon-Sat and hourly 0900-1800 Sun, £3.60 per passenger, bicycles free.

🔾 Directory

Mull *p136*
Banks Clydesdale Bank, Main St, is Mull's only permanent bank. There's also a mobile bank which tours the island; for details T08457-826818.

Coll, Tiree and Colonsay

The low-lying, treeless and windswept island of Coll offers the simple pleasures in life. There's little to do here other than stroll along the magnificent, deserted beaches. Tourism, though, remains low on the list of priorities, and those who do come prefer it that way. Even by Hebridean standards there are few facilities, and accommodation is scarce. Tiree, meanwhile, claims to be the sunniest place in Scotland, but it's also one of the windiest places in the country. So windy, in fact, that Tiree has become the windsurfing capital of Scotland and is known as the 'Hawaii of the North'. The wild weather, however, contrasts sharply with the warm kindness of the islanders. Colonsay is the epitome of the island haven: remote, tranquil and undemanding. It has abundant wildlife, beautiful plants and flowers, dazzling white beaches and even a miniature mountain range, all packed into its modest 17 square miles. All this has become accessible to daytrippers, with a ferry round trip (see below), leaving you six hours ashore. This does scant justice to the island's peculiar charms, however, and judging by the ever-growing number of holiday homes and self-catering accommodation on Colonsay, it's a view shared by many. ▸▸ *For Sleeping, eating and other listings, see page 149.*

Coll → *Phone code: 01879. Colour map 3, grid B2-3.*

The best of Coll's beaches are on the west coast, at **Killunaig, Hogh Bay** and **Feall Bay**. The latter is separated from the nearby **Crossapool Bay** by giant sand dunes up to 100 ft high. These are now owned by the RSPB to protect the resident corncrake population. The CalMac ferry from Oban calls in at Coll's only village, **Arinagour**, where half of the island's population live and where you'll find the post office and a few shops. There's no petrol station, but you should leave the car behind anyway. The island is only 13 miles long by four miles wide and the best way to get around is on foot or by bike. It's worth taking a walk up **Ben Hogh** (341 ft), the island's highest point, overlooking Hogh Bay on the west coast, to get a good overview. The east coast, north from Arinagour to Sorisdale, is an uninhabited wilderness which is ideal for some gentle hillwalking.

Tiree → *Phone code: 01879. Colour map 3, grid B2.*

Tiree is a low, flat island, only about 11 miles long and six miles across at its widest, and is also known by the nickname *Tir fo Thuinn*, or 'Land below the waves'. When seen from a distance most of it disappears below the horizon, save its two highest hills, **Ben Hynish** (462 ft) and **Beinn Hough** (390 ft), on the west coast. Being flat and small, it obviously makes good sense to explore it by bicycle, but remember that the constant wind varies from strong to gale force. The ferry port is at **Gott Bay**, half a mile from **Scarinish**, the island's main village and home to a **Co-op** supermarket, post office and bank (there's a garage at the pier head). About four miles from Scarinish, is Vaul Bay,

❧ *If you are a windsurfing fan, you must come to Tiree – it is one of the best places to surf in the British Isles.*

where the well-preserved remains of **Dun Mor**, a Pictish Broch built around the first century AD, stand on a rocky outcrop to the west of the bay.

The island's main road runs northwest from Scarinish, past the beautiful beach at **Balephetrish Bay** to Balevullin, where you can see some good examples of restored traditional thatched houses. Just to the south, at Sandaig, is the **Thatched House Museum** ① *Jun-Sep Mon-Fri 1400-1600*, which tells of the island's social history.

In the southwestern corner of the island is the most spectacular scenery of all, at the headland of **Ceann a'Mara**, or Kenavara. The massive sea cliffs are the home of thousands of sea birds and you can see seals on the rocky shore. East from here, across the golden sands of Balephuil Bay, is the island's highest hill, **Ben Hynish**, topped by a radar-tracking station resembling a giant golf ball. Despite this, it's worth the climb to the top for the magnificent views over the island and, on clear days, across to the Outer Hebrides. Below Ben Hynish, to the east, is the village of **Hynish**, where you'll find the **Signal Tower Museum**, which tells the fascinating story of the building of the **Skerryvore Lighthouse** (1840-1844) by Alan Stevenson, an uncle of Robert Louis Stevenson. This incredible feat of engineering was carried out from Hynish, where a dry dock/reservoir was built for shipping materials by boat to the Skerryvore reef, 10 miles to the southwest.

Colonsay → *Phone code: 01951. Colour map 3, grid C3.*

Colonsay's population lives in the three small villages, the largest of which is **Scalasaig**, the ferry port. A few miles north of the ferry, in the middle of the island, is **Colonsay House**, dating from 1772. The house was sold, along with the rest of the island, in 1904 to Lord Strathcona, who had made his fortune in Canada with the Hudson Bay Company and went on to found the Canadian Pacific Railway. The house is not open to the public but the lovely gardens and woods, full of rhododendrons, giant palms and exotic shrubs, are worth a stroll. The estate cottages are now self-catering holiday homes.

There are several standing stones, the best of which are **Fingal's Limpet Hammers**, at Kilchattan, southwest of Colonsay House. There are also Iron Age forts, such as **Dun Eibhinn**, next to the hotel in Scalasaig (see below). Colonsay is also home to a wide variety of wildlife. You can see choughs, one of Britain's rarest birds, as well as corncrakes, buzzards, falcons, merlins and perhaps even the odd golden eagle or sea eagle. There are also otters, seals and wild goats (said to be descended from the survivors of the Spanish Armada ships wrecked in 1588). The jewel in the island's crown, though, lies six miles north of Scalasaig, past Colonsay House, at

Kiloran Bay. The beach here is described as the finest in the Hebrides, and who could argue. Just a glimpse of this magnificent half mile of golden sands, backed by tiers of grassy dunes, with massive breakers rolling in off the Atlantic, is worth the two-hour ferry crossing alone.

Just off the southern tip of Colonsay is the island of Oronsay, two miles square with a population of six and one of the highlights of a visit to Colonsay. The name derives from the Norse for 'ebb-tide island', which is a fitting description as Oronsay can be reached on foot at low tide, across the mud flats known as 'The Strand'. It takes about an hour to walk from the south end of Colonsay to the ruins of a 14th-century **Augustinian Priory**. This was the home of some of the most highly skilled medieval craftsmen in the Western Highlands. A surviving example of their work is the impressive Oronsay Cross and the beautifully carved tombstones, on display in the **Prior's House**. Make sure you take wellies for the walk across the Strand and check on the tides. Tide tables are available at the hotel or shop. Spring tides (new and full moon) allow about three to four hours to walk across and back, which is just enough time to see the priory but little else.

● Sleeping

Coll *p147*
C **Coll Hotel**, Arinagour, T01879-230334.
A family hotel with a good restaurant.
E **Achamore**, T01879-230430. A lovely old farmhouse a few miles west of the village.

Tiree *p148*
C **Kirkapol House**, in a converted church overlooking Gott Bay, T/F01879-220729.
D **The Glassary Guest House & Restaurant**, at Sandaig, T/F01879-220684. 4 en suite rooms, open all year, very good food (**££**).

Colonsay *p148*
Accommodation on Colonsay is limited and must be booked up well in advance. Even self-catering options are hard to come by, because the same families return year after year (and who can blame them?). Try **Colonsay Cottages**, T01951-200312, www.colonsay.org.uk/estate
B **Isle of Colonsay Hotel**, T01951-200316, www.colonsay.org.uk. A few 100 yds from the ferry, 11 rooms, a cosy inn with a friendly bar and excellent food; they also arrange various trips around the island.
E **Seaview**, T01951-200315, at Kilchattan, near the standing stones. Open Apr-Oct.
F **Colonsay Backpacker's Lodge**, T01951-200312, www.colonsay.org.uk. An old keeper's cottage 2km from the ferry, sleeps 16 and open all year, phone for lift from ferry.

▲▲ Activities and tours

Tiree *p148*
Windsurfing tuition is available at Loch Bhasapol, T01879-220559 (summer only). The major windsurfing event is the **Wave Classic**, held annually in Oct.

● Transport

Coll *p147*
Some 13 miles long by 4 miles wide, Coll is best navigated on foot or by bike. CalMac car/ passenger ferries leave from **Oban**, 2 hrs 40 mins, 1 daily, £12.30 per person and £72 per car.

Tiree *p148*
Air Tiree has an airport with 1 flight daily Mon-Sat (45 mins), all year round to Glasgow. The airport is at The Reef, Crossapol, T01879-220309.
Bicycle Bicycle hire is available at the **Tiree Lodge Hotel**, or contact Mr N Maclean, T01879-220428.
Bus There's a postbus service around the island, and to and from the airport. The timetable is available at Scarinish Post Office.
Ferry CalMac car/passenger ferries sail to the island from **Oban**, via **Coll** once daily (3 hrs 50 mins, £12.30 per passenger, £72 per car) once daily and, occasionally, **Tobermory**. From Coll to Tiree (50 mins) costs £3.20 per passenger and £18.45 per car. The ferry port is at Scarinish (T01879- 220337).

Taxi There's a shared taxi service which operates on request Mon-Fri 0930-1500 (limited service on Sat), also Mon-Wed and Fri 1600-1730, and a Tue evening service for arriving ferries in the summer. For private taxi hire call **Island Cabs**, T01879-220344 (evenings and weekends only).

Colonsay *p148*

Bicycle As the island is only 8 miles long by 3 miles wide, you might want to consider hiring a bicycle. Bike hire from **A McConnel**, T01951-200355.

Bus There's a limited bus and postbus service around the island Mon-Sat, for those without their own transport. On Wed in the summer, a tour bus meets the ferry and takes visitors round the island.

Ferry There are ferry sailings from **Oban** (2 hrs, £10.90 one way per passenger, £53 per car) once daily Mon, Wed, Thu Fri and Sun, arriving at Scalasaig on the east coast. From **Kennacraig** there is 1 sailing (3 hrs 35 mins) on Wed. From **Port Askaig** there is 1 sailing (1¼ hrs, £4.10 per passenger, £21.20 per car) also on Wed. Ferries need to be booked well in advance during the summer months.

Islay and Jura

Islay (pronounced eye-la), the most southerly of the Hebridean islands and one of the most populous, with around 4,000 inhabitants, has one very important claim to fame – single malt whisky. Islay produces a very distinctive, peaty malt and connoisseurs are in for a treat, as the island has no fewer than seven working distilleries. Aside from whisky, people also come here to watch birds. The island is something of an ornithologists' wonderland, and from October to April plays host to migrating barnacle and white-fronted geese flying down from Greenland in their thousands for the winter. The short ferry crossing from Islay takes you to Jura, a primeval and uncompromising place; a lost world, pervaded by an almost haunting silence. The words 'wild' and 'remote' tend to get overused in describing the many Hebridean islands, but in the case of Jura they are, if anything, an understatement. Jura has one road, one hotel, six sporting estates and 5,000 red deer, which outnumber the 200 people by 25:1, the human population having been cleared to turn the island into a huge deer forest. Rather appropriately, the name Jura derives from the Norse 'dyr-ey', meaning deer island. ▶▶ *For Sleeping, Eating and other listings, see page 155-156.*

Ins and outs

Islay's only official tourist information centre is in **Bowmore** ① *T01496-810254, Apr-Sep daily, Sep and Oct Mon-Sat, Oct-Mar Mon-Fri*. They'll find accommodation for you. ▶▶ *For Transport details, see page 156.*

Islay → *Phone code: 01496. Colour map 5, grid A1.*

Port Ellen and around

Port Ellen is the largest place on Islay and the main ferry port, yet it still has the feel of a sleepy village. There are many day trips from Port Ellen. A road runs east out to **Ardtalla**, where it ends. Along the way, it passes three distilleries, first **Laphroaig**, then **Lagavulin** and lastly, **Ardbeg**, all of which offer guided tours, see page 151. Between the Lagavulin and Ardbeg distilleries is the dramatically sited 16th-century ruin of **Dunyvaig Castle**, once the main naval base and fortress of the Lords of the Isles. A mile further on is the impressive **Kildalton Cross**, standing in the graveyard of the ruined 13th-century chapel. The eighth-century cross is well preserved and one of Scotland's most important Early Christian monuments, and the carvings depict biblical scenes.

Islay's malts distilled

Though the whisky distilling process is basically the same everywhere, some distilleries have more beautiful locations and more interesting tours. Islay's seven distilleries enjoy the most scenically stunning settings and are full of character and history. Islay also offers the unique opportunity to visit several of Scotland's most impressive distilleries in one day, and their distinctive peaty malts are considered to be among the finest.

Laphroaig, *T01496-302418, www.laphroaig.com, tours all year by appointment only 1015 and 1415, free*, (pronounced 'la-froyg'), is the closest to Port Ellen, and its wonderful setting is summed up by its name, meaning 'The beautiful hollow by the broad bay' in Gaelic. According to many this is the ultimate in malt whisky and is at its best after dinner.

Lagavulin, *T01496-302400, www.malts.com, tours all year Mon-Fri by appointment 1000, 1130 and 1430, £4*, (pronounced 'laga-voolin') is a mile along the shore by the romantic ruin of Duny-veg Castle. Their 16-year-old single malt is one of the classics and also makes the ideal after-dinner tipple. A very interesting tour.

Ardbeg, *T01496-302244, www.ardbeg.com, tours all year Mon-Fri 1030, 1130, 1430 and 1530, Jun-Aug daily, £2*, is a mile further east and produces a robust and powerful single malt. Established in 1815, it was closed for a while, but was recently acquired by Glenmorangie.

Bowmore, *T01496-810441, www.bowmore.com, tours winter Mon-Fri 1030 and 1400, Sat 1030; summer Mon-Fri 1030-1130, 1400 and 1500, Sat 1030 and 1400, £2*, is the oldest distillery on Islay and still uses all the old traditional methods to produce its fine single malt, also at its best after dinner. Their hour-long tours are the most professionally done and even include a video.

Caol Ila, *T01496-302760, www.malts.com, tours by appointment Apr-Oct Mon-Thu 1000, 1115, 1330 and 1445, £4*, (pronounced 'coal-eela') was founded in 1846 and lies close to Port Askaig, with great views across the Sound of Islay to Jura. Unlike most of its island peers, this single malt is best before dinner.

Bunnahabhain, *T01496-840646, www.brunstewartdistillers.com, tours Mar-Oct Mon-Fri 1030, 1300 and 1500, other times by appointment only, free*, (pronounced 'bun-a-havan') is the most northerly of the distilleries, set in a secluded bay with great views across to Jura.

Bruichladdich, *T01496-850221, www.bruichladdich.com, tours Mon-Fri 1030, 1130 and 1430, Sat (booking required) 1030 and 1430, £3*, (pronounced 'brook-laddie') is in the village of the same name on the road south to Port Charlotte. Recently voted distillery of the year by the readers of America's Malt Advocate.

Southwest of Port Ellen a road runs out to a little, rounded peninsula known as **The Oa**, an area of varied beauty, both wild and pastoral, and with a wonderful coastline. The road runs as far as **Upper Killeyan**, from where it's about a mile uphill to the spectacular headland at the **Mull of Oa**. Here you'll see the strange-looking **American monument**. The obelisk commemorates the ship-wrecks offshore of two US ships, the *Tuscania* and the *Ontranto*, both of which sank in 1918 at the end of the war. There's a great walk north from the Mull of Oa up to Kintra, but it's best to start out from Kintra.

A turn-off from the road to The Oa leads north to **Kintra**, at the south end of **The Big Strand** at Laggan Bay, with five miles of sands and dunes. There's a restaurant and accommodation here, and it's a great place for camping. The restaurant is at the end of the road, with the beach on one side and on the other a wild and spectacular coastal walk to the **Mull of Oa**. There's a detailed map of the route in the restaurant. Just to the north of Kintra is the **Machrie golf course**, a golfing experience that shouldn't be missed.

Islay & Jura

Bowmore and the Rinns of Islay

The A846 runs north from Port Ellen, straight as a pool cue, to Bowmore, the island's administrative capital and second largest village. Founded in 1768 by the Campbells, it's an appealing place, laid out in a grid plan with the main street running straight up the hill from the pier to the unusual round church, designed to ward off evil spirits, who can hide only in corners. Thankfully, the nice spirit stayed behind and can be found at the **Bowmore**

> ‼ If you are a golfer then tee off at the Machrie golf course, for a memorable golfing experience.

Distillery, just to the west of Main Street. This is the oldest of the island's distilleries, founded in 1779, and the most tourist-friendly.

North of Bowmore, at **Bridgend**, the A846 joins the A847 which runs west to the hammerhead peninsula known as the Rinns of Islay (*rinns* is derived from the Gaelic for promontory). A few miles west of Bridgend the B8017 turns north to the **RSPB Reserve** at **Loch Gruinart**. The mudflats and fields at the head of the loch provide winter grazing for huge flocks of barnacle and white-fronted geese from Greenland, arriving in late October. There's an RSPB visitor centre at **Aoradh** (pronounced *oorig*) which houses an observation point with telescopes and CCTV, and there's a hide across the road. There are about 110 species of bird breeding on Islay, including the rare chough and corncrake.

The coastal scenery around the Rinns is very impressive, particularly at **Killinallan Point**, a beautiful and lonely headland at the far northeast of Loch Gruinart. Also impressive is **Ardnave Point**, west of Loch Gruinart, and further west along the north coast, **Sanaigmore.** The best beaches are at **Saligo** and **Machir Bay** on the west coast, past Loch Gorm. Both are lovely, wide, golden beaches backed by high dunes, but swimming is forbidden due to dangerous undercurrents.

Port Charlotte is without doubt the most charming of Islay's villages, with rows of well-kept, whitewashed cottages stretched along the wide bay. Here, the **Islay Wildlife Information and Field Centre** ① *T01496-850288, Easter-Oct Mon, Tue, Thu, Fri and Sun 1000-1500, £2,* is a must for anyone interested in flora and fauna. It's very hands-on, with good displays on geology and natural history, a video room and reference library. It's also a great place for kids, and has activity days when staff take tours of the surrounding area. Also worth visiting is the compact **Museum of Islay Life** ① *Easter-Oct Mon-Sat 1000-1700, Sun 1400-1700, £2,* to

Argyll & Inner Hebrides Islay & Jura

⦂ Weapon of mass drunkeness

The US Defence Threat Reduction Agency (DTRA), whose mission is "to safeguard the US and its allies from weapons of mass destruction" has been monitoring the Bruichladdich Distillery on Islay.

The distillery installed webcams to show the world that their whisky is made using traditional methods, but in September 2003 discovered that the DTRA was spying on them. According to the agency, it only takes a 'tweak' – their words – in the process of whisky making and Bruichladdich could be producing deadly chemical weapons, hence their interest. The DTRA had emailed the distillery to inform them that one of their webcams was faulty and when the distillery replied to thank them and inquire who they were, the agency went right ahead and revealed who they were and what they were doing.

Once they had been 'outed', the DTRA had to admit that the distillery posed no threat to world peace, though many would contest that excessive consumption of the amber liquid has been known to contribute to the occasional breach of local peace in the island's bars.

Mark Reynier, the managing director of the Port Charlotte distillery, took it all in good humour: "we're a sinister-looking bunch, so I can see how we might be mistaken for Al-Qaeda", he quipped.

As they say, only in America.

the east of the village, where you can find out all about illegal whisky distilling on the island. It also has interesting archival material. At the southern end of the Rinns is the picturesque little fishing and crofting village of Portnahaven, its Hebridean cottages rising steeply above the deeply indented harbour.

Port Askaig and around

Port Askaig is Islay's other ferry port, with connections to the mainland and to the islands of Jura and Colonsay. It's little more than a dock, a car park and a few buildings huddled at the foot of a steep, wooded hillside. A short walk north along the coast is the **Caol Ila distillery**, and a couple of miles further north, at the end of the road which branches left before you enter Port Askaig, is the beautifully situated **Bunnahabhain Distillery**.

The A846 runs east from Bridgend out to Port Askaig passing through **Ballygrant**, just to the south of **Loch Finlaggan**. Here, on two *crannogs* (artificial islands), were the headquarters of the Lords of the Isles, the ancestors of Clan Donald. The MacDonalds ruled from Islay for nearly 350 years, over a vast area covering all of the island off the west coast and almost the whole of the western seaboard from Cape Wrath to the Mull of Kintyre. There's a **visitor centre** ① *Easter-Oct Tue, Thu and Sun 1400-1630, £1.50*, to the northeast of the loch, where you can see some of the archaeological remains. You can walk across the fen to **Eilean Mor**, where there's a collection of carved gravestones near the ruins of a medieval chapel. A smaller island, **Eilean na Comhairle** (The Council of the Isle), is where the Lords of the Isles met to decide policy.

● *In the 1940s one-legged Bill Dunn became the first man to swim across the Corryvreckan,*
● *his brother-in-law, author George Orwell, meanwhile, almost drowned in the whirlpool when it capsized his dinghy.*

▲ Jura → *Phone code 01496. Colour map 3, grid C4.*

Jura is one of the last, great wildernesses in the British Isles and perfect for some real off-the-beaten-track walking. Its main attractions are the beautiful **Paps of Jura**, three breast-shaped peaks that dominate not only the island itself but also the view for miles around. From Kintyre, Mull, Coll and Tiree, and from the mountains of mainland Scotland from Skye to Arran, they can be seen on the horizon. The Paps provide some tough hillwalking and require good navigational skills, or a guide. It takes a good eight hours to cover all three peaks, though during the Paps of Jura fell race they are covered in just three hours.

A good place to start is by the three-arch bridge over the Corran River, north of Leargybreack. The first pap you reach is Beinn a'Chaolais (2,408 ft), next is the highest, Beinn an Oír (2,571 ft) and the third is Beinn Shiantaidh (2,476 ft). To find out about guides, ask at **Jura Hotel**, see Sleeping. The island's west coast is completely uninhabited and inaccessible to all but the hardiest and most dedicated of walkers.

One of the island's main draws is the **Corryvreckan whirlpool** at the very northern tip, between Jura and the uninhabited island of **Scarba**. The notorious whirlpool, the second largest in the world, is in fact a tidal race that creates an action like a gigantic washing machine. It is seen at its awesome best during spring tides, especially with a westerly gale, when this most treacherous stretch of water creates oar falls of 25 ft and the terrible roar can be heard for up to 10 miles away. A two-hour tidal difference between the sound on the east and the Atlantic flood tides combine with the gulf of Corryvreckan's steep sides and underwater pinnacle, the Hag, to create the vortex. The Royal Navy officially says it's unsailable, but that doesn't stop several local boat tours actually going over the top of it. It is named after a Viking, Bhreacan, who anchored his boat here for three days and nights by a rope woven from the hair of virgins. Unsurprisingly, the rope parted under the strain, casting doubt on the status of one of the contributors, and Bhreacan drowned. To get there, follow the rough track from **Ardlussa** to **Kinuachdrach**, or get someone to drive you, then it's a two-mile walk. Before setting out, ask at the hotel for information and directions.

Also in the north of the island is **Barnhill**, the completely isolated and forlorn-looking cottage where **George Orwell** wrote *1984*. He finished it in 1948, and the title was derived from a reversal of the last two numbers. Though the house attracts literary pilgrims, it remains closed, but can be rented, see Sleeping, over.

The only village on Jura is Craighouse, eight miles from Feolin Ferry on the southeast coast. Here you'll find the **Jura distillery** ① *T01496-820240, www.isleof jura.com, all year round, tours by appointment only, free*, which is not particularly attractive but makes up for it with a friendly and informative tour. Three miles south of the village, at Ardfin, is **Jura House** ① *daily during daylight hours, £2*, with its beautiful walled garden, filled with wild flowers and Australasian plants and trees.

Argyll & Inner Hebrides Islay & Jura Listings

🛏 Sleeping

Islay *p150*
A-B Kilmeny Farmhouse, Ballygrant, 4 miles from Port Askaig, T/F01496-840668, www.kilmeny.co.uk. A working beef farm with stylish, comfortable rooms, excellent food and a warm, friendly atmosphere. The only drawback is that there are only 3 rooms, so book well in advance.

B Glenmachrie, Machrie golf course, T/F01496-302560. 5 rooms. A genuine farmhouse offering genuine hospitality and superb food. The price includes dinner, and you'd be crazy to book only B&B.
C Port Charlotte Hotel, Port Charlotte, T01496-850361, F850361. 10 rooms. Restored Victorian inn with gardens and

conservatory on seafront; their restaurant features local seafood and is one of the best around.

D Harbour Inn, Main St, Bowmore, T01496-810330, www.harbourinn.com. 4 rooms. Completely refurbished to a high standard, great views across the bay and superb food in their acclaimed restaurant (£££) where you can watch your seafood being landed.

D Lochside Hotel, Shore St, Bowmore, T01496-810244, F810390. 8 rooms. Friendly and good-value hotel with a mind-boggling selection of single malts.

E The Bothy, 91 Lennox St, Port Ellen, T01496-302391, mickstuart@thebothyislay. freeserve.co.uk. Run by Mick Stuart who hires out bikes and acts as a wildlife guide.

Self catering

Islay Estate Company, T01496-810221, has houses of varying sizes, such as Octovullin Farmhouse, which sleeps up to 10 and costs £750/week.

Jura *p155*

C Jura Hotel, T01496-820243, www.hometown.aol.com. The island's one and only hotel, overlooking the small isles bay. They'll provide information on island walks, and the pub is the social hub.

Barnhill, can be rented through **Scotts Cottages**, T0131-229 7111, www.scotts cottages.com, for £590 for 4 people, £710 for 5, and £830 for 6. Closed Nov-Mar.

Camping

Ask about camping at the **Jura Hotel**.

▲ Activities and tours

Jura *p155*

Mike Richardson, T07899-912116, guides hill walks and Orwell trails from £20 per person (minimum charge of £55 if fewer than 3 people) and runs a landrover taxi service on Jura.

⊖ Transport

Islay *p150*

Air Islay can be reached by air from Glasgow (for details, see p108). The airport is at Glenegedale, a few miles north of Port Ellen on the road to Bowmore.

Bus For those without their own transport, there's a regular bus service around Islay, with **Islay Coaches**, T01496-840273, and post buses, T01246-546329. There are buses from **Portnahaven** to **Port Ellen**, via **Port Charlotte**, **Bridgend**, **Bowmore** and the airport; from **Port Askaig** to **Port Ellen** via **Ballygrant**, **Bridgend**, **Bowmore** and the airport; from **Port Ellen** to **Ardbeg**, **Bowmore**, **Port Askaig** and **Portnahaven**, and also a postbus to **Bunnababhain**. Buses run regularly at least from Mon-Sat, but only once on Sun.

Ferry The ferry to Islay (and Jura) from **Kennacraig** to **Port Ellen** (2 hrs 10 mins, £7.75 one way per passenger, £56 per car) sails twice daily on Mon, Tue, Thu, Fri and Sun, once on Wed and 3 times on Sat. A ferry also sails from **Kennacraig** to **Port Askaig** (2 hrs, same prices as above) once daily on Tue and Thu, twice daily on Wed, Fri, Sat and Sun, and 3 times on Mon. The Wed ferry sails via **Colonsay**. The ferry from **Oban** to Port Askaig sails on Wed (4¼ hrs, £10.90/£53). CalMac offices are in Kennacraig, T01880-730253; Port Ellen, T01496-302209.

Jura *p155*

There is a bus service on Jura, which runs from **Feolin Ferry** to **Craighouse** several times a day, Mon-Sat. A few buses continue to **Lagg** and **Inverlussa** and return to Craighouse. Note that some journeys are by request only and must be booked the day before. Contact Alex Dunnichie, T01496-820314, or visit www.scotland-inverness. co.uk/jura.htm, for an online timetable.

A small car and passenger ferry makes the regular 5-min crossing daily to Jura, from **Port Askaig** on Islay to Feolin Ferry (£2.10 return per passenger, £11.80 per car. For times, contact **Argyll & Bute Council** , T01496-840681.

North & Northwest

☷ Footprint features

Introduction

The Northwest Highlands is the part of Scotland that best reflects the romantic image of the country, with mist-shrouded castles on every headland, a spooky tale around each corner and an enthusiastic welcome waiting behind every door.

Inverness, the largest settlement in the region and 'capital of the Highlands', became a city in 2000. It lies at the north-eastern end of the Great Glen, which cuts diagonally across the southern Highlands to Fort William like a surgical incision, linking deep and mysterious Loch Ness with the west coast and giving access to Glencoe, one of the most beautifully evocative Highland glens and a major climbing and skiing centre.

Inverness is also ideally situated for exploring the northeast coast, with its charming old fishing ports, and the storm-lashed north coast, running west from John O'Groats to Cape Wrath, as wild and remote a place as you could ever wish for.

The main town on the northwest coast is Fort William, which lies in the shadow of Britain's highest mountain, Ben Nevis. North from here stretches a dramatic shoreline of deep sea lochs and sheltered coves of pure, white sand backed by towering mountains and looking across to numerous Hebridean islands. West of Fort William, via the lyrical 'Road to the Isles', is Mallaig, the main departure point for ferries to Skye. Further north is Ullapool, one of the main ferry ports for the Outer Hebrides and the ideal base from which to explore the wild and near-deserted far northwest.

★ Don't miss...

① **Moray Firth** Cruise with the dolphins in the Moray Firth, page 169.

② **West Highland line** Get on board the Jacobite Steam Train and ride the West Highland line, one of the world's great train journeys, page 185.

③ **Glenelg** Drive from Shiel Bridge to this splendidly isolated village, home of Gavin Maxwell's famous otters, page 208.

④ **Applecross** Travel the vertigo-inducing route over the mountains to this village where you can sit with a pint of fresh prawns washed down with Red Cuillin ale in the cosy Applecross Inn, page 217.

⑤ **Sandwood Bay** Go for a walk along the beach here and watch the sun set with a bottle of single malt and a loved one, page 226.

Ins and outs

Getting there

There are daily flights to Inverness airport from London, Glasgow and Edinburgh. Inverness is linked to the south by the fast A9 from Edinburgh and Perth, to Aberdeen by the A96 and to Fort William by the A82, and is well served by buses. Wick, Thurso, Ullapool and Kyle of Lochalsh can all be reached by bus from Inverness. The rail line from Edinburgh closely follows the A9 to Inverness, and there are connections north to Wick and Thurso, west to Kyle of Lochalsh and east to Aberdeen. Fort William is easily reached from Glasgow by buses and trains which continue to Mallaig for the ferry to Skye.

Getting around

Getting around in the Highlands is a lot easier with your own transport, especially in the more remote parts, but it's not difficult to reach the main tourist centres by bus or train. Getting off the beaten track can be a little more complicated, but with forward planning is easily achievable. Much of the time you'll need to rely on the local postbus service, www.royalmail.com/postbus, which runs between the various remote post offices throughout the region. Timetables are available at most post offices or tourist information centres. A good idea is to purchase the *Public Transport Travel Guides for South Highland and/or North Highland and Orkney*. These are available at main tourist offices for £1. Details of ferries from the mainland ports to Skye, the Outer Hebrides and Orkney are given in the respective island chapters. **Highlands Council** ① *T01463 702458, public.transport@high land.gov.uk,* produces guides showing timetables for all modes of transport for the Highland area

● By far the most scenic route to the Highlands is the spectacular West Highland Railway, one of the world's great rail journeys, particularly the section from Fort William to Mallaig.

Tourist information

Roughly speaking, this chapter covers the northern half of mainland Scotland and is covered by the **Highlands of Scotland Tourist Board** ① *www.visithighlands.com, T0845-2255121,* which publishes free accommodation guides for the region. They will also book accommodation for a nominal fee. Note that many of the smaller offices are closed during the low season.

Climate

The beauty of the northwest Highlands is only enhanced by the notoriously unpredictable weather and that ever-present travelling companion, the midge. That's a lie. The midge is the scourge of many a Highland holiday: a ferocious, persistent and unbelievably irritating little beast who will drive you to the edge of sanity. For details on how best to combat this little terror, see page 63.

The only predictable thing about the weather is its unpredictability. You can have blazing sunshine in April, pouring rain in July and a blizzard in May. So, you'll need to be prepared for everything. Climbers and walkers especially must take heed of all weather warnings. It can be hot enough for bikinis in the car park at the foot of a 2,000-ft mountain, and two hours later near the summit you're faced with driving, horizontal hail, rain or snow and unable to see further than the end of your nose. People die every year on the Scottish mountains simply because they are ill-prepared, and it is essential to take proper precautions, see page 56. Even those who are not intent on bagging the odd Munro should remember the old adage, that there's no such thing as bad weather, only inadequate clothing.

Inverness → *Phone code: 01463. Colour map 2, grid C2. Population: 42,000.*

Inverness is the only city in the Highlands and the busy and prosperous hub of the region. All main routes through the Highlands pass through here at some point, so it's a hard place to avoid. The town's position at the head of the Great Glen and on the shores of the Moray Firth have made it a firm favourite with tourists, who flock here in their legions during the summer months to look for the evasive Loch Ness Monster. Though Inverness has little in the way of major sights, it's a pleasant place to base yourself as you explore the other, more visible attractions on offer in the surrounding area, including the resident population of dolphins in the Moray Firth. The city, though, is not without its own appeal, particularly the leafy banks of the River Ness, which runs through its heart, linking Loch Ness with the Moray Firth. ▸▸ For Sleeping, Eating and other listings, see pages 164-169.

Ins and outs

Getting there

There are daily flights to and from London Gatwick, Glasgow and Edinburgh with **British Airways,** and daily flights to and from London Luton and London Gatwick with **easyJet.** There are also flights to and from Birmingham and Manchester (Monday and Friday) with **Eastern Airways,** and to and from Stornoway (Monday to Saturday) with **British Airways Express.** The **airport** ⓘ *T01667-464000, www.hial.co.uk* is seven miles east of the town at Dalcross. A twice-daily airport bus to and from the town centre connects with London and Stornoway flights. It takes 20 minutes and costs £2.50. A taxi to/from the airport costs £10-13. The bus station is nearby, just off Academy Street, T01463-233371. Left luggage costs £2-3 per item, open Monday to Saturday 0830-1800, Sunday 1000-1800. The train station is at the east end of Academy Street, T01463-239026. Left-luggage lockers at the train station cost £2-4 per 24 hours. ▸▸ *For further details, see page 168.*

Getting around

Inverness town centre is compact and easy to explore on foot, and most of the hotels and guest houses are within a 15-minute walk of the TIC. Loch Ness is not within walkable distance, so you'll need your own transport, or alternatively book a tour, see pages 167 and 183.

Tourist information

Tourist information centre ⓘ *T01463-234353, open daily Easter-Nov, Mon-Sat Nov-Easter,* or **National Contact Centre** ⓘ *T0845- 2255121,* is on Castle Wynd, near Ness Bridge, a five-minute walk from the train station. It stocks a wide range of literature on the area, can book accommodation and transport and gives out free maps of the town and environs. Tickets for all the tours listed on the next few pages are available from the TIC.

History

One of the old town's first visitors was that much-travelled cleric, St Columba, who came in AD 565 to confront the Pictish King Brude, whose fortress was reputedly at Craig Phadraig, a few miles west of Inverness. Around the mid-12th century King David I built the original castle and made Inverness a royal burgh on the strength of its growing importance as a trading port. Furs, hides, wool and timber were all exported as far afield as the Mediterranean. The town's economic prosperity and status as the

Inverness

To Moray Firth Cruises, Black Isle, Wick & Edinburgh (A9)

To Black Isle (A9) & Nairn & Aberdeen (A96)

Library
Eastgate Shopping
Old High
Dunbar's Hospital
Abertaff House
Footbridge
Shopping Centre
Shopping Centre
Kiltmaker Centre
Ness Bridge
Tolbooth Steeple
Town House
Museum & Art Gallery
St Andrews Cathedral
Eden Court Theatre
Footbridge

To Beauly (A862)

To Loch Ness, Fort William & Jacobite Cruises (A82)

To Culloden Moor

To Bught Park & Ness Islands

N

0 metres 200
0 yards 200

Sleeping
Bazpackers Hostel 1
Brae Ness 2
Culloden House 10
Dionard Guest House 16
Dunain Park 13

Eastgate Backpackers Hostel & Zanzibar 3
Felstead House 4
Glenmoriston Town House 5
Ho Ho Hostel 6
Inverness Hostel 7
Ivybank Guesthouse 8
Kinkell House 9
Melness Guest House 15
Moyness House 12
SYHA Hostel 11
Wetherspoon's Lodge 14

Eating
Café No 1 1
Castle 2
Chez Christophe 10
Dickens 3
Glen Mhor Hotel 4
Jimmy Chung's Chinese Buffet 8
Lemon Tree 5
Mustard Seed 16
Pizza Express 18
Raja 6
Red Pepper 20

River Café & Restaurant 19
River House 21
Rocpool 22
Shapla 7

Bars & clubs
Blackfriars 9
Chilli Palmers 14
Gellions 17
Hootenanny & Sofa Bar 15
Johnny Foxes 11
Phoenix Bar 13
Shot's 12

North & Northwest Inverness

most important northern outpost, however, made it a prime target for marauding
Highland clansmen, and during the Wars of Independence in the 13th century
Inverness was also a regular target for both English and Scots armies.

The town's renaissance came with the completion of the Caledonian Canal and
rail links with the south in the 19th century. These improved communications
heralded something of a tourist boom amongst the wealthy and fashionable who
came north to the Highlands to shoot anything that moved in the name of sport. In the
mid-19th century Queen Victoria decided to embrace all things Scottish, which only
boosted the town's popularity. Over recent decades Inverness has grown rapidly, not
only as a prime base for visiting tourists, but also as the main administrative and
commercial centre for the Highlands. In 2000 it was given city status, a move which
has given it a considerable boost.

Sights

The city is dominated by its red sandstone **castle** ① *T01463-243363, Mar-Nov
Mon-Sat (Sun only in Jul/Aug) 1030-1730, £4, concession/child £3. Built in 1834*, this
Victorian edifice is very much the new kid on the block in terms of Scottish castles.
The original castle dates from the 12th century and was built on a ridge to the east of
the present structure. Nothing remains of the old castle, which is
unsurprising given its bloody and eventful history. It was here
that King Duncan of Scotland was slain by Macbeth, an event
dramatically (and erroneously) portrayed in Shakespeare's
eponymous work. The castle was occupied three times during

> Nairn is only 5 miles from
> the airport and makes a
> pleasant alternative to
> staying in Inverness.

the Wars of Independence in the 13th century, and when Robert the Bruce recaptured
it in 1307 he destroyed it. In the mid-17th century Cromwell ordered his men to build a
stone version on the same site. In 1715 James Francis Edward was proclaimed king
there, but not long after it was destroyed by the Jacobites to prevent it from falling into
enemy hands following the defeat of Bonnie Prince Charlie at Culloden, see page 179.
The present castle houses the Sheriff Court and also stages the Castle Garrison
Encounter, where you can sign up as a mid-18th-century soldier. New recruits (that's
you) pass through the Quartermaster's Store and are introduced to the Sergeant of
the Guard, before being accosted by a female camp follower and finally led out
through the garrison shop. On the castle terrace is a statue of Flora MacDonald, to
honour her part in helping the prince escape, see box page 256.

Below the castle is **Inverness Museum and Art Gallery** ① *Mon-Sat 0900-1700,
free, Castle Wynd beside the TIC*. The museum gives a decent overview of the history
of the town and the region, while the gallery hosts some special exhibitions that
have included paintings by the Scottish colourist JD Fergusson. Just around the
corner, on High Street, is the Gothic-style **Town House**, where Prime Minister
Lloyd George held an emergency cabinet meeting in 1921, the first ever to be held
outside London.

Opposite, on the corner of Bridge Street and Church Street, is the **Tolbooth
Steeple** which dates from 1791 and which had to be repaired after an earth tremor in
1816. Church Street also boasts the town's oldest building, **Abertarff House**
① *T01463-250999*. Built around 1592, it is now a contemporary art and jewellery
gallery. Almost opposite is the much-restored **Dunbar's Hospital**, built in 1688 as an
almshouse for the town's poor. At the end of Church Street, where it meets Friar's
Lane, is the **Old High Church** ① *Fri 1245-1315, mid Jun-mid Sep Fri 1200-1400, guided
tour at 1230*, founded in the 12th century and rebuilt in 1772, though the 14th-century
vaulted tower remains intact. In the adjoining graveyard prisoners taken at Culloden
were executed, and you can still see the bullet marks left by the firing squads on some
of the gravestones.

At the corner of Huntly Street and Ness Bridge, is the **Kiltmaker Centre** ① *T01463-222781, www.hector-russell.com, Mid-May-end Sep Mon-Sat 0900-2100, Sun 1000-1700, Oct-mid-May Mon-Sat 0900-1700, £2, concession £1*, where you can learn everything you ever wanted to know about tartan (including what Scotsmen wear under their kilts). You can also see kilts being made in the factory and, in the shop downstairs, be measured up for one of your own. Nearby, directly opposite the castle, is the neo-Gothic **St Andrews Cathedral** which dates from 1869, and is worth a peek if you're passing by. Continuing south along Ness Bank, past the **Eden Court Theatre**, see Entertainment page 166, you reach **Bught Park**, see Sleeping page 165, which overlooks the Ness Islands, joined by footbridge to both banks. The islands are attractively laid out as a park and are a favourite with local anglers. This also happens to be a lovely place for a peaceful evening stroll.

● Sleeping

Inverness *p161, map p162*
You shouldn't have much trouble finding somewhere to stay in Inverness, though in Jul and Aug it's advisable to book ahead. This can be done through the TIC, or less cheaply, at the train station at the Thomas Cook booth; you'll be charged a booking fee, see p41.

There are several good quality hotels in and around town and plenty of B&Bs. The best places to look are along both banks of the river south of the Ness Bridge, Old Edinburgh Rd and Ardconnel St (east of the castle) and around Bruce Gardens, Ardross St, Kenneth St and Fairfield Rd(the west bank). There are also several budget hostels in and around the centre, and a couple of campsites.

L Culloden House Hotel, Milton of Culloden, 3 miles east of town near the A9. T01463-790461, www.cullodenhouse.co.uk. 28 rooms. Superb Georgian mansion with 1st-class facilities, service and restaurant.

A Dunain Park Hotel, about 3 miles southwest of the town centre, just off the A82 Fort William Rd, T01463-230512, www.dunainparkhotel.co.uk. 11 rooms. An elegant Georgian mansion house with its own grounds, lovely and peaceful with an excellent restaurant, see Eating p165, and its own indoor pool.

B Glenmoriston Town House Hotel, 20 Ness Bank, T01463-223777. 15 rooms. Recently refurbished and now one of the classiest places in town, with a superb Italian restaurant, see Eating p165.

B Inverness Marriot, Culcabock Rd, 1 mile south of the town centre near A9, T01463-237166, F225208. 82 rooms. Large, modern hotel with excellent rooms, service and facilities.

C Brae Ness Hotel, 17 Ness Bank, T01463-712266, www.braenesshotel.co.uk. 10 rooms. No smoking. Family-run Georgian hotel overlooking the river and Eden Court, with a licensed restaurant for residents.

C Felstead House, 18 Ness Bank. T/F01463-231634, felsteadgh@aol.com. 8 rooms, 5 with en suite. Family-run Georgian guest house, large and comfortable rooms, good breakfast and overall good value.

C Glenruidh House Hotel, Old Edinburgh Rd South, 2 miles from the town centre (phone for directions). T01463-226499, www.cozzee-nessie-bed.co.uk. 5 rooms. No smoking. Comfortable and peaceful hotel in secluded setting, with friendly service and excellent food.

C Highland Voyages, Eala Bhan tall ship, T01463-404441, www.highlandvoyages.co.uk. When moored at Seaport Marina has on board accommodation in 3 and 2 bunk cabins, evening meals available.

C Ivybank Guesthouse, 28 Old Edinburgh Rd, T/F01463-232796, www.ivybankguest house.com. 5 rooms, 3 with en suite bath- room. Georgian house with lots of character, nice garden and friendly welcome.

C Melness Guest House, 8 Old Edinburgh Rd, T01463-220963, www.melness@visit-inverness.com. 2 rooms, 1 en suite. Very clean and comfortable accommodation.

C Moyness House Hotel, 6 Bruce Gardens, T/F01463-233836, www.moyness.co.uk. Fine Victorian villa in a quiet area near the theatre, with very clean and comfortable en suite rooms and nice touches like Body Shop products in the bathrooms. No smoking.

D Dionard Guest House, 39 Old Edinburgh Rd, T01463-233557, www.dionardguest house.co.uk. 4 rooms, friendly and comfortable B&B a few mins walk from the centre of the city.
D Kinkell House, 11 Old Edinburgh Rd, T01463-235243, clare@kinkell.freeserve.co.uk. 7 rooms, 3 with en suite bathroom. Comfortable Victorian family home with spacious rooms, decent value (£2 charge for credit card payment).
D Wetherspoon's Lodge, 72-74 Church St, T01463-251800, invernesslodge@ jdwetherspoon.co.uk. 27 en suite rooms. Great value central rooms, if rather lacking in character, breakfast not included but available in the bar.
F Bazpackers Hostel, 4 Culduthel Rd (at the top of Castle St), T01463-717663, bazmail@ btopenworld.com. 48 beds in dorms of 4-8, twin and double rooms available, cooking facilities and garden for barbecues, also has laundrette, good atmosphere.
F Eastgate Backpackers Hostel, 38 Eastgate T/F01463-718756, www.hostelsaccommod ation.com. 38 beds, free tea and coffee, and continental breakfast for £1.50.
F Ho Ho Hostel, 23a High St, T01463-221225, www.hohohostel.force9.com, is another cheap option.
F Inverness Student Hotel, 8 Culduthel Rd, next door to **Bazpackers**, T01463-236556. 9 dorms with 54 beds, some dorms have good views. Friendly and laid-back atmosphere with all the usual facilities.
F SYHA Youth Hostel, Victoria Drive, off Millburn Rd, T0871-3308529. 166 beds. Huge hostel in former school hall of residence.

Camping
Bught Caravan and Camping Site, Bught Park, on the west bank of the river near the sports centre, T01463-236920. The largest and most centrally located campsite, with good facilities, £4.30-11.40 per pitch.

🍴 Eating

Inverness *p161, map p162*
As you'd expect in a major tourist centre, there's the usual plethora of pubs, cafés and restaurants serving cheap and basic food for the non-discerning palate, but those looking for a high standard of cuisine won't be disappointed either. Takeaways are plentiful particularly on Academy St, Eastgate, around the train station and on Young St, just across the Ness Bridge.
£££ Chez Christophe, 16 Ardross St, T01463-717126. High quality French cuisine a few minutes from the city centre.
£££ Dunain Park Hotel, see Sleeping. Award-winning Scots-French cuisine in elegant surroundings, with a superb list of malts. Take a stroll in the lovely gardens afterwards.
£££ Glen Mhor Hotel, 9-12 Ness Bank, T01463-234308. Their **Riverview** restaurant at the front is good, especially for seafood and the bistro, **Nico's** offers a cheaper alternative.
£££ La Riviera, Glenmoriston Town House Hotel, see Sleeping. Excellent Italian food.
£££ River House Restaurant, 1 Greig St, T01463-22203. Green tartan outside is a clue to the fact that this restaurant serves good quality Scottish produce. Dishes might include sea bass, or Highland game stew. 3 courses for £27.95. Tue-Sat 1200-1400, 1830-late.
££ Café No 1, 75 Castle St, T01463-226200. Nice contemporary decor, good selection of vegetarian options. Mon-Sat 1200-1400 and 1800-2130.
££ Dickens, 77 Church St, T01463-713111. Offers a mix of oriental and international dishes with an emphasis on fish, set lunch for £6.50. Daily 1200-1400 and 1730-2300.
££ The Mustard Seed, 16 Fraser St, T01463-220220. Lovely contemporary restaurant, with cheery yellow walls and sculptural flowers as well as an imaginative menu. Lunch choices like spinach and gorgonzola polenta, dinner might include salmon or guinea fowl. Daily 1200-1500, 1800-2200.
££ Pizza Express, Falcon Sq, T01463-709700. New branch of the dependable pizza chain. Mon-Sat 1130-2200, Sun 1200-2200.
££ The River Café and Restaurant, 10 Bank St, T01463-714884. Offers high teas and traditional dishes like haggis. Mon 1000-2030, Tue-Sat 1000-2130, Sun 1200-2030.

 For an explanation of sleeping and eating price codes used in this guide, see inside the front cover. Other relevant information is found in Essentials, see pages 41-49.

££ Rocpool, 1 Ness Walk, T01463-717274.
Very popular contemporary restaurant with
wooden floors and crisp white tablecloths.
Serves dishes like fillet of beef or lemon and
herb risotto. Daily 1200-1430, 1800-2200.
££ Shapla, 2 Castle Rd, T01463-241919.
Good Indian restaurant with Tandoori and
Balti menu and good views of the river in the
upstairs lounge. Daily 1200-2330.
£ Castle Restaurant, 41 Castle St. Clean, no
nonsense café serving huge portions of
stodgy, filling grub at low prices, convenient
for backpacker's hostels. Daily till 2100.
£ Jimmy Chung's Chinese Buffet, 28-36
Union St, T01463-237878. Cheap Chinese
food served daily 1145-1445 and 1700-2300.
£ The Lemon Tree, 18 Inglis St. Located in
the pedestrianized town centre, family-run
café offering good home-baking and basic
but filling meals.
£ The Red Pepper, Bow Court, 74 Church St,
T01463-237111. Bustling little café/takeaway
offering fresh paninis, sandwiches, soups
and salads. Mon-Sat 1930-1630.

Bakeries
For picnic supplies check out **Gourmet's
Lair**, 8 Union St, a great deli with all sorts of
goodies. **Ashers**, Church St, is a good bakery.

Bars and clubs

Inverness *p161, map p162*
Blackfriars, Academy St, a decent pub.
Chilli Palmers, on the corner of Queensgate
and Church St, is a trendy bar offering decent
food and a DJ at weekends, and you can enjoy
a Jazz Lunch on Sun at No 27, on Castle St.
Gellions, Bridge St, has varied live music
throughout the week.
Hootananny, 67 Church St. A great bet for
atmosphere and all things Scottish, has live
music every night and anyone is welcome to
get involved with the Mon and Tue sessions.
They have ceilidhs 1500-1700 on Sat and
Gaelic speaking meetings 1930-2030 on Mon.
Johnny Foxes, 26 Bank St, has Irish folk music
every night in summer as well as boasting one
of the most unusual pub menus around.
Phoenix, 108 Academy St. One of the best
pubs in town and always lively.
Shot's, Academy St, a sports pub.
Sofa Bar, above **Hootenanny**, for a younger
crowd, with live bands, DJs and comfy sofas.

Entertainment

Inverness *p161, map p162*
Cinema The cinema attached to
Eden Court Theatre, see below, shows a
programme of art house and newly released
movies, for information: T01463-234234.
Prices vary depending on the performance.
Warner Village, A96 Nairn Rd, about 2 miles
from the town centre, The 7-screen. Tickets
cost from £4.
Theatre Eden Court Theatre, Bishops Rd,
overlooking the River Ness. It offers a varied
programme of theatre, dance and all kinds of
music. There's also a bar and self-service
restaurant with good food and views over
the river.

Festivals and events

Inverness *p161, map p162*
There are numerous events held in and
around Inverness throughout the year. These
range from a humble pub ceilidh and a food
festival and to a full-blown Highland Games.
For details contact the tourist information
centre or visit their website.
Feb/Mar Inverness Music Festival,
T01463-716616.
Easter The best of the local folk festivals
are held over the Easter weekend,
T01738-623274.
Jun Highland Festival is excellent and
taking place over several days at the end of
the month, T01463-711112,
www.highlandfestival.demon.co.uk.
Jul The Inverness Tattoo is held in the
Northern meeting Park.

Shopping

Inverness *p161, map p162*
Inverness is a good place to buy a kilt, or
practically anything else in tartan. To find
your own clan tartan, head for the Scottish
Kiltmaker Visitor Centre, see Sights.
Bookshops There are several bookshops
in town.
Leakey's, Castle St, is a brilliant second-hand
bookshop which has about 100,000 books
with a huge wood burning stove in the
middle of the shop and a café upstairs.
Waterstone's, 50-52 High St.

Highland dress and traditional gifts
Chisholm's Highland Dress, 47-51 Castle St, T01463-234599, 0900-1730 and 1900-2130 in Jul and Aug.
Hector Russell, 4-9 Huntly St, T01463-222781.
James Pringle Weavers, Holm Mills, Dores Rd, T01463-223311.
Mall Eastgate Shopping Centre has all the usual high-street branches like **Gap** and Marks and Spencer.
Market Victorian Market, Church St, has a wide range of shops.

▲ Activities and tours

Inverness *p161, map p162*
Boat tours Fingal of Caledonia, T01397-772167, www.fingal-cruising.co.uk, run all-inclusive 4- and 6-day cruises in a converted Dutch 'spitz' barge that gently ploughs its way through the 60-mile waterway of the Great Glen. During this time guests can make use of mountain bikes, canoes, sailing dinghies and windsurfers lashed to the deck. Guides and instructors are included. Cruises operate from Apr to Oct and cost from £250-525 per person.
Bus tours Guide Friday run open-topped bus tours around the city and to Culloden. Tours leave from Bridge St near the TIC at 1000 and then every 45 mins till 1645 from May to Oct. Tickets can be bought at their booth in the train station, T01463-224000, Mon-Fri 0900-1730, Sat 0830-1745, or on board the bus. Full-day tour costs £7.50, concession £6, children £2.50. They also run half-day bus tours around Loch Ness.
Cycling The recently opened **Great Glen Way** (see Walking below) can be cycled. The stretch alongside the **Caledonian Canal** is flat and good for families. For a free leaflet, T01320-366322.
Golf The best golf course in the area is at Nairn (see p171). There's an 18-hole public course at Torvean, 2 miles from town on the A82 to Fort William, T01463-711434.
Ghost tours Inverness Terror Tour leaves from outside the tourist office at 1900 nightly and tells the tale of the town's horrific past, complete with witches, ghosts, torture and murders.
Horse riding Highland Riding Centre, Borlum Farm, Drumnadrochit, T01456-450892, www.borlum.com.

Iceskating There's an Ice Centre at Bught Park, T01463-235711, www.inverness-ice -centre.org.uk.
Leisure centre Aquadome Leisure Centre, Bught Park, T01463-667500, Mon-Fri 0730-2200, Sat-Sun 0730-2100. Competition-sized pool, flumes, wave machine and kiddies' pool, also health suites, gym and other indoor sports facilities.
Loch Ness tours Jacobite Cruises, T01463-233999, www.jacobite.co.uk, run a variety of coach tours, boat cruises and combined coach and cruise trips around the loch.
Discover Loch Ness, T0800-7315564 (freephone), www.discoverlochness.com, run cultural tours which include a cruise and entry to Urquhart Castle. Tours leave Inverness at 1030 all year round. Summer prices: half-day tour from £22, or £12 without a boat trip or castle entry; full-day tour £30.
George Edwards, contact Loch Ness Cruises, T01456-450395, www.lochness-cruises.com, or Original Loch Ness Monster Visitor Centre, see p175, takes would-be monster-spotters out on the loch in his boat, Nessie Hunter, which is based near Drumnadrochit. He not only once caught a glimpse of Nessie but also discovered the deepest part of the loch (812 ft), now known as Edward's Deep. Cruises run from Apr to Oct 0930-1800. They last 1 hr and cost £9 per adult and £5 per child.
Orkney tours Orkney Islands Day Tours leave from Inverness every day throughout the summer. The tour departs daily 1 Jun-2 Sep from Inverness bus station at 0730; returns 2100. Booking essential; £44 per person, under 16 half price. Details from the tourist office, or contact **John O'Groats Ferries**, Ferry Office, John O'Groats, Caithness. T01955-611353, F611301, www.jogferry.co.uk (for tours from John O'Groats, see p235).
Tennis and squash Inverness Tennis and Squash Club, Bishop's Rd, T01463- 230751.
Ten-pin bowling Roller Bowl, 167 Culduthel Rd, T01463-235100, Mon-Fri 1200 till late, Sat-Sun 1100 till late.
Walking Great Glen Way is a new, waymarked walking trail that runs for 73 miles between Inverness and Fort William. Panoramic views of Loch Ness can be seen at many of the sections between Fort Augustus and Inverness. Although a relatively easy walk, there are some fairly tough sections around Loch Ness and you'll

North & Northwest Inverness Listings

need to be properly equipped and have a good map. OS Landranger Nos 26, 34 and 41 cover the entire route. The route should take 4-5 days to complete, depending on your level of fitness. It is probably better to walk it in 'reverse', from Fort William to Inverness, as the easiest section is then at the start. The Great Glen Way also has its own website at www.greatglenway.com.

⊖ Transport

Inverness *p161, map p162*
Bus There are regular daily buses to **Glasgow** and **Edinburgh** (via **Aviemore**), **Pitlochry** and **Perth** with Scottish Citylink, T0990-505050. Change at Perth for **Dundee**. There are regular daily **Citylink** buses to **Ullapool**, connecting with the ferry to **Stornoway**; also to **Fort William** and **Oban**. There are daily **Citylink** buses to **Kyle of Lochalsh**, **Portree** and **Uig** (connecting with ferries to **Tarbert** and **Lochmaddy**). There are regular **Citylink** buses to **Fort Augustus** via **Drumnadrochit** and **Urquhart Castle** (also with Highland Bus & Coach, T01463-233371), and to **Scrabster**, for the ferry to **Stromness**, via **Wick** and **Thurso**; also with Morrison's Coaches, T01847-821241.
To **Ullapool** via **Gairloch** and **Aultbea**, there are daily buses with Spa Coaches, T01997-421311, Bluebird Northern, T01463-239292 and Westerbus T01445-712255. To **Tain** and **Lairg** there are daily services with Bluebird and Rapson's. To **Tain** and **Helsmdale**, via **Dornoch** there are regular daily buses with Citylink, Morrison's and Bluebird. To **Lochinver** via **Ullapool** there's a daily service with Spa coaches and Rapson's of Brora, T01408-621245. To **Durness** via **Lairg** and **Tongue**, or via **Ullapool** (not in winter) there's a daily service with Royal Mail postbuses, T0131-2287407. To **Grantown- on-Spey**, daily service with Highland Country Buses, T01463-233371, and Highland Bus & Coach. Inverness Traction and Highland Country Buses have services to places around **Inverness**, including **Nairn**, **Forres**, **Culloden**, **Beauly** and **Dingwall**. Bluebird have regular buses to **Aberdeen**, via **Nairn**.
Boat For details of connections to **Stornoway** (Lewis) see p278, or contact the CalMac office in Inverness, T01463-717681. For **Scrabster** to **Stromness**, run by

Northlink Ferries, T01856-851144, www.northlinkferries.co.uk, see p312.
Car hire **Avis** is at the airport (T01667-462787); **Budget** is on Railway Terr behind the train station (T01463- 713333); **Europcar** has an office at 16 Telford St (T0870-0500289), and at the airport (0870-8700120); **Sharps Reliable Wrecks**, Railway Station, Academy St, T01463-236694 and at the airport T01463-461212, www.sharpsreliable wrecks.co.uk. **Thrifty** is at 33 Harbour Rd, T01463-T224466. Expect to pay from around £30 per day.
Cycle hire **Barney's Bicycle Hire & Shop**, 35 Castle St, T01463-232249. Daily 0900- 2100 in season. Mountain bike hire from £12 per day. **Highland Cycles**, Telford St, T01463-234789. Mon-Sat 0900-1730 all year, range of bikes available from £11 per day. Also bikes for hire from **Bazpacker's Hostel**, see Sleeping p164.
Taxi Rank Radio Taxis, T01463-221111; Tartan Taxis, T01463-233033. For a Taxi Tour of the area, T01463-220222.
Train For more information, T0845-7484950. There are direct trains to/from **Aberdeen**, **Edinburgh** (via **Aviemore**) and **Glasgow**. There are several daily services to/from **London King's Cross** (via **Perth**) and **Edinburgh**, and a Caledonian Sleeper service from **London Euston** to **Inverness** and **Fort William**, ScotRail, T08457 550033, www.scotrail.co.uk. There is also a regular service to **Wick** and **Thurso**, via **Tain**, **Lairg** and **Helmsdale**. The journey from Inverness to **Kyle of Lochalsh** (for Skye) is one of the most scenic in Britain. There are 3 trains daily (none on Sun).

⊕ Directory

Inverness *p161, map p162*
Banks All the major banks can be found in the town centre. The **Royal Bank** is on the High St; the **Bank of Scotland** is opposite the Town House on the High St; the **Clydesdale** is opposite the train station; and **Lloyds TSB** is on Church St. **Currency exchange** Money can be changed at the TIC at 2.5% commission. Also **Thomas Cook**, 9-13 Inglis St, T711921, Mon-Fri 0900-1700; and **Alba Travel** (American Express agents), 43 Church St, T01463- 239188, Mon-Sat 0900-1700.
Cultural centres Inverness library is

opposite the bus station. It has an excellent genealogical research unit. Consultations with the resident genealogist cost £12 per hr; T236463. The library also houses the Highland archives, where you can research the history and culture of the region. Open Mon-Fri 1100-1300 and 1400-1700; Oct-May 1400-1700 only. **Internet** Available from the **TIC**, the **Launderette**, Young St, **The Mail Box**, Station Sq and at the **library**. **The Gate café bar**, opposite the post office, has internet facilities and serves drinks and snacks, 1000-2100. **Medical Services Hospitals** **Raigmore Hospital**, on the southeastern outskirts of town near the A9, T01463-704000, for accidents and emergencies. **Pharmacies** **Boots**, Eastgate Shopping Centre; daily 0900-1730, Thu till 1900. The main branch is at 14-16 Queensgate, T01463-234111. Mon-Thu 0900-1730, Fri 0930-1730, Sat 0900-1320.

Around Inverness → *Colour map 2, grid C2.*

East of Inverness along the Moray Firth stretches a long coastline of cliff-top walks, fine beaches, attractive old towns and many historic sites and castles. The Moray Firth is perhaps best known for its large resident population, the largest dolphins in the world. Over 100 of these beautiful and intelligent mammals live in the estuary, the most northerly breeding ground in Europe, and there's a very good chance of seeing them, particularly between June and August. The Moray Firth dolphins have become a major tourist attraction and several companies run dolphin-spotting boat trips. You can also see them from the shore. Two of the best places are, on the southern shore of the Black Isle, see page 238, and Fort George, on the opposite shore, see below. The Kessock Bridge, which crosses the Moray Firth to the Black Isle, is another good dolphin-spotting location and also has a visitor centre, where you can listen in to their underwater conversations.

West of Inverness, the Moray Firth becomes the Beauly Firth, a relatively quiet little corner despite its proximity to Inverness, as most traffic heading north crosses the Kessock Bridge on the main A9. The A862 west to Beauly offers a more scenic alternative, and the chance to visit a 13th-century priory and a distillery. South of Beauly, the A831 leads to two of Scotland's most beautiful glens, Glen Strathfarrarand Glen Affric. ➽ For Sleeping, Eating and other listings, see pages 173-174.

▸ The attractions that follow can be visited as day trips from Inverness.

The Moray Firth

Culloden → *Colour map 2, grid C2.*

① *T01463-790607. Site open daily all year. Visitor centre open Feb-31 Mar and 1 Nov to 31 Dec daily 1100-1600, 1 Apr-30 Jun, 1 Sep-31 Oct daily 0900-1800, Jul, Aug daily 0900-1900. Visitor centre, including audio-visual presentation, and Old Leanach cottage £5, concession £3.75, children £1. Wheelchair access, bookshop, restaurant.*

The eerie and windswept Culloden Moor, five miles to the east of Inverness on the B9006, was the site of the last major battle fought on the British mainland. The Jacobite cause was finally lost here, on 16 April 1746, when the army of Prince Charles Edward Stuart was crushed by the superior Government forces, led by the Duke of Cumberland, whose savagery earned him the nickname 'Butcher'. Contrary to popular myth this was not a battle between the Scots and the English, more a civil war: there were actually English Jacobites while many Scots fought for the Government. It is now owned by the National Trust for Scotland.

The battlefield has been restored to its original state (minus the dead bodies). The visitor centre is the obvious starting point and gives a graphic audio-visual description of the gruesome episode. From the visitor centre paths lead across the

Battle of Culloden

The second Jacobite rebellion of 1745 was ill-fated from the start. Bonnie Prince Charlie's expedition south lacked sufficient support and was turned back at Derby. After their long and dispiriting retreat north, the half-starved, under-strength army – exhausted after an abortive night attack on Hanoverian forces at Nairn – faced overwhelmingly superior forces under the command of the ambitious Duke of Cumberland at Culloden.

The open, flat ground of Culloden Moor was hopelessly unsuitable for the Highlanders' style of fighting, which relied on steep hills and plenty of cover to provide the element of surprise for their brave but un-disciplined attacks. In only 40 minutes the Prince's army was blown away by the English artillery, and the Jacobite charge, when it finally came, was ragged and ineffective. Cumberland's troops then went on to commit the worst series of atrocities ever carried out by a British Army. Some 1,200 men were slain, many as they lay wounded on the battlefield. Prince Charlie, meanwhile, fled west where loyal Highlanders protected him until he made his final escape to France.

But the real savagery was to come. Cumberland resolved to make an example of the Highlands. Not only were the clans disarmed and the wearing of Highland dress forbidden, but the Government troops began an orgy of brutal reprisals across the region. Within a century the clan system had ended and the Highland way of life changed forever. For further information see page 365.

field to the clan graves, marked by simple headstones which bear the names of the clans who fought. Next to the visitor centre, the restored cottage of Old Leanach – which was used by the Jacobites as a headquarters, and where 30 Highlanders were burnt alive – is arranged as it would have been at the time of the battle. A memorial cairn, erected in 1881, is the scene each April of a commemorative service organized by the Gaelic Society of Inverness.

Clava Cairns

This impressive and important Bronze-Age site lies only a mile southeast of Culloden and is well worth a short detour. The 5,000 year-old site consists of three large burial cairns encircled by standing stones, set in a grove of trees. The less imaginative visitor may see it as merely a pile of stones but no one can fail to be affected by the spooky atmosphere of the place. This is even more perceptible when no one else is around. To get there, continue on the B9006 past Culloden Moor, then turn right at the Culloden Moor Inn and follow the signs for Clava Lodge. Look for the sign on the right of the road.

Fort George → Colour map 2, grid C2.
ⓘ T01667-460232, Apr-Oct daily 0930-1830, Oct-Mar Mon-Sat 0930-1630, Sun 1400-1630, £6, concession £4.50, children £1.50. Wheelchair access, café.

Standing proudly on a sandy spit that juts out into the Moray Firth is Fort George, Europe's finest surviving example of 18th-century military architecture. Begun in 1748, it was the last in a chain of three such fortifications built in the Highlands – the other two being Fort Augustus and Fort William – as a base for George II's army to prevent any potential threats to Hanoverian rule. It was completed in 1769, by which time the Highlands were more or less peaceful, but was kept in use as a military barracks. Today it remains virtually unchanged, and there are even armed sentries at the main gate. You can walk along the ramparts to get an idea of the sheer scale of the

place and also enjoy the sweeping views across the Moray Firth. You may even be
lucky enough to see a school of dolphins. Within the fort are the barracks, a chapel,
workshops and the Regimental Museum of the Queen's Own Highlanders, which
features the fascinating Seafield Collection of arms and military equipment, most of
which dates from the Napoleonic Wars.

Cawdor Castle → *Colour map 2, grid C2.*
① *To1667-404401, May to mid-Oct daily 1000-1730, £6.50.*
Though best known for its legendary association with Shakespeare's *Macbeth*,
Cawdor Castle post-dates the grisly historical events on which the great Bard based
his famous tragedy. The oldest part of the castle, the central tower, dates from 1372,
and the rest of it is mostly 16th or 17th century. But despite the literary
disappointment, the castle is still one of the most appealing in Scotland. It has been
in the hands of the Cawdor family for over six centuries and each summer they clear
off, leaving their romantic home and its glorious gardens open for the enjoyment of
ordinary folks like us. There's also a nine-hole golf course.

According to family legend, an early Thane of Cawdor, wanting a new castle,
had a dream in which he was told to load a donkey with gold, let it wander around
for a day and watch where it lay down, for this would be the best spot for his new
castle. He duly followed these instructions and the donkey lay down under a thorn
tree, the remains of which can still be seen in the middle of a vaulted chamber in the
14th-century tower.

Just to the west of Cawdor is **Kilravock Castle** ① *To1667-493258, gardens Mon-Sat
1000-1600, free*. This lovely 15th century stately home (pronounced *Kilrawk*) is still the
seat of the Rose family and is closed to the public but can be visited by prior
appointment. You can also stay here, in the guest house, which is run on strictly
Christian principles. The castle gardens are open to the public and worth visiting.

Nairn and around → *Phone code: 01667. Colour map 2, grid C2. Population: 11,190.*
The genteel seaside resort of Nairn claims the driest and sunniest climate in the
whole of Scotland. This alone should be reason enough to pay a visit, but there are
other attractions besides the sunshine. There are miles of sandy beach stretching
east to the Culbin Forest, a championship golf course (which hosted the 1999 Walker
Cup), and two of the best castles in the country are within easy reach – Cawdor Castle,
see above, and Brodie Castle, see below.

Nairn Museum ① *May-Sep Mon-Sat 1000-1630, £1*, at Viewfield House on
Viewfield Drive, gives an insight into the area's history with interesting account of the
building of the harbour and subsequent decline of the herring industry.

About two miles east of Nairn, in the little village of **Auldearn**, is a 17th-century
doocot (dovecote) from where the royal standard was flown, in 1645, by the victorious
troops of Charles I led by the Marquis of Montrose against the Covenanters. Displays
in the *doocot* ① *£1.50*, tell of the battle.

Ten miles south of Nairn on the A939 to Grantown is **Dulsie Bridge**, a very popular
local beauty spot which is a great place for a summer picnic or to swim in the River
Findhorn. On the southern shores of the Moray Firth, just east of Nairn, is **Culbin
Sands**, a stretch of sand home to a host of birdlife. The best time to visit is from
autumn to spring when bar-tailed godwits, oystercatchers, knots, dunlins, ringed
plovers, redshanks, curlews, shellducks, red breasted mergansers, greylag geese
and snow buntings, to name but a few, come here in their droves.

Brodie Castle
① *To1309-641371. Castle Apr, Jul, Aug daily 1200-1600, May, Jun, Sep, Sun-Thu 1200-
1600; grounds all year daily 0930-sunset. Castle £5, concession £3.75, children £1;
grounds only £1 (honesty box).*

Big blue

The waters in this area are renowned for their populations of the well-loved mammal, the dolphin. Buckie is the home of the Moray Firth Wildlife Centre, which houses a dolphin exhibition, where you can find out evrything you ever wanted to know about them. There are various dolphin-spotting cruises around the Moray Firth, but there is a code of conduct for boat operators. Before you choose a cruise, make sure the company is part of the accreditation scheme.

Moray Firth Dolphin Cruises, Inverness, T01463-717900, morayfirth.cruises@virgin.net, are accredited and offer trips for £10 (£8 concession) that last 1½ hours and leave from Shore Street Quay (at the far end of Chapel St). Buses run from the TIC 15 minutes before sailings. **McAuley Charters**, Harbour offices, Longman Drive, Inverness, T01463-717337, are also accredited and offer dolphin-spotting cruises which leave from Cromarty (see page 238) and Buckie.

Brodie Castle, 8 miles east of Nairn, just off the main A96 to Forres, is one of Scotland's finest castles. The oldest part of the castle, the Z-plan tower house, is 16th-century, with additions dating from the 17th and 19th centuries, giving it the look of a Victorian country house. The interior of the house is the epitome of good taste, with some fabulous ceilings, and you can look round several rooms, including the huge Victorian kitchen. The collections of furniture and porcelain are wonderful but most notable are the outstanding paintings, which include Edwin Landseer and Scottish Colourists. The grounds, too, are a delight, especially in spring when the daffodils are in bloom. There's also a tearoom.

Highlights include the impressive paintings and tapestries, the fascinating kitchen and the genuinely witty captions that have visitors laughing all over the castle.

The Beauly Firth

Beauly and around → *Phone code: 01463. Colour map 2, grid C1.*
The sleepy little market town of Beauly is 10 miles west of Inverness, where the Beauly river flows into the Firth. It's a lovely wee place – hence its name. According to local legend, when Mary, Queen of Scots stayed here, at the priory, in 1564, she was so taken with the place that she cried (in French, of course) "Ah, quel beau lieu!" (What a beautiful place!).

At the north end of the marketplace is the ruin of **Beauly Priory** ① *Jun-end 30 Sep daily 0930-1830, £1.20, concession £0.90, children £0.50*, founded in 1230 for the Valliscaulian order, but like so much else of Scotland's ecclesiastical heritage, destroyed during the Reformation.

Four miles east of Beauly, at Balchraggan just off the main Inverness road, is **Moniack Castle Winery** ① *Mon-Sat 1000-1700 summer, 1100-1600 winter*, where you can try a whole range of wines, including elderflower and birch. Four miles to the north is the **Glen Ord Distillery** ① *T01463-872004, www.malts.com, Nov-Feb, Wed-Fri 1130-1500, Mar-Jun, Mon-Fri 1000-1700, Jul-Sep Mon-Sat 1000-1700, Sun 1200-1600, Oct Mon-Fri 1100-1600, £4, take a bus or train from Inverness, on the outskirts of Muir of Ord*, just off the A832. It offers a fairly good basic tour and a wonderful de-luxe tour for whisky aficionados. The River Beauly is one of Scotland's best salmon-fishing rivers, and five miles south of Beauly at **Aigas** is a fish lift ① *Mon-Fri 1000-1500*, where you can watch salmon bypass the dam with the aid of technology.

Glen Strathfarrar → *Colour map 1, grid C6.*

Southwest of Beauly are glens Affric and Strathfarrar. Glen Strathfarrar, the lesser known of the two, is unspoiled and considered by some to be the more beautiful. To get there, take the A831 nine miles south from Beauly to Struy and follow the signs. Access to the glen is restricted by the owners, Scottish Natural Heritage, to 12 cars at a time and you have to leave by 1900. The glen is also closed from mid-August to October. But once you're in there is a tremendous feeling of peace, and there's good climbing, fishing and walking. The little ungraded road runs for 14 miles all the way to the impressive **Monar Dam** at the head of the glen. Glen Strathfarrar can also be reached from Drumnadrochit, via Cannich (see below). Most of the walks and cycle routes here are covered by OS Landranger Nos 25 and 26.

Glen Affric → *Colour map 3, grid A6. OS Landranger Nos 25 and 26.*

The A831 continues south from Struy through Strathglass to the village of **Cannich**, gateway to glorious Glen Affric, a dramatic and beautiful gorge, with the River Affric rushing through it, and surrounded by Caledonian pine and birch forest – in fact this is one of the few places where you can still see the native Scots pine. There are few, if any, more stunning sights in the Scottish Highlands and it's perfect for walking, or even just to drive through and stop for a picnic on a nice, sunny day.

▲ Beyond Loch Affric the serious walking starts. From **Affric Lodge**, nine miles west of Cannich, begins a 20-mile trail west to **Morvich**, near Shiel Bridge, on the west coast near Kyle of Lochalsh, see page 208. This strenuous walk is for experienced hikers only, and takes around 10 hours. You can stop off halfway at one of the most remote youth hostels in Scotland, **Glen Affric Youth Hostel**, at Allt Beithe (no phone, open mid-March till end October).

> ✱ *Glen Affric reaches west into the very heart of the Highlands and is great for a spot of Munro-bagging, see further page 57.*

▲ There are also many shorter, easier walks around Glen Affric. There are some short, circular marked trails at the end of the road which runs west from Cannich almost to Loch Affric, and also from the car park at the impressive **Dog Falls**, 4½ miles from Cannich and a great place to stop for a picnic and swim. Cycling in the forests around Cannich is good too – you can hire bikes at Cannich Caravan and Camping Park.

▲ Glen Affric can also be reached from **Drumnadrochit**, see page 175, by heading west on the A831 through Glen Urquhart to Cannich. Just before Cannich, on the road from Drumnadrochit, a single track road leads left (south), past the Caravan and Camping Park, to the tiny village of **Tomich**. From here, it's a three-mile hike up a woodland trail to a car park. A few hundred yards down through the trees takes you to the lovely Plodda Falls. An old iron bridge affords a spectacular view of the waterfall as it plunges 150 yards into the foaming waters below.

North & Northwest Around Inverness Listings

● Sleeping

Nairn and around *p171*

L The Golf View Hotel, Seabank Rd, next to the golf course, T01667-452301, scotland@ morton-hotels.demon.co.uk. 47 rooms. The most luxurious here, with pool, sauna, spa, gym, tennis courts and fine restaurant.
E Bracadale House, Albert St, T01667-452 547, neil.macleod@lineone.net. Very fine B&B.

Camping

Spindrift Caravan & Camping Park, Little Kildrummie, T01667-453992, open Apr-Oct. A good campsite 1½ miles from town.

Beauly and around *p172*

L The Priory Hotel, on the main street, T01463-782309. The most expensive place to stay.
C Lovat Arms Hotel, at the opposite end of the main street from **The Priory Hotel**, T01463-782313, lovat.arms@cali.co.uk. A relaxed and comfortable place with an excellent restaurant and great bar food, lots of tartan and the occasional ceilidh. Best place to stay in town.
F Ellengowan, Croyard Rd, T01463-782273, open Apr-Oct. A cheaper B&B option.

B The Tomich Hotel, Tomich, T01456-415399, F415469. The price includes dinner, and it's a comfortable place with good food and free use of the nearby indoor heated pool; also great for fishing holidays.
C-D Kerrow House, Cannich village, T01456-415243, stephen@kerrow-house.demon.co.uk. An excellent B&B.
F Cougie Lodge, near Tomich, T01456-415459, www.cougie.org, Apr-Sep. An independent hostel with 6 beds. Valerie or John will pick you up from Tomich or Cannich if you phone ahead.
F Glen Affric Backpackers, Cannich, T/F01456-415263, open all year. Slightly cheaper than Cannich Youth Hostel and independent.
F SYHA Cannich Youth Hostel, Cannich, T01456-415244, open mid-Mar to end Oct. Clean hostel accommodation.

● Eating

Cawdor Castle *p171*
££-£ Cawdor Tavern, in the village of Cawdor, close by the castle, T/F01667-404777, a traditional country pub serving excellent food in a friendly atmosphere. Perfect for lunch or dinner after visiting the castle.

Nairn and around *p171*
££ Boath House, T01463-455469, 2 miles east of Nairn in the little village of Auldearn. Aside from the hotels in town, this is one of the best places to eat.
£ Friar Tuck's, at 30 Harbour St, if you fancy a fish supper.
£ Asher's Bakery, 2 Bridge St, recommended for a hot snack. Run by the same folk as the one in Inverness.

Beauly and around *p172*
£££-£ Lovat Arms Hotel, serves up the best food around. Offers bar meals (£) or dinner in the restaurant (£££).
Beauly Tandoori, The Square, T01463-782221, for a cheap curry.
Friary for an even cheaper fish supper.

▲ Activities and tours

Nairn and around *p171*
Cycling The Bike Shop, High St, Nairn. For bike hire.

Horse riding Heatherfield Riding Centre, Lochloy Rd, Nairn, T01667-456682, offer pony trekking.

● Transport

Culloden *p169*
Highland Country Bus No 7 leaves from Inverness – pick it up outside the Post Office Mon-Sat (last bus back about 1830).
Guide Friday tour buses leave from Bridge St, Inverness, May-Sep (see p167).

Fort George *p170*
Fort Highland Bus and Coach No 11 from the Post Office in Inverness, several daily except Sun, also buses from Nairn.

Cawdor Castle *p171*
Highland Country Buses No 12 leaves from **Inverness** Post Office and runs several times daily (except Sun), the last bus returns around 1800, also regular buses from **Nairn**.

Brodie Castle *p171*
Bluebird buses run to Brodie from Inverness, via Culloden and Nairn, 45 mins.

Nairn and around *p171*
There are regular daily buses to Nairn from **Inverness** (30 mins) with Highland Country Buses and Bluebird, see p168. Nairn is on the **Inverness-Aberdeen** rail line, and there are several trains daily from **Inverness** (20 min).

Beauly and around *p172*
There are **Inverness Traction** buses, T01463-239292, every hour to **Beauly**, and on to **Muir of Ord**, from **Inverness** and from **Dingwall**. There's also a Ross's Minibus service from Beauly 3 days a week, T01463-761250. The train station at Beauly (with the shortest platform in the UK, so take care getting off) is now open; trains between **Inverness** and **Thurso** stop here.

Glen Affric *p173*
Highland Bus & Coach, T01463-233371, runs buses 3 days a week Mon-Fri from **Inverness** to **Cannich** and **Tomich**, via **Drumnadrochit**. There are also buses from **Inverness** to **Cannich** and **Tomich**, via **Beauly** (2 on Tue and Fri, and 1 on Sat).

Loch Ness and around

One of Scotland's biggest attractions is the narrow gash of Loch Ness, Britain's deepest body of fresh water, stretching 23 miles from Fort Augustus in the south almost to Inverness in the north. The loch is scenic in its own right, with rugged hills rising steeply from its wooded shores, but visitors don't come here for the views. They come every year, in their hundreds of thousands, to stare across the dark, cold waters in search of its legendary inhabitant, the Loch Ness Monster. A huge tourist trade has grown up around 'Nessie', as the monster is affectionately known, and every summer the main A82 which runs along its western shore is jam packed with bus-loads of eager monster-hunters, binoculars trained on the loch surface, desperate for one glimpse of the elusive beast. ▸▸ *For Sleeping, Eating and other listings, see pages 180-184.*

Ins and outs

The best way to see the loch is on a cruise from Inverness, see page 183 and page 178. There are also boat trips from Drumnadrochit and Fort Augustus. Most of the tourist traffic uses the congested A82, which offers few decent views of the loch. By far the best views of the loch are from the quiet and picturesque B862/852 which runs along its eastern shore from Fort Augustus up to Inverness. It's possible to make a complete circuit of the loch, which is best done in an anti-clockwise direction heading south from Inverness on the A82, but you'll need your own transport (or take a tour), as there are no buses between Fort Augustus and Foyers. There are regular daily bus services between Inverness and Fort William, with additional buses between Invergarry and Fort Augustus. ▸▸ *For further details, see Activities and tours page 182 and Transport, page 183.*

Around the loch

Drumnadrochit → *Phone code: 01456. Colour map 2, grid C1.*

The Nessie tourist trade is centred on the village of Drumnadrochit, 15 miles south of Inverness, where the canny locals have cashed in on the enduring popularity of the monster myth. The monster hype is almost overpowering, with two rival Monster Exhibitions and the inevitable souvenir shops selling all manner of awful tartan tack, including those scary-looking tartan dolls with flickering eyelids, the "See-You-Jimmy" tartan bonnet, complete with ginger 'hair', and not forgetting the Loch Ness Monster novelty hat. There's a TIC in the car park ① *T01456-459086.*

One of the two Monster Exhibitions is the revamped **'Original' Loch Ness Monster Visitor Centre** ① *T01456-450342, www.lochness-centre.com, Apr to end of Oct daily 1000-1800 (Jul-Aug till 2100), £3.50, students £3, children/OAPs £2.75,* which features a wide-screen cinema multi-lingual translator, plus gift shop, restaurant and internet café. Loch Ness Cruises operate from here, see page 182. The rival exhibition is **Loch Ness 2000 Exhibition** ① *T01456-450573, Easter-end May 0930-1700, Jun and Sep 0900-1800, Jul-Aug 0900-2000, Oct 0930-1730, Nov-Mar 1000-1530, £5.95, students/seniors £4.50, children £3.50.* Though it's considerably more expensive, it gives a detailed description of the many eye-witness accounts over the years and also explains the recent research projects carried out in the loch.

If it all gets too much, then fear not, for Drumnadrochit gives easy access to one of the most beautiful corners of Scotland. The A831 heads west from the village through **Glen Urquhartto Cannich**, about 12 miles away, at the head of Glen Affric, a great place for walking or enjoying a picnic, see page 173.

Castle Urquhart

ⓘ *T01456-450551, Apr-Sep 0930-1830, Oct-Mar 0930-1630, £6, concession £4.50, children £1.20.*

A few miles south of Drumnadrochit are the ruins of Castle Urquhart. The castle bears the scars of centuries of fighting but its setting, perched on a rocky cliff on the loch's edge, is magnificent and, not surprisingly, one of the most photographed scenes in Scotland. Dating from the 14th century, the castle was a strategic base, guarding the Great Glen during the long Wars of Independence. It was taken by Edward I, held by Robert the Bruce against Edward II, and was then almost constantly under siege before being destroyed in 1692 to prevent it from falling into Jacobite hands. Most of the existing buildings date from the 16th century, including the five-storey tower, the best-preserved part of the complex, from where you get great views of the loch and surrounding hills. There's also a new visitor centre, which is not to everyone's taste, so if you really like it, best keep it to yourself.

Invermoriston → *Phone code: 01320. Colour map 4, grid A1.*

Between Drumnadrochit and Fort Augustus is the tiny village of Invermoriston, probably the nicest spot on the entire Inverness to Fort Augustus stretch of the A82. It's a beautiful little piece of Highland scenery, with a photogenic old stone bridge over foaming river rapids. There are marked woodland trails leading off into the hills past some lovely waterfalls.

At Invermoriston the A887 heads west through Glen Moriston to meet the A87, which runs from Invergarry (below) all the way through the rugged and dramatic Glen Shielto, the awesome mountains of Kintailon to the west coast near Kyle of Lochalsh.

Fort Augustus → *Phone code: 01320. Colour map 4, grid A1.*

At the more scenic southern end of Loch Ness stands the village of Fort Augustus, originally set up as a garrison after the Jacobite rebellion of 1715, and headquarters of General Wade's campaign to pacify the Highlands. Today, Fort Augustus is a busy little place, full of monster-hunting tourists and boats using the flight of five locks to enter or leave Loch Ness on their journey along the Caledonian Canal. The tourist information centre ⓘ *T01320-366367, Apr-Oct*, is in the car park next to the petrol station and Bank of Scotland.

On the shores of Loch Ness is **Fort Augustus Abbey**, a Benedictine Monastery founded in 1876 on the site of the original fort. The abbey closed in 1998. By the canal locks is **The Clansman Centre** ⓘ *T01320-366444, Apr, May, Jun and Sep daily 1100-1700, Jul-Aug 1000-1800, £3, concession £2.50*, where young guides in traditional dress provide a lively and entertaining presentation of 17th-century Highland family life in an old turf house. There follows a display of weaponry and a mock sword fight in the garden. You can even have your picture taken wearing traditional Highland costume. There's also a craftshop selling the more tasteful kind of souvenirs.

Fort Augustus to Dores → *Colour map 4, grid A1-2.*

A worthwhile detour from Fort Augustus is to take the B862/852 up the east shore of Loch Nesson, a mostly single-track road that skirts the loch for much of its length to the village of Dores. It's a much quieter and more scenic route than the busy A82 and follows General Wade's original (and very straight) military road which linked Fort Augustus with Fort George. Though it makes a more interesting alternative to the more popular A82 route from Inverness to Fort Augustus, it's best done from south to north, if you have the time.

The road winds its way up into rugged hills before returning to the lochside at **Foyers**. It's worth stopping here to see the impressive waterfall where the River Foyers plunges into Loch Ness. To get there, follow the steep (and slippery) track down from opposite the shops. Three miles further north, at **Inverfarigaig**, is the spooky and

• Great Monster Hunt

In a country full of myths and legends, the Loch Ness Monster is the greatest of them all. As elusive as a straight answer from a politician, Nessie has single-handedly sold more tins of tartan-wrapped shortbread to foreign visitors than Edinburgh Castle.

Tales of Nessie go way back to the sixth century, when St Columba is said to have calmed the beast after she had attacked one of his monks. But the monster craze only really took off with the completion of the A82 road along the loch's western shore in 1933. Since then there have been numerous sightings, some backed up with photographic evidence, though the most impressive of these – the famous

black-and-white movie footage of Nessie's humps moving through the water, and the classic photograph of her head and neck – have been exposed as fakes.

In recent decades determined monster hunters have enlisted the help of new technology, such as sonar surveys, but have failed to come up with conclusive evidence. Enter Cyber Nessie, the latest attempt to end the years of rumours, hoaxes and speculation. Nessie's very own website – www.lochness.scot land.net/camera.htm – is a 24-hour real-time video watch of Loch Ness, and has already produced a couple of claimed sightings. But nothing could compare with the excitement of seeing the monster in the flesh.

sinister **Boleskine House**, once home of Alastair Crowley, who is said to have practised devil worship here. In the 1970s the house was bought by Jimmy Page of Led Zeppelin, but sold some years later after the tragic death of his daughter. Those of a nervous disposition may wish to pass on quickly and continue to the little village of **Dores**, at the northeastern end of the loch, where you can enjoy a good pint of ale and some decent grub at the **Dores Inn**.

You can then continue to Inverness, or return via the beautiful hill road that leads up to **Loch Mhorand** back to Fort Augustus via the **Stratherrick Valley**. From **Errogie**, at the northern end of Loch Mhor, there's a dramatic section of road that winds down to the loch through a series of tight, twisting bends, reminiscent of an Alpine pass, and great for cyclists. There are also interesting marked woodland trails around Errogie.

Fort Augustus to Fort William

South of Fort Augustus, the A82 leaves behind Loch Ness and runs along the west shore of Loch Oich and then the east shore of Loch Lochy, till it reaches Spean Bridge. Here the A82 continues south to Fort William, while the A86 branches east through Glen Spean to join the A9 Perth to Inverness road finally at Kingussie. All along this route are many opportunities to get off the beaten track and explore huge chunks of real wilderness, deserted since the Clearances and soaked in the blood of history.

▸▸ *For Sleeping, Eating and other listings, see pages 180-184.*

Invergarry and around → *Phone code: 01809. Colour map 4, grid A1.*

The old village of Invergarry stands where the A82 turns west to meet the A87. There's not much to see or do in the village, but the surrounding area merits some exploring, particularly the route west through Glen Garry, and there are several places to stay.

Inside the entrance to the **Glengarry Castle Hotel**, see Sleeping page 183, stand the ruins of **Invergarry Castle**, once the stronghold of the MacDonnells of Glengarry

⁞ Old as the hills

The Great Glen, which splits the Scottish mainland from Fort William in the south to Inverness in the north, is one of the world's major geological fault lines. The Glen was formed millions of years ago when the northern part of the Caledonian mountains 'slid' more than 60 miles south, leaving behind a massive glen with four freshwater lochs – Loch Linnhe, Loch Lochy, Loch Oich and Loch Ness.

The most famous of these is Loch Ness, which attracts hordes of visitors eager to catch a glimpse of its elusive monster.The renowned engineer, Thomas Telford, succeeded in connecting all these lochs when he built the impressive Caledonian Canal. The canal took 22 years to complete, and when it was opened in 1822 was the first in Britain to take ships from one coast to the other. It remains the only

canal in the country capable of carrying ships of up to 500 tons. The best way to appreciate the glen is by boat, through the 38 miles of natural lochs and rivers and the 22 miles of canal, and every summer pleasure craft of all shapes and sizes ply its length. The main A82 runs from Inverness south to Fort William. The southern section, from Fort Augustus, follows the original line of the road constructed in 1727 by General Wade to link the military garrisons at Fort William and Fort Augustus (hence their names).

Another way to travel through the Great Glen is along the excellent cycle route, which follows the canal towpaths, forest trails and quiet minor roads to avoid the busy main road. The route is outlined in the Forestry Commission leaflet, available from most tourist information centres.

and later destroyed by the Duke of Cumberland as he wreaked revenge on the Highlands in the aftermath of Culloden, see page 41. The hotel was later built as the main house of the Ellice family, who made their fortune from the Hudson Bay Company in Canada and who were the main driving force behind the creation of the Victorian planned village.

A mile or so south of the village, at **North Laggan**, is a monument by the side of the road standing over **The Well of the Seven Heads**. This tells the grisly story of the **Keppoch Murders**, one of the most infamous clan murders which took place at **Roy Bridge** (see below) in the 17th century. It all began when the chief of the clan MacDonnell died, leaving two young sons, who were sent away to complete their education before returning to Roy Bridge to celebrate the elder brother's accession to the chiefship. Another branch of the clan present at the celebrations started a fight in which both brothers were killed. Believing they had been murdered, one of their cousins persuaded a fellow clan member to raise 50 men and march on the murderers' house at nearby Inverlair. The accused murderers – a father and his six sons – were duly slaughtered and their heads cut off, to be displayed before the local laird at Glengarry. On the way to his lodge, the heads were washed here in this well.

A few miles further south, at **Laggan**, where the A82 crosses to the east bank of Loch Lochy, is the site of the **Battle of the Shirts**, see box. The A87 leads west from Invergarry through Glen Shiel to Shiel Bridge, on the way to Kyle of Lochalsh on the west coast, see page 208. About seven miles along the A87, past the turning for Kinloch Hourn (see below), is the **Glen Garry viewpoint**, from where you get one of the most stunning, and famous, of all Highland views. From this angle Loch Garry looks uncannily like a map of Scotland, so get out the camera for that classic holiday snap.

Glen Garry to Kinloch Hourn → *Colour map 3, grid A5-6.*

A mile or so before the Glen Garry viewpoint, where the A87 begins to leave the shores of Loch Garry, is the turning left for the road through Glen Garry, described as the longest and most beautiful cul-de-sac in Britain. The little single-track road turns and twists for 22 glorious miles along the shores of Loch Garry and Loch Quoich all the way to Kinloch Hourn, at the head of Loch Hourn, a sea loch on the west coast.

Glen Garry is now virtually deserted but was once home to some 5,000 people who were driven out during the infamous Highland Clearances in the 19th century. The road passes the tiny hamlet of **Tomdoun**, once the junction of the main road to Skye, until the massive post-war hydroelectric schemes changed the landscape. Experienced hillwalkers can still follow the old route to Skye, through Glen Kingie, along Loch Hourn and then across the wild Knoydart peninsula till they reach the tiny settlement of **Inverie**. From here a little ferry runs twice a day (Monday to Wednesday and Friday) to Mallaig, see page 202.

Beyond Tomdoun the road passes a huge dam, built in the 1950s, which raised the waters of **Loch Quoich** by over 100 ft, flooding many of the old settlements. Also flooded was **Glen Quoich Lodge**, which can count Edward VII and Sir Edward Landseer among its notable guests. It was reputedly Glen Garry that gave Landseer the inspiration for his famous painting *The Monarch of the Glen*. The road then reaches its highest point, at 1,200 ft, before descending to **Kinloch Hourn**, once a thriving fishing village but now remote and isolated. Incredible as it may seem, you can actually stay here, see Sleeping page 183.

Spean Bridge → *Phone code: 01397. Colour map 3, grid B6.*

The main A82 runs down the east shore of Loch Lochy to the village of Spean Bridge, at the head of Glen Spean, beneath the towering Lochaber Mountains. The village gets its name from Thomas Telford's bridge across the River Spean. Two miles west are the remains of the old 'Highbridge', built in 1736 by General Wade, and the site of the first clash between Government troops and the Jacobites, three days before Prince Charles raised his standard at Glenfinnan.

Spean Bridge is only eight miles north of Fort William so gets busy in the summer, but it still makes a more peaceful and attractive alternative base for exploring this astoundingly beautiful part of the Highlands. There's a tourist information centre ① *T01397-712576, Easter-Oct*, just off the main road behind the post office. Spean Bridge is also the starting point for the excellent **Grey Corries ridge walk** (OS Landranger Map No 41).

Loch Arkaig and around → *Phone code: 01397. Colour map 3, grid A6.*

A mile north of Spean Bridge on the A82 is the **Commando Memorial**, which commemorates the commandos who trained here during the Second World War. It's worth lingering for a few moments to appreciate the fantastic views all around. From here the B8004 branches west to **Gairlochy**, crossing the Caledonian Canal, then the B8005 heads north to Loch Arkaig, a long, deep and mysterious loch stretching west through the mountains. Bonnie Prince Charlie passed this way, before and after Culloden, through an area which has, for centuries, been the seat of the Camerons of Lochiel. The Camerons were fervent supporters of the Jacobite cause and when Prince Charles landed at Loch nan Uamh, on the road from Fort William to Mallaig, he called on Cameron of Lochiel to join him at Glenfinnan.

In the tiny township of **Achnacarry**, nestled between the shores of Loch Lochy and Loch Arkaig, you can find out about the Camerons and their involvement in the Jacobite rebellion of 1745 at the **Clan Cameron Museum** ① *T01397-712480, Easter to mid-Oct daily 1330-1700, Jul-Aug 1100-1700, £3, concession £1.50, children free.* This museum is housed in an old cottage, rebuilt after being burned by government troops in 1746.

⦂ Getting shirty

One the bloodiest battles in Scottish clan history was the Battle of the Shirts, fought in 1544. It was so named because it was fought on a hot day and the combatants took off their shirts before proceeding to butcher each other. One side – the Frasers – were almost wiped out and their opponents – a combined force of MacDonalds, MacDonnells and Camerons – suffered less heavy losses and claimed victory. Over 1,000 were killed and a plaque beside the canal locks describes the terrible events.

Beyond the turn-off to Achnacarry, the single-track road runs through the Clunes Forest and The Dark Mile, a long line of beech trees which completely cuts out daylight. At the east end of Loch Arkaig, a stone bridge crosses the Caig Burn. Beside the bridge is a car park, from where a path leads up to the spectacular **Cia-Aig Falls** which tumble into a deep, dark pool known as **The Witch's Cauldron**. It was here that an old hag was accused of casting her evil eye over Lochiel's cattle, causing them to fall ill and die. But when she fell into the pool and drowned, the cattle miraculously began to recover from their illness. The road runs along the north shore of Loch Arkaig all the way to the head of the loch, from where experienced and well-equipped hill walkers can hike through the glens to Loch Nevis and Knoydart.

Glen Roy and Loch Laggan → *Phone code: 01397. Colour map 4, grid A-B1.*

From Spean Bridge the A86 runs east through Glen Spean to meet the A9 Perth to Inverness road which leads to Aviemore, see page 98. The road passes through Roy Bridge, which is the turn-off for Glen Roy, noted for its amazing 'parallel roads'. These are not in fact roads, but three gravel ledges etched on to the mountains at different heights. The 'roads' marked the shorelines of a glacial lake formed during the last Ice Age. Roy Bridge was also the site of the infamous Keppoch Murders, see page 177.

The road continues east towards Loch Laggan. After a couple of miles it passes **Cille Choirille**, an ancient church built by a 15th-century Cameron chief as penance for a life of violence. The church fell into disrepair but was restored and reopened in 1932 and now attracts people of all creeds as it's said to inspire peace and spiritual healing. Further east, at the eastern end of Loch Laggan, is the massive **Laggan Dam**, built in 1933 to provide water for the aluminium smelter at Fort William. The water is piped through tunnels up to 15 ft in diameter carved through the core of Ben Nevis. The road runs along the north shore of the loch, past the **Creag Meagaidh National Nature Reserve**, where you can see herds of red deer right by the reserve car park. A track leads from here up to **Lochan a' Choire** (about four hours).

⬤ Sleeping

Drumnadrochit *p175*

B Polmaily House Hotel, 3 miles from Drumnadrochit on the A831 to Cannich, in Glen Urquhart, T01456-450343, polmailyhousehotel@btinternet.com. 10 rooms. If you can afford it, this is your best bet. A comfortable, child-friendly country house far away from the crowds with peace and quiet, many walks nearby, also tennis courts, horse riding and covered pool, and a good restaurant.

D The Benleva Hotel, T01456-450288, F450781. Small, family-run hotel with bar and dining room.
D Gillyflowers, T/F01456-450641, gillyflowers@cali.co.uk. Good value.
D-E Woodlands, East Lewiston, T01456- 450356, www.woodlands bandb.net. 3 en suite rooms. Open Mar-Oct. Refurbished to a high standard, plush, spacious bathrooms and very comfortable. Recommended.

E Drumbuie Farm, T01456-450634,
F450595. Modern farmhouse on the right as
you enter the village from Inverness, with its
own herd of Highland cattle. Recommended.
F Loch Ness Backpackers Lodge, Coiltie
Farmhouse in East Lewiston, T01456-450807,
immediately south of Drumnadrochit, on the
left. It's open all year, has excellent facilities,
and arranges boat trips and local walks.

Invermoriston *p176*
F SYHA Loch Ness Youth Hostel,
T0871-3308537, mid-Apr to end Oct. A few
miles to the north on the main A82
overlooking Loch Ness.
Loch Ness Caravan & Camping Park, 1½
miles south of Invermoriston, and 6 miles
north of Fort Augustus, is the T01320-351207,
right on the shores of the loch with great
views and excellent facilities (Easter-Oct).

Fort Augustus *p176*
There are lots of B&Bs to choose from here.
D Lovat Arms Hotel, T01320-366206,
www.ipv.com/lovatarms. 23 rooms. This
beautiful old mansion house standing above
the village is the best place to stay around
here. It also has a good restaurant (dinner £15
per person) and a warm welcome awaits.
D-E Mrs Service, Sonason the Inverness Rd,
T01320-366291. Lives up to its name.
E Kettle House, Golf Course Rd, T01320-
366408, open Feb-Nov. Another B&B with a
good name. Friendly, too.
F Morag's Lodge, T01320-366289. Newly
converted, this place offers backpacker
accommodation between Mar and Oct.

Fort Augustus to Dores *p176*
E-F Intake-House, Foyers, T01456-482258,
open Apr-Oct.
F Foyers House, Foyers, T01456-486623.
Small independent youth hostel.

Invergarry and around *p177*
A Glengarry Castle Hotel, T01809-501254,
www.glengarry.net, open Mar-Nov. Set in 60
acres of woodland running down to Loch
Oich. 26 rooms. There are various options for
sleeping in and around Invergarry, but none
can match the splendour of this place. The
hotel has been in the MacCallum family for
over 40 years and continues to be one of the
best in the Highlands.

C-D Invergarry Hotel, T01809-501206,
hotel@invergarry.net. Rather less luxurious
but still comfortable and good value.
D Forest Lodge, South Laggan, south of
Invergarry, T01809-501219, www.flgh.co.uk.
7 rooms. Welcoming and comfortable B&B
run by Janet and Ian Shearer. Well-equipped
rooms with good views and a 4-course
dinner is available.
F Invergarry Lodge, Mandally Rd,
Invergarry, T01809-501412,
www.invergarrylodge.co.uk. Independent
hostel sleeping up to 26 in 4-6 bed rooms.
Open all year. Fully-equipped kitchen and
safe cycle shed.
F SYHA Loch Lochy Youth Hostel,
South Laggan, T01809-501239, mid-Mar
to end-Oct.

Camping
There are a couple of campsites near the
village: **Faichem Park**, T01809-501226, Easter-
Oct; and **Faichemard Farm Camping Site**,
T01809-501314, Apr-Oct, which is off the A87.

Glen Garry to Kinloch Hourn *p179*
B Skiary, T01809-511214, open May-Sep,
phone ahead to arrange for a boat to meet
you. This is perhaps the most remote guest
house in the Highlands. It is accessible only
by boat or foot and has no mains electricity.
There are 3 rooms and prices are for full
board, and include the boat trip both ways.
The food is wonderful and the setting is
simply magnificent.

Spean Bridge *p179*
There's no shortage of accommodation in
Spean Bridge. There are lots more guest
houses and B&Bs than are listed here.
A Old Pines Restaurant with Rooms, just
past the Commando Memorial on the
B8004, T01397-712324, www.oldpines.
co.uk. 8 rooms, price includes dinner. Pick
of the bunch in Spean Bridge. This
Scandinavian- style chalet run by Bob and
Sukie Barber is a great place to stay,
especially if you have kids in tow, features
include a large playroom, a barn with
snooker and table tennis and a trampoline
in the garden. Sukie's exceptional,
award-winning Scottish cuisine is also a
major draw. The 5-course dinner (**£££**) is
also available to non-guests.

A Corriegour Lodge Hotel, 9 miles north of Spean Bridge on the A82, T01397-712685, www.courriegour-lodge-hotel.com. 9 rooms, open Feb-Dec. Lovely Victorian hunting lodge on the shores of Loch Lochy, with fine views and an excellent restaurant (non-residents dinner only £££).

D Corriechoille Lodge, T/F01397-712002, www.corrie1.demon.co.uk. Open Mar-Nov. A good stop for a night.

D Invergloy House, on the shores of Loch Lochy, T01397-712681. Very good B&B.

E Smiddy House, in Spean Bridge village, T01397-712335, F712043. A comfortable guest house with a bistro attached, serving good, cheap meals.

Camping

There are a couple of campsites, north of the village at **Stronaba Caravan & Camping**, T01397-712259, open Apr-Oct; and west towards Gairlochy at **Gairlochy Holiday Park**, T01397-712711, F712712, open Apr-Oct.

Glen Roy and Loch Laggan *p180*

There are several hotels in Roy Bridge and 3 independent hostels, listed below.

C Stronlossit Hotel, T0800-0155321, www.stronlossit.co.uk, which serves good meals all day from 1100 (££-£).

F Aite Cruinnichidh, Achluachrach, 1½ miles from the village, T01397-712315, is the cheaper hostel.

F Grey Corrie Lodge, T01397-712236, is handy for shops and transport, serves cheap bar meals and also has laundry facilities.

F Station Lodge, 5 miles east at Tulloch train station, T/F01397-732333, is this option which serves meals (including vegetarian).

❶ Eating

Drumnadrochit *p175*

The hotels all tend to serve decent bar food and some B&Bs offer evening meals.
££ Fiddler's Bistro, T01456-450678, which offers generous portions of staples such as salmon steak and good service. Open for lunch and dinner, last orders 2100.

Fort Augustus *p176*

££-£ Bothy, T01320-366263, a cosy choice down by the canal bridge, serves simple but tasty bistro-style meals in a rustic setting from 1000-2000.

£ Loch Inn, by the canal, is the best place for a drink, and also serves decent pub grub.

Spean Bridge *p179*

£££ Old Station Restaurant, T01397-712535. In a converted railway station. Has a very good reputation, lunch by prior arrangement only, open Apr-Oct, Tue-Sun 1800-2100.

£££ The Coach House Restaurant, 3 miles north of town on the right-hand side, at Glenfintaig, T01397-712680, crann_tara@ bigfoot.com. It's a popular place and small, so you'll have to book ahead for lunch or dinner, open late Apr to late Oct, daily 1200-1500 and 1800-2100.

Glen Roy and Loch Laggan *p180*

£££-££ Glenspean Lodge Hotel, T01397-712223. Lunch served 1230-1430 and dinner 1830-2100. A good place to eat.

❀ Festivals and events

Fort Augustus *p176*

Late Jun and Jul, mid-Aug and early Sep is the period when Fort Augustus hosts **Highland Gatherings**, featuring traditional dancing and piping competitions, tossing the caber and sheep dog trials.

▲ Activities and tours

Loch Ness and around *p175*
Climbing

Nevis Guides, Bohuntin, Roy Bridge, T01397-712356.

Cycling

Hiring bikes in Drumnadrochit and cycling into Glen Affric makes for a great day out. You can hire mountain bikes at **Fiddler's Bistro**, see Eating. In Fort Augustus you can hire bikes at **Loch Ness Ferry Co Ltd**.

Fishing

Fishing Scotland, T/F01397-712812, www.fishing-scotland.co.uk, runs fishing courses and trips on the surrounding lochs. Loch Arkaig in particular is renowned for its trout fishing.

Horse riding

Fort Augustus Riding Centre, Pier House, Fort Augustus, T01320-366418.
Highland Icelandic Horse Trekking beyond the falls at Loch Arkaig, T01397-712427, hihot@compuserve.com, offers 1-hr, 2-hr and day rides in the surrounding hills.
Highland Riding Centre, T01456-450358, Borlum Farm, Drumnadrochit.

Loch Ness tours

There are various monster-spotting tours of Loch Ness which leave from the tourist office in Drumnadrochit or Fort Augustus.
Cruise Loch Ness, Fort Augustus, T01320-366277, www.cruiselochness.com, on board the *Royal Scot*, set off from the canal in the centre of Fort Augustus, Apr-Oct hourly from 1000. The trip lasts 50 mins and costs £6 per adult. Also boat and bike hire.
Guide Friday, at the train station, Drumnadrochit, T01456-224000. Half-day coach trips right round the loch, at 1030 and 1430, lasting 3 hrs. Tickets cost adult £14.50, concession £11.50, children £6.50, available from booking office at the station or TIC.
Jacobite Cruises, Drumnadrochit, T01456-233999, jacobite@cali.co.uk, offers coach tours, boat cruises and combined coach and cruise trips round the loch. Half-day cruises cost £10, half-day coach and cruise trips cost £14.50 (including entry to the Loch Ness Monster Exhibition and Castle Urquhart). Trips run from Apr-Oct and leave from Tomnahurich Bridge on Glenurquhart Rd, 1½ miles south of the town centre in Drumnadrochit. Free buses leave from the TIC, 20 mins before sailing, if tickets are bought here. Otherwise, to get there take Inverness Traction buses Nos 3, 3A, 4 and 4A every 15 mins from Church St.

Tour operators

Glengarry Mini Tours, Invergarry, T01809-501297, runs various minibus day tours in Great Glen, Glen Coe and Glen Nevis.

Watersports

Great Glen Water Park, east shore of Loch Oich, near North Laggan, T01809-501381. An outdoor activities centre offering adventure sports including whitewater rafting, canoeing, mountain biking, rock climbing, sailing, windsurfing, hill walking and water skiing. Self-catering lodges for rent too.

⊖ Transport

Drumnadrochit *p175*

Citylink buses between **Inverness** and **Fort William** stop at here several times daily in either direction. Additional services run between **Inverness** and **Urquhart Castle** during the summer months. There are also buses from **Inverness** to **Cannich** and **Tomich**, via Drumnadrochit (see p174). Citylink buses between **Inverness** and **Kyle of Lochalsh** stop at Invermoriston.

Fort Augustus *p176*

Fort Augustus is a convenient stopover between **Fort William** and **Inverness**, and there are several buses daily (No 919) in either direction. It takes 1 hr to both towns. There is an additional service between **Fort Augustus** and **Invergarry** (see below) once a day Mon-Sat.

Fort Augustus to Dores *p176*

This route is only possible if you have your own transport. There are buses south from **Inverness**, but they only run as far as **Foyers** (3 times Mon-Fri, twice on Sat). Alternatively, it can be done by bike, as a full-day circular trip from Fort Augustus or from Inverness.

Invergarry and around *p177*

Invergarry is on the **Fort William** to **Inverness** bus route (see Fort Augustus above). It is also on the main **Fort William** to **Kyle of Lochalsh** (and Skye) Citylink route (Nos 915, 916) and a couple of buses pass through daily in both directions. For times T0990-505050.

Glen Garry to Kinoch Hourn *p179*

There's a postbusfrom **Invergarry** on Mon, Wed and Fri, which runs to **Kingie**, which is halfway to Kinloch Hourn. A 4-seater post car runs all the way to Kinloch Hourn from **Invergarry** on Tue, Wed, Thu and Sat.

North & Northwest Loch Ness & around Listings

● *For an explanation of sleeping and eating price codes used in this guide, see inside the*
● *front cover. Other relevant information is found in Essentials, see pages 41-49.*

A more scenic return would be to take the ferry from Kinloch Hourn to **Arnisdale** (summer only; daily by arrangement) and then head to **Glenelg** (see p208), from where you can take a ferry across to **Kylerhea** on Skye.

Spean Bridge *p179*
There are regular buses to and from **Fort William** and **Inverness** (£6 single). Spean Bridge is also on the **Fort William-Glasgow** railline (see p192).

Loch Arkaig and around *p179*
There's no public transport beyond Achnacarry, and there's only 1 busa day to Achnacarry from Lochaber High School in Fort William.

Glen Roy and Loch Laggan *p180*
There are busesfrom **Fort William** to **Roy Bridge** (3 times daily Mon-Fri; 1 on Sat). **Roy Bridge** is also on the **Fort William-Glasgow** rail line.

Fort William and around

Fort William is the gateway to the Western Highlands and one of the country's main tourist centres. It stands at the head of Loch Linnhe, with the snow-topped mass of Ben Nevis towering behind. You could be forgiven for assuming that it's quite an attractive place, but you'd be wrong. Despite its magnificent setting, Fort William has all the charm of a motorway service station. A dual carriageway runs along the lochside, over a litter-strewn pedestrian underpass and past dismal 1960s concrete boxes masquerading as hotels. Most of the good things about Fort William are outside the town. The surrounding mountains and glens are amongst the most stunning in the Highlands and attract hikers and climbers in their droves: Ben Nevis – Britain's highest peak at 4,406 ft – and also the very beautiful Glen Nevis, which you may recognize from movies such as Braveheart *and* Rob Roy. *There's also skiing and snowboarding at nearby Aonach Mor, one of Scotland's top ski areas and top-class mountain biking around the Leanachan Forest.* ►► *For Sleeping, Eating and other listings, see pages 189-193.*

Ins and outs

Getting there
Fort William is easily reached by bus, from Inverness, Glasgow and Oban, and by train, direct from Glasgow via the wonderful West Highland Railway, see page 185. The train station is at the north end of the High Street, next to the Safeway supermarket. The bus station is also here but closed for refurbishment at the time of going to press. Buses leave from temporary stances opposite the Nevis Centre. If you're driving, parking can be a problem. There's a big car park beside the loch at the south end of town, and another behind the tourist office. You can also walk to Fort William, if you have a week to spare, from just north of Glasgow, along the 95 mile-long West Highland Way, see page 55.

Getting around
The town is strung out for several miles along the banks of Loch Linnhe. The centre is compact and easy to get around on foot. Many of the guest housesand B&Bs, and a few youth hostels, are in Corpach, 1½ miles to the north, but there are frequent buses from the town centre. There are also buses to the youth hostel in Glen Nevis. ►► *For further details, see Transport page 192.*

Riding the rails

Running from Glasgow to Mallaig via Fort William, the **West Highland Railway** is only 164 miles long but is widely acknowledged as one of the most scenic railway journeys in the world. The great thing about this journey is its variety, taking you from the distinctive red tenements of Glasgow and the former shipbuilding areas of the River Clyde, to the windy wilderness of Rannoch Moor and the chilly splendour of the hills. It's about an hour after leaving Glasgow that you get your first taste of highland scenery when the train hugs the eastern bank of sinewy Loch Long. Then it's on past the 'bonnie banks' of Loch Lomond, Britain's largest body of inland water. It's impossible not to pass this serene loch without thinking of the famous ballad about two Jacobite soldiers captured after the '45 rebellion. The soldier taking 'the low road' is due to be executed, his companion taking the 'high road' is due to be released.

After Ardlui, at the top of Loch Lomond, the countryside gets more rugged. Wherever you look you see something of interest: a waterfall gushing down a hillside, a buzzard surfing on the breeze, perhaps a herd of Highland Cattle wallowing in a river.

The **West Highland Way**, the long-distance footpath from Glasgow to Fort William, is close to the line now and at stations such as Crianlarich, Upper Tyndrum and Bridge of Orchy you can often spot footsore walkers with muddy boots – who get on the train looking slightly guilty and collapse on their seats with sighs of relief.

The landscape gets wilder and bleaker as the railway crosses the lonely, peaty wastes of Rannoch Moor and on to Corrour, which featured in the film version of Irvine Welsh's cult book *Trainspotting*. Then you descend to the lusher country around Tulloch, before pulling in to Fort William. This is a popular visitor centre as it's close to Ben Nevis, Britain's highest mountain, and beautiful Glen Nevis, which has featured in films such as *Braveheart* and *Rob Roy*. Now comes the most spectacular part of the journey, for the West Highland Line leaves the best till last. Leaving Fort William, the train crosses Thomas Telford's Caledonian Canal – where you can see an impressive series of eight locks known as 'Neptune's Staircase' – hugs the shore of Loch Eil, then crosses the magnificent Glenfinnan Viaduct, a masterpiece in concrete. You soon get superb views of the evocative Glenfinnan Monument that commemorates the start of the 1745 rebellion, before pulling in to Glenfinnan Station. The train now takes you through a landscape of craggy hills and glacial lochs etched with birch and pine trees. You pass Loch nan Uamh, from where Bonnie Prince Charlie fled for France after his defeat at Culloden, then draw in to Arisaig, the birthplace of the man who inspired RL Stevenson's Long John Silver. Next is beautiful Loch Morar, Britain's deepest inland loch and home – so legend has it – to a mysterious monster. Soon you get great views across the water to the craggy islands of Eigg and Rùm, before finally pulling in to the port of Mallaig.

Tourist information

The overworked **TIC** ① *Cameron Sq, just off the High St, T01397-703781, F705184, open year round, Apr-late Oct daily, Nov-Mar Mon-Sat*, stocks a good range of books, maps and leaflets covering local walks. They will also help arrange transport to more remote Highland parts.

Fort William → *Phone code: 01397. Colour map 3, grid B6. Population: 10,774.*

Though it's not a pretty sight, Fort William is the largest town hereabouts and has all the services and facilities you'd expect. There are banks with ATMs on the pedestrianized High Street, as well as a couple of good supermarkets and well-stocked outdoor-equipment shops.

Sights

There's little of real interest in the town, though the **West Highland Museum** ⓘ *Cameron Sq by the TIC, T01397-702169, Jun-Sep Mon-Sat 1000-1700, Oct-May 1000-1600, Jul-Aug also Sun 1400-1700, £3, £2 concession, £0.50 child (12-18, under 12 free)*, is a worthwhile exception. It contains excellent exhibits of Jacobite memorabilia, including a bed in which Prince Charles slept, and a 'secret' portrait of the prince which is revealed only when reflected in a cylindrical mirror. There are also fine displays of Highland clans and tartans, wildlife and local history. The fort from which the town gets its name was built in 1690 by order of William III to keep the rebellious Scottish clans in order. The garrison fought off attacks by Jacobites during the rebellions of 1715 and 1745 but was then demolished to make way for the railway line. The scant remains of the fort can be seen on the lochside, near the train station.

Ben Nevis Distillery ⓘ *T01397-700200, www.bennevisdistillery.com, Mon-Fri 0900-1700, Jul-Aug till 1800 and also Sun 1200-1600, Easter-Sep also Sat 1000-1600, tours £2*, is at Lochy Bridge, at the junction of the A82 to Inverness and the A830 to Mallaig, about a mile north of the town centre. It's a bit too polished for some tastes but kids will enjoy the company of Hamish McDram. Just before the distillery, on the left, are the 13th-century ruins of **Inverlochy Castle**.

Three miles from the town centre along the A830 to Mallaig, in the suburb of Banavie, is **Neptune's Staircase**, a series of eight linked locks on the Caledonian Canal. The locks lower the canal by 90 ft in less than two miles between Loch Lochy and Loch Eil and comprise the last section of the

Sleeping
6 Caberfeidh 1
Alexandra Milton 2
Bank Street Lodge 10
Calluna 3
Crolinnhe 4
Distillery House 5
Lauriestone Guesthouse 7
Fort William Backpackers 6
Glenlochy Guesthouse 11
Grange 8
Guisachan House 9

Eating
Crannog Seafood 2
Grog & Gruel 3
McTavish's Kitchens 5
No 4 Cameron Square 4

canal which links the North Sea with the Irish Sea. It's a pretty dramatic sight, with equally dramatic views of Ben Nevis and its neighbours behind Fort William. From here you can walk or cycle along the canal towpath. For details on the new Great Glen Way, which links Fort William with Inverness, see page 191.

Further along the A830 to Mallaig, in the village of Corpach, is **Treasures of the Earth** ① *T01397-772283, May-Sep daily 0930-1900, Oct-Apr 1000-1700, £3.50, £3 concession, £2 child*, an exhibition of crystals, gemstones and fossils displayed in a huge simulated cave.

Glen Nevis → *Colour map 3, grid B6.*

Only 10 minutes' drive from Fort William is one of Scotland's great glens, the classic Glen Nevis. The sparkling Water of Nevis tumbles through a wooded gorge, closed in by steep, bracken-covered slopes, with the massive hulk of Ben Nevis watching over. The whole scene is both rugged and sylvan, and the nearest you'll get to a Himalayan valley in the Scottish Highlands. It's not surprising, then, that this is a favourite with movie directors and has featured in films such as *Rob Roy, Braveheart, Highlander III* and *Harry Potter and the Philosopher's Stone*.

There are many walks in and around the glen, not least of which is the trek up to the summit of Britain's highest mountain. Aside from the walks described below, there are several easy, marked forest walks which start from the car park at Achriabhach. Pick up a leaflet at the TIC (£0.35) for more scenic walks aroun the area. There are buses into Glen Nevis, as far as the youth hostel, from Fort William bus station, see Transport page 192.

▲ Ben Nevis → *OS Landranger No 41.*
Every year many thousands of people make the relatively straightforward ascent of Ben Nevis, and every year a frighteningly high percentage end up injured, or lost, or dead. More people die annually on the 'Ben' than Everest, so this is a mountain that needs to be taken seriously. Though it may be around 20°C in the car park when you set off, the weather changes with alarming speed and you can find yourself in a blizzard at the summit, or, as is usually the case, in a blanket of cloud or hill fog. It goes without saying that you need to be well prepared. You will need a good, strong pair of boots, warm clothing, waterproofs, food and drink. You should also take a map and a compass. Allow six to eight hours for the return trip. In the winter the top part of the mountain is covered in snow and you should not attempt the walk unless you are an experienced hill climber.

The main tourist path, built as a pony track to service the now-dilapidated observatory on the summit, starts from the car park at Achintee Farm, on the north side of the river, reached by the road through Claggan. It climbs gradually at first across the flank of Meal an t-Suidhe, before joining the alternative path from the youth hostel. This latter route is shorter but much steeper.

The trail continues to climb steadily as it begins to follow the Red Burn, until it reaches a junction, with Lochan Meal an t-Suidhe down to the left. Here, an alternative route down from the summit heads left under the north face of the mountain (see below). This is the halfway point of the main route. The path crosses the Red Burn and then climbs by a series of long and seemingly neverending zigzags up to a plateau. The path splits in two, but both paths take you up to the summit, marked by a cairn and emergency shelter, on the ruins of the old observatory. Note that on the upper sloping plateau the path can 'disappear' in mist and snow, and some cairns and beacons have been removed by vandals masquerading as purists. If conditions deteriorate, a compass is a life-saver. There is a shelter on the summit and at least two others on the mountain.

To return simply retrace your steps all the way. If the weather is settled enough and you have time, you can follow the alternative route below the north face. This leads right round the mountain to the Charles Inglis Clark mountain hut, then heads down into the Allt a' Mhuilinnglen which leads all the way down to the distillery on the A82, a mile north of the town centre. Note that this route adds an extra three or four miles to the descent and should only be attempted by fit and experienced hillwalkers.

▲▲ Steall Falls → OS Landranger No 41.

A fairly easy low-level walk is to the spectacular 300 ft-high Steall Falls at the head of the glen. It's a popular walk, especially in the summer when the trail can resemble the queue for the ladies at a Robbie Williams gig, but this doesn't detract from its stunning natural beauty.

The path starts at the end of the road, at the second car park. Before setting off you might like to note the sign by the steep waterfall that cascades down to the edge of the car park. It reads 'Warning! This is not the path to Ben Nevis'. If you need to be warned against attempting to climb up Ben Nevis through a waterfall, you probably shouldn't be left alone in possession of this book, never mind let loose on the Scottish mountains. Once you've shaken your head in disbelief at the apparent mind-numbing stupidity of some of your fellow travellers, follow the track alongside the Water of Nevis. The path climbs steadily through the woods and becomes rocky, with the river thundering below through the steep gorge. It runs close to the river before emerging from the gorge and opening up into a wide, flower-filled meadow, with a high waterfall at the far end. It's a beautiful, tranquil place and ideal for a picnic. Follow the path across the valley floor till it crosses the river via a precarious bridge that consists of three ropes of thick wire in a V-shape. The path then leads to the bottom of the falls. You can also head left at the bridge and continue up the valley to some ruins. From here the path leads to Corrour station, 14 miles away, but it's for fit and experienced hillwalkers

Sleeping 🛏
Achintee Farm
Guesthouse 1

Ben Nevis Inn 2
SYHA Youth Hostel 3

Eating 🍴
Café Beag 1
Glen Nevis Restaurant 2

Nevis Range

① *To1397-705825, www.nevis-range.co.uk, the gondola is open all year, except early Nov to the week before Christmas, 1000-1700, Jul-Aug 0930-1800, Thu-Fri till 2100, £7.75 return, concessions £7, children (5-17, under 5 free) £4.75; day ticket £9.50, child £6. Wheelchair access, guide dogs ride free. Dry ski slope open open Jul-Aug Sun-Thu 1100-1230.*

The Nevis Range Mountain Experience, seven miles north of Fort William at Torlundy, just off the A82 to Inverness, situated on the mountain of **Aonach Mhor** (4,006 ft), is Scotland's highest skiing and snowboarding area and has the longest ski season, running from Christmas to May. It also boasts the country's only mountain gondola. The 1½-mile (15-minute) ride is a popular attraction not only with skiers and snowboarders in the winter but also during the summer off-season period, when it's used by hillwalkers to gain easy access to the mountains, and mountain bikers who come for some of Britain's best downhill track (see page 192). For most tourists, though, it's an easy way to climb to over 2,000 ft and enjoy the wonderful views from the terrace of the self-service **Snowgoose** restaurant at the top. A couple of easy walks lead from the centre to Sgurr Finnisgaig (40 minutes) and Meal Beag (one hour), both of which offer stunning views from the top. The ski and snowboarding school offer instruction and packages including equipment hire. There's also a snowpark with quarterpipe for snowboarding freestylers and a dry slope for summer skiing in July and August .

🛏 Sleeping

Fort William has plentiful accommodation, ranging from large luxury hotels to modest guest houses and B&Bs. Many of the B&Bs are in Corpach and Banavie to the north of town. Achintore Rd, which runs south along the loch, is packed with B&Bs and hotels, many of which are large and characterless. Running parallel is Grange Rd, which is lined with B&B accommodation. There are also plenty of B&Bs which are closer to the bus

Steall Falls walk

and train stations, mostly on and around Fassifern Rd and Alma Rd. As a main tourist centre, Fort William gets very busy in the high season and you'll need to book ahead at this time. The tourist office will book a room for you, for a small fee, or you can ask for their *Freedom of the Highlands Accommodation Guide* and phone around yourself.

South of Fort William, on the A82, are the villages of Onich and North Ballachulish, which make an attractive alternative to staying in the town.

Fort William *p185, map p186*

L Inverlochy Castle Hotel, 3 miles north of town on the A82 to Inverness, T01397-702177, www.inverlochy.co.uk. 16 rooms. One of the best hotels in the country, and everything you'd expect to find in a real castle: unsurpassed elegance, impeccable service and superb food (see Eating p191), all set in 500 acres of beautiful grounds.

B Crolinnhe, Grange Rd, T01397-702709, open Mar-Nov. One of the best B&Bs on this road.

B The Grange, Grange Rd, T01397-705516, open Mar-Nov. Another of this road's superb B&Bs.

B The Moorings Hotel, 3 miles out of town in Banavie, on road to Corpach and Mallaig, T01397-772797, www.moorings-fortwilliam. co.uk. 21 rooms. Overlooks 'Neptune's Staircase'; well situated and comfortable with an excellent restaurant, though guests can dine at sister restaurant No 4 Cameron Square (see Eating below) .

C Alexandra Milton Hotel, The Parade, T0808-1005556, www.miltonhotels.com. 97 rooms. Large established hotel right in the centre of town, with restaurant.

C Glenloy Lodge Hotel, about 6 miles from town on the B8004 north from Banavie, T/F701397-12700. 9 rooms. Open mid-Dec to late Oct. Friendly and comfortable little hotel tucked away in a quiet, secluded location, and with a good restaurant.

C Highland Hotel, Union Rd, T01397- 702291, www.british-trust-hotels.com. Traditional Highland hotel overlooking the town, with great views across Loch Linnhe. Good restaurant, comfortable; cheaper off-season.

D Distillery House, across the road from the Glenlochy Guesthouse (opposite the road into Glen Nevis), T01397-700103, www.fort -william.net/distillery-house. 6 rooms. Comfortable, upmarket guest house.

D Glenlochy Guesthouse, Nevis Bridge, North Rd, T01397-702909, www.glenlochy guesthouse.co.uk, is recommended.

D Guisachan House, Alma Rd, T/F01397- 703797; and **D 6 Caberfeidh**, Fassifern Rd, T01397-703756, are both recommended.

D Lawriestone Guesthouse, Achintore Rd, T/F01397-700777, www.lawriestone.co.uk. More appealing than most of the other guest houses on this road.

E-F Bank Street Lodge, Bank St, T01397-700 070, www.accommodation-fortwilliam.com. 48 beds, open all year.

F Calluna, T01397-700451, www.fortwilliamholiday.co.uk, is at Heathercroft, about a 15-min walk from the tourist office (see map). Run by experienced mountain guide, Alan Kimber, 22 beds, open all year.

F Fort William Backpackers, Alma Rd, 500 yds from the train station, T01397-700711, www.scotlands-top-hostels.com, has 38 beds and is open all year.

F The Smiddy Bunkhouse & Blackmiths Backpackers Lodge, next to the Corpach train station, 4 miles west of Fort William on A8309 to Mallaig, T01397-772467, www. highland-mountain-guides.co.uk. Alpine-style bunkhouse accommodation for up to 12 plus hostel for 14, fully self-catered. They also run the Snowgoose Mountain Centre (see below), which organizes mountaineering, rock climbing, canoeing, kayaking, skiing and mountain biking tours and hire.

Glen Nevis *p187*

E Achintee Farm Guesthouse, T01397-702240, mcy@btinternet.com, by the start of the path to Ben Nevis. For details of how to get there, see Transport p192.

F Ben Nevis Inn, at Achintee Farm, across the river from the visitor centre (see above), T01397-701227, www.ben-nevis-inn.co.uk. This independent operation is a good bet.

F Farr Cottage Hostel is at the Farr Cottage Activity Centre, Corpach,

For an explanation of sleeping and eating price codes used in this guide, see inside the front cover. Other relevant information is found in Essentials, see pages 41-49.

T01397-772315, www.farrcottage.com, which also organizes hillwalking trips and rents out mountain bikes.

F SYHA Youth Hostel, T0870-0041120, www.syha.org.uk, 3 miles out of town in Glen Nevis, near the start of the path up Ben Nevis, this large hostel gets very busy in summer.

F SYHA Loch Lochy Youth Hostel, T01809-501239, open mid-Mar to late Oct. Convenient for the end of the Steall Falls walk.

Camping

Glen Nevis Caravan & Camping Park, T01397-702191, www.glennevisholidays .co.uk, is 2 miles up the Glen Nevis Rd, open mid-Mar to late Oct, has excellent facilities.

❶ Eating

Fort William *p185, map p186*

Fort William isn't exactly the culinary capital of the Highlands, but there are some top quality restaurants and a decent choice across the range. Most of the hotels offer lunch and dinner. Few restaurants open on Sun.

£££ Crannog Seafood Restaurant, on the Town Pier, T01397-705589, www.crannog.net. By far the best option is this excellent restaurant housed in an old smokehouse. The seafood is as fresh as you can get and the surroundings are unpretentious. It gets very busy and service can be slow, so book ahead and take your time.

£££ Inverlochy Castle, see Sleeping. This is the best hotel to eat at. It's expensive but the food is superb and the surroundings are the last word in grandeur. Daily 1230-1345, 1900-2115.

££ An Crann, T01397-772077, 4 miles from town, take the A830 to Mallaig, turn right to Banavie on the B8004. This converted barn is a local favourite and offers good Scottish cooking in a friendly atmosphere. Mon-Sat 1230-1500, 1700-2100. Apr-mid Oct.

££-£ No 4 Cameron Square, Cameron Sq, T01397-704222, www.no4-fortwilliam.co.uk. Bright, airy dining room with garden for those rare al fresco opportunities, good for a light lunch (£4-6) or bistro-style dinner menu of fish, pasta, game or vegetarian dishes.

££ The Grog & Gruel, 66 High St, T01397-705078, is a pub-cum-restaurant offering good-value pizza, pasta and Tex Mex, and a wide range of superb cask ales. Open til 2400.

Glen Nevis *p187*

££-£ Glen Nevis Restaurant, near the SYHA hostel, T01397-705459, serves a 2-course lunch, 3-course dinner. Daily 1200-2200, Apr-Oct.

£ Café Beag, T01397-703601, a cosy place with log fire. Good vegetarian food.

▲ Activities and tours

Fort William *p185, map p186*
Boat trips

Seal Island Cruises, T01397-705589, runs trips of 1½ hrs from Apr-Sep. One of several cruises which leave from the Town Pier in Fort William which give you the chance to spot local marine wildlife including seals, otters and seabirds. Another is **Crannog Cruises**, T01397-700714, www.crannog.net, who run daily trips from mid-Mar to Oct, £7.50, child £4.

Sea Ventures, T01397-701687, www.seaventures-scotland.com. Run thrilling fast-boat trips of varying lengths to Oban, Mull and the Small Isles, leaving from the town pier. Prices start from £14 (child £10) for 1-hr trip, up to £45 (£30) for the 5-hr trip which stops in Tobermory for lunch.

Canoeing and kayaking

There are several good whitewater rivers around Fort William ranging in difficulty from Grade I to VI, or you can paddle the Caledonian Canal.

Nevis Canoe Club, T01397-705388.
Snowgoose Mountain Centre, attached to **The Smiddy Bunkhouse** (see Sleeping above), runs canoe courses.
Rhiw Goch, Top Locks, Banavie, T01397- 772 373, www.rhiwgoch.co.uk. Close to Neptune's Staircase, hires out canoes, sea kayaks and mountain bikes, £25 per day for canoes.

Fishing

Torlundy Trout Fishery, Torlundy Farm in Tomacharich, 3 miles north off the A82, T01397-703015, has 3 lakes filled with rainbow trout and hires out rods. Also pony trekking from £15/hr, book in advance.

Hiking and climbing

Fort William is a mecca for hikers and climbers. For information on the climb up Ben Nevis and walks around Glen Nevis, see p187.

Nevis Range offers some of the most accessible winter climbs in the country for experienced climbers. For details of the gondola ride see p189. If you want to hire a guide, try **Lochaber Walks**, 22 Zetland Av, T01397-703828; **Fort William Mountain Guides**, T01397-700451; **Alba Walking Holidays**, T01397-704964; and **Snowgoose Mountain Centre** (see above). Fort William has 2 good outdoor activity equipment shops: **Nevisport**, T013967-704921, is on the High St, and has a huge selection of books, maps and guides, a bureau de change and bar-restaurant. At the other end of the High St is **West Coast Outdoor Sports**, T01397-705777. There's an indoor climbing wall at the **Lochaber Leisure Centre** (below). See also page 198 for Ice Factor in Kinlochleven.

Mountain biking
Fort William hosted the World Cup in 2003 so no surprise that mountain biking here is just about as good as it gets. The Leanachan Forest, below Aonach Mhor, 7 miles north of town, covers a huge area with over 25 miles of mountain bike trails, ranging from easy to demanding, including **The Witch's Trails**, free cross-country routes run by the Forestry Commission (www.forestry.gov.uk). You can even take your bike up on the Nevis Range gondola and ride it back down the 2.6-km course. Access is via the road to Nevis Range (see page 189). This is only recommended for skilled riders, open mid-May to mid-Sep daily 1100-1500, £9.75 single trip, £17.50 multi trip. A more gentle alternative is the new **Great Glen Cycle Route**, mainly off-road, running from Fort William to Inverness. See p189 and p167. For bike hire, sale, repair and advice visit Off Beat Bikes at 117 High St, T01397-704 008, www.off beatbikes.co.uk, or at the base station in Jul-Aug. Bikes from £15 per day. Specialist bikes, helmets and armour also available.

Paragliding
Take the gondola up to 650 m and fly among Britain's highest peaks. **Active-highs**, T01397-712188, www.active-highs.co.uk, run courses and tandem flights from the top station.

Skiing
Nevis Range ski centre, see page 189. For ski equipment, try **Nevisport**, see above.

Stream train
Jacobite Steam Train, contact West Coast Railway Company, T01463-239026, www.steamtrain.info, runs from Fort William to Mallaig from early Jun to early Oct, departing Fort William at 1020, arriving in Mallaig at 1225, departing Mallaig at 1410 and arriving back in Fort William at 1600. Day return £25, child £14.50; 1st class return £38/£19 (see box on page 185).

Swimming
There's an indoor pool at **Lochaber Leisure Centre**, off Belford Rd, T01397-704359. Open Mon-Fri 1000-2100, Sat and Sun 1000-1800.

⊖ Transport

Fort William *p185, map p186*
Boat
There is a passenger-only ferry service to **Camusnagaul**, on the opposite bank of Loch Linnhe, from the Town Pier. It sails several times daily (Mon-Sat) and takes 10 mins. The Corran Ferry to **Ardgour** (see p199) is 8 miles south of Fort William, just off the A82. The ferry makes the 5-min crossing every 20-30 mins in the early morning and every hr thereafter till 2015 (last one at 2130) Apr-Oct. For further details contact Highland Council, T01463-702695, or ask at the TIC.

Bus
There are local buses every 10-20 mins to and from **Caol** and **Corpach**, and every hour on Sun and in the evening. There is an hourly service to **Glen Nevis**, Mon-Sat 0800-2300, Jun to Sep only (fewer on Sun). Four buses daily to **Aonach Mhor** during the ski season.

Long-distance services include several daily Citylink buses to **Inverness** (1 hr, £8.20); to **Oban** (1¾ hrs, £7.60) via **Glencoe** (30 mins); and to **Uig** (3½ hrs), via **Portree** and **Kyle of Lochalsh** (1 hr 50 mins). Citylink buses also go several times daily to **Glasgow** (3¼ hrs), via **Glencoe** and **Tyndrum**, and to **Edinburgh** (4 hrs, £18.50), via **Stirling** (3 hrs). There is a bus to **Mallaig** (1½ hrs, £4) daily except Sun with Shiel Buses, T01967-431272. Highland Country Buses, run several times a day to **Kinlochleven** (50 mins) via **Glencoe**. There is also a postbus service (Mon-Sat) to **Glen Etive**.

Car hire

Easydrive, at Lochy Bridge, T01397-701616; Volkswagen Rental, at Nevis Garage, Argour Rd, Caol, T01397-702432; Budget, at North Rd, T01397-702500, or Practical Car & Van Hire, at Slipway Autos, Corpach, T01397-772404. Prices start from around £35 per day.

Taxi

You can call a taxi on T01397-706070.

Train

There are 2-3 trains daily from Glasgow to Fort William (3¾ hrs) via Crianlarich. These continue to Mallaig (1 hr 20 mins) where they connect with ferries to Armadale on Skye (see p252). There are no direct trains to Oban; you need to change at Crianlarich. There is a sleeper service from London Euston (see p32), but you'll miss the views.

● Directory

Fort William *p185, map p186*
Banks Plenty with ATMs on the High St.
Internet The library on the High St and Thing King, on High St.

Glen Coe → *Phone code: 01855. Colour map 3, grid B5-6.*

There are many spectacular places in the Scottish Highlands, but few, if any, can compare to the truly awesome scenery of Glen Coe. No-one could fail to be moved by its haunting beauty, with imposing mountains, their tops often wreathed in cloud, rising steeply on either side from the valley floor. The brooding atmosphere of the landscape is only enhanced by the glen's tragic history. Once you've heard of the Glen Coe Massacre it sends a shiver down the spine every time you pass this way. Scotland's most famous glen is also one of the most accessible, with the A82 Glasgow to Fort William road running through it. Much of the area is owned by the National Trust for Scotland and virtually uninhabited, leaving huge tracts of glen and mountain which provide out- standing climbing and walking. There's also skiing at the Glencoe Ski Centre, and canoeing on the rivers Coe and Etive. ▶▶ For Sleeping, Eating and other listings, see pages 197-199.

Onich, North Ballachulish and Kinlochleven

The A82 south from Fort William passes through the collection of guesthouses and B&Bs known as Onich before the B863 turns east at North Ballachulish and heads to Kinlochleven, at the head of Loch Leven. It can also be reached on the same road from Glencoe Village, seven miles west. It's an unlikely place to find a huge aluminium factory, but it kept the village alive for many years, until its recent closure. It has since been turned into an indoor mountaineering centre (see Activities and tours below). You can find out all about the long and often tragic history of aluminium-working in Lochaber at **The Aluminium Story** ① *Linnhe Rd, T01855-831663, Apr-Oct Tue-Fri 1030-1800, Sat-Sun 1100-1500, free,* in the Kinlochleven Visitor Centre and Library.

The **West Highland Way** passes through the village and many walkers spend the night here before setting out on the last stretch before Fort William. There are also good walks in the surrounding hills and glens, a few of which are described below.

▲▲ Walks around North Ballachulish

About a mile north of the village of North Ballachulish, there's an easy 40-minute circular walk up to **Inchree Waterfall**. It starts from the car park at the end of the road beyond the tiny hamlet of Inchree and is clearly marked. The waterfall is impressive and divided into three sections. The views from the top, down the length of Loch Linnhe, are worth the walk alone. The path continues up past the waterfall to the forest road which leads back downhill to the car park.

There are some fairly easy short walks from Kinlochleven up the glen of the River Leven, including the one to the impressive **Grey Mare's Tail waterfall**. It's a short walk of under an hour, signposted from the village.

A fairly easy but rewarding half-day walk is to follow the **West Highland Way** south from the village to the top of the **Devil's Staircase**, where it meets the A82 at the eastern end of Glen Coe. The route starts from the **British Aluminium Visitor Centre**, runs around the side of the aluminium factory, then crosses a wooden bridge and climbs gradually on a dirt jeep-track up to **Penstock House**, at 1,000 ft. At the top, near the house, the track forks to the right and continues on a rough footpath to the Devil's Staircase. The path is marked with the West Highland Way thistle sign, so it's easy to follow uphill to the top of the pass (1,804 ft), from where you get great views of Loch Eilde Mór and the Mamores to the north. The path then descends down the staircase to Glen Coe, with breathtaking Buachaille Etive Mór in front of you all the way. You'll have to return to Kinlochleven by the same route, or you could carry on to the **Kingshouse Hotel** (see below). The return trip from Kinlochleven should take four to five hours, or you can start out from Glencoe (see below). This section of the West Highland Way was once part of the old military road which ran from Fort William to Stirling.

Another good hike, though more strenuous, is to **Beinn na Callich** (2,507 ft). You'll need to be fairly fit for this steep climb, and allow around six to seven hours for the return trip. The route is well marked and starts from the West Highland Way footpath opposite the school, which is on the road heading out of the village towards Fort William. The path climbs steeply at first, crosses the tarmac road to **Mamore**

Glen Coe & Loch Leven

Sleeping 🛏
Ballachulish **1**
Ballachulish House **2**
Clachaig Inn **3**
Isles of Glencoe **4**
Kingshouse **5**
Red Squirrel Campsite **7**
SYHA Hostel **8**

⁝ A stab in the back

Glen Coe is probably best known as the scene of one of the most shameful and notorious incidents in Scottish history.

Following his succession to the throne, William III wanted all the clans to swear an oath of allegiance by 1 January 1692. After much hesitation, the Jacobite clans of the West Highlands agreed to do so. However, Maclain of Glencoe, chief of a small branch of the MacDonalds, was not only late in setting off on the journey, but mistakenly went to Fort William to sign, instead of Inveraray. By the time he reached Inveraray it was 6 January and the deadline had passed.

The government decided that the rebellious clan be punished, in order to set an example to other clans, some of whom had not taken the oath. A company of 120 soldiers, under the command of Campbell of Glenlyon, were sent to Glen Coe and, since their leader was related by marriage to Maclain, the troops were billeted in MacDonald homes, in keeping with the long-standing Highland tradition of hospitality.

There they stayed for almost two weeks, until the cold-blooded order came through to '... put all to the sword under seventy'. And so, on a cold winter's night, in the early hours of 13 February 1692, the Campbells ruthlessly slaughtered their hosts. Maclain and 37 men, women and children were slain in their beds, while many others fled into the hills, only to die of hunger and exposure. It was a bloody incident which had deep repercussions and proved to be the beginning of the end of the Highland way of life. For further information, see page 365.

There's a monument to the fallen MacDonalds in the village of Glencoe, where members of the clan still gather on 13 February each year. For a powerful and evocative account of the Massacre, read *Glencoe* by John Prebble (Penguin, first published 1966).

strenuous, but you'll still need a map, good boots, warm clothing, food and water, and you should take the usual precautions, see page 53.

One of the most popular walks is the relatively straightforward hike up to the **Lost Valley**, a secret glen where the ill-fated MacDonalds hid the cattle they'd stolen. Allow around three hours for the return trip. Start from the car park by the large boulder (see map), opposite the distinctive **Three Sisters**. Head down to the valley floor and follow the gravel path which leads down to a wooden bridge across the River Coe. Cross the bridge and follow the path up and over the stile. From here there's a choice of two routes. The less obvious route heads right and offers an easier climb into the valley. This eventually meets the lower, well-worn track, which involves a bit of scrambling but is more exciting as it follows the rushing waters of the **Allt Coire Gabhail**. The upper and lower paths meet a few miles further up and here you cross the river by some stepping stones. Proceed up the steep scree slope till you reach the rim of the **Lost Valley**, where many of the MacDonalds fled on the night of the infamous massacre. Once in the valley there are great views of Bidean nam Bian, Gearr Aonachand Beinn Fhada and you can continue for a further 20-30 minutes to the head of the valley. From here it's possible to climb **Bidean**, but you'll need to be fit, experienced and well equipped.

● The Devil's Staircase was named by the 400 soldiers who had to endure severe hardship
● while building it in the 17th century.

Glen Coe also offers one of the world's classic ridge walks, the **Aonach Eagach**. It's not for the inexperienced or faint-hearted as there are some fairly exposed pinnacles. The ridge runs almost the entire length of the glen, starting at **Am Bodach** and ending at **Sgor nam Fiannaidh**. Don't make the mistake of descending from the last summit straight down to the Clachaig Inn. This is not the correct route.

Another difficult route is to the summit of **Buachaille Etive Mór**, one of the most photographed mountains in Scotland and one you'll probably recognize immediately the first time you see it from the A82 on the way to or from Glencoe. The mountain is best viewed from the **Kingshouse Hotel** and the route starts from Altnafeadh, a couple of miles west of the hotel. This is also the start or finish point for the fairly easy half-day walk over the **Devil's Staircase**, which is part of the West Highland Way. For a description of the route, see page 194. **Glen Etive** runs southwest from the hotel. It's a very beautiful and little-visited place, and great for wild camping. There's a postbus service once a day from Fort William.

Finally, there are some short, pleasant walks around **Glencoe Lochan**, an artificial loch created in the mid-19th century by Lord Strathcona for his homesick Canadian wife. Take the left turning off the minor road to the youth hostel just beyond the bridge over the River Coe. There's a choice of three walks of between 40 minutes and an hour, all detailed at the car park.

Glencoe Ski Centre

① *T01855-851226, www.ski.scotland.net, chair lift operates 0930-1700, full day pass with lifts, costs £17 (children £9.50), combined 5-day pass for Glencoe and Nevis Range.* The Glencoe Ski Centre is just over a mile from the **Kingshouse Hotel**, on the other side of the A82, on **Meall A'Bhuiridh** (3,636 ft). This is Scotland's oldest ski centre, established in 1956, and remains one of the best, with the longest single descent. At the base station is the **Museum of Scottish Skiing and Climbing** ① *May-Sep 0900-1700, restaurant and café*, where you can see the ice axe used by Chris Bonnington, among other things.

● Sleeping

Onich, North Ballachulish and Kinlochleven *p193, map p194*

There's a wide selection of places to stay in the villages of Onich and North Ballachulish, mostly with good views of the loch. They make an attractive alternative to Fort William.
L Allt-nan-Ros Hotel, Onich, T01855-821210, www.allt-nan-ros.co.uk. Price includes dinner. James and Fiona Macleod's Victorian country house overlooks Loch Linnhe with views across to Appin and the hills of Ardgour and Morvern, with pretty gardens and great food.
L The Lodge on the Loch Hotel, Onich, T01855-821237, www.freedomglen.co.uk, open Feb-Dec. High-quality hotel with great views and good restaurant (**£££**).
B Cuilcheanna House, Onich, T01855-821226, open Easter-Oct. A comfortable guest house just off the main road, a good place to dine, but for residents only.
B Onich Hotel, Onich, T01855-821214. Loch views and good meals (**££**) in its busy bar.

D MacDonald Hotel, Fort William Rd, Kinlochleven, T01855-831539, open Mar-Dec, serves cheap bar lunches and moderately priced dinners.
E Tailrace Inn, Riverside Rd, Kinlochleven, T01855-831777, does cheap bar meals all
F Blackwater Hostel, Lab Rd, Kinlochleven, T01855-831253, www.blsckwaterhostel.co.uk.
F Inchree Hostel, T/F01855-821287, www.hostel-scotland.com, at Inchree, on the A82 to Fort William. Buses stop 100 m from the hostel. Accommodation dorms and twin and double rooms. All facilities and on-site bistro and bar.

Ballachulish *p195, map p194*

As well as one of the most historic hotels in Scotland, there's a wide selection of cheaper B&Bs and guest houses in the village.
L The Isles of Glencoe Hotel, T01855-811602, www.freedomglen.co.uk/ig. 39 rooms. A modern hotel and leisure

complex on the shores of the loch, and facilities include heated pool, sauna and gym. The restaurant serves a 3-course lunch (££) and 3-course dinner (£££).

L Ballachulish Hotel, South Ballachulish by the bridge, T01855-821582, www.freedom glen.co.uk/bh. 54 rooms. Grand old hotel, handily placed for Glen Coe, Fort William or Oban, restaurant serves meals throughout the day (£££-££).

L Ballachulish House, T01855-811266, www.ballachulishhouse.com, open Mar-Oct. 8 rooms. Some 200 yds beyond the **Ballachulish Hotel** on the A828 to Oban. This comfortable and elegant hotel/guest house is steeped in history. The seat of the Stewarts of Ballachulish since the 16th century, this was where the final order for the Glencoe Massacre was signed. The decor is plush but understated, the hospitality second-to-none and the food is superb. Even if you're not staying you can enjoy the experience of dining here (£44 a head for the 5-course dinner), but book ahead.

E Fern Villa, T01855-811393. A good value guesthouse.

Glencoe Village p195, map p194
There are several B&Bs and guest houses in the village and quite a few options around.

C-D Clachaig Inn, about 3 miles south of the village, on the old road which leads from the village to the NTS visitor centre, T01855-811252, www.clachaig.com. 19 rooms. Good-value accommodation and one of the great Highland pubs. It's a favourite haunt of climbers and there's a lively atmosphere as well as some fine real ales and decent cheap food. There are also 3 chalets which can be rented on a weekly basis (phone for details), and mountain bike hire (see below).

D Kingshouse Hotel, at the east end of the glen, almost opposite the turn-off to the Glencoe Ski Centre, T01855-851259. 22 rooms. This is Scotland's oldest established inn and such a landmark that it even appears on maps, marked as 'hotel'. It's on the West Highland Way and is popular with hikers, climbers and skiers who frequently drop in for a refreshing drink in the bar and some good-value food.

E The Glencoe Guesthouse, T01855-811244. On the outskirts of the village, at Upper Carnoch.

E Scorrybreac Guesthouse, T/F01855-811354, www.scorrybreac.co.uk, Dec-Oct. In the village, this is a pleasant guest house.

F Glencoe Bunkhouses, nearby SYHA Youth Hostel, T01855-811256, squirrels@amserve. net, offers cheap, basic accommodation in 2 bunkhouses and an alpine barn. The same people also run the **Red Squirrel Campsite** further along the road.

F SYHA Youth Hostel, on the same road as Clachaig Inn, about 2 miles from the village, T01855-811219. An excellent hostel, open all year and very popular with climbers, so you should book ahead.

Camping
Invercoe Caravans, T/F01855-811210. To the east of the village, on the shores of Loch Leven. See also **Glencoe Bunkhouses** above.

● Eating

Onich, North Ballachulish and Kinlochleven p193, map p194
££ Four Seasons Bistro and Bar, Inchree, T01855-821393, a friendly and informal place that looks like a log cabin. It's open daily except Tue, 1800-2130.
£ Fishnet fish and chip shop, Kinlochleven Superb rendition of Scotland's favourite dish.

Glencoe Village p195, map p194
Apart from the places listed under Sleeping:
££-£ The Glencoe Hotel, in the village T01855-811245, serves decent bar food.

● Bars and clubs

Onich, North Ballachulish and Kinlochleven p193, map p194
Tail Race Inn, Kinlochleven, serves beer from the local Atlas micro-brewery.

▲ Activities and tours

Glen Coe p193
Climbing
Ice Factor, Kinlochleven, T01855-831100, www.ice-factor.co.uk. The world's largest indoor ice climbing facility has opened in the former aluminium factory with rock climbing wall, bouldering hall, outdoor equipment shop, café and restaurant, sauna, steam room and hot tub. Annual membership costs

£5 and daily rates range from £6.50 to £14. Also climbing courses available. Mountain guides can be found at **Hadrian Mountaineering**, 19b Carnoch, T/F01855-811472, www.glencoe-mountain-sport.co.uk; **Glencoe Guides**, T01855-811402; **Dave Hanna**, Ballachulish, T01855-811620.

Cycling
Glencoe Mountain Bike Centre, at the Clachaig Inn (see Sleeping), has bike hire, £12 for a full day, £8 for a half day.

Skiing
Glenco Ski Centre, see p197, is one of Scotland's best. It's also home to the Museum of Scottish Skiing and Climbing.

Outdoor activities
Alfresco Adventure, T01855-821248, just to the east of North Ballachulish on the B863 to Kinlochleven, offers boat hire and various outdoor activities such as mountain biking and canoeing.
Lochaber Watersports, West Harbour, West Laroch, Ballachulish, T07831-846025,

www.lochaberwatersports.co.uk. Sailing courses (£325 for 5 days), kayaking (£25 for 3 hrs), mountain bike hire (£15 per day) and power boat cruises (£30/half day).
Vertical Descents, Inchree Falls, Onich, T01855-821593, www.activities-scotland.com. Extreme sport enthusiasts can try the growing sport of canyoning, or funyaking, a mix of rafting and kayaking.

⊖ Transport

Onich, North Ballachulish and Kinlochleven *p193, map p194*
Highland Country Buses, T01397-702373, runs 6 times a day (Mon-Sat) between **Fort William** and **Kinlochleven** (50 mins).

Glencoe Village *p195, map p194*
Highland Country Buses run several times daily from Fort William to Glencoe Village (30 mins, £3.40). There are **Citylink** buses to **Glasgow** (2½ hrs) and **Fort William**. The daily **postbus** service from **Fort William** to the **Kingshouse Hotel** and **Glen Etive** stops at the Glencoe crossroads.

West of Fort William → *Colour map 3, grid B4-5 & A4.*

West of Fort William lie some of the Britain's most extravagantly scenic landscapes and some of the its most remote places. From southernmost Morvern, through the ruggedly-handsome Ardnamurchan Peninsula, across the evocatively named 'Road to the Isles', through the haunting and tragic 'Rough Bounds' and on to the hopelessly isolated and utterly wild lands of Knoydart, this is serious wilderness, with little pockets of accessible and user-friendly Highlands thrown in for good measure. ➤➤ *For Sleeping, Eating and other listings, see pages 204-207.*

Ardgour, Ardnamurchan and Morvern

This lonely, southwestern corner features a dramatic landscape of rugged mountains, desolate moorland and near-deserted glens, fringed by a coastline of sparkling white beaches and clear turquoise seas with wonderful views across to the isles of Mull and Skye. This is one of the least-populated areas in Britain, mainly due to the legacy of the Highland Clearances in the mid-19th century, when whole communities were evicted by landlords in favour of more profitable sheep. With so few people around, this is an area noted for its wildlife, with a huge variety of birds and animals, such as deer, pine martens, wildcats and eagles. If you have both the time and the energy, it's worth exploring on foot. There's a series of footpaths throughout the area, particularly around Ardnamurchan.

North & Northwest West of Fort William

Raising standards

It all started on 19 August 1745 at Glenfinnan, 19 miles west of Fort William at the head of Loch Shiel. Less than a month earlier, Prince Charles Edward Stuart had landed on the Scottish mainland for the first time, on the shores of Loch nan Uamh, between Lochailort and Arisaig (see below). He had come to claim the British throne for his father, James, son of the exiled King James VII of Scotland and II of England.

The clan chiefs had expected French support, but when the Prince arrived with only a handful of men they were reluctant to join the cause. Undeterred, the prince raised his standard and his faith was soon rewarded when he heard the sound of the pipes and Cameron of Lochiel, along with 800 men, came marching down the valley to join them. It must have been an incredible moment.

Ins and outs

Getting around Once you leave the A830 Fort William to Mallaig road, buses are few and far between, so it's not easy to get around quickly without your own transport. You'll need your own transport to reach Ardnamurchan Point and Sanna Bay as there are no buses beyond Kilchoan. It's an area of few roads. » *For further details, see Transport page 199.*

Tourist information The website www.ardnamurchan.com, has lots of information on walks, as well as local events and attractions. Some 40 walks in the area are listed in a local guidebook *Great Walks* (£3.75) available at tourist offices. OS Explorer Maps 383, 390 and 391 cover the entire region. See also Activities and tours on page 206.

Ardgour → *Phone code: 01967. Colour map 3, grid B5.*

The name Ardgour means 'height of the goats', and you can still see feral goats in this huge, sparsely populated wilderness bordered by Loch Shiel, Loch Eil, Loch Linnhe and Loch Sunart. Access is via the A861 south from Kinlocheil, or on the Corran Ferry to the tiny lochside villages of **Corran** and **Clovulin**.

The attractive little village of **Strontian** on the shores of Loch Sunart gave its name to the element strontium, which was first discovered in the nearby lead mines in 1790. These now-abandoned mines also produced most of the lead shot used in the Napoleonic wars. Strontian is the largest settlement in these parts and has a couple of shops, a post office and a **tourist information centre** ⓘ *T01967-402131, Apr-Oct Mon-Fri 0900-1700, Sat 1000-1600, Sun 1000-1400.* About two miles north of the village is the **Ariundle Nature Reserve**, which offers a pleasant two-hour nature trail through the glen and a 40-minute forest walk.

Morvern → *Phone code: 01967. Colour map 3, grid B6.*

Just east of Strontian the A884 leads south through the bleak, desolate landscape of Morvern to the tiny remote community of **Lochaline** on the Sound of Mull, departure point for the CalMac ferry to Fishnish. About three miles before Lochaline is the turning left for the track which leads down the side of Loch Aline to the 14th-century ruins of **Ardtornish Castle**. First you'll come to **Kinlochaline Castle** (keys available at the cottage) and **Ardtornish House**. This house stands on the site of the original house, which was visited on several occasions by Florence Nightingale, who was a family member of the original owners. The author John Buchan spent many summers here in the 1930s. There's a path which leads from

During the stalking season (1 July-20 October) check at the estate office before setting out on the walk to Loch Tearnait.

the estate office uphill across open moorland for an hour till it reaches **Loch Tearnait**.
In the centre of the loch is a 1,500 year-old crannog, an artificial island built for
defensive purposes. This walk is detailed in the tourist board's leaflet, along with the
Ariundle Nature Trail (see above).

Ardnamurchan Peninsula and Moidart→ *Phone code: 01972 & 01967.*
Colour map 3, grid B4.
The main places of interest in this area are to be found on the rugged Ardnamurchan
peninsula (from the Gaelic *Aird nam Murchan*, meaning 'Point of the High Seas'), the
end of which is the most westerly point on the British mainland. The winding A861
runs west from Strontian along the north shore of Loch Sunart to **Salen**, where the
single-track B8007 branches west and runs all the way out to the tip of the peninsula.
The A861 meanwhile turns north to Acharacle.

The first settlement you reach heading west out to Ardnamurchan Point is
Glenborrodale. Before you reach the tiny hamlet look out on the left for the castellated
late-Victorian towers of **Glenborrodale Castle**, once the property of a certain Jesse Boot,
who founded a chain of chemist shops which you may have heard of. Just west of
Glenborrodale is the excellent **Glenmore Natural History Centre** ① *T01967-500254,
Apr-Oct 1030-1730 (Sun 1200-1730), £2.50, concession £2, children £1.50*, local
photographer Michael McGregor's interactive exhibition which features some of his
most stunning photographs of local wildlife. The centre is designed to interact with the
environment and there's live video action of the surrounding wildlife, including pine
martens, birds and even fish in the nearby river. It's a good place for kids, and a
life-saver when the weather is just too bad to venture outside. There's a good little café
(£) serving snacks and light lunches, and a decent gift shop. A mile to the east is the
RSPB Reserve where you can see golden eagles, otters and seals. You can take a
two-hour wildlife trip to the seal colonies – or further afield to Tobermory on Mull or
Staffa and the Treshnish Islands, see Activities and tours page 206. A few miles west of
the centre, the B8007 turns away from the coast. Here you'll see the beautiful bay of
Camas nan Geall (Bay of the stranger or pledge, the precise meaning is unclear). It's
worth stopping at the car park to admire the fantastic views, or take the path down to
the beach. Between Glenborrodale and Kilchoan, a road runs to the north coast of the
peninsula and the beautiful beaches at **Fascadale, Kilmory** and **Ockle**.

The straggling crofting village of **Kilchoan** is the main settlement on
Ardnamurchan. Shortly after passing the sign for the village, you can turn left to the
scenic ruin of **Mingary Castle**, built around the 13th century. There's a tourist
information centre ① *T01972-510222, Easter-Oct daily*, which provides information on
local scenic walks and will help with accommodation. Beyond Kilchoan the road leads
to the lighthouse at mainland Britain's most westerly point, with stunning views (on a
clear day) across to the small Isles of Rùm, Eigg, Muck and Canna, with the Cuillins of
Skye rising behind Rùm. The former lighthouse was designed by Alan Stevenson, father
of Robert Louis, and built in 1849. The buildings have been converted into the
Ardnamurchan Visitor Centre ① *T01972-510210, www.ardnamurchan.u-net.com,
1 Apr-31 Oct daily from 1000-1800 (1700 in Oct), £2.50, concession/children £1.50*,
where you can learn about the history and workings of lighthouses. There's also
self-catering accommodation, a café and gift shop.

A mile northwest of Kilchoan a road branches to the right to the beautiful long,
white beach at **Sanna Bay**. It's worth making the trip here just to walk on the beach,
but this is also a good place to spot whales and dolphins. On the road to Sanna Bay is
the tiny settlement of **Achnaha**, which is famed for its rare 'ring-dyke' system, a huge,
natural rock formation which is the crater of an extinct volcano.

North of Salen on the A861 is the scattered crofting township of **Acharacle**, at the
western end of Loch Shiel surrounded by rolling hills. The village has several shops, a
post office, garage and plenty of places to stay. A couple of miles to the west a road

leads to beautiful **Kentra Bay**. Cross the wooden bridge, follow the footpath round the side of Kentra Bay and then follow the signs for Gortenfearn, where you'll find the famous 'singing sands'. Not only is the beach music to the ears as you walk its length, but the view across to Skye and the small isles is a feast for the eyes.

Three miles north of Acharacle is **Loch Moidart**. Here, perched on a rocky promontory in the middle of the loch, is the 13th-century ruin of **Castle Tioram** (pronounced 'Cheerum'), one of Scotland's best-loved castle ruins. This was the seat of the MacDonalds of Clanranald, until it was destroyed by their chief in 1715 to prevent it from falling into Hanoverian hands while he was away fighting for the Jacobites. There are plans to restore the castle, but you can visit it (free) via the sandy causeway that connects it to the mainland at low tide. The A861 follows the shores of Loch Moidart, into the region of the same name, before joining the A830 Fort-William Mallaig road at Lochailort.

The Road to the Isles

The 46-mile stretch of the A830 from Fort William to Mallaig is evocatively named 'The Road to the Isles'. It's a very beautiful journey, particularly by train – see page 185 – through a landscape that resonates with historical significance. This is Bonnie Prince Charlie country, where the ill-fated Jacobite Rising not only began, but also ended, with the Prince's flight to France. It's also one of the most stunning stretches of coastline in Britain, especially the last bit, between Arisaig and Morar: a continuous string of glorious beaches the colour of vanilla ice cream (with temperatures to match), backed by machair and washed by turquoise seas, with views across to Rùm, Eigg and the Cuillins of Skye. This is a sight to bring a smile to the face and shouts from your passengers to keep your eyes on the road.

Glenfinnan → *Phone code: 01397. Colour map 4, grid B5.*

Some 17 miles west of Fort William, at the head of Loch Shiel, is tiny Glenfinnan. There's a powerful sense of history here. You don't have to be Scottish to feel a shiver run down the spine and a tear well in the eye as you gaze across eerily beautiful Loch Shiel stretching into the distance, veiled by steep mountains. You can almost hear the wail of the bagpipes in the distance, through the mist. A commemorative tower stands proudly at the head of the loch, erected in 1815 by Alexander MacDonald of Glenaladale in memory of the clansmen who fought and died for the Prince. You can climb to the top of the tower (mind your head, though) for even better views down the loch. The **Glenfinnan Games** are held here in mid-August. On the other side of the road is the **National Trust for Scotland Visitor Centre** ① *T01397-722250, 1 Apr-18 May and 1 Sep-31 Oct daily 1000-1700, 19 May-31 Aug 0930-1800, £2.50, concession £1, café*, which has displays and an audio programme of the Prince's campaign, from Glenfinnan to its grim conclusion at Culloden.

A mile away, in Glenfinnan Village, is the **Station Museum** ① *T01397-722295, Jun-Oct daily 0930-1630, other times by appointement, £0.50*, which is housed in the railway station on the magnificent Fort-William to Mallaig railway line. It has displays of memorabilia from the line's 100-year history. You can also sleep and eat here (see below). The 1,000-ft span of the **Glenfinnan Viaduct**, between the visitor centre and the village, is one of the most spectacular sections of the famous West Highland Railway, see page 185.

About 10 miles west of Glenfinnan the road passes through the village of **Lochailort**, where the A861 branches south to the remote Ardnamurchan Peninsula, see above. A couple of miles further on, is **Loch nan Uamh**, where Prince Charles first landed on the Scottish mainland and from where, a year later, he fled for France following the disastrous defeat at Culloden, see page 170. A path leads down from the car park to the Prince's Cairn, which marks the beginning and the end of the Jacobite cause.

At the western end of the Morar Peninsula is the little village of Arisaig, scattered around the head of a sheltered bay with An Sgurr's knobbly peak peering above the narrow mouth. The village has sleeping and eating options, as well as a post office, general store (with ATM) and doctor's surgery and is a useful service centre for the many self-catering cottages and caravans that line this stretch of coastline. There are some nice beaches around, and the road west from the village out to the **Rhue Peninsula** is great for seal spotting. You can also take a cruise from Arisaig to the islands of Rùm, Eigg and Muck, see Transport page 207.

This was the birthplace of Long John Silver, who worked on the construction of the nearby lighthouse at **Barrahead**, one of many such lighthouses designed by the father of Robert Louis Stevenson. Silver met Robert Louis on a few occasions, and so impressed the young writer that he immortalized him in his classic *Treasure Island*.

The main A830 bypasses Arisaig on its way to Mallaig, while a wiggly single-track road hugs the coast and heads north, past the golf course and on past luscious Camusdarach beach (which featured in the film *Local Hero*) before joining the main road by the tiny village of Morar. A single-track road leads up behind the village of Morar to dark, mysterious **Loch Morar**, the deepest inland loch in the country and home of Morag, Scotland's other, lesser-known (and more attractive, according to the locals) monster. Two locals reported seeing her in August 1969 and a scientific investigation two years later uncovered a remarkable number of eye-witness accounts. You could always try to elicit further information from the locals over a wee dram in the bar of the **Morar Hotel**. The road runs along the north shore of the loch for three miles till it reaches the pretty little hamlets of **Bracora** and **Bracorina**. Here the road stops, but a footpath continues all the way to **Tarbet** on the shores of Loch Nevis, from where it's possible to catch a boat back to Mallaig, see Transport page 207. It takes about three hours to walk to Tarbet – where there's now a bothy – and you'll need to get there by 1530 for the boat.

Mallaig → *Phone code: 01687. Colour map 4, grid A4.*

The end of the road is Mallaig, a busy fishing port huddled round its harbour and main departure point for the ferry to Skye. It's very much a working fishing port, with tourist facilities attached, and there's not a huge amount to do, but it's always busy with people waiting for the ferry or the train to Fort William. The train and bus stations and CalMac ferry office are all within a few yards of each other. Also close by are banks with ATMs and the post office. The tourist information centre is by the harbour ① *To1687-462170, Apr-Oct daily, Nov-Mar Mon, Tue, Fri.* It has a café and internet terminal but staff are not well informed.

There are great views over the Sound of Sleat from the indoor swimming pool at the top of Frank Brae.

If you have some time to kill you could visit **Mallaig Marine World** ① *To1687- 462292, Jun-Sep Mon-Sat 0900-2100, Sun 1000-1800, Oct-May Mon-Sat 1200-1730, £2.75, children £1.35*, an aquarium with indigenous marine creatures as well as displays on the history of the local fishing industry. Beside the train station is the **Mallaig Heritage Centre** ① *To1687-462085, Apr, May, Jun and Oct Mon-Sat 1100-1600, Jul-Sep Mon-Sat 0930-1630, Sun 1230-1630, Nov-Mar Wed, Thu, Fri and Sat 1200-1700, £1.80, children £1*, with interesting descriptions of the local Clearances, the railway line and the fishing industry.

▲▲ For something a bit more energetic, there are a couple of good walks around the village. An easy one, which should take around 45 minutes, goes to the little village of **Mallaig Bheag** (Mallaigviag), further east along the coast. Just before the car park at the eastern end of the harbour you'll see a sign, on the right as you head east,

 Glenfinnan Viaduct featured in Harry Potter and the Chamber of Secrets, in the famous scene where he tried to board the Hogwarts Express from a flying Ford Anglia.

which points you towards the old road to Mallaig Bheag. Follow the path up behind the houses and continue into a small glen behind the hill that overlooks the port. The path then rises gradually till you're rewarded with great views of Loch Nevis. It continues through Mallaig Bheag then joins up with the main road back to Mallaig. Follow this till the end of the row of houses on your right, turn right and then left and back down to Mallaig bay and the start of the walk.

Knoydart Peninsula → *Phone code: 01867. Colour map 3, grid A5.*

The Knoydart Peninsula, the most remote and unspoilt region in Britain and one of Europe's last great wildernesses, literally lies between Heaven and Hell, for it is bordered to the north by Loch Hourn (Loch of Hell) and to the south by Loch Nevis (Loch of Heaven). Knoydart is not for wimps. It can only be reached on foot, or by boat from Mallaig, and consequently attracts walkers, who can wander for days around a network of trails without seeing another soul.

▲▲ A two-day hiking route starts from Kinloch Hourn, reached by bus from Invergarry, see page 177. The trail winds its way around the coast to Barrisdale and on to Inverie. Another route into Knoydart starts from the west end of Loch Arkaig, see page 179, and runs through Glen Dessarry. Both are tough hikes and only for fit, experienced and well-equipped hillwalkers. An easier way in is by boat, see Transport page 207.

The peninsula's only settlement of any size is tiny **Inverie**, with just 60 inhabitants, one of only a few villages in Scotland which can't be reached by road, but still has a post office, a shop, a few places to stay and Britain's most remote pub. Much of the peninsula is mountain, with four peaks over 3,000 ft. Its 85 square miles is a mix of private sporting estate, conservation trust and community partnership. Five years ago one chunk of the peninsula, the 17,000 acre **Knoydart Estate**, was rescued from a succession of indifferent landlords by a community buy-out, funded by public money and individual donations. The Knoydart Foundation's trustees include the conservationist Chris Brasher and impresario Cameron Mackintosh, and if you sit outside the Old Forge long enough, one of them might pass by, or stop for a chat. Equally possible is the sighting of otters in the Sound of Sleat or golden eagles soaring overhead.

● Sleeping

Ardgour *p200*
L-A Kilcamb Lodge Hotel, Strontian, T01967-402257, www.kilcamblodge.com, open mid-Feb to end Dec. Luxurious Victorian country house standing in its own grounds on the shores of Loch Sunart with its own private beach. The perfect bolthole with only the occasional otter or eagle to disturb the peace, also serves superb food.
E Heatherbank, Upper Scotstown, Strontian, T01967-402201, www.heatherbankbb.co.uk. Open all year. 3 en suite rooms. Modern house with great views to the Ardgour hills. Spacious guest lounge with log fire. Non smoking. Discounts for longer stays.

Ardnamurchan Peninsula and Moidart *p201*
A Feorag House, Glenborrodale, T01972-500248, admin@feorag.co.uk. Superb guesthouse set in 13 acres of

grounds. Great views out to sea and top-class cuisine. Price includes dinner.
A-B Meall Mo Chridhe, Kilchoan, T/F01972-510328. Open Apr-Oct. A beautiful 18th-century converted manse with great sea views and fine cooking. Full board also available. Dinner available for non-residents (£££), but booking essential.
B Far View Cottage, Kilchoan, T01972-510357, www.ardamurchan.com/farview. Mar-Nov. Superior and friendly B&B with great views and excellent food (££, also for non-residents, but booking is essential).
B Water's Edge, Kilchoan, T01972-510261, www.ardnamurchan.com/watersedge. As intimate and private as it gets, accommodation for 2 in an open-plan suite only yards from the water's edge. TV/video/CD and excellent home cooking (bring your own wines). Price includes dinner. Non smoking.

B-F Glen Uig Inn, Glen Uig, by loch Ailort, T01687-470219, www.glenuig.com. 18th century inn offering bunkhouse accommodation for £7 per person in adjoining chalet. Also has en suite accommodation for families or groups. Local fare served in the Inn's restaurant and a good night's entertainment in the lively bar.

C Loch Shiel House Hotel, Acharacle, T01967-431224. 8 en suite rooms. Comfortable hotel and decent bar meals (£££-£). Contact them for details of cruises on Loch Shiel.

D Kilchoan House Hotel, Kilchoan, T01972-510200, www.kilchoanhotel.co.uk. 7 en suite rooms. Comfortable option with views of Mull from most of the rooms. Also good meals served 1200-1400 and 1800-2030, in the bar (£) and dining room (££).

D Sonachan Hotel, a few miles beyond Kilchoan, on the road to Ardnamurchan Point, T/F01972-510211, www.sonachan.u-net.com. Open all year. The most westerly hotel on the UK mainland, close to the lighthouse and beaches and surrounded by 1000 acres of grounds with walking and fishing opportunities. Good food available and children welcome. Also has a 4-bedroom self catering house and 2 rooms.

D-E Cala Darach, Glenmore by Glenborrodale, T01972-500204. Open Mar-Oct. 3 en suite rooms. Lovely country house with views across Loch Sunart.

D-E Salen Inn, Salen, T01972-431661, www.thesalen-ardnamurchan.co.uk. Open all year. Decent hotel accommodation and food (££), cosy bar and information on local walks.

Camping and self catering

Glenmore House and Cottage, Port An Aiseig, Glenborrodale, T01972-500263, www.michael-macgregor.co.uk. Luxury self-catering cottage and lodge on shores of Loch Sunart, facilities include whirlpool baths and sauna. Available all year, £275-775 per week.

Glenbay Cottages, Glenborrodale, T01972-500201, ll@nacyp.org.uk. 2 well-equipped self catering cottages, with games room and boats for hire. £250-690 per week. Also available is a round tower for 2.

Resipole Farm Caravan Park, a mile or so east of Salen, Resipole, T01967-431235, www.resipole.co.uk. Self-catering chalets, caravan and tent pitches and caravans for rent, also a restaurant and bar on site.

A The Prince's House, on the main road, half a mile past the monument on the right, heading west, T01397-722246, princes house@glenfinnan.co.uk. 9 rooms, open Mar-Nov. Comfortable old coaching inn which offers good food (££).

B-C Glenfinnan House Hotel, just off the main road, T/F01397-722235. 17 rooms, open Apr-Oct. Historic house with lots of charm, which is more than can be said for the staff. Overpriced. Dinner served from 1930 (£££). You can also walk in the vast grounds or fish on the loch.

F Glenfinnan Sleeping Car, at the train station, T01397-722400. Bunkhouse accommodation for 10 people, also mountain bike hire. You can eat here, too, in the **Glenfinnan Dining Car** (££-£).

Arisaig and Morar *p203*

Arisaig has plenty of accommodation and a decent range of services.

B Arisaig Hotel, Arisaig, T01687-450210, www.arisaighotel.co.uk. 8 en suite rooms. Open all year. 18th century former coaching inn with good sea views. Meals (££) served in the restaurant, 1200-1400 and 1800-2100, and bar (£). Child-friendly, with separate playroom. Bike hire also available for £10/day.

B The Old Library Lodge, Arisaig, T01687-450651. Open Apr-Oct. Highly-acclaimed restaurant (£££) with well-furnished rooms. The owner is like a Highland version of Basil Fawlty and very entertaining with it. Recommended.

Mallaig *p203*

C Marine Hotel, T01687-462217, www.marinehotel-mallaig.co.uk. Next to the train station and much nicer inside than it appears. Their restaurant also serves the best food in town (££).

E Glencairn, T01687-462412, open Apr-Sep. Decent B&B but there are lots of others to choose from. The TIC should just about be able to help should these ones be booked up.

E-F Western Isles Guesthouse, T/F01687-462320, open Jan-Nov. Follow the road round the harbour to East Bay, where you'll find this excellent-value guesthouse which serves dinner to guests.

F Sheena's Backapackers Lodge, T01687-462764. The cheapest place to stay is this friendly, easy-going independent hostel, with dorm beds, double rooms and kitchen facilities.

Knoydart Peninsula *p204*
B Doune Stone Lodge, 3-4 miles up the peninsula's only road, standing in splendid isolation, T01687-462667, www.doune-marine.co.uk. 3 en suite rooms, all with bunk beds for 2 children. Minimum stay 3 nights. Price includes breakfast, packed lunch and dinner. The food is superb and cannot be praised highly enough. Guests are picked up by boat from Mallaig, where you can leave your car. The owners also run the nearby **Doune Bay Lodge**, with shared facilities, for parties of up to 14. Can be self-catered, fully-catered, or somewhere in between. £40 per person for fully-catered.
C Pier House, Inverie, T01687-462347, www.thepierhouseknoydart. 4 rooms, 2 en suite, 2 with extra beds for children. Price includes dinner. Good, old-fashioned hospitality and wonderful local seafood (££).
F Torrie Shieling, T01687-462669. It's a bit more expensive than most other hostels, but is very comfortable, and popular with hikers. They also have their own transport for trips around the peninsula and will collect guests from Mallaig by arrangement.
F Knoydart Hostel, T01687-462242, near Inverie House. This is the only alternative hostel to **Torrie Shieling**. Much cheaper, but less appealing.

❶ Eating

Ardgour *p200*
££ The Inn at Ardgour, Corran, T01855-841225, www.ardgour.biz. Family-run inn serving bar meals, full a la carte and takeaway snacks. Dogs and children welcome.
££ Ariundel Centre, Strontian, T01967-402279, www.ariundle.co.uk. Open 0900-1730. Licensed tearoom/restaurant serving soups, salads and snacks. Also does candelit suppers during the summer; phone for details.

Morvern *p200*
££ Lochaline Hotel, Lochaline, T01967-421657. Hotel serving decent bar meals.

Ardnamurchan Peninsula and Moidart *p201*
All the hotels in Sleeping serve good food.
££-£ Clanranald Hotel, at Mingarry, T01967-431202. Food is also available here.
Arisaig and Morar
Very good meals can be had at the Arisaig Hotel and Old Library Lodge and Restaurant, see Sleeping above.
£ Rhu Café, Arisaig, next door to the Spar store, T01687-450707. Open daily 1000-1800. Snacks, soups, filled rolls and burgers, also takeaway, internet terminal £1/hr. Friendly and good with kids.

Mallaig *p203*
££ Cabin Seafood Restaurant, by the harbour, serves decent meals and a great value 'teatime special'.
£ Tea Room, below Sheena's Backpackers (see above under Sleeping), serves decent meals and snacks at reasonable prices.

Knoydart Peninsula *p204*
££ The Old Forge, T01687-462267. The most remote pub on mainland Britain, where you can enjoy some tasty local seafood and a pint of real ale in front of an open fire. There's even the occasional impromptu ceilidh. Dress code is 'wellies, waterproofs and midge cream'.

▲ Activities and tours

West of Fort William *p199*
Boat trips and wildlife cruises
Ardnamurchan Charters, T01972-500208, offers a 2-hr wildlife trip to the seal colonies – or further afield to Tobermory on Mull or Staffa and the Treshnish Islands.
Arisaig Marine, T01687-450224, www.arisaig.co.uk, sail from Arisaig pier to Rum, Eigg and Muck daily Mon-Fri all year and also Sat-Sun during Apr-Sep. The islands are visited on different days, though there is a boat to Eigg every day except Thu in summer. You can visit all three islands in a day, allowing between 2 and 5 hrs ashore. Fares range from £15 to Eigg and Muck to £19 return to Rum (children under 3 free to all islands, 4-12 are £6 and 13-16 £9). See also p274 These trips cater for the island's residents as much as tourists, so don't expect a running commentary, though hot and cold drinks are served on board.

The Brightwater Experience,
T07747-034767, www.seaotter.co.uk. This fast RIB (rigid inflatable boat) cruises to Eigg (£25, under 8s £20), Skye (£25/£20), Tobermory (£50/£40) and Eilean Donan (£25/£20) at breakneck speeds, slowing down to check out the local marine life.
Loch Shiel Cruises, T/F01687-470322, www.highlandcruises.co.uk, run a variety of cruises down Loch Shiel, from Glenfinnan to Acharacle. Sailings most days from Apr-Oct. Parking available at the **Glenfinnan House Hotel**, see Sleeping p204. Prices from £10 for a 2-hr cruise up to £13 for 3½ hrs.
MV Grimsay Isle, T01687-482652, www.lochaber.com/grimsayisle. Available for fishing charters and ferry service.

Outdoor activities
The Achnanellan Centre, cross from Dalilea Pier, T02967- 431265, is an outdoor activities centre on the south shore of Loch Shiel at the foot of Beinn Resipol (2,772 ft). They hire out mountain bikes, canoes, sail boats and camping equipment, as well as providing cheap, basic bunkhouse accommodation (F). It was from Dalilea Pier that Bonnie Prince Charlie left to sail up Loch Shiel to raise his standard at Glenfinnan, see p200.

Swimming
Indoor pool in Mallaig, next to the school on Frank Brae, £2 per session.

☉ Transport

Ardgour, Ardnamurchan and Morvern *p199*
Boat For details of the ferry from Lochaline to Fishnish on Mull and from Kilchoan to Tobermory, see p146.
Bus Shiel Buses, T01967-431272, run most of the bus services. There's a bus once a day on Tue, Thu and Sat from **Fort William** to **Lochaline** (2 hrs), via the **Corran Ferry**. There's a bus once a day (Mon-Sat) from **Fort William** to **Acharacle** (1½ hrs), via Lochailort. There's also a bus (Mon-Fri) to **Acharacle** from **Mallaig** (1½ hrs). There's a bus once a day (Mon-Sat) from **Fort William** to **Kilchoan** (2 hrs 25 mins), via **Strontian** (1 hr), **Salen** and **Glenborrodale.**

Car If you're travelling by car, access is via the A861, leaving the A830 before Glenfinnan or at Lochailort. You can also make the 5-min ferry crossing to Ardgour from the Corran Ferry, about 8 miles south of Fort William on the A82, see p192.

Mallaig *p203*
Boat CalMac, T01687-462403, ferries run throughout the year to **Armadale** on Skye (see p252), to **Lochboisdale** and **Castlebay** (see p278), and to the **Small Isles** (see p270).
Bus Shiel Buses, T01967-431272, run 2 buses daily Mon-Sat from **Mallaig** to **Fort William** (1½ hrs, £4.50) from Jul-Sep, and on Mon, Thu and Fri the rest of the year. Oban Minibus Services (T01852-314247) run a new direct service from Oban to Mallaig daily leaving Oban at 0945, arriving in Mallaig at 1215 for the 1300 sailing to Skye and returning at 1810, arriving in Oban at 2040; £15 single, £25 return, bikes £3/5. Possible to get off and on at Onich, Fort William and Glenfinnan but book in advance.
Train The best way to arrive in **Mallaig** is by train. There are several services daily (1 on Sun) to and from **Fort William**, with connections to **Glasgow** (see p192). There's also a steam train which runs in the summer months (see p185).

Knoydart Peninsula *p204*
Boat Bruce Watt Sea Cruises, T01687-462320, have trips to the remote village of **Inverie**, on the Knoydart Peninsula, and **Tarbet** on Loch Nevis. They sail on Mon, Wed and Fri throughout the year, departing at 1015 (to Inverie only) and 1415, and returning at 1200 and 1745. They also sail on Sat during Jun-Aug to **Inverie**, departing at 1030 and returning at 1215. Though billed as a wildlife cruise, this is essentially a working ferry. Fares are £9 return and £14 for the afternoon sailing. There's also a ferry service from **Arnisdale**, on the north shore of Loch Hourn, to **Barrisdale**. To arrange a crossing, contact Len Morrison, Croftfoot, Arnisdale, T01599-522352. It's a small open boat which takes 5 passengers, and all sailings are subject to weather.

Great Glen to Kyle of Lochalsh

The A87 is one of the main Highland tourist routes, connecting the Great Glen with the west coast and the Isle of Skye. It runs west from Invergarry between Fort Augustus and Fort William, through Glen Moriston and Glen Shiel to Shiel Bridge, at the head of Loch Duich, and on to Kyle. At Shiel Bridge a road branches off to Glenelg, from where you can sail across to Skye. It's a beautiful journey and by far the best way to reach the island. ▸▸ *For Sleeping, Eating and other listings, see pages 210-212.*

▲▲ Glen Shiel → *Colour map 3, grid A5. OS Landranger No33.*

The journey from Invergarry to Shiel Bridge is worth it for the views alone. Glen Shiel is a sight to make the heart soar as high as the 3,000 ft-high peaks that tower overhead on either side. This is one of the most popular hiking areas in Scotland, with the magnificent and much-photographed Five Sisters of Kintail on the north side of the glen, and the equally beautiful South Glen Shiel Ridge on the other.

There are several excellent hiking routes in Glen Shiel, but these mountains are to be treated with great respect. They require fitness, experience and proper equipment and planning. None of the routes should be attempted without a map, compass and detailed route instructions. You should be aware of the notoriously unpredictable weather conditions and also check locally about deer stalking. The season runs from August to October, but for more details contact the local stalkers ① *T01599-511282*. A good trekking guide is the *SMC's Hill Walks in Northwest Scotland*.

The **Five Sisters Traverse** is a classic ridge route. It starts at the first fire break on the left as you head southeast down the glen from Shiel Bridge and finishes at Morvich, on the other side of the ridge. Allow a full day (eight to 10 hours). You can also hike from Morvich to **Glen Affric Youth Hostel** at Cannich. It's a strenuous 20-mile walk, but you can stop off midway at the remote **Allt Beithe Youth Hostel**. For details, see Glen Affric page 173.

The magnificent **South Glen Shiel Ridge** is one of the world's great hikes. It starts from above the **Cluanie Inn**, see Sleeping. From here, follow the old public road to Tomdoun which meets up with a good stalking path which climbs to the summit of the first Munro, Creag a' Mhaim (3,108 ft). The ridge then runs west for almost nine miles and gives you the chance to pick off no fewer than seven Munros. Allow a full day for the walk (nine to 10 hours), and you'll need to set off early.

Glenelg and around → *Phone code: 01599. Colour map 3, grid A5.*

One of the most beautiful journeys in Scotland is the road from Shiel Bridge to the picturesque little village of Glenelg on the Sound of Sleat, only a short distance opposite Kylerhea on Skye, for Transport details see page 211. The unclassified single-track road turns off the A87 and climbs steeply and dramatically through a series of sharp switchbacks to the top of the **Mam Ratagan Pass** (1,115 ft). From here the view back across Loch Duich to the Five Sisters of Kintail is simply amazing, and the all-time classic calendar shot.

The road then drops down through Glen More to Glenelg, the main settlement on the peninsula, which lies on the old drovers' route which ran from Skye to the cattle markets in the south. This little-known corner of the Western Highlands is Gavin Maxwell country and was featured in *Ring of Bright Water*, his novel about otters. He disguised the identity of this beautiful, unspoiled stretch of coastline, calling it Camusfearna, and today it remains a quiet backwater.

You can see the famous otters at **Sandaig**, on the road running from Glenelg, where Gavin Maxwell lived. The site of his cottage is now marked with a cairn. As well as otters, you can see numerous seabirds, seals and porpoises in the Sound of Sleat, and around the peninsula you may be lucky enough to catch a glimpse of wildcats, pine martens, golden eagles and the recently reintroduced sea eagles. The village itself consists of a row of whitewashed cottages surrounded by trees and overlooked by the ruins of the 18th-century **Bernera Barracks**. Just before the village the road forks. The right turning leads to the Glenelg-Kylerhea ferry, which makes the ten-minute crossing to Skye, see page 211.

A road runs south from Glenelg to Arnisdale. About a mile and a half along this road, a branch left leads to the **Glenelg Brochs** – Dun Telve and Dun Dun Troddan – two of the best-preserved Iron-Age buildings in the country. Dun Telve stands to a height of over 30 ft and the internal passages are almost intact. The road south from Glenelg continues past Sandaig Bay and runs along the north shore of unearthly Loch Hourn, with great views across the mountains of Knoydart. The road ends at the impossibly cute little fishing hamlet of **Arnsidale**, from where you can take a boat across the loch to Barrisdale on the Knoydart Peninsula. For details, see page 204. A bit further along the coast, the road ends at the even tinier hamlet of **Corran**.

Eilean Donan Castle → *Phone code: 01599. Colour map 3, grid A5.*
① *To1599-555202, Apr-Oct 0900-1700. £3.95, concession £3.20, group rates £2.95.*
Some 10 miles west of Shiel Bridge on the A87 is the little village of Dornie, home to the one of Scotland's most photographed sights, the stunningly located Eilean Donan Castle. It stands on a tiny islet at the confluence of Loch Duich and Loch Alsh, joined to the shore by a narrow stone bridge and backed by high mountains. This great calendar favourite has also featured in several movies, including *Highlander*, which starred Sean Connery.

The original castle dates from 1230 when Alexander III had it built to protect the area from marauding Vikings. It was destroyed by King George in 1719 during its occupation by Spanish Jacobite forces sent to help the 'Old Pretender', James Stuart. It then lay in ruins, until one of the Macraes had it rebuilt between 1912 and 1932. Inside, the Banqueting Hall with its Pipers' Gallery is most impressive, and there's an exhibition of military regalia and interesting displays of the castle's history. The views from the battlements are also worthwhile.

Kyle of Lochalsh → *Phone code: 01599. Colour map 3, grid A5.*
Before the coming of the controversial Skye Bridge a mile to the north, see page 252, the little town of Kyle, as it is known, was the main ferry crossing to Skye and consequently a place which attracted a busy tourist trade. Now though, the tourist traffic bypasses Kyle, which is probably the most sensible thing to do as it's not the most attractive of places. There are a couple of banks with ATMs, two small supermarkets and a post office in the village. The **tourist information centre** ① *To1599-534276, Apr-late Oct*, is at the main seafront car park.

Plockton → *Phone code: 01599. Colour map 3, grid A4.*
If there were a poll taken of visitors' favourite Highland villages then you can bet your bottom dollar that Plockton would come top with most folk. If you look for a definition of picturesque in your dictionary, it'll say 'see Plockton'. Maybe not – but it should.

Plockton's neat little painted cottages are ranged around the curve of a wooded bay, with flowering gardens and palm trees. Yachts bob up and down in the harbour and there are views across the island-studded waters of Loch Carron to the hills beyond. Even on the telly Plockton's charms proved irresistible, and millions of viewers tuned in each week to watch the TV series *Hamish Macbeth*, which featured Robert Carlyle as the local bobby. Plockton's a popular place with artists who are drawn by the village's setting and the wonderful light. A good place to find some of their work, as well as other souvenirs, is **The Studio Craft Shop**, on the corner of the seafront and the road leading out of town.

▲ There are lots of good walks around the village. One of the best ways to appreciate it is to head up to **Frithard Hill,** from where there are great views of the bay. Another good walk is along the beach, starting from the High School playing fields at the top of the village.

🛏 Sleeping

Glen Shiel *p208*
C **Cluanie Inn**, 9 miles east of Shiel Bridge, T01320-340238. This is one of the Highlands' classic hotels. It's a firm favourite with hikers and climbers and it's easy to see why. After a hard day's ridge walking, what could be better than jumping into the jacuzzi, then having a hot dinner and a good pint beside a log fire.
C-F **Kintail Lodge Hotel,** T01599-511275, www.kintaillodgehotel.co.uk. Small, cosy hotel, dinner also available. Bunkhouse attached with 12 beds. You can also camp nearby, but why deny yourself the pleasure if you can afford it?
E **Fisherbeck**, 3 Macinnes Place, T01599-511365. One of the several B&Bs in the village of Ratagan.
F **Ratagan Youth Hostel,** T01599-511243, just outside Shiel Bridge. A less salubrious option than the above but it's popular with hikers, and is open all year except Jan.

Camping
Morvich Caravan Club Site, T01599-511354, open late Mar to late Oct. **Shiel Bridge**, T01599-511211.

Glenelg and around *p208*
E **Glenelg Inn,** T01599-522273. It's worth stopping in Glenelg, if you've got the time, to experience a night in this wonderfully cosy place. Even if you can't spend the night, at least spend an hour or two enjoying the atmosphere, good ale and fine seafood. It's one of those places that almost makes you glad it's raining. If you're really lucky, you may even chance upon an impromptu folk jam.
E-F **Mrs Nash,** T01599-522336. B&B accommodation in Arnisdale where there's also a tea hut serving cakes and hot drinks.

Eilean Donan Castle *p209*
There are several places to stay in the nearby village of Dornie.
B **Conchra House Hotel**, cross the bridge in Dornie and turn right for Killilan, a tiny hamlet at the head of Loch Long, the hotel is about ¾

mile up this road, T01599-555233, conchra@ aol.com. 6 rooms. This historic 18th-century hunting lodge is peaceful, has lovely views and boasts a reputation for good food.
D **Dornie Hotel**, T01599-555205, is a good option and serves very good food (**££**).
D **Loch Duich Hotel**, across the bridge from Dornie Hotel, T01599-555213. It offers comfortable accommodation, meals and live music in the bar on a Sun evening.
E **Tigh Tasgaidh**, T01599-555242, and
F **Fasgadale**, T01599-588238, are two of the several B&Bs in the village.
F **Silver Fir Bunkhouse**, Carndubh, T01599-555264. The cheapest place to stay is this 6-bed bunkhouse.
F **Tigh Iseabeal**, near Cochra House Hotel, at Camasluinie, T01599-588205, a 6-bed independent hostel.

Kyle of Lochalsh *p209*
It's a good idea to get the TIC to book a room for you, as there's not much choice.
B **Lochalsh Hotel**, T01599-534202. The most luxurious of the of couple of hotels here. Great views across to Skye and good food.
D **Old Schoolhouse**, Erbusaig, T01599-534 369. A very comfortable option offering dinner for guests (24 hrs notice required).
E **Crowlin View**, T01599-534286. A mile and a half north of Kyle.
F **Cuchulainn's**, T01599-534492, on Station Rd. Cheap hostel accommodation.

Camping
Reraig Caravan Site, T01599-566215, 4 miles east of Kyle, at Balmacara.

Plockton *p209*
C **The Haven Hotel**, Innes St, T01599-544223. 15 rooms, open Feb-Dec. The best place to stay and the food in the restaurant is quite superb (**£££**).
D **Plockton Hotel**, T01599-544274. There are quite a few places on Harbour St along the waterfront, including this wonderful and busy hotel. Serves good food (**££**) and has a

great little beer garden at the front where you can sit and enjoy a drink on a balmy summer evening.

D Plockton Inn, T01599-544222. Near The Haven Hotel is this cosy, comfortable place.

E An Caladh, T01599-544356. This B&B is on the seafront.

E Craig Highland Farm, T01599-544205, on the road to Achmore, this farm offers B&B accommodation and self-catering cottages from £235 per week. The farm is also a conservation centre, where you can see and feed rare and ancient breeds of domestic animals.

E Shieling, T01599-544282, at the far end of the harbour. There are lots of B&Bs to choose from, this is one of the nicest.

F Plockton Station Bunkhouse, Nessun Dorma, Burnside, T01599-544235. A few miles out of Plockton. Cheapest option.

● Eating

Eilean Donan Castle *p209*
Aside from the hotels listed above, there are a couple of places in Dornie serving decent food.

££ Clachan Pub where you can enjoy a good-value 3-course evening meal.

££ Jenny Js, across the bridge, T01599-555362.

Kyle of Lochalsh *p209*
£££-££ Seagreen Restaurant & Bookshop T01599-534388. Just outside the village, on the road to Plockton is this bistro-cum-bookshop and gallery serving wholefood and local seafood throughout the day.

£££-££The Seafood Restaurant at the railway station, T01599-534813, has a good reputation for seafood, open Easter-Oct 1000-1500 and 1830-2100.

Plockton *p209*
Apart from the hotels listed above, this option is a good place to eat in Plockton.

££ Off the Rails, at the railway station, T01599-544423. It's open from 0830 for breakfast, snacks, lunch and evening meals.

▲ Activities and tours

Kyle of Lochalsh *p209*
Boat trips There are a couple of interesting boat trips from Kyle. One is on

board the *Seaprobe Atlantis*, which is fitted with underwater windows. Check sailing times at the pier. If you prefer, you could take a seafood cruise – a 2½-hr wildlife-spotting and seafood-eating boat trip. Contact **Neil MacRae**, T01599-577230.

Plockton *p209*
Leisure Marine, T01599-544306, runs 1-hr seal- and otter-watching cruises in the summer. They also hire out boats.
Sea Trek Marine, T01599-544346. Similar trips are run by this outfit.

● Transport

Glen Shiel *p208*
Citylink buses between **Fort William**, **Inverness** and **Skye** pass through Glen Shiel several times daily in each direction. There's a postbus service between **Kyle** and **Glenelg** (see below) and Highland Country Buses run from **Ratagan Youth Hostel** to **Kyle** (30 mins) and on to **Plockton** (50 mins), on schooldays only, departing at 0755 and returning at 1640.

Glenelg and around *p208*
There's a postbus service from **Kyle of Lochalsh** to **Arnisdale** and **Corran** via Glenelg at 0945 Mon-Sat. It takes 3¾ hrs. The return bus from **Corran** departs at 0725. The Glenelg-Kylerhea ferry provides the most scenic connection to Skye. 10-min crossing from Oct Mon-Sat 0900-1800 till mid-May; Mon-Sat 0900-2000, Sun 1000-1800 from mid-May to end-Aug; Mon-Sat 0900-1800, Sun 1000-1800 end-Aug to end-Oct. Per car with up to 4 passengers, £6; day return £10, T01599-511302.

Eilean Donan Castle *p209*
Citylink buses between **Fort William** and **Inverness** and **Skye** stop by the castle.

Kyle of Lochalsh *p209*
Bus Scottish Citylink buses, T0990-505050, run to Kyle from **Inverness** (3 daily, 2 hrs); **Glasgow** via **Fort William** (4 daily, 5 hrs); and **Edinburgh** via **Fort William** (1 daily, 6½ hrs). These buses continue to **Portree** (a further hour) and **Uig** (1½ hrs), for ferries to **Tarbert** on Harris and Lochmaddy on North Uist. There's also a regular shuttle service across the bridge to **Kyleakin** (every 30 mins).

The train journey from **Inverness** to
Kyle, though not as spectacular as the West
Highland line, is very scenic. It runs 3-4 times
Mon-Sat (2½ hrs) and once or twice on Sun
from May to Sep. There's also an observation
car and dining car in the summer.

Wester Ross

*From Loch Carron north to Ullapool, is the region of Wester Ross, an area of dramatic
mountain massifs, fjord-like sea lochs and remote coastal villages. Here lies some of
Europe's most spectacular scenery, from the isolated peninsula of Applecross to
Tolkien-esque peaks of Torridon, which offer some of Scotland's best climbing and
hillwalking. There are also gentler attractions such as the vast, sprawling gardens at
Inverewe and the beguiling pink sands of Gruinard Bay.* ▸▸ *For Sleeping, Eating and other
listings, see pages 217-221.*

Loch Carron and around

Along Loch Carron
East of Plockton, just before the road meets the A890 at **Achmore** is the **West
Highland Dairy**, where you can pick up some good local cheese for a picnic – weather
permitting of course. The road passes the turn-off for Stromeferry and continues along
the east shore of Loch Carron to **Strathcarron** at its northeastern end, on the
Inverness to Kyle of Lochalsh rail line.

Lochcarron village → *Phone code: 01520. Colour map 1, grid C4. Population: 870.*
Lochcarron village consists of little more than a main street along the shore of the loch,
but it has more facilities and services than most other places in these parts. Here you
should take the opportunity to withdraw cash at the Bank of Scotland ATM, fill up with
petrol and buy some supplies at the small self-service store. The TIC ① *T01520-722357,
Apr-Oct,* has details of some excellent walks in the surrounding hills.

Two miles south of the village on the road to the 15th-century ruins of **Strome
Castle** is **Lochcarron Weavers**, where you can see tartan being made and also buy
from a vast range of woven goods.

Loch Kishorn to Applecross → *Colour map 1, grid C4.*
There are many scenic routes in the Highlands but the road from Kishorn, west of
Lochcarron to Applecross beats them all. The **Bealach na Ba** ('Pass of the Cattle') is the
highest road in Scotland and is often closed during the winter snows. It climbs
relentlessly and dramatically through a series of tortuous switchbacks – both
spectacular and terrifying in equal measure. The high plateau, at 2,053 ft, is cold and
desolate, but from here you have the most amazing views: from Ardnamurchan
Peninsula to Loch Torridon, taking in Eigg, Rùm, the Cuillins of Skye, the Old Man of
Storr and the Quirang.

The narrow, single-track road then begins its gradual descent to the isolated
little village of **Applecross**, site of one Scotland's first Christian monasteries,
founded in AD 673. The village consists of a row of whitewashed fishermen's
cottages looking across to the island of Raasay and backed by wooded slopes. It's a
beautifully tranquil place where you can explore beaches and rock pools or enjoy a
stroll along sylvan lanes – and then of course there's the peerless **Applecross Inn**,
see Sleeping page 217.

Torridon and around → *Phone code: 01445. Colour map 1, grid C4.*

Torridon is perhaps the most striking skyline in the Scottish Highlands. The multi-peaked mountains of Beinn Alligin, Liathach (pronounced *Lee-ahakh*) and Beinn Eighe (*Ben-eay*) form a massive fortress of turrets, spires and pinnacles that provides an awesome backdrop to Loch Torridon, as well as the most exhilarating walking and climbing on the Scottish mainland. The straggly little village of Torridon makes the ideal base from which to tackle these mountains.

Ins and outs
Torridon offers some of the most spectacular walking on the Scottish mainland but also presents some of the most serious challenges. You need to be fit, experienced and well prepared and also be aware of the notoriously unpredictable weather, see page 56. You should have a compass and the relevant map. OS Outdoor Leisure series No 8 covers the area. For recommended mountain guides, see page 220.

Around Loch Torridon
The coast road from Applecross meets the A896 from Lochcarron at the lovely little village of **Shieldaig** on the southern shore of Loch Torridon. There's a shop, a post office, a campsite, a couple of B&Bs. Several miles east, a side road turns off the A896 by **Torridon village** and winds its way along the northern shore of the loch, then climbs through dramatic scenery before dropping to the beautiful little village of **Diabaig** (pronounced *Jee-a-beg*), 10 miles from Torridon village. It's a worthwhile side trip, as the views across to the Applecross peninsula and Raasay are fantastic. There's also a great seven mile coastal walk from Diabaig to Redpoint (see below).

Much of the Torridon massif is in the care of the National Trust for Scotland, and just before Torridon village is the **NTS countryside centre** ① *T01445-791221*, where you can get information and advice on walks in the area, as well as books and maps. About 400 yards past the centre is the **Deer Museum**, which has a small display describing the management of red deer in the Highlands as well as some live specimens outside.

▲▲ Beinn Alligin
Beinn Alligin (3,232 ft) is the most westerly of the Torridon peaks and probably the least demanding. The **Allt a'Bhealaich Walk** is a steep but short walk of about two hours. It starts from the car park just beyond the stone bridge that crosses the Abhainn Coire Mhic Nobuil. Follow the path that runs beside the river gorge until you reach the first bridge, cross it and follow the east bank of the Allt a' Bhealaich burn. Higher up, cross the second bridge and continue to follow the track up to the 380-m contour line, then turn back retracing your steps. This walk doesn't include the ascent of the peak but the views are magnificent. Those who wish to climb the three **Horns of Beinn Alligin** can continue from the 380-m contour line above the second bridge. The track that follows their ridge is exposed and requires rock scrambling experience.

▲▲ Liathach
Seven-peaked Liathach (3,460 ft) stretches over five miles, and the magnificent ridge walk is considered by many to be the most impressive in Britain. This walk requires a high level of stamina and will take at least seven to eight hours. It also helps if you have a car waiting at the end.

A good place to start this long and strenuous challenge is about half a mile or so east of Glen Cottage, which is just over two miles east of the Countryside Centre. A steep climb takes you to a point just west of Stuc a'Choire Dhuibh Bhig (3,000 ft). Then retrace your route to climb the twin tops of Bidein Toll a'Mhuic (3,200 ft), linked by a narrow ridge. The path from here descends to the head of a deep ravine and keeps to the crest of the ridge around the rim of Coireag Dubh Beag which plunges steeply to the north. The ridge then rises across a field of huge and unstable boulders to the highest peak – Spidean a'Choire Leith. The view from this point is stunning, with Coire na Caime before you, surrounded by 2,000 ft sheer cliffs. From here, the path follows a narrow exposed ridge for over a mile towards Mullach an Rathain (3,358 ft). Unless you are an experienced scrambler with a good head for heights, the best way from here is to take the path to the south, below the sharp pinnacles. Beyond the pinnacles the climb to Mullach an Rathain is straightforward. The track from here to Sgorr a'Chadail is a long but fairly easy walk and ends on the path in Coire Mhic Nobuil, see Beinn Alligin above.

▲ Coire Walk

A less difficult walk, but still requiring a fair degree of fitness and taking most of the day, is the Coire Walk. It follows the River Coire Mhic Nobuil to its watershed and down again by the Allt a'Choire Dhuibh Mhoir to the main road in Glen Torridon. Again, two cars will shorten the distance considerably.

The walk starts at the same point as the Beinn Alligin walk above. It follows the path up to the first bridge then branches east and continues on the path that runs north of the river, all the way to its source in the pass between Liathach and Beinn Dearg. Here the ground is boggy between the string of pools and lochans and the path is less distinct, but it becomes clear again in the upper reaches of the Coire Dubh Mor, a huge gully that separates Liathach from Beinn Eighe. A little further on, the track joins a stalkers' path which curves round Sail Mhor to the famous Coire Mhic Fhearchair, considered to be the most spectacular corrie in Scotland (see Beinn Eighe below). The Coire path leads to a ford, which is crossed by stepping stones, then descends following the west side of the burn down to the car park on the Torridon road, from where it's about 4½ miles to Torridon village.

▲ Diabaig to Red Point Walk → OS Landranger No 19.

An excellent low-level coastal walk is from Diabaig to Red Point. It is far less strenuous or daunting than the others described above and there is a clear path. It starts at the wooden gate to the right of the post office in Diabaig and ends at Red Point Farm, seven miles away.

After four miles the coastal path reaches the derelict croft houses in the Craig Valley. One of these has been converted into a **SYHA Hostel**. There are two possible routes from here. You can follow the footpath above the coastline, or leave the footpath after crossing the wooden bridge over the Craig river and climb through an area of woodland. Take a reference from your OS map and you'll reach the highest point, Meall na h-Uamha, from where there are superb views. You can then descend to rejoin the coastal path and continue till you reach the glorious golden sands of Red Point, with wonderful views across to Skye and Raasay. Keep to the path through the farm till you reach the car park. Unless you've arranged your own transport here, you'll have to walk back the way you came, or catch the schoolbus to Gairloch, see page 220.

▲ Beinn Eighe National Nature Reserve

While most of the Torridon massif is managed by the National Trust of Scotland, Beinn Eighe (which means 'File Peak' in Gaelic) is under the control of Scottish Natural Heritage. It is Britain's oldest National Nature Reserve, set up in 1951 to protect the ancient Caledonian pine forest west of Kinlochewe. It has since been designated an International Biosphere Reserve and extended to cover 30 square miles. The reserve is the home of a great variety of rare Highland wildlife, including pine martens, wildcats, buzzards, Scottish crossbills and golden eagles. There's also a wide range of flora which can best be appreciated on the excellent mountain trail described below which climbs from the ancient pine woods through alpine vegetation to the tundra-like upper slopes.

About half a mile northwest of Kinlochewe on the A832, is the Beinn Eighe Visitor Centre, which has information on the flora and fauna in the reserve and sells pamphlets on the trails described below.

Beinn Eighe (3,309 ft) has nine peaks and is the largest of the Torridon Mountains. To traverse its ridge is a mighty undertaking and can take two days. A much shorter and easier walk around the base of the mountain is described here. The mountain and woodland trails both start and end in the car park at the side of Loch Maree, about two miles beyond the visitor centre. The woodland trail heads west along the lochside then crosses the road and climbs for about a mile up to the Conservation cabin before descending back to the starting point. It should take about an hour and is easy to follow, though quite steep in parts, and you'll need a good pair of walking boots. The mountain trail is four miles long and rough and steep in parts. You should be well equipped with good walking boots, waterproofs, food and warm clothing. It should take three to four hours. The route is well marked with cairns and you should not stray from the path. The trail heads south from the car park and begins a gentle ascent through woodland to a boggy area and then begins to zigzag up a very steep and rugged section, climbing to over 1,000 ft in less than half a mile. This is the steepest section of the trail, but the views back across Loch Maree to Slioch are fabulous. The summit of the mountain trail is Conservation cairn (1,800 ft) from where you can see the tops of 31 Munros on a clear day and enjoy a close-up view of the impressive Beinn Eighe ridge a few miles to the south. The trail now begins to descend as it heads northwest towards An t-Allt (1,000 ft), turns northwards down to a small enclosure, then heads east to the deep Allt na h-Airidhe gorge. From here the trail continues down to the treeline and runs through woodland to join up with the top of the Woodland Trail. Follow the path to the right to get back to the car park.

Kinlochewe and Loch Maree → *Phone code: 01445. Colour map 1, grid C5.*

On the north side of the Torridon Mountains is the sprawling village of Kinlochewe, at the southeastern end of beautiful Loch Maree. The loch is dotted with islands and bordered by the mass of Slioch (3,215 ft) to the north and ancient Caledonian pine forest to the south. Running along its northern shore, from **Slioch** almost as far as **Poolewe**, is the remote **Letterewe Estate**, one of Scotland's great deer forests. The A832 skirts the south shore of the loch, running northwest from Kinlochewe, and passes the **Victoria Falls**, a mile or so beyond Talladale. The falls commemorate Queen Victoria's visit in 1877. To find them, look for the Hydro Power signs.

Gairloch and around → *Phone code: 01445. Colour map 1, grid C4.*

Gairloch consists of a string of tiny crofting townships scattered around the northeastern shore of the loch of the same name. It's a great place which attracts a large number of visitors who come for the many beautiful beaches, excellent walks, golf and fishing, and the chance of seeing seals, porpoises, dolphins and whales in the surrounding waters. ►► *For Sleeping, Eating and other listings, see pages 217-221.*

Ins and outs

Getting there and around There are buses to and from Inverness three times a week, also buses to Kinlochewe and a local postbus service. A passenger ferry service now operates from Gairloch to Portree on Skye. ►► *For further details, see Transport page 219.*

Tourist information TIC① *To1445-712130, open year round, Apr-Oct daily*, at the car park in Auchtercairn, where the road branches to Strath. They book accommodation and sell books and maps. There are shops and takeaways in Strath and Auchtercairn, a petrol station in Auchtercairn, and a bank near the harbour at Charleston.

Gairloch Heritage Museum
① To1445-712287, Apr-Oct Mon-Sat 1000-1700, £2.50, concession £2, children £0.50.
If you are interested in local history, or the weather is bad – not unknown – then this
museum may entertain for a hour or so. Included are archaeological finds, a mock-up
of a crofthouse room, schoolroom and shop, the interior of the local lighthouse and
an archive of old photographs. It is found beside the tourist office on the A832 to
Poolewe, a few yards beyond the turn-off to Strath.

Big Sand, Melvaig and Midtown
The beach by the golf course at Gairloch is nice, but the beach at Big Sand, a few miles
northwest of Strath, is better, and quieter. Further north is Melvaig, from where you
can walk to **Rubha Reidh Lighthouse**, see Sleeping page 217. Around the headland
from the lighthouse is the beautiful, secluded beach at **Camas Mor**. This is a good
place for spotting sea birds, and there's a great walk from here on a marked footpath
to Midtown, four miles northwest of Poolewe. You'll have to walk or hitch from here as
there's no public transport to Poolewe.

The waters around Gairloch are home to a wide variety of **marine mammals** such
as seals, otters, porpoises, dolphins, minke whales and even killer whales. For
details of wildlife cruises, see page 220.

Destitution Road
Many of the roads in the area were built during the Potato Famine of 1840 in order to
give men work, with funds supplied by Dowager Lady Mackenzie of Gairloch. These
became know as the 'Destitution Roads', and one of these is the narrow B8056 which
runs west for nine miles to Red Point from the junction three miles south of Gairloch, at
Kerrysdale. This is a lovely little side trip and well worth it, especially on a clear evening
to enjoy the magnificent sunsets at **Red Point beach**. The beach itself is extremely
seductive, backed by steep dunes and looking across to the Trotternish peninsula on
Skye. So romantic is this spot that some people (naming no names) have been known
to plight their troth here. Red Point is also the start or finish point for the excellent
coastal walk to or from Diabaig, see page 214. On the road to Red Point is the
picturesque little hamlet of **Badachro**, tucked away in a wooded, sheltered bay with
fishing boats moored in its natural harbour. It's worth stopping off here on the way back
from Red Point for a wee dram at the **Badachro Inn**.

There are lots of other good walks in the area, including to **Flowerdale Falls** and
the **Fairy Lochs** and the **USAAF Liberator**. The TIC has a selection of walking guides
and OS maps.

Poolewe → *Phone code: 01445. Colour map 1, grid B4.*
Five miles east of Gairloch on the other side of the peninsula is the neat little village of
Poolewe, straddling the mouth of the River Ewe, where it cascades into sheltered
Loch Ewe. There are some good walks around Poolewe, including the one around
Loch Kernsary described below. There's also a nice little drive up the side road
running along the west shore of Loch Ewe to Cove. You can walk from Midtown,
midway along the road, to Rubha Reidh, north of Gairloch (see above).

▲ Loch Kernsary → *OS Landranger Map No 19.*
This straightforward but rewarding walk covers six miles and should take around 2½
to three hours. The track is very boggy underfoot in places, especially after rain, so
you'll need good boots.

Start in Poolewe, from the car park by the school near the bridge over the Ewe.
Head up the single-track road with the river on your right. Go through the gate, then the
track heads away from the river and up into woodland. At the Letterewe Estate gate
cross the stile and continue to the next fork. Turn left here to Kernsary Estate, with views

of Loch Maree and Beinn Eighe to the south. Follow the track to the next gate, go through and cross the wooden bridge. Continue along the track and you'll see Loch Kernsary on your left. At the next fork, turn left over the bridge and pass Kernsary Cottage on the right. Beyond the cottage, go through the gate and immediately head left down towards the burn, where the ground may be boggy. There's no path here, but cross the wooden footbridge and continue straight on, past the piles of stones on your left. Cross the stile, and the path follows the length of Loch Kernsary. At the head of the loch, the path climbs to give you views down to Poolewe. Follow the path down till it eventually takes you to the main road. Turn left and follow the road back to the car park.

Inverewe Garden

ⓘ T01445-781200, garden 15 Mar-31 Oct daily 0930-2100, 1 Nov-14 Mar daily 0930-1700 (guided garden walks 15 Apr to 15 Sep Mon-Thu at 1330); visitor centre 15 Mar to 31 Oct 0930-1730, £7, concession £5.25, family £19.

The reason most people come this way is to visit Inverewe Garden where you'll find an astonishing collection of exotic subtropical plants growing on the same latitude as Siberia, thanks to the mild climate created by the North Atlantic Drift. This wonderful 50-acre oasis of colour is a mecca for garden lovers, but even those who flinch at the mere sight of a lawn-mower will be bowled over by the sheer scale and diversity of plants and flowers on view. The garden was created from a treeless wilderness by Osgood Mackenzie, starting in 1862. By the time of his death in 1922 he had produced an internationally renowned walled and woodland garden. His work was continued by his daughter, who then gave the garden to the National Trust for Scotland in 1952. Since then, the plant collection has diversified even more and an intricate maze of paths leads you through ever-changing displays of Himalayan rhododendrons, Tasmanian eucalyptus, many Chilean and South African species, together with a large collection of New Zealand plants.

The garden is well worth visiting in any weather and at any time of the year, but especially from the end of April through the summer when the rhododendrons are in bloom. You should allow at least a couple of hours to do it justice. The garden is about a mile north of Poolewe on the main A832. There's a visitor centre and gift shop and a good restaurant, which serves snacks and hot meals.

Gruinard Bay → Phone code: 01445. Colour map 1, grid B5.

North of Poolewe the A832 passes Aultbea on its way to Laide, where it then skirts the shores of Gruinard Bay, with its lovely coves of pink sand. From Laide Post Office a side road branches north to **Mellon Udrigle** and **Opinan**, both with great beaches. Between Laide and Mellon Udrigle, at **Achgarve**, a road branches left for about half a mile. From the end of this road you can walk all the way to **Slaggan**, a ruined village on the other side of the peninsula. It's a nice spot for a picnic but don't be tempted to swim in the sea as the tidal race makes it dangerous.

Gruinard Bay is a very beautiful part of the northwest coast but will always be synonymous with **Gruinard Island**, standing ominously in the middle of the bay. The island was used as a testing ground for biological warfare during the Second World War and was contaminated with anthrax spores. The Ministry of Defence finally agreed to decontaminate it in 1990 and it has now been declared 'safe'.

⏺ Sleeping

Loch Carron and around p212
There's a wide range of accommodation and several places to eat.
B **Applecross Inn**, Applecross, T01520-744262. There are, sadly, too few

authentic Highland hostelries where you could quite happily while away a few hours, or even an entire afternoon, but if you have to be holed up somewhere to escape the rotten weather, then this place is as good as

any and better than most. The welcome is warm, the craic is good and the seafood is so fresh you can almost see it swimming past as you order (try a half pint of prawns for a fiver or scallops for £7.50). Bar food served 1200-2100, children welcome till 2030, ceilidhs on Fri evening. The rooms upstairs have recently been refurbished to a high standard and all have sea views. If there's no room at the Inn there are a few B&Bs a mile to the south, see Torridon and around below.
C **Shore House**, Ardarroch, Kishorn, a few miles west of Lochcarron on the A896, T01520-733333, www.shorehouse.co.uk. 3 rooms. Comfortable with traditional Celtic character and superb food also on offer. Best of the bunch.
D **Rockvilla Hotel**, Lochcarron village T01520-722379, rockvilla@btinternet.com. Small, family-run hotel offering very good food (**££**).
E **Bank House**, Lochcarron village, T01520-722332, in the same building as the Bank of Scotland.

Self catering
Jam Factory, contact **Cottages and Castles**, T01463-226990, www.cottages -and-castles. Co.uk. An excellent self-catering option is this 18th-century building once used for jam making, 10 mins walk from Lochcarron village. It sleeps 2 and costs from £170-235 per week.

Torridon and around p213
L **Loch Torridon Hotel**, a mile south of the turn-off to Torridon village, T01445-791242, www.lochtorridonhotel.com. 22 rooms. This fairytale Gothic pile sits on the lochside surrounded by mountains and offers the ultimate in style and comfort. Rooms are sumptuous, with enormous beds and romantic bathrooms. Breakfast is positively Olympian in proportion and the restaurant is one of the finest in the area (**£££**). The views cap it all, though.
A **The Old Mill Highland Lodge**, on Loch Maree at Talladale, halfway between Kinlochewe and Gairloch, T01445-760271, open mid-Dec to mid-Oct. The best accommodation around here is this converted mill set in its own gardens.

It's friendly and comfortable, offers great food (price includes dinner), seclusion and great views.
B **Loch Maree Hotel**, on Loch Maree, T01445-760288, lochmaree@easynet.co.uk. This beautifully located hotel is being returned to its former glory. Queen Victoria was here! It also offers superb cuisine (**A** including dinner).
B **Tigh-an-Eilean Hotel**, in Shieldaig, T01520-755251, where you can get reasonable meals.
D **Cromasaig**, Torridon Rd, Kinlochewe, T01445-760234, cromasaig@msn.com. A decent B&B.
E **Kinlochewe Hotel**, T01445-760253, offers B&B as well as cheaper bunkhouse beds and cheap bar meals. Kinlochewe is a good base for walking in and around Loch Maree. It has a post office, shop and garage.
E **Upper Diabaig Farm**, T01445-790227, open Apr-Sep, in Upper Diabaig. This an excellent choice.
F **SYHA hostels**, T01445-791284. There are two of these. One is in Torridon village, open 29 Jan-31 Oct, with an adjacent campsite. The other is much smaller and more basic, 4 miles north of Diabaig on the trail to Redpoint, at the disused crofting township of Craig (no phone; open 14 May-3 Oct).

Camping
There is a basic campsite at Taangan Farm, at the head of Loch Maree.

Gairloch and around p215
There are numerous B&Bs scattered through-out the area. Most of the owners will provide maps and information on local walks.
L **Pool House Hotel**, Poolewe, T01445-781272, poolhouse@inverewe.co.uk, open Mar-Dec. On the Cove road by the lochside is this former home of Osgood Mackenzie. It has great views and serves good food (**£££**).
B-C **Myrtle Bank Hotel**, T01445-712004, MyrtleBank@email.msn.com. 12 rooms. Modern hotel in the centre of Gairloch overlooking the loch, very good food and service in the restaurant (**£££-££**).
C **The Old Inn**, by the harbour, T01445-712006, www.theoldinn.co.uk. 14 rooms.

Staying here gives the advantage of not having to move far after enjoying the best pint of real ale and pub grub (**££**) for miles around.

D Old Smiddy Guest House, in Laide, near Gruinard Bay, T01445-731425, www.old smiddy.co.uk. Open Apr-Oct. Its excellent restaurant (**£££**) is open to non-residents, but it's best to book well in advance.

E Bruach Ard, near Poolewe, T01445-781214, open Apr-Oct. At Inverasdale, a few miles up the Cove road.

E Lochside, T01445-741295. Further afield, at Badachro, south of Gairloch on the road to Red Point, is this B&B.

E Mrs A MacIver, T01445-712388, open Feb-Nov. In Charleston, B&B by the harbour.

E Mrs MacDonald, T01445-781354, open Apr-Oct. Further up this road from Bruach Ard, near Cove. B&B.

E Mrs MacIver, T01445-781389, open Apr-Oct. Above Poolewe, reached by a path that leads from the road beside the campsite. B&B.

E-F Duisary, T01445-712252, open Apr-Oct. On the road that turns off to the right by the Millcroft Hotel, beyond the fire station.

F Auchtercairn Hostel, T01445-712131, open Mar-Nov, is at Gairloch Sands Apartments, just before the turn-off to Strath.

F Badachro Bunkhouse, T07760-344008. Also at Badachro, is this cheap bunkhouse.

F Bains House, T01445-712472. On the main street in Strath, near the shops, is this friendly and great value B&B.

F Carn Dearg Youth Hostel, T01445-712219, open 15 May-3 Oct. 3 miles beyond Gairloch, on the road to Melvaig.

F Rubha Reidh Lighthouse, T/F01445-771263, ruareidh@netcomuk.co.uk. 3 miles north of Gairloch, at the end of the road is this comfortable B&B (**D** including dinner) and hostel accommodation. It's best to book ahead in the high season. They also have a tearoom serving home baking, snacks and light lunches; open Easter-Oct Sun, Tue and Thu 1100-1700. Self-catering is also available for private rooms or the hostel. There are buses from Gairloch as far as Melvaig (see below), then it's a 3-mile hike along the road to the lighthouse.

F Sail Mhor Croft Independent Hostel south of Ullapool in Camusnagaul, T01854-633224, sailmhor@btinternet.com. Call before arriving.

There are a couple of campsites: **Gairloch Caravan & Camping Park**, T01445-712373, is at Strath, with full facilities and close to all amenities; **Sands Holiday Centre**, T01445-712152, open Easter-Oct, is at Big Sand, about a mile beyond Strath.

Camping and Caravan Club Site, T01445-781249, is between Poolewe village and Inverewe Garden. An excellent site.

Gruinard Bay Caravan Park, in Laide near Gruinard Bay, T01445-731225, open Apr-Oct.

Badrallach Bothy & Camp Site, T01445-633281. Near Gruinard Ba, this campsite is situated in the tiny, remote hamlet of Badrallach. A few miles east of Dundonnell, take a side road which branches left and runs for 7 miles.

● Eating

Loch Carron and around *p212*
££ Carron Restaurant, T01520-722488. About 5 mins' drive from the village, across the loch on the A890, is this excellent option.

Gairloch and around *p215*
£££ The Creel, Charleston House, Gairloch, T01445-712497, www.charlestonhouse .co.uk. Open Mar-Dec, dinner only. Guesthouse restaurant with a reputation for high quality food, especially the local seafood. Also delicious home-made bread and ice cream. No smoking. Booking is normally essential.

££-£ Badachro Inn, Badachro, T01445-741319, www.badachroinn.com. Good food in this handily-placed hotel on the road to Red Point. Try the local fish and seafood. Nice views from the dining room.

££-£ Inverewe Garden, see Sights, daily 1000-1700. The best place to eat in Poolewe is probably the licensed restaurant here.

££ Scottish Seafood Restaurant, T01445-712137, next to Gairloch filling station, is good for seafood but is unlicensed.

££-£ Myrtle Bank Hotel, see Sleeping, serves very good, expensive, meals, and good value bar lunches.

£ Bridge Cottage Café, left at the turn-off to Cove, Poolewe. If you need to grab a quick snack, or fancy a coffee, try here.

£ Gino's Italian Restaurant at the friendly Millcroft Hotel in Strath, T01445-712376.

£ **Mountain Restaurant**, Strath Sq, Gairloch,
T01445-712316, has a terrace overlooking
Gair Loch. It is run by mountaineers and
offers an interesting menu, as well as
accommodation in several themed rooms.

▲ Activities and tours

Wester Ross *p212*
Climbing and hillwalking
For those who are not experienced
hillwalkers, there's a Ranger Service for
visitors. During Jul and Aug the ranger,
Seamus McNally, takes guided walks up
into the mountains 3 times a week. For more
details call, T01445-791221. A recommended
local mountain guide is **Steve Chadwick**,
T01445-712455. For guided walks around
Lochcarron, contact **Island Horizons**, Kirkton
Rd, T01520-722238.

Fishing
For information on sea angling trips, contact
the chandlery shop at the harbour,
T01445-712458.

Quad biking
For those who prefer dry land, try a quad
bike tour of the Flowerdale Deer Forest with
Highland Trails. Book at The Anchorage
post office/craft shop at the harbour or at
Flowerdale estate office, T01445-712378.

Wildlife cruises
You can take a wildlife-spotting cruise with **Sail
Gairloch**, T01445-712636. The cruise lasts 2 hrs
and leaves daily from Gairloch Pier (subject to
weather conditions). It can be booked at the
Gairloch Marine Life Centre by the pier.

⊖ Transport

Loch Carron and around *p212*
There's a postbus service from **Strathcarron** to
Shieldaig and **Torridon** twice a day Mon-Sat.
It's possible to reach **Applecross** by public
transport, but only just. A postbus service
leaves **Strathcarron** train station daily
(except Sun) at 0955, arriving in **Shieldaig** at
1040. Another postbus then leaves
Shieldaig at 1130 and arrives in Applecross
at 1300, via the beautiful and winding coast
road. No buses run over the Bealach na Ba.
A postbus leaves **Applecross** at 0915 and

arrives in **Shieldaig** at 1010. It continues to
Torridon (see below) and arrives at 1030.
Another postbus leaves **Shieldaig** at 1045
and arrives at **Strathcarron** train station at
1130. There are train connections from
Strathcarron to **Inverness** and **Kyle** (for
times T08457-484950).

Torridon and around *p213*
The postbus from **Applecross** to **Shieldaig**
continues to **Torridon village** (see above).
There's a postbus from **Strathcarron** station
at 0955 which arrives in **Shieldaig** at 1040.
Duncan Maclennan buses, T01520-755239,
have a service which leaves **Strathcarron** at
1230 and arrives in **Torridon** at 1330 (daily
except Sun). There's also a daily (Mon-Sat)
postbus service from **Diabaig** to **Kinlochewe** and **Achnasheen**, via **Torridon**, at 0955.
There are also Duncan Maclennan buses
between **Torridon** and **Shieldaig**
and **Strathcarron**.
For **Loch Maree**, **Kinlochewe** is 9 miles
west of **Achnasheen** rail station which is on
the Inverness-Kyle line. There's a daily
(except Sun) postbus service. There's also a
postbus (Mon-Sat) from **Kinlochewe** to
Torridon and **Diabaig**, and a bus to
Torridon and **Shieldaig**, T01520-755239.
Buses between **Gairloch** and **Inverness** (see
below) stop in **Kinlochewe**.

Gairloch and around *p215*
Boat
The MV Spirit of Skye passenger ferry sails
between **Gairloch** and **Portree** (Skye) twice
daily Apr-Oct, leaving Gairloch at 0930 and
1600, returning to Gairloch at 1300 and
1930, 1½ hrs, £10 each way. It is operated by
West Highland Seaways, T01445-712777,
www.overtheseatoskye.com.

Bus
There's a bus from **Inverness** to **Gairloch**
3 times a week (Mon, Wed and Sat) at 1705
with **Westerbus**, T01445-712255. The return
bus is at 0805. **Westerbus** also have services
to **Kinlochewe** (Mon-Sat, 0730) and to
Mellon Charles/Laide, via **Poolewe**
(Mon-Sat). There's a **Melvaig-Gairloch-Red
Point** postbus service Mon-Sat which leaves
Gairloch at 0820 heading north to **Melvaig**
and leaves Gairloch heading south to **Red
Point** at 1035. On Fri only there's a taxi

service between **Gairloch** and **Melvaig** 1030-1230 (to book T01445-712559).

For **Gruinard Bay**, daily buses go to **Laide** from **Gairloch** with Westerbus, T01445-712255. Some continue to **Mellon Udrigle**.

Buses between **Laide** and **Inverness** 3 times a week (Tue, Thu and Fri), leaving at 0805 and returning at 1705. There are also buses on other days between **Gairloch** and **Inverness** which stop at **Laide** (see above).

Ullapool and around

The attractive little fishing port of Ullapool, on the shores of Loch Broom, is the largest settlement in Wester Ross. The grid-pattern village, created in 1788 at the height of the herring boom by the British Fisheries Society, is still an important fishing centre as well as being the major tourist centre in the northwest of Scotland and one of the main ferry terminals for the Outer Hebrides. At the height of the busy summer season the town is swamped by visitors passing through on their way to or from Stornoway on Lewis, heading north into the wilds, or south to Inverness. It has excellent tourist amenities and services and relatively good transport links, making it the ideal base for those exploring the northwest coast and a good place to be if the weather is bad.

North of Ullapool you enter a different world. The landscape becomes ever more dramatic and unreal – a huge emptiness of bleak moorland punctuated by isolated peaks and shimmering lochs. A narrow and tortuously twisting road winds its way up the coast, past deserted beaches of sparkling white sand washed by turquoise sea. There's not much tourist traffic this far north and once you get off the main road and on to the backroads, you can enjoy the wonderful sensation of having all this astonishingly beautiful scenery to yourself. ‣‣ *For Sleeping, Eating and other listings, see pages 227-231.*

Ins and outs

Getting there and around Ullapool is the mainland terminal for ferries to Stornoway (Lewis). **Scottish Citylink** buses, T08705-505050, to and from Inverness (twice daily Monday to Saturday, just under 1½ hour; £12.10 return) connect with the ferry to and from Stornoway, see page 278. The local **CalMac** office on Shore Street, opposite the pier, T01854-612358, also has details. There are also buses to places further north, and south along the coast. Buses stop at the pier near the ferry dock. ‣‣ *For further details, see Transport page 230.*

Tourist information The **tourist information centre** ① *6 Argyle St, T01854-612135, Easter-Oct daily, Nov-Easter Mon-Fri 1300-1630*, is well run and provides an accommodation booking service as well as information on local walks and trips, and has a good stock of books and maps. To find out what's on locally, tune in to Loch Broom FM (102.2 and 96.8) or pick up a copy of the *Ullapool News* on Fridays.

Ullapool ‣ *Phone code: 01854. Colour map 1, grid B5. Population: 1,800.*

Sights

Ullapool's attractions are very much of the outdoor variety and include the Falls of Measach, Achiltibuie and Stac Pollaidh. However, whist in town it's worth taking a stroll around the harbour to watch the comings and goings of the fishing fleet and you might even see the occasional seal or otter swimming close to the shore. The only real 'sight' as such is the **Ullapool Museum and Visitor Centre** ① *T01854-612987, Apr-Oct Mon-Sat 0930-1730, Jul and Aug also 1930-2130, Nov-Mar 1200-1600, £3, children free*, in a converted church in West Argyle Street. It has some interesting displays on local history, including the story of those who set sail from here in 1773 on board *The Hector*, the first ship to carry emigrants from the Highlands to Nova Scotia in Canada.

There are several good walking trails which start in Ullapool. One of these is to the top of **Ullapool Hill**, or **Meall Mhor** (886 ft). Starting from the tourist office, head to the end of Argyle Street, turn left on to North Road and then cross the road at the Far Isles Restaurant. Walk down the lane between Broom Court and the Hydro sub-station and then follow the path which zigzags up the hillside. There's a good cairned path up to the top of the hill. The views from the top over Glen Achall, and on a clear day, the mountains of Sutherland, are superb. You can return by traversing the hillside to the top of the Braes, or take a track leading to Loch Achall and follow the Ullapool river through the quarry road back to the village. The return trip takes one to two hours.

A relatively easy, but much longer walk, of five to six hours, is to **Rhidorroch Estate**. Take the A835 north out of Ullapool. Opposite the petrol station and before the bridge, take the road on the right signed 'Quarry'. Go through the quarry keeping to the left, and follow the Ullapool river till you see Loch Achall. Continue along the north bank of the loch for another six miles. East Rhidorroch Lodge is on the right; cross the bridge to get there, then skirt the lodge fences and cross to the track which leads up the southwestern hill. This brings you out to Leckmelm, about four miles south of Ullapool on the A835. This last section offers wonderful views across Loch Broom to An Teallach. From Leckmelm you can also climb Beinn Eilideach (1,837 ft).

Ullapool

North & Northwest Ullapool & around

N

| 0 metres | 100 |
| 0 yards | 100 |

Sleeping
Brae Guest House 1
Broomfield
  Holiday Park 2
Ceilidh Place 3

Eilean Donan 4
Ferry Boat Inn 5
Harbour Lights 6
Morefield &
  Mariner's Restaurant 7

Point Cottage
  Guest House 8
Strathmore Guest House 11
SYHA Youth Hostel 9
Ullapool Tourist Hostel 10

Eating
Jade House 1

A good coastal walk is to **Rhue Lighthouse** and back. From the north end of Quay
Street go down the steps to the river. Cross the bridges and head left by the football
field. Follow the path to the left by the duck pond and cross in front of the bungalow.
Then follow the shoreline north for about two miles, climbing up the hillside when the
tide is high. Follow the path till you reach the little white lighthouse at Rhue Point. To
return, take the single-track road out of Rhue back to the main road and up over the
hill to Ullapool. It's about six miles in total.

There are many more strenuous hiking routes around Ullapool. The A835 south of
town gives access to **Beinn Dearg** (3,556 ft) and the **Fannichs**, a range of hills on the
southern side of Dirrie More. There's also **An Teallach**, a favourite with Scottish
climbers, see page 223. North of Ullapool are the mountains within the Inverpolly
National Nature Reserve (see below).

All routes require hillwalking experience and you should be well prepared for the
unpredictable weather conditions. A good guidebook is *The Northern Highlands*,
SMC District Guide, by Tom Strang.➤ *For details of a tour operator offering trips, see page 230.*

South of Ullapool → *Colour map 1, grid B5.*

On the southern shore of Little Loch Broom is the village of **Dundonnell**, from where
there are spectacular views of awesome An Teallach (3,483 ft), a mountain of almost
mythical status amongst Scottish climbers and spoken of in hushed, reverential
tones. The path to the highest of its summits is clear and begins southeast of the
Dundonell Hotel. It will take a full day and you'll need to be well prepared (OS map No
19) and heed the usual advice.

The A832 coastal road meets the A835 Ullapool-Inverness main road at
Braemore junction, 12 miles south of Ullapool. Before heading on to Ullapool it's
worth stopping at the very impressive **Falls of Measach**, just by the junction. The falls
plunge 150 ft into the spectacular **Corrieshalloch Gorge** (or 'ugly/fearsome gorge' in
Gaelic) and can be crossed by a distinctly wobbly suspension bridge (not for vertigo
sufferers). The falls can be reached from the A835, but the most dramatic approach is
from the A832 Gairloch road.

North of Ullapool → *Colour map A5, B5-6.*

The region immediately north of Ullapool is called Assynt, and is heaven for serious
hillwalkers and climbers. Though most are not Munros, and not particularly difficult by
Scottish standards, they can attract some of the worst weather imaginable, even in the
height of summer, see page 56. Amongst the most spectacular of Assynt's distinctive
'island peaks' are Suilven (2,398 ft), Ben More Assynt (3,275 ft), Quinag (2,650 ft) and
Canisp (2,775 ft). Much of this region is protected in the Inverpolly and Inchnadamph
National Nature Reserves, home to an extremely rich and diverse wildlife.

Inverpolly National Nature Reserve → *Phone code: 01854. OS Landranger No 15.*
About 12 miles north of Ullapool on the main A835 is the exceptional **SNH Visitor Centre**
① *T01854-666234, open all year round 24 hours a day*, at Knockan Crag. It's an
interactive display of the geology, flora and fauna of the area. From the visitor centre
there's a marked trail which leads up to the **Crag**, and the views from the clifftop are
excellent, across to Inverpolly's 'island' peaks of Cul Mór, Cul Beag and Stac Pollaidh.

A few miles north of here is the village of **Knockan**. Nearby, at **Elphin**, is the
Highland and Rare Breeds Farm ① *mid-May to end of Sep, 1000-1700*. Beyond Elphin
is **Ledmore**, where the A837 branches east towards Lairg and Bonar Bridge. There's a
good craft shop at Ledmore where you can buy hand-knitted sweaters.

▲ Between Ullapool and Knockan Crag is the turn-off west (left) to the distinctive craggy peak of **Stac Pollaidh**. A path has been established by the John Muir Trust, which takes you on a circular walk around the peak from the car park. Take the right-hand path and go round at the same level, or climb up the rear to the top, go around the summit and descend by the same path. You'll need a head for heights to reach the summit as much of the route is exposed, but the stunning views are worth it. Be careful not to stray from the path; it's been put there because of the damage inflicted by tens of thousands of pairs of boots each year, resulting in serious erosion on the south face. It's a fairly easy 2½-hour walk.

Achiltibuie → Phone code: 01854.

The unclassified single-track road winds its way west past Stac Pollaidh to the turn-off for Achiltibuie. This old crofting village, with whitewashed cottages set back from the sea views across to the beautiful Summer Isles, is home to one of the northwest's main tourist attractions, **Hydroponicum** ① T01854-622202, www.thehydroponicum, Apr-Sep daily 1000-1800, guided tours every hour on the hour, £4.75, concession £3.50, children £2.75. This 'Garden of the Future' is a gigantic greenhouse which is pioneering the system of hydroponics to grow plants from all over the world. Hydroponics uses water instead of soil to carry nutrients to the plants and can be carried out anywhere. Here you can see an incredible variety of subtropical trees, orchids, flowers, vegetables, herbs and fruits. A guided tour takes you through the different climatic zones, and you can taste their produce, including the famous strawberries, in the **Lilypond Café**, which serves meals and snacks.

Another worthwhile attraction is the **Achiltibuie Smokehouse** ① T01854-622353, May-Sep Mon-Sat 0930-1700, free, 5 miles north, at Altandhu. Here you can watch the salmon, herring, trout and other fish being cured before buying some afterwards.

Lochinver and around → Phone code: 01571.

The road from Achiltibuie north to Lochinver is known locally as the 'wee mad road', and you'd be mad to miss this thrilling route which twists and winds its way through some the northwest's most stunning scenery. The village of Lochinver is a working fishing port and the last sizeable village before Thurso. It has a good tourist office, lots of accommodation, a bank with ATM, post office and petrol station.

The best place to start is the **Assynt Visitor Centre** ① T01854-844330, Apr-Oct Mon-Fri 1000-1700 and Sun 1000-1600, which houses the tourist information centre. It has displays on the local geology, history and wildlife and there's also a ranger service with guided walks throughout the summer. Those looking for local souvenirs should head for **Highland Stoneware**, see page 229.

▲▲ A few miles south of Lochinver, beyond Inverkirkaig, is the trail along the river to the **Kirkaig Falls**. The path starts near the **Achins Bookshop**, which has a good stock of Scottish titles and a café. Follow the path for about two miles till it branches right to the falls in the gorge below. Continue along the main path for about another ¾ mile till you reach Fionn Loch, with superb views of mighty Suilven. The walk up to the falls and back should take around 1½ hours. This is one of the main approaches to the foot of the mountain.

Loch Assynt and Inchnadamph → Phone code: 01571.

The area east of Lochinver is a remote wilderness of mountains and moorland dotted with lochs and lochans. As well as being a favourite haunt of hardy climbers and walkers, Assynt is a paradise for anglers. Most of the lochs are teeming with brown trout, and fishing permits are readily available throughout the area from the TIC in Lochinver or at local hotels, guest houses and B&Bs. There's also salmon fishing on the River Kirkaig, available through the **Inver Lodge Hotel** and on Loch Assynt through the **Inchnadamph Hotel**, see Sleeping page 227.

The A837 Lochinver-Lairg road meets the A894 to Durness 10 miles east of Lochinver at Skiag Bridge by Loch Assynt. Half a mile south of here, by the loch, are the ruins of **Ardvreck Castle**. The castle dates from 1597 and was the stronghold of the Macleods of Assynt until a siege of the castle in 1691, when it was taken by the Seaforth Mackenzies. Before that, the Marquis of Montrose had been imprisoned here following his defeat at Carbisdale in 1650. Access to the castle is free, but the ruins are in a dangerous state and should be approached with care.

To the east of the road lies the **Inchnadamph National Nature Reserve**, dominated by the massive peaks of Ben More Assynt and Conival, which should only be attempted by experienced hillwalkers. A few miles south of the village of Inchnadamph, at the fish farm, is a steep, but well-marked footpath up to the **Bone Caves**. This is one of Scotland's oldest historical sites, where the bones of humans and animals such as lynx and bear were found together with sawn-off deer antlers dating from over 8,000 years ago.

Lochinver to Kylesku → *Phone code: 01571.*

The quickest way north from Lochinver is the A837 east to the junction with the A894 which heads to Kylesku. But by far the most scenic route is the B869 coast road that passes moorland, lochs and beautiful sandy bays. It's best travelled from north to south, giving you the most fantastic views of Suilven. Untypically, most of the land in this part of Assynt is owned by local crofters who, under the aegis of the Assynt Crofters' Trust, bought 21,000 acres of the North Assynt Estate, thus setting a precedent for change in the history of land ownership in the Highlands.

The trust now owns the fishing rights to the area and sells permits through local post offices and the tourist office in Lochinver. It has also undertaken a number of conservation projects, including one at **Achmelvich**, a few miles north of Lochinver, at the end of a side road which branches off the coast road. It's worth a detour to see one of the loveliest beaches on the west coast, with sparkling white sand and clear turquoise waters straight out of a Caribbean tourist brochure.

▲ From the beach car park below the hostel a path leads northwest along the coast. Bear left off the sandy path shortly after the white cottage on the hill ahead comes into view, and follow the footpath until the road is reached at Alltan na Bradhan, where there are the remains of an old meal mill. Continue north from here along the coast for about a mile till you reach a small bay just before Clachtoll, the **Split Rock**. Close by are the remains of an Iron-Age Broch, but don't cause further damage by clambering over the ruins. Return to the beach by the same path. The walk there and back should take about 1½ hours.

Old Man of Stoer

▲ A side road turns left off the B869 north of Stoer and runs out to **Stoer lighthouse**. From here you can walk across the Stoer Peninsula to the **Old Man of Stoer**, a dramatic rock pillar standing offshore, surrounded by sheer cliffs. Allow about three hours for the circular walk which starts and ends in the lighthouse car park. There is no public transport to the lighthouse, but the Lochinver-Drumbeg postbus runs to Raffin, one mile away. A clear path runs from the car park to the cliffs then follows the line of the cliffs northwards. The path heads inland for a short distance as it bypasses a deep gully then meets the clifftop again, and after a mile or so you can see the Old Man tucked away in a shallow bay, battered by huge waves. Beyond the Old Man the path continues to the headland, the **Point of Stoer**, from where it turns back on itself and climbs **Sidhean Mór** (532 ft). The views from here are fantastic, across to Harris and Lewis and south to the mountains of Assynt. From here, follow the faint path south, back towards the lighthouse, passing a small loch below Sidhean Beag on your left and an obvious

Remember to check access locally during the deer-stalking season which runs from mid-August to mid-October.

cairn on your right. Then you pass a radio mast and follow the clear track back to the lighthouse car park. OS Landranger Map No 15 covers the route. Nine miles further on, in beautiful **Eddrachillis Bay**, is **Drumbeg**, a popular place for anglers who come to fish in the many lochs of North Assynt.

Kylesku → *Phone code: 01971. Colour map 1, grid B5.*

The road runs east from Drumbeg, under the shadow of towering Quinag (2,654 ft), to meet the A894 heading north to Kylesku, site of the sweeping modern road bridge over Loch a'Cháirn Bháin. From Kylesku you can visit Britain's highest waterfall, the 650-ft high **Eas a'Chùal Aluinn**, near the head of Loch Glencoul. Cruises leave from the old ferry jetty below the **Kylesku Hotel** to the falls, see Activities and tours page 230.

▲ There's also a trail to the top of the falls. It starts at the south end of Loch na Gainmhich, about three miles north of Skiag Bridge. Skirting the loch, follow the track in a southeasterly direction up to the head of the Bealach a Bhuirich (the Roaring Pass). Continue until you meet a stream, with several small lochans on your right. Follow this stream until it plunges over the Cliffs of Dubh (the Dark Cliffs). You can get a better view of the falls by walking to the right about 100 yards and descending a heather slope for a short distance. Allow about three to four hours for the round trip.

Scourie and Handa Island → *Phone code: 01971. Colour map 1, grid A5.*

Ten miles north of Kylesku is the little crofting community of Scourie, sitting above a sandy bay. Anyone remotely interested in wildlife is strongly advised to make a stop here to visit Handa Island, a sea bird reserve run by the Scottish Wildlife Trust, and one of the best places in the country for bird life. The island is now deserted, except for the warden, but once supported a thriving community of crofters, until the potato famine of 1846 forced them to leave, most emigrating to Canada's Cape Breton. Now it's home to huge colonies of shags, fulmars, razorbills, guillemots and puffins, in season. The best time to visit is during the summer breeding season, from late May to August. There's a footpath right round the island, which is detailed in the free SWT leaflet available at the warden's office when you arrive. You should allow three to four hours. There's a ferry service to the island, see Transport page 230.

Another excellent wildlife boat trip leaves from Fanagmore, a mile from Tarbet on the other side of the peninsula, see Activities and tours page 230.

Kinlochbervie and around → *Phone code: 01971. Colour map 1, grid A5.*

The road north from Scourie passes Laxford Bridge, where it meets the A838 running southeast to Lairg, see page 242. The A838 also runs north to Durness, on the north coast (see page 231). At Rhiconich, the B801 branches northwest to Kinlochbervie, a small village with a very big fish market. This is one of the west coast's major fishing ports, and huge container lorries thunder along the narrow single-track roads carrying frozen fish and seafood to all corners of Europe. It's worth heading down to the fish market in the evenings to see the day's catch being landed and sold.

A few miles beyond Kinlochbervie is **Oldshoremore**, a tiny crofters' village scattered around a stunning white beach, and a great place to swim. The less hardy can instead explore the hidden rocky coves nearby.

At the end of the road is **Blairmore**, from where a footpath leads to **Sandwood Bay**, the most wonderful beach on the entire west coast. It's a long walk, but because of its isolation you'll probably have this glorious mile-long stretch of white sand all to yourself. The beach is flanked at one end by a spectacular rock pinnacle and is said to be haunted by the ghost of an ancient shipwrecked mariner. Allow three hours for the walk there and back, plus time at the beach. You could take a tent and watch the sunset. Sandwood Bay can also be reached from Cape Wrath, a day's hike to the north, see page 232.

🚌 Sleeping

Ullapool *p221, map p222*

There is no shortage of places to stay in Ullapool ranging from one of the very finest hotels in the UK to numerous guest houses and B&Bs, a couple of good youth hostels and a campsite. Garve Rd, heading south out of town, has several guest houses, and there are lots of B&Bs along Seaforth Rd and Pulteney St. Unfortunately the famous **Altnaharrie Inn** has closed though the ferry from Ullapool to the other side of Loch Broom is running; for details T01854-612656.

A Tanglewood House, T01854-612059, www.tanglewoodhouse.co.uk. 3 rooms. Chalet-style house overlooking Loch Broom. Part of the Wolsey Lodge scheme so you dine with the hostess, Anne Holloway, who offers superb cooking in a civilized atmosphere. Wonderful views across the loch.

B The Ceilidh Place, 14 West Argyle Pl, T01854-612103, www.theceilidhplace.com. 23 rooms. This former boat-shed has grown over the years to become one of the most refreshingly different hotels in the country, with comfortable bedrooms, cosy lounge, bookshop, restaurant, bar and coffee shop. They also host a varied programme of arts events such as live music, plays, poetry readings, exhibitions and ceilidhs (see below); a great place to relax and soak up some local culture. Across the road is their clubhouse, with basic but comfortable dorms (**E-F**).

C-D Harbour Lights Hotel, Garve Rd (on the left, heading into Ullapool on the A835), T01854-612222, harbour-lights.co.uk. 22 rooms, 1 Mar-31 Oct. Modern hotel offering good service and very good food available all day (**££**).

C-D Morefield Hotel, North Rd, T01854-612161. Open May-Oct. On the edge of town heading north, in the middle of a housing estate, motel-style accommodation and a superb seafood restaurant, see Eating below.

D Ferry Boat Inn, Shore St, T01854-612366, www.ferryboat-inn.com. On the lochside, decent accommodation and food and the best pub in town.

D Point Cottage Guest House, 22 West Shore St, T01854-612494, www.pointcott age.co.uk. Lovely old fishing cottage at the quieter end of the loch-front.

E Brae Guest House, Shore St, T01854-612421. 8 rooms, open May-Oct. Comfortable guest house on the loch-front.

E Eilean Donan Hotel, 14 Market St, T01854-612524. Friendly and central.

E Strathmore House, Strathmore, Morefield, 1 mile north of town, T01854-612423, murdo @strathmore.fsnet.co.uk. Open Apr-Oct. Friendly, comfortable and good value.

F SYHA youth hostel on Shore St, T01854-612254, open Mar-Dec, is very good. You can pick up some information on local walks, also bike hire, internet and laundry facilities.

F Ullapool Tourist Hostel, West House, West Argyle St, T01854-613126, open all year. This independent hostel has the full range of facilities, including free internet for guests, hires mountain bikes and runs local bus tours.

Camping

Broomfield Holiday Park, T01854-6120020, on Shore St at the west end of the village, the only campsite, has great views across to the Summer Isles and a laundrette on site. It's open Easter-Sep.

South of Ullapool *p223*

B Dundonnell Hotel, south of Ullapool, T01854-633204, selbie@dundonnellhotel. co.uk, open Feb-Dec, good meals (**£££-££**).

E Mrs Ross, T01854-633237, south of Ullapool in Camusnagaul, a few miles back up the loch. B&B.

Achiltibuie *p224*

L Summer Isles Hotel, near the Hydroponicum, T01854-622282, www.summerisleshotel.com. Open Easter to mid Oct. This relaxing, civilized hotel enjoys magnificent views across to the Summer Isles. Mark and Geraldine Irvine also boast a Michelin-starred restaurant serving some of the best seafood on the planet. Dinner will set you back around £40 a head but you can enjoy delicious bar lunches for a fraction of the price. Even if you're not staying or eating here, it's worth stopping to have a drink on

---

🔴 *For an explanation of sleeping and eating price codes used in this guide, see inside the*
⚫ *front cover. Other relevant information is found in Essentials, see pages 41-49.*

the terrace and watch the sun set over the islands.

ECulross, T01854-622426, 2 rooms, a vegetarian B&B run by Mary King, who also runs the **Picture Shack**, a gallery featuring highland landscapes. The best bet for an option in the lower ranges.

FSYHA Youth Hostel, a few miles south at Achininver, T01854-622254, open mid-May to early Oct. Basic and very cheap.

Lochinver and around *p222*
LInver Lodge Hotel, Iolaire Rd, T01571-844496, stay@inverlodge.com. 20 rooms, open Apr-Oct. A modern luxury hotel standing above the village with great views and excellent restaurant (**£££-££**).

LThe Albannach Hotel, Baddidaroch, T01571-844407, F844285. This wonderful 18th-century house overlooking Loch Inver is one of the very best places to stay in the northwest, and the food offered in the award-winning restaurant is sublime. The price includes dinner. Non-residents are also welcome but booking is essential.

EArdglas Guest House, T01571-844257, ardglass@btinternet.com. Comfortable.

EPolcraig, T01571-844429, cathelmac@ aol.com. Clean and friendly.

ETigh-Na-Sith, T01571-844740, Apr-Sep. A comfortable choice.

Loch Assynt and Inchnadamph *p224*
CInchnadamph Hotel, T01571-822202, www.inchnadamphhotel. co.uk. An old-fashioned Highland hotel on the shores of Loch Assynt, catering for the hunting and fishing fraternity, see p224.

FInchnadamph Lodge, T01571-822218, assynt@presence.co.uk, or Assynt Field Centre, offers basic hostel accommodation in bunk rooms, as well as twin, double and family rooms. Continental breakfast is included. It's open all year, but phone ahead Nov-Mar. It's ideally situated for climbing Ben More Assynt and guides are available.

Lochinver to Kylesku *p225*
There's not much accommodation around here other than self-catering cottages.
Camping
Shore Caravan Site, T01571-844393, open Apr-Sep.

Kylesku *p226*
BKylesku Hotel, T01971-502231, kyleskuhotel @lycos.co.uk. Mar-Oct. Comfortable rooms and renowned for its delicious and great-value pub seafood. There's also a more formal and expensive restaurant next door.

DNewton Lodge, T/F01971-502070, newtonlge@aol.com, mid-Mar to mid-Oct. Non-smoking hotel with great views.

FKylesku Lodges, T01971-502003, open Easter-Oct. A small hostel.

Scourie and Handa Island *p226*
There are lots of options in this area.
CEddrachilles Hotel, Badcall Bay, T01971-502080, www.eddrachilles.com. Mar-Oct. 11 rooms, this is one of the most magnificently situated hotels in the country. The 200 year-old building stands in 300 acres of grounds overlooking the bay, the food on offer is superb, though the atmosphere is a little stuffy (their Eddrachilles heel, you might say).

BScourie Hotel, T01971-502396, www.scourie-hotel.co.uk, open Apr-Oct. 17th-century former coaching inn popular with anglers. Also an excellent place to eat (lunch **££** dinner **£££**).

CScourie Lodge, T01971-502248, open Mar-Oct. There are several B&Bs in the village, but none better than this welcoming lodge. Also does good evening meals.

Camping
A campsite, T01971-502060, Harbour Rd.

Kinlochbervie and around *p226*
BThe Kinlochbervie Hotel, T01971-521275, F521438, www.kinlochberviehotel.com. In Kinlochbervie village, a decent hotel.

CRhiconich Hotel, Rhiconich, T01971-521224, www.rhiconichhotel.com. 10 en suite rooms. Modern functional hotel with good facilities and surrounded by superb scenery. **B**for half board.

DOld School Hotel, halfway between Kinlochbervie and the A838 at Rhiconich, T/F01971-521383, www.host.co.uk. This is the best place to stay. It used to be a school, as the name implies, and this only adds to the charm. They also serve great food (**££**) daily 1200-1400 and 1800-2000.

EBenview, T01971-521242, open Apr-Sep. A friendly B&B.

Camping
There's a good campsite at Oldshoremore, T01971-521281.

● Eating

Ullapool *p221, map p222*
££ Mariner's Restaurant, Morefield Hotel, see Sleeping. The setting may be a little incongruous but there's nothing wrong with the food. The seafood is sensational, which is why people travel from miles around and it's always busy. Excellent value.
££ The Ceilidh Place, see Bars and clubs, is one of those places that tourists seem to hang around for hours or even days. It exudes a laid-back, cultured ambience. The self-service coffee shop does cheap wholefood all day during the summer, while the restaurant serves more expensive full meals, with an emphasis on vegetarian and seafood at night. There's even outdoor seating. Open 1100-2300. Also live music and various other events, see Bars and clubs.
££ Jade House, beside Safeway, Latheron La, good Chinese food at reasonable prices.
£ Ferry Boat Inn, the **Seaforth Inn** and the **Arch Inn**, see Bars and clubs, for cheap pub food at lunchtime and early evening.
£ Mountain Man supplies, see Shopping, has a good coffee shop above the shop. Serves snacks and light meals.
£ Ullapool Catering, T01854-612969, make up great picnics from local organic produce at good value prices.
£ There's a good 'chippie' on West Shore St.

Lochinver and around *p224*
££ Lochinver's Larder Riverside Bistro, T01571-844356, on the way into town on the A837. Apart from the hotels listed above, the best food is here. Eat in or takeaway.
£ Caberfeidh, T01571-844321. Near to the bistro, this option is the cheap and cheerful

Scourie and Handa Island *p226*
££ Seafood Restaurant, just above the jetty at Tarbet. Run by Julian Pearce, who also runs **Laxford Cruise**, see Activities and tours. If you're up this way, don't miss a visit to this restaurant which serves seafood caught by Julian during his boat trips. It's a great place and you can stay here, in the self-catering caravan next door, which sleeps up to six.

● Bars and clubs

Ullapool *p221, map p222*
Arch Inn, Shore St, is good place for a drink.
The Ceilidh Place, see Sleeping, for something a wee bit more sedate and civilized than the other choices, head here where you can enjoy a quiet drink in the cosy **Parlour Bar** or take advantage of their varied programme of events. There's live music nightly (except Sun) throughout the summer and on a Mon in winter, also ceilidhs and poetry readings. The clubhouse opposite stages plays.
Ferry Boat Inn (or 'FBI' as it's known locally), on Shore St. Is Ullapool's favourite pub. It has a Thu night live music session year round and during the summer you can sit outside on the sea wall and watch the sun go down as you drain your glass
Seaforth Inn, Quay St, has live music on a Fri night, which has been described by one local as 'raucous'.

● Shopping

Ullapool *p221, map p222*
The town is well supplied with shops.
The Captain's Cabin, on the corner of Quay St and Shore St, also sells books, as well as crafts and souvenirs.
The Ceilidh Place, see Bars and clubs, has the best bookshop in the northwest.
Highland Stoneware, T01854-612980, on Mill St, heading north towards Morefield. Look no further than here for pottery. You can wander round the studios before browsing in their gift shop, which is pricey but you may have luck in their bargain baskets. They also have a factory in Lochinver, T01854-844376, www.highland trail.co.uk/stoneware, Mon-Fri 0900-1800 (Easter-Oct also Sat 0900-1700), a local pottery factory just outside the village of Lochinver. See p224.
Knockan Studio, opposite the TIC on Argyle St, T01854-613365, open Mar-Oct, Mon-Sat 0900-1800, is an excellent jewellers.
Mountain Man Supplies, opposite the museum on West Argyle St, is a good outdoor equipment shop.

▲ Activities and tours

Ullapool *p221, map p222*
During the summer the *MV Summer Queen* runs 4-hr cruises to the Summer Isles, with a 45-min landing on Tanera Mór. These leave Mon-Sat at 1000 from the pier and cost £14 per person. There are also 2-hr wildlife cruises around Loch Broom, Annat Bay and Isle Martin, which leave daily at 1415 and also on Sun at 1100, and cost £8 per person. Cruises can be booked at the booth by the pier or by calling, T01854-612472. Walking tours around Ullapool and throughout the Northwest Highlands can be arranged daily with **Northwest Frontiers**, NWF@compuserve.com, ourworld. compuserve.com/homepages/NWF, T01854-612628, with the very experienced Andy Cunningham, and **Celtic Horizons**, T01854-612429.

Achiltibuie *p224*
I Macleod, Achiltibuie Post Office, T01854-622200, or at home, T018754-622315, for cruises to the Summer Isles from Achiltibuie pier on board the *Hectoria*. Cruises leave Mon-Sat at 1030 and 1415 and last 3½ hrs, with 1 hr ashore on the islands. They cost £12 per person (half price for children). There are also deep-sea angling trips (1800-2100).

Kylesku *p226*
On board the *MV Statesman*, T01571-844446, cruises go to Eas a'Chùal Aluinn waterfall leaving from the old ferry jetty below the **Kylesku Hotel**. You can also see porpoises, seals and minke whales en route. The 2-hr round trip runs Apr-Sep daily at 1100 and 1400 (Jul and Aug also at 1600), and costs £9, children £3. You may be able to get closer to the falls by getting off the boat and walking to the bottom, then getting on the next boat.

Scourie and Handa Island *p226*
Laxford Cruises, T01971-502251, sail around beautiful Loch Laxford, where you can see lots of birds from nearby Handa Island, as well as seals, porpoises and otters. Trips leave Easter till the end of Sep daily except Sun at 1000, 1200 and 1400 (also at 1600 in Jul and Aug). The trips last 1¾ hrs and cost £10 for adults, £5 for children. For bookings contact Julian Pearce, who also runs the wonderful **Seafood Restaurant**, see Eating, just above the jetty at Tarbet.

⊖ Transport

Ullapool *p221, map p222*
Scottish Citylink buses run 2-3 times daily (except Sun) between Ullapool and **Inverness**, connecting with the ferry to **Stornoway**. There are also buses daily (except Sun) to and from **Inverness** with **Rapson's Coaches**, T01463-710555, and **Spa Coaches**, T01997-421311. There's a service to **Lochinver** (1-2 times daily except Sun, 1 hr) with **Spa Coaches** and **Rapson's of Brora**, T01408-621245, and to **Achilitibuie** (twice daily Mon-Thu, once on Sat, 1 hr) with **Spa Coaches**. There's also a daily bus to and from **Gairloch**, which continues to **Inverness**, during the summer only.
  Car hire from **Daley's Deals**, Morefield Industrial Estate, T01854-612848. Cycle hire at the hostels, (see Sleeping p227.

Achiltibuie *p224*
There are 2 buses daily (Mon-Thu) to **Ullapool** with **Spa Coaches**, T01997-421311, leaving Achiltibuie Post Office at 0800 and 1300. The early bus starts in Reiff (at 0740) and the other one leaves from Badenscallie. The journey takes an hour. There's also a bus on Sat, leaving at 0750.

Lochinver and around *p224*
There's a postbus service from **Lochinver** to and from **Drumbeg**, via the coast road, which continues to **Lairg**. It runs once a day, Mon-Sat. There are also buses to and from **Drumbeg** and on to **Ullapool**, once or twice daily except Sun, with **Rapsons of Brora**, T01408-621245, and **Spa Coaches**, T01997-421311.

Scourie and Handa Island *p226*
There's a postbus service to Scourie from **Durness** and **Lairg** once a day, Mon-Sat. It leaves Durness at 0820 and arrives at 0935 and continues to Lairg. It returns at 1245 and arrives at 1420. There's also a postbus service between Scourie and **Elphin**, with connections to **Lochinver**. There's a ferry

service to Handa Island from **Tarbet Beach**, 3 miles northwest off the A894, about three miles north of Scourie. It sails continuously, depending on demand, Apr-Sep Mon-Sat 0930-1700. The 15-min crossing costs £7.50 return, T01971-502077.

Kinlochbervie and around *p226*
A postbus leaves Kinlochbervie harbour at 0900 and goes to **Scourie** (35 mins) and on to Lairg (1 hr 50 mins) from where there are

connections to Inverness. The same postbus returns from **Lairg** at 1245, arrives in Kinlochbervie at 1448, then continues to **Durness** (35 mins).

❶ Directory

Ullapool *p221, map p222*
Bank Royal Bank of Scotland on Ladysmith St, and **Bank of Scotland** with ATM, on West Argyle St.

North coast

Scotland's rugged north coast attracts few visitors, but those who do venture this far find that's there's plenty to write home about. This is some of Britain's most spectacular and undisturbed coastline from the wild and remote Cape Wrath in the far northwest to John O'Groats, that perennial favourite of sponsored walkers, in the far northeast. In between lie over 100 miles of storm-lashed cliffs, sheer rocky headlands and deserted sandy coves, all waiting to be explored. It's also a great place for birdwatching, with vast colonies of seabirds, and there's a good chance of seeing seals, porpoises and minke whales in the more sheltered estuaries. ▸▸ *For Sleeping, Eating and other listings, see pages 235-237.*

Ins and outs

Getting there and around
Getting around the far north without your own transport can be a slow process. Getting to Thurso, the main town, by bus or train is easy, but beyond that things get more difficult. ▸▸ *For further details, see Transport page 236.*

Tourist information
Durness TIC ① *T01971-511259, Apr-Oct Mon-Sat, daily Jul and Aug*, arranges guided walks and has a small visitor centre with displays on local history, flora and fauna and geology. The **Thurso tourist information centre** ① *Riverside Rd, T01847-892371, Apr-Oct Mon-Sat 0900-1800, Jul and Aug also Sun 1000-1800*, has a leaflet on local surfing beaches.

Durness and around → *Phone code: 01971. Colour map 1, grid A5.*

Durness is not only the most northwesterly village on the British mainland, but also one of the most attractively located, surrounded by sheltered coves of sparkling white sand and machair-covered limestone cliffs. It's worth stopping here for a few days to explore the surrounding area.

Smoo Cave
A mile east of the village is the vast 200 ft-long Smoo Cave. A path from near the youth hostel leads down to the cave entrance which is hidden away at the end of a steep, narrow inlet. Plunging through the roof of the cathedral-like cavern is an 80-ft waterfall which can be seen from the entrance, but the more adventurous can take a boat trip into the floodlit interior.

A few miles east of the Smoo Cave are a couple of excellent beaches, at **Sangobeg** and **Rispond**, where the road leaves the coast and heads south along the west shore of stunning **Loch Eriboll**.

Balnakeil

About a mile northwest of Durness is the tiny hamlet of Balnakeil, overlooked by a ruined 17th-century church. In the south wall is a graveslab with carved skull-and-crossbones marking the grave of the notorious highwayman Donald MacMurchow. If you're looking for souvenirs, or an escape from the rat race, then head for the **Balnakeil Craft Village** ① *Apr-Oct daily 1000-1800*, an alternative artists' community set up in the 1960s in a former RAF radar station. Here you can buy weavings, pottery, paintings, leatherwork and woodwork in the little prefab huts. There's also a café. Balnakeil has also become well-known in golfing circles. The nine-hole course, T511364, is the most northerly in mainland Britain, and its famous ninth hole involves a drive over the Atlantic Ocean. The beach here is glorious, especially in fine weather when the sea turns a brilliant shade of turquoise. Even better, walk north along the bay to **Faraid Head**, where you can see puffin colonies in early summer. The views from here, across to Cape Wrath in the west and Loch Eriboll in the east, are stupendous.

Cape Wrath

There are several excellent trips around Durness, but the most spectacular is to Cape Wrath, Britain's most northwesterly point. It's a wild place and the name seems entirely appropriate, though it actually derives from the Norse word *hwarf*, meaning 'turning place'. Viking ships used it as a navigation point during their raids on the Scottish west coast. Now a lighthouse stands on the cape, above the 1,000 ft-high Clo Mor Cliffs, the highest on the mainland, and breeding ground for huge colonies of seabirds.

▲You can walk south from here to **Sandwood Bay**, see page 226. It's an exhilarating but long coastal walk, and will take around eight hours. It's safer doing this walk from north to south as the area around the headland is a military firing range and access may be restricted, which could leave you stranded.

Tongue to Thurso → *Phone code: 01847-01641. Colour map 2, grid A1-2.*

The road east from Durness runs around Loch Eriboll on its way to the lovely little village of **Tongue**. A causeway runs across the beautiful Kyle of Tongue, but a much more scenic route is the single-track road around its southern side, with great views of Ben Hope (3,041 ft) looming to the southwest. The village of Tongue is overlooked by the 14th-century ruins of **Varick Castle**, and there's a great beach at **Coldbackie**, two miles northeast.

The A836 runs south from Tongue through Altnaharra to Lairg, see page 242. It also continues east to the crofting community of **Bettyhill**, named after the Countess of Sutherland who ruthlessly evicted her tenants from their homes in Strathnaver to make way for more profitable sheep. The whole sorry saga is told in the interesting **Strathnaver Museum** ① *T01641-521418, Apr-Oct Mon-Sat 1000-1300 and 1400-1700, £1.90, concession £1.20, children £0.50*, housed in an old church in the village. There are also Pictish stones in the churchyard behind the museum.

The museum sells a leaflet detailing the many prehistoric sites in the Strathnaver Valley which runs due south from Bettyhill. There are a couple of great beaches around Bettyhill, at **Farr Bay** and at **Torrisdale Bay**, which is the more impressive of the two and forms part of the **Invernaver Nature Reserve**. There's a small tourist information centre in Bettyhill ① *T01641-521342, Easter-Sep Mon-Sat*.

● Loch Eriboll, Britain's deepest sea loch, was used by the Royal Navy during the Second
● World War as a base for protecting Russian convoys.

East from Bettyhill the hills of Sutherland begin to give way to the fields of Caithness. The road passes the turn-off to Strathy Point before reaching **Melvich**, another wee crofting settlement overlooking a lovely sandy bay.

South from Melvich the A897 heads to Helmsdale, see page 242, through the **Flow Country**, a vast expanse of bleak bog of major ecological importance. About 15 miles south of Melvich at Forsinard is an **RSPB Visitor Centre** ① *T01641-571225, Easter-Oct daily 0900-1800*, guided walks through the nature reserve leave from the visitor centre. The peatlands here are a breeding ground for black- and red-throated divers, golden plovers and merlins as well as other species. Otters and roe deer can also be spotted.

Thurso and around

Thurso is the most northerly town on the British mainland and by far the largest settlement on the north coast. In medieval times it was Scotland's chief port for trade with Scandinavia, though most of the town dates from the late 18th century when Sir John Sinclair built the 'new' extension to the old fishing port. The town increased in size to accommodate the workforce of the new nuclear power plant at nearby Dounreay, but the plant's demise has threatened the local economy. Today Thurso is a fairly nondescript place, mostly visited by people catching the ferry to Stromness in Orkney, or the occasional hardcore surfer.

Thurso

Sleeping ⬤	Sandra's Backpackers 4	Eating ❶
Murray House 1	Thurso Youth	Johnston's 1
Royal 2	Club Hostel 3	Pentland Hotel 2

0 metres 100
0 yards 100

Thurso → *Phone code: 01847. Colour map 2, grid A3. Population: 9,000.*

There's little of real interest in the town centre. Near the harbour are the 17th-century ruins of **Old St Peter's Church**, which stand on the site of the original 13th-century church founded by the Bishop of Caithness. In the town hall on the High Street is the **Heritage Museum** ① *T01847-892459, Jun-Sep Mon-Sat 1000-1300 and 1400-1700, £0.50*, which features some Pictish carved stones. There may little in the way of activity in the town, but 10 miles west of Thurso you might say there's plenty of radioactivity at the **Dounreay Nuclear Power Station**. Though its fast breeder reactors were decommissioned in 1994, the plant is still a major local employer and now reprocesses spent nuclear fuel. There's a permanent exhibition at the visitor centre ① *T01847-802572, Easter-Sep daily 1000-1700, free*, where you learn all about the 'benefits' of nuclear power.

▲ Strathmore to Braemore → *OS sheet No 11 covers the route.*

This walk gives a flavour of the bleak but beautiful landscape of the Caithness hinterland. The 16-mile linear route starts from **Strathmore Lodge**. To get there, head south from Thurso on the B874. After a short distance turn on to the B870 and follow it for 10 miles to the little hamlet of Westerdale, which stands on the River Thurso. Turn right here on to an unnumbered road and follow this road for about five miles. Just past the white **Strathmore Lodge** the road splits. Follow the right-hand track which runs through commercial forestry, before emerging on to open moor with Loch More on the left.

Where the forestry begins again on the right, the track swings left across an arm of the loch and heads southwards. At the southern end of the loch a track runs left to **Dalnaha**, but keep going straight ahead, along the valley of the River Thurso. You then reach a cluster of buildings at **Dalnawillan Lodge**. Ignore the track which heads off to the right and carry straight on, past the house at **Dalganachan**, over Rumsdale Water and on to the junction before **The Glutt**, which is a series of buildings. Turn left here and follow the track for a further four miles till you reach the junction beside Lochan nan Bò Riabach. Continue down the valley of Berriedale Water to Braemore. There is no public transport from here, so you'll have to arrange your own transport if you don't want to retrace your steps.

Dunnet Head → *Phone code: 01847. Colour map 2, grid A3-4.*

About 10 miles northeast of Thurso is the most northerly point on the British mainland. No, not John O'Groats, but Dunnet Head. It's reached by turning off the Thurso-John O'Groats road at Dunnett, at the east end of Dunnett Bay, a three-mile-long sandy beach that's popular with surfers who come to tackle the gigantic waves of the Pentland Firth, the wild and treacherous strait between the mainland and Orkney. Dunnet Bay has an excellent reef break and there's another good reef break, at Brims Ness to the west. Further west, at Strathy Bay you'll find rollers that can match anything in Hawaii (though the water's a lot colder). Dunnett Head is a much nicer place than John O'Groats, with marvellous views across to Orkney and along the entire north coast (on a clear day). There's a Victorian lighthouse out at the point, and the dramatic seacliffs are teeming with seabirds. There's also a great little café, see Eating page 236.

The area's newest attraction are the **Castle and Gardens of Mey** ① *T01847-851473, www.castleofmey.org.uk, mid May-end Sep (closed from 29 Jul-11 Aug) Tue-Fri 1100-1630, Sun 1400-1700, £7, concessions £6, children £3, under 12 free, family £18, 15 miles east of Thurso*. This was the holiday home of the late Queen Mother and Prince Charles still holidays here each summer.

If you still feel inclined to visit this dreary tourist trap, then that's your prerogative, but don't say we didn't warn you. It's boring at best and pretty miserable most of the time. It gets its name from the Dutchman Jan de Groot, who was commissioned by King James IV to run a ferry service to Orkney in 1496. Ferries still operate from here to Burwick in Orkney, see Transport page 236. There's a **tourist information centre** ① *To1955-611373, Apr-Oct Mon-Sat*, as well as a post office, craft shops and a chippie.

Two miles east of John O'Groats is **Duncansby Head**, which is far more rewarding. South of the headland a path leads to the spectacular **Duncansby Stacks**, a series of dramatic rock formations. The 200-ft cliffs are home to countless seabirds and you can see the narrow, sheer-sided inlets known locally as geos.

● Sleeping

Durness and around *p231*
B-CPort-Na-Con Guest House, T01971-511367, www.portnacon.info, on the west shore of Loch Eriboll, 7 miles from Durness. This has to be the best value around Durness. It's popular with anglers and divers so you'll need to book ahead to take advantage of such comfort amidst all this great scenery. The food in the adjoining restaurant is superb and also great value, especially the seafood. Non-residents are welcome but should book.
B-CTongue Hotel, Tongue, T01847-611206, is a former hunting lodge of the Duke of Sutherland. It overlooks the Kyle of Tongue and does good food.
CBen Loyal Hotel, Tongue, T01847-611216, benloyalhotel@htinternet.com, is also recommended for its food.
CMackays Rooms & Restaurant, Durness, T01971- 511202, www.visitmackays.com. Open Mar-Nov. 6 en suite rooms. Good quality accommodation.
DBighouse Lodge, Melvich, T01641-531207, open May-Oct. 18th-century mansion sitting at the mouth of the Halladale river in 4 acres of its own grounds.
ECloisters, Talmine, T01847-601286, www.cloisteral.demon.co.uk, is a lovely 19th-century converted church.
EFarr Bay Inn, Bettyhill, T01641-521230, www.bettyhill.com, decent bar food too.
EPuffin Cottage, Durness, T01971-511208, www.puffincottage.com, open Apr-Sep. Best of the B&Bs in Durness.
ERhian Cottage, Tongue, T01847-611257, jenny.anderson@tesco.net. Excellent value.
EShieling Guest House, Melvich, T/F01641-531256, theshieling@btinternet .com, open Apr-Oct. Recommended.

FBruachmor, Bettyhill, T01641-521265, open Apr-Oct. A good value B&B.
FSYHA Youth Hostel, at Smoo, to the east of the village, T01971-511244; open mid-Mar to early Oct. Basic.
FSYHA Youth Hostel, Tongue, T01847-611301, open mid-Mar to late Oct, beautifully situated at the east end of the causeway.

Camping
Kincraig Camping and Caravan Site, Tongue, T01847-611218, just to the south of the village.
Salgo Sands Caravan Park, T01971-511222, caravans and camping.
Talmine, T01847-601225, 5 miles north of Tongue by the beach.

Thurso and around *p233, map p233*
Thurso has a wide variety of accommodation, most of it fairly average.
AForss Country House Hotel, 4 miles out of Thurso at Bridge of Forss, T01847-861201, www.forsshousehotel.co.uk. The nicest place to stay by far. Price includes dinner. This small family-run hotel is set in 20 acres of lovely woodland and has an excellent restaurant, open to non-residents (**£££**).
BRoyal Hotel, Traill St, Thurso, T01847-893191, www.british-trusthotels.com. 102 rooms. Central, well-appointed rooms but often fully booked with bus tours.
CPark Hotel, at the south end of town, 10 mins walk from train station. T01847-893251, www.parkhotelthurso.co.uk. 11 rooms. Modern and rather functional building but clean, comfortable and friendly with good food at reasonable prices.
EAnnandale, 2 Rendel Govan Rd, Thurso, T01847-893942, thomson@annandale2.

freeserve.co.uk. 3 rooms. Open all year. Good value B&B.

E Bencorragh House, Upper Gills in Canisbay, a few miles west of John O'Groats, T01955-611449, www.bencorraghhouse. com, open Mar-Oct. A very decent B&B.

E Murray House, 1 Campbell St, Thurso, T01847-895759, www.murrayhousebb. com. 4 rooms. Open all year. Dinner B&B also available (**C**).

F SYHA Youth Hostel, John O'Groats, T01955-611424, open 19 Mar-31 Oct.

F Sandra's Backpackers, 24-26 Princes St, Thurso, T01847-894575, www.sandras-back packers@ukf.net. A decent hostel.

F Thurso Youth Club Hostel, Old Mill, Millbank, Thurso, T/F01847-892964, www. tyc-hostel.com, open 1 Jul-30 Aug.

Camping

Thurso Camping Site, T01847-607771, north of town on the road to Scrabster is the nearest to Thurso. There are a couple of campsites, John O'Groats and further west by the beach at Huna. Ask at the TIC.

✿ Eating

Durness and around *p231*
See Sleeping for options.

Thurso and around *p233, map p233*
£££ The Bower Inn, T01955-661292, between Thurso and Wick. This comes a close second to the hotel. To get there, turn off the coast road at Castletown and follow the B876 till you see the sign for Gillock.

£££ Forss Country House Hotel, see Sleeping, is the best place to eat in the area.

££ The Upper Deck, Scrabster, T01847-892814, by the harbour. A surf'n'turf menu.

£ Dunnett Head Tearoom, Dunnett Head, T01847-851774, open Apr-Oct daily 1500-2000, a few miles from the lighthouse, which serves snacks and meals.

£ Johnston's, Traill St, Thurso, a decent café.

£ Pentland Hotel, Thurso, T01847-893202. Does a decent bar meal.

£ There are also the ubiquitous Indian and Chinese restaurants and fish and chip shops in Thurso.

✿ Entertainment

Thurso and around *p233, map p233*
Bowling Viking Bowl, Ormlie Rd, T01847-895050.
Cinema At Viking Bowl, see above.

▲ Activities and tours

Thurso and around *p233, map p233*
John O'Groats Ferries, Ferry Office, John O'Groats, T01955-611353, www.jogferry. co.uk, operate **Orkney Islands Day Tours**, which leave daily 1 May-30 Sep at 0900, and return at 1945 (£35, children £17.50, under 5 free). A shorter day tour goes daily from 1 Jun-2 Sep 1030, and returns at 1800 (£32, children £16). There's also a wildlife cruise 20 Jun-31 Aug, which departs at 1430, £14, children £7.

✿ Transport

Durness and around *p231*
A daily bus runs to and from **Thurso**, via **Tongue** and **Bettyhill** (Jun-Aug, Mon-Sat) with **Highland Country Buses**, T01847-893123, leaving Thurso at 1130 and Durness at 1500. There's also a daily bus service (May to early Oct) to and from **Inverness** via **Ullapool** and **Lochinver**, with Bluebird/Inverness Traction, T01463-239292. There's a postbus service to **Lairg** via **Tongue** and **Altnaharra**, Mon-Sat at 1115; also via **Kinlochbervie** and **Scourie** Mon-Sat at 0820.

To get to **Cape Wrath**, first take the passenger ferry across the Kyle of Durness from Keoldale, 3 miles south of Durness, T01971-511376. It runs May-Sep hourly 0930-1630. The ferry connects with a minibus, T01971-511287, for the 11 miles to the cape (40 mins).

Thurso and around *p233, map p233*
Boat Northlink Ferries, www.northlink ferries.co.uk, to **Stromness** in **Orkney** leave from **Scrabster**, 2 miles north of Thurso. For details, see p312). **John O'Groats Ferries** (see above for details) sail to **Burwick** (Orkney) twice daily from Jun to Sep (45 mins, £16 one way). A connecting bus takes pass- engers on to **Kirkwall** (40 mins, price incl in ferry ticket).
Bus Citylink buses run to and from **Inverness** (3½ hrs) 4 times daily, T0870-

5505050, continuing to **Scrabster** to connect with the ferries to and from **Stromness** in **Orkney**. Citylink buses to **Inverness** connect with buses to **Edinburgh**. Highland Country Buses, T01847-893123, run local services to **Bettyhill** (3 times daily Mon-Thu, twice on Sat; 1 hr 10 mins) and to **Reay** (4 times daily Mon-Thu, 3 times on Sat). There are regular daily buses to and from **Wick** via **Halkirk** or **Castletown**. Highland Country Buses also run the service between Thurso train station and **Scrabster** ferry pier (5-10 mins). **Harrold Coaches**, T01955- 631295, run a service to and from **John O'Groats** (4 times daily Mon-Thu, twice on Sat; 1 hr). Also from **Wick** (5 daily Mon-Fri, 4 on Sat) with **Highland**

Country Buses. There's also a **postbus** service to Wick airport, leaving Riverside Rd at 0920 and arriving at 1000. Buses arrive at Sir George's St Port Office and depart from Sir George's St Church.

Car hire William Dunnett & Co, T01847-893101.

Cycle hire The Bike & Camping Shop, the Arcade, 34 High St, T01847-896124, rents mountain bikes for £8 per day.

Train Three trains leave daily from **Inverness** (3½ hrs), 2 of them connecting with the ferries from **Scrabster** to **Stromness** in **Orkney**. Trains continue to **Wick** (30 mins) and return trains to **Inverness** leave from **Wick**. The train station is at the south end of Princes St.

237

East coast

The east coast of the Highlands, from Inverness north to Wick, doesn't have the same draw as the west coast and attracts far fewer visitors, but it has its own, gentler appeal, and there are many lovely little seaside towns to explore. The sea lochs and estuaries of the inner Moray Firth are fringed with fields and woods, a fertile lowland landscape dotted with farms and crofts. Fast-flowing rivers drop from the hills through deep, wooded straths. The bulk of Ben Wyvis dominates the horizon northwest of Dingwall.
➤➤ *For Sleeping, Eating and other listings, see pages 246-248.*

The Black Isle → *Phone code: 01381. Colour map 2, grid C2.*

Across the Kessock Bridge from Inverness is the Black Isle, which is neither an island nor black. It shares with the Moray coast long hours of sunshine and low rainfall, rolling acres of barley and stately woods of oak and beech dropping down to the shores. It also has a compelling atmosphere – a combination perhaps of its soft microclimate, lush vegetation and attractive architecture. Its main attractions are the picturesque town of Cromarty and Chanonry Point, on the southern side near Rosemarkie, which is one of the best dolphin-spotting sites in Europe. ➤➤ *For Sleeping, Eating and other listings, see pages 246-248.*

North Kessock to Tore
On the north side of the Kessock Bridge, just north of the village, is the **North Kessock Tourist Information Centre** ① *T01463-731505, daily from Easter to Oct.* Next door is the Dolphin and Seal Visitor Centre, which gives details of accredited dolphin cruises. You can see dolphins from the village of North Kessock just to the south.

One of the many sacred wells (and caves) in the area is the unmissable **Clootie Well**, on the verge of the main road between Tore and Munlochy Bay Nature Reserve. It was once blessed by St Curitan (see below under Rosemarkie) and is thought to cure sick children. Thousands of rags still flutter from the surrounding trees, though well-worshippers are in danger of being mown down by traffic. Despite the presence of traffic, it's an eerie place. Go at night – if you dare.

North & Northwest East coast

Further east on this road, beyond Munlochy and Avoch (pronounced *Och*) is the village of Fortrose, on the east shore. The magnificent cathedral at Fortrose is now largely a ruin where rainwashed carved faces of rose-coloured sandstone peer down from roof bosses, and snapped-off stumps of window tracery are redolent of Reformation vandalism. On the golf course at **Chanonry Point**, see box, page 239, overlooking the Moray Firth, a plaque marks the spot where the Brahan Seer was boiled in a barrel of tar. Chanonry Point is also a great place for seeing dolphins. They come close to shore at high tide and there's a good chance of seeing them leaping above the waves.

Rosemarkie

A few miles from Fortrose on the north side of Chanonry Point is the tiny village of Rosemarkie. Celtic saints Curitan and Boniface selected this sheltered spot on the southern shore for their Christian mission in the seventh century. St Boniface is remembered at nearby St Bennet's Well. **Groam House Museum** ① *T01381-620961, Easter-Sep Mon-Sat 1000-1700, Sun 1400-1630, Oct-Apr Sat and Sun 1400-1600, free*, houses a huge collection of Pictish sculptured stones found locally, imaginatively displayed alongside contemporary artwork inspired by them. A year-round programme of events and lectures is devoted to the study of Pictish culture.

Beware of fairies, last sighted in the 1970's in Fairy Glen, now a nature reserve. A lovely marked trail leads into the glen from the top end of the High Street, through a wooded gorge where you may spot woodpeckers and treecreepers.

Cromarty → *Phone code: 01381.*

On the northeastern tip of the Black Isle Peninsula, at the mouth of the Cromarty Firth, is the gorgeous village of Cromarty, one of the east coast's major attractions. Its neat white-harled houses interspersed with gracious merchants' residences are almost unchanged since the 18th century when it was a sea port thriving on trade as far afield as Russia and the Baltic. Many emigrants bound for the New World embarked here. A prosperity based on textiles and fishing led to decline and dereliction. Although restored and much inhabited, Cromarty now has the atmosphere of a backwater, but a very attractive one at that, where you feel as if you're stepping back in time, in stark contrast to the numerous oil rigs moored on the opposite shore in Nigg Bay.

For a fascinating insight into the history of the area, visit the 18th-century **Cromarty Courthouse** ① *Church St, T01381-600418, Apr-Oct daily 1000-1700, Nov, Dec and Mar daily 1200-1600, £3, concession/children £2, includes loan of headset for recorded tour of the town's other historic buildings*, which houses the town's museum. Next to the courthouse is the thatch-roofed **Hugh Miller's Cottage** ① *T01381-600245, 1 May-30 Sep daily 1100-1300 and 1400-1700 (Sun afternoon only), £5, concession £2.50, family £10*, birthplace of the eminent local geologist and author. Also worth seeing is the elegant 17th-century **East Church**.

There's a good walk along a coastal path from the east end of the village through woodland to the top of the South Sutor headland, one of the two steep headlands guarding the narrow entrance to the Cromarty Firth. There are excellent views from here across the Moray Firth. Leaflets describing this and other local walks are available at the Cromarty Courthouse.

One of Cromarty's main attractions is its **dolphins**. They can be seen from the shore, or with a boat trip, see Activities and tours page 247. To the west, the mudflats of **Udale Bay** are an RSPB reserve and a haven for wading birds and wintering duck and geese, which can be viewed from a hide. In the winter other birds such as pinkfooted geese and whooper swans use the bay as a roost.

Poyntzfield Herb Garden is an organic plant nursery specializing in rare and native medicinal herbs. Worth visiting if only for a glimpse of the house, and the view from the car park over the Cromarty Firth through massive beech trees.

⁝ A seerious crime

The Brahan Seer was boiled in a barrel of tar in 1660 but not before he had foretold the building of the Caledonian Canal and Kessock Bridge, the Highland Clearances and the Second World War. He also predicted the demise of the local lairds and the Seaforths. It was Lady Seaforth who ordered his execution, after the seer had a vision of her husband in the arms of another woman. Apparently the precise spot where he met his end is now the 13th hole of the golf course at Chanonry Point, which just goes to prove that it is indeed unlucky for some.

The Cromarty Firth → *Colour map 2, grid C1-2.*

Dingwall and around → *Phone code: 01349.*
Dingwall, at the head of the Cromarty Firth, has two major claims to fame. Not only is it believed to be the birthplace of Macbeth, it was also the home for many years of Neil Gunn (1891-1973), perhaps the Highlands' greatest literary figure, see also page 375. It's a fairly dull, though functional town, with good shops and banks lining its long main street. **Dingwall Museum** ① *To1349-865366, May-Sep Mon-Sat 1000-1700, £1.50, concession £1, children £0.50*, tells the history of this Royal Burgh.

East of Dingwall, before Evanton, is **Clanland and Sealpoint** ① *To1349-830033, all year daily 0930-1730*, which has history and wildlife exhibitions and offers the chance to see the local seal population. Standing on a hill above **Evanton** is the Fyrish Monument, a replica of the Gate of Negapatam in India, built by local men and funded by local military hero, Sir Hector Munro, to commemorate his capture of the Indian town, in 1781. To get there, turn off the B9176 towards Boath. It's a stiff two-hour climb up to the top.

The Cromarty Firth is a centre for repairing North Sea oil rigs, and many of the villages along its north shore have benefited from the oil industry. One of these is **Invergordon**, just west of Nigg Bay, which has suffered in recent years due to the closure of the local aluminium factory. Beyond Invergordon, a road branches south to Nigg Ferry. The ferry from Cromarty to **Nigg** was once a major thoroughfare, and now a tiny two-car ferry makes the 20-minute crossing in the summer months, see Transport page 247. From the ferry you get a good view of Nigg Bay, a vast natural harbour used in both world wars by the Royal Navy. Its entry is guarded by the dramatic headlands of the Sutors, identified in folklore as friendly giants. Also gigantic are the oil rigs ranged along the firth and the oil terminal at Nigg, a dramatic and not unpleasant contrast with Lilliputian Cromarty.

Strathpeffer and around → *Phone code: 01997.*
Just along from the Cromarty Firth is Strathpeffer, which gets busy in the summer with coach parties, but it's a pleasant place and there are some excellent walks in the surrounding hills. The little village gained recognition in 1819 when Doctor Morrison, a physician from Aberdeen, bathed in its sulphur springs and cured himself of rheumatoid arthritis. He quickly spread the word and Strathpeffer became a fashionable spa resort attracting thousands of visitors. Two world wars intervened and the town's popularity declined. Today the only reminder of its past is the **Water Sampling Pavilion** in the square where you can test the waters. There's a seasonal **TIC** ① *main square, To1997-421415, Easter-Nov Mon-Sat 1000-1700.*

Just outside Strathpeffer on the road to Dingwall is the **Highland Museum of Childhood** ① *To1997-421031, Mar-Oct Mon-Sat 1000-1700, Sun 1400-1700, Jul and Aug Mon-Thu 1000-1700 and 1900-2100, Sat 1000-1700, Sun 1400-1700, £1.50,* *concession £1,* which has many historical displays on childhood in the highlands, as well as collections of dolls, toys and games.

▲▲ A fine walk is to **Knock Farrel** and the **Touchstone Maze**, site of an Iron-Age vitrified fort which lies at the north end of a ridge known locally as the **Cat's Back**. A marked trail starts from Blackmuir Wood car park. Head up the hill from town, turn left up a road immediately before the youth hostel, and the car park is on the left. The walk is six miles in total and takes about three hours. Aside from OS Landranger sheet 26, the route is also described in a Forestry Commission leaflet Forests of Easter Ross, available from tourist offices.

Another excellent side trip is to **Rogie Falls**, near Contin, which is three miles southwest of Strathpeffer on the main A835 Inverness-Ullapool road. The short walk up to the falls starts from the car park three miles north of Contin on the A835. There are also some pleasant woodland walks around here. Experienced hikers can tackle magnificent **Ben Wyvis** (3,432 ft). The route to the summit starts four miles north of Garve, seven miles northwest of Contin.

Tain and around → *Phone code: 01862. Colour map2, grid B2-C2.*

Squeezed between the Cromarty Firth to the south and the Dornoch Firth to the north is the Tain Peninsula, whose largest town is Tain, a place with a 1950's time-warp feel. It has an impressive historical portfolio. Its backstreets are an intriguing jigsaw of imposing merchants' houses, steep vennels, secret gardens and dormer windows. The town of Tain serves a vast hinterland. Inland the hills are little-visited backwoods and farm towns, narrow valleys lined with crofts where cattle graze in boggy haughs and, to the west, glens and moorland. Along the seaboard are the windswept fields of the Tarbat Peninsula. Good sea angling is to be had from the harbours of the otherwise dull coastal villages such as Balintore, and at Shandwick is a massive Pictish stone. It is said that unbaptized children were buried near the stone which is now in the Museum of Scotland in Edinburgh. ▶▶ *For Sleeping, Eating and other listings, see pages 246-248.*

Tain

The **Collegiate church**, see box, is on Castle Brae, just off the High Street, and inside is a 17th-century panel painted with the badges of the trade guilds, a reminder of the town's busy international trade. Another reminder is the imposing 16th-century **Tolbooth** in the High Street. Next to the church is **Tain through Time** ⓘ *T01862-894089, Apr-Oct daily 1000-1800, Nov, Dec and Mar 1200-1600, £3.50, concession £2.50,* a museum housed in the Pilgrimage which charts the town's medieval history. One of Tain's main attractions is the very fine **Glenmorangie whisky distillery** ⓘ *T01862-892477, www.glenmorangie.com, all year Mon-Fri 0900-1700, Jun-Aug also Sat 1000-1600 and Sun 1200-1600, tours from 1030-1530, £2,* just off the A9 to the north of town, where you can see how the world-famous whisky is made and try a sample. Also out of town, just to the south off the A9, is the **Aldie Water Mill**, a restored 16th-century mill in working order, with various high-quality craft shops attached. Nearby is **The Tain Pottery** ⓘ *T01862-893786, 1000-1700,* which you can also visit.

Portnahomack

The seaside village of Portnahomack, or 'port of Colman', is named after the missionary who was keen as mustard to found a religious settlement here. Archaeological work is revealing the importance of this area in Pictish times. The **Tarbat Discovery Centre** ⓘ *T01862-871790,* in Tarbat Old Church, displays recently discovered Pictish stonecarving. From the harbour, with its 18th-century girnals (grain warehouses) and sheltered sandy beach, you can see a huge stretch of the Sutherland coast, and the great sandbanks – the 'gizzen brigs' – at the mouth of the

⁝ Saintly beginnings

Tain was the birthplace of the 11th-century missionary St Duthac. Pilgrims flocked here in the Middle Ages to his shrine, and a ruin near the links is thought to be the original chapel. His head and heart, encapsulated in gold and silver reliquaries, were later kept in the still extant medieval Collegiate church until their disappearance during the Reformation. The shrine was much favoured by the Stewart kings, notably James IV who on one of his frequent pilgrimages reputedly approached walking penitentially barefoot along the King's Causeway. Tain's status as a place of sanctuary probably explains why Bruce's family fled here during the Wars of Independence.

Dornoch Firth. Boat trips are available from the harbour for sea angling. A worthwhile trip is out to Tarbat Ness lighthouse, about three miles north.

Hill of Fearn

South from Portnahomack, just west of the junction of the B9165 and the B9166, is Hill of Fearn. Fearn Abbey was moved here around 1250 from its original site near Edderton, where it was too vulnerable to sea raiders. It later became the parish church, but in 1742 lightning struck the roof which fell in, killing 38 Sunday worshippers. A tragedy was preceded by a fairy harbinger sighted at nearby Loch Eye. In Hill of Fearn is the excellent **Anta Factory Shop** ① *Mon-Sat 1000-1700, Jun-Sep also Sun 1000-1600*, one of the very best places in the country for classy tartan furnishing fabrics, as well as tartan rugs and throws, and pottery.

The Dornoch Firth → *Colour map 2, grid B2.*

Fairies were said to cross the Dornoch Firth on cockle shells and were once seen building a bridge of fairy gold, perhaps a forerunner of the Dornoch Bridge which carries the A9 across the Firth just north of Tain. A more pleasant and interesting route is to follow the A836 along the south shore. From The Struie, reached by the B9176 which branches south at Easter Fearn, there's a panoramic view over the Dornoch Firth and the Sutherland hills. ►► *For Sleeping, Eating and other listings, see pages 246-248.*

Edderton to the Kyle of Sutherland

In the churches of Edderton and Kincardine are Pictish stones. Another stands in a field northwest of Edderton, but don't disturb the crops or livestock. A quartz boulder at **Ardgay**, the 'Clach Eiteag', commemorates the cattle tryst and fair which once took place locally.

Ten miles from Ardgay, at the end of lovely Strathcarron, is the isolated **Croick church**, one of the most poignant reminders of the infamous Clearances. Here in 1845, 90 local folk took refuge in the churchyard after they had been evicted from their homes in Glencalvie by the Duke of Sutherland to make way for flocks of sheep. A reporter from *The Times* described the 'wretched spectacle' as men, women and children were carted off, many never to return. The report is there to read. Far more evocative and harrowing, though, are the names and messages the people scratched in spidery copperplate in the window panes.

North of Ardgay is the **Kyle of Sutherland**, where several rivers converge to flood into the sea through lush water meadows. Montrose was defeated here, at Carbisdale, in 1651. Overlooking the Kyle, at Culrain, is the 19th-century **Carbisdale**

Castle, once home of the exiled King of Norway, which now houses a youth hostel, see Sleeping page 246. After the Dornoch Ferry disaster of 1809, a bridge was built over the Kyle at **Bonar Bridge**, from where the A949 runs eastwards to join the main A9 just before Dornoch, while the A836 continues north to Lairg (see below). A few miles north of Invershin are the **Falls of Shin**, an excellent place to watch salmon battling upstream on their way to their spawning grounds (best seen June to September). A visitor centre and café/shop – which serves food daily till 1730 – has information about six easy walks in the immediate area; all are under an hour long.

Lairg → *Phone code: 01549.*

Eleven miles north of Bonar Bridge is the uninspiring village of Lairg, the region's main transport hub. Lairg is best known for its annual lamb sale, when young sheep from all over the north of Scotland are bought and sold. It is said that all roads meet at Lairg, and it's certainly a hard place to avoid. From here the A839 heads east to meet the A9 between Dornoch and Golspie, and west to meet the A837 which runs out to Lochinver. The A836 heads north to Tongue, and south to Bonar Bridge. The A838 meanwhile heads northwest to Laxford Bridge and on to Durness, near Cape Wrath. There's a **tourist information centre** ① *T01549-402160, Apr-Oct daily.*

There are several interesting walks around the village, some of which lead to prehistoric sites such as the Neolithic hut circles at nearby **Ord Hill**. These walks, and many others in the region, are described with maps in the Forestry Commission's leaflet Forests of the Far North, which is available at the Ferrycroft Countryside Centre and the TIC.

Dornoch and around → *Phone code: 01862. Colour map 2, grid B2.*

Dornoch is another architectural delight, with its deep, golden sandstone houses and leafy cathedral square. Bishop Gilbert of Moravia (Moray) built the cathedral circa 1245. His family's success in gaining a foothold in Northeast Scotland against the Norsemen was rewarded with the Earldom of Sutherland. It was trouble with the Jarls which prompted Gilbert to move his power base here from Caithness, mindful that his predecessor had been boiled in butter by the locals. The tourist information centre ① *T01862-810400, Apr-Oct Mon-Sat,* is on the main square.

The 13th-century **cathedral** ① *Mon-Fri 0730-2000, you can climb the cathedral tower during Jul and Aug,* was badly damaged in 1570, then subjected to an ill-conceived 'restoration' by the Countess of Sutherland in 1835. Among the few surviving features is a series of gargoyles, including a green man, and the effigy of an unknown knight. Opposite the cathedral is the 16th-century Bishop's Palace, now a hotel, see Sleeping page 246.

Nowadays Dornoch is famous for its links golf course, one of the world's finest and relatively easy to get on. It overlooks miles of dunes and pristine sandy beach. A stone near the links marks the spot where the last witch in Scotland was burned in 1722. Folklore recounts a bloody battle against raiding Vikings in 1259 on the beach at Embo, just to the north, in which Sir Richard Murray was killed. The battle is commemorated at the Earl's Cross. Trout fishing is available on Dornoch Lochans; enquire locally.

Straggling crofting townships such as **Rogart** are scattered through the glens and around the coast, all occupied and worked vigorously. The coastal population was swollen in the 19th century by tenants evicted from the inland glens, resettled here and encouraged to try fishing at such villages as Embo. Others joined the eager flood of emigrants to the New World already under way. Crofting tenancies still exist, but crofters now enjoy more protection, see page 285.

North of Dornoch is **Loch Fleet**, a river estuary with a ferocious tide race at its mouth and an SNH reserve protecting rare birds and plants. The rotting skeletons of the fishing fleet abandoned in the First World War lie in the sand on the south shore west of the car park. Nearby **Skibo Castle** is where Madge and Mr Ritchie tied the knot, in relative

Far northeast coast

North of Dornoch, the A9 follows the coast of Sutherland into the neighbouring county of Caithness through a series of straggling villages, still haunted by the memories of the Duke of Sutherland, one of Scotland's most odious landowners. The chief town in these parts is Wick, once the busiest herring port in Europe. ▸▸ *For Sleeping, Eating and other listings, see pages 246-248.*

Golspie → *Phone code: 01408. Colour map 2, grid B2. Population: 1,650.*
There is little to recommend the dull little town of Golspie, though it does have a couple of banks and supermarkets. There's an 18-hole golf course, and the **Orcadian Stone Company** has a large display of fossils and geological specimens from the Highlands and beyond. The town lives in the dark shadow of the Sutherlands. On **Beinn a'Bhraggaidh** (1,293 ft), to the southwest, is a huge, 100 ft-high monument to the Duke of Sutherland. Those who make it up to the monument and who know something of the Duke's many despicable acts may find the inscription risible, as it describes him as "a judicious, kind and liberal landlord". There's no reference to the fact that he forcibly evicted 15,000 tenants from his estate. Not surprisingly, locals would like to see this eyesore removed from the landscape, broken into tiny pieces and then scattered far and wide. Unfortunately, they have thus far been unsuccessful.

The aptly named **Dunrobin Castle** ① *T01408-633177, Apr-May and 1-15 Oct Mon-Sat 1030-1630, Sun 1200-1630, 1 Jun-30 Sep Mon-Sat 1030-1730, Sun 1200-1730, £6.70, 1 mile north of the village*, is the ancient seat of the Dukes of Sutherland, who once owned more land than anyone else in the British Empire. Much enlarged and aggrandized in the 19th century with fairytale turrets, the enormous 189-room castle, the largest house in the Highlands, is stuffed full of fine furniture, paintings, tapestries and objets d'art and bears witness to their obscene wealth. The castle overlooks beautiful gardens laid out with box hedges, ornamental trees and fountains. In stormy weather you should listen to the sea crashing on the beach beyond the walls. The museum is an animal-lover's nightmare and almost a caricature of the aristocracy, with a spectacular Victorian taxidermy collection. There are also local antiquities, some from ancient brochs, and Pictish stonecarvings.

Brora → *Phone code: 01408. Colour map 2, grid B2. Population: 1,860.*
Brora sits at the mouth of the River Brora which, as everywhere on this coast, is the site of a once-lucrative salmon netting industry. At the harbour, the ice house is a relic of the herring boom. Coal mines, opened in the 16th century, salt pans and a brickworks are all defunct. Still very much alive, however, is **Hunter's**, the local weavers of heavyweight traditional tweeds, and a good place to invest in some natty headwear. A mile or so north of town is the fairly ordinary **Clynelish distillery** ① *T01408-623000, Easter-Sep Mon-Fri 1000-1700, Oct 1100-1600, Nov-Easter by appointment, £4*. **Castle Cole** in lovely Strath Brora, eight miles northwest, is one of several ruined brochs. Another, **Carn Liath** (signposted), is by the main road, three miles south of Brora.

Helmsdale → *Phone code: 01431. Colour map 2, grid B2.*
North of Brora is the former herring port of Helmsdale, which gets busy in the summer. The village is most notable for its excellent **Timespan Heritage Centre** ① *T01431-821327, Easter-Oct Mon-Sat 0930-1700, Sun 1400-1700, £4, concession £2, children £1.75*, which brings the history of the Highlands to life through a series of high-tech

North & Northwest East coast

⠸ After the goldrush

A short drive from Helmsdale, up the Strath of Kildonan (or Strath Ullie), is Baile an Or (Gaelic for 'goldfield'), site of the great Sutherland Gold Rush of 1869. It all started after local man Robert Gilchrist returned home from the Australian gold fields only to discover gold here, on his doorstep. His success brought others rushing to Kildonan, and soon a shanty town had sprung up to accommodate them.

Within a year the gold rush was over, but small amounts are still found today. Anyone who fancies their luck can try a bit of gold panning in the Kildonan Burn at Baile an Or, about a mile from Kildonan train station. You can rent out gold panning kits at Strath Ullie Crafts & Fishing Tackle, opposite the Timespan Heritage Centre in Helmsdale, for £2.50 per day, and licences are free.

displays, sound effects and an audiovisual programme. The TIC ① *T01431-821640, Apr-Sep Mon-Sat 1000-1700*, is on the south side of the village, by the A9.

North from Helmsdale the A9 climbs spectacularly up the **Ord of Caithness** and over the pass enters a desolate, treeless landscape; an area devastated during the Clearances. To get some idea of the hardships people had to endure, stop at the ruined crofting village of **Badbea**, just beyond Ousdale. At **Berriedale**, a farm track leads west to the Wag, from where you can climb **Morven** (2,313 ft), the highest hill in Caithness, with amazing views across the whole county.

Dunbeath → *Phone code: 01593. Colour map 2, grid B3.*

The A9 coast road then drops down into Dunbeath, a pleasant little village at the mouth of a small *strath* (or glen). This was the birthplace of one of Scotland's foremost writers, Neil Gunn (1891-1973). His finest works, such as *The Silver Darlings* and *Highland River*, reflect his experiences of growing up in the northeast and are fascinating accounts of life here during the days of the herring boom, though the sleepy harbour of today is barely recognizable as the erstwhile bustling fishing port. The villages of Dunbeath, and Latherton to the north, are included on the Neil Gunn Trail, as is the beautiful walk up the glen, described in the leaflet available at the **Dunbeath Heritage Centre** ① *T01593-731233, Apr-Sep daily 1100-1700, £2, concession £1, children free*. Here, you can learn all about the life and works of the famous novelist as well as the history of Caithness. Just outside the village is the **Laidhay Croft Museum** ① *T01593-731370, Apr-Oct daily 1000-1800, £1, children £0.50*, a restored traditional longhouse with stable, house and byre all under the same roof.

Wick and around → *Phone code: 01955. Colour map 2, grid A4.*

A century ago Wick was Europe's busiest herring port, its harbour jam-packed with fishing boats and larger ships exporting tons of salted fish to Russia, Scandinavia and the West Indian slave plantations. The fishing industry has long since gone, and the demise of the nearby nuclear power station at Douneray has only added to the sense of a place that's past its best. However, there are some interesting archaeological sites in Caithness, as well as the dramatic landscapes, and Wick makes a useful base for exploring the area. There is a **tourist information centre** ① *Whitechapel Rd (just off the High St), T01955-602596, all year Mon-Fri 0900-1700, Sun 0900-1300.*

Wick is actually two towns. On one side of the river is Wick proper and on the other is Pulteneytown, the model town planned by Thomas Telford for the British Fisheries Society in 1806 to house evicted crofters who came to work here. Now it's

The light fantastic

A feature of visiting the far north of Scotland in winter is the chance of seeing the *Aurora Borealis*, or Northern Lights, which decorate the night skies like a gigantic laser show. The best time to see them is between October and March – especially during December and January. Try to get as far north as you can, though there are no guarantees of a sighting as cloud cover can obscure visibility. Any of the north-facing coastal villages are a good bet.

one great living museum of fishermen's cottages and derelict sheds and stores around the near-deserted quays. It gives a good idea of the scale of the herring trade during its heyday in the mid-19th century, when over 1,000 boats set sail to catch the 'silver darlings'. Here, on Bank Row, is the superb **Wick Heritage Centre** ① *T01955-605393, May-Sep Mon-Sat 1000-1700, £2, children £0.50*. The highlight of the centre is its massive photographic collection dating from the late 19th century.

Whether you're staying or just passing through don't miss Capaldi's, on the High Street, for exquisite home-made Italian ice cream.

Three miles north of Wick are the impressive 15th-century clifftop ruins of **Sinclair and Girnigoe Castle**. On the A99 heading north out of town is the **Caithness Glass Visitors Centre** ① *T01955-602286, Mon-Thu 0900-1630*, where you can watch the famous glass being blown. There is a good walk along the rocky shore east of town to The Trinkie, and about a mile further on to the Brig o' Trams. Ask for details at the TIC. Before Wick, at Ulbster, is another archaeological site, the **Cairn o' Get**. Opposite the sign are the precipitous **Whaligoe Steps**, which lead to a tiny, picturesque harbour.

Archaeological sites around Caithness

Caithness may lack the impressive henges of other parts of the UK but it does boast a number of stone rows: areas covered by large numbers of small stones arranged in geometric patterns. These are thought to date from circa 2000 BC. The best and most easily accessible is the **Hill o' Many Stanes**. To get there, drive nine miles south of Wick. On the A9 and turn right onto a minor road where you see the signpost. A short way up this road is a signposted gate into the field, on the left-hand side. A path leads to the curious fan-shaped configuration of Bronze Age standing stones; 200 of them in 22 rows. No one yet knows their precise purpose but studies have shown that there were once 600 stones here.

There are also a couple of Pictish Brochs in Caithness. These were almost entirely unique to the north and northwest of Scotland and were windowless, dry-stone towers, between 3-15 m in height, with a circular ground plan. The walls were hollow in places to allow staircases and small chambers. These were built between 2000 BC and 200 AD, though they continued in use after that time, and were used for both domestic and defensive purposes. There are remains of a broch at **Nybster**, seven miles south of John o' Groats on the A9. Look out for the sign for the harbour and broch on the right heading north. Turn onto the minor road which leads down to a small car park. Follow the path along the cliff-top to the broch, which stands on a headland surrounded by steep cliffs on three sides. Just to the south of here, at Keiss, are the remains of another broch.

One of the most fascinating archaeological sites in the north are the well-preserved **Grey Cairns of Camster**. These chambered cairns, dating from the third and fourth millenia BC, are burial mounds of stone raised around carefully structured circular chambers with narrow entrance passages. To get there, head a mile east of

Lybster on the A9, then turn left on to the minor road leading north to Watten. The cairns are five miles along this road, on the left-hand side. They comprise two enormous prehistoric burial chambers dating from 2500 BC. They are amazingly complete, with corbelled ceilings, and can be entered on hands and knees through narrow passageways.

● Sleeping

Cromarty p238
For such an appealing place, there's precious little accommodation, so it's advisable to book ahead during the summer months.
C Royal Hotel, Marine Terr, T01381-600217, www.royalcromartyhotel.co.uk. The best place to stay, with a good restaurant (£££), and cheaper meals are available in the bar.
E Beechfield House, 4 Urquhart Ct, T01381-600308, faericketts@btinternet.com. Out of a couple of B&Bs, this is a very good option.

Dingwall and around p239
B Tulloch Castle Hotel, T01349-861325, www.tullochcastle.co.uk. This 12th-century castle is the smartest place around.
F Blackrock Bunkhouse, Evanton, T01349-830917, open 1 Apr-31 Oct. Basic.

Strathpeffer and around p239
The best accommodation is in Contin, 3 miles southwest of Strathpeffer.
B Coull House Hotel, T01997-421487, www.milford.co.uk/go/coulhouse.html. Top of the list is this elegant 19th-century country house offering fine food. Excellent choice.
C Brunstane Lodge Hotel, Golf Course Rd, Strathpeffer, T01997-421261, www.brunstanelodge.com, open Mar-Dec, which serves decent cheap bar meals.
D Craigvar, on the Square, Strathpeffer, T01997-421622, www.craigvar.com. Elegant, good value B&B.
D-E Dunraven Lodge, Golf Course Rd, T01997-421210, sandra.iddon@ntlworld.com. Good value B&B.
E Inver Lodge, T01997-421392, open Mar-Dec. A decent B&B.
E Taigh an Eilein, T01997-421009, lorna.mac@talk21.com, open Apr-Sep. There are several B&Bs in Contin, including the very grand-looking house.

Tain p240
L Mansfield House Hotel, Scotsburn Rd, T01862-892052, www.mansfield-house.co.uk. 19th-century baronial splendour and superb cuisine. Restaurant also open to non-residents (£££).
C Morangie House Hotel, Morangie Rd, T01862-892281, www.morangiehotel.com. It's popular locally for its food (££) and is open for lunch and dinner. Excellent value.
E Golf View House, at 13 Knockbreck Rd, T01862-892856, www.golfview.co.uk. A modest B&B.

Lairg p242
D-E The Nip Inn, on the main street, T01549-402243, www.nipinn.co.uk. Also does bar meals.
F Sleeperzzz.com, T01408-641343, www.sleeperzzz.com. There are several B&Bs and a campsite too, but the most interesting place to stay is 9 miles east at Rogart train station, where you can get cheap hostel accommodation at the 2 old rail carriages that have been converted to sleep 16 people. There's a 10% discount for bike or train users.

Dornoch and around p242
There are also lots of good B&Bs and a campsite, in addition to these options.
L The Royal Golf Hotel, T/F01862-810283, www.morton-hotels.com, next to the first tee. Plush hotel catering to golfers. Good restaurant (£££-££).
B The Two Quails, Castle St, T01862-811811, www.2quail.com. 3 rooms. Restaurant with rooms run by Michael and Kerensa Carr. Well-equipped rooms and superb cuisine (£££).
B-D Dornoch Castle Hotel, T01862-810216, www.dornochcastle.com, open Apr-Oct. Formerly the Bishop's Palace, this 16th-century building is full of character and boasts excellent food (£££).
F Carbisdale Castle Youth Hostel, T01549-421232, open end Feb-end Oct (except the first 2 weeks in May). The largest

and most sumptuous hostel in Scotland, and possibly anywhere else, is half a mile up a steep hill from the station.

Brora *p243*
D **Glenaveron**, on Golf Rd, T/F01408-621601, www.glenaveron.com. Among the many B&Bs here this is excellent.

Helmsdale *p243*
B-C **Navidale House Hotel**, T01431-821258, open Feb-Nov. A good place to eat.
D **Broomhill House**, T01431-821259. A B&B with a distinctive turret.
E **Torbuie**, T01431-821424, Navidale.
F **SYHA Youth Hostel**, T01431-821577, open mid-May to early Oct.

Wick and around *p244*
A-B **Portland Arms Hotel**, 15 miles south, in Lybster, T01593-721208, www.portland arms. co.uk. Best around, a 19th-century coaching inn, full of character serving great food (£££).
C **Mackay's Hotel**, Union St, T01955-602323, www.mackayshotel.co.uk. Nothing fancy but handy for getting to the train station.
The best of the guest houses and B&Bs are:
E **The Clachan**, on South Rd, T01955-605384; and
E **Wellington Guest House**, 41-43 High St, T01955-603287, open Mar-Oct.

● Eating

Cromarty *p238*
££ **Binnie's Tearoom**, Church St, a great place for tea and scones.
££ **Cromarty Arms**, opposite the Cromarty Courthouse, for cheap bar food. Also has live music some nights.
££ **Thistle's Restaurant**, Church St, T01381-600471. Has an imaginative menu, including interesting vegetarian dishes.

Portnahomack *p240*
££ **The Oyster Catcher**, T01862-871560. A great place to eat out here is this small café-restaurant serving snacks and lunches, and dinner from 1930 (if booked). Crêpes are a speciality, but it also does pasta, seafood and fish.

££ **La Mirage**, opposite the TIC. Daily 1200-2045 (Dec-Apr till 1900). Famous tearoom whose erstwhile proprietress, the inimitable Nancy Sinclair, modelled herself, and her tearoom, on Barbara Cartland, queen of romantic novels. The whole effect is pure kitsch. Good fish and chips.

Wick and around *p244*
The best places to eat are out of town.
££ **Bower Inn**, see p235.
££ **Old Smiddy Inn**, in Thrumster, 5 miles south of Wick, T01955-651256, open daily 1200-2100.
££ **Queen's Hotel**, Francis St, T01955-602992. Probably the best place in town, varied menu.
£ **Cabrelli's**, 134 High St, also in town is a great caff serving pizza and fish and chips.

● Shopping

Tain *p240*
Bannerman's, a fish and seafood wholesalers, sells local mussels.
Brown's Gallery, Castle Brae. Showcases work by Highland artists.

Dornoch and around *p242*
The Dornoch Bookshop, High St, T01862-810165, is the only bookshop in the area and stocks local books.

▲ Activities and tours

Cromarty *p238*
Dolphin-spotting boat trips leave from Cromarty, but make sure you go with an accredited operator.
Dolphin Ecosse, T01381 600323. Half- and full-day trips leave from the harbour to see porpoises, seals, dolphins, and perhaps even killer whales further out. Accredited operator.

● Transport

Cromarty *p238*
Highland Bus & Coach, T01463-233371, runs a bus service from **Inverness** to **Fortrose** and **Cromarty** (4-7 times daily Mon-Sat). There is also a bus service to and from **Dingwall** on Wed and Thu. A 2-car ferry crosses to **Nigg** every half hour from Apr to Oct, 0900-1800.

Dingwall and around *p239*

There are hourly buses between **Inverness** and **Invergordon**, via Dingwall. There are also hourly buses between **Inverness** and Dingwall via **Muir of Ord**. There are buses between Dingwall and **Rosemarkie** (twice a day Mon-Thu), and between Dingwall and **Cromarty** (Wed and Thu).

Dingwall is on the rail line between **Inverness** and **Kyle of Lochalsh** and **Thurso**. There are several trains daily in each direction (30 mins to Inverness).

Strathpeffer and around *p239*

There are regular buses between Strathpeffer and **Dingwall** (see above).

Tain *p240*

Citylink buses between **Inverness** and **Thurso** pass through Tain 4 times a day. There are also buses to **Portmahomack** (4 times daily Mon-Thu), **Balintore** (5-6 times daily Mon-Sat), **Lairg** via **Bonar Bridge** (3 times daily Mon-Sat) and **Dornoch** via **Bonar Bridge** (once a day Mon-Thu) with Inverness Traction, T01463-239292, and Rapson's of Brora, T01408-621245.

Tain is on the **Inverness-Thurso** rail line and there are 3 trains daily in each direction.

Lairg *p242*

Inverness Traction buses, T01463-239292, run from here to **Ullapool**, with connections to **Lochinver** and **Durness**, from May to early Oct (Mon-Sat). Lairg is also the central point for several **postbus** routes, T01463-256228.

Trains between **Inverness** and **Thurso** stop at Lairg and Rogart stations 3 times daily.

Dornoch and around *p242*

Buses (hourly Mon-Sat, 5 times on Sun) between **Inverness** and **Lairg** stop in **Ardgay** and **Bonar Bridge**. Citylink buses between Inverness and Thurso also stop in Dornoch 4 daily.

Trains between **Inverness** and **Thurso** stop at **Ardgay** and **Culrain**.

Helmsdale *p243*

Buses and trains are the same as for Wick (see below). Helmsdale is on the Inverness-Wick/Thurso rail line.

Wick and around *p244*

Air A few miles north of town, is Wick airport, T01955-602215. Daily direct flights to and from **Kirkwall** (Orkney), **Sumburgh** (Shetland), **Aberdeen** and **Edinburgh** with and British Airways Express, T08457-733377. Also direct flights to/from **Newcastle** with Eastern Airways, T01955-603914. There's a postbus service to Wick airport Mon-Sat at 1015.
Bus Scottish Citylink, T08705-505050, buses between **Inverness** and **Thurso** stop en route in **Wick** (3 daily). There are also regular local buses to **Thurso**, via **Halkirk** or **Castletown**, and buses to **Helmsdale** (2-6 times daily Mon-Sat, 1-4 on Sun) and **John O'Groats** (5 daily Mon-Sat, 4 on Sun). The train and bus stations are next to each other behind the hospital.
Car/bike hire **Richard's Garage**, Francis St, T01955-604123.
Train Trains leave for **Inverness** (3 daily Mon-Sat, 2 on Sun; 3¾ hrs) via **Thurso**, **Helmsdale**, **Golspie**, **Lairg** and **Dingwall**. The train station is behind the hospital.

Skye & the Small Isles

⦂ Footprint features

Introduction

The Isle of Skye (An t-Eilean Sgitheanach), the most scenically spectacular of all the Scottish islands, gets its name from the Norse word for cloud (skuy) and is commonly known as Eilean a Cheo (the Misty Isle), so it obviously rains a lot here. But when the rain and mist clear, the views make the heart soar. Despite the unpredictable weather, tourism is an important part of the island's economy, and has been since Victorian times when climbers returned home extolling its beauty. In the busy summer months the main roads become choked with coach tours and caravans, but the island is large enough to escape the worst of the crowds if you take the time to explore it. It offers a range of excellent walks from low-level strolls to tougher routes requiring experience and a head for heights. In the centre of the island stand the proud, implacable Cuillins, the greatest concentration of peaks in Britain. They provide Scotland's best climbing and are a real attraction for all serious and experienced walkers. Equally spectacular, but easier to negotiate, are the bizarre rock formations of the Trotternish Peninsula in the north.

The Small Isles is the collective name given to the four islands of Eigg, Muck, Rùm and Canna, lying south of Skye. Seen from the mainland, they look a very tempting prospect, especially the jagged outline of Rùm and the curiously shaped Eigg. But visiting the islands is not easy, as ferry transport is purely designed for the inhabitants and not geared towards the convenience of island-hopping tourists. Furthermore, the island populations are small, and accommodation and facilities are limited. But the determined traveller with time on their hands will be well rewarded, particularly on mountainous Rùm, with its superb walking and abundant wildlife.

★ Don't miss...

❶ **Loch Coruisk** Take a boat trip into the gaping mouth of this loch, page 261.

❷ **Raasay** Sail to this island, only a few miles off Skye's east coast yet well off the beaten track, and climb to the top of Dun Caan, page 262.

❸ **Three Chimneys restaurant** Sample some of the finest food in the country, page 268.

❹ **Eigg** Walk across the 'Singing Sands' on this tiny island, page 270.

❺ **Rùm** Brave the wilds of this island, home to the rare white-tailed sea eagle, and then explore the bizarre and extravagant interior of Kinloch Castle, page 271.

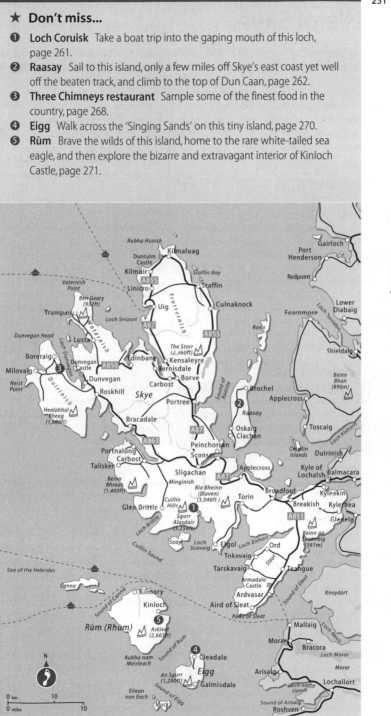

Skye & the Small Isles

Isle of Skye

Skye is one of the best places in Scotland for outdoor types. It offers air, sea land and light in their purest form and any visitor will return home physically refreshed and spiritually uplifted. Aside from swooning at the island's natural beauty, the most popular destination is Dunvegan Castle, stronghold of the Macleod clan, while their old enemies, the MacDonalds, hail from the Sleat Peninsula in the south of the island. The most famous Macdonald, Flora, who helped Bonnie Prince Charles flee to France, hailed from the northern tip of the island and is buried there. ▶▶ *For Sleeping, Eating and other listings, see pages 264-270.*

Ins and outs

Getting there
The most popular, and quickest, route to Skye is across the bridge (£6 toll), from Kyle of Lochalsh to Kyleakin. Coach services run to Skye from Glasgow and Inverness, with connections to all main cities in the UK (**Citylink**, T08705-5505050; **National Express**, T08705-808080). There is also a train service from Kyle of Lochalsh to Inverness, see page 211.

A more scenic approach is by ferry from Mallaig to Armadale, on the southern Sleat Peninsula. The car and passenger ferry makes the 20-minute crossing eight to nine times daily each way (Monday-Saturday only from mid September to mid May). Booking is recommended during the summer months, T08705-650000. The one-way trip costs £3.05 per passenger and £16.90 per car. Five-day saver return is £5.25 and £29. Trains to and from Fort William and Glasgow Queen Street connect with some of the ferries, see page 203.

The best way to Skye is from Glenelg to Kylerhea, south of Kyleakin. The tiny private car ferry makes the 10-minute crossing when required from Easter to October daily, see page 211 for details. There is also a passenger ferry from Gairloch to Portree, sailing twice daily, see page 219. For more details and ticket bookings, visit www.overtheseatoskye.com. ▶▶ *For further details, see Transport page 269.*

Getting around
Skye is the largest of the Hebridean islands, at almost 50 miles long and between seven and 25 miles wide. It is possible to run up a hefty mileage as the extensive road system penetrates to all but the most remote corners of its many peninsulas. It is possible to get around by public transport midweek, with post buses supplementing the normal services, but, as everywhere in the Highlands and Islands, buses are few and far between at weekends, especially Sunday, and during the winter months. Buses run between Portree, Broadford, Uig (for ferries to the Western Isles), Kyleakin, Armadale (for ferries to Mallaig), Dunvegan and Carbost, and a more limited service runs from Broadford to Elgol and Portree to Glen Brittle. Getting around by public transport is virtually impossible in winter (October-March) as bus and post bus services are severely limited. ▶▶ *For further details, see Activities and tours page 268 and Transport page 269.*

Tourist information
Skye is well served by all types of accommodation: B&Bs, guest houses, hostels, bunkhouses, campsites and some very fine hotels. During the peak summer months advance bookings are recommended. These can be made directly or through the island's tourist information centres in Portree (open all year), Broadford, Uig and Dunvegan. See also www.isleofskye.com. For local tourist information centres see individual sections.

Portree → *Phone code: 01478. Colour map 1, grid C3.*

Portree is the island's capital and main settlement. It's a fairly attractive little fishing port, built around a natural harbour, with a row of brightly painted houses along the shorefront and the rest of the town rising steeply up to the central Somerled Square.
▶▶ *For Sleeping, Eating and other listings, see pages 264-270.*

Ins and outs

Getting there and around Portree is ideally placed for trips to all parts of the island. Buses leave from the bus station in Somerled Square to Dunvegan, Uig, Broadford, Kyleakin, Armadale, the Talisker Distillery and Glenbrittle. There are also services to the mainland. The **CalMac ferry office** ① *T01478-612075*, is on Park Road, just off Somerled Square. The town is compact enough to get around easily on foot,

Portree

Sleeping
Bosville 1
Mr & Mrs Mathieson's B&B 2
Portree Backpackers Hostel 3
Portree House 8
Portree Independent Hostel 4
Rosedale 5
Torvaig Campsite 7
Viewfield House 6

Eating
Ben Tianavaig 1
Chandlery Seafood 2
Lower Deck Seafood 3
Spicehut 5
Steve's Kitchen Takeaway 6

Bars & clubs
Pier Hotel 7
Royal Hotel 8

Skye & the Small Isles Isle of Skye

though there is a regular town bus service for those needing to get into the centre from the outskirts.

Tourist information The **TIC** ① *Bridge St, T01478-612137, mid-May to mid-Aug daily, mid-Aug to mid-May Mon-Sat*, has bus timetables and a good selection of books and maps.

Sights

Aros Experience ① *Viewfield Rd, T01478-613649, www.scotlandcreates.com/aros, daily 0900-2100 (off season 0900-1800), £3, concession £2, children £1, under 12 free, half a mile from the town centre on the road to Broadford*, is an exhibition and audio-visual display of the island's history and cultural heritage. The island's only theatre is housed here and features a varied programme of events, including drama, traditional music and movies, see Entertainment page 268. There's also a restaurant with good value snacks and meals, a shop and a network of forest trails to explore.

An Tuireann Arts Centre ① *Struan Rd, T01478-613306, www.antuireann.org.uk, Mar-Oct Mon-Sat 1000-1700, Nov-Feb Tue-Sat 1000-1700, free*, hosts exhibitions of contemporary visual arts and crafts. It has a fine café, see Eating page 267.

▲▲ A nice, gentle introduction to walking in the area, and an opportunity to stretch your legs before tackling more strenuous routes such as the Old Man of Storr or the Quiraing, starts out from Bosville Terrace. Follow the street as it curves round then take the right fork at the first junction, down towards the shore. Just after the car park to the right the road splits: follow the path to the right along the northern shore of the bay. The path follows the shore and passes a viewpoint and flagpole. It then becomes rougher as it swings round the headland and reaches a gate in a dyke. Go through the gate and cross the muddy field, then follow the fence up to the left till you reach another gate. Climb over the gate and continue along the edge of the next field, then cross a stile at the top of the field. Walk up the slope to the clear track and follow this left as it heads uphill. You'll then see some houses; take the track beyond the house on the left and follow it down between two large farm buildings. The path heads down across rough moorland towards Portree. Cross the stile and continue downhill through some woods, then you'll see a hotel on your left before rejoining the original road near the car park. It's about 2½ miles and takes about an hour and a half at an easy pace. The path can get very muddy in places.

Trotternish Peninsula → *Phone code: 01470. Colour map 1, grid C3.*

North from Portree is the 30-mile long Trotternish Peninsula, sticking out like a giant thumb hitching a lift from a passing ferry. The interior of the peninsula is a basaltic lava wilderness full of bizarre rock formations. A 20-mile long escarpment of sheer cliffs and towering pinnacles dominates the landscape. The best known of these strange formations, the **Quiraing** and **Old Man of Storr**, can be explored on foot (see below). The A855 and A87 roads follow the coast around the peninsula, and a spectacular minor road bisects the ridge from Staffin Bay to Uig. Trotternish is best explored with your own transport, but there a few daily buses covering the circular route from Portree. ►► *For Sleeping, Eating and other listings, see pages 264-270.*

Uig

The A87 runs northwest from Portree to the tiny ferry port of Uig, dramatically set in a horseshoe bay and the departure point for ferries to **Tarbert** (Harris) and **Lochmaddy** (North Uist). Everything in the village revolves around the ferry timetables, and the regular bus service to and from Portree coincides with the arrival and departure of the ferries. The **TIC** ① *T01470-542404, 1 Apr-31 Oct, Mon-Sat, also Sun Jul-Sep*, is inside the CalMac office at the ferry pier, and will book accommodation anywhere on the island.

66 99 It's almost inconceivable that these are natural formations and the inevitable mist only adds to the spooky strangeness of the place...

Just outside the village is the magical **Fairy Glen**. Turn right just before the **Uig Hotel** coming down the hill from the Portree direction. About a mile up the single track road you enter an eerie, mysterious world of perfect conical hills, some up to 60-ft high. It's almost inconceivable that these are natural formations and the inevitable mist only adds to the spooky strangeness of the place.

Uig to Duntulm

At **Kilmuir**, is the **Skye Museum of Island Life** ① *Easter to Oct Mon-Sat 0930-1700, £2, children £1*. The group of thatched houses give a fascinating insight into the way of life of a crofting community at the end of the last century, and is the most authentic of several such museums on Skye. Behind the museum, at the end of the road, is **Flora MacDonald's Monument**, which marks the grave of Skye's most famous daughter, with her husband buried alongside. The rather austere memorial is inscribed with Dr Johnson's poignant tribute, see box page 256.

At the northwest tip of the peninsula, 15 minutes' drive from Uig, is **Duntulm Castle**, a fairytale ruin dramatically perched on a steep cliff. This 15th-century structure, built on the site of an ancient Norse stronghold, became the chief Skye residence of the powerful MacDonalds and was the most imposing castle in the Hebrides. According to local legend, the castle was abandoned around 1732 when a nursemaid accidentally let the baby heir fall from a window on to the cliffs below.

▲ The Quiraing

Beyond Duntulm the A855 heads across the tip of the peninsula to the east coast, where the famous bizarre rock scenery is found. At the north end of **Staffin Bay**, a minor road cuts across the peninsula to Uig. This road is the access point for the Quiraing, the famous jumble of strangely shaped hills and rocks that is one of the island's classic walks. This four-mile walk is quite demanding, but the dramatic scenery more than compensates. To get to the starting point, drive 19 miles north from Portree on the A855. At Brogaig, just north of Staffin, take the single-track road to Uig. Follow it and, just after the road has zigzagged its way up the face of the ridge, park in the car park to the left. Cross the road and follow the well-defined path along the base of the cliffs, with a steep grassy slope down to the right. After about one mile you'll start to see some of the well-known rocky features on the far side of a rough valley. The most imposing of these is **The Prison**, a huge, tilted square block. On the left, among the towering cliffs, is **The Needle**, a shaft of rock about 120-ft high. Scramble up the narrow gully to the left of The Needle to reach **The Table**, an area of flat grassland surrounded by high cliffs (local shinty teams used to play here!). From The Table continue along the path at the foot of the cliffs, past a small lochan on the right and through a stone dyke, until you reach the lowest point of the ridge on your left. Scramble up on to the ridge and make your way back along the tops of the cliffs (take care at this point). There's a hard climb up the slopes of Meall na Suiramach, but the views from the top are spectacular. Continue along the top of the cliffs for just over a mile and you'll see the car park.

‼ *Even if you don't attempt the walk, the road over the back of the Trotternish ridge from Uig makes a worthwhile detour.*

Skye & the Small Isles Isle of Skye

Faithful Flora

In Kilmuir graveyard is the memorial which marks the grave of Flora MacDonald, one of the most famous characters in Skye's long history. The memorial bears Dr Johnson's fitting epitaph: *A name that will be mentioned in history, and if courage and fidelity be virtues, mentioned with honour.*

It was Flora MacDonald who helped Bonnie Prince Charlie to escape capture following the Jacobite defeat at Culloden in 1746. Pursued by government troops, the prince fled from South Uist 'over the sea to Skye' aboard Flora's boat, disguised as an Irish servant girl by the name of Betty Burke. He then made his way to Portree, where he bade his farewell to the young woman who had risked her own life to protect his.

When Flora's part in the prince's escape became known, she was immediately arrested and sent to the Tower of London. She was released a year later, married a Skye man and then emigrated to North Carolina where she spent the next 12 years of her life. They returned to her husband's house in Kingsburgh in 1786. Flora died in Skye in 1790, and it is said that her funeral was the largest ever witnessed in the Highlands.

Kilt Rock

A few miles south of Staffin Bay is Kilt Rock, an impressive sea cliff which gets its name from the vertical columnar basalt strata overlying horizontal ones beneath. A rather tenuous comparison perhaps, but the cliffs south of Staffin are particularly spectacular, as are the **Lealt Falls**, a torrent of mountain water at the head of a gorge, a few miles south of Kilt Rock. The falls are signposted by the road, so all you have to do is park the car and peer over. Just before the turn for Kilt Rock is a wee museum sporting such finds as a dinosaur bone and bronze age artefacts (open May-October).

▲▲ Old Man of Storr

A few miles further south, and seven miles north of Portree, is a car park which is the starting point for another of Skye's famous walks: up to the Old Man of Storr, the distinctive pinnacle which has detached itself from the cliffs of the Storr behind. This basalt finger of rock, 165 ft high, stands beneath the steep cliffs of The Storr (2,360 ft) and is visible from the A855. The starting point for the 3½-mile walk up and back (1½ hours) is the car park on the left, just over six miles north of Portree, near the northern end of Loch Leathan, which can be reached by bus from Portree. Cross the stile over the wall by the Forestry Commission sign and follow the clear track up through the conifer plantation. The track is a gradual uphill climb until you come out into open grassland. Go through the gate in the fence and then it's a steep climb up the grassy slope with the massive pinnacle towering overhead. Once at the top you enter an area of weird and impressive rock formations. You can follow any of the dozens of paths that lead between the rocks, or just enjoy the fantastic views across to Raasay and the mainland beyond. You can follow the same path back down to the car park.

Waternish, Dunvegan and Duirinish → *Phone code: 01470.*

Colour map 1, grid C2-3.

In the northwest of Skye the peninsulas of Waternish (or Vaternish) and Duirinish point out into the Minch towards the Western Isles. The larger Duirinish Peninsula

Take no prisoners

Violent conflict between neigh-bouring clan chiefs was so common-place on Skye and in the rest of the Western Highlands that it was almost accepted as part of the very fabric of society. One particularly gruesome example took place on Eigg in 1577. The Macleod's had taken refuge in a cave but their presence was discovered by the MacDonalds, who piled brushwood at the entrance and set fire to it, burning alive the 395 people sheltering inside, almost the entire population of the island. Revenge came the following year, at Trumpan church in Ardmore Bay on Skye. The Macleods landed under cover of the early morning fog and set light to the church, burning the congregation inside.

holds more interest for the visitor, featuring the beautiful green valley of **Glendale**, an area brimming with history, the dramatic walk to **Neist Point** and **Dunvegan Castle**, Skye's most famous landmark. ▸▸ *For Sleeping, Eating and other listings, see pages 264-270.*

Edinbane

The turn-off to this much-visited part of the island is four miles northwest of Portree. The A850 swings west towards Dunvegan, by-passing the tiny village of Edinbane, where there's a campsite, two hotels, several B&Bs, a petrol station and the renowned **Edinbane Pottery** ① *T01470-582234, Easter-Oct 0900-1800 workshop and showroom*, which is a must for souvenir hunters.

Waternish Peninsula

The A850 continues west, and those with their own transport and time on their hands might wish to make an interesting little detour at the **Fairy Bridge**, where the B886 runs north to **Trumpan**, near the tip of the Waternish Peninsula. If the weather's good (and it is, occasionally) this is the best place to watch the sun set, in a blaze of red over the Outer Hebrides. If there's no sunset, then you could always visit **Skyeskins** ① *T01470-592237, www.skyeskins.co.uk, daily 1000-18000*, in Loch Bay, the country's only traditional exhibition tannery. While here, you could also pop into the island's oldest pub at **Stein**.

The ruined church at Trumpan, at the end of the road, has some grisly skeletons in its cupboard (see box, above). In the graveyard is the 'trial stone'. A hole in the stone was used to test whether or not an accused person was telling the truth. If they could quickly find the hole and stick their arm through it while blindfolded, they were found innocent, but if not, they were guilty. The church is also the starting point for the strenuous eight-mile walk out to **Waternish point** and back.

Dunvegan

A few miles further on from the turn-off to Waternish is the little village of Dunvegan. Just to the north of the village is proud **Dunvegan Castle** ① *www.dunvegancastle. com, mid-Mar to Nov daily 1000-1730, rest of the year 1100-1600, castle £6.50, £3.50 children, gardens only £4.50*, the island's most important tourist attraction. This is the home of the chiefs of the Clan Macleod who have lived here for over seven centuries, making it the oldest inhabited castle in Britain. The present structure dates from the 15th and 16th centuries and, though the Victorian restoration has left it looking more like a baronial house, a look inside reveals its true age. Among the few genuinely interesting relics on display is Rory Mor's horn, a huge drinking vessel which the chief's heir must drain 'without setting down or falling down', when filled with claret (about 1½ bottles). There's also a lock of Bonnie Prince Charlie's hair,

Things to do on Skye when it's raining

Just in case you didn't know, it can rain quite often on Skye and unless you're one of those hardy souls who's prepared to brave the elements, you'll need to know about the island's main indoor attractions. There are numerous opportunities to shelter from the rain, but most of them cost money, and many will leave you regretting it, so here's our list of the top ten things to do. Details of opening times and admission prices are given under each relevant destination.

Beginning in Portree, there's the **Aros Experience**, which gives a good introduction to the island's history. North of Uig, at Kilmuir on the Trotternish Peninsula, is the **Skye Museum of Island Life**, which pretty much does what it says on the sign. Northwest from Portree is **Dunvegan Castle**, home of the Clan Macleod and top of most visitors' itineraries. On the road to Dunvegan is **Edinbane Pottery**, where you can buy pots of every shape and size and watch them being made.

Travelling south from Dunvegan, you'll reach the turn-off to the **Talisker Distillery**, the island's only whisky distillery, where you can sample the distinctive peaty taste. While you're there you can visit nearby **Carbostcraft Pottery**, in the village of Carbost, and indulge in some more gift buying. If you're in need of some refreshment after all that culture and shopping, you could do a lot worse than the bar at the **Sligachan Hotel**, which boasts an impressive array of whiskies and climbers' beards. In the southern peninsula of Sleat, near the Armadale ferry terminal, is **Armadale Castle**, with a visitor centre that is actually worth visiting. Nearby is one of the branches of **Skye Batiks**, with a huge selection of these 'new age' style fabrics in a range of original Celtic designs (the other branch is in Portree). And for that final drink before boarding the ferry to Mallaig, why not pop into the cosy bar of the **Hotel Eilean Iarmain**, which also happens to serve wonderful food.

clipped from his head by Flora MacDonald as a keepsake, but pride of place goes to the Fairy Flag. The flag has been dated to between the fourth and seventh centuries and is made of Middle Eastern silk. It is said to have been given to the clan chief by a fairy, and has the power to ensure victory in battle for the clan on three occasions. It has been used twice so far. The lovely castle gardens lead down to the lochside jetty, from where you can take a seal-spotting cruise or a boat trip around the loch. There's also a busy restaurant and gift shop by the castle gates.

In the village of Dunvegan is **Giant Angus MacAskill Museum** ⓘ *T01470 -521296, Mar-Oct daily 0930-1830, £1*, housed in a thatched, whitewashed cottage, which relates the life story of the tallest ever Scotsman, Angus MacAskill, who grew to 7 ft and 9 ins tall. He emigrated to Novia Scotia and toured the United States with the midget General Tom Thumb, who is said to have danced on his outstretched hand. More interesting than the museum, though, are the stories of its owner, Peter MacAskill, in particular the one about the replica coffin, which is worth the admission fee alone. Peter is a descendent of Angus and also runs the museum at Colbost (see below).

Duirinish Peninsula

West of Dunvegan is the Duirinish Peninsula. The northern half is populated along the western shores of **Loch Dunvegan** and in the beautiful and green **Glendale**, an area brimming with history but with hardly an island family left. Glendale is now dubbed 'Little England', owing to the large number of incoming settlers from the south. The area is famed throughout the Highlands and Islands, for it was here in 1882 that local crofters, spurred on by the **Battle of the Braes**, see page 262, resisted the cruel and petty tyranny of their estate manager. The authorities sent a gunboat to deal with the uprising and arrested the ringleaders, some of whom were imprisoned in Edinburgh and became known as 'the Glendale Martyrs'. This episode sparked a radical movement throughout the Highlands and led to the **Crofter's Holdings Act of 1886** which gave the crofters a more secure tenure and fair rent, see page 285. The uninhabited southern half of the peninsula is dominated by the flat-topped hills, Healabhal Bheag (1,601 ft) and Healabhal Mhor (1,538 ft), known as **Macleod's Tables**.

The **Glendale Visitor Route** is signposted from just before Dunvegan village and leads westwards along the shores of the loch and across the peninsula. There are several interesting little sights along the way. Those interested in finding out more about the region's history, and crofting on the island, should head for the fascinating **Colbost Folk Museum** ⓘ *Easter-Oct daily 0900-1800, £1.50, children free*, housed in a restored 'black house' and with a peat fire burning and an illicit still out the back. The museum is four miles from Dunvegan on the B884 to Glendale. A little further on is **Skye Silver** ⓘ *www.skyesilver.com, daily 1000-1800*, where you can buy silver jewellery in traditional Celtic designs. Further north is the **Borreraig Park Exhibition Croft** ⓘ *daily 0900-1800, £1.50*, which features a huge display of farm equipment from days gone by.

At **Borreraig** is the **MacCrimmon Piping Heritage Centre** ⓘ *T01470-511369, daily all year 1000-1700, £1.50*, a fascinating place which is more of a shrine to the famous MacCrimmons, who were hereditary pipers to the Macleod Chiefs and the first composers, players and teachers of *piobaireachd* (pibroch), which can be heard in the museum (there's an annual recital at Dunvegan Castle in early August). Opposite are the ruins of the ancient piping college. Moving from the sublime to the ridiculous, in the village of **Glendale** is a **Toy Museum** ⓘ *T01470-511240, Mon-Sat 1000-1800, £2.50, children £1*, which should appeal to kids of all ages.

▲ The B884 continues west, then a road turns off left for Waterstein. At the end of this road (just over two miles) is a car park which is the starting point for the walk out to the lighthouse at **Neist Point**, the most westerly point on Skye and one of the most pleasant walks on the island. It's about 1½ miles there and back and well worth the effort. The path is easy to follow and the views of the sea cliffs are wonderful. There are lots of nesting seabirds around and you might even spot whales offshore. The **lighthouse**, built in 1909, is now unmanned, and you can stay in one of the self-catering cottages ⓘ *T/F01470-511200*.

The Cuillins and Minginish → *Colour map 3, grid A3-4. OS Landranger No 32 & OS Outdoor Leisure No 8.*

The district of Minginish is the wildest and least-populated part of the island, but for many it is the greatest attraction, for this is where the Cuillins are to be found. This hugely impressive mountain range, often shrouded in rain or cloud, is the spiritual heartland of the island, and when it's clear their heart-aching grandeur can be appreciated from every other peninsula on Skye. Though officially called the Cuillin 'Hills', these are the most untamed mountains in Britain. The magnificent scenery and vast range of walks and scrambles have attracted climbers and walkers for centuries, but have also claimed many lives. It cannot be stressed too strongly that the Cuillins are the most dangerous mountains in Britain and only for experienced climbers, see further page 56. ▸▸ *For Sleeping, Eating and other listings, see pages 264-270.*

● Macleod's Tables are so named because legend has it that the clan chief held a huge
● open-air feast for King James V on one of the hilltops.

⁞ Law of the land

One of the most significant incidents in the island's history took place in April 1882, when a group of around 100 local crofters and their families fought a pitched battle against a force of 60 police sent by the government from Glasgow. The 'Battle of the Braes', as it became known, was caused, like many other such uprisings throughout the Highlands and Islands, by threatened evictions. The local crofters were so incensed by the injustice of the eviction notices served on them that they destroyed the offending documents, leading the government to dispatch its police force. The defeat of the government forces of law and order by a bunch of men, women and children with sticks and stones is often described as the last battle fought on British soil, and led eventually to the establishment of a Royal Commission to look into the crofters' grievances.

▲ The Cuillins

There are three routes into the Cuillins: from the Sligachan Hotel, from Glen Brittle, and from Elgol. The eastern part of the range is known as the **Red Cuillins**. Their smoother, conical granite peaks contrast sharply with the older, darker gabbro of the jagged-edged **Black Cuillins** to the west. The latter are particularly suitable for rock climbing and best approached from Glen Brittle, while the former are accessed from the Sligachan Hotel. There are 20 'Munros' (mountains over 3,000 ft in height) in the Cuillins, with the highest being Sgurr Alasdair, at 3,251 ft. Though the sheer majesty of the mountains can only be appreciated at close quarters by the climber, there are impressive views from Elgol, from the road into Glen Brittle and, more distantly, from the west coast of Sleat. **Glen Sligachan** is one of the most popular routes into the Cuillin range and the main access point for the more forgiving Red Cuillins, the walk to **Loch Coruisk**, or the ascent of **Marsco**.

Glen Brittle → *Phone code: 01478.*

Six miles along the A863 to Dunvegan from Sligachan is a turning left to Portnalong, Carbost and the Talisker Distillery (B8009), which soon leads to the entrance to Glen Brittle. The road down Glen Brittle affords great views of the western side of the imposing Black Cuillins, until it ends at the campsite and shore at the foot of the glen. From Glen Brittle there are numerous paths leading up to the corries of the Black Cuillins. There are many alternative options for those wishing to continue up to the upper corries or to the Main Ridge. One of the finest of the Cuillin corries is **Coire Lagan**. This walk starts from the beach at Glen Brittle village and takes you up to the lochan in the upper coire, with Sgurr Alasdair, the most difficult of the Munros, towering overhead. A fine Cuillin sampler is the short walk to the spectacular **Eas Mor** waterfall.

Talisker → *Phone code: 01478.*

A recommended trip for whisky drinkers, or if it's raining, is to the excellent **Talisker Distillery** ① *T01478-614308, www.malts.com, Easter-Oct Mon-Sat 0930-1700, Nov-Easter Mon-Fri 1400-1700, tours every 15-20 mins, £4,* at **Carbost** on the shores of Loch Harport, on the B8009 (not in the village of Talisker itself, which is on the west coast). This is Skye's only whisky distillery and produces a very smoky, peaty single malt.

Near the distillery is **Carbostcraft Pottery** ① *T01478-640259, Mon-Sat 0900- 1700 from Feb-Dec, also Sun in summer,* which produces a wide range of traditional and original pottery, including the famous 'torn pots'. They also have a shop in Portree.

 Every year there's a hill race up Glamaig, near Glen Sligachan. In 1899, it was climbed in 55 minutes (up and down) by a Gurkha soldier – in bare feet!

Elgol → *Phone code: 01471.*

One of the most rewarding drives on Skye is the 14-mile single-track road from Broadford to Elgol (Ealaghol), a tiny settlement near the tip of the Strathaird Peninsula, from where you can enjoy the classic view of the Cuillins from across Loch Scavaig and of the islands of Soay, Rùm and Canna. It was from here, on 4 July 1746, that the Young Pretender finally left the Hebrides. Before leaving, he was given a farewell banquet by the MacKinnons in what is now called **Prince Charlie's Cave**. There's also the added attraction of a dramatic boat trip, see page 269, to the mouth of **Loch Coruisk**, in the heart of the Black Cuillin. The glacial sea loch, romanticized by Walter Scott and painted by Turner, is over two miles long but only a few hundred yards wide, closed in by the sheer cliffs on either side and overshadowed by the towering mountains of black basalt and gabbro. The road to Elgol also gives great views of Bla Bheinn (pronounced Blaven), best seen from Torrin, at the head of Loch Slapin.

▲▲ Elgol to Camasunary Bay

Elgol is the starting point for the walk to Camasunary Bay. This nine-mile coastal walk is quite demanding, but on a clear day the views of the Cuillins make it well worth the effort. It starts from the car park in Elgol. From here, walk back up the road for a short distance, then turn left along a track behind some houses, signposted for 'Garsbheinn'. Beside the last of these houses is a sign for the path to Coruisk. Follow this path along a steep grassy slope. The views across Loch Scavaig to the island of Soay and the Cuillins behind are marvellous. The slope gets even steeper beneath Ben Cleat, and you'll need a good head for heights to continue, across the foot of Glen Scaladal, crossing a burn in the process (which can be tricky if it's in spate). Then it's on along the path beyond Beinn Leacach to Camasunary Bay, with its backdrop of mighty Sgurr na Stri and Bla Bheinn. The shortest way back is to retrace your steps, but as an alternative, follow the clear track from Camasunary up the right side of Abhainn nan Lean over the hills to the east until it joins the B8083 from Broadford. From here it's about 3½ miles back along the road to Elgol.

Broadford and the east coast → *Colour map 3, grid A4-5.*

Broadford (An t-Ath Leathann), Skye's second largest village, basically consists of a mile-long main street strung out along a wide bay. The village may be low on charm but it's high on tourist facilities and makes a good base for exploring the south and east of the island. The road north from Broadford to Portree passes through Sconser, departure point for the short ferry ride to the little-visited island of Raasay. ➤➤ *For Sleeping, Eating and other listings, see pages 264-270.*

Broadford

Broadford has plenty of accommodation and places to eat. Next to the Esso station is a Co-op, and there's a laundrette in the petrol station shop (open 24 hours), and bank with ATM. There is no tourist office as such, just an information point housed in the **Otter Shop** in the main car park (with erratic opening hours). It is also home to one of the most incongruous attractions on the island, or elsewhere in the Highlands, the **Skye Serpentarium** ① *T01471-822209, www.skyeserpentarium.org.uk, Apr-Oct Mon-Sat 1000-1700 (also Sun in Jul/Aug), £2.50, children £1.50*, where you can see, and touch, all kinds of snakes, lizards and other reptiles. A welcome retreat if it's raining. When the weather's clear you can take a trip on a glass-bottomed boat from the pier, see Activities and tours page 268.

The opening of the Skye Bridge, linking the island with the Kyle of Lochalsh, see page 209, has turned the former ferry terminal of Kyleakin (Caol Acain) into something of a backwater, as well as infuriating the locals with its £6 per car toll. The absence of road traffic, though, makes it a quiet place to stay, and it's now a favourite with backpackers, judging by the number of hostels. The bridge is supported in the middle on the small islet of **Eilean Ban**, erstwhile home of author and naturalist, Gavin Maxwell, and now home to an otter sanctuary. It can be visited as part of tour from the **Bright Water Visitor Centre** ⓘ *T01599-530040, Apr-Oct Mon-Fri 1000-1700, free (tour costs £8)*, in Kyleakin. The centre is worth a visit, especially if you have kids. There's precious little else to do here, other than look at the small ruin of **Castle Moil**.

Kylerhea

About four miles out of Kyleakin a road turns left off the A87 and heads southeast to Kylerhea (pronounced Kile-ray). The bridge may be the most convenient route to Skye, but the best way to cross is on the small car and passenger ferry that makes the 10-minute crossing to Kylerhea from Glenelg, see page 208. For full details of times and prices, see page 252. Near Kylerhea is the Forestry Commission **Otter Haven** ⓘ *T01320-366322, daily 0900 till 1 hr before dusk, free.* An hour-long nature trail takes you to an observation hide where you can look out for these elusive creatures.

Broadford to Portree

The road north to Portree runs between the fringes of the Red Cuillins and the coast, giving good views across to the **Isle of Scalpay**. The road then turns west along the shores of Loch Ainort to the turn-off for the **Luib Folk Museum** ⓘ *0900-1800, £1*, another of Peter MacAskill's island museums. The restored croft house has a smoky atmosphere and has old newspaper cuttings telling of the 'Battle of the Braes' and the 'Glendale Martyrs'.

The road runs north to **Sconser**, departure point for the ferry to Raasay (see below), then runs around Loch Sligachan and heads north to Portree. On the opposite side of the loch from Sconser are the crofting communities known as **The Braes**, who successfully opposed their landlords' eviction notices and brought the crofters' cause to the public's attention.

Isle of Raasay → *OS Landranger No 24.*

The lush and beautiful island of Raasay lies only a few miles off the east coast of Skye yet remains completely off the tourist trail. The island is a nature conservancy, and you may see seals, eagles and otters. Its hilly terrain and superb cliff scenery also offer numerous walking opportunities and the views from the highest point, **Dun Caan** (1,456 ft), with the Cuillins on one side and Torridon on the other, are simply beyond compare.

▲ The walk to the distinctive flat-topped summit of the extinct volcano, Dun Caan, via an old iron mine, is relatively straightforward and one of the most rewarding anywhere in the islands. So much so, in fact, that Boswell was inspired to dance a Highland jig on reaching the top, in 1773, during his grand tour with Dr Johnson. Another excellent walk starts from North Fearns, at the end of a road running east from **Inverarish**, to the deserted township of **Hallaig**, down the side of Beinn na Leac and back to North Fearns. The circular route is five miles long.

Raasay was for much of its history the property of the Macleods of Lewis, whose chief residence was the ruined **Brochel Castle**, before moving to **Clachan**, where **Raasay House** is now located (see below). The original Raasay House was torched by government troops after Culloden, along with all the island's houses and its boats, as punishment for the Macleods giving refuge to Bonnie Prince Charlie. After the Macleods sold the island in 1843, the Clearances began in earnest and Raasay suffered a long period of emigration, depopulation and poverty. It is not surprising,

Gaelic spread

Outside the Outer Hebrides, Skye is the most important centre of Gaelic culture, with a large proportion of the island's population speaking the Gaelic language in everyday life. This in itself is remarkable given the significant drop in population during the Clearances and the continued undermining of the Gaelic culture ever since, especially through the State education system.

Today, as in other parts of the Hebrides, the native culture is again under threat, this time from the huge influx of 'white settlers' from the south, but there is also a new-found pride and interest in the Gaelic language. This has been helped by the existence of the Gaelic college on Sleat, through Gaelic writers such as the late Sorley Maclean, a radical local newspaper (*The West Highland Free Press*), economic support from Highlands and Islands Enterprise, and spiritual underpinning from the Sabbatarian Free Church. Gaelic is being taught again in schools and can be heard on television. The ancient heritage of the Highlands and Islands is fighting back and reasserting itself as a major European culture.

then, that the island's most famous son, the great poet **Sorley Maclean**, wrote so passionately about this lost society. Born in Oskaig in 1911, he wrote in his native Gaelic as well as in English, and is highly regarded internationally. He died in 1996. Raasay's population now numbers around 150 and the island is a bastion of the Free Church, whose strict Sabbatarian beliefs should be respected by visitors.

Those who make it to the north of the island may wish to note that the two miles of road linking **Brochel** to **Arnish** were the work of one man, Calum Macleod. He decided to build the road himself after the council turned down his requests for proper access to his home. He spent between 10 and 15 years building it with the aid of a pick, a shovel, a wheelbarrow and a road-making manual which cost him three shillings. He died in 1988, soon after its completion, and it coninues to be known as 'Calum's Road'.

Sleat Peninsula → *Phone code: 01471. Colour map 3, grid A4.*

East of Broadford is the turn-off to the peninsula of Sleat (pronouned 'slate'), a part of the island so uncharacteristically green and fertile that it's known as 'The Garden of Skye'. Sleat is another entry point to the island. Ferries cross from Mallaig on the mainland to Armadale on the southeastern shore of the peninsula. While the rest of the island is the preserve of the Macleods, Sleat is MacDonald country. The MacDonalds of Sleat are one of the major surviving branches of Clan Donald, and have the right to use the title Lord MacDonald (but not Lord of the Isles, which is now used by the heir to the throne). ▶▶ *For Sleeping, Eating and other listings, see pages 264-270.*

Isle Ornsay

South of Duisdale is the signed turning for Isle Ornsay, or Eilean Iarmain (pronounced *eelan yarman*) in Gaelic, a very beautiful place in a small rocky bay overlooking the tidal Isle of Ornsay with the mountains of Knoydart in the background. This was once Skye's main fishing port, and the neat whitewashed cottages and tiny harbour are still there. It is also largely Gaelic-speaking, thanks mainly to the efforts of its landlord, Sir Iain Noble, who owns the hotel and his own local Gaelic whisky company as well as the northern half of the peninsula, which is known as Fearan Eilean Iarmain. ▶▶ *See Sleeping, page 266.*

A few miles further on is a turn-off to the left to the villages of **Ord**, **Tokavaig** and **Tarskavaig**, on the west coast of the peninsula, from where, on a clear day, there are views across to the Cuillins. Near Tokavaig is the ruin of **Dunsgaith Castle**, home of the MacDonalds of Sleat until the 17th century. Tarskavaig is a typical crofting township. In the early 19th century the MacDonalds wanted the more fertile glens inland for their sheep farms and so evicted the people to coastal townships like Tarskavaig. Just beyond the turn-off to Ord are the remains of **Knock Castle**, yet another MacDonald stronghold.

Ostaig

At Ostaig is the Gaelic College, **Sabhal Mor Ostaig** ① *T01471-844373*, where all subjects are taught in Gaelic, including full-time courses in business studies and media, as well as short courses in Gaelic music and culture during the summer months. The bookshop has a good selection of books and tapes for those wishing to learn the language. The college was founded by Sir Iain Noble. Ostaig is also the beginning or end (depending on which direction you're heading) of the detour to Tarskavaig, Tokavaig and Ord.

Armadale to the Point of Sleat

Just before the ferry pier at Armadale is **Armadale Castle** ① *T01471-844305, www.high landconnection.org/clandonaldcentre.htm, Apr-Oct daily 0930-1730, £4.50*, which was built in 1815 as the main residence of the MacDonalds of Sleat. Most of the castle is now a roofless ruin but the servants' quarters contain an excellent exhibition and accompanying video explaining the history of the Lordship of the Isles. The Clan Donald Lords of the Isles took over from their Norse predecessors in ruling the Hebrides until their power was broken in 1493. The former stables at the entrance comprise offices, a restaurant and bookshop, while the estate manager's house has been converted to accommodate an extensive library and archives. The castle is surrounded by 40 acres of handsome gardens and woodland, and there are ranger-led walks along nature trails with fine views across to the mainland.

Just beyond Armadale Castle is the tiny village of **Armadale** which is strung out along the wooded shoreline and merges into the neighbouring village of **Ardvasar** (pronounced Ard-vaa-sar), which has a post office, general store. Armadale's raison d'être is the ferry pier and there's not a huge amount to keep you occupied, but there are a couple of good handicraft shops. At the turn-off to the pier is **Skye Batiks** ① *T01471-844396*, which also has a shop in Portree, see page 268. Here you'll find the colourful cotton garments which make a unique souvenir of the island. They also now have B&B accommodation. On the ferry pier is **Ragamuffin** ① *T01471-844217, daily 0900-1800*, which sells a wide range of knitwear. About four or five miles past the ferry port, at the end of the road, is **Aird of Sleat**, a crofting township, from where you walk out to the lighthouse at the **Point of Sleat**. It's a five-mile walk on a clear path across moorland with fine coastal scenery.

● Sleeping

Portree *p253, map p253*
There are numerous hotels, guest houses and B&Bs in Portree, but accommodation can be hard to find in the busy summer season. There are several guest houses on Bosville Terr and many B&Bs on Stormyhill Rd and the streets running off it.

For a small fee the tourist office will book accommodation for you. Prices tend to be slightly higher in Portree than the rest of the island, though B&Bs on the outskirts of town are usually cheaper.

B Rosedale Hotel, Beaumont Cres, T01478-613131. 23 rooms. Open May-Sep. Cosy little hotel by the harbour, converted from fishermen's houses.

C Bosville Hotel, Bosville Terr, T01478-612846, www.macleodhotels.co.uk/bosville

18 rooms. Comfortable and stylish accommodation with friendly service. Boasts 2 award-winning restaurants (see Eating).
C Viewfield House Hotel, on the road into Portree from the south, T01478-612217, www.skye.co.uk/viewfield. 9 rooms. Open mid-Apr to mid-Oct. Grand old country house full of antiques, set in 20 acres of woodland garden. Log fire adds to the welcoming atmosphere; great value.
E Mr & Mrs Mathieson, 'Grenitote', 9 Martin Cres, T01478-612808, on Viewfield Rd heading south out of town. Good value.
E Portree House, Home Farm Rd, T01478-613713, nigel@potreehouse.demon. co.uk. 5 rooms. B&B with reduction on meals in the restaurant.
F Portree Backpackers Hostel, 6 Woodpark, Dunvegan Rd, T01478-613641, F613643. 26 beds.
F Portree Independent Hostel, Old Post Office, The Green, T01478-613737. 60 beds. Right in the centre of town, with laundrette (£3 per wash) and email facilities (£3 per hr).

Camping
There's a campsite at Torvaig, just outside the town, T01478-612209, open Apr-Oct.

Trotternish Peninsula *p254*
A Flodigarry Country House Hotel, a few miles north of Staffin and 20 miles north of Portree, T01470-552203, F552301. Beautifully located at the foot of the mighty Quiraing and with stunning views across Staffin Bay, this is one of the great country house hotels, with a relaxing old-world atmosphere and excellent restaurant. Flora MacDonald's actual cottage is in the grounds and has been tastefully refurbished, giving the chance to stay in a place steeped in the island's history. The lively bar is a good place to enjoy a laugh and a jig.
B Uig Hotel, on the right of the road into the village from Portree, beside a white church and opposite Frazer's Folly, Uig, T01470-542205, F542308. 17 rooms, open year round. Classy accommodation with great views across the bay, good food and a friendly island welcome. Offers clay pigeon shooting and fly fishing.
C Duntulm Castle Hotel, near Duntulm Castle, T01470-552213, www.duntulm castle.co.uk. Open Mar-Nov. Friendly and

homely with great views across the Minch to the Outer Hebrides. Idyllic and good value. Restaurant is open to non-residents.
D The Ferry Inn, Uig, T01470-542242, joycemary@supanet.com. Close to the ferry pier and serves bar meals.
D Glenview Inn and Restaurant, at Culnacnoc, just north of the Lealt Falls, T01470-562248. 5 rooms. Cosy and relaxed accommodation with a very fine restaurant.
E Idrigill House, Uig, T01470-542398, s.watkins@lineone.net. Good value B&B.
F Dun Flodigarry Backpackers Hostel T/F01470-552212. 66 beds. Open Mar-Oct. Only 100 yds from the bar of the **Flodigarry Country House Hotel**. Those who can't afford the luxury of the **Flodigarry House Hotel** can always opt for this more modest alternative. Laundry facilities, breakfast.
F SYHA Youth Hostel, Uig, T01470-542211, is high above the port on the south side of the village and is open mid-Mar to Oct.

Camping
There's a campsite south of Staffin Bay, T01470-562213, open mid Apr-end Sep.

Waternish, Dunvegan and Duirinish *p256*
There are numerous places to stay in and around Dunvegan, and the tourist information centre in the village will arrange accommodation for you, T01470-521581
A The House Over-By, a few yards away from the very wonderful **Three Chimneys**, see Eating, on Duirnish Peninsula, and run by the same folk. 6 sumptuous rooms, all with sea views.
B Atholl House Hotel, Dunvegan, T01470-521219, www.athollhotel.co.uk. Very comfortable accommodation.
B Harlosh House Hotel, just beyond Roskhill is a turning south off the A863 to T/F01470-521367, harlosh.house@virgin.net. 6 rooms. Open Easter to mid-Oct. Cosy, comfortable, great views and a reputation for superb food (evenings only).
C Lyndale House, Edinbane, T01470-582329, www.lyndale.net. 2 rooms. Quiet, delightful retreat hidden down a private drive off the A850 to Dunvegan. 300-year old house with lovely views and sunsets from the sitting room. Nice touches such as fresh flowers and bathrobes.

D Roskhill House, 3 miles south of Dunvegan Castle on the A863, T01470- 521317, stay@roskhill.demon.co.uk. 5 cosy rooms, peaceful setting, great food. Recommended.

The Cuillins and Mininish *p259*

C Sligachan Hotel, 7 miles south of Portree, where the A87 Kyleakin-Portree road meets the A863 to Dunvegan, T01471-8650204, F650207. The legendary rallying point for climbers who come to Skye for the Cuillins. The hotel's **Seamus** bar stocks an impressive selection of malts and also serves the island's real ales as well as meals.

C Talisker House, in the village of Talisker, T01471-640245, jon_and_ros.wathen@ virgin.net. 4 rooms. This excellent guest house makes an ideal retreat from the summer hordes, and serves fine food.

D Coruisk House, on the righthand side just after the Elgol village sign on the road from Broadford, T01471-866330, www.seafood-skye.co.uk. Restaurant with rooms. No smoking, all rooms en suite. Worth coming here for the freshest of seafood (lunch ££, dinner £££). Also have a self-catering cottage and traditional crofthouse for rent.

D Rowan Cottage, a mile east at Glasnakille, T01471-866287, www.rowancottage-skye.co.uk. Open mid-Mar to end Nov. Attractive B&B offering the best of home cooking (lunch ££, dinner £££, restaurant closed Tue).

F Croft Bunkhouse & Bothies, north of Carbost, near Portnalong, T/F01471-640254, pete@skyehostel.free-online.co.uk. Sleeps 26. Also room for camping, transport from Sligachan or Portree, rents mountain bikes, pub and shop nearby.

F Skyewalker Independent Hostel, T640250, skyewalker@easynet.co.uk. In a converted school beyond Portnalong on the road to Fiscavaig. 32 beds.

F SYHA Hostel, Glen Brittle, T01471-640278, in the village. It's open mid-Mar to end of Oct and has 39 beds.

Camping

The campsite opposite **Sligachan Hotel** is the most popular place to stay in the area. There's also a campsite by the shore in Glen Brittle, T01471-640404.

Broadford and the east coast *p261*

D Lime Stone Cottage, 4 Lime Park (behind the Serpentarium), Broadford, T01471-822142, kathielimepark@btinternet.com. One of the best places to stay around here, full of rustic charm.

D Ptarmigan, Broadford, T01471-822744, www.ptarmigan-cottage.com. Modern and comfortable B&B overlooking the bay.

E Churchton House, Isle of Raasay, T01478-660260, open all year.

E Isle of Raasay Hotel, on the Isle of Raasay nearby to the Outdoor Centre, T/F01478-660222. Open all year.

E Mrs Mackay, at Oskaig on the Isle of Raasay, T01478-660207. A good B&B including dinner.

E Raasay Outdoor Centre, T01478-660266, the main settlement on the island is Inverarish, a 15-min walk from the ferry dock. Half a mile further is this centre housed in the huge Georgian mansion that was Raasay House, which runs many and various adventure courses, from climbing to windsurfing, as well as offering basic accommodation from Mar to mid-Oct, and a campsite.

F Dun Caan Hostel, near the old ferry quay, Kyleakin, T01599-534087, www.skyerover.co.uk. Open all year and also hires bikes.

F Fossil Bothy, a mile or so south of Broadford, at Lower Breakish off the A87 to Kyleakin, T01471-822297. Has 8 beds and is open Easter-Oct, book in advance.

F SYHA Hostel, Broadford, is by the new pier, T01471-822442. Open all year.

F SYHA Hostel, Kyleakin, T01599-534585. Large, modern building a few hundred yards from the pier. Open all year.

F Skye Backpackers Hostel, Kyleakin, T/F01599-534510, skye@scotlands-top-hostels.co.uk. More relaxed option. Open all year, breakfast £1.50.

F SYHA Hostel, T01478-660240, open mid-Mar to end-Oct. Reached via a rough track leading up a steep hill from tiny Oskaig.

Sleat Peninsula *p263*

L Hotel Eilean Iarmain, at Isle Ornsay, T01471-833332, www.eileanarmain.co.uk. 12 rooms. Award-winning Victorian hotel full of charm and old-world character, with wonderful views. It is utterly lovely and romantic and an absolute must if you're in the area and can afford it. Award-winning restaurant features local shellfish landed only yards away (open to non-residents). A cheaper option is to eat in the cosy bar next door, which serves pub grub of an impossibly high standard in a more informal atmosphere. The hotel also offers winter shooting on the local estate, and you can enjoy a tasting of the local whisky.

L Kinloch Lodge, at the head of Loch na Dal, T01471-833214, www.kinloch-lodge.com. Lord and Lady MacDonald's family home is also an award-winning restaurant, offering the rare chance to enjoy superb food in the grandest of settings. The track that leads to the 19th-century Sporting Lodge turns off the A851 about 8 miles south of Broadford. Lady Claire MacDonald is one of the best known cooks in Scotland and author of several cookbooks, and if you do decide to treat yourself make sure you leave enough room for their exquisite puddings. The 5-course fixed menu is in our expensive range, but well worth it. Accommodation is in 10 en suite rooms. Open Mar-Nov.

B Duisdale Hotel, Duisdale, T01471-833202, www.duisdale.com. 19 rooms (2 with 4-poster beds). Country house hotel set in lovely grounds with great views across the Sound of Sleat. The restaurant serves good traditional Scottish cooking, and a 5-course meal is in the expensive range.

C Ardvasar Hotel, in Ardvasar, near the ferry terminal, T01471-844223, www.ardvasar. com. Traditional whitewashed coaching inn with 9 rooms, an excellent restaurant and the liveliest pub in the vicinity.

F Flora MacDonald Hostel, at Kilmore, between the turning for Isle Ornsay and Armadale, T01471-844440, www.isle-of skye -tour-guide.co.uk. Newly refurbished with all facilities, 32 beds, open all year, and free transport to and from Armadale Pier.

F SYHA Hostel, just before the turn-off to the ferry pier, T01471-844260. 42 beds. Open mid-Mar to end Oct, rents bikes.

● Eating

With the notable exception of the magnificent **Three Chimneys** restaurant the best food on Skye is normally served in hotel dining rooms, so also check the Sleeping section for places to eat. Many B&Bs also provide evening meals on request.

Portree p253, map p253
£££ Chandlery Seafood Restaurant, next door to the **Bosville Hotel**, see Sleeping. Superb French/Scottish cuisine using local produce.
£££ Lower Deck Seafood Restaurant, on the harbour front at the foot of Quay Brae, T01478-613611. Freshest of seafood and a contender with the **Chandlery** for the best food in town. Open Apr-Oct daily 1100-2200. For a budget treat try the excellent fish and chips from their takeaway next door.
£££ Skeabost House Hotel, 4 miles north of Portree on the Dunvegan Rd, T01470-532202, skeabost@sol.co.uk. This peaceful country house in lovely grounds on the shores of Loch Snizort has a reputation for fine food using the best local produce.
££ Ben Tianavaig, 5 Bosville Terr, T01478-612152. Excellent vegetarian bistro. Seating is limited so you'll need to book. Open for lunch at weekends, and Tue-Sun 1800-2130.
££ Bosville Restaurant, in the Bosville Hotel, see Sleeping. Also recommended. They offer a lunchtime special (soup, sand-wich and coffee for £5) which is great value.
£ Portree House, Home Farm Rd, see Sleeping, serves good value food, daily 1200-1545, 1730-2000.
£ Spicehut, Bayfield Rd, T01478-612681. Indian restaurant and takeaway. Open daily 1200-1430 and 1700-2400.
£ Steve's Kitchen Takeaway, on Bayfield Rd, opposite the library. For cheap Chinese takeaway food.
£ Tuireann Café, part of the arts centre, see Sights p253. Natural whole-foods and organic produce, home-made bread, cakes and pastries. Excellent quality and value. Open Mar-Oct Mon-Sat 1000-1800, Nov-Feb Tue-Sat 1000-1630.

Trotternish Peninsula p254
££ Oystercatcher Restaurant, in the village of Staffin, T01470-562384, closed Sun. A good place for food.

Skye & the Small Isles Isle of Skye Listings

● For an explanation of sleeping and eating price codes used in this guide, see inside the
● front cover. Other relevant information is found in Essentials, see pages 41-49.

£ **Pub on the Pier**, Uig, has cheap bar meals, and the famous Cuillin ales are brewed at the nearby Skye Brewery.You can also change foreign currency here. Open till 2300.

Waternish, Dunvegan and Duirinish *p256*

£££ **The Three Chimneys**, Duirinish Peninsula, T01470-511258, www.three chimneys.co.uk. Considered by many to be the best restaurant in the north of Scotland and, judging by the numerous awards they've won, that judgement can't be far wrong. Local seafood, meat, veg and dairy produce and a great wine list. Open daily 1230-1400 (except Sun) and 1830-2130.
££ **Lochbay Seafood**, Waternish Peninsula, T01470-592235. You should finish off the day with a meal at the this wonderful restaurant where you can almost see your dinner being landed. Open Apr-Oct for lunch and till 2030 (closed Sat).

Broadford and the east coast *p261*

£££ **Rendezvous**, at Breakish, south of Broadford on the main road to Kyleakin, T01471-822001. Expensive place to eat but excellent food.
££-£ **Claymore Bar-Restaurant**, at the south end of the village, T01471-822333. Decent bar meals.
££ **The Crofter's Kitchen**, outside the village of Kyleakin on the road to Broadford, T01599-534134. Good food, from snacks to 3-course meals. Open Mon-Sat 1000-2100, Sun 1230-2100.

⊕ Bars and clubs

Portree *p253, map p253*
The town's nightlife is mainly confined to eating and drinking.
Pier Hotel, Quay St, T01478-612094, by the harbour. The bar in this hotel is a real fishermen's drinking den.
Royal Hotel, Bank St, T01478-612525. Also popular is the bar here.

⊕ Entertainment

Portree *p253, map p253*
Portree Community Centre, Camanahd Sq, Park Rd, T01478-613736. This is the place to come if you fancy a wild Fri night ceilidh.

Aros Experience, see Sights p253, has a theatre which shows drama, movies and live music. Call the box office for details of their monthly programme, T01478-613750.

⊛ Festivals and events

Portree *p253, map p253*
Early Aug Highland Games are a 1-day event held in Portree.

⊙ Shopping

Portree *p253, map p253*
Carbostcraft Pottery, Bayfield Rd, which sells pottery with a huge variety of designs (they also have a shop near the Talisker Distillery, see p260).
Jackson's Wholefoods, at Park Pl, opposite the council offices, a wholefood store.
Outdoor Sports, Bridge Rd, next to **Skye Batiks**, Portree. Good for mountain gear.
Over the Rainbow, at the top of Quay Brae, T01478-612555. Open 0900-2200 in the high season. A good place to buy woollens.
Safeway supermarket, diagonally opposite the Bosville Hotel.
Skye Batiks, The Green, near the TIC, T01478-613331. Sells handmade 'batiks' (colourful cotton fabrics), which are pricey but unique souvenirs of Skye, see also p264.
Skye Woollen Mill, Dunvegan Rd, T01478-612889. Knitwear and tartan souvenirs can be found here.

The Cuillins and Minginish *p259*
Cioch Direct, 4 Ullinish, Struan, T01470-572307. For mountain gear.

⛰ Activities and tours

Portree *p253, map p253*
If the weather's good, Portree offers opport-unities for a wide variety of outdoor activities.
Boat trips, T01478-613718, or ask for Peter Urquhart at the pier, can be made to the island of Rona, north of Raasay, with the *MV Brigadoon*. Trips leave from the pier (Apr- Sep) and cost from £10 per person. Full-day charters are also available for £75-150 (12 passengers).
Island Cycles, on The Green, Mon-Sat 1000-1700, T01478-613121. Mountain bikes for hire here.

Portree Riding and Trekking Stables,
T01478-582419, are a couple of miles from
the town centre. Follow the Struan Rd (B885)
for 2 miles, then bear right at the fork
towards Peiness. Offer horse riding.
Skye Riding Centre, T01470-532439, 2 miles
north of Portree, at Borve on the road to Uig.
Offer horse riding.
Swimming pool, Camanahd Sq,
T01478-612655.

Trotternish Peninsula *p254*
Whitewave Activities, a few miles north of
Uig, on the A855 at Linicrowhere, T01471-
542414, info@white-wave.co.uk. Here you
can try windsurfing and sea kayaking. There's
also a café specializing in vegetarian, seafood
and celtic music, and a B&B.

The Cuillins and Minginish *p259*
The Bella Jane, T0800-7313089 (freephone
0730-2200), www.bellajane.co.uk, makes the
spectacular trip from Elgol into the gaping
maw of Loch Coruisk, one of the highlights
of any trip to Skye. It lasts 3 hrs, including
about 1½ hrs ashore, and cost £15, £7.50
children. You should be able to see seals and
porpoises en route. There's also a one-way
trip for experienced walkers/climbers who
wish to make the return journey on foot or to
explore the Cuillins. There are also trips on
the **Aquaxpolre** to Rùm or Canna.
For **climbing** the following guides have all
been recommended:
Colin Threlfall, Outdoor Sports (see below).
Cuillin Guides, Gerry Achroyd, Stac Lee, Glen
Brittle, T01478-640289.
Hugh Evans, 4d Wentworth St, Portree,
T01478-612682.
Richard MacGuire, 4 Matheson Place,
Portree, T01478-613180.
Skye Highs, Mike Lates, 3 Luib, Broadford,
T01471-822116.

Broadford and the east coast *p261*
Wildlife cruises, T0800-7832175, www.glass
bottomboat.co.uk, run from Broadford pier.
You can choose the glass-bottomed *Family's
Pride II*, or the much faster *SkyeJet*, a Rigid
Inflatable Boat (RIB) which has the
advantage of taking you farther afield.
Kyleakin Private Hire, T01599-534452, run a
taxi service and guided tours of the island.

Portree *p253, map p253*
There are 4 buses daily (Mar-Oct) Mon-Fri
(2 on Sat) around the Trotternish Peninsula, in
each direction, via **Uig**. There are daily buses
(4 Mon-Sat, 3 on Sun) to **Kyleakin**, and 3
buses daily Mon-Sat to **Armadale** via
Broadford. There are 2 daily buses to **Carbost**
(for the Talisker Distillery) and Mon-Fri (1 on
Sat), and 2 daily buses to **Glenbrittle** (in the
summer only). There are 3 buses daily Mon-Fri
to **Glendale** via **Dunvegan** (1 on Sat), and 3
buses to **Waternish** via **Dunvegan** (Mon-Sat).
For taxis call **Ace Taxis**, T01478-613600 or
A2B Taxis, T01478-613456.
　There's a **Scottish Citylink** service from
Inverness (3 Mon-Sat, 2 on Sun, 3 hrs) and
also from **Glasgow** via **Fort William** to
Kyleakin, **Portree** and **Uig** 3-4 times daily
(3 hrs from Fort William to Portree). Winter
services are severely limited with only a few
buses in each direction each day.

Trotternish Peninsula *p254*
Bus Scottish Citylink runs a service to/from
Inverness, **Fort William** and **Glasgow**.
Ferries leave from **Uig** to **Lochmaddy** on
North Uist (1¾ hrs) and to **Tarbert** on
Harris (1¾ hrs). For details see p252, or
contact Uig, T01470-542219.

**Waternish, Dunvegan and
Duirinish** *p256*
There are 3 buses daily (Mar-Oct, Mon-Fri) from
Glendale to and from **Portree** via **Dunvegan**.
The bus leaves Portree at 1000, arrives at the
castle at 1048 and returns at 1252 (Mar-Oct
only). There is 1 bus on Sat and a daily bus from
Dunvegan to Glendale (not Sun).

The Cuillins and Minginish *p259*
There are 2 daily buses from **Portree** to **Glen
Brittle** Mon-Sat during the summer only.
Otherwise, take the **Portree-Carbost-
Fiscavaig** bus, which leaves twice Mon-Fri
and once on Sat, and get off at the turn-off,
then walk the remaining 7 miles, or hitch,
though it can be slow. The only public
transport to **Elgol** is the postbus from
Broadford, which runs twice Mon-Sat and
once on Sun, and takes 2 hrs. There's a
regular bus service (weekdays only) from

Portree and Sligachan to Portnalong,
T01470-532240.

Broadford and the east coast *p261*
Daily **Citylink** buses run from **Broadford** to
and from **Portree**, **Inverness** and **Fort
William**. Waterloo buses run daily to and
from **Kyleakin**, **Portree** (£6 return) and
Armadale/Ardvasar. There are buses from
Kyleakin to **Portree** via **Broadford** (4 daily),
to **Armadale** and **Ardvasar** via Broadford
(3 daily Mon-Sat) and half hourly to **Kyle of
Lochalsh**, see p209, via the Skye Bridge.

CalMac car and passenger ferry runs from
Sconser to Raasay daily Mon-Sat every hour. It
takes 15 mins and costs £4.45 per person
return, plus £17.95 per car and £1 per bicycle.

Car hire at **Sutherlands** at the Esso Garage,
Broadford, T01471-822225. From £30 per
day. Bikes can be hired from **Fairwinds
Bicycle Hire**, just past the Broadford Hotel,
T01471-822270. Mar-Oct

Sleat Peninsula *p263*
For full details of ferry crossings to Mallaig,
see p252. There are 3 buses daily, except
Sun, from **Armadale Pier** to **Portree** (1 hr
20 mins) and **Kyleakin** (1 hr) via **Broadford**
(40 mins). The first bus leaves at 0935.

⊙ Directory

Portree *p253, map p253*
Banks **Bank of Scotland** and **Clydesdale
Bank**, both on Somerled Sq. **Royal Bank of
Scotland** is on Bank St. All have ATMs.
Internet **Portree Independent Hostel**,
see Sleeping p264, at the post office and at
Portree Backpacker's Hostel, Dunvegan Rd.
Laundry At the **Portree Independent
Hostel. Post** At the top of Quay Brae.

Broadford and the east coast *p261*
Banks **Bank of Scotland** by the shops
opposite the road to the new pier in Broadford.

The Small Isles

*These four tenacious little siblings are a world away from the Scottish mainland and
not for the faint or fickle traveller. It takes longer to reach them from London than it
does to fly to Australia, so you have to be pretty determined. Those who do make it
this far are rewarded with perfect peace and an almost primeval silence and
solitude. This is nature in its purest form, a slow-moving, sepia-tinged counterpoint
to the frenetic pace and special effects of 21st century life.* ‣‣ *For Sleeping, Eating and
other listings, see pages 273-274.*

Ins and outs
Getting there A CalMac passenger-only ferry sails from Mallaig to all four islands
once daily Monday to Thursday and twice on Friday and Saturday, returning on the
same days. For more details contact the CalMac office in Mallaig, T01687-462403. At
Muck passengers are transferred to small boats as there are no suitable piers. There
aren't any transport connections with Skye.

From Apr-Sep the CalMac ferries from Mallaig are supplemented by cruises from
Arisaig with **Arisaig Marine** ⓘ *T01687-450224, www.airsaig.co.uk.* There's a good
chance of seeing dolphins, porpoises, and even whales, during the bumpy ride. For
details, see page 207. ‣‣ *For further details, see Transport page 274.*

Eigg → *Phone code: 01687. Colour map 3, grid A3-B3.*

Little Eigg (pronounced *egg*), only five miles long by three miles wide, has had
something of a chequered past. In 1577 it was the scene of one of the bloodiest
episodes in the history of Clan warfare, when 395 MacDonalds, almost the entire
population, were trapped in a cave and suffocated by a raiding party of Macleods

from Skye, who lit a fire at the entrance. More recently it has been at the heart of a bitter land ownership debate. Having endured a succession of absentee landlords, ranging from the merely eccentric to the criminally negligent, the 70 remaining islanders seized the moment in 1997 and bought the island themselves, in conjunction with the Scottish Wildlife Trust. Now everyone can enjoy the island's wildlife, which includes otters, seals, eagles and many other birds, such as the Manx shearwater, guillemots and black-throated divers. It's worth tagging along on one of the regular walks organized by the Scottish Wildlife Trust warden, John Chester.

The island is dominated by **An Sgurr**, a distinctive 1,289 ft flat-topped basalt peak with three vertical sides. It can be climbed fairly easily by its western ridge, though the last few hundred feet is precipitous, and there are superb views of the Inner Hebrides and mountains of Knoydart from the summit. Sitting in the shadow of the Sgurr, at the southeastern corner, is the main settlement, **Galmisdale**. This is where the ferries drop anchor (passengers are transferred to a smaller boat), and there's a post office, shop and tearoom, all by the pier. At the northern end is the small township of **Cleadale**, on the Bay of Laig. Just to the north are the **'Singing Sands'**, a beach that makes a strange sound as you walk across it. At the end of the island's only road you'll find its most famous property, **Howlin' House**, which apparently once belonged to JRR Tolkien. More details on the island are available at www.isleofeigg.org. ›› *For Sleeping, Eating and other listings, see pages 273-274.*

Muck → *Phone code: 01687. Colour map 3, grid B3.*

Tiny Muck, just two miles long by one mile wide, is the smallest of the four islands and is flat and fertile, with a beautiful shell beach. It has been owned by the MacEwan family since 1879. The island gets its unfortunate name (*muc* is Gaelic for pig) from the porpoises, or 'sea pigs', that swim round its shores. The ferry drops anchor near **Port Mór**, where there's accommodation. The tearoom here does snacks and sells fresh bread. Visit the island's website, www.islemuck.com. ›› *For Sleeping, Eating and other listings, see page 273.*

Rùm → *Phone code: 01687. Colour map 3, grid A3.*

Diamond-shaped Rùm, known as the Forbidden Island, is the largest of the group and the most wild, beautiful and mountainous. The island is owned and run by Scottish Natural Heritage as an enormous outdoor laboratory and research station, and most of the 30 or so inhabitants are employed by them. Studies of the red deer population are among the most important areas of their work, and access to parts of the island is restricted. This is not prohibitive, though, and there are many marked nature trails, walks and birdwatching spots. The island is a haven for wildlife, and perhaps its most notable resident is the magnificent white-tailed sea eagle, successfully re-introduced on to Rùm in the 1980s and now spreading beyond the island. Rùm is also home to golden eagles, Manx shearwaters and, less appealingly, millions of midges. The island is the wettest of the Small Isles and a haven for the little pests. ›› *For Sleeping, Eating and other listings, see page 273.*

Ins and outs
Ferries are anchored at the new pier, at the mouth of Loch Scresort, from where it's a 15-minute walk to Kinloch Castle. The castle stands at the head of narrow Loch Scresort by the little hamlet of **Kinloch**, where you'll find the one-and-only shop and the community hall which sometimes operates as a café.

The end of an era

George Bullough and his wife, Lady Monica, brought a slice of Belgravia to the tiny Hebridean island of Rùm. Every autumn the family showed up to stalk deer and throw lavish parties for the glitterati and aristocracy of the day. Guests would be met at the pier by chauffeur-driven Albion cars while those arriving by ferry would step into a horse-drawn carriage, or be given a piggy-back by the castle staff when the tide was out. The outrageously wealthy Bulloughs guarded their privacy with a level of ruthlessness that would make even today's pop and film stars blush. Guns were routinely fired at passing boats to warn off any unwanted commoners and discourage the curious.

All this frivolous excess ended suddenly with the outbreak of war in 1914. George Bullough was appointed to a military post, the island's able-bodied staff were sent to the trenches to die for their country and the family's 220-ft steam-yacht, Rhouma, became a minesweeper. After the war, the Bulloughs visited less and less and the castle began to show signs of neglect. Even the poor hummingbirds died when the heating failed. Sir George himself died in 1939 and Lady Monica abandoned the place in 1954 – literally – leaving musical instruments on the stands in the ballroom and wine in the cellar. In 1957 the Bullough family sold Rùm to the Nature Conservancy for £23,000.

Kinloch Castle
① By guided tour only; Mon at 1330, Tue-Thu and Sat/Sun at 1400 and Fri at 1200, £2, children free.

Though it looks like a wilderness, Rùm once supported a population of 300. Most of them were shipped off to Canada in the mid-19th century, leaving behind an uninhabited deer forest for sporting millionaires. One of these, John Bullough, a cotton millionaire from Accrington, bought it in 1888 and passed it on to his son, Sir George Bullough, who built the extravagant and extraordinary Kinloch Castle. No expense was spared on this massive late-Victorian mansion, built, in 1900 at a cost of £250,000 (which equates to £15 mn today). It took 300 men nearly 3 years to build Bullough's dream, using red Annan sandstone from Dumfrieshire shipped by puffer from the mainland. For the gardens, 250,000 tons of soil was shipped from Ayrshire and used for planting exotic specimens collected from around the world. A nine-hole golf course and bowling green were laid out, along with a Japanese-style garden and huge walled garden. Hothouses were built to grow tropical fruits and palm houses were home to hummingbirds, turtles and even alligators. One of these creatures escaped, only to be shot by Bullough to prevent them 'interfering with the comfort of the guests'. As well as the elaborate carvings, wood panelling, furniture and flooring, the castle also incorporarated many state-of-the-art features such as an electricity generator, central heating, air conditioning and an internal telephone system (the first private residence in Scotland to do so). Pride of place, however, went to the magnificent Orchestrion, a fantastical mechanical contraption that simulated a 40-piece orchestra and belted out military marches, polkas, operatic excerpts and popular tunes of the day from its position under the main staircase. It is still in working order and visitors today will be treated to a gloriously surreal rendition of The Liberty Bell March (the Monty Python theme tune to you and me). Michael Palin would heartily approve.

Kinloch Castle was a finalist in the BBC's first Restoration series and is currently undergoing a major refurbishment. Visitors must take off their shoes as they are escorted round the lavish rooms, many of them fading, peeling or leaking. The castle

is a genuinely fascinating testament to Edwardian wealth and extravagance and the **273**
tour is worth the boat trip alone. You can even stay at the castle, in the hostel which
occupies the former servants' quarters (what else did you expect?).

Island walks

Rùm's other great attraction is its mountain range, which offers some of the best
island mountain treks outside the Cuillins of Skye. The highest point is **Askival**
(2,664 ft), which can be reached by the main ridge from **Hallival**, though the route
involves some rock scrambling and is only advised for fit and experienced walkers.
Before setting out, ask permission from the manager of the reserve office at the White
House ① *T01687-462026, Mon-Fri 0900-1230.*

The Bullough family mausoleum, built in the style of a Greek Doric temple, stands
incongruously on the west coast at **Harris Bay**. It's an interesting 7½-mile walk across
to the mausoleum from Kinloch. A less strenuous alternative is the **Kinloch Glen Trail**
which is signposted by the stone bridge as you head from the castle to the farm
steading. The circular route is 4 km and takes a leisurely 1 ½ hrs.

Canna → *Colour map 3, grid A3.*

Canna is the most westerly of the Small Isles and is owned by the National Trust for
Scotland. It's a small island, five miles long by one mile wide, bounded by cliffs and
with a rugged interior, fringed by fertile patches. It's attached to its smaller neighbour,
Sanday, by a narrow isthmus which is covered, except at low tide. The main attraction
for visitors is some fine walking. It's about a mile from the ferry jetty up to the top of
Compass Hill (458 ft), so called because its high metallic content distorts compasses.
The highest point on the island is **Carn a' Ghaill** (690 ft). During the summer, a day trip
from Mallaig allows you over nine hours in which to explore Canna and enjoy the
fantastic views across to Rùm and Skye.

The population of 20 mostly work on the island's farm. Canna was gifted to the
National Trust by its benevolent owner, the late Dr John Lorne Campbell, a notable
Gaelic scholar. The island continues to be run as a single working farm and, since it was
sold in 1938, has been an unofficial bird sanctuary with 157 recorded bird species,
including Manx shearwater and puffins. ▶▶ *For Sleeping, Eating and other listings, see page 273.*

⊜ Sleeping

Eigg *p270*
D Kildonan House, T01687-482446. The
island's only guest house, price includes
dinner and the food is superb.
F The Glebe Barn, T01687-482417,
www.glebebarn.co.uk. 24-bed
independent hostel and outdoor centre.
Open Apr-Oct (all year for groups).
Comfortable accommodation in twin,
family and bunk rooms. Sitting room
with log stove. Residencial courses
and retreats, self-catering or
fully-catered options for groups and
exclusive lets.
Self-catering cottages are also available,
for details visit www.isleofeigg.org.

Muck *p271*
D Port Mór House, T01678-462365. The
price includes dinner which is also available
to non-residents. Alternatively, you can ask
permission to camp at the tearoom.

Rùm *p271*
E Bay View, T01687-462023. The only B&B.
Book well in advance.
E-F Kinloch Castle, T01687-462037,
castleman ager@rumcastle.free_/online.
co.uk. Open Mar to end-Oct. 42-bed hostel in
the old servants' quarters, with twin, 4-bed
and 6-bed dorms, also 3 double rooms and 1
family room (**D**) available for B&B. Also has
café selling snacks and meals to guests only.

Camping

F **Bothies**, and camping is allowed at Kinloch. Contact the reserve manager at the White House, T01687-462026.

Canna *p273*
Those wishing to stay can **camp rough**, with permission from the **National Trust for Scotland**, or rent out their self-catering cottage, T0131-226 5922, www.nts.org.uk.

❼ Eating

There is a tearoom and shop on each island with the exception of Canna, where there are no shops so you'll need to bring your own supplies. Most of the B&Bs and guest houses serve food. The well-stocked shop on Eigg is at the jetty, T01687-482432, open Mon-Sat. The café/tearoom on Rùm is housed in the village hall, it serves hot drinks, cakes, soup and other home-made food and is open several afternoons a week during summer. The shop has limited opening hourse, depending on the requirements of island life, but is always open after 1700. Call the Reserve Office, T01687-462026, to check in advance. The village hall is always open as an escape from the rain or midges.

▲ Activities and tours

Guided walks are organized on all Eigg (Sat and Sun) and Muck (Wed), ranging in length and difficulty, for groups of 4-10. All cost £4.50. Book through **Arisaig Marine**, T01687-450224, www.arisaig.co.uk, 0900-1730.

❸ Transport

Boat CalMac operates the passenger-only ferry from **Mallaig** to all 4 islands once daily Mon-Thu and twice on Fri and Sat, returning on the same days. There's also a **non-landing cruise** around all the islands which costs £13 but you can sail to all 4 islands if you catch the 0620 ferry on Sat. A second ferry leaves on Sat, making it possible to spend time on one of the islands. Bicycles cost £2 for any trip.

To **Eigg** 1 hr 10 mins direct, £5.15 one way) on Mon, Tue (via **Muck**), Thu, Fri and Sat. To **Muck** (1 ½ hrs direct, £7.90 one way) on Tue, Thu (via Eigg), Fri and Sat (via Eigg). To **Rùm** (1 hr 10 mins direct, £7.75 one way) on Mon (via Eigg), Wed, Fri and Sat. To **Canna** (2 hrs direct, £9.80 one way) on Mon (via **Eigg** and **Rùm**), Wed (via **Rùm**), Fri (via Rùm) and Sat.

Bus For a bus/taxi service on Eigg, call **Davie Robertson**, T01687-482494.

Bike hire from Eigg Bikes, call Stuart Thomson, T01687-482469.

Outer Hebrides

⁞ Footprint features

Introduction

The Outer Hebrides – or Long Island as they are also known –
consist of a narrow 130-mile long chain of islands, lying
40 miles off the northwest coast of the Scottish mainland.
Relentlessly battered by fierce Atlantic winds, the islands can
seem a hostile environment and an unappealing proposition,
particularly if you happen to be stuck there on a wet Sunday
without your own means of transport. Much of the interior is
bleak peat bog, rocks and endless tiny lochs, and the long,
straggling crofting communities only add to the feeling of
desolation. But there are also miles of superb beaches, wild
mountain scenery, numerous archaeological treasures and
long hours of summer daylight in which to appreciate it all.

Despite the frequency of transport connections with the
mainland, the Outer Hebrides remain remote in every sense.
Unlike Skye and the Inner Hebrides, tourism is of far less
importance to the local economy. In many ways, the islands
are the last bastion of the old Highland life. Though newer
industries such as fish farming have been introduced, the
traditional occupations of crofting, fishing and weaving still
dominate, and outside Stornoway on Lewis (the only
decent-sized town in the islands) life is very much a traditional
one, revolving around the seasons and the tides. Almost every
islander has more than one occupation, so don't be surprised
if the landlady of your guest house also weaves Harris Tweed,
or if her husband drives the postbus as well as doing a bit of
fishing on the side. This creates a network of relationships
where everyone knows everyone else.

★ Don't miss...

1 **Calanais** Visit the standing stones here, preferably at night when there's a spooky atmosphere, page 286.

2 **Uig sands** Take a stroll along these wonderful sands, the loveliest beach on Lewis page 288.

3 **Bays** Hire a car and drive through the weird lunar landscape at Bays, on the east coast of Harris, page 295.

4 **Barra** Fly to this island, where the planes land on the beach, page 302.

5 **St Kilda** Take a trip here, home to some of the largest seabird colonies in Europe, page 307.

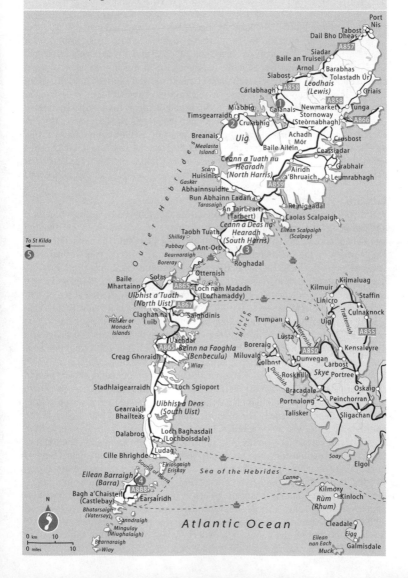

Outer Hebrides

Ins and outs

Getting there

British Airways/Loganair flies from Glasgow to Stornoway on Lewis, Barra and Benbecula on North Uist. There are also flights from Edinburgh to Stornoway, Inverness to Stornoway, and from Benbecula to Barra and Stornoway. **CalMac** car and passenger ferries sail to and from Stornoway (Lewis), Tarbert (Harris), Lochmaddy (North Uist), Lochboisdale (South Uist) and Castlebay (Barra). Ferry details are given under each respective destination, but note that times change according to the day of the week and time of the year. For full details of ferry timetables contact **CalMac**, T01475-650100, www.calmac.co.uk. Car space is limited during the summer months, so it's advisable to book ahead, T0990-650000. For details of bus connections on Skye and on the mainland, contact **Scottish Citylink**, T0990-505050. A much cheaper way to get around the islands with a car is with one of **CalMac**'s Island Hopscotch tickets. There are various route options, and tickets give you 30 days unlimited travel on each route. For example, a ticket for the Oban-Lochboisdale-Berneray-Leverburgh-Stornoway-Ullapool route allows you to visit South and North Uist, Harris and Lewis and costs £36 per passenger and £151 per car. See the **CalMac** guide or call the numbers above for full details of the Island Hopscotch Tickets, and the Island Rover Ticket, which gives unlimited travel on most **CalMac** routes for eight or 15 days and costs £47.50/69 per passenger and £228/341 per car. ▸▸ *For further details, see Transport pages 290, 296 and 306.*

> ✿ *Weather conditions are so changeable that flights are prone to delay and can be very bumpy. Flights to Barra have an added complication. They land on the beach, meaning that the runway disappears twice a day under the incoming tide.*

Getting around

You should allow plenty of time to explore the islands fully. With your own transport and travelling from top to bottom, a week would be enough time for a whistle-stop tour but not enough to explore in any depth or scratch beneath the surface. You will need to allow for the lack of public transport on Sundays on most islands (taxi is the only way around), and for the fact that weather conditions frequently affect ferry and flight timetables. **British Airways/Loganair** fly between Barra, Benbecula and Stornoway daily. A ferry sails to Berneray from Leverburgh (Harris) three or four times daily. Several ferries sail daily from Barra to the island of Eriskay. There's also a regular passenger ferry from Ludag in South Uist to Eoligarry on Barra. Bus services have improved and now run regularly to most main towns and villages on the islands. Most of the islands' roads are single track but in good condition and, unlike other parts of the Highlands and Islands, not too busy. On Sunday you'll barely meet another soul. Petrol stations are few and far between, expensive and closed on Sundays. The normal rules for single track roads apply and, as elsewhere in the Highlands, you need to look out for wandering sheep. Distances are greater than most people imagine. For example, the distance from Nis (Ness) at the northern tip of Lewis to Leverburgh in the south of Harris is 85 miles. From Stornoway to Tarbert is 37 miles. And the distance from Otternish in the north of North Uist to Lochboisdale, the main ferry port on South Uist, is 50 miles. Several local car hire agencies offer reasonable rental deals. Expect to pay around £15-25 per day, depending on the size of engine and age of the car. You cannot take a rented car off the islands. Cycling is a great way to explore the islands. You can fully appreciate the amazing scenery around, and it only costs a few pounds to transport a bike by ferry. There is, of course, the major problem of strong winds, which can leave you frustrated and exhausted, especially when cycling into the prevailing easterly wind. ▸▸ *For further details, see Transport pages 290, 296 and 306.*

☃ Never on a Sunday

The islands are the *Gaidhealtachd*, the land of the Gael. Gaelic culture has remained more prominent here than in any other part of Scotland, and the way of life and philosophy of the islanders will seem totally alien and fascinating to many visitors. Gaelic is the first language for the majority of the islanders – and the only one for the older generation – but the all-pervading influence of the English media has taken its toll and the language is under threat. Though Gaelic is still taught in schools, the younger generation tends to speak to each other in English. Visitors will not have any language problems, as the Gaelic-speaking inhabitants are so polite they will always change to English when visitors are present, though place names and signposts are in Gaelic.

The church is also an important factor in preserving the language, and services are usually held in Gaelic. In fact, religion is one of the most pervasive influences of Hebridean life, and the islanders' faith is as strong as the winds that pound their shores. The islands are split between the Presbyterian Lewis, Harris and North Uist, and the predominantly Roman Catholic South Uist and Barra. Benbecula, meanwhile, has a foot in either camp. On Lewis and Harris the Free Church is immensely powerful and the Sabbath is strictly observed. Don't expect to travel anywhere by public transport, shops and petrol stations will be closed and you'll be hard pressed to find a place to eat. Even the swings in the playgrounds are padlocked! Things are changing, however, and October 2002 saw the revolutionary move to allow Loganair to fly to Stornoway on a Sunday. Despite protests of tsunami-like proportions from the church, who described the idea as "a breach of God's moral law", Loganair's tourist-friendly flights went ahead.

Tourist information

The Outer Hebrides are made up of more than 200 islands, only 10 of which are populated: Lewis and Harris; Scalpay; Berneray; North Uist; Benbecula; South Uist; Eriskay; Barra; and Vatersay; giving a total population of just under 30,000. The main population centre is Stornoway on Lewis, the only major town in the islands. The rest of the population is scattered throughout the islands in much smaller villages, mostly strung out along the coast. There are tourist information centres in Stornoway and Tarbert which are open all year round, and also in Lochmaddy, Lochboisdale and Castlebay which are open early April to mid October. Full details are given under each destination. The Western Isles Tourist Board produces an accommodation brochure as well as the essential *Western Isles Official Tourist Map* (Estate Publications; £3.95), which gives place names in English and Gaelic. They also have their own website which provides lots of information on the islands, including up and coming events, www.visithebrides.com. You should also invest in a copy of the *Highlands & Islands Travel Guide* which is available from the local tourist information centres. Accommodation on the islands is generally not difficult to find, except perhaps at the height of the summer when you should book in advance, either directly or through the local tourist office. It's also a good idea to book ahead if you're staying on a Sunday, and if you're staying in the countryside, you should check if there's a convenient pub or hotel to eat in, and if not, make arrangements to eat at your B&B. ▸▸ *For further accommodation information, see page 44.*

Leodhas (Lewis) → *Phone code: 01851. Colour map 1.*

Lewis constitutes the northern two thirds of the most northerly island in the Outer Hebrides. It is by far the most populous of the Outer Hebridean islands and, with over 20,000 inhabitants, makes up two thirds of the total population. Just over 8,000 people live in Stornoway, the largest town in the Hebrides and the administrative capital of the Western Isles. The majority of the rest of the population live in the long line of crofting townships strung out along the west coast between Port Nis (Ness) and Càrlabhagh (Carloway). The west coast is also where you'll find the island's most interesting sites: the prehistoric remains of Dùn Chàrlabhaigh (Carloway) Broch, the impressive Calanais (Callanish) Standing Stones, the restored blackhouse village of Garenin and the Arnol Blackhouse. These can all be visited as a day trip from Stornoway, either as an organized tour or on the 'West Side Circular' bus service. The interior of the northern half is flat peat bog, hence the island's name which means 'marshy' in Gaelic. Further south, where Lewis becomes Harris, the scenery is more dramatic as the relentlessly flat landscape gives way to rocky hills, providing the backdrop to the sea-lochs that cut deep into the coast and the beautiful beaches around Uig. → *For Sleeping, Eating and other listings, see pages 288-290.*

History

Lewis was dominated by the Vikings, and the Norse influence can be seen in many of the place names, such as Uig (which is Norse for 'a bay'). After the end of Norwegian sovereignty in 1266, the island was ruled by the Macleods, said to be descendants of early settlers from Iceland. Control of the island was wrested from them by the Mackenzies, who then proceeded to sell it, in 1844, to Sir James Matheson. The new owner built Lews Castle in Stornoway and began to develop the infrastructure of the island as well as investing in new industries. Though many crofts were cleared and families sent to Canada, the people of Lewis fared well and certainly much better than their counterparts in the Southern Isles.

The next proprietor was Lord Leverhulme, founder of Lever Brothers, who bought the island (along with Harris) in 1918. He planned to turn Lewis into a major fishing centre and ploughed money into developing the infrastructure. He was forced to abandon his plans, however, partly because of the decline of the fishing industry, and partly owing to the growing conflict between him and the islanders returning from the war who wanted land of their own to farm. As a final benevolent gesture, Lord Leverhulme offered Lewis to the islanders, but only Stornoway Council accepted. The island was then divided into estates and sold, and hundreds of people emigrated.

Today the economy of Lewis is still based on the traditional industries of crofting, fishing and weaving, though there are other economic activities such as fish farming, which is now a major employer, service industries, tourism, construction and the onshore oil yard at Stornoway.

Steòrnabhagh (Stornoway) → *Colour map 1, grid B3. Population: 8,132.*

The fishing port of Stornoway, the only town in the Outer Hebrides, is the islands' commercial capital and as such boasts more services and facilities than you might expect in any town of comparable size. It's not a pretty place, dominated as it is by the oil industry, but has the full range of banks, shops, hotels, guest houses, pubs and

restaurants, garages, car hire firms, sports facilities, an airport and ferry terminal, and **281**
for the visiting tourist it presents a rare opportunity to stock up on supplies.

Stornoway is also the administrative capital and home to the Comhairle nan
Eilean (Western Isles Council), which has done much to broaden the local economy
and to promote and protect Gaelic language and culture, but is probably best known
for its disastrous financial dealings with the Bank of Credit and Commerce
International (BCCI), which collapsed in 1991, losing the islands a cool £23 million.
▸▸ *For Sleeping, Eating and other listings, see pages 288-290.*

Ins and outs

Getting there and around Stornoway is the island's transport hub. The airport is
4 miles east of the town centre, a £5 taxi ride away. The **CalMac** ferry terminal is just
beyond the bus station, which is on South Beach, a short walk from the town centre.
Buses leave from Stornoway to all parts of the island and also to Tarbert and Leverburgh

Sleeping
Cabarfeidh **6**
Laxdale Holiday Park **7**
Mrs Anne Macleod's B&B **1**

Mrs MacMillan's B&B **2**
Park Guest House **3**
Royal **4**
Stornoway Backpackers Hostel **5**

Eating
Stornoway
  Balti House **2**

on Harris. Bus timetables are available from the tourist office. The town is compact and most of what you need is within easy walking distance of the tourist office. Some of the B&Bs in the residential areas are quite a distance from the centre, but there's an hourly town bus service, or hire a taxi. ▶▶ *For further details, see Transport page 290.*

Tourist information The TIC ① *26 Cromwell St, T01856-703088, Apr-May and Sep-Oct Mon-Fri 0900-1800, Sat 0900-1700, Jun-Aug Mon-Fri 0900-2000, Oct-Mar Mon-Fri 0900-1700*, stocks maps, bus timetables and various books and brochures, and sell tickets for minibus tours to Calanais and for wildlife trips around Lewis and Harris.

Sights

Stornoway is short on conventional tourist sights and once you've been to the tourist office and bought the necessities from the local supermarkets, there's not much else to do. The focal point of the town has always been its sheltered deep-water **harbour** and, though the fishing industry has declined since its peak at the end of the last century, there's still a fair amount of activity, especially at the fish market on North Beach on Tuesday and Thursday evenings. The harbour is usually full of seals, giving the town its nickname of Portrona (port of seals). There's a good view across the harbour to **Lews Castle**, a 19th-century edifice built by Sir James Matheson with money earned from opium and tea. The castle now houses a college and its real attraction is the wooded grounds, the only place you'll see trees on the islands.

    Museum nan Eilean ① *Francis St, T01851-703773, Apr to Sep Mon-Sat 1000- 1730, Oct-Mar Tue 1000-1700 and Sat 1000-1300, free*, features a range of temporary exhibitions on island life and history. Anyone remotely interested in Harris Tweed should visit the **Lewis Loom Centre** ① *T01851-703117, Mon-Sat 1000-1700, £2*, housed in the Old Grainstore at the northern end of Cromwell Street, just off Bayhead. The 40-minute guided tour includes demonstrations of traditional methods of warping, dyeing and spinning, and offers a detailed history of Harris Tweed. There's also a craft shop.

    The impressive baronial Town Hall on South Beach currently houses the **An Lanntair Art Gallery** ① *T01851-703307, www.lanntair.co.uk, Mon-Sat 1000-1730, free*, though plans are afoot to move the gallery into a new arts centre. The gallery features the work of local, national and international artists and also stages various musical events. The coffee shop serves home baking and tasty snacks.

North to Nis (Ness) → *Colour map 1, grid A3.*

The A857 leaves Stornoway and runs northwest through barren, treeless and relentlessly bleak moorland to **Barabhas (Barvas)**. The landscape is scarred by deep gashes caused by peat digging, and the unfamiliar smell you detect in your nostrils is peat burning – a strange mixture of burning grass, whisky and coffee. Peat is the main source of domestic fuel used on the islands, and outside most houses you'll see large stacks of peat, or *cruachs*.

    The road from Barabhas northeast to Nis runs through a series of forlorn-looking, scrawny settlements that all look identical and merge into one. They consist of modern, characterless grey pebble-dash cottages with the ubiquitous piles of peat in the gardens, and the abandoned cars and vans scattered around everywhere only adds to the ugly and depressing scene.

    Just beyond Barabhas a sign points left to the **Morvern Art Gallery**, which has a café, making it a welcome refuge in bad weather. A few miles further on is a turning right to **Baile an Trùiseil (Ballantrushel)**, site of the huge **Clach an Trùiseil**, a 20-ft monolith (the largest in Europe), which was the scene of the last major battle on the island, fought between the Morrisons of Nis and the MacAuleys of Uig. This is the first of a number of prehistoric sights between here and **Siadar (Shader)** which may be of

Gatliff Trust

The Gatliff Hebridean Hostels Trust (GHHT) is a non-profit-making charitable organization run entirely by volunteers, working with the island community to establish, maintain and develop a chain of 'value-for-money' hostels offering clean, cheap, simple, safe, welcoming and traditional croft-style accommodation in dramatic and beautiful locations for visitors to the Outer Hebrides.

The GHHT is independent of the SYHA but has adopted status. Visitors do not have to be members of either organization to use and stay in the hostels. First established as the Gatliff Trust in 1961 by Herbert Gatliff, the Trust was originally intended to provide young persons of limited means with the opportunity to meet local people and enjoy the unique natural environment and cultural heritage of the islands. However, in recent years visitors of all incomes, ages, nationalities and interests have been encouraged to use the facilities.

The Trust is currently involved in the operation of four hostels situated at Garenin (Isle of Lewis), Rhenigidale (Isle of Harris), Berneray (Isle of North Uist) and Howmore (South Uist). Further hostels may be opened on other islands in the future.

The hostels are open all year and looked after by non-resident wardens who live and practise crofting nearby. No advance bookings are accepted but it is very unlikely that visitors will find themselves turned away and without a bed for the night. There is also limited space for camping at the hostels. Hostels provide bunk/camp beds, cooking facilities and cutlery, piped water, toilets and coal/wood fires, but visitors should bring their own food and a sleeping bag is recommended.

Charges for 2005 are: £8 per night, under 18 £5.50, camping £4.50, day visitors £1. Annual membership £10, under 18 £7.50. Further information, including membership and contact details, hostel locations and photographs, a reading list and places of interest to visit in the surrounding area can be found at the GHHT website: www.gatliff.ic24.net.

interest to the keen archaeologist, but otherwise there's little of note on the road north to Nis as it passes through the typical crofting townships of **Coig Peighinnean Buirgh** (Five Penny Borve), **Gàbhsann bho Dheas** (South Galson), **Dail** (Dell), **Suainebost** (Swainbost), **Tàbost** (Habost) and **Lional** (Lionel). In saying that, those interested in buying souvenirs should look in at the **Borgh Pottery** ⓘ *T01856-850345, Mon-Sat 0930-1800*, by the bridge at Coig Peighinnean. Here you'll find a wide range of beautiful and original domestic and decorative ware.

The road continues north, passing through a number of villages that collectively make up **Nis (Ness)**, until it ends at the fishing village of **Port Nis (Port of Ness)**. It's a lovely spot, with a picturesque little harbour and golden sweep of beach enclosed by steep cliffs. Each September the locals head out to the island of **Sula Sgeir**, 30 miles to the north, for the annual cull of young gannets (or *gugas*), which are considered something of a delicacy by the people of Lewis. A few minutes to the northwest, the Butt of Lewis lighthouse forms the most northerly tip of the Outer Hebrides.

▲ Just before Port Nis, is Lional, where the B8015 turns off right and leads to the start of the 10-mile coastal trail to **Tòlstadh (Tolsta North)** and the beautiful beaches of Traigh Mhor and Garry. Numerous shielings pepper the landscape from an earlier era when local crofters drove their cattle to the summer pastures in the island's interior. The beaches can be reached much more easily by road north from Stornoway. For details of the coastal walk, see the tourist information centre in Stornoway.

Another minor road heads northwest to the tiny hamlet of **Eòropaidh (Eoropie)** (pronounced *Yor-erpee*). By the road junction that leads to Rubha Robhanais is the ancient **Teampull Mholuaidh (St Moluag's Church)**, thought to date from the 12th century and restored to its present state in 1912. It is now used on certain Sundays by Stornoway's Episcopal Church. From Eòropaidh a narrow road runs to the lighthouse at **Rubha Robhanais (Butt of Lewis)**, which marks the nothernmost tip of the Outer Hebrides. It's a great place for spotting seabirds or whales and dolphins, but also very wild and windy. Just don't tell any visiting Americans where you've been. Half a mile back down the road a path leads to the tiny beach of **Port Sto**, which is more sheltered.

The West Coast → *Phone code: 01851. Colour map 1, grid A2-3 & B2.*

Arnol

At the end of the village of Arnol is the **Blackhouse Museum** ① *To1851-710395, Apr-Sep Mon-Sat 0930-1830 Oct-Mar Mon-Sat 0930-1630, Sun 1400-1630, £3, concession £2.30, children £1*, one of the best surviving examples of an original blackhouse in Scotland and well worth visiting. These traditional thatched houses were once common throughout the Highlands and Islands, and inhabited until the 1960s. They were built in the tradition of 'longhouses' which can be traced back 1,000 years to the time of the Viking invaders. The name 'blackhouses' dates back to the 1850s when modern buildings were introduced. These were known as 'white houses' and the older style houses were called 'blackhouses'. The blackhouses were well adapted to the harsh local climate. They had no windows or chimney and were built with local materials – stone, turf and thatch of oat, barley or marram grass, and with a peat fire burning continually in the central hearth – and attached to the living quarters was the cattle byre. This particular blackhouse was built in 1885 and lived in until 1964. **Hebridean Replicas** ①*To1851-710562, in the village, offers quality handmade Lewis chess sets from local stone, and provides a welcome alternative to much of the tacky tourist paraphernalia to be found in Stornoway.*

> ‼ *The west coast of Lewis contains most of what you'll want to see and can be covered in a day trip from Stornoway, either with your own transport, by public bus or as part of a minibus tour.*

Siabost and around

Two miles south of the Arnol turn-off, at **Bragar**, look out for an archway, formed from the jawbone of a blue whale which was washed up on the coast nearby in 1920. A few miles further on is the township of Siabost (Shawbost), where the charmingly ramshackle **folk museum** ① *Mon-Sat 0900-1800, free*, which was started as a project by local schoolchildren, now contains an interesting collection of Hebridean artefacts.

Just south of Siabost, beside a small loch, is the sign for the recently restored **Norse Mill and Kiln**, which are a half-mile walk over the hill from the car park. There's not much to see as yet, but it's worth getting out of the car if you want to stretch your legs. A little further on is the turning for **Dail Beag (Dalbeg)**, a lovely secluded beach.

Gearrannan (Garenin)

The landscape gradually becomes more undulating and scenically interesting as the road then passes through the village of **Càrlabhagh (Carloway)**, Lord Leverhume's proposed fishing port. Here, a branch road leads to the ruined and deserted 'blackhouse' village of Gearrannan (Garenin). The old village has been undergoing extensive renovation in recent years with the aid of EU funding, and several derelict crofts have now been painstakingly restored to their original style of stone walls and thatched roofs. An old cart track leads down to the bay and wonderful sunsets out at sea. The village now boasts a Gatliff Trust hostel, heritage centre, café and holiday dwellings. Above the village a footpath can be followed through the lazybeds and

Croft conversion

The word 'croft' is derived from the Gaelic *croit*, meaning a small area of land, and crofting has been the traditional way of life in the Scottish Highlands for many centuries. Its emotive hold on the psyche of the Highlander comes from the long, hard struggle for security of tenure, see page 365.

A croft is aptly described as a parcel of land entirely surrounded by regulations. Most crofts consist of a few acres of arable land with a proportion of grazing land shared with other crofts. Each crofter is, in effect, a kind of small tenant-farmer, the distinction being that he has almost absolute security of tenure and has the right to assign the croft to a member of his family whether the landlord agrees or not. In fact, over the years the crofter has managed to acquire most of the rights of ownership with few of the disadvantages.

The croft is the area of land involved and not the house which is called the 'croft house'. Crofts can vary in size, from a quarter of an acre upwards. Those on Lewis are small and relatively unproductive, with an average size of only about five acres, while on the Uists, where the land is more fertile, crofts are up to 50 acres or more.

As well as having the sole tenancy of the croft, the crofter usually also has a share in a huge area of 'common grazing' along with the other members of the crofting community – commonly called a township. They also work together in such activities as fencing, sheep dipping or cutting peat.

In reality, crofting does not provide a viable means of living. Very few crofters rely solely on their smallholding for an income and most need to have several occupations (including running a B&B) to make ends meet. But without the family croft whole communities would just pack up and leave, so crofting functions as a means of preventing the depopulation of remote rural areas.

The crofter's lot may change for the better, however, thanks to the Scottish Parliament's new Land Reform Bill which includes a special right to buy for the crofting communities.

above the sea cliffs to reveal a stunning view of beautiful **Dal More Bay**. The Atlantic waves seem to break relentlessly on golden sands and the beach is, not surprisingly, a favourite haunt of surfers from Stornoway and farther afield. Swimmers and bathers should be careful, however, because as with many of the west coast beaches there can be a fierce rip-current carrying the unwary into deeper water out at sea.

Dùn Chàrlabhaigh (Doune Carloway) Broch

A little further on, standing a few hundred yards from the main road, is the Dùn Chàrlabhaigh Broch, the best-preserved building of its type in the Outer Hebrides. The impressive 2,000 year-old drystone habitation is beautifully situated on a rocky outcrop, commanding great views across Loch Carloway to the sea beyond. The remaining outer wall is 30-ft high and slopes inwards, with an inner wall which rises vertically, leaving chambers between the walls. Parts of the inner wall have collapsed, revealing the interior stairs and galleries. There's also the **Doune Broch Visitor Centre** ① To1851-643338, Apr-Oct Mon-Sat 1000-1800, free, which tastefully complements the architectural style of the site, and which gives a good audio-visual description of how life must have been in one of these structures around 50 BC.

Music to your ears

As the heartland of Gaelic culture, the Outer Hebrides are host to many music events throughout the year ranging from a spontaneous ceilidh to one of the three local mods. Mods usually consist of three days of competition in piping, singing, instrumental music, drama and poetry, and are an opportunity to see the best of the local talent. More information can be obtained from An Comunn Gaidhealach, T01851-703487.

Also listed below are the various Highland Games and agricultural shows, where you can also see piping competitions and Highland dancing.

Late March Feis nan Coisir, Stornoway, Lewis.

First Friday in April Donald Macleod Memorial Piping Competition, Stornoway, Lewis.

May-June Highland Festival, held in various locations.

Early June Harris Mod, Tarbert, on Harris.

Second week in June Lewis Mod, Stornoway, Lewis.

Mid June Uist Mod, Iochdar, on South Uist.

May-June Lochmaddy Boat Festival, Lochmaddy, North Uist.

Mid July Berneray Week, Bearnaraigh (Berneray), North Uist.

July Ceolas Music School, South Uist.

Early July Barra Festival for 2 weeks.

Early/mid July Feis Tir an Eorna, Paibeil, North Uist; Barra Highland Games, Borgh (Borve), Barra, lasting for a week.

11-14 July Hebridean Celtic Music Festival, Stornoway, Lewis.

Mid July North Uist Highland Games, Hosta, North Uist.

Mid/late July Harris Gala; South Uist Highland Games, Aisgeirnis (Askernish), South Uist; Lewis Highland Games, Tong, Lewis.

Mid July Barra Highland Games.

Third week of July Harris Festival

Late July Barra Live, Barra; West Side Agricultural Show, Barabhas (Barvas), Lewis; South Uist Agricultural Show, Iochdar, South Uist; South Harris Agricultural Show, Leverburgh,.

July Feis Eilean an Fhraoich, Stornoway, Lewis.

Late July/early August North Uist Agricultural Show, Hosta, North Uist.

Early August Carloway Agricultural Show, Càrlabhagh (Carloway), Lewis; Fies Tir a Mhurain, Lionacleit, Benbecula; Lewis Carnival, Stornoway; Fish Festival, Stornoway; Twin Peaks Hill Race, North Uist.

Second week August Harris Arts Festival, Tarbert.

Calanais (Callanish)

① *T01851-621422, site Apr-Sep 1000-1900, Oct-Mar 1000-1600, free; visitor centre closed Sun, £1.75, concession £1.25, children £0.75.*

Five miles south of Dun Chàrlabhaigh is the jewel in the islands' prehistoric crown, the Calanais **Standing Stones**, which are unique in Scotland and the equal of Stonehenge in historical value. The stones are in a beautiful setting overlooking Loch Roag and are very atmospheric, especially at sunset or at night, when no one's around. They are in the form of a Celtic cross, and in the centre is a circle of 13 stones with a central monolith over 12-ft tall, and a chambered burial cairn. The oldest part of this great ceremonial site – probably the stone circle – dates from around 3,000 BC (older than Stonehenge) and continued in use until about 800 BC. The full significance of the site is not yet known, though it is probably connected to the seasonal cycle, as many of the stones are aligned with the rising and setting moon. There are also a number of smaller and more isolated stone circles a few miles south of Calanais on the road to Gearraidh na h-Aibhne (Garynahine).

⁞ Ratpacker hostel

Lying about five miles off the east coast of Lewis, due east of Scalpay, are the Shiant (pronounced *shant*) islands, a group of three small, uninhabited, wild and rugged islands comprising Garbh Eilean (Rough Island), Eilean an Tighe (House Island) and Eilean Mhuire (Mary Island). Though unknown to most, they do have one rather dubious claim to fame: they boast the largest black rat population in the British Isles. The islands are currently owned by writer, Adam Nicolson, who inherited them from his father, renowned novelist Nigel Nicolson, who bought them for £1,400 after his mother, Vita Sackville-West, saw them advertised for sale in *The Telegraph*. The owner has written eloquently and informatively about his beloved

islands in *Sea Room* (Harper Collins, 2001) and at the end of the book he actually invites readers to go and visit. All they have to do is email him at adam@shiantisles.net and he'll send the keys. The sole accommodation on the islands is described by Nicolson as "extremely basic, rarely clean and at times rat-ridden", but the bonus is that there's no charge for staying there. It's recommended you sleep in tents and use the house as kitchen-cum-sitting rooms. The catch is (aside from the rats) that there's only one boat licensed to take passengers to the Shiants, from Stornoway. The price is negotiable but expect to pay around £500 return – although up to 10 people can travel for that price. For details, T01895-540250, woodfootloose@sol.com.

Next to the stones is the **Calanais Visitor Centre**, which features 'The Story of the Stones' exhibition, a restaurant and shop. On the other side of the stones is the Blackhouse tearoom and craft shop, run by the MacBears and better value for a bite.

The Uig Peninsula → *Colour map 1, grid B2.*

From Gearraidh na h-Aibhne the main A858 runs back to Stornoway, while the B8011 forks west to the remote Uig Peninsula in the southwest of the island. Here are some of the Outer Hebrides' finest beaches and most dramatic coastal scenery, and you'll barely see another soul. ▶ *For Sleeping, Eating and other listings, see pages 288-290.*

Bearnaraigh (Great Bernera) to Cnip

Four miles down this road is a turning to the right onto the B8059, which leads to the island of Bearnaraigh, now connected to the mainland of Lewis by a single-track road bridge. The main settlement on the island is **Breacleit (Breaclete)**, where you can find out about the island's history in the **Bernera Museum** ① *Jun-Sep Mon-Sat 1100-1800, £1.50*. The rest of the island is fairly interesting with tiny fishing villages, and one or two brochs and some standing stones. The nicest part, though, is on the north coast, near the tiny hamlet of **Bostadh (Bosta)**, where a lovely little sandy bay looks out to the nearby island of **Bearnaraigh Beag (Little Bernera)**.

The B8011 continues across bleak moorland, then cuts north to **West Loch Roag**, which is fringed by some fine sandy beaches and backed by a much hillier landscape. Just beyond **Miabhag (Miavaig)** is the turn-off right to **Cliobh (Cliff)**, with its picturesque beach which is unsafe for swimming. A mile further on is the little village of **Cnip (Kneep)**, to the east of which is the beautiful **Traigh na Berie**, a long sandy beach backed by flat machair which is ideal for camping.

Beyond Miabhag, the eerie peninsula of Gallan Head provides a setting befitting of a science fiction drama or Cold War Orwellian novel, with empty, decaying Ministry of Defence buildings battered by the Atlantic storms. Wandering around the abandoned site it is easy to form ideas of bizarre, top-secret government experiments and early-warning missile tracking in this seemingly edge-of-the-world place far removed from the unwanted prying eyes of everyday society.

Mangersta and the Flannan Islands

Beyond Ardroil the road continues to Mangersta where at Aird Fenish is some of the most spectacular and photogenic coastal scenery in the Outer Hebrides. The cliffs plunge dramatically beyond the road to the inaccessible beach below with a series of crumbling sea stacks battered by the fearsome waves and seabirds riding the updraughts adding to the sense of natural beauty, energy and power. Further south at **Brenish**, about a 10-minute walk from the road, is a menacing blowhole connected to the sea by an underground passage.

Far out into the Atlantic are the haunting Flannan Islands, scene of an unsolved mystery in 1900 following the disappearance of three lighthouse keepers. Various explanations have been put forward over the years, ranging from a freak-wave in stormy weather to a monster sea serpent or even a dispute and fight between the men, but whatever the real reason the legend continues. See page 290 for boat trips.

Timsgearraidh (Timsgarry)

At Timsgearraidh (Timsgarry) are the **Traigh Chapadail (Uig sands)** at the village of **Eadar Dha Fhadhail (Adroil)**. This is the loveliest of all the beaches on Lewis, with miles of sand dunes and machair, but it is famous for an entirely different reason. It was here in 1831 that a crofter dug up the 'Lewis Chessmen', 78 pieces carved from walrus ivory and belonging to at least eight incomplete chess sets from 12th-century Scandinavia. Some are now in the Museum of Scotland in Edinburgh, but most can be found in the British Museum in London.

⬤ Sleeping

Stornoway *p280, map p281*
As the largest settlement on the islands, Stornoway has a good selection of accommodation from which to choose, though you should book in advance in the peak summer season. The TIC will do this for you, for a small fee.
B Cabarfeidh Hotel, Perceval Rd South, T01851-702604, F705572. 46 rooms. On the outskirts of town and not as convenient as the **Royal** but with the full range of facilities and a decent restaurant.
B Park Guest House, 30 James St, T01851-702485, F703482. 10 rooms. This Victorian townhouse is comfortable, only 500 yds from the ferry terminal, and the best of the guest houses. It also has an excellent restaurant, recommended even if you're not staying.
B Royal Hotel, Cromwell St, T01851-702109, www.calahotels.com. 24 rooms. Best of several centrally located hotels. Good value,

and good food in its restaurant and bistro (see Eating below).
There are many B&Bs in and around the town centre, most of which offer a 'room only' rate for those requiring an early start to catch the first ferry. There are several along Matheson Rd, which is close to the town centre and the ferry terminal, including:
E Mrs Anne Maclead, at No 12, T01851-702673; and
E Mrs M MacMillan, 'Fernlea' No 9, T01851-702125. **F** room only.
F Fairhaven, 17 Keith St, T01851-705862, which can also do meals.
F Laxdale Holiday Park, Laxdale La, about a mile out of town on the road to Barabhas, T01851-703234. This bunkhouse has 16 beds, basic facilities and is open all year.
F Stornoway Backpackers Hostel, 47 Keith St, T01851-703628. Includes breakfast, open all year. Basic.

North to Nis *p282*

D Galson Farm Guest House, Gàbhsann bho Deas (South Galson), halfway between Barabhas and Port Nis, T01851-850492, www.galsonfarm.freeserve.com. Friendly and beautifully restored 18th-century house.

D Ms Catriona Macleod, at Coig Peighinnean Bulrgh (Five Penny Borve), T01851-810240.

F Galson Farm Bunkhouse, is cheaper, more basic accommodation run by the same owners.

The West Coast *p284*

If you want to stay near the stones and visit them after dark, there are several inexpensive B&Bs in the village of Calanais.

E Aros, T01851-621266, kateblue@yahoo.com. Again convenient for the stones, owned by Kate Kirby.

E Debbie Nash, a few miles north at 19 Tolsta Chaolais, T01851-621321. Recommended vegetarian B&B .

E-F Mrs Morrison, 27 Callanish (200 yds from the site), T01851-621392 (open Mar-Sep). Friendly.

Uig Peninsula *p287*

C Baile Na Cille Guest House, Timsgarry, T01851-672242, F672241. Apr-Sep. Best of the places to stay around Uig bay, this restored 18th-century manse is beautifully located overlooking a 2-mile stretch of sand. Superb home cooking and one of the warmest welcomes in the islands.

There are a couple of B&Bs on the island of Great Bernera which both evening meals:

E Mrs Macauley, in Circebost (Kirkibost), on the east coast, T01851-612341.

E Mrs MacDonald, in Tobson, on the west coast, T01851 612347.

🍴 Eating

Stornoway *p280, map p281*

The pubs and hotels serve the usual range of bar meals. Note that pubs are closed on Sun and hotels cater only for residents. There are plenty of takeaways offering the standard fare of pizza, kebabs, fish and chips etc.

£££ The Boatshed, in the Royal Hotel, see Sleeping above. Also recommended, specializes in seafood. Less upmarket and cheaper is their **Barnacle Bistro**.

£££-££ Park Guest House, see Sleeping above. Probably the best restaurant in town. Top-class modern Scottish cooking using local fish, lamb and venison. It also caters for vegetarians. Open Tue-Sat.

£ Ann Lanntair Gallery, see Sights p280. Good, cheap snacks and light lunches.

£ Co-op supermarket. If you are on a budget the all-day breakfast served here is one of the cheapest dishes on the island.

£ Deep Sea Fishermen's Mission, North Beach. A cheap cafeteria.

£ Stornoway Balti House, near the bus station on South Beach. For a touch of non-Scottish fare.

North to Nis *p282*

£ Harbour View Gallery & Café, Port Nis, T01851-810735. Also offers B&B.

The West Coast *p284*

££ Copper Kettle, overlooking a small lochan beside the car park at Dalbeg, T01851-710592. An unassuming little house which is actually a superb restaurant. Meals must be booked at least 24 hrs in advance (last booking 2000). Open 1030 till 1730 for tea, coffee, snacks and home baking (all year Mon-Sat). Next door is a self-catering bungalow for rent (same phone number).

££ Tigh Mealros, a few miles south of the stones, Gearraidh na h-Aibhne, T01851-621333. They serve good local grub in a cosy, relaxed atmosphere, with scallops a speciality (closes at 2100).

£ Calanais Visitor Centre and the **Blackhouse tearoom**, are places to eat near the stones.

The Uig Peninsula *p287*

££ Bonaventure, north of Timsgarry, at Aird Uig, T01851-672474. Restaurant and B&B serving lunches and dinners of a French/Scottish style.

🛍 Shopping

Stornoway *p280, map p281*

Safeway is beside the ferry terminal and the **Co-op** is by the first roundabout on the road out to Barabhas. There's also a smaller supermarket opposite the TIC.

Outer Hebrides Leodhas (Lewis) Listings

▲ Activities and tours

Stornoway *p280, map p281*
Elena C, 5a Knock, Point, T01851-870537,
F706384. Wildlife trips that leave from
Stornoway harbour.
Galson Motors, T01851-840269, leaving
from Stornoway bus station they run day
trips to Calanais.
Hebridean Exploration, 19 Westview Terr,
T01851-705655, T0374-292746 (mob). Sea
kayak tours.
Island Cruising, Uig, T01851-672381. For
boat trips to the Flannan Islands.
MacDonald's Coaches, at the Ferry
Terminal, T01851-706267. Coach tours.
W. MacDonald, T01851-706267, day trips to
Calanais leaving from the pier.

⊙ Transport

Lewis *p280*
Air British Airways/Loganair,
T08708-509850, www.ba.com, flies from
Glasgow to Stornoway (Mon-Sat 2 daily,
1 hr). There are also flights from **Edinburgh**
to Stornoway (Mon-Sun 1 daily, 1 hr), **Inverness** to Stornoway (Mon-Sat 4 daily, 40 mins).
Bus Buses leave from Stornoway to all parts
of the island. Note that buses do not run on
Sun. To **Port Niss (Ness)** via **Barabhas
(Barvas)** 4-6 times per day; to **Arnol**, **Siabost
(Shawbost)**, **Càrlabhagh (Carloway)**,
Calanais (Callanish), and back to Stornoway
('West Side Circular') 4-6 times per day; to
Bearnaraigh (Great Bernera) via **Gearraidh
na h-Aibhne (Garynahine)** 4 per day; to **Uig
District** 3-4 per day; to **Ranais (Ranish)** 6-8
times per day. Contact the tourist office in

Stornoway, or the bus station, T01851-704327, for further details. There are also
buses from Stornoway to **Tarbert** and on to
Leverburgh (for the ferry to North Uist) 4-5
times per day, T01859-502441.
Boat CalMac ferry runs a service from
Ullapool to Stornoway (2 hrs 40 minutes)
2-3 times daily Mon-Sat in the summer
(Jun-Sep) and twice daily Mon-Sat in the
winter. One-way ticket costs £14.05 per
passenger and £69 per car. A 5-day saver
return costs £24.05 per passenger and £117
per car. Contact **CalMac** offices Ullapool,
T01854-612358, and Stornoway,
T01851-702361, for further details.
Car Car and bike rental is available at good
rates from **Lewis Car Rentals**, 52 Bayhead St,
T01851-703760, F705860. Also **Arnol Motors**,
in Arnol (see p284), T01851-710548,
T0831-823318 (mob).
Cycle hire You can rent bikes at **Alex
Dan's Cycle Centre**, 67 Kenneth St,
T01851-704025, F701712.
Taxis from **Central Cabs**, T01851-706900.

⊙ Directory

Stornoway *p280, map p281*
Banks **Bank of Scotland** is directly
opposite the tourist office and has an ATM.
The other major banks are also in the centre
of town and also have ATMs.
Internet **Captions**, 27 Church St, T01851-702238, www.captions.co.uk. Open Mon- Sat
till late in the summer months. Internet
facilities also available at the public library on
Cromwell St.
Post Main post office is on Francis St.

Na Hearadh (Harris) → *Phone code: 01859. Colour map 1.*

*Harris is not an island, but together with Lewis forms the largest of the Outer Hebrides,
with Harris taking up the southern third. The two parts are divided by the long sea
lochs of Loch Seaforth in the east and Loch Resort in the west, though this division is
rarely shown on maps. Though joined, the two are very different in terms of
geography. Harris is largely mountain and rock whereas Lewis is flat moorland.*

*The largest town and site of the ferry terminal is An Tairbeart (Tarbert). To the
north are the highest peaks in the Outer Hebrides, surrounded by some of the finest
unspoilt wilderness in the whole country, while to the south are miles of wonderful
sandy beaches and, on the east coast, a preternaturally strange lunar landscape*

straight out of a science fiction film. With your own transport you could 'do' Harris in
a day quite comfortably, but if the weather's good enough you'll want to spend more
time and appreciate its precious natural beauty. ➤➤ *For Sleeping, Eating and other listings,*
see pages 295-296.

Background

The separation of Harris and Lewis dates back to Norse times, when the island was
divided between the two sons of Leod, progenitor of the Macleods. Harris remained in
Macleod hands until 1834. The recent history of Harris is closely bound up with that of
Lewis. Both were bought by the soap magnate, Lord Leverhulme, see page 280,
whose grandiose schemes for Lewis came to nothing. Leverhulme then turned his
attentions to Harris, where the peaceful little village of An t-Ob (Obbe) was renamed
Leverburgh and transformed into a bustling port with all manner of public works
programmes under development. His death in 1925 brought an end to all his plans for
Harris, and instead of becoming a town with a projected population of 10,000,
Leverburgh reverted to being a sleepy village, with only the harbour, the roads and the
change of name to show for it all.

Since the Leverhulme era there has been no main source of employment for the
population of 2,400 on Harris, though a successful fishing industry continues on
Scalpaigh (Scalpay). There is still some crofting supplemented by the Harris Tweed
industry, though most production is now in Lewis, and whatever employment can be
found: road-works, crafts and tourism. The most recent project proposed for Harris, to
create one of Europe's largest superquarries, is highly controversial and would
involve destroying an area of outstanding natural beauty for the sake of perhaps only
a few dozen jobs, see page 295, with potentially disastrous consequences for the
island's fragile tourist economy.

Ceann a Tuath na Hearadh (North Harris)

➜ *Phone code: 01859. Colour map 1, grid B2.*

North Harris is the most mountainous part of the Outer Hebrides and its wild, rugged
peaks are ideal for hillwalking. The A859 south from Lewis gets progressively more
scenic as it skirts **Loch Siophort (Seaforth)** and the mountains rise before you like a
giant barrier. The road then climbs past **Bogha Glas (Bowglass)** and **Aird a Mhulaidh
(Ardvourlie)** with **Clisham** (2,619 ft), the highest peak in the Outer Hebrides, and
Sgaoth Aird (1,829 ft) towering overhead on either side.

Just off the A859 near Ardvourlie is **Ardvourlie Castle Guest House**, see Sleeping
page 295. If you can't afford such luxury but still crave the isolation, then carry on
south until you reach the turn-off to **Reinigeadal (Rhenigidale)**, which was the most
remote community on Harris and accessible only by sea or by a rough hill track until
the access road was built. Here you'll find a **Gatliff Trust youth hostel**, see Sleeping
page 295. From Reinigeadal an ascent of shapely **Toddun** (528 m) provides
exhilarating exercise rewarded with fine views east across the Minch to the mainland
and in the other direction to the mountain wilderness of North Harris.

The A859 continues west across the crest of the craggy hills then drops down to
the turn-off for the single-track B887 which winds its way all the way out to Huisinis
(Hushinish) between the impressive mountains of the Forest of Harris on one side
and the northern shore of West Loch Tarbert on the other, with views across to the
Sound of Taransay and the beaches of South Harris. Immediately beyond the turn-off
you pass through **Bun Abhainn Eadarra (Bunavoneadar)**, which was a thriving
whaling station until 1930 and one of Lord Leverhulme's many schemes for the

⁞ Right to buy

The Forest of Harris is a vast tract of mountain wilderness extending north from West Loch Tarbert to Loch Resort that forms the de facto boundary with Lewis. It is one of the most isolated and unspoilt upland landscapes in Scotland and, because of its remoteness, receives very few visitors. For experienced hillwalkers, however, it is a paradise offering rugged mountains, dramatic escarpments, airy ridges and desolate glens. There are endless walking possibilities including a horseshoe walk around Clisham and a long walk through Glen Ulladale to Kinlochresort, a former crofting community now abandoned, but once described as the remotest habitation in Britain. Known as the North Harris Estate, this 22,000 acre tract of land was owned and managed by the family of the Bulmer cider empire – until 2003. In a move that had Scottish lairds incandescent with rage, the 800 residents of the estate were granted the right to take over the land on which they live, for more than £2 million, and finally throw off the shackles of feudal rule. Now that they have become masters of their own destiny, the community can relish the thought of a prosperous future, with energy development plans, sporting rights and tourism top of the agenda.

island. The old whaling station is worth a visit even though the site has not been developed as a tourist attraction.

▲▲ Just before the village of **Miabhag (Meavaig)**, a defined footpath heads north into the hills up Glen Meavaig to Loch Voshimid. Further on, though, is a better opportunity for walking. Just before the gates of **Amhuinnsuidhe Castle** (pronounced 'Avan-soo-ee') is a signpost for Chliostair Power Station. From here you can walk two miles up to the dam, then follow the right-hand track round the reservoir and the left-hand track round the upper loch, before you arrive in a wild and remote glen. Just beyond the castle gates you'll see a beautiful waterfall spilling straight into the sea. The road then runs right past the front door of the castle, built in 1868 by the Earl of Dunmore, and still a private residence, before passing through an archway and continuing to the tiny crofting township of **Huisinis (Hushinish)**, beautifully situated in a sandy bay. This is where the road ends; next stop the USA. Follow the track to the right across the machair where a footpath above the jetty and rocky beach can be followed to the old fishing lodge at **Cravadale** and Loch Cravadale beyond. Make a detour to the golden sands and turquoise waters of **Traigh Mheilein** overlooking Scarp. From the coast strong walkers can follow Glen Cravadale inland eventually rejoining the main road near Amhuinnsuidhe Castle.

The rocky island of **Scarp** supported a population of more than 100 as late as the 1940s but was abandoned in 1971, and now the crofters' cottages are used as holiday homes. The island was the scene of a bizarre experiment in 1934, when a German rocket scientist, Gerhard Zucher, tried to prove that rockets could be used to transport mail and medical supplies to remote communities. His theory went up in smoke, however, when the rocket exploded before it even got off the ground, with 30,000 letters on board.

An Tairbeart (Tarbert) and around

→ *Phone code: 01859. Colour map 1, grid B2. Population: 500.*

Tarbert, the largest settlement on Harris, lies in a sheltered bay on the narrow isthmus that joins North and South Harris. It's a tiny place and there's not much to do, but as

:: Tweed the world

Few visitors to Harris will not have heard of its most famous export. Harris Tweed was originally made by fishermen's wives to clothe their own families until the Countess of Dunmore, who owned a large part of Harris in the mid-19th century, took great interest and introduced many of her aristocratic friends to the local cloth. Very soon, much of the surplus was being sold and becoming quite a fashion statement in high places. Since its heyday as a de rigeur item of clothing for any self-respecting aristocrat, however, the future of Harris Tweed has largely been determined by the vagaries of the world's top fashion designers. The industry can produce around 5,000,000 yards of tweed annually, depending on demand, but that demand has been low of late. Step forward Nike, the US plimsoll manufacturer. Their new range of retro trainers will incorporate a swatch of Harris Tweed in the design, and so introduce the durable yet stylish material to a whole new generation of younger wardrobes. The trainers will not only carry the Nike logo but also the famous Harris Tweed orb, thus carrying the name around the world (again). Can we expect to see gangs of teenagers loitering on grouse moors instead of their customary shopping malls?

it's the main ferry port for Harris it has more facilities than anywhere else, with shops, a bank and post office. Tarbert's relatively wide range of accommodation and location makes it the ideal base from which to explore. The **TIC** ① *T01859-502011, Apr-Oct Mon-Sat 0900-1700, also in winter (check times)*, is close to the ferry terminal.

An interesting little excursion from Tarbert is the 10-mile return route that runs east through the tiny villages of **Urgha** and **Caolas Scalpaigh** to **Carnach** at the end of the road. Just beyond Urgha, on the north side of the road, is a path which leads across the hills to the **Reinigeadal**. It was originally used by the community in Reinigeadal, and the children would make the daily journey across the hills to Tarbert before the village was connected to the A859 by the new road. The wonderfully engineered zigzag path passes through enchanting scenery above **Loch Trollamarig** in a setting more reminiscent of Scandinavia's fjordland. A visit can easily be made to the deserted village of **Molinginish** nestled snugly in a small valley above the loch.

The island of **Scalpaigh (Scalpay)**, now connected to Harris by a road bridge opened by Prime Minister Tony Blair in 1998, is a thriving fishing community with a population of over 400. It's a pleasant three-mile walk across the island to Eilean Glas Lighthouse, built by the Stevensons and the first ever on the Outer Hebrides. There are diving trips here, see page 296.

Ceann a Deas na Hearadh (South Harris)

An absolute must while you're in the Outer Hebrides is the 45-mile circular route around South Harris. If you only do one thing while you're here, then make sure this is it, for the change in scenery from the west coast to the east is utterly astounding. One thing you're sure to puzzle over as you travel round is the fact that most people live on the harsh and inhospitable east coast, known as Na Baigh (Bays), while the beautiful west

 Rumour has it that during the Castaway television series, the bar in the Harris Hotel in Tarbert had never seen such good business, suggesting that some participants were more committed than others.

Outer Hebrides Na Hearadh (Harris)

coast with its miles of glorious golden sands is scarcely populated. This is not through choice. The fertile west coast housed most of the population until the end of the 18th century when they were cleared to make way for sheep farms. Some emigrated to Cape Breton, while others chose instead to stay in Harris and moved to the east side.

The West Coast

The main road from Tarbert runs south, skirting East Loch Tarbert, then cuts inland and heads west through a dramatic lunar landscape of rocks dotted with tiny lochans. It then begins to descend towards the sea and you can see the vast expanse of **Losgaintir (Luskentyre)** beach directly ahead. A single-track road turns off to the right and runs out to the tiny settlement of Losgaintir. The road cuts through the rich machair as it follows the magnificent stretch of bleached white sand that fills the entire bay, washed by turquoise sea and backed by steep dunes. All this set against the backdrop of the mountains to the north. Paradise!

A short distance offshore is the island of **Tarasaigh (Taransay)**, which was well populated at the beginning of the 1900s but was recently abandoned. The island gained national prominence a few years ago as the setting for the popular BBC television series *Castaway* where an assortment of supposedly normal people from a variety of backgrounds were challenged to pit their wits against the elements and themselves for a period of a full year in 2000.

The road follows the coast, passing through the tiny settlements of **Seilebost**, **Horgabost** and **Burgh (Borve)**. There's B&B accommodation at Seilebost and Horgabost, but a few miles further on is another beautiful stretch of white sands at **Sgarasta Bheag (Scaristabeg)**.

Beyond Sgarasta Bheag, the village of **Taobh Tuath (Northton)** provides access to the scenic promontory of **Toe Head**, almost cut off from the rest of Harris by the huge expanse of the golden sands of Sgarasta. At the **MacGillivary Machair Centre** you can learn about the ecology of the local machair which forms such a distinctive and attractive element of the landscape of the west coast of the Hebrides. A ruined chapel of 16th-century origin is situated on the machair below **Chaipaval** (365 m), whose heathery slopes can be climbed for one of the best views out to sea towards St Kilda some 40 miles distant.

Ant-Ob (Leverburgh)

The road then runs along the south shore till it reaches An t-Ob (Leverburgh), site of Lord Leverhulme's ambitious plan to turn a sleepy crofting township into a major fishing port, see page 291. The present village consists of little more than a row of incongruous Scandinavian-style wooden houses. A few of the original buildings can be seen near the pier, which is the departure point for CalMac's car ferry to Berneray.
▶▶ For further details, see Transport page 296.

Ròghadal (Rodel)

Three miles east of Leverburgh, at the southeastern tip of Harris, is Ròghadal (Rodel), dominated by the beautiful 12th-century **St Clement's Church**, something of an unusual sight in such a remote spot and one of the most impressive religious building in the Hebrides (only the Benedictine abbey on Iona is larger). The church stands on a site which goes back 1,500 years and was built by Alastair Crotach (Hunchback) Macleod of Harris in the 1520s. Though impressive from the outside, particularly the huge tower, the real interest lies inside, with a collection of remarkable carved wall tombs. There are three tombs, the most notable of which is that of the founder, Alastair Crotach. The one in the south wall of the choir is also worth a close look.

Running north from Ròghadal up the east coast of South Harris is the **Golden Road**, so named by the locals because the of the huge expense of building it. This twisting, tortuous single-track road runs through a bizarre and striking moonscape, and driving through it is a unique experience (but keep your eyes on the road or you'll end up in one of the many narrow sea lochs). It seems inconceivable that anyone could survive in such an environment, but the road passes through a string of townships created in the 19th century by the people evicted from the west coast, see page 293. People here have spent years eking a meagre living from the thin soil by building 'lazy beds' (thin strips of piled-up earth between the rocks) for planting potatoes. Weaving and fishing also provide much-needed income.

At **Lingreabhagh (Lingarabay)** the road skirts the foot of **Roinebhal**, the proposed site of one of the largest superquarries in Europe, which would demolish virtually the entire mountain over many decades. Local people and environmentalists are up in arms at the prospect of losing precious fishing grounds, not to mention a precious natural asset. The road passes through a succession of tiny settlements before joining the A859 just south of Tarbert.

● Sleeping

North Harris *p291*

B Ardvourlie Castle Guest House, just off the A859 near Ardvourlie, T01859-502307, F502348. 4 rooms. Open Apr-Oct. This lovingly-restored Victorian hunting lodge on the shores of Loch Seaforth just oozes charm and elegance and can't be recommended highly enough. As if that weren't enough, they also happen to serve excellent food. There can be no better end to a day spent walking in the surrounding mountains.
F Gatliff Trust youth hostel, Reinigeadal (Rhenigidale). Here you'll find a converted croft house (no phone) which sleeps 11 and is open all year (for details on how to get there on foot, see Sights p291).

Tarbert and around *p292*

C Harris Hotel, on the main road from Stornoway on the left before the turning for the ferry, Tarbert, T01859-502154, F502281. An old established favourite, but more importantly the only place serving food on a Sun, see Eating. The bar next door also serves meals and is the social hub of the village.
C Leachin House, 1 mile out of Tarbert on the Stornoway road, T/F01859-502157. Luxurious Victorian home with great views and superb home cooking (for residents only). **B** including dinner. Only 2 rooms so book ahead.

D Allan Cottage Guest House, on the left after the turning into Tarbert, T01859-502146. Open Apr-Sep. Close to the ferry, very comfortable rooms and exceptional food. **B** including dinner. Book ahead.
E Hirta House, Scalpay, T01859-540394. 3 en suite rooms. Lovely location, spacious rooms and guest lounge and library.
E Macleod Motel, right beside the ferry pier, T01859-502364. Very handy for the early-morning ferry, also has room-only rate.
E Mrs Mackinnon, Tarbert, T01859-502095. Very friendly and welcoming B&B within 5 mins' walk of the ferry pier.
E Mrs Morrison, Tarbert, T01859-502334. . Comfortable B&B near the pier.
E Mrs Miller, Tarbert, T01859-502140. A friendly and clean B&B.
E Seafield, Scalpay, T01859-540250, seafieldscalpay@hotmail.com. 3 rooms. Open Feb-Nov. Comfortable, good sea views, fishing trips available.
E-F Mrs Flora Morrison, Tigh na Mara, Tarbert, T01859-502270. A B&B within 5 mins' walk of the ferry pier, very friendly.
F Rockview Bunkhouse, on the main street, Tarbert, T/F01859-5022211. Open all year.

South Harris *p293*

There is a wide range of accommodation in Leverburgh but on the east coast it is limited.

For an explanation of sleeping and eating price codes used in this guide, see inside the front cover. Other relevant information is found in Essentials, see pages 41-49.

Outer Hebrides Na Hearadh (Harris) Listings

B **Scarista House**, Scaristabeg, T01859-550238, www.scaristahouse.com. 5 rooms, open May-Sep. Overlooking the beach in a wonderful setting, To add to the peace and quiet, there's no TV, only an extensive library and drawing room with open fires. The food on offer is amongst the best on the islands, particularly the seafood. Even if you're not staying, you should treat yourself to dinner here. Breakfast is a majesterial feast of kippers, kedgeree, Stornoway black pudding and Ayrshire bacon. Expensive but well worth it. There are also self-catering cottages in the grounds. The golf course over the road is so scenic the views may put you off your swing.

E **Mrs Paula Williams**, Leverburgh, T01859-520319, F520146. Caters for vegetarians.

E **Mrs Catherine Mackenzie**, Leverburgh, T01859-520246, situated on Ferry Rd, a few mins from the ferry terminal.

E **Shieldaig House**, Leverburgh, T01859-520378, kwhettall@aol.com. More secluded and with free cycle hire.

E-F **Caberfeidh House**, Leverburgh, T01859-520276. Close to the ferry and also offers room only (**F**). One of the best B&Bs.

E-F **Hillhead**, T01859-511226, at Scadabhagh (Scadabay), Bays, between Stocinis and Drinisiadar. Good value B&B option, as are the 2 listed below.

E-F **Moravia**, Luskentyre, T01859-550262, open Mar-Oct. B&B.

E-F **Seaview**, Luskentyre, T01859-550263, open Apr-Oct.

F **Am Bothan Bunkhouse**, Leverburgh, T01859-520251, close to the ferry, has full facilities, space for tents and is open all year.

F **Drinishader Bunkhouse**, at Drinisiader (Drinishader), 3 miles south of Tarbert, Bays, T01859-511255, open all year.

Camping

In Luskentyre, you can camp on the machair, but ask for permission at the first house.

❼ Eating

Options on places to eat are limited. Most guesthouses and B&Bs provide dinner on request, check if they do so on a Sun.

Tarbert and around *p292*

££ Firstfruits Tearoom, Tarbert, T01859-502349. Aside from the guest houses, this is probably the best food here, a cosy joint by the ferry pier. Open Apr, May and Sep Mon-Sat 1030-1630 and till 1830 Jun, Jul and Aug.

££ Harris Hotel, see Sleeping, serves food every day till around 2030. They do a 3-course fixed menu or basic and cheap bar meals, as does the bar next door Mon-Sat.

£ Fish and chip shop next door to the **Rockview Bunkhouse**, the only other option in Tarbert, open for lunch and in the evening.

South Harris *p293*

£ An Clachan, Leverburgh, T01859-520370, café/restaurant and shop, not far from the bunkhouse.

▲ Activities and tours

Tarbert and around *p292*
Scalpay Diving Services, T01859-540328, for diving.

❺ Transport

Harris *p290*

Bus There's a regular bus service between **Tarbert** and **Stornoway** (1¼ hrs, which continues to **Leverburgh** (for the ferry to North Uist) via the west coast of South Harris. There's a also bus service 3-4 times per day from **Tarbert** to **Leverburgh** via the east coast (45 mins), along the so- called 'Golden Road'. There are also services to **Huisinis** (2-4 per day on school days, 45 mins), to **Reinigeadal** (2 per day on school days) and to **Scalpaigh** (2-5 per day, 10 mins). Bus timetables are available at the TIC.

Ferry Ferries sails from **Uig** (Skye) to **Tarbert** (1 hr 35 mins) 1-2 times daily Mon-Sat. One-way ticket £9.15 per passenger, £44 per car (£15.65 and £75 for 5-day saver return). Contact Uig, T01470-542219, or Tarbert, T01859-502444. A ferry sails from **Leverburgh** to **Berneray** 3 or 4 times daily. The trip takes 1 hr 10 mins and a one-way ticket costs £5.20 per passenger, £23.70 per car (£8.85 and £40.50 for 5-day saver return). See above for details of services to Leverburgh.

The Uists, Benbecula and Barra

South from Harris lies the southern 'half' of the Outer Herbides. The Uists, north and south, and Benbecula, are all connected by a series of causeways and you can drive their length, past a never-ending series of fish-filled lochs and windswept beaches, tiny, straggling crofting communities and the bizarre giant 'golf balls' of Space City, on South Uist. The road ends at the southerly tip of South Uist, where you'll have to board a ferry to cross to the more relaxed island of Barra, or, better still, fly there from Glasgow, landing on the famous cockle strand – at low tide, of course! ▸▸ *For Sleeping, Eating and other listings, see pages 304-306.*

Uibhist a Tuath (North Uist) → *Phone code: 01876. Colour map 1, grid C1. Population: 1,815.*

North Uist is the largest of the southern chain of the Outer Hebrides, about 13 miles from north to south and 18 miles east to west at its widest point. At first sight it comes as something of a disappointment after the dramatic landscapes of Harris. In fact, it's barely a landscape at all, as over a third of the island's surface is covered by water. The east coast around Lochmaddy, the main settlement, is so peppered with lochs it resembles a giant sieve. But heading west from Lochmaddy the island's attractions become apparent, particularly the magnificent beaches on the north and west coast. Also on the west coast, the Balranald Nature Reserve is the ideal place for bird watching. You're also likely to see otters. There are numerous prehistoric sites scattered across the island, and with all that water around there's obviously plenty of good fishing to be had. ▸▸ *For Sleeping, Eating and other listings, see pages 304-306.*

Ins and outs
Getting there There are three car ferry services to North Uist. One is to Otternish from Leverburgh on South Harris, the others are to Lochmaddy from Uig on Skye, and from Tarbert on Harris. North Uist is joined to the islands of Benbecula and South Uist to the south by causeway and bridge. There are several buses daily (Monday-Saturday) from Otternish to Lochmaddy and on to Lochboisdale on South Uist. ▸▸ *For further details, see Transport pages 278 and 306.*

Getting around There are four to six buses per day (except Sunday) from Otternish to Lochmaddy. These buses continue to Baile a Mhanaich (Balivanich) on Benbecula, where there is an airport, see page 299, and Lochboisdale and Ludag on South Uist, see page 300. There are four to seven buses per day from Lochmaddy to Otternish. These continue via the new causeway to the island of Bearnaraigh (Berneray) just off the north coast in the sound of Harris. There are three buses per day from Lochmaddy to Clachan na Luib (Clachan-a-Luib) which run in an anti-clockwise direction around the north and west coasts. Two buses per day connect Clachan-a-Luib with Baile Sear (Baleshare) and also with Saighdinis (Sidinish). There are also postbuses linking the main settlements. Bus timetables are available at the tourist office in Lochmaddy.

Loch nam Madadh (Lochmaddy)
Lochmaddy, the island's main village and ferry port, is a tiny place, so small you're almost through it before you realize. Though it's on the east coast and not close to the beaches, it is the best base for exploring the island as it boasts most facilities. It has a bank (next to the tourist office), a hotel and pub, a tourist office, a few shops, post office, hospital and petrol station.

Outer Hebrides The Uists, Benbecula & Barra

❖ A prickly issue

In a classic David and Goliath struggle, the hedgehogs of the Western Isles took on the might of the Scottish Executive, and lived to tell the tale – or so we think. The decision of the SNH to cull the island's hedgehogs was made in order to protect the dwindling numbers of wading birds. Hedgehogs, you see, just love eating their eggs for breakfast. So, while hedgehog numbers have soared to around 5,000 since first being introduced by a South Uist man as a means of slug control, numbers of birds such as ringed plover and red shank have plummeted by up to 60%. SNH scientists believe it to be more humane to exterminate the spiky little imposters using gas and lethal injection rather than let them starve on the mainland, and so began the controversial cull, with the backing of the RSPB. But by the middle of 2003 only 66 had been killed, and only 6 weeks later, a further 60 baby hedgehogs had been born to take their place. At a total cull cost of £26,000, the cost per animal was nearly £4,500. Meanwhile, animal welfare groups, including Mrs Tiggywinkle's Hedgehog Refuge, organized a massive rescue operation which resulted in 150 of the little blighters being relocated to southern Scotland and 50 to Bristol University – not to enrol on a degree course, but to be electonically tagged to find out if they can survive the trauma of relocation and adapt to their new habitat. The world waits for the answer with bated breath.

If you have time the **Taigh Chearsabhagh Museum and Arts Centre** ① *T/F01876-500293, www.taigh-chearsabhagh.com*, is worth visiting and has a café. The tourist information centre ① *near the ferry pier, T01876-500321, Mid-Apr to mid-Oct Mon-Sat 0900-1700, and for the arrival of the evening ferry*, will provide transport timetables.

Around the island

There are a number of interesting archaeological sites of different periods dotted around the island. The most notable is **Barpa Langass**, seven miles southwest of Lochmaddy on the slope of Ben Langass, just off the A867 which cuts across the bleak peaty hinterland of North Uist. This is a huge chambered burial cairn dating from around 3,000 BC. Unfortunately, it is now too dangerous to enter. About a mile away, on the southern side of Ben Langass, is the small stone circle known as **Pobull Fhinn**, standing on the edge of Loch Langass. Three miles northwest of Lochmaddy on the A865 are three Bronze Age standing stones called **Na Fir Bhreige** (The False Men), said to be the graves of three spies who were buried alive.

The real charms of North Uist, though, are its fabulous beaches on the north and west coasts. Heading anti-clockwise from Lochmaddy, the A865 runs northwest, passing the turning for Otternish and Bearnaraigh (see below), which is now connected to North Uist by a causeway. It continues west through the township of **Sollas (Solas)**, where there are a couple of B&Bs, and then past the beautiful sands of **Bhalaigh (Vallay) Strand**. Near the northwestern tip of the island is **Scolpaig Tower**, standing on an islet in Loch Scolpaig, a 'folly' built for famine relief in the 19th century.

▲ Three miles south of here is the turning to Balranald RSPB Reserve, an area of rocky coast, sandy beaches and dunes, machair and lochs. The reserve is ideal for bird watching, especially waders. A two-hour guided walk along the headland allows you to see Manx shearwaters, gannets, skuas and storm petrels, and during the summer you can listen out for the distinctive rasping call of the corncrake, one of the rarest birds in Britain. There's a basic visitor centre ① *Apr-Sep*.

In Ceann a Bhaigh is the **Uist Animal Visitors Centre** ① *Mon-Sat 1000-2200, £2,* where you can see Highland cattle and other rare native breeds, as well exotic species such as llamas. The road continues south to **Clachan na Luib**, at the crossroads of the A865 and A867 which heads east back to Lochmaddy. Offshore is the tidal island of **Baile Sear (Baleshare)**, now connected by a causeway to North Uist, with its three-mile long beach on the west coast. A further five miles west are the **Monach Isles** (also known by their old Norse name of *Heisker*), which were once connected to North Uist at low tide, until the 16th century when a huge tidal wave swept away the sand bridge, thus isolating them. Even so, the islands were still populated until as recently as the 1930s. Now they are populated by the largest breeding colony of grey seals in Europe.

South of Clachan, the road runs past **Cairinis (Carinish)** over a series of causeways to the little-visited lobster-fishing island of **Griomasaigh (Grimsay)**, before heading across another causeway to Benbecula. Near Cairinis is **Feith na Fala** (Field of Blood), site of the last battle fought in Scotland solely with swords and bows and arrows, in 1601, between the MacDonalds of Sleat and Macleods of Harris. The bloodshed was provoked by one of the MacDonalds divorcing his Macleod wife. When 60 Skye Macleods set off to North Uist to wreak revenge, they were met by 16 MacDonalds who literally chopped them to pieces, proving that divorce was a messy affair even then.

Bearnaraigh (Berneray) → *Phone code: 01876. Colour map 1, grid C1.*
Ferries from Leverburgh on Harris arrive at the low-lying island of Bearnaraigh, now connected by a causeway to North Uist. The island is famous as the place where Prince Charles spent a holiday helping out on a croft. It's also the birthplace of the giant Angus MacAskill, see page 258. Its real attraction, though, apart from the splendid isolation, is the three-mile-long sandy beach along its north and west coast.

▲▲ A *Western Isles Walks* booklet for Bearnaraigh, available from Lochmaddy TIC, describes an enjoyable eight-mile walk around the island visiting all the main places of interest including the 16th-century gunnery at **Baile**, the beaches and machair of the north and west coast, and archaeological sites dating from the Viking period near **Borgh**.

Beinn na Faoghla (Benbecula)
→ *Phone code: 01870. Colour map 1, grid C1. Population: 1,803.*

Tiny Benbecula may be suffering from delusions of stature. Its Gaelic name means 'mountain of the fords', but the highest point is a mere 407 ft, with the rest of the island as flat as a pancake. It lies between Protestant North Uist and Catholic South Uist, and most visitors use it solely as a means of getting from one to the other via the A865 which cuts straight through the middle.

Ins and outs
Benbecula's airport is at Balivanich and there are direct flights to Glasgow, Barra and Stornoway, see page 306. The island is connected by causeways to both North and South Uist, and buses travelling to and from Lochmaddy and Lochbois- dale pass through the villages of Balivanich, Lionacleit (Liniclate) and Creag Ghoraidh (Creagorry). There are also regular island buses which run between these settlements.

Sights
Like North Uist, the east of the island is so pitted with lochs that most people live on the west coast. A large percentage of the population are Royal Artillery personnel and their families stationed at **Baile a Mhanaich (Balivanich)**, a sprawling army base of

utilitarian buildings in the northwest of the island. The influx of so many English-speakers has had a less than positive impact on Gaelic culture, and the military facilities have blighted much of the island's natural beauty, but Benbecula has benefited economically from the army's presence. Not only is there an airport here, but also a relatively large number of shops and amenities, including the only NAAFI (military) supermarket in the UK that's open to the public, a Bank of Scotland (with ATM) and post office. There are worries, however, that the base may be scaled or closed, which would have a devastating effect on the local economy.

South of Balivanich the B892 runs around the west coast before joining the main A865 at the southern end of the island. It runs past **Culla Bay**, overlooked by **Baille nan Cailleach (Nunton)**. It was from here in 1746 that Bonnie Prince Charlie set off with Flora MacDonald over the sea to Skye, disguised as her maid, see page 256. To the south is **Poll-na-Crann**, better known as 'stinky bay' because of the piles of seaweed deposited there by fierce Atlantic storms. From the mid-18th century this kelp was used extensively in making glass, and provided a source of income for many communities. By 1820 the so-called kelp boom was over, but it is still gathered today and used for fertilizer.

The B892 ends at **Lionacleit (Liniclate)**, where the new community school serves the Uists and Benbecula. It has extensive facilities, including internet, a swimming pool, library, theatre and even a small local history **museum** ① *Mon, Tue and Thu 0900-1600, Wed 0900-1230 and 1330-1600, Fri 0900-2000, Sat 1100-1300 and 1400-1600, free.*

Uibhist a Deas (South Uist) → *Phone code: 01870. Colour map 3, grid A1.*
Population: 2,285.

South Uist is the largest of the southern chain of Outer Hebridean islands and the most scenically attractive. Like its southern neighbour, Barra, South Uist is Roman Catholic and generally more relaxed about Sunday openings. Its 20 miles of west coast is one long sandy beach, backed by dunes with a mile or two of beautiful, flowering machair behind. To the east of the main A865 that runs the length of the island rises a central mountainous spine of rock and peat dotted with numerous lochs. Its two highest peaks, **Beinn Mhor** (2,034 ft) and **Hecla** (1,988 ft), tower over the rocky cliffs of an inaccessible eastern coastline indented by sea lochs. ▶▶ *For Sleeping, Eating and other listings, see pages 304-306.*

Ins and outs
Getting there The island's main ferry port is Lochboisdale, which is reached from Oban (via Castlebay on Barra), arriving late at night. A private passenger-only ferry sails from Barra to Ludag, at the southern tip of South Uist . There are passenger ferry sailings on Sunday to and from Barra and a car ferry to Castlebay and Oban, but no ferry arrival from Oban or Castlebay and no bus services. ▶▶ *For further details, see Transport pages 278 and 306.*

Getting around A causeway connects South Uist to Benbecula by road and regular buses (four to six per day daily except Sunday) run between Lochboisdale and Lochmaddy on North Uist, stopping en route at Dalabrog (Daliburgh), Tobha Mòr (Howmore) and Lionacleit and Balinavich on Benbecula. There is also a regular bus service between Lochboisdale and Ludag (for ferries to Barra). A new causeway links Eriskay to South Uist. There are ferries to Eriskay from Barra, see page 306.

History
The dominant family in South Uist was Clanranald, who also owned Benbecula. They were descendants of the first Lord of the Isles, who was a MacDonald. The island's

Tight little island

Between Eriskay and South Uist is the wreck of the famous *SS Politician*, the island's other claim to fame. In 1941 the 12,000 ton ship went aground just off the island of Calvey and sank with its cargo, which included 20,000 cases of whisky. This not only provided many islanders with a supply of whisky for many years, but also provided the plot for Compton Mackenzie's book *Whisky Galore!*, which was later made into the famous Ealing comedy of the same name (it was called *Tight Little Island* in the US) and filmed on Barra. Part of the wreck can be seen at low tide, and there's more information on the famous incident on display in the appropriately named Am Politician pub (open 1230-1430), in the main settlement of Baile (Balla).

connections with Clanranald came to a sorry end, however, in 1837 when it was sold, along with Benbecula, to pay off bad debts, and became the property of the infamous Lieutenant-Colonel John Gordon Cluny. Though all the southern isles suffered during the brutal clearances of the 19th century, the experiences of people on South Uist were particularly cruel and inhumane. Between 1849 and 1851 over 2,000 were forcibly shipped to Quebec in Canada. Those who refused to board the transport ships were hunted down by dogs and bound, before being thrown on board and shipped to Canada, where they were left to starve.

Loch Baghasdail (Lochboisdale) → *Phone code: 01878. Colour map 3, grid A1.*
South Uists's largest settlement is set on a rocky promontory in a beautiful island-dotted sea loch. The imposing entrance is guarded by Calvay Island with its 13th-century castle ruin. Lochboisdale is a tiny place, with little in the way of tourist sights, though it does have a hotel, bank, post office and tourist information centre ① *Pier Rd, To1878-700286, early Apr to mid-Oct.*

About 10 miles south of Lochboisdale, on the southern coast of the island, is **Ludag jetty**, the departure point for the small private passenger ferry to **Eòlaigearraidh (Eoligarry)** on Barra. At **Cille Bhrìghde (West Kilbride)** nearby is **Hebridean Croft Originals** ① *open daily*, which has a wide range of local crafts on show, as well as a photographic display of local history and a tearoom.

Around the island
At the north of the island a causeway leads across **Loch Bi** (pronounced 'Bee') to the distinctive modern statue of **Our Lady of the Isles**, standing by the main road on the lower slopes of **Rueval Hill**. Further up the hill is the Royal Artillery control centre, known by the locals as 'Space City', due to its forest of aerials and 'golf balls', which tracks the missiles fired from a range on the northwestern corner of the island out into the Atlantic.

Just to the south of here is **Loch Druidibeag Nature Reserve**, on the site of the large freshwater loch, one of the largest breeding grounds in the British Isles for greylag geese and also a favourite haunt for mute swans (there's a warden nearby at Groigearraidh Lodge). From here the main road runs down the spine of the island, and all along the way little tracks branch off to the west, leading down to lovely beaches.

Not far south of Loch Druidibeag is the turning to the tiny village of **Tobha Mòr (Howmore)**, where you can see a collection of old traditional thatched 'blackhouses' beside the seemingly endless stretch of golden sand. One of the houses has been converted into a **Gatliff Trust Youth Hostel**, see Sleeping page 304. From the hostel it's a five-minute walk across the machair to the sandy beach which stretches almost the entire length of South Uist.

From Tobha Mòr, there are superb walks through the lonely hills of **Beinn Mhor** (620 m), **Beinn Corodale** (527 m) and **Hecla** (606 m) to the picturesque and dramatic valleys of Glen Hellisdale, Glen Corodale and Glen Usinish on the east coast. In 1746 that ubiquitous troglodyte, Bonnie Prince Charlie is reputed to have taken refuge in a cave above **Corodale Bay** for three weeks after his defeat and escape from Culloden.

Near **Bornais (Bornish)** another minor road can be followed east of the A865 to **Loch Eynort** that penetrates far inland from the Minch. An old stalkers path can be followed along the north shore of the loch towards the sea, with views of numerous seals and the occasional otter and the steep upper slopes of Beinn Mhor towering above to the north.

A few miles south, at **Gearraidh Bhailteas (Milton)**, a cairn marks the birthplace of that famous Hebridean lass, Flora MacDonald, see page 256. Nearby is the **Kildonan Museum**, which has a tearoom. The A865 continues south for a few miles to the village of Dalabrog (Daliburgh), then heads east to the island's main ferry port, **Lochboisdale**.

Eirisgeidh (Eriskay) → *Phone code: 01878. Colour map 3, grid A1.*

The tiny island of Eriskay, with a population of less than 200, gives its name to the native breed of pony, said to have been ridden by King Robert the Bruce at the Battle of Bannockburn in 1314. In the late 1970s it nearly became extinct, but one surviving stallion saved the breed and numbers are growing. A series of paths take you around the island in about three hours. For more details, see the Cuairt Eirisgeidh leaflet published by the Western Isles Tourist Board and available at the Lochboisdale Tourist Information Centre.

Most people come to Eriskay to pay a visit to **Coilleag a' Phrionnsa (Prince's beach)**, the sandy beach on the west coast. This is where Bonnie Prince Charlie first stepped on to Scottish soil on 23 July 1745, at the start of the ill-fated Jacobite Rebellion. The rare pink convolvulus which grows there today is said to have been planted by the Prince himself from seeds brought from France. A small memorial cairn in the dunes behind the beach was erected by the local school to commemorate the occasion.

As well as the wreck of the *SS Politician*, see box page 301, another sight worth seeing is **St Michael's**, the Roman Catholic church built in 1903 and funded by the local fishing fleet.

Bharraigh (Barra) → *Phone code: 01871. Colour map 3, grid A1. Population: 1,316.*

It may be tempting to overlook the little island of Barra, only about eight miles long by five miles wide, but that would be a mistake, as it's one of the most beautiful of all the islands in the Outer Hebrides – 'Barradise' indeed. Here you'll find the best of the islands in miniature – beaches, machair, peat-covered hills, tiny crofting communities and Neolithic remains – and a couple of days spent on Barra gives a real taster of Hebridean life. Gaelic culture is also strong here but, with its Catholic tradition, Barra is more laid-back than many of the other islands in the Outer Hebrides and doesn't follow the others' strict Sabbatarianism. ▶▶ *For Sleeping, Eating and other listings, see pages 304-306.*

Ins and outs
Getting there The best way to arrive is by air at Tràigh Mhòr ('Cockle Strand'), the famous airstrip on the beach at the north end of the island. This is the only airport in the UK where flight schedules are shown as 'subject to tides'. Barra is reached by car ferry from Oban on the mainland, by car ferry from Lochboisdale on South Uist, and from Tiree. A private passenger-only ferry sails from Ludag on South Uist. ▶▶ *For further details, see Transport pages 278 and 306.*

There is a regular bus/postbus service (five to eight times per day
Monday-Saturday) that runs from Castlebay to the ferry port of Eòlaigearraidh, via the
airport. There are also buses (three to four per day Monday-Saturday) from Castlebay
to Bhatarsaigh (Vatersay). You can also hire a car or a bicycle to tour the island at your
leisure. ▶▶ *For further details, see Transport pages 278 and 306.*

Bàgh a' Chaisteil (Castlebay)

The main settlement is Castlebay, on the southern side of the island, situated in a
wide sheltered bay and overlooked by **Sheabhal** (383 m), on top of which is a marble
statue of the Blessed Virgin and Child. It's a short but steep walk up to the top from
the town, and the views are well worth it. The once-thriving herring port is also
overlooked by the large Roman Catholic church, Our Lady, Star of the Sea.

As the main ferry port, Castlebay provides the full range of services: hotels, B&Bs,
shops, a bank (with ATM) and post office. The tourist information centre ① *T01871-
810223, Apr to mid-Oct Mon-Sat 0900-1700, also open for the arrival of the evening
ferry*, is on the main street near the ferry terminal. It has information on local walks
and will book accommodation.

Castlebay's most notable feature is the impressive 15th-century **Kisimul Castle**
① *T01871-810313, Apr-Sep daily 0930-1830, Oct Mon-Wed 0930-1630, Thu
0930-1230, Sat 0930-1630, Sun 1400-1630, £3.30, concession £2.50, children £1*,
reached by boat from Castlebay pier (five minutes), weather permitting, built on an
island in the middle of the harbour. This was the ancient home of the Chief of the
MacNeils, one of the oldest Scottish clans, who owned the island from 1427 till 1838. It
was then sold to the notorious Colonel Gordon of Cluny, along with neighbouring South
Uist and Benbecula, see page 300, and the poor people of Barra suffered the same
cruel fate, 600 of them being shipped to Canada to starve. One hundred years later the
castle and much of the island was bought back for the MacNeils by an American
architect, Robert Lister MacNeil, who became the 45th Clan Chief and restored the
castle to its present state before his death in 1970. His son, Ian Roderick MacNeil, used
it as his residence when visiting the island, before handing it over to Historic Scotland
in 2000 on a 1,000-year lease, in exchange for a rent of £1 and bottle of whisky.

If you're interested in finding out about the island's history, you should visit the Barra
Heritage Centre, known as **Dualchas** ① *T01871-810403, Apr-Sep Mon-Fri 1100-1700, £1*.

Around the island

The A888 follows a circular route of 14 miles around the island, making an ideal
day's bike tour from Castlebay. Heading west, it passes the turning for the
causeway to **Vatersay** (see below), then runs northwest between two hills
(Sheabhal to the east and Beinn Tangabhal to the west) to the west coast, where
you'll find the nicest beaches. One of these is at **Halaman Bay**, near the village of
Tangasdal (Tangasdale), overlooked by the **Isle of Barra Hotel**, see Sleeping page
304. At the turning for **Borgh (Borve)** there are standing stones. Next is the turning
for the small settlement of **Baile Na Creige (Craigston)**, where you'll find the
Thatched Cottage Museum ① *Easter-Oct Mon-Fri 1100-1700, £1*, an original
'blackhouse' and the chambered burial cairn of **Dun Bharpa**. From Dun Bharpa
there are pleasant walks into the surrounding hills, with the summit of **Sheabhal**
offering tremendous views from the highest point on the island.

North of the turning, near **Allathsdal (Allasdale)**, is another lovely beach, and just
beyond are the remains of **Dun Cuier**, an Iron-Age fort. Make a short detour at Greian,
and follow the headland to the rugged cliffs at **Greian Head**.

The A888 then heads east to **Bagh a Tuath (Northbay)**, where a branch left leads
to the village of **Eòlaigearraidh (Eoligarry)**, near the northern tip, surrounded by
sandy bays washed by Atlantic rollers. A private passenger ferry leaves from here to
Ludag on South Uist.

The road to Eoligarry passes the island's airport at **Tràigh Mhòr**, the 'cockle strand', which once provided 100 to 200 cartloads of delicious cockles each day. Now the cockleshells are gathered and used for harling, the roughcast wall covering used on many Scottish houses. By the beach is the house that was once the home of Compton MacKenzie, author of *Whisky Galore!*, see page 302. He lies buried at **Cille Bhara**, to the west of the village of Eòlaigearraidh, along with members of the MacNeil clan. This was one of the most important religious complexes in the Outer Hebrides, built in the 12th century, and consists of a church and two chapels. One of these, St Mary's, has been re-roofed and houses several carved medieval tombstones and a copy of a runic stone. The original stone is in the **Museum of Scotland** in Edinburgh.

Bhatarsaigh (Vatersay) and Mingulay

A worthwhile trip from Castlebay is to the island of Vatersay, now linked to Barra by a causeway built in an effort to stabilize the island community (the present population is around 70). The island boasts two shell-sand beaches backed by machair, only a few hundred yards apart on either side of the narrow isthmus that leads to the main settlement of Vatersay. On the west beach, Bagh Siar, is the **Annie Jane Monument**, commemorating the terrible tragedy in 1853, when the emigrant ship Annie Jane was wrecked off the coast of Vatersay, with the loss of 333 lives, many of them islanders.

On a clear day from Vatersay you can enjoy the view of the smaller islands to the south – Sandray, Pabbay and Mingulay. The latter was inhabited until 1912, and can still be visited from Barra. It has recently been acquired by the National Trust for Scotland. ▶▶ *For details of tours, see Activities and tours page 306.*

● Sleeping

North Uist *p297*
B Langass Lodge, near Pobhull Fhinn (see above), T01876-580285, langars@btinternet.com. Their restaurant specializes in local seafood and game.
C Lochmaddy Hotel, Lochmaddy, T01876-500332, F500210. Right by the ferry terminal. Open all year. Their restaurant serves great seafood, and the lively bar serves snacks. This is also the place to ask about fishing, as they rent out boats and sells permits for trout and salmon fishing.
C Temple View Hotel, at Grimsay, T01876-580676.
D-E The Old Courthouse, Lochmaddy, T01876-500358. One of a couple of good B&Bs.
D-E The Stag Lodge, Lochmaddy, T01876-500364, F500417, is a restaurant which also does B&B.
E Mrs Kathy Simpson, near Balranald, in Hogha Gearraidh (Houghgarry), overlooking the beautiful beach, T01876-510312.
E The Old Bank House, Lochmaddy, T01876-500275. Another good choice and also open all year.

E-F Mrs Morag Nicholson, in Ceann a Bhaigh (Bayhead), T01876-510395.
F Lochmaddy Uist Outdoor Centre, half a mile from the ferry pier, Lochmaddy, T01876-500480. Independent hostel, open all year, offers a wide range of outdoor activities including kayaking, windsurfing and rock climbing.
F Taigh Mo Sheannair, a few miles south of Clachan, at Cladach a Bhaile Shear (Claddach-baleshare), T01876-580246. Renovated crofthouse on a working farm which offers good hostel accommodation all year round, rents out bicycles and has space for those who want to camp.

Berneray *p299*
There are a couple of options for those wishing to stay.
E Burnside Croft, T01876-540235, splashmackilloop@burnsidecroft.fsnet.co.uk. Here you can share the prince's crofting experience with Donald (Splash) MacKillop. It also offers cycle hire and stories round the fire for evening entertainment.

F **Gatliff Trust Hostel**, in 2 restored blackhouses overlooking a lovely sandy beach and old Viking pier about a mile up the east coast from the old ferry pier. 12 beds, no phone, open all year.

Benbecula *p299*

A **Dark Island Hotel**, Lionacleit, T01870-603030, F602347. Functional hotel but a lot nicer inside than its name may suggest, has a good restaurant.
D **Inchyra Guest House**, Lionacleit, T01870-602176. Reliable and much cheaper alternative to the hotel.
F **Tigh-na-Cille Bunkhouse**, Balivanich, T01870-602522, open all year and sleeps 10 in 2 dorms and 2 twin rooms.

Camping
Shellbay Caravan and Camping Park
Lionacleit, T01870-602447, open Apr-Oct.

South Uist *p300*

You should book accommodation in advance, as the ferry arrives in Lochboisdale late in the evening.
C **Lochboisdale Hotel**, Lochboisdale, T01870-700332, F700367. This fishing hotel is right by the ferry terminal, and the best place to stay and the only place to have a drink or a meal.
C **Polachar Inn**, a few miles to the west of Ludag, at Pol a' Charra (Pollachar), T01870-700215, F700768. Charming place with great views across the Sound of Barra and its own beach close by.
D **Brae Lea Guest House**, about a mile from the terminal, Lochboisdale, T/F01870-700497. Will collect you from the ferry.
D **Orosay Inn**, T01870-610298, www.orosayinn.com. Small, modern hotel at Loch a' Chairnain (Lochcarnan). Open all year and offers fine Scottish cooking (££).
E **Bayview**, Lochboisdale, T01870-700329. B&B accommodation at the ferry terminal.
E-F **Lochside Cottage**, Lochboisdale, T01870-700472. B&B at the ferry terminal.
F **Gatliff Trust Youth Hostel**, at Tobha Mòr (Howmore), converted blackhouse which overlooks the ruins of an ancient church and graveyard, beside the seemingly

endless stretch of golden sand, 13 beds, open all year, no phone. The warden lives at Ben More House, at the junction with the main road.

Barra *p302*

It's a good idea to book in advance if arriving on the evening ferry from Oban.
B-C **Isle of Barra Hotel** a few miles west of Castlebay, T01871-810383, www.barra hotel.com. 30 rooms, open Apr-Oct. Modern, purpose-built hotel overlooking a lovely beach with fantastic sea views.
D **Castlebay Hotel**, by the ferry terminal in Castlebay, T01871-810223. 14 rooms. The best place to stay on the island. Friendly, good food, good value and a great bar.
D **Craigard Hotel**, in Castlebay, T01871-810200, is a family-run hotel with hearty home cooking.
E **Ceol Mara**, T01871-810294, one of several B&Bs in and around Castlebay.
E **Terra Nova**, T01871-810458, a 10-min walk from the ferry in Nask.
At the moment there are no independent hostels or a Gatliff Trust Hostel on Barra.

Camping
Although there are also no official campsites on Barra, there are endless opportunities for wild camping across the island, with the most popular spots to be found on the machair at Traigh Mhor (north Barra), Borve Point (west Barra) and Ledaig (Castlebay). Generally no permission is required from the landowner, but ensure all waste and litter is removed when you leave the site. For campers, there are 2 or 3 well-stocked mini-supermarkets in Castlebay

Eriskay *p302*
There is a **B&B**, T01870-720232, and a **self-catering flat**, T01870-720274, or you can wild camp – though there are few amenities, other than a shop, pub and post office.

● Eating

See Sleeping for further options.

For an explanation of sleeping and eating price codes used in this guide, see inside the front cover. Other relevant information is found in Essentials, see pages 41-49.

Outer Hebrides The Uists, Benbecula & Barra Listings

305

Benbecula *p299*
£££-££ Stepping Stone Restaurant,
Balivanich, T01870-603377. By far the best
place to eat on the island. Good wholesome
Scottish food every day from 1000 till 2100.
Snacks, sandwiches, takeaways and home
baking are all available, as well as 3- or
5-course meals.

Barra *p302*
££ Castlebay Hotel and **Isle of Barra Hotel**,
both offer excellent local fish and seafood.
£ Kismul Galley, on the main street in
Castlebay, T01871-810645, offers all-day
breakfasts, snacks and home baking, and is
open Mon-Sat 0900-2100 and Sun 1000-1800.
£ There's also a tearoom at the airport.

▲ Activities and tours

North Uist *p297*
Uist Outdoor Centre, is based in Lochmaddy,
T01876-500480, www.seakayakouter
hebrides.co.uk. They run week-long kayaking
courses as well as weekend beginners' trips
from £140, including tuition, food and
accommodation. For those wishing even
more solitude there are overnight expeditions
to Pabbay and Boreray. Wildlife on view
includes dolphins, porpoised, minke whales,
grey seals and basking sharks. The centre also
provides accommodation for 20 people in
4-person dorms.

Barra *p302*
Mr John Allan MacNeil in Castlebay,
T01871-810449 (approximately £15 per
person), can arrange boat trips to Mingulay.
He sails to the island in settled weather when
sufficient people can be found to fill the boat.
It is one of the most rewarding excursions in
the Outer Hebrides, particularly during the
puffin season from Jun to early Aug. The trip
normally includes a 2-hr sail from Barra past
the neighbouring islands of Sandray and
Pabbay, a circumnavigation of Mingulay to
view the spectacularly high western sea cliffs,
and a landing on the east coast for a 3-hr
exploration of the beautiful beach of Mingulay
Bay, the deserted village and surrounding hills
and coast. There are also fine views to the
lighthouse on Barra Head, the most southerly
outpost of the Outer Hebrides island chain.

Mr George McLeod, at the Castlebay Hotel,
T01871-810223, can arrange a similar tour to
that outlined above, or ask at the tourist
office in Castlebay.
Hatcher's Taxis, T01871-810486; and
Nellie's Taxi, T01871-810302, conduct
island tours.

● Transport

The Uists, Benbecula and Barra *p297*
Air
British Airways/Loganair, T08708-509850,
www.ba.com, flies from **Glasgow** to **Barra**
(Mon-Sat 1 daily, 1 hr 5 mins) and
Benbecula on North Uist (Mon-Sat 1 daily,
1 hr). There are also flights from **Benbecula**
to **Barra** (Mon-Fri 1 daily, 20 mins).

Ferry
To North Uist From **Uig** to **Lochmaddy** (1
hr 40 mins) 1-2 times daily. One-way ticket
£9.15 per passenger, £44 per car. Contact
Lochmaddy, T01876-5000337.
To Barra and South Uist From **Oban** to
Castlebay (5 hrs) and on to **Lochboisdale**
(a further 1 hr 40 mins) once daily except
Wed, plus an extra sailing on Thu to
Castlebay only, via **Tiree**. **Oban** to
Castlebay or **Lochbois- dale**, one-way
ticket £20.20 per passenger, £74 per car,
5-day saver return £34.50 and £126.
Castlebay to **Lochboisdale**, £5.75 one
way per passenger, £33.50 per car. **Tiree**
to **Castlebay**, £9.50 per passenger, £42
per car.
  There's also a regular passenger ferry
from **Ludag** in **South Uist** to **Eoligarry** on
Barra, T01878-720238. Ferries sail from
Barra to **Eriskay** 5 times daily (4 on Sun). A
one-way ticket costs £5.50 per passenger
and £16.25 per car. 5-day return £9.40 and
£28. Bikes £1.

Car and bike hire
Car hire at **Maclennan Self Drive**, Balivanich
on Beinn na Faoghla, T01870-602191,
F603191. Also at **Ask Car Hire**, Lionacleit,
Beinn na Faoghla, T01870-602818, F602933.
Car hire on South Uist is possible from **Laing
Motors**, Lochboisdale, T01870-700267, and
cycle hire from **Rothan Cycles**, Lochboisdale,
T01870-620283.

St Kilda

More than 40 miles west of the Outer Hebrides lie the spectacular and isolated islands of St Kilda, Scotland's first UNESCO World Heritage Site. St Kilda consists of several islands and manages to capture the imagination of most visitors to the Outer Hebrides, whether they actually get there or just dream about romantic voyages to mysterious lands across perilous seas. Owned by the National Trust for Scotland, St Kilda is a National Nature reserve. Each year, during the brief summer months when travel to the islands is possible, teams of volunteers work on Hirta, maintaining what remains of the abandoned houses, studying the wildlife and glorying in the peace and isolation of the place.

Ins and outs

The biggest problem apart from accessibility is cost, although it is definitely possible if you're prepared to break the bank. **Island Cruising** in Uig, on Lewis, T01851-672381, F672212, arranges boat trips to St Kilda from April to October starting from about £300 (four-day all-inclusive). The tour comprises the journey to and from St Kilda and a landing on Hirta with a visit to the museum, the old village and a wider exploration of the island including a climb up to the highest sea cliffs in the British Isles at Conachair (430 m). A 70-ft converted lifeboat also makes the trip, operated by **Northern Light** in Oban, T01680-814260. A seven-day expedition costs £650 per person. For more details of tours, ask at one of the main tourist information centres in the Outer Hebrides.

    National Trust for Scotland also organizes two-week long voluntary work parties throughout the summer every year to undertake restoration, maintenance and archaeology projects around the old village on Hirta. The groups are very popular, and each volunteer must complete an application form, so apply early. The fortnight costs between £450 and £500 and this covers transport from Oban to St Kilda and all food and lodging costs while on the island. For details contact **National Trust for Scotland** ⓘ *Oban, T01631-570000, stkilda@nts.org.uk.* For more information, contact **Scottish Natural Heritage** ⓘ *135 Stilligarry, South Uist, HS8 5RS, T01870-620238.*

Sights

In 1957 the islands become the property of the National Trust for Scotland, who in turn leased them to the Nature Conservancy (the forerunner of Scottish Natural Heritage) as a National Nature Reserve. St Kilda is the most important seabird breeding station in northwest Europe. The islands are home to the largest colony of gannets in the world, the largest colony of fulmars in Britain, and one the largest colonies of puffins in Scotland. These huge numbers of seabirds were vital to the islanders' survival. Their eggs provided food in the summer, and gannets and fulmers were caught each season to be plucked, dried and stored for the winter. Their feathers and oil were kept for export to generate income, whilst their bones were shaped into useful tools and their skins into shoes.

    The largest of the islands, **Hirta**, was the remotest community in Britain, if not Europe, until 1930, when the remaining 36 Gaelic-speaking inhabitants were evacuated at their own request, in one of the most poignant episodes of Scottish history. Today Hirta is partly occupied by the army as a radar-tracking station for the rocket range on South Uist and managed by Scottish Natural Heritage. Across a narrow channel lies **Dun**. Nearby **Boreray** is home to the world's largest colony of gannets, and **Soay** virtually completes the group. There are several dramatic 'stacs' rising sheer from the Atlantic Ocean. At 430 m, the sea cliffs at Conachair are the highest in the British Isles.

How St Kilda was killed off

Friday 29 August 1930 was the end of the life of St Kilda as it had been for centuries. For a least 1,000 years the inhabitants of this remote group of islands had been tenants of the Macleods of Dunvegan on Skye. In earlier days the trip from Skye, undertaken in longboats, would require 16 hours of rigorous rowing and sailing. Even now, the trip to St Kilda is no easy matter.

Until 1930 the islanders had been supported by the mainland by the provision of a nurse and a post office. But the Scottish Office decided that their subsidy of the islands was no longer economic. This meant that life for the residents without those facilities would be untenable.

But in 1930, to the younger of the 36 residents, including a man with nine children, evacuation was an attractive prospect. There would be better schooling for the children, and better health care. Although many had never seen a tree, a new life in forestry appealed. The more elderly residents, most of whom had never left the island and who could not speak English, must have viewed the drastic change with alarm. But the younger majority view prevailed and evacuation was planned.

There were 500 Soay sheep to be moved first. Their coats of fine wool were not sheared but plucked by the inhabitants using only a penknife. The resultant locally-woven tweed, either shipped ashore or sold to rare visitors, had provided the inhabitants' only contact with actual money. No taxes on income or on anything else were paid. Their internal economy took the form of barter. The plentiful supply of gannets, when dried, provided winter food. No inhabitant had ever fought in any war. Their distance and isolation earned them no consideration by the rest of Scotland.

Despite protestations by The Canine Defence League, all dogs were destroyed. Just two were put down by injections of hydrocyanic acid. The rest, at the islanders' insistence, had stones tied around their necks and were hurled from the jetty. Small boats, holding only a dozen or so sheep, were used to ferry them out to the *SS Dunara Castle*. Ten cows with four calves were also evacuated. Then *HMS Harebell*, of the Fishery Protection Service, came on the final day to take the islanders to the mainland. The Under Secretary of State for Scotland imposed a ban on photography, thus ensuring the people of St Kilda privacy during the evacuation. It was not possible to house all of the inhabitants in Argyll, as had been hoped, so the community was split, their communal lives coming to an end.

The history of the island has been documented in a number of scholarly works, including *The Life and Death of St Kilda* by Tom Steel, and *Island on the Edge of the World* by Charles Maclean.

Orkney & Shetland

⁝ Footprint features

Introduction

To some these two archipelagos will never be anything more than distant and overlooked specks of land peppering the wild north Atlantic, above an already distant north coast of mainland Scotland. They certainly are remote and they have maintained a social and political, as well as geographical, distance from the rest of Scotland, which goes a long way to explaining the relatively few visitors each year. Both were under Norse rule until the mid-15th century and, somehow, seeing them as a part of Scotland can be very misleading. Each must be seen within the context of its own unique cultural background and unusual geography.

Shetland's northern islands, on the same latitude as Alaska, are as strange and different as Britain gets, while beguiling Orkney just smiles serenely as the rest of world goes mad. It is these qualities that make the islands worth visiting and the ones that the tourist boards are keen to plug. Both Orkney and Shetland are also littered with outstanding archaeological evidence, not just of Norse occupation, such as at Jarlshof at the very southern tip of Shetland, but also of life back in 3000 BC at Skara Brae and the Knap of Howar in the Orkneys. They are also the best places in Britain to see wildlife as yet untamed by the 21st century. Here you can sail alongside porpoises and seals, and watch a million migratory seabirds nest and bring up their young during the summer months. And, thanks to fast and frequent transport links, it doesn't take an Arctic expedition to get here.

★ Don't miss...

❶ **Stromness** Explore the winding streets of one of the most fascinating fishing villages in Scotland, page 317.

❷ **Maes Howe and Skara Brae** Visit these amazing archaeological wonders, page 319.

❸ **Island of Lamb Holm** Visit the incredible little Italian Chapel, page 323.

❹ **Old Man of Hoy** Take the spectacular clifftop walk to meet the Old Man of Hoy, page 325.

❺ **Westray to Papa Westray** Fly to one island from the other, it takes all of two minutes, page 329.

❻ **Mousa** Visit the best-preserved broch in Scotland, page 343.

❼ **Fair Isle** Brave the white-knuckle boat trip to one of the best places on earth for birdwatching, page 345.

❽ **Hermaness National Nature Reserve** Explore the dramatic coastal scenery of this nature reserve, page 348.

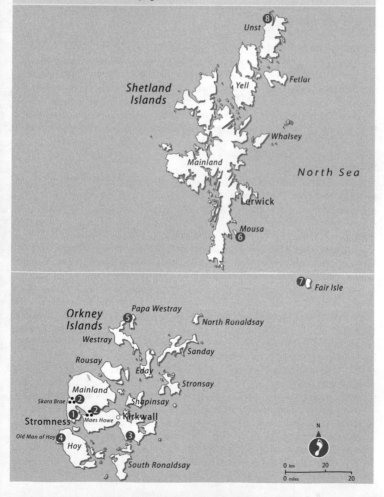

Orkney & Shetland

Orkney

Orkney may only be a short step away from John O' Groats, but to the fiercely independent Orcadians, 'Mainland' means the largest of the Orkney islands and not the Scottish mainland. Mainland is also the site of the two main towns and ferry terminals: the capital Kirkwall and the beautiful old fishing port of Stromness. Here, you'll also find many of Orkney's most precious archaeological treasures: the Stones of Stenness, Maes Howe, the Broch of Gurness and the remarkable Neolithic village of Skara Brae, all of which give the Orkney a rare continuity of past and present. Aside from Mainland, there are a dozen smaller islands to explore, including Hoy, with its wild, spectacular coastal scenery. The even more remote northerly islands offer miles of deserted beaches, and nothing but the calls of myriad birds to shatter the peace and quiet. Quiet also describes the taciturn locals. They aren't unfriendly, but Orcadians will rarely use one word where none will do. ▸▸ *For Sleeping, Eating and other listings, see pages 330-337.*

Ins and outs

Getting there
There are direct flights to Kirkwall airport daily except Sunday from Aberdeen, Edinburgh, Glasgow, Inverness and Shetland, with connections to London Heathrow, Birmingham, Manchester and Belfast. There are several ferry routes to Orkney from the mainland: Aberdeen-Kirkwall (7½ hours); Scrabster, near Thurso, to Stroness; John o' Groats to Burwick, on South Ronaldsay (40 minutes, from May to September) and Gill's Bay, near John o' Groats, to St Margaret's Hope. There's also an 'Orkney Bus', which leaves daily from Inverness, direct to Kirkwall. ▸▸ *For further details, see page 334.*

Getting around
There are inter-island flights which are operated by **Loganair** ① *To1856-872494, www.loganair.co.uk.* They are very reasonable, starting from £12 one way to many of the islands. There are sightseeing flights in July and August which fly over all the islands costing £30. There's also an Orkney Adventure ticket which allows you to fly to three islands for £68.

Orkney Ferries ① *To1856-872044,* operates daily car and passenger ferries to Rousay, Egilsay and Wyre from Tingwall; to Shapinsay, Eday, Stronsay, Sanday, Westray and Papa Westray from Kirkwall; to Graemsay and Hoy from Stromness; and to Hoy and Flotta from Houton. There's a ferry on Friday to North Ronaldsay from Kirkwall. Fares to Rousay, Egilsay, Wyre, Shapinsay, Hoy, Graemsay and Flotta cost £5.80 return per passenger and £17.50 per car. To Eday, Stronsay, Sanday, Westray, Papa Westray and North Ronaldsay fares cost £11.60 return per passenger £26 per car. An inter-island fare is £2.90 one-way per passenger and £6.55 per car. Those travelling by car should book all ferry journeys in advance.

Only the main population centres on Mainland are served by public transport, and having a car is essential to visit many of the most interesting sights. Bringing a car to Orkney is expensive, but there are several car hire firms on the Mainland and on the other islands. An alternative could be taking to a bike. Orkney is relatively flat and most of its roads are quiet, which makes it ideal for touring on two wheels, though the wind can make it difficult if it's blowing in the wrong direction. Bicycles can be hired in Kirkwall, Stromness and on many of the other islands. Those with limited time may prefer to book a tour of the islands. ▸▸ *For further details, see Activities and tours page 333 and Transport page 334.*

⦂ Learning the lingo

Despite the disappearance of the Norse language, many of the Viking place names have survived. Here are some of the most common Old Norse elements which will help explain the meaning of many place names:

A(y)	island	*holm*	small island
a, o	stream	*howe*	mound
aith	isthmus	*kirk*	church
ayre	beach	*lax*	salmon
bard	headland	*ler*	mud, clay
bister	farm	*lyng*	heather
brae, brei	broad	*minn*	mouth
fell, field	hill	*mool, noup*	headland
fors	waterfall	*setter*	farm
garth	farm	*thing*	parliament
geo	creek	*toft*	house site
grind	gate	*voe*	sea inlet
ham(n)	anchorage	*wick, vik*	bay

Tourist information

Orkney Tourist Board ① *www.visitorkney.com*, has tourist offices in Kirkwall and Stromness. They will book accommodation for you, or provide a list of what's available, though many B&Bs are not included in the tourist board scheme. They can also provide information on various sights, walks and the islands' wildlife. Those wishing to leave Mainland and visit the smaller islands should pick up a free copy of the tourist board's excellent information and travel guide, *The Islands of Orkney*.

Many of Orkney's monuments are managed by **Historic Scotland**. They include the Bishop and Earl's Palaces, Broch of Gurness, Maes Howe, Skara Brae and Skaill House, Brough of Birsay and Hackness Martello Tower. If you plan to visit all or most of these sights, it may be cheaper to buy a three, seven or 10-day Historic Scotland Explorer Ticket, which costs £16, £22 and £25 respectively.

Kirkwall → *Phone code: 01856. Population: 7,000.*

Orkney's rugged, Nordic-feeling capital is built around a wide sheltered bay and is the main departure point for ferries to the northern islands. First impressions are a little misleading, as the harbour area has been blighted by modern development. More appealing, however, are the narrow winding streets and lanes of the old town, which has not changed much over the centuries. There are many houses dating from the 16th, 17th and 18th centuries, as well as Kirkwall's greatest attraction, its magnificent cathedral, the finest medieval building in northern Scotland. *▶▶ For Sleeping, Eating and other listings, see pages 330-337.*

Ins and outs

Getting there and around The **airport** ① *To1856-872421*, is three miles southeast of Kirkwall on the A960. There are no buses to and from town. A taxi will cost around £6. The bus station is five minutes' walk west of the town centre. The town is compact and it's easy to get around on foot. The main street changes its name from Bridge Street to Albert Street, to Broad Street and Victoria Street as it twists its way south from the

busy harbour. The cathedral is on Broad Street, and most of the shops and banks are on Broad Street and Albert Street. ▶▶ *For further details, see Transport page 334.*

Tourist information On Broad Street, near the cathedral, is the very helpful **TIC** ① *To1856-872856, info@otb.ossian.net, Apr-Sep 0830-2000, Oct-Mar Mon-Sat 0930-1700*. Service they provide include booking accommodation and changing money, and they also has various useful free leaflets including *The Islands of Orkney and the Kirkwall Heritage Guide*. They also stock a wide range of guidebooks and maps, and have details of forthcoming events. Another good source is the weekly newspaper *The Orcadian*.

Sights

The town's outstanding sight is the huge and impressive red sandstone **St Magnus Cathedral** ① *Apr-Sep Mon-Sat 0900-1800, Sun 1400-1800, Oct-Mar Mon-Sat 0900-1300 and 1400-1700, Sun service at 1115*, built by masons who had worked on Durham Cathedral in the north of England. It was founded in 1137 by Rognvald Kolson, Earl of Orkney, in memory of his uncle, Magnus Erlendson, who was slain by his cousin, Haakon Paulson, on Egilsay in 1115. Magnus was buried at Birsay and it is said that heavenly light was seen over his grave. It soon became a shrine, attracting pilgrims from as far afield as Norway. Magnus was canonized in 1133, and four years later his nephew commissioned construction of the cathedral. The building wasn't completed until the 14th century, and major additions were made during the intervening centuries. The most recent addition was a new west window for the nave, to celebrate the cathedral's 850th anniversary in 1987. The bones of St Magnus now lie in the north choir pillar, while those of St Rognvald lie in the south one. There's also a memorial to John Rae, the 19th-century Arctic explorer who is buried in the graveyard, as well as a monument to the 833 men of the *HMS Royal Oak* who died when it was torpedoed in Scapa Flow in 1939.

Orkney & Shetland Orkney

N

0 km   5
0 miles   5

Looming impressively nearby are the ruins of the **Bishop's Palace**, built in the 12th century as the first Kirkwall residence of the Bishop of Orkney. Here King Haakon of Norway died in 1263 after his defeat at the Battle of Largs. The palace was repaired and extended in the mid-16th century by Bishop Reid, and most of what you see dates from that period. There's a good view of the town from the top of the 'Moosie Too'r'.

The adjacent **Earl's Palace** ① *To1856-871918, Apr-Sep daily 0930-1830, £2.20, concession £1.60, children £0.75*, was built around 1600 by the notorious Patrick Stewart, Earl of Orkney, using forced labour. Still very much intact, it is one of Scotland's most elegant Renaissance buildings and was occupied by the tyrannical Stewart only for a very short time, until he was imprisoned and later executed. Wandering around both these spectacularly impressive, and solid, buildings is a very good way to get a feel for a period of Orkney's history that is very often ignored.

Kirkwall

Sleeping
Albert 1
Ayre 2
Foveran 5
SYHA Hostel 3
West End 4
Whiteclett 6

Eating
Mumatz 1
Mustard Seed Café 2

Opposite St Magnus Cathedral is **Tankerness House and Gardens,** a 16th-century former manse which has been restored and now houses the **Orkney Museum** ① *To1856-873191, Oct-Mar Mon-Sat 1030-1230, 1330-1700, Apr-Sep 1030-1700, May-Sep also Sun 1400-1700, free*, which features various archaeological artefacts from Neolithic times to the Vikings. If you are spending any time in Kirkwall at the beginning of your stay, then this is an exceedingly worthwhile exhibition. It is a great way to whet your appetite for the archaeological gems that are lying in wait for you all over the islands, and it also puts them into a useful chronological context.

Old radio buffs should not miss the **Orkney Wireless Museum** ① *Apr-Sep Mon-Sat 1000-1630, Sun 1400-1630, £2, children £1*, at Kiln Corner, at the harbour end of Junction Road, which houses a jumble of domestic and wartime communications equipment from the 1930s onwards.

A mile south of the town centre on the road to South Ronaldsay is the 200-year-old **Highland Park Distillery** ① *To1856-874619, www.highlandpark.co.uk, tours every half hour Apr, Sep and Oct Mon-Fri 1000-1700, May-Aug Mon-Sat 1000-1700, Sun 1200-1700, Nov-Mar Mon-Fri at 1400 only, £4*, the most northerly of Scotland's whisky distilleries and one of the very best. It's one of the few that still has its own floor maltings – as well as its own mouser cat – and there's a dram of this particularly fine single malt at the end.

Stromness and West Mainland → *Phone code: 01856.*

Ferries from Scrabster arrive in Stromness, and the newcomer is greeted by rows of stone-built houses hugging the shore, each with their own jetty. Stromness is a much more attractive town than Kirkwall, and its narrow, winding main street, its *wynds* and *closes*, its fascinating shops, and its unique atmosphere make it the ideal base for exploring the West Mainland, the name given to everything west of Kirkwall. It's an area of rich farmland, rolling hills and moorland, fringed by spectacular cliffs along the Atlantic coastline and with the greatest concentration of prehistoric monuments in Britain. Here you'll find, amongst many others, the well-preserved Neolithic village of **Skara Brae,** silent monuments to human endeavour in the form of the standing **Stones of Stenness** and the **Ring of Brodgar,** and the chambered tomb of **Maes Howe,** with its many still unresolved mysteries. ▸▸ *For Sleeping, Eating and other listings, see pages 330-337.*

Ins and outs

Stromness Tourist Information Centre ① *To1856-850716, Apr-Oct Mon-Sat 0800-1800, Sun 0900-1600, Nov-Mar Mon-Fri 0900-1700*, is at the new ferry terminal. Its exhibition, *This Place Called Orkney,* is a useful introduction to the islands, and its free *Stromness Heritage Guide* takes you round all the buildings of interest in the town. ▸▸ *For details of Transport, see pages 312 and 324.*

Stromness

Stromness is a classic Scottish fishing towns and a perfect introduction to Orkney. Though referred to in the Viking Saga as *Hamnavoe,* the town dates from the 17th century. Its importance as a trading port grew in the 18th century when wars and privateers made the English Channel too dangerous and ships used the northern route across the Atlantic, calling in at Stromness for food and water and to hire a crew. Until the late 19th century, ships of the Hudson Bay Company made Stromness their main base for supplies. Whaling ships bound for Greenland also hired local labour. By the late 19th century the herring boom had reached Stromness and there were 400 boats using its harbour, but within two decades the boom was over due to over-fishing. Today Stromness remains a fishing port, as well as Orkney's main ferry terminal and the headquarters of the Northern Lighthouse Board.

Scandanavian settlements

The history of Orkney and Shetland is bound up with the history of the Vikings, who first came to the islands in the latter half of the ninth century and stayed for about 650 years. This was part of a great Viking expansion westwards, and in less than a century emigrants from Norway and Denmark settled in Orkney, Shetland, Iceland, Greenland, Caithness, the Western Isles, Isle of Man and parts of Ireland and the northern half of England.

In 872 the King of Norway set up a Norse earldom in Orkney, from which the Vikings ruled Orkney, Shetland and the Western Isles and took part in raids around Britain and Europe, creating the popular image of Vikings as aggressive, bloodthirsty invaders. At home, however, they lived a peaceful life, adhering to the laws of their parliament, the 'thing', and many converted to Christianity.

In the late 14th century Norway, Denmark and Sweden were united under a Danish king. In 1469 the Royal estates and prerogatives in Orkney and Shetland were pledged to Scotland as part of the marriage dowry of Margaret, daughter of the King of Denmark, on her marriage to Prince James of Scotland, later to become King James III. Orkney and Shetland were to revert to rule by the kings of Norway when the debt was paid, but the pledge was never redeemed and the islands remained under Scottish control.

Soon after assuming control, the Scots began to change the old Norse laws which they had agreed to maintain, and Scottish influence grew. In 1564 Mary, Queen of Scots granted the control and revenues from Orkney and Shetland to her half-brother, Robert Stewart. His prime motivation, however, was to extract as much money as possible through taxes. He was succeeded by his son, the infamous Patrick Stewart, who demanded even more rents, dues and fines. Earl Patrick eventually got his come-uppance when he was executed in Edinburgh for treason, but the changes he had made continued and Scots and English gradually began to usurp Old Norse as the native language of the islands.

Stromness consists largely of one narrow, winding main street, paved with flagstones, which hugs the shoreline. Running off the street are numerous little lanes and alleyways, many with fascinating names such as **Khyber Pass**, and full of interesting buildings which reflect the town's proud maritime heritage. The houses on the seaward side of the street are gable end to the waterfront and each has its own jetty. The town is not designed for the car, so you'll have to park by the harbour and explore its delights on foot. The main street changes its name from Victoria Street to Graham Place, Dundas Street, Alfred Street and South End as it runs south from the harbour.

Stromness Museum ① *52 Albert St, T01856-850025, May-Sep daily 1000-1700, Oct-Apr Mon-Sat 1030-1230 and 1330-1700, £2.50, children £0.50*, has exhibitions on natural and maritime history, and contains artefacts from Scapa Flow and the days of the Hudson Bay company. Opposite the museum is the house where **George Mackay Brown** (1921-1996), Orkney's most famous poet and story-writer, spent the last two decades of his life, see also page 375. On a jetty to the south of the new harbour is the excellent **Pier Arts Centre** ① *Tue-Sat 1030-1230 and 1330-1700, Jul and Aug also Sun 1400-1700, free*, housing a permanent collection of works of the St Ives school, including Barbara Hepworth, Ben Nicholson and Patrick Heron, amongst others, in a lovely gallery.

Skara Brae and Skaill House

① To1956-841815, Apr-Sep daily 0930-1830. £5, concession £3.75, children £1.30. Oct-Mar (Skara Brae only) Mon-Sat 0930-1630 and Sun 1400-1630. £4, concessions £3, children £1.20.

Eight miles north of Stromness, in the magnificent setting of the dazzling white sands of the Bay of Skaill, is Skara Brae, the best-preserved Stone-Age village in northern Europe. First revealed in 1850 after a violent storm blew away the dunes, the site dates from around 5,000 years ago and was occupied for about 600 years.

The houses contain stone furniture, fireplaces, drains, beds, dressers and even have damp-proof coursing in the foundations. The whole complex presents a unique picture of the lifestyle of its inhabitants, and there's also a replica 'house' that you can wander around in through the gloom, empathizing with that 3000 BC lifestyle.

The swish, modern visitor centre has a useful introductory video and exhibition which is definitely worth seeing before you look round the site (and it's also worth buying their guidebook). After leaving the visitor centre, you walk down a 'path of time', which takes you back through landmark achievements of the last seven millennia, gradually building up the suspense and putting the achievements of Skara Brae in perspective – they may only be rudimentary buildings that once had turf for their rooves, but they were built 2,000 years before the pyramids of Egypt, and in one of the world's most northerly outposts.

During the summer a ticket to Skara Brae includes admission to nearby **Skaill House**, an early 17th-century mansion which contains a few old artefacts, including Captain Cook's dinner service from the Resolution, but is a bit of a let-down after what you will have just witnessed, not 300 yards away at Skara Brae.

Sandwick and Yesnaby

A short distance inland from here, at Sandwick, is Orkney's only brewery, housed in the old Quoyloo School. It brews the island's Raven Ale and various bottled beers, including Skull-splitter, named after the Viking Earl, Thorfinn Skull-splitter.

South of the Bay of Skaill is Yesnaby, one of the most spectacular places on the islands, where the cliffs have been eroded into a series of stacks and geos by the fierce Atlantic seas. An exhilarating, and precarious, half-mile walk south from the car park and old Second World War lookout post brings you to **Yesnaby Castle**, a huge sea stack similar to the Old Man of Hoy. It's a dramatic sight, especially in a full force gale.

Standing Stones of Stenness and Ring of Brodgar

Northeast of Stromness on the road to Kirkwall is the tiny village of **Stenness**, near some of Orkney's most interesting prehistoric sites. The Standing Stones of Stenness comprise the four remaining stones from an original circle of 12 stones, dating from 3000 BC. The largest of the stones stands over 15 ft high. A path leads from the stones to the nearby **Barnhouse Settlement**, a recently excavated Neolithic village.

About a mile northwest of Stenness is another stone circle, the **Ring of Brodgar**. This is a particularly impressive henge monument. It is over 100 yards in diameter and 27 of the original 60 stones are still standing, some of them up to 15 ft high. Given the importance of these sites, it is particularly refreshing to realize when you get there that you can walk about amongst the stones in the calm of a summer evening, with only a few oyster catchers for company, but both get busy with coach parties during the day.

Maes Howe

① To1856-761606, Apr-Sep daily 0930-1830, Oct-Mar Mon-Sat 0930-1630 and Sun 1400-1630. £3, concession £2.30, children £1, tickets bought from Tormiston Mill, on the other side of the road, where there's an exhibition, introductory video and café.

Less than a mile northeast of the Stones of Stenness is Maes Howe, the finest Neolithic burial chamber in Europe. It was built around 2750 BC, making it contemporary with the Standing Stones and Skara Brae, and is amazingly well preserved. A huge mound covers a stone-built entrance passage which leads into a central chamber – over 12 ft square and the same in height – with three smaller cells built into the walls of the tomb.

When it was opened in 1861, no human remains or artefacts were found, giving no clues as to its usage. However, in the 12th century Vikings returning from the Crusades broke into the tomb searching for treasure. They found nothing but left behind one of the largest collections of runic graffiti anywhere in the world, as well as carvings of a dragon, serpent and walrus. Many of the inscriptions are pretty basic, along the lines of 'Thorfinn wrote these runes', but some are more intriguing, such as 'Many a woman has come stooping in here no matter how pompous a person she was'.

A guide gives you an excellent overview of the chamber's mysterious architectural attributes, but the fact remains that the history of this extraordinary place is still largely unsolved – something that obviously adds to the site's attraction. Unfortunately, you do not get the chance to spend very much time in the chamber, so you are unlikely to uncover any great secrets.

Orphir

On the southern shores of West Mainland, overlooking Scapa Flow, is the scattered community of Orphir, which has a few sights worth visiting, especially if you're heading across to Hoy from the ferry terminal at **Houton**, a little further west. The main point of interest in Orphir is the **Orkneyinga Saga Centre** ① *all year daily 0900-1700, free*, where a small exhibition and video introduces the saga, written circa 1200, possibly by an Icelander, which tells the history of the Viking Earls of Orkney from around AD 900 to AD 1200, when the islands became a part of Scotland rather than Norway. As you would expect, there's plenty of gore and Machiavellian goings-on, including an assassination attempt that went disastrously wrong, when a poisoned shirt meant for Earl Harold was unwittingly and fatally worn by his brother Paul instead.

‼ For details of ferries to Hoy and Flotta, see page 324. For details of buses to Houton, see page 334.

Behind the centre is **The Earl's Bu**, looking out across Orphir Bay south to Cava Island. These are the 12th-century foundations of the home of the Norse Earls of Orkney written about in the saga. Inside the cemetery gates is a section of the circular church built by Haakon and modelled on the rotunda of the Church of the Holy Sepulchre in Jerusalem.

Markwick Head

At the southern end of Birsay Bay are the wild and spectacular 300 ft-high cliffs of Marwick Head, topped by the distinctive **Kitchener Memorial**, erected after the First World War to commemorate Lord Kitchener and the crew of the *HMS Hampshire*, which was sunk by a German mine off the coast in 1916 with the loss of all but 12 of her crew. Marwick Head is also an **RSPB Reserve**, and during the nesting season in early summer is home to many thousands of guillemots, razorbills, kittiwakes and fulmars, as well as a few puffins.

A mile inland, by the Loch of Isibister, is another RSPB reserve, **The Loons**, an area of marshland where you can see breeding and migrating wildfowl and waders. Further east, between Boarhouse Loch and Hundland Loch, is the **Kirbuster Farm Museum** ① *Mar-Oct Mon-Sat 1030-1300 and 1400-1700, Sun 1400-1900, free*, the last surviving Orkney 'black house' which was inhabited till the 1960s and gives an insight into 19th-century rural life on the islands.

● A fascinating feature of Maes Howe is that the winter solstice sun sets directly over the Barnhouse Stone, half a mile away, and shines down the entrance passage of Maes Howe and on to the back wall of one of the cells.

Sitting pretty

One of Scotland's most distinctive pieces of furniture is the Orkney chair. Starting as a 'needs must' object, the chairs were originally made of driftwood and backed with oat straw. Their half-moon shape ingeniously gave protection from the many draughts in a house. Very often the back was extended upwards into a cowl, so that the chair looked rather like an upended cradle. This gave added protection. It was often been said that what an Orkney man could not make from straw was not worth having. The straw, which came from black oats, was particularly important as trees are not plentiful on Orkney. Even today bringing timber from across the Pentland Firth is an expensive business. Heavy storms still yield windfall wood but not such a variety as in the days of wooden ships which too often perished in these waters.

Birsay

At the far northwestern corner of the Mainland is the parish of Birsay, which was a favourite residence of the Earls of Orkney in Viking times as well as the first seat of the Bishop, before the building of St Magnus Cathedral in Kirkwall. Earl Thorfinn the Mighty lived here (1014-1064) and built Orkney's first cathedral, **Christchurch**, for the new Bishop.

In the centre of the village are the ruins of the **Earl's Palace** ① *T01856-721205, open at all times, free,* built by the infamous Earl Robert Stewart in the late 16th century, and once described as "a sumptuous and stately dwelling". Not much remains today, but enough to give some idea of the sheer scale of the place. Close by is **St Magnus church**, built in 1760 on the site of an earlier church, which in turn was built on the foundations of what is believed to be the original Christchurch. Also in Birsay, just south of the A966 and A967 junction, is **Barony Mills** ① *Apr-Sep daily 1000-1300 and 1400-1700, £1.50,* the last working water-powered mill in Orkney.

Lying half a mile off the coast near the village is the **Brough of Birsay** ① *open (when tides permit) 11 Jun-30 Sep daily 0930-1830, £1.80, concession £1.30, children £0.50, phone the Earl's Palace (see above).* The tidal island, managed by Historic Scotland, jutts out into the north Atlantic and is visible from several other points all the way down the west cost of the mainland. It is only accessible for a couple of hours at low tide (times available from Kirkwall and Stromness tourist offices) but, if possible, it is best seen at the end of the day, as the sun sets – and you'll probably have the whole island to yourself. Pick your way over the causeway and wander at your leisure (but don't forget the tide!) amongst the remnants of a Pictish, and then Viking, community. The island was an important Pictish settlement from around the sixth century, and many artefacts have been found here. Some of these can be seen at the small ticket office at the entrance to the island. The Brough was also the site of an important Viking settlement, and there are extensive remains, including the 12th-century **St Peter's church** where St Magnus was buried after his murder on Egilsay. You can also walk out to the island's lighthouse along the top of the cliffs and see puffins – amongst other migrating seabirds – and possibly Minke whales, Pilot whales and Killer whales.

Evie and the Broch of Gurness

Nine miles northwest of Kirkwall is the tiny village of Evie. A track leads from the village towards the coast, past a sandy beach, to the **Broch of Gurness** ① *T01856-751414, Apr-Sep daily 0930-1830, £3, concession £2.30, children £1.* Standing on a lonely, exposed headland on the north coast, with warm, gentle views across towards the island of Rousay, this is the best-preserved broch on Orkney, thought to date from around 100 BC. It is surrounded by an Iron-Age village whose houses are also remarkably well-preserved, with the original hearths, beds, cupboards and even a toilet still in evidence. The broch and village were occupied by the Picts right up till Viking times, around AD 900. Many Pictish artefacts have been found on the site, and the grave of a ninth-century Norse woman was also discovered.

To the southwest of Evie is the **Birsay Moors RSPB Reserve**, and at **Lowrie's Water** on Burgar Hill there's a bird-hide from where you can watch breeding red-throated divers. Also on Burgar Hill you'll see several huge aerogenerators built to take advantage of Orkney's fierce winds.

East Mainland and South Ronaldsay → *Phone code: 01856.*

The East Mainland is mainly agricultural land and though it contains little of the amazing archaeological wealth of its western counterpart, there are some attractive fishing villages, fine coastal walks and many poignant reminders of Orkney's important wartime role. Linked to East Mainland by a series of causeways, South Ronaldsay is the southernmost of the Orkney islands, only six miles from the Scottish mainland across the stormy Pentland Firth, the most dangerous stretch of water in the British Isles. A small passenger ferry crosses to Burwick on the southern tip of the island from John O' Groats. ▸▸ *For Sleeping, Eating and other listings, see pages 330-337.*

Deerness

There is not much to see inland on the road running southeast from Kirkwall past the airport, but head on towards the Deerness Peninsula and you will be richly rewarded by a truly serene, gentle beauty. There are sandy bays, which make for very pleasant short walks and picnics (if you can find a sheltered spot), jutting cliffs and a great variety of birdlife. The peninsula makes the West Mainland seem positively crowded by comparison, and is one of the best places on the Mainland to 'get away from it all'.

▲▲ When the weather's good, the view southwest from Sandside Bay to the Isle of **Copinsay** (an RSPB reserve) is glorious, and is a perfect example of the whale-like properties that have been attributed to the Orkneys by the islands' most famous poet George Mackay Brown. There is a footpath following the coast from Sandside Bay to Mull Head (a Nature Reserve) and round the tip of the peninsula to the Covenanters Memorial (1679), a five-mile circular walk.

▲▲ If you continue along the B9050, the road ends at The Gloup car park at Skaill Bay, from where it's a 200-yd walk to **The Gloup**, a dramatic collapsed sea cave, separated from the sea by a land bridge about 80 yards wide. The word comes from the Old Norse 'gluppa', meaning chasm, the local name for a blow-hole. A network of signposted footpaths covers the northeastern part of the peninsula and there are circular walks of between two and five miles which start from The Gloup car park. At the northeastern tip is **Mull Head**, a clifftop nature reserve which is home to guillemots, shags, fulmars, razorbills, terns and skuas.

On the south coast of East Mainland, near the northern end of the Churchill Barriers, is the old fishing village of **St Mary's**, once a busy little place but largely forgotten since the building of the causeways. To the east of the village is the **Norwood Museum** ⓘ *T01856-781217, May-Sep Tue-Thu and Sun 1400-1700 and 1800-2000, £3, children £1*, which features the large and eclectic antique collection of local stonemason Norris Wood.

The Churchill Barriers

East Mainland is linked to a string of islands to the south by four causeways, known as the Churchill Barriers, built on the orders of Prime Minister Winston Churchill during the Second World War as anti-submarine barriers to protect the British Navy

of the battleship *HMS Royal Oak* in October 1939 by a German U-boat which had
slipped between the old blockships, deliberately sunk during the First World War to
protect Scapa Flow, and the shore. After the war, a road was built on top of the
causeways, linking the islands of Lamb Holm, Glimps Holm, Burray and South
Ronaldsay to Mainland.

On the island of **Lamb Holm** camps were built to accommodate the men working
on the construction of the barriers, many of whom were Italian Prisoners of War. The
camps have long since gone, but the Italians left behind the remarkable **Italian Chapel**
ⓘ *open all year during daylight hours, free*, fittingly known as 'The Miracle of Camp 60'.
It is difficult to believe that such a beautiful building could have been using two
Nissen huts, concrete and bits of scrap metal, and the chapel's enduring popularity
with visitors is a tribute to the considerable artistic skill of the men involved. One of
them, Domenico Chiochetti, returned in 1960 to restore the interior paintwork.

Burray

On the island of Burray the road passes the **Orkney Fossil and Vintage Centre**
ⓘ *Apr-Sep daily 1000-1800, Oct Wed-Sun 1030-1800, £2*, which houses a bizarre
collection of old furniture, various relics and 350 million-year-old fish fossils found
locally. There's also an archive room where you can browse through old books and
photographs, and a coffee shop. Not really something to go out of your way for, but
worth a look if it's raining.

South Ronaldsay

The main settlement is the picturesque little village of **St Margaret's Hope** on the
north coast. It is said to be named after Margaret, Maid of Norway, who died near here
in 1290 at the age of seven while on her way to marry Prince Edward, later Edward II of
England. She had already been proclaimed Queen of Scotland, and her premature
death was a major factor in the long Wars of Independence with England. The word
'hope' comes from the Old Norse word *hjop* meaning bay.

The village smithy has been turned into the **Smiddy Museum** ⓘ *May and Sep
daily 1400-1600, Jun-Aug 1200-1600, Oct Sun 1400-1600, free*, with lots of old
blacksmith's tools to try out. The museum also features a small exhibition on the
annual **Boys' Ploughing Match**, a hugely popular event first held circa 1860. Each
year in August, boys from the village (and now girls as well) dress up as horses and
parade in the village square (prizes are given for the best costume). Afterwards the
boys and their fathers, or grandfathers, head for the **Sand of Wright**, a few miles west,
and have a ploughing match with miniature ploughs, which are usually family
heirlooms. The categories are: best ploughed ring, best feering or guiding furrow,
neatest ends and best kept plough. This sheltered beach is well worth a visit anyway,
ploughing or no ploughing. The views stretch in a spectacular 180 degree panorama,
south across the Pentland Firth to Caithness on mainland Scotland, west to South
Walls and Cantick Head on Hoy, and northwest to Flotta and the west Mainland. It is
also yet another good place to spot snipe, lapwing, curlew and redshank. Arctic terns
also nest nearby and you can spot them diving dramatically as they fish in the bay.

To the north of the beach is the **Howe of Hoxa**, a ruined broch where Earl Thorfinn
Skull-Splitter was buried in AD 963, according to the Orkneyinga saga. South
Ronaldsay is a good place to buy local arts and crafts, and there are several
workshops dotted around the island. One of these is the **Hoxa Tapestry Gallery**
ⓘ *T/Fo1856-831395, Apr-Sep Mon-Fri 1000-1730, Sat and Sun 1400-1800, £2,
concession £1.50, children under 12 free*, three miles west of the village on the way to
Hoxa Head. Local artist Leila Thompson's huge tapestries are well worth a visit; you
may not like the style, but you cannot help but marvel at the extraordinary amount of
work and dedication involved in their creation; many of them take years to finish.

⁙ The graveyard of Scapa Flow

The huge natural harbour of Scapa Flow has been used since Viking times, and in the years leading up to the First World War the Royal Navy held exercises there, sometimes involving up to 100 ships. But Scapa was vulnerable to attack, and over the course of the war defences were improved with 21 blockships sunk at the eastern approaches. Scapa Flow continued to be used as the main naval base in the Second World War, but the blockships were not enough to prevent a German U-boat from torpedoing *HMS Royal Oak*, and the huge task of building the Churchill Barriers began, see page 322.

Scapa Flow's most famous incident happened at the end of the First World War, when, under the terms of the Armistice, Germany agreed to surrender most of her navy. Seventy-four German ships were interred in Scapa Flow, awaiting the final decision, but as the deadline approached the German commander, Admiral Von Reuter, gave the order for all the ships to be scuttled, and every ship was beached or sank.

The scuttled German fleet, however, proved a hazard for fishing and a massive salvage operation began. Today seven German ships remain at the bottom of Scapa Flow – three battleships and four light cruisers – along with four destroyers and a U-boat and the Royal Navy battleships *HMS Royal Oak* and *HMS Vanguard*, which blew up in 1917.

At the southeastern corner of South Ronaldsay is the **Tomb of the Eagles** ① *Apr-Oct daily 1000-2000, Nov-Mar 1000-1200, £3.50*, one of the most interesting archaeological sights on Orkney. The 5,000-year-old chambered cairn was discovered by local farmer and amateur archaeologist, Ronald Simison, whose family now runs the privately owned site and museum. The interior contents of the tomb were practically intact and there were up to 340 people buried here, along with carcasses and talons of sea eagles, hence the name. Various objects were also found outside the tomb, including stone tools and polished stone axes.

Before visiting the tomb you can handle the skulls and various other artefacts at the small 'museum' in the family home, which actually means their front porch! Then you walk for about five to 10 minutes through a field to visit a **burnt mound**, a kind of Bronze-Age kitchen, where Ronald Simison will regail you with all manner of fascinating insider information about the excavation process, before walking out along the cliff edge to the spectacularly sited tomb which you must enter by lying on a trolley and pulling yourself in using an overhead rope. It is particularly eerie being here because there is generally no-one else around, and as you haul yourself into the tomb, with the sound of the North Sea crashing into the cliffs nearby, you wonder to yourself how those buried here met their fate. There is also a lovely, but generally wild and windy, walk back along the cliffs, via a different route, to the car park.

Hoy → *Phone code: 01856.*

To the southwest of the Mainland is Hoy, the second largest of the Orkney islands. The name is derived from the Norse *Ha-ey*, meaning High Island, which is appropriate as much of the island is more reminiscent of the Scottish Highlands than Orkney, with only the southern end being typically low and fertile. ⟫ *For Sleeping, Eating and other listings, see pages 330-337.*

There are two ferry services to Hoy, both run by Orkney Ferries, To1856-850624.
Transport on Hoy is limited to a minibus between Moaness Pier and Rackwick. ▸▸ *For
further details, see Transport page 334.*

Sights

Orkney's highest point, **Ward Hill** (1,571 ft) is in the north of the island, and the north
and west coasts are bounded by spectacular cliffs. At **St John's Head**, the sheer
cliffs rise out of the sea to a height of 1,150 ft, the highest vertical cliffs in Britain. The
island is most famous for its **Old Man of Hoy**, a great rock stack rising to 450 ft. This
northern part of Hoy forms the **North Hoy RSPB Reserve** which has a variety of
habitats ranging from woodland to tundra-like hill-tops and sea cliffs. The reserve is
home to a huge variety of birds including great skuas and Arctic skuas, Manx
shearwaters and puffins. On the hills there are red grouse, curlews, golden plovers
and dunlins, peregrine falcons, merlins, kestrels and even golden eagles. Mountain
hares are quite common and, if you are lucky, you can also see otters along the
Scapa Flow coastline.

On the southeast coast of the island is **Lyness**, site of a large naval base during
both world wars when the British fleet was based in Scapa Flow. Many of the old
dilapidated buildings have gone, but the harbour area is still scarred with the
scattered remains of concrete structures, and there's also the unattractive sight of
the huge oil terminal on **Flotta**. Lyness has a large **Naval Cemetery**, last resting place
of those who died at Jutland, of Germans killed during the scuttle and of the crew of
HMS Royal Oak. The old pump house opposite the new ferry terminal is now the
Scapa Flow Visitor Centre ① *To1856-791300, Mon-Fri 0900-1630, Sat and Sun
0930-1630, free*, a fascinating naval museum with old photographs, various
wartime artefacts, a section devoted to the scuttling of the German Fleet, and an
audio-visual feature on the history of Scapa Flow. Well worth a visit. At South Walls,
overlooking Longhope Bay, is **Hackness Martello Tower and Battery**
① *To1856-811397, Apr-Sep daily 0930-1830, £3, concessions £2.50, children £1*,
which, along with another tower on the north side at Crockness, was built in 1815 to
protect British ships in Longhope Bay against attack by American and French
privateers while they waited for a Royal Navy escort on their journey to Baltic ports.

▲▲ Hoy's great attraction is its many excellent walking opportunities. A minibus
runs between **Moaness Pier**, where the ferry from Stromness docks (see Transport
page 334), and **Rackwick**, on the opposite side of the island, but it's a lovely two-hour
walk by road through beautiful **Rackwick Glen**, once populated by crofters and
fishermen, but now quiet and isolated. On the way you'll pass the **Dwarfie Stone**, a
huge, lonely block of sandstone which is the only rock-cut tomb in Britain, dating from
around 3000 BC. Be careful, though, because according to Sir Walter Scott this is the
residence of the Trolld, a dwarf from Norse legend. On your return you can take a
different route through a narrow valley between the **Cuilags** (1,421 ft) and **Ward Hill**
and **Berriedale Wood**, the most northerly woodland in Britain. The most popular walk
on Hoy is the spectacular three-hour hike from Rackwick to the cliffs facing the **Old
Man of Hoy**. The path climbs steeply westwards from the old crofting township, then
turns northwards before gradually descending to the cliff edge.

Rousay, Egilsay and Wyre

These three islands lie a short distance off the northeast coast of Mainland and,
together with Shapinsay to the southeast, are the closest of Orkney's North Isles to
Kirkwall. ▸▸ *For Sleeping, Eating and other listings, see pages 330-337.*

Rousay is a hilly island about five miles in diameter and known as the 'Egypt of the North' due to the large number of archaeological sites. It also has the important **Trumland RSPB Reserve**, home to merlins, hen harriers, peregrine falcons, short-eared owls and red-throated divers, and its three lochs offer good trout fishing.

A road runs right around the island, and makes a pleasant 13-mile bike run, but most of the sights are within walking distance of the ferry pier on the southeast side of the island, where most of the 200 inhabitants live. A short distance west of the pier by the road is **Tavershoe Tuick**, an unusual two-storey burial cairn, which was discovered in the late 19th century by Mrs Burroughs, wife of General Traill Burroughs who lived at nearby Trumland House. A mile further west, to the north of the road, is **Blackhammer**, a stalled Neolithic burial cairn. Further west, and a steep climb up from the road, is **Knowe of Yarso**, another stalled cairn, which contained the remains of at least 21 people. The tomb dates from around 2900 BC.

Most of the island's archaeological sights are to be found along the **Westness Walk**, a mile-long walk which starts from Westness Farm, about four miles west of the ferry pier, and ends at the remarkable Midhowe Cairn. The walk is described in detail in a leaflet available from the tourist offices on Mainland. **Midhowe Cairn** is the largest and longest thus far excavated on Orkney – over 100 ft long and 40 ft wide – and, like the others, dates from around 3000 BC. Housed in a large building to protect it, the 'Great Ship of Death', as it is known, contained the remains of 25 people in crouched position on or under the eastern shelves of the chamber, which is divided into 12 sections. Standing nearby, with fine views across to Eynehallow island, is **Midhowe Broch**, one of the best-preserved brochs on Orkney, occupied from around 200 BC to AD 200. The outer walls are about 60 ft in diameter and up to 14 ft high in places.

Another fine walk on the island is around the **RSPB Reserve**. A footpath leads from beside Trumland House and heads up towards the island's highest point, **Blotchnie Field** (821 ft). A leaflet describing the walk is available from the tourist offices on Mainland or the **Trumland Orientation Centre** by the pier.

Egilsay and Wyre

These two small islands lie to the east of Rousay and have a couple of interesting sights of their own. Egilsay's claim to fame is the murder here of St Magnus in 1115, and a **cenotaph** marks the spot where he was slain. The island is dominated by the 12th-century **St Magnus church**, built on the site of an earlier church, possibly as a shrine to St Magnus. It is the only surviving example on Orkney of a round-towered Viking church. Much of Egilsay has been bought by the RSPB as a reserve to preserve the habitat of the very rare **corncrake**, whose distinctive rasping call may be heard.

Tiny Wyre features strongly in the Viking saga as the domain of Kolbein Hruga, and the remains of his 12th-century stronghold, **Cubbie Roo's Castle**, and nearby **St Mary's chapel** can be still be seen. Kolbein's home, or Bu, was on the site of the nearby Bu Farm, where the poet Edwin Muir (1887-1959) spent part of his childhood. The far westerly point of the island, known as **the Taing**, is a favourite haunt of seals, and a great place to enjoy a summer sunset.

Shapinsay → *Phone code: 01856.*

Less than 30 minutes by ferry from Kirkwall is the fertile, low-lying island of Shapinsay. The main attraction is **Balfour Castle** ① *guided tour only which leaves from Kirkwall on Wed and Sun, May-Sep, 1415 ferry, arrange in advance at the tourist office in Kirkwall, cost £15 per person including ferry ticket, guided tour of the castle* *and gardens (at 1500) and complimentary tea and cakes in the servants' quarters*, an imposing baronial pile which is in fact a Victorian extension to a much older house called 'Cliffdale'. The house, and the rest of the island, was bought by successive generations of the Balfour family who had made their fortune in India. Today the castle is the home of the Zawadski family and can only be visited as part of an inclusive half-day tour. You can take an earlier ferry if you wish to explore the island.

In the village, built by the Balfours to house their estate workers, is the **Shapinsay Heritage Centre** ① *T01856-711258, Mon, Tue and Thu-Sat 1200-1630, Wed and Sun till 1730, free*, in the old Smithy. It has displays on the island's history and a tearoom upstairs. There's a pub in the village, in the old gatehouse. Also a couple of shops and a post office.

A mile north of the village is the **Mill Dam RSPB Reserve**, where there's a hide overlooking a loch from which you can see many species of wildfowl and waders. Four miles from the pier, at the far northeast corner of the island, is the well-preserved **Burroughston Broch**, with good views of seals sunning themselves on the nearby rocks. West of here, at **Quholme**, is the original birthplace of the father of Washington Irving, author of *Rip Van Winkle*.

Eday → *Phone code: 01857.*

The long, thin and sparsely populated island of Eday lies at the centre of the North Isles group. It is less fertile than the other islands, but its heather-covered hills in the centre have provided peat for the other peatless Orkney islands. Eday's sandstone has also been quarried, and was used in the building of St Magnus Cathedral in Kirkwall. ▸▸ *For Sleeping, Eating and other listings, see pages 330-337.*

Ins and outs

There are flights from Kirkwall to Eday airport, called London Airport. There are also ferries from Kirkwall. The ferry pier is at Backaland, on the southeast of the island, a long way from the main sights. **Orkney Ferries** ① *T01856-872044*, also run the Eday Heritage Tour. ▸▸ *For further details, see Transport page 334.*

Sights

The island has numerous chambered cairns and these, along with the other attractions, are concentrated in the northern part. They are all covered in the signposted five-mile **Eday Heritage Walk**, which starts from the Community Enterprises Shop and leads up to the Cliffs of Red Head at the northern tip. The walk takes about three hours to complete, and it's worth picking up the *Eday Heritage Walk* leaflet.

The walk starts at Mill Bay and heads past **Mill Loch**, where an RSPB hide allows you to watch rare red-throated divers breeding in spring and summer. Further north is the huge, 15-ft tall **Stone of Setter**, the largest standing stone in Orkney and visible from most of the chambered cairns. Close by are the **Fold of Setter**, a circular enclosure dating back to 2000 BC, and the **Braeside** and **Huntersquoy** chambered cairns. Further north along the path is **Vinquoy Chambered Cairn**, one of the finest in Orkney and similar to the better-known tomb at Maes Howe, dating from around the same time. An acrylic dome provides light to the main chamber, which can be entered by a narrow underground passage.

The path continues to the summit of **Vinquoy Hill**, which commands excellent views of the surrounding islands of Westray and Sanday. From here you can continue north to the spectacular red sandstone cliffs at **Red Head**, home to nesting guillemots, razorbills and puffins in summer, or head southeast along the coast to **Carrick House** ① *T01856-622260, Mid-Jun to mid-Sep guided tour at 1400, £2*. Built for Lord Kinclaven, Earl of Carrick, in 1633, the house is best known for its associations with the pirate, John Gow, whose ship ran aground during a failed attack on the house. He was captured and taken to London for trial and hanged. Sir Walter Scott's novel, *The Pirate*, is based on this story.

Sanday → *Phone code: 01857.*

Sanday is the largest of the North Isles, 12 miles long and flat as a pancake except for the cliffs at Spurness. It is well-named, as its most notable feature is its sweeping bays of sparkling white sand backed by machair, and turquoise seas.

There are numerous burial mounds all over the island, the most impressive being **Quoyness Chambered Cairn**, a 5,000 year-old tomb similar to Maes Howe. The 13 ft-high structure contains a large main chamber with six smaller cells opening through low entrances. Most of the burial tombs remain unexcavated, such as those at **Tofts Ness** at the far northeastern tip, where there are over 500 cairns, making it potentially one of the most important prehistoric sites in Britain. At **Scar**, in Burness, a spectacular Viking find was made, and at **Pool** a major excavation has uncovered the remains of at least 14 Stone-Age houses.

Sanday is known for its **knitwear**, though the factory unfortunately closed down. You can still visit the **Orkney Angora craft shop**, in Upper Breckan, near the northern tip of the island.

Stronsay → *Phone code: 01857.*

The peaceful, low-lying island of Stronsay has some fine sandy beaches and cliffs which attract large colonies of grey seals and nesting seabirds. There are few real sights on this largely agricultural island, but the coastline has some pleasant walks. One of the best is to the **Vat of Kirbister** in the southeast, a spectacular 'gloup' or blow-hole spanned by the finest natural arch in Orkney. To the south of here, at **Burgh Head**, you'll find nesting puffins and the remains of a ruined broch, and at the southeastern tip, at **Lamb Head**, is a large colony of grey seals, lots of seabirds and several archaeological sites.

The main settlement is the quiet village of **Whitehall**, on the northeast coast where the ferry arrives. It's hard to believe it now, but this was one of the largest herring ports in Europe. During the boom years of the early 20th century 300 steam drifters were working out of Whitehall and nearly 4,000 fishing crew and shore workers were employed. In the peak year of 1924 over 12,000 tons of herring were landed here, to be cured (salted) and exported to Russia and Eastern Europe. Whitehall developed considerably and the Stronsay Hotel was said to have the longest bar in Scotland. On Sundays during July and August there were so many boats tied up that it was possible to walk across them to the little island of Papa Stronsay. By the 1930s, however, herring stocks were severely depleted and the industry was in decline. The old Fish Mart by the pier houses a **heritage centre** ① *T01856-616360, May-Sep 1100-1700, free*, with photos and artefacts from the herring boom days. It also has a café and hostel. ➤➤ *For Sleeping, Eating and other listings, see pages 330-337.*

● *Prior to the herring boom, Stronsay's economic mainstay was the kelp industry. By the end of the 18th century 3,000 people were employed in the collection of seaweed and production of kelp for export, to be used in making iodine, soap and glass.*

Westray → *Phone code: 01857.*

Westray is the second largest of the North Isles, with a varied landscape of farmland, hilly moorland, sandy beaches and dramatic cliffs. It is also the most prosperous of the North Isles, producing beef, fish and seafood, and supports a population of 700.

The main settlement is **Pierowall**, in the north of the island, but, though it has one of the best harbours in Orkney, the main ferry terminal is at Rapness, on the south coast. Pierowall is a relatively large village for the North Isles and there are shops, a post office, a hotel and the **Westray Heritage Centre** ① *early May to late Sep Tue-Sat 0930-1230 and 1400-1700, £2*, with displays on local and natural history, and a tearoom. Also in the village is the ruined 17th-century **St Mary's church**. About a mile west of the village is Westray's most notable ruin, **Noltland Castle**, a fine example of a 16th-century fortified Z-plan tower-house. To explore inside, pick up the key from the back door of the nearby farm.

• There are guided minibus tours of Westray which connect with the ferry at Rapness. See page 333.

There are some great coastal **walks** on the island, particularly to the spectacular sea cliffs at **Noup Head**, at the far northwestern tip, which are an **RSPB Reserve** and second only to St Kilda in terms of breeding seabirds, with huge colonies of guillemots, razorbills, kittiwakes and fulmars, as well as puffins. The cliffs on the west coast of Westray are five miles long and there's an excellent walk down the coast from Noup Head, past **Gentleman's Cave**, used as a hiding place by four Jacobite lairds in 1746. Near the southern end of the walk is **Fitty Hill** (554 ft), the highest point on the island, which you can climb for great views, and the walk ends at **Inga Ness**, where you can also see puffins. The best place to see puffins is at **Castle o' Burrian**, a sea stack on **Stanger Head**, on the southeastern coast near the Rapness ferry terminal.

▸▸ *For Sleeping, Eating and other listings, see pages 330-337.*

Papa Westray → *Phone code: 01857.*

Tiny Papa Westray, known locally as 'Papay', is best known as being the destination for the world's shortest scheduled flight, from Westray – all of two minutes, or less with a good following wind, and there's no shortage of that.

But there are other reasons to visit this little island, one of the most remote of the Orkney group. Papay is home to Europe's oldest house, the **Knap of Howar** ① *open at all times, free*, which was built around 5,500 years ago and is still standing (they knew how to build 'em in those days). It's on the west coast, just south of the airport. Half a mile north is **St Boniface Kirk**, one of the oldest Christian sites in the north of Scotland, founded in the eighth century, though most of the recently restored building dates from the 12th century. Inland from the Knap of Howar is **Holland Farm**, former home of the lairds of the island, where you can rummage around the farm buildings and museum.

Papay is famous for its birds, and **North Hill**, on the north of the island, is an important RSPB Reserve. The cliffs are home to many thousands of breeding seabirds, and at **Fowl Craig** on the east coast you can see nesting puffins. The interior is home to the largest arctic tern colony in Europe, as well as many arctic skuas. If you wish to explore you have to contact the warden at **Rose Cottage** ① *T01857-644240*, who runs regular guided walks.

It's worth taking a boat trip to the even tinier, deserted **Holm of Papay**, off the east coast. This is the site of several Neolithic burial cairns, including one of the largest **chambered cairns** on Orkney. You enter the tomb down a ladder into the main chamber which is nearly 70 ft long, with a dozen side-cells. Contact Jim Davidson, T01856-644259, for boat trips between May and September. ▸▸ *For Sleeping, Eating and other listings, see pages 330-337.*

North Ronaldsay

Remote and storm-battered, North Ronaldsay is the most northerly of the Orkney islands and a place where old Orcadian traditions remain. It seems remarkable that anyone should live here at all in these extreme conditions, but 'North Ron' – as it is known locally – has been inhabited for many centuries and continues to be heavily farmed. The island's sheep are a hardy lot and live exclusively off the seaweed on a narrow strip of beach, outside a 13-mile stone dyke which surrounds the island. This gives their meat a unique, 'gamey' flavour.

This small, flat island, only three miles long, has few real attractions, except to keen ornithologists who flock here to catch a glimpse of its rare migrants. From late March to early June and mid-August to early November there are huge numbers of migratory birds. The **Bird Observatory**, in the southwest corner of the island by the ferry pier, gives information on which species have been sighted, as well as providing accommodation. There are also colonies of grey seals and cormorants at **Seal Skerry**, on the northeast tip of the island. ▸▸ *For Sleeping, Eating and other listings, see pages 330-337.*

● Sleeping

Kirkwall *p313, map p315*
There are plenty of cheap B&Bs, though most rooms are small without en suite.
B-C Ayre Hotel, on the harbour front, T01856-873001, www.ayrehotel.co.uk. The best hotel in Kirkwall, very comfortable.
B-D Albert Hotel, Mounthoolie La, T01856-876000, enquiries@alberthotel .co.uk. Another good option, in the centre of town with a restaurant and a couple of lively bars.
D Foveran Hotel, 2 miles from town on the A964 Orphir road at St Ola, T01856-872389, www.foveranhotel.com. Overlooking Scapa Flow. It is friendly and comfortable, and also offers very good food, including vegetarian.
D West End Hotel, Main St, T01856-872368, www.orkneyisles.co.uk/westendhotel. Central and serves good bar meals.
E Whiteclett, St Catherine's Pl, T01856-874193. This B&B is a 200-year-old listed house near the harbour.
E-F Arundel, Inganess Rd, T01856-873148. A modern bungalow offering B&B on a quiet road about a mile from the town centre.
F SYHA Youth Hostel, Old Scapa Rd, T01856-872243, open Apr-Sep. This large, well-equipped youth hostel about 15 mins' walk from the town centre.

Camping
Pickaquoy Caravan & Camping Site, on the western outskirts of Kirkwall, off the A965, T01856-873535. Open May-Sep.

Stromness and West Mainland *p317*
B Merkister Hotel, on the shores of Loch Harray, Stenness, T01856-771366, merkister hotel@ecos.co. A favourite with anglers. It has a very good restaurant and a popular bar.
C-D Standing Stones Hotel, on the shores of Loch Stenness, Stenness, T01856-850449, standingstones@sol.co.uk.
C-D Stromness Hotel, Stromness, T01856-850298, www.stromnesshotel.com. The best hotel in town is this imposing old building overlooking the harbour. Recently refurbished and offering good-value meals.
D-E Barony Hotel, on the north shore of Boardhouse Loch, Marwick Head, T01856-721327, baronyhotel@btinternet.com. May-Sep. It specializes in fishing holidays and is about the only place offering food round here.
D-E Mill of Eyreland, Stenness, T01856-850136, ww.orknet.co.uk/mill. A lovely converted mill 3 miles from Stromness.
D-E Stenigar, T01856-850438. Open Apr-Oct. Converted boatyard on Ness Rd, just before the campsite, with views of Hoy.
E Ferry Inn, near the ferry terminal, John St, T01856-850280, www.ferryinn.com. Serves food and has a lively bar.
E Kierfield House, near Loch Harray, T/F01856-841583. There are a few B&Bs close to Skara Brae, including this one.
E Orca Hotel, on Victoria St near the harbour, T01856-850447, www.theoak leigh.com. Also has a cellar bistro, **Bistro 76**, serving good food.

E **Thira**, a few miles behind Stromness, at Innertown, T01856-851181. Comfortable, friendly and non-smoking modern bungalow with spectacular views of Hoy. Also serves an excellent cooked breakfast, and will provide a fantastic dinner made from the finest local ingredients on request.

E-F **Netherstove**, I/F01856-841625, ann.poke@virgin.net. A B&B near Skara Brae, overlooking the Bay of Skaill.

E-F **Primrose Cottage**, Marwick Head, T/F01856-721384, i.clouston@talk21.com. A comfortable B&B overlooking Marwick Bay.

F **Brown's Hostel**, 45 Victoria St, T01856-850661. This popular independent hostel has no curfew and is open all year round.

F **SYHA Hostel**, on Hellihole Rd, a 10-min walk south from the ferry terminal, T01856-850589. Open Mar-Oct.

Camping
F **Eviedale Centre**, beside the junction of the road to Dounby, T01856-751270, Apr-Oct, has a small bothy and campsite. There's a **campsite**, T01856-873535, open May to mid-Sep, at Ness Point, a mile south of the ferry terminal. It's well equipped and has incomparable views, but is very exposed.

East Mainland and South Ronaldsay *p322*
There's a good selection of accommodation in St Margaret's Hope.

D **Creel Restaurant & Rooms**, Front Rd, St Margaret's Hope, T01856-831311, www.thecreel.co.uk. Best of the lot. Offers comfortable rooms and superb, though expensive, food using deliciously fresh, locally grown ingredients. Dinner only.

E **Bellevue Guest House**, St Margaret's Hope, T01856-831294. Good B&B choice.

E **Commodore Motel**, Deerness, T01856-781319. Only place to stay or eat in Deerness.

E **The Fisher's Gill**, St Margaret's Hope, T01856-831711. Another good B&B and also offers seafood dishes.

E **Murray Arms Hotel**, Back Rd, St Margaret's Hope, T01856-831205. Good value bar meals.

E **Vestlaybanks**, Burray village, on the south coast, T01856-731305, vestlaybanks@btinternet.com. B&B also providing evening meals.

F **Wheems Bothy**, at Wheems, Eastside, a few miles southeast of St Margaret's Hope, T01856-831537, open Apr-Oct. Organic farm offering cheap and basic hostel accommodation.

Hoy *p324*
There's not much accommodation in the north of the island, except for the 2 SYHA hostels. There are a few very good B&Bs in the south of the island.

E **The Hoy Hotel**, near the ferry terminal in Lyness, T01856-791377. Open Apr-Oct. Also serves meals.

E **Stoneyquoy**, south of Lyness, T/F01856-791234, www.visithoy.com. The owner, Louise Budge, also runs guided tours of the island for £40 for up to 4 people with lunch.

E-F **Burnhouse**, on the other side of the bay in Longhope, T01856-701263.

E-F **Old Custom House**, also in Longhope, T01856-701358.

F **Hoy Youth Hostel**, is the larger hostel, about a mile from Moaness Pier. Open May-Sep.

F **Rackwick Youth Hostel** in Rackwick Glen (open mid-Mar to mid-Sep). To book ahead for both hostels, contact Orkney Council, T01856-873535, ext 2404.

Rousay, Egilsay and Wyre *p325*
Accommodation is very limited on Rousay, and non-existent on Egilsay and Wyre.

D-E **Taversoe Hotel**, near Knowe of Yarso, about 2 miles west of the pier, T01857-821325. Offers excellent-value meals. Seafood is particularly recommended (closed Mon to non-residents).

F **Rousay Hostel**, Trumland Organic Farm, T01857-821252, open all year and half a mile from the ferry. With laundry and camping.

Shapinsay *p326*
C **Balfour Castle**, T01857-711282, www.balfourcastle.co.uk. Stay here and enjoy all that Victorian splendour. The price includes dinner. The castle has a private chapel and a boat is available for bird watching and fishing trips for residents.

E **Girnigoe**, T01857-711256, near the northern end of Veantro Bay. This B&B is a little humbler but comfortable. Also offers evening meals.

Orkney & Shetland Orkney Listings

● *For an explanation of sleeping and eating price codes used in this guide, see inside the*
● *front cover. Other relevant information is found in Essentials, see pages 41-49.*

E Mrs Poppelwell's, T01857-622248, Blett, Carrick Bay, opposite the Calf of Eday. Very friendly. Evening meal and packed lunch provided if you wish. Mrs Poppelwell also has a self-catering cottage for up to 3 nearby.

D Mrs Cockram, T01857-622271. Open Jun-Mar, at Skaill Farm, just south of the airport. Price includes dinner.

F Youth Hostel, T01857-622206, open Apr-Sep, run by Eday Community Enterprises, just north of the airport. Basic lodging.

Sanday *p328*

E Belsair Hotel, Kettletoft, where the ferry used to dock, T01857-600206, joy@sanday. quista.net. Serves meals.

E Kettletoft Hotel, Kettletoft, T/F01857-600217. Serves meals and has a lively bar.

E-F Quivals, T01857-600467. One of a handful of B&Bs, this one is run by Tina and Bernie Flett. In addition to the B&B between them they operate a ferry service, run a car and bike hire service (T01857-600418), and Bernie also takes out tours, see Activities and tours p333.

Stronsay *p328*

F Stronsay Fish Mart Hostel, T01857-616360. Open all year, is well-equipped and comfortable, see p328. Their café does cheap meals.

E Stronsay Hotel, T01857-616213, www.stronsayhotel.com, has been refurbished and offers cheap bar food.

F Stronsay Bird Reserve, Mill Bay, south of Whitehall, T01857-616363. B&B or you can camp overlooking the wide sandy bay.

F Torness Camping Barn, at the southern end of the island, on the shore of Holland Bay near Lea-shun Loch, T01857-616314. Very basic and very cheap. They also organize nature walks to the nearby seal-hide. Phone for pick-up from the ferry.

Westray *p329*

C-D Cleaton House Hotel, about 2 miles southeast of Pierowall, T01857-677508, www.orknet.co.uk/cleaton. This converted Victorian manse is the best place to stay. It serves excellent meals in the restaurant (1900-2100) and in the bar (1200-1400, 1800-2100).

E Pierowall Hotel, in the village, T01857-677208, www.orknet.co.uk/pierwall. Less

stylish, but comfortable and friendly. It also serves good-value bar meals.

E-F Sand o' Gill, T01857-677374. One of several B&Bs. You can also camp or hire their self-catering caravan.

Papa Westray *p329*

D-E Beltane House Guest House, T01857-644267. A row of converted farm workers' cottages to the east of Holland House. It offers dinner (**££**). Run by the island community co-operative.

F Papa Westray Hostel, T01857-644267. Open all year, housed in the same complex at Beltane. A 16-bed hostel run by the island community co-operative which also runs a shop and restaurant serving lunch and evening meals. They have a minibus which takes ferry passengers from the pier to anywhere on the island.

North Ronaldsay *p330*

E North Ronaldsay Bird Observatory, T01857-633200, alison@nrbo.prestel.co.uk. Offers wind-and solar-powered full-board accommodation in private rooms or dorms.

D-E Garso House, T01857-633244, christine. muir@virgin.net, about 3 miles from the ferry pier. Full-board. They also have a self-catering cottage (up to 5 people) and can arrange car hire, taxis or minibus tours.

Camping

Phone T01857-633222, for information.

❼ Eating

Eating options are very limited on the islands but most B&Bs and guest houses will provide evening meals. Even in Kirkwall you'll be hard-pushed to find a decent meal.

Kirkwall *p313, map p315*

£££-££ Foveran Hotel, see Sleeping, is probably the best place to eat in town. Friendly service but not the quickest.

££-£ Albert Hotel, see Sleeping, serves bar meals made with home-grown produce.

££ Mumtaz, on Bridge St. The islands' only Indian restaurant.

£ The Mustard Seed Café, 65 Victoria St. The best place for a snack is this cafeteria-style café, serving substantial soups and main courses in a bustling and very friendly atmosphere.

Stromness and West Mainland *p317*
££ Hamnavoe Restaurant, 35 Graham Pl, Stromness, T01856-850606. The best place to eat in town. It specializes in local seafood but also offers good vegetarian dishes. Open Mar-Oct Tue-Sun from 1900.
££ Julia's café and bistro, opposite the ferry terminal, Stromness. Home-cooked food in pleasant surroundings. Open for à la carte Thu-Sat evenings.
££-£ Stromness Hotel, see Sleeping, Stromness, good bar meals.
£ Ferry Inn, see Sleeping, Stromness, also serves decent bar food.

Hoy *p324*
££-£ Hoy Inn, near the pier and post office, T01856-791313, a bar and restaurant which serves good seafood (closed Mon). There's also an RSPB information centre here.
£ Anchor Bar, T01856-791356, in Lyness serves lunches.
There are shops/petrol stations in Lyness and Longhope.

Rousay, Egilsay and Wyre *p325*
££-£ Pier Restaurant, beside the pier, serves food at lunchtime.

North Ronaldsay *p330*
Burrian Inn and Restaurant is the island's pub, and also serves food.

🍸 Bars and clubs

Kirkwall *p313, map p315*
Nightlife in Kirkwall revolves around its lively pubs. Check in *The Orcadian* for folk nights etc.
Ayre Hotel is quiet and relaxed but also stages folk music nights.
Bothy Bar, Albert Hotel, is a good place for a drink, and sometimes has live folk music.
Matchmakers Bar, also at the Albert Hotel, has a disco at weekends.

Stromness and West Mainland *p317*
Stromness Hotel, the **Ferry Inn** and the bar of the **Royal Hotel** are the best places for a drink are in Stromness.
The Mistra, Evie, is the local village shop, post office and pub.

😀 Entertainment

For details of what's going on, buy *The Orcadian*, which comes out on Thu, or pick up a free copy of the Tourist Board's guide.

Kirkwall *p313, map p315*
The town's **New Phoenix cinema** is housed in the **Pickaquoy Leisure Centre**, Pickaquoy Rd, T01856-879900. It also has sports and fitness facilities, and a café and bar.

🎉 Festivals and events

There are numerous events which take place throughout the year.
May Orkney Folk Festival This excellent event takes place for 3 days at the end of May at various locations throughout the islands. It is one of the most entertaining events of all.
Jun St Magnus Festival This acclaimed festival is the most prestigious and popular. Held in Kirkwall, it consists of 6 days of music, drama, literature and the visual arts, with many internationally renowned performers.
Jul Regattas During this month there are several regattas held on most of the islands.
Aug Festival of the Horse and Boys' Ploughing Match on South Ronaldsay There are numerous agricultural shows in Aug which culminate in this festival, see p323.
Sep Orkney Science Festival on the first week in Sep, T01856-876214.
Christmas Day and New Year's Day The Ba' (ball) in Kirkwall Amongst the best-known annual events it is a bit like rugby, basketball and a full-scale riot all rolled into one, and is contested between two sides – the Uppies and the Doonies – representing different districts of the town. As many as 200 'players' may be involved, and a game can last up to 7 hrs as both sides attempt to jostle the ball along the streets until one reaches their 'goal' to win the prized ba'.

⛰ Activities and tours

Both general sightseeing tours and special interest tours are available.
Go-Orkney, South Cannigall, St Ola, T01856-871871, www.orknet.co.uk/orkney-tours, runs a series of tours of Mainland, and also to Hoy and Rousay.

To dive for

Orkney offers some of the best scuba diving in the world, thanks to the part played by Scapa Flow in both world wars, see page 139. The wreckage on the sea bed, combined with the wildlife that teems around it – sea anemones, seals, whales and porpoises – make for great diving. Visibility is sharp and the water is not as cold as you expect, thanks to the Gulf Stream. Several companies offer diving courses for beginners and wreck diving for more experienced divers. This can be as a dive package, including accommodation, meals and boat charter, or simply as a boat charter. Most companies are based in Stromness. See page 333.

For a full list of dive operators, check out www.subaqua.co.uk.

Wildabout Orkney, 5 Clouston Corner, Stenness, T01856- 851011, www.wildabout.orknet.co.uk, offers highly rated wildlife, historical, folklore and environmental tours of Mainland for £16 per person for a full day.
Discover Orkney Tours, T/F01856-872865, offers tours of Mainland as well as trips to Westray and Papa Westray.

Stromness and West Mainland *p317*
The Diving Cellar, 4 Victoria St, Stromness, T01856-850055, divescapaflow.co.uk, and **Scapa Flow Diving Holidays**, Stromness, T01856-851110, offer liveaboard packages or day trips on the *MV Invincible*, complete with its own bar.

East Mainland and South Ronaldsay *p322*
Orkney Divers, based at the Crowsnest bunkhouse, St Margaret's Hope, South Ronaldsay, T01856-831205, www.orkney divers.com. Scuba diving.

Rousay, Egilsay and Wyre *p325*
Rousay Traveller, T01856-821234, run very informative minibus tours from Jun-early Sep Tue-Fri, meeting the 1040 ferry from Tingwall, they last 6 hrs and cost £15, children £6.

Eday *p327*
Orkney Ferries, T01856-872044, also run the Eday Heritage Tour every Sun from mid-Jun to mid-Sep. It leaves Kirkwall at 0920 and return at 1955 and costs around £30 per person, which includes ferries, guided walks or minibus tour, entry to Carrick House and lunch. Book with **Orkney Ferries** or at the tourist office in Kirkwall.

Sanday *p328*
Quivals, see also Sleeping, T01856-600467. A B&B, the owners also run full-day tours of the island, on Wed and Fri, from mid-May to early Sep, departing from Kirkwall pier at 1010 and returning at 1940 (around £30 per person, minimum of 4 people).

Westray *p329*
Discover Orkney, T/F01856-872865, run day tours on a Sun to Westray from Kirkwall, leaving at 0940 and returning at 2015, and costing around £30 per person including ferry. They also run a day tour on a Mon to Papa Westray.
Island Explorer, T01856-677355. There are guided minibus tours of Westray with Alex Costie. They connect with the ferry at Rapness and cost £20 for a full day.
J & M Marcus, Pierowall, also runs bus tours and offers car hire.
Tom Rendall, T01856-677216, for boat trips to Papa Westray.

Transport

Kirkwall *p313, map p315*
Air
Daily flights from **Scotland** and **England** are operated by **Loganair/ British Regional Airlines** and can be booked through **British Airways**, T08708-509850 or **Loganair**, T01856-872494. 8-seater aircraft fly from Kirkwall daily except Sun to **Stronsay**, **Sanday**, **North Ronaldsay**, **Westray** and **Papa Westray**, and on Wed to **Eday**. To Papa Westray and North Ronaldsay costs only £15 one way (£12 with a one-night stay), and to the other islands listed costs £31 one way.

Bus

There's a limited bus service around the Mainland. **Peace Coaches**, T01856-872866, runs regular buses Mon-Sat from Kirkwall bus station to **Stromness**, 30 mins. They also run 3-5 buses a day, Mon-Sat, to **Houton**, 30 mins, which connect with ferries to **Hoy**; and a daily bus, Mon-Sat, to **East Holm**, 25 mins, and **Stromness** via **Dounby**, 55 mins. **Causeway Coaches**, T01856-831444, runs 2-4 buses a day, Mon-Sat, to **St Margaret's Hope**, 30 mins. **Rosie Coaches**, T01856-751227, runs buses to **Tingwall** and **Evie**. The bus service between Kirkwall and **Burwick** is run by Shalders Coaches, T01856-850809. Note that there is no Sun bus service on Orkney.

Car

Scarth Car Hire, Great Western Rd, T01856-872125; **WR Tullock**, Castle St, T01856-876262, and Kirkwall airport, T01856-875500.

Cycle hire

Cycle hire from **Bobby's Cycle Centre**, Tankerness La, T/F01856-875777. Mountain bikes from £8 per day.

Ferry

Northlink Ferries, T01856-885500, www.north linkferries.co.uk, sail from **Aberdeen** to **Kirkwall** (7½ hrs) on Tue, Thu, Sat and Sun at 1700, returning to Aberdeen on Mon, Wed and Fri at 2330. A return passenger fare costs from £32 up to £48 (peak season, Jul-Aug). A car and driver costs from £142 up to £200, plus £25-40 per additional passenger.

Northlink Ferries also sail from **Lerwick** (Shetland) to **Kirkwall** (7 hrs) on Mon, Wed and Fri at 1800, returning on Tue, Thu, Sat and Sun at 2345. A passenger fare costs £26-39 return. A car with driver costs £112-178, plus £22-20 per additional passenger. Single fares are 50 per cent of return fares and children under 16 travel for 50% discount. Cars should be booked in advance and all passengers must check in at least 30 mins before departure. 2- and 4-berth cabins are available on all journeys, from £42 up to £78 per trip.

John O'Groats Ferries, T01955-611353, www.jogferry.co.uk, operate a passenger-only (and bicycles) ferry service from **John O' Groats** to **Burwick** (twice a day, 4 times Jul-Aug, 40 mins) on South Ronaldsay, from

May to Sep. There are bus connections between **Burwick** and **Kirkwall** (45 mins) for all ferry sailings. Return fare including bus is £26 (bicycles an extra £3). No bookings required. A free bus meets the afternoon train from Thurso at 1445 and connects with the 1600 or 1800 ferry to Orkney. They also operate the **Orkney Bus**, a daily direct bus/ferry/bus service between **Inverness** and **Kirkwall**, via **John o' Groats**. It leaves Inverness at 0730 and 1420 from Jun-Sep (at 1420 only in May). It costs £40 return. Journey time 5 hrs. Advance booking is essential.

Stromness and West Mainland *p317*
Bus

There are several buses daily (Mon-Sat) between **Stromness** and **Kirkwall**, 30 mins. On Mon there's a bus between Kirkwall and Birsay with **Shalder Coaches**, T01856-850809. To get to Skara Brae you'll need your own transport, or you can visit as part of a guided tour (see the TIC), or walk north along the coast from Stromness, via Yesnaby.

Car and bicycle

Car hire from **Brass's Car Hire**, Blue Star Garage, North End Rd, Stromness, T01856-850850. Cycle hire from **Orkney Cycle Hire**, 54 Dundas St, Stromness, T01856-850255.

Ferry

Northlink Ferries sail from **Scrabster** to **Stromness** (1½ hrs) 3 times a day Mon-Fri and twice a day on Sat and Sun. Passenger fare is £27-33 return and a car costs £98-112 with a driver plus £20-22 per additional passenger. A shuttle bus links Scrabster with the nearby town of Thurso, on the north coast. There are regular bus and train services to Thurso from Inverness, see p235.

East Mainland and South Ronaldsay *p322*
Ferry

See Kirkwall Transport section for the ferry service from **John o' Groats** to **Burwick**. Pentland Ferries, T01856-831226, www.pentlandferries.co.uk, sail from Gill's Bay (between John o' Groats and Thurso) to St Margaret's Hope, 4 times daily Jun-Sep, 3 daily Oct-May, £12 return, £6 child 5-16, car £28.

Hoy *p324*

Bus Transport on Hoy is very limited. North Hoy Transport, T01856-791315, runs a minibus service between **Moaness Pier** and **Rackwick**, which meets the 1000 ferry from Stromness. Call the same telephone number for a taxi around the island.

Car and bicycle Car and bike hire is available from **Halyel Car Hire**, Lyness, T01856-791240.

Ferry A passenger ferry sails between **Stromness** and **Moaness Pier** in the north (30 mins) 3 times a day Mon-Fri and twice on Fri evenings, twice daily Sat and Sun. There's a reduced winter service (mid-Sep to mid-May). There's also a car and passenger service between **Houton** and **Lyness** and **Longhope** (45 mins) up to 6 times daily (Mon-Sat). There's a limited Sun service from mid-May to mid-Sep.

Rousay, Egilsay and Wyre *p325*
Ferry A small car ferry sails from **Tingwall** (20 mins) to **Rousay** 6 times a day (Mon-Sat; 5 times on Sun). Most of the ferries call in at **Egilsay** and **Wyre**, but some are on demand only and should be booked in advance, T01856-751360. A bus connects **Tingwall** and **Kirkwall** (see p334).
Cycle hire is available from **Arts, Crafts & Bike Hire**, at the pier, T01856-821398.

Shapinsay *p326*
The small car ferry makes 6 sailings daily (including Sun in summer) from Kirkwall (25 mins).

Eday *p327*
Air There are flights from **Kirkwall** to Eday with **Loganair**, T01856-872494, on Wed only. There are ferries from **Kirkwall** (1¼ hr to 2 hrs) twice daily via **Sanday** or **Stronsay**.
Taxi You can hire a taxi from **Mr A Stewart** by the pier, T01857-622206, or hire bikes from **Mr Burkett** at Hamarr, near the post office south of Mill Loch.

Sanday *p328*
Air There are **Loganair** flights to Sanday from **Kirkwall** twice daily Mon-Fri and once on Sat.

Ferry There's a ferry service twice daily from **Kirkwall** (1½ hrs). The ferry arrives at Loth, at the southern tip of the island, and is met by a minibus which will take you to most places.

Stronsay *p328*
Air There are **Loganair** flights to Stronsay from **Kirkwall**, twice daily Mon-Fri. A ferry service runs from **Kirkwall** (1½ hr) twice daily Mon-Sat (once on Sun), and once daily Mon-Sat from Eday (35 mins).
Taxi Taxis and island minibus tours are available from **M Williamson**, T01857-616255. Car hire and taxis are available from **DS Peace**, T01857-616335.

Westray *p329*
Air Flights to Westray with **Loganair** depart Kirkwall twice daily Mon-Fri and once on Sat.
Cycle hire For cycle hire contact **Mrs Groat** at Sand o' Gill (see above); or **Mrs Bain** at Twiness, T01856-677319.
Ferry There's a car ferry service from **Kirkwall** to **Rapness**, on the south coast of the island (1½ hrs). It sails twice daily in summer (mid-May to mid-Sep) and once daily in winter. There's also a passenger ferry from **Pierowall** to **Papa Westray** (see below).

Papa Westray *p329*
Air The famous 2-min flight from Westray leaves twice daily Mon-Sat (£14 one-way). There is also a direct flight to Papay from **Kirkwall** daily Mon-Sat, except Fri (£15 one-way).
Ferry There's a passenger ferry from **Pierowall** on Westray 3-6 times daily (25 mins). The car ferry from **Kirkwall** to Westray continues to Papa Westray on Tue and Fri (2¼ hrs).

North Ronaldsay *p330*
Air There are **Loganair** flights from **Kirkwall** twice daily Mon-Sat, T01856-872494.
Ferry There's a car and passenger ferry which sails from **Kirkwall** (2 hrs 40 mins) once a week (usually Fri) and also on some Sun between May and Sep. Contact **Orkney Ferries** for details, T01856-872044.

● Directory

Kirkwall p313, map p315
Banks Branches of the 3 main Scottish banks with cash machines are on Broad St and Albert St. Exchange also at the tourist office. **Laundry The Launderama**, Albert St, T01856-872982. Open Mon-Fri 0830-1730, Sat 0900-1700.
Medical services Balfour Hospital, Health Centre and Dental Clinic, New Scapa Rd, T01856-885400. **Post** Junction Rd. Open Mon-Fri 0900- 1700, Sat 0930-1230.

Stromness and West Mainland p317
Banks There are branches of **Bank of Scotland** and **Royal Bank of Scotland**, both with ATMs, on Victoria St, Stromness.
Laundry Next to the Coffee Shop, Stromness, T01856-850904. Self-service or service washes.

Shetland

Shetland is so far removed from the rest of Scotland it can only be shown as an inset on maps. It is closer to the Arctic Circle than it is to London and it's easier and quicker to get there from Norway than it is from the UK's capital. This seems entirely appropriate, for Shetland is historically and culturally closer to Scandinavia than Britain. Many of its place-names are of Norse origin, and people here still celebrate the vikings in the annual Up Helly-Aa festival. Modern-day visitors tend to come by plane rather than longboat, and usually bring binoculars, for Shetland is a birdwatchers' paradise. It is home to countless species, many of them seeking refuge from the madding crowds. And, let's face it, there's no better place than here to get away from it all. ➤➤ For Sleeping, Eating and other listings, see pages 348 354.*

Ins and outs

Getting there

Shetland has good air connections with the rest of the UK. There are regular flights to and from several mainland airports which are operated by British Airways' franchise partners Loganair and British Regional Airlines. There are daily car ferry sailings from Aberdeen to Lerwick taking 12 hours and as well as ferries arriving from Kirkwall (Orkney). ➤➤ *For further details, see Transport page 352.*

Getting around

There is a regular scheduled inter-island service from Tingwall Airport near Lerwick with Loganair to Foula, Fair Isle, Papa Stour and Out Skerries. There are also frequent ferry service links many of the islands with the Shetland Mainland. Booking is essential for all journeys. Shetland has around 500 miles of good roads, and an extensive public bus service links Lerwick with all towns, villages and tourist sights. There are several bus operators. A Shetland Transport Timetable, published by Shetland Islands Council, contains details of all air, sea and bus services throughout the islands. It is available from the tourist office in Lerwick. The best way to explore the islands is with your own private car. It is cheaper to hire a car in Lerwick rather than at the airport. Hitching is a feasible way to get around and is relatively safe. Cycling is a good way to experience the islands, though most places are very exposed and the winds can be strong. ➤➤ *For further details, see Transport page 352.*

Orkney & Shetland Shetland

Muckle Flugga
Hermaness
Saxa Vord
Burraforth
Norwick
Unst
Haroldswick
Baltasound
Gloup
Cullivoe
Westing
Gutcher
Uyeasound
Muness
Sellafirth
Haaf Gruney
Yell
Hascosay
Fetlar
Fethaland
Isbister
Oddsta
Houbie
North Voe
Mid Yell
Tresta
Funzie
West
Ronies Hill
Sandwick
(1,477ft)
Aywick
Otterswick
Hamnavoe
Gossabrough
Heylor
Ollaberry
Urafirth
Ulsta
Hamnavoe
Esha Ness
Hillswick
Sullom Voe
Burravoe
Stenness
Oil Terminal
The
Mossbank
Out
Drongs
Firth
Skerries
Lunna
Housay
Mavis
Brae
Lunning
Grind
Skaw
Busta
Brough
Muckle Roe
Laxo
Vidlin
Isbister
Voe
Huxter
Symbister
Papa Stour
Whalsey
Hurdiback
East
North
Laxfirth
Burrafirth
Nesting
Clausta
Mainland
Skellister
Sandness
West
Aith
Weisdale
Eswick
Burrafirth
Bixter
Gletness
Bridge of Walls
Tresta
Wats
Girlsta
Walls
Stanydale
Ness
Whiteness
Burrastow
Gruting
Tingwall
Vaila
Garderhouse
Sand
Gott
Skeld
Reawick
Heogan
Dale
Maryfield
Scalloway
LERWICK
Westerwick
Noss
Bressa
Tondra
Gulberwick
The
Quarff
Ord
Hamnavoe
Burra Isle
Fladdabister
Ocraquoy
Cunningsburgh
Maywick
Leebitton
Mousa
Channerwick
Hoswick
St Ninian's Isle
Bigton
Sandwick
Levenwick
Scousburgh
Fitful Head
Southvoe
Quendale
Sumburgh
Grutness
Jarlshof
Sumburgh Head

To Foula
To Norway
To Aberdeen
To Fair Isle

N

0 km 5
0 miles 5

Lerwick and around → *Phone code: 01595. Population: 7,600.*

Lerwick is the capital and administrative centre of Shetland and the only sizeable town, containing more than a third of the islands' 22,000 population. Though the islands have been inhabited for many centuries, Lerwick only dates from the 17th century, when it began to grow as a trading port for Dutch herring fishermen, thanks to its superb natural sheltered harbour, the Bressay Sound. The town spread along the waterfront, where merchants built their lodberries, which were houses and warehouses with their own piers so that they could trade directly with visiting ships. By the late 19th century Lerwick had become the main herring port in northern Europe. Lerwick has continued to grow and is now home to a third of Shetland's population. The discovery of oil in the North Sea in the early 1970s led to the building of the Sullom Voe Oil Terminal, and the effect on Lerwick has been dramatic. It is now the main transit point to the North Sea oil rigs and there have been major extensions to the harbour area, bringing increased shipping and prosperity to the town. ▸▸ *For Sleeping, Eating and other listings, see pages 348-354.*

Ins and outs

Getting there and around Ferries from Aberdeen arrive at the main Holmsgarth terminal, about a mile north of the old harbour. There's a regular bus service between Lerwick and Sumburgh airport (50 minutes) run by John Leask & Son, T01595-693162. Taxis (around £25) and car hire are also available. All island bus services start and end at the Viking bus station, which is on Commercial Road, a short distance north of the town centre. The town is small and everything is within easy walking distance.

Tourist information The main **TIC** ① *Market Cross, Commercial St, T01595-693434, www.shetland-tourism.co.uk, May-Sep Mon-Fri 0800-1800, Sat 0800-1600, Sun 1000-1300, Oct-Apr Mon-Fri 0900-1700,* are an excellent source of information, books, maps and leaflets. They will also change foreign currency and book accommodation.

Lerwick

The town's heart is the attractive **Commercial Street**, which runs parallel to the Esplanade. At the southern end are many old houses and lodberries, and you can continue south along the cliffs to the **Knab** or to lovely **Bain's beach**. *Lerwick Walks* is a leaflet detailing many interesting walks in and around town.

Overlooking the north end of Commercial Street is **Fort Charlotte** ① *Jun-Sep daily 0900-2200, Oct-May 0900-1600, free,* built in 1665 and later rebuilt in 1780 and named after Queen Charlotte, George III's consort. It has since been used as a prison and Royal Naval Reserve base and, though there's little to see in the fort, there are fine views of the harbour from the battlements. One of Lerwick's most impressive buildings is the Victorian **town hall** ① *Mon-Fri 1000-1200 and 1400-1530, free,* on Hillhead. The stained-glass windows of the main hall depict episodes from Shetland's history. Opposite the town hall, above the library, is the **Shetland Museum** ① *T01595-695057, Mon, Wed and Fri 1000-1900, Tue, Thu and Sat till 1700, free,* which gives a useful introduction to the islands' history. Amongst the artefacts on display is a replica of the St Ninian's Isle treasure.

Also in town is the **Up Helly-Aa Exhibition** ① *mid-May to mid-Sep Tue 1400-1600 and 1700-1900, Fri 1700-1900, Sat 1400-1600, £3, concession £1.50,* in the Galley Shed off St Sunniva Street. This gives a taste of the famous fire festival held annually in Lerwick on the last Tuesday in January, when a torch-lit procession through the town by hundreds of people dressed in Viking costumes (*guizers*) is followed by a replica Viking longship built especially for the event. At the end of the procession the ship is set ablaze when the guizers throw their flaming torches on to it.

Orkney & Shetland Shetland

A mile west of town are the substantial remains of **Clickimin Broch**, a fortified site occupied from 700 BC to around the fifth or sixth century AD. A path leads to the site from opposite the Safeway supermarket on the A970. About a mile north of the ferry terminal is the **Böd of Gremista** ① *Jun to mid-Sep Wed and Sun 1000-1300 and 1400-1700*, free, a restored 18th-century fishing *böd* (booth) which was the birthplace of Arthur Anderson (1791-1868), co-founder of the Peninsular and Oriental Steam Navigation Company, now P&O. One of the rooms features an exhibition on Anderson's life and involvement with P&O.

Bressay

Lying to the east of Lerwick across the Bressay Sound is the island of Bressay (pronounced 'bressah'), which creates a sheltered harbour for the capital and led to its establishment as a major trading port. Seven miles long by three miles wide, it makes an ideal day trip for cyclists. Another good way to get around is on foot, and there's a fine walk to the top of **Ward Hill** (742 ft), the highest point, from where you get great views of the island and as far afield as Foula and Out Skerries. There are also good coastal walks, particularly along the cliffs from Noss Sound south to **Bard Head**, **The Ord** and **Bressay Lighthouse**, where you can see large colonies of seabirds.

Noss

Serious birdwatchers should head for Noss, a tiny, uninhabited island off the east coast of Bressay, which is a **National Nature Reserve** with over 100,000 pairs of breeding seabirds. A walk around the perimeter of the island takes at least three hours but is highly recommended. At the east side is the **Noup of Noss**, where the 600-ft cliffs are packed full of nesting gannets. The reserve is managed by Scottish Natural Heritage who have a small visitor centre at Gungstie.

Lerwick

Sleeping		
Alder Lodge Guest House 1	Kveldsro House 5	Eating
Carradel Guest House 2	Old Manse 6	Monty's Bistro 1
Fort Charlotte Guest House 3	Queen's 7	Osla's Café 2
Grand 4	SYHA Hostel 9	

0 metres 200
0 yards 200

Central Mainland → *Phone code: 01595.*

The Central Mainland is Shetland's slim waist, and only a few miles of land separates the east and west coast. There's not a huge amount of tourist interest here but the area's history is fascinating and the Scalloway Museum is certainly worth a visit. ▶▶ *For Sleeping, Eating and other listings, see pages 348-354.*

Scalloway and around

Six miles from Lerwick on the west coast is Scalloway, once the capital of Shetland and now a fishing port and fish-processing centre. In 1942, during the Second World War, Scalloway became the headquarters of the **Shetland Bus** operations. This was the name given to the Norwegian fishing boats which sailed to Shetland during the night from German-occupied Norway, bringing refugees to safety and returning with ammunition and resistance fighters. An interesting exhibition on the 'Shetland Bus' can be seen at **Scalloway Museum** ① *Main St, May to Sep Tue-Thu 1400-1630, Sat 1000-1230 and 1400-1630, free.*

The harbour is dominated by the ruins of **Scalloway Castle**, built in 1600 by the notorious Earl Patrick Stewart using local slave labour, see page 318. After his execution the castle fell into disrepair, though the four-storey main block and one wing remain. Inside, an interpretative display explains its history.

South of Scalloway lie the islands of **Trondra** and **Burra**, now connected to the Mainland by bridges. At Burland on Trondra is the **Spirit of Shetland**, where you can buy knitwear, while on West Burra is the attractive little fishing village of **Hamnavoe**.

Tingwall

North of Scalloway, the B9074 runs through the fertile Tingwall Valley, past a nine-hole **golf course** at Asta, and the **Loch of Tingwall**, which is good for brown trout fishing and also home to swans and otters. At the northern end of the loch is a promontory called **Law Ting Holm**, which was the site of the Althing, or parliament, during the period of Norse rule. Overlooking the loch is **Tingwall Kirk**, built in the late 18th century on the site of the earlier church of St Magnus which dated back to the early period of Norse Christianity. In the graveyard is the old burial vault with several interesting old grave slabs. Nearby is **Tingwall Agricultural Museum** ① *Jun-Aug Mon-Sat 1000-1300 and 1400-1700, £1.50*, which houses a collection of old crofting implements.

Weisdale

The A971 continues northwest towards Weisdale, a district with some worthwhile attractions. At the head of **Weisdale Voe** the B9075 branches north to **Weisdale Mill** ① *T01595-830400, Wed-Sat 1030-1630, Sun 1200-1630, free*, which now houses the **Bonhoga Gallery**, a purpose-built art gallery featuring varied exhibitions of local, national and international works. There's also a nice café serving snacks. Weisdale Mill was part of the Kergord Estate, known until 1945 as Flemington, and was built from the stones of evacuated crofthouses. Over 300 crofters were forcibly evicted in the mid-19th century during the 'Clearances', when lairds expanded their more profitable sheep-farming activities. In 1940 the mill was requisitioned as the intelligence and administrative HQ for the **Shetland Bus** operations (see Scalloway above). The Kergord estate today is the largest area of woodland in Shetland, and attracts a variety of migratory birds.

On the west shore of Weisdale Voe, south of the mill, are the ruins of the house where **John Clunies Ross** (1786-1854) was born. He settled in the Cocos Islands in the Indian Ocean in 1827 and the islands were owned by the Estate of the Clunies Ross family until purchased by the Australian government in 1978. In 1984 the islanders voted to become part of Australia.

The Westside → *Phone code: 01595. OS Landranger Nos 3 & 4.*

The western Mainland of Shetland, stretching west from Weisdale to Sandness, is known as The Westside. This part of Shetland is notable for its varied landscape of spectacular sea cliffs, rolling green hills, bleak moorland, peaty freshwater lochs and numerous long sea lochs, or voes. This is excellent **walking** country, with many fine coastal routes, especially around **Culswick** and **Dale of Walls**. It is also great for birdwatching and trout fishing, and there are many opportunities for spotting whales, dolphins and otters. ▶ *For Sleeping, Eating and other listings, see pages 348-354.*

Stanydale, Walls and Sandness

There are a few interesting archaeological sites here, too. At Stanydale, signposted from the road between the villages of **Bixter** and **Walls**, is the site of a Neolithic settlement with the remains of houses, field boundaries and clearance cairns. Near the **Brig o' Waas**, just north of Walls, is the **Scord of Brouster**, a prehistoric farm site which has been excavated.

The pretty little village of **Walls** (pronounced *waas*) is set around a sheltered natural harbour and is a popular spot with visiting yachts. It also attracts many visitors during its **Agricultural Show** in August, the biggest such event on Shetland. Walls is the departure point for ferries to the remote island of Foula, below.

Northwest of Walls, the A971 crosses bleak moorland before descending to the crofting township of **Sandness** (pronounced *saa-ness*), surrounded by fertile land and facing little Papa Stour, about a mile offshore. There's a good beach here and also a **woollen spinning mill** ① *Mon-Fri 0800-1700, free*, where you can watch how they spin the famously fine wool into yarn.

Foula

Lying 15 miles west of the Shetland Mainland, tiny Foula – whose name derives from the Norse *fugl ey*, meaning 'bird island' – is the second most remote inhabited island after Fair Isle. It supports a population of around 40 people, who are greatly outnumbered by the many thousands of seabirds, including a small colony of gannets and the rare Leach's petrel. There are also about 2,500 pairs of great skuas, the largest colony in the UK. The island is dominated by its sheer cliffs, which reach their most peak at **The Kame** (1,220 ft), the second highest sea cliffs in Britain after St Kilda.

An interesting feature of the island's people is that they still observe the old **Julian calendar**, replaced in 1752 in Britain by the present Gregorian system which deleted 11 days from the year. Remote areas of the country kept to the old calendar, adding an extra day in 1800, which was a leap year, and some parts of Shetland continued to observe festivals 12 days after the dates in the new calendar. The most remote areas kept to the old calendar longest, and the people of Foula still celebrate Christmas on 6 January and New Year's Day on 13 January.

Papa Stour

A ferry sails from West Burrafirth on the Westside, near Sandness, to the little island of Papa Stour, only a mile offshore. The island, which has a population of around 30, is mostly made up of volcanic rock which has been eroded to form an amazing coastline of stacks, arches and caves, most spectacular of which is **Kirstan's Hole**. The island is home to large colonies of auks, terns and skuas, and also has a fascinating history of its own. Pick up the island trails leaflet from the tourist office in Lerwick.

 Catpund Quarries, 10 miles south of Lerwick, to the south of Cunningsburgh, is where soft soapstone was quarried from Neolithic to medieval times, making a variety of stone implements and utensils for these times.

South Mainland → *Phone code: 01950.*

From Lerwick a long, narrow finger of land points south. The main road runs down the east coast for 25 miles till it ends at Sumburgh Head, near Shetland's main airport. This southern part of the Shetland Mainland holds the islands' two most important archaeological sights and main tourist attractions. ▶▶ *For Sleeping, Eating and other listings, see pages 348-354.*

Isle of Mousa

① *T01950-431367, www.mousaboattrips.co.uk, entry to the broch is free, a ferry sails to the island from Leebitton harbour in Sandwick twice daily from mid-Apr to mid-Sep, weather permitting, allowing visitors 2½ hours to see the island, the trip takes 15 mins and costs £8 per adult.*

Fifteen miles south of Lerwick, the scattered crofting communities of Sandwick look across to the Isle of Mousa, site of the best-preserved broch in Scotland. This fortified tower was built around 2,000 years ago and still stands close to its original height of 45 ft. It's a very impressive structure when you see it from the inside and has chambers, galleries, an internal staircase and a parapet. The broch features in a Viking saga of the 12th century when the mother of Harald, Earl of Orkney, took refuge there with her lover. The Earl, who did not approve of the liaison, laid siege to the broch, but it proved impregnable and he gave up.

Mousa island is also home to many seabirds and waders, most notably the Storm Petrel, which is best seen at dusk as they return to their nests amongst the beach rocks. You can also see seals on the white sand beach at West Voe. If you have time, it's a good idea to walk right around the coast, starting from the landing stage at West Ham and first heading south to the broch. Watch out for dive-bombing terns.

South of Sandwick

At Hoswick, between Sandwick and Levenwick, is **Da Warp and Weft Visitor Centre** ① *May-Sep Mon-Sat 1000-1700, Sun 1200-1700, free,* which houses an exhibition on weaving, crofting, fishing and island life. Next door is the **Shetland Woollen Company,** where you can buy knitwear. Further south on the east coast, at Boddam, is the **Shetland Crofthouse Museum** ① *May-Sep daily 1000-1300 and 1400-1700, £2,* a restored thatched crofthouse with 19th-century furniture and utensils.

St Ninian's Isle to Quendale

On the west coast, near Bigton village, a signposted track leads to the spectacular sandy causeway (known as a tombolo) which leads to St Ninian's Isle. The tombolo is the best example of its kind in Britain, and you can walk across to the island which is best known for the hoard of Pictish treasure which was discovered in 1958 in the ruins of the 12th-century church. The 28 silver objects included bowls, a spoon and brooches, probably dating from around AD 800, and are now on display in the Royal Scottish Museum in Edinburgh, though you can see replicas in the Shetland Museum in Lerwick.

The west coast south of Bigton is beautiful with long, sandy beaches interspersed with dramatic cliff scenery. On the other side of the road from the long, sheltered beach at **Scousburgh Sands** is the **Loch of Spiggie RSPB Reserve**. The loch is an important winter wildfowl refuge, particularly for Whooper Swans, and during the summer you can see various ducks, waders, gulls, terns and skuas. There's a hide on the northern shore with an information board. Nearby is the **Spiggie Hotel** which offers bar meals, afternoon tea or dinner.

A few miles south of the loch is the village of **Quendale**, overlooking a wide, sandy bay. Here you'll find the beautifully restored and fully working 19th-century

Close encounters of the bird kind

Shetland is famous for its birds. As well its huge seabird colonies, the islands attract Arctic species and are an important crossroads for migrating birds. Over 340 species have been recorded on Fair Isle, including rare and exotic birds from Asia and America. Twenty-one out of the 24 seabirds common to Britain breed in Shetland. These can be found around the coastline, but the largest colonies are at the Hermaness and Noss reserves.

Amongst the many species which can be seen are the puffin. About one fifth of Scotland's puffins breed in Shetland. Its cousins in the auk family, guillemots, and razorbills, are also here in abundance during the summer months, along with kittiwakes, shags and that most common of seabirds, the fulmar. Britain's largest seabird, the gannet, can be seen diving spectacularly for fish at Hermaness, Noss, Fair Isle and Foula, while its smallest seabird, the storm petrel, is best seen around dusk on the tiny island of Mousa.

Summer heralds the return of the Arctic tern which breeds along low coastlines, as do the eider, oystercatcher, ringed plover and black guillemot, or tystie, which stays here all year round. The best place to see waders and shelduck are the nutrient-rich tidal mudflats at the Pool of Virkie in the South Mainland.

Many birds breed on agricultural land, and these include the lapwing, skylark, meadow pipit and wheater. The hills and moorland provide breeding grounds for many summer visitors such as that pirate of the skies, the great skua, or bonxie, and the Arctic skua. Another Arctic species, the whimbrel, also nests here, mainly in Unst, Yell and Fetlar. Moorland habitats are also favoured by the curlew, golden plover and merlin, Shetland's only bird of prey, while the lochs are home to large numbers of red-throated divers. Fetlar is home to 90 per cent of the population of one of Britain's rarest birds, the red-necked phalarope.

Many of Shetland's bird habitats are protected as RSPB Reserves and National Nature Reserves, and it is an offence to disturb the birds and their young at or near their nests. You also risk being dive-bombed by some of the more aggressively protective species. For a full list of all species recorded on the islands and more practical birdwatching information, be sure to get a copy of the *Shetland Bird Chart* by Joyce Gammack, available from the tourist office in Lerwick.

Quendale Mill ① *May-Sep daily 1000-1700, £2*, the last of Shetland's watermills. Not far from here, between Garth's Ness and Fitful Head, lies the wreck of the Braer oil tanker which ran on to the rocks in 1993. A disaster of epic proportions was averted by the hurricane-force gales which dispersed the huge oil spillage.

Sumburgh and Jarlshof

At the southern tip of Mainland is the village of Sumburgh, site of Shetland's main airport for external passenger flights and for helicopters and planes servicing the North Sea oil industry. South of the airport is Shetland's prime archaeological site, **Jarlshof** ① *T01950-460112, Apr-Sep daily 0930-1830, £3.30, concession £2.50, children £1*, a hugely impressive place which spans 4,000 years of occupation from Neolithic times through Norse settlement to the 16th century. The original Stone-Age dwellings are topped by a broch, Pictish wheelhouses, Viking longhouses and, towering over the whole complex, the ruins of a 16th-century mansion. This remarkable site was only discovered at the end of the 19th century when a violent

storm ripped off the top layer of turf. Jarlshof is, in fact, not a genuine name, but the
exotic invention of Sir Walter Scott in his novel *The Pirate*. A helpful guidebook
available from the visitor centre helps to bring the place to life.

South of Jarlshof the Mainland ends abruptly at **Sumburgh Head**, an RSPB
Reserve. The **lighthouse** on top of the cliff was built by Robert Stevenson in 1821, and
the keepers' cottages are now rented out as self-catering accommodation. The
lighthouse isn't open to the public, but from its grounds you can see many nesting
seabirds such as puffins, kittiwakes, fulmars, guillemots and razorbills. Just to the
east of the airport is **Pool of Virkie**, another good birdwatching area.

Fair Isle → *Phone code: 01595.*

Fair Isle, 24 miles southwest of Sumburgh and 27 miles northeast of North Ronaldsay in
Orkney, is the most isolated of Britain's inhabited islands. Only three miles long by 1½
miles wide, the island has a population of around 70 and is best known for its intricately
patterned knitwear, which is still produced by a co-operative, **Fair Isle Crafts**.
Co-operative could be said to sum up the friendly islanders, whose lifestyle is based on
mutual help and community effort. ▶▶ *For Sleeping, Eating and other listings, see pages 348-354.*

Ins and outs
Getting to Fair Isle requires patience, persistence and a strong stomach to survive the
white-knuckle 4½-hour ferry sailing. There are also flights from Tingwall Airport. For
more information visit on Fair Isle visit www.fairisle.org.uk, or call the **National Trust
for Scotland** ① *T0141-616 2266, www.thenationaltrustforscotland.org.uk.* ▶▶ *For further
details, see Transport page 352.*

Sights
Fair Isle is a paradise for birdwatchers, and keen ornithologists form the majority of
the island's visitors. Celebrity birdwatcher and former Goodie, Bill Oddie, has
dubbed it the "the Hilton of the bird world". It stands in the flight path of many
thousands of migrating birds, and over 340 species have been recorded here at the
Fair Isle Bird Observatory, which also offers accommodation and where visitors are
welcome to take part. As well as the almost obscenely rich birdlife there are around
240 species of flowering plants, making the island an especially beautiful haven for
naturalists. Fair Isle's coastline, especially in the north and west, also boasts some
outstanding cliff scenery.

The bird observatory was the brainchild of George Waterston, an ornithologist
who first visited in 1935 and then bought the island in 1948 to begin his task of
building the observatory. The island was given to the National Trust for Scotland in
1954 and declared a National Scenic Area. It was recently designated a place of
outstanding natural beauty and cultural heritage by the Council of Europe. The
George Waterston Memorial Centre ① *May to mid-Sep Mon and Fri 1400-1600, Wed
1030-1200, donations welcome*, has exhibits and photographs detailing the island's
natural history, as well as the history of crofting, fishing, archaeology and knitwear.

North Mainland → *Phone code: 01806.*

The main road north from Lerwick branches at **Voe**, a peaceful and colourful little
village nestling in a bay at the head of the Olna Firth. One branch leads to the Yell car
and passenger ferry terminal at **Toft**, past the turn-off to the massive **Sullom Voe Oil
Terminal**, the largest oil and liquefied gas terminal in Europe. The other road heads
northwest to Brae (see below). ▶▶ *For Sleeping, Eating and other listings, see pages 348-354.*

Brae is not a very pretty place and was built to accommodate workers at the nearby Sullom Voe oil terminal. It does boast a good selection of accommodation and decent facilities, though, and makes a good base from which to explore the wild and wonderful coastal scenery around the Northmavine peninsula to the north. There's also good walking and spectacularly good westerly views around the island of **Muckle Roe** to the southwest, and up the island's small hill, **South Ward** (554 ft). But be careful of the overly protective bonxies, or great skuas, which will attack if you get too close. The island is attached to the mainland by a bridge.

Northmavine

Mavis Grind, the narrow isthmus where it's claimed you can throw a stone from the Atlantic to the North Sea, leads into Northmavine, the northwest peninsula of North Mainland. It is one of Shetland's most dramatic and beautiful areas, with rugged scenery, spectacular coastline and wide empty spaces. This is wonderful walking country, and it's a good idea to abandon the car and explore it on foot. **Hillswick Ness**, to the south of **Hillswick** village, is a nice walk, but further west, around the coastline of **Eshaness**, is the most spectacular cliff scenery and amazing natural features, all with unusual and evocative names.

North of the lighthouse are the **Holes of Scraada**, **Grind o' da Navir** and the **Villians of Hamnavoe**, which are not the local gangs but eroded lava cliffs with blowholes, arches and caves. East of Eshaness are the **Heads of Grocken** and **The Drongs**, a series of exposed sea stacks, which offer superb diving. Further north, overlooking the deep sea inlet of **Ronies Voe**, is the dramatic red granite bulk of **Ronies Hill** (1,477 ft), with a well-preserved burial cairn at the summit. The coastal scenery to the north and west of here is even more breathtaking, but very remote and exposed. You should be well equipped before setting out.

Between Eshaness and Hillswick, a side road leads south to the **Tangwick Haa Museum** ① *May-Sep Mon-Fri 1300-1700, Sat and Sun 1100-1900, free*, which features displays and photographs on the history of fishing and whaling and the hardships of life in these parts.

Whalsay and Out Skerries → *Phone code: 01806.*

South of Voe, the B9071 branches east to Laxo, the ferry terminal for the island of **Whalsay**, one of Shetland's most prosperous small islands owing to its thriving fishing industry, which helps support a population of around 1,000. The fleet is based at **Symbister**, the island's main settlement. Beside the harbour at Symbister is the **Pier House** ① *Mon-Sat 0900-1300 and 1400-1700, Sun 1400-1700, free*, a restored böd which was used by the Hanseatic League, a commercial association of German merchants who traded in Shetland from the Middle Ages to the early 18th century. Inside is an exhibition explaining the history of the Hanseatic trade, and general information on the island. One of Scotland's great poets, **Hugh McDiarmid** (Christopher Grieve), spent most of the 1930s in Whalsay, where he wrote much of his finest poetry, until he was called for war work in 1942, never to return. His former home, at Sodom near Symbister, is now a camping böd, see Sleeping page 349.

The Out Skerries is a small group of rocky islands about five miles from Whalsay and 10 miles east of Shetland Mainland. It's made up of three main islands: the larger islands of **Housay** and **Bruray**, which are connected by a road bridge; and the uninhabited island of **Grunay**. The Skerries boast some spectacular and rugged sea cliffs which are home to many rare migrant seabirds in spring and autumn. ▸▸ *For Sleeping, Eating and other listings, see pages 348-354.*

Yell, Fetlar and Unst → *Phone code: 01957.*

Yell

Yell, the second largest of the Shetland islands, was described rather damningly by Shetland-born writer Eric Linklater as 'dull and dark'. And it's true that the interior is consistently desolate peat moorland. But the coastline is greener and more pleasant and provides an ideal habitat for the island's large **otter** population. Yell is also home to a rich variety of birds, and offers some good coastal and hill walks, especially around the rugged coastline of **The Herra**, a peninsula about half way up the west coast.

At **Burravoe**, about five miles east of the ferry terminal at **Ulsta**, is the **Old Haa Museum** ① *T01957-722339, late Apr-Sep Tue-Thu and Sat 1000-1600, Sun 1400-1700, free*, housed in Yell's oldest building which dates from 1672. It contains an interesting display on local flora and fauna and history.

The island's largest village, **Mid Yell**, has a couple of shops, a pub and a leisure centre with a good swimming pool. About a mile northwest, on the hillside above the main road, are the reputedly haunted ruins of **Windhouse**, dating from 1707. To the north is the **RSPB Lumbister Reserve**, where red-throated divers, merlins, great and Arctic skuas and many other bird species come to breed. The reserve is also home to a large number of otters. A pleasant walk leads along the nearby steep and narrow gorge, known as the **Daal of Lumbister**, filled with many colourful flowers. The area to the north of the reserve provides good walking over remote moorland and coastline.

The road continues north past the reserve and around **Basta Voe**, where you can see otters. North of **Gutcher**, the ferry port for Unst, is the village of **Cullivoe**, with some good walks along the attractive coastline.

Fetlar

Fetlar is the smallest of the North Isles but the most fertile, and known as 'the garden of Shetland'. Indeed, the name derives from Norse meaning 'fat land', as there is good grazing and croftland and a rich variety of plant and bird life. The whole island is good for birdwatching, but the prime place is the 1,700 acres of **North Fetlar RSPB Reserve** around Vord Hill (522 ft) in the north of the island. This area has restricted access during the summer months, and visitors should contact the warden at Bealance, T01957-733246. The warden will also let you know if and when you can see the one or two female Snowy Owls which sometime visit.

The north cliffs of the reserve are home to large colonies of breeding seabirds, including auks, gulls and shags, and you can also see common and grey seals on the beaches in late autumn. Fetlar is home to one of Britain's rarest birds, the **red-necked phalarope**, which breeds in the loch near **Funzie** (pronounced 'finnie') in the east of the island. You can watch them from the RSPB hide in the nearby marshes. Red-throated divers and whimbrel also breed here. The island is also good for walking, and a leaflet describing some of the walks is available from the tourist office in Lerwick.

The main settlement on the island is **Houbie**; on the south coast. Here you'll see a house called Leagarth, which was built by the island's most famous son, Sir William Watson Cheyne, who with Lord Lister pioneered antiseptic surgery. Nearby is the excellent **Fetlar Interpretive Centre** ① *May-Sep Tue-Sun 1200-1700, free*, which presents the island's history and gives information on its bounteous birdlife.

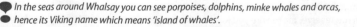 *In the seas around Whalsay you can see porpoises, dolphins, minke whales and orcas, hence its Viking name which means 'island of whales'.*

⁞ A böd for the night

There is only one youth hostel in Shetland, but budget travellers shouldn't panic. Shetland Camping Böd project has developed a network of camping böds (pronounced 'burd') which provide basic and cheap digs throughout the islands.

A böd was a building used to house fishermen and their gear during the fishing season and the name has been used to describe these types of accommodation which are similar to English 'camping barns'. They are all located in scenically attractive places and each has its own fascinating history. They are very basic and the more remote ones have no electricity or lighting. You'll need to bring a stove, cooking and eating utensils, sleeping bag and torch (flashlight). All böds must be booked in advance through the tourist office in Lerwick. They cost £5 per person per night, though they can also be booked for exclusive use by large groups. They are open from the beginning of April till the end of September. There are at present six camping böds on Shetland and these are listed in the relevant places.

Unst

Unst is the most northerly inhabited island in Britain, but there is more to the island than its many 'most northerly' credentials. It is scenically one of the most varied of the Shetland islands, with spectacular cliffs, sea stacks, sheltered inlets, sandy beaches, heather-clad hills, fertile farmland, freshwater lochs and even a sub-arctic desert. Such a variety of habitats supports over 400 plant species and a rich variety of wildlife. Unst is a major breeding site for gannets, puffins, guillemots, razorbills, kittiwakes, shags, Arctic and great skuas and whimbrels, amongst others, and in the surrounding waters you can see seals, porpoises, otters and even killer whales.

In the east of the island, north of **Baltasound**, is the **Keen of Hamar National Nature Reserve**, 74 acres of serpentine rock which breaks into tiny fragments known as 'debris', giving the landscape a strange, lunar-like appearance. This bleak 'desert' is actually home to some of the rarest plants in Britain. Baltasound is the island's main settlement, with an airport, hotel, pub, post office, leisure centre with pool and Britain's most northerly brewery, the **Valhalla Brewery** which can be visited by appointment, To1975-711348.

To the north of here is the village of **Haroldswick**, home of Britain's most northerly post office, where your postcards are sent with a special stamp to inform everyone of this fact. Here also is **Unst Boat Haven** ⓘ *May-Sep daily 1400-1700, free*, where you can see a beautifully presented collection of traditional boats and fishing artefacts. A little way further north is the **Unst Heritage Centre** ⓘ *same opening hours as Boat Haven and also free*, which has a museum of local history and island life. Nearby is an RAF radar-tracking station at Saxa Vord. The road ends at Skaw, where there's a lovely beach and Britain's most northerly house. The road northwest from Haroldswick leads to the head of **Burra Firth**, a sea inlet flanked by high cliffs, and site of Britain's most northerly golf course.

To the west of Burra Firth is the remote **Hermaness National Nature Reserve**, 2,422 acres of dramatic coastal scenery and wild moorland which is home to over 100,000 nesting seabirds including gannets, and the largest number of puffins and great skuas (or 'bonxies') in Shetland. There's an excellent **visitor centre** ⓘ *To1975-711278, daily late Apr to mid-Sep 0830-1800*, in the former lighthouse keeper's shore station, where you can pick up a leaflet which shows the marked route into the reserve, and see the artistic efforts of many of Unst's children. Whilst in the reserve, make sure you keep to the marked paths to avoid being attacked by

Orkney & Shetland Shetland

66 99 With nothing between you and the North Pole but water, this is the place to sit and contemplate what it feels like to be at the end of the world...

bonxies; they are highly protective and they will attack if they think that their territory is being threatened.

The views from Hermaness are wonderful, out to the offshore stacks and skerries including **Muckle Flugga**, and then to the wide open north Atlantic Ocean. Muckle Flugga is the site of the most northerly lighthouse in Britain, built in 1857-1858 by Thomas Stevenson, father of Robert Louis Stevenson. The writer visited the island in 1869, and the illustrated map in his novel *Treasure Island* bears a striking similarity to the outline of Unst. Beyond the lighthouse is **Out Stack**, which marks the most northerly point on the British Isles. With nothing between you and the North Pole but water, this is the place to sit and contemplate what it feels like to be at the end of the world.

● Sleeping

Lerwick and around *p339, map p340*
Shetland's best accommodation is outside Lerwick, whose hotels are mostly geared towards the oil industry. During the peak months of Jul and Aug and the Folk Festival in Apr, it's a good idea to book in advance.
B Grand Hotel, Commercial St, T01595-692826. Features Shetland's only nightclub.
B Kveldsro House Hotel, Greenfield Pl, T01595-692195, www.kghotels.co.uk. The most luxurious hotel in town. Pronounced 'kel-ro', it overlooks the harbour and has an upmarket (and £££) restaurant as well as cheaper bar food.
B Lerwick Hotel, 15 South Rd, T01595-692166, reception@lerwickhotel.co.uk. 10 mins from the centre, has a reputation for fine cuisine.
B Shetland Hotel, directly opposite the ferry terminal, T01595-695515. Modern and functional.
B-C Queen's Hotel, Commercial St, T01595-692826. By the harbour. Rather faded.
There are several pleasant guest houses and B&Bs, including:
D Alder Lodge Guest House, 6 Clairmont Pl, T01595-695705;
D The Old Manse, 9 Commercial St, T01595-696301;
D-E Carradel Guest House, 36 King Harald St, T01595-692251;

D-E Fort Charlotte Guest House, 1 Charlotte St, T01595-695956;
D-E Maryfield House Hotel, on the little island of Bressay, T01595-820207, near the ferry terminal.
D-E Solheim Guest House, next door to Maryfield House Hotel, T01595-695275.
F SYHA hostel, Islesburgh House, King Harald St, T01595-692114, open Apr-Sep. Clean and well-run.

Camping
Clickimin Caravan & Camp Site, T01595-741000, near Clickimin Leisure Centre and loch on the western edge of the town.

Central Mainland *p341*
E Hildasay Guest House, Scalloway, in the upper part of the village, T01595-880822. Has disabled facilities and arranges fishing trips.
C Herrislea House Hotel, Tingwall, near the airport, by the crossroads, T01595-840208, www.herrislea-house.shetland.co.uk. Offers good home cooking daily till 2100, and live music in its Starboard Tack bar.
C-D Westings Hotel, in Wormadale, near Tingwall, T01595-840242, www.westings. shetland.co.uk. Modern hotel which is a good place to stop for lunch.

The best accommodation is in Walls.

B Burrastow House, 2 miles southwest of Walls, T01595-809307, burr.hs.hotel @zetnet.co.uk. A restored 18th-century house in a stunning location overlooking Vaila Sound, it's full of character and has a reputation for serving superb cuisine (some say the best on the islands, so you'll need to book ahead).

D North House, Papa Stour, T01595-873238, offers full board (there's no shop on the island).

E Leraback, Foula, T01595-753226, which includes dinner in the price.

E Skeoverick, a mile or so north of Walls, T01595-803349. Friendly B&B.

E-F Pomona, Gruting, east of Brig o' Waas, T01595-810438.

Camping

Voe House, Walls, is a camping **böd** – a restored 18th-century house overlooking the village. Open Apr-Sep. Book through Lerwick tourist office.

Self catering

There is self-catering accommodation available on Foulla, £90-150 per week for a cottage sleeping 4-6 people. Contact Mr R Holbourn, T01595-753232.

South Mainland *p343*

There's accommodation in Sandwick, around Sumburgh however it is limited.

C Sumburgh Hotel, T01950-460201, next to Jarlshof, in a converted laird's house, has a bar and restaurant.

E Barclay Arms Hotel, Sandwick, T01950-431226, offers evening meals.

Camping

Betty Mouat's Cottage, next to a excavated site at Scatness, next to the airport, is this camping böd. It sleeps up to 8 and is open Apr-Sep. Book through Lerwick tourist office.

Fair Isle *p345*

There are a few places to stay on the island, but accommodation must be booked in advance and includes meals. There are no hotels, pubs or restaurants.

C Fair Isle Lodge and Bird Observatory, T01595-760258, www.fairislebirdobs.co.uk, offers full-board accommodation in private rooms or in a dormitory (**E**).

D Schoolton, T01595-760250. Full board.

D Upper Leogh, T01595-760248, kathleen.coull@lineone.net. Full board.

Self-catering cottage, T01595-760248, for 4 from £210 weekly.

North Mainland *p345*

B Busta House Hotel, Brae, T01806-522506, www.bustahouse.com. The best place to stay around Brae, or anywhere else on Shetland, is this luxurious and wonderfully atmospheric 16th-century country house overlooking Busta Voe about 1½ miles from Brae village. The superb restaurant (**£££**) is the finest on Shetland, with a selection of malts to match, and there are also meals in the bar.

D Valleyfield Guest House, Brae, T01806-522563. B&B with the option of dinner.

E Almara, T01806-503261, Upper Urafirth. Comfortable B&B.

E Drumquin Guest House, Brae, T01806-522621, dinner available.

E Westayre, T01806-522368. On Muckle Roe, a working croft.

Camping

Sail Loft, in Voe by the pier, is this former fishing store and now Shetland's largest camping böd. Open Apr-Sep.

Johnny Notion's Camping Böd, in Hamnavoe, Northmavine, is reached by a side road which branches north from the road between Hillswick and Eshaness. This is birthplace of John Williamson, known as 'Johnny Notion', an 18th-century craftsman who developed an effective innoculation against smallpox. It's open Apr-Sep and has no electricity. Book through Lerwick TIC.

Whalsay and Out Skerries *p346*

Hugh Mc Diarmid's Camping Böd, near Symbister, open Apr-Sep, with no electricity. The former home of this great poet, see p346.

For an explanation of sleeping and eating price codes used in this guide, see inside the front cover. Other relevant information is found in Essentials, see pages 41-49.

Yell, Fetlar and Unst *p347*

There's a decent selection of accommodation on Unst.

D Buness House, 101975-711315,Unst, buness@zetnet.co.uk. Top choice has to be this lovely old 17th-century Haa in Baltasound. Staying here is a bizarre and rather surreal experience, given that you are on the most northerly island in Britain. The house is crammed full of Indian Raj relics, and the stuffed eagle, tiger and leopard skins hanging in the hallway are a wildlife close up almost as impressive, though considerably more unsettling and un-'PC', as the Hermaness Nature Reserve in the north of the island that the family own. The food is excellent and accommodation comfortable.

E Cligera Guest House, Baltasound, Unst, T01975-711579. Friendly.

E Gerratoun, Haroldswick, Unst, T01975-711323. B&B.

E The Glebe, Fetlar, T01975-733242, a lovely old house overlooking Papil Water.

E The Gord, in Houbie, Fetlar, T01975-733227.

E Hillhead, in Burravoe, Yell, T01975-722274.

E Pinewood Guest House, in South Aywick, between Burravoe and Mid Yell,Yell, T01975-702427.

E Prestegaard, Unst, T01975-755234. Another good place is this Victorian house at Uyeasound on the south coast near the ferry.

E-F Post Office, in Gutcher, Yell, T01975-744201. Friendly and welcoming.

F Gardiesfauld Hostel, Baltasound, Unst, T01975-755259; open Apr-Sep. An independent hostel which also hires bikes.

Camping

Windhouse Lodge, Yell, a camping böd below the ruins of haunted Windhouse. It's well-equipped and open Apr-Sep.

Gerth's Campsite, Fetlar, T01975-733227, overlooks the beach at Tresta and has good facilities.

● Eating

Lerwick and around *p339, map p340*
Despite a ready supply of fresh local produce, Shetland is a gastronomic desert. The hotels and guesthouses listed above under Sleeping are far and away the best options.

££ Kveldsro Hotel and **Lerwick Hotel** (see Sleeping) are the next best choices after Monty's for dinner or bar lunch.

£££ Monty's Bistro & Deli, 5 Mounthooly St, T01595-696655. The best place to eat in Lerwick. It offers good modern Scottish cooking in a cosy, informal setting. Closed Sun.

£ Osla's Café, 88 Commercial St, T01595-696005. Cosy café serving a wide range of coffees, pancakes and other snacks and boasting the islands' only beer garden. Open Mon-Sat till at least 1900, Sun 1200-1600.

Central Mainland *p341*
£ Da Haaf Restaurant, T01595-880328, is a canteen-style restaurant in the North Atlantic Fisheries college and specializes in (yes, you guessed it) seafood. Does a good fish supper, as well as having a more up-market menu for the evenings. Open Mon-Fri 0900-2000.

£ Scalloway Hotel and **Kiln Bar**, both offer bar meals.

North Mainland *p345*
££ Busta House, Brae, see Sleeping, serves fine food.

££-£ Mid Brae Inn, Brae, is a good place to eat serving great food daily till 2100.

££-£ Pierhead Restaurant and Bar, Voe, T01806-588332, serves meals.

££ The Booth, Hillswick, is Shetland's oldest pub serving food daily in summer.

Yell, Fetlar and Unst *p347*
Eating options on very limited, though most B&Bs will serve evening meals on request.
Baltasound Hotel, Unst, T01975-711334, serves meals and drinks to non-residents.
Hilltop Restaurant and Bar, **Old Haa Museum Café** , and **Seaview Café**, are all on Yell.

● Bars and clubs

Lerwick and around *p339, map p340*
Lounge, Mounthooly St near the tourist office. The upstairs bar here is best place for a drink. Local musicians usually play on Sat lunchtimes and some evenings.
Posers, at the **Grand Hotel**, is the town's only nightclub.

❀ Festivals and events

Lerwick and around *p339, map p340*
For details of both events, contact the Folk Festival office, 5 Burns La, Lerwick, T01595-694757. The *Shetland Times* (Fri), www.Shetland-times.co.uk, also details what is going on. Also check the tourist board's Events phoneline, T01595-694200.
Folk music has a strong following in Shetland and the islands play host to 2 of Scotland's top folk events.
Jan Up Helly Aa. Annual fire festival celebrated on the last Tue in Jan with torch-lit processions, Viking costumes and the burning of a Viking longboat. See also sights, p339.
Apr Shetland Folk Festival The islands are alive with the sound of music as musicians from around the globe come to play at this event. See also www.shetlandfolkfestival.com.
Mid-Oct Shetland Accordion and Fiddle Festival.

◐ Shopping

Lerwick *p339, map p340*
Ninian, 110 Commercial St, Lerwick, T01595-696655. Stocks a wide range of Shetland-made products and 'alternative' gifts.

Central Mainland *p341*
Shetland Woollen Company, next to Scalloway Castle, T01595-880243, where you can buy the famous Shetland wool and Fair Isle sweaters.

▲ Activities and tours

Lerwick and around *p339, map p340*
Shetland Wildlife Tours,T01950-422483, www.shetland-wildlife-tours.zetnet.co.uk. Offer a number of guided tours to see the islands' outstandingly rich selection of wildlife; ranging from the excellent-value £20 trip around Noss and Bressay, where, if you go at the right time of year, you are almost guaranteed to see seals, porpoises and the astounding gannetry on the spectacular cliffs of Noss' east coast, to the more upmarket week-long 'Ultimate Shetland' tour, at around £700.

Noss & Bressay Wildlife Cruises, with Bressaboats, T01595-693434, and **Shetland Sea Charters** (same phone number), also offer cruises which cost around £20.
Bressa- boats and **Shetland Wildlife Tours** both run a full-day Hermaness and Muckle Flugga Cruise which costs around £70 per person.
John Leask & Son, The Esplanade, Lerwick, T01595-693162, offers a variety of bus tours costing from around £10 up to £20 depending on the destination.
Seabirds-and-seals, T07831-217042, www.seabirds-and-seals.com, run by Jonathan Wills, trips to Noss, weather permitting, £30, £20 under 16, under 5 free.

⊜ Transport

Lerwick and around *p339, map p340*
Air
Getting to Shetland by air is expensive. From Aberdeen fares range from around £150 one way, depending on the day and time of year. A return flight from Orkney is around £186. For details of the excellent value Highland Rover Pass, see p37. Flights from several mainland airports in Scotland and England can be booked through **British Airways**, T08708-509850, or by calling **Loganair** in Lerwick, T01595-840246. Shetland's main airport is at Sumburgh, 25 miles south of Lerwick, T01950-460654. Bus services operate linking Sumburgh with Lerwick. There are direct daily flights from **Aberdeen** (4 Mon-Fri; 2 on Sat and Sun), which has frequent services to all other major British airports. There are also direct flights from **Glasgow** (daily), **Edinburgh** (daily except Sun), **London Heathrow** (daily), **Inverness** (Mon-Fri), **Orkney** (daily except Sun), **Wick** (Mon-Sat) and **Belfast** (daily except Sat). There are also international flights to and from **Bergen** and **Oslo** (Norway) on Thu and Sun.

Bus
For detailed information on all bus services, call T01595-694100 (Mon-Sat 0900-1715). There are regular daily buses (Nos 3 and 4) to and from **Sumburgh airport** which connect with flights. These buses also stop at several main sights, including **Jarlshof**, **Sandwick** (for Mousa Broch) and **St Ninian's Isle**. Bus No 2 runs to **Scalloway**

(Mon-Sat). There are also buses (daily except Sun) to **Walls**, **Sandness**, **Aith**, **Skeld**, **North Roe**, **Hillswick**, **Vidlin**, **Toft** and **Mossbank**. Buses depart from the Viking bus station.

Car

There is car hire at **Bolts Car Hire**, Toll Clock Shopping Centre, 26 North Rd, T01595-693636; **John Leask & Son**, Esplanade, T01595-693162; and **Star Rent-a-Car**, 22 Commercial Rd, T01595-692075. They have offices at Sumburgh Airport too.

Cycle hire

Grantfield Garage, North Rd, T692709, Mon-Sat 0800-1300 and 1400-1700.

Ferry

Ferry links with the UK are provided mostly by **Northlink Ferries**, T0845-6000449, www.northlinkferries .co.uk. They operate car ferries to **Lerwick** from **Aberdeen** (and to Kirkwall, Orkney). There are sailings from Aberdeen once a day Mon-Sun at 1900, the journey takes 12 hrs. Passenger fares for a seat with no accommodation cost from £43-63 return, depending on the times of year. A car and driver costs from £190-263 return. A 2-berth cabin costs £50-78 per journey. Children aged 4-16 travel for half price and under 4s go free. There are also ferries from **Norway**, **Iceland** and the **Faroe Isles**, see p33.

There are regular daily car ferries between **Lerwick** and **Bressay** (5 mins), **East Mainland** and **Whalsay** (30 mins), **North Mainland** and **Yell** (20 mins), **Yell** and **Unst** (10 mins), and **Yell** and **Fetlar** (25 mins). **Noss** can only be visited from late May to late Aug daily, except Mon and Thu, from 1000-1700. From the 'Wait here' sign overlooking Noss sound on the east side of Bressay an inflatable dinghy shuttles back and forth to Noss during the island's opening hours. The trip costs £3 return. In bad weather, call the tourist office, T01595-693434, to check if it's sailing. A postcar service runs once a day (except Sun) from Maryfield ferry terminal to Noss Sound, T01595-820200. There's a less frequent car ferry service between **East Mainland** and **Skerries** (Mon, Fri, Sat and Sun; 1½ hrs),

and **Lerwick** and **Skerries** (Tue and Thu; 2½ hrs). There's also a passenger/cargo ferry service between **West Mainland** and **Papa Stour** (Mon, Wed, Fri, Sat and Sun; 40 mins), **West Mainland** and **Foula** (Tue, Sat and alternate Thu; 2 hrs), **Scalloway** and **Foula** (alternate Thu; 3 hrs), **South Mainland** and **Fair Isle** (Tue, Sat and alternate Thu; 2½ hrs), and **Lerwick** and **Fair Isle** (alternate Thu; 4 ½ hrs). These services are operated by Shetland Council, T01595- 744866, www.shetland.gov.uk. Fares vary according the route. Bookings are also essential. Times and fares are also available from the TIC in Lerwick (see below).

Taxi

There are several taxi companies in Lerwick: **6050 Cabs**, T01595-696050; **Sheilds Taxis**, T01595-695276; and **Abbys Taxis**, T01595-696666.

Central Mainland *p341*

Tingwall Airport, T01595-840246, has flights to most of the smaller islands, see the Lerwick transport. Getting to and from the airport is straightforward, as regular buses between Lerwick and Westside (see below) stop in Tingwall. There are several daily buses (except Sun) between **Lerwick** and **Scalloway**, operated by **Shalder Coaches**, T01595-880217.

The Westside *p342*

Air Loganair, T01595-840246, operates a regular service from Lerwick to the islands of **Foula** (£43.60 return), **Fair Isle** (£76 return), **Papa Stour** (£33 return) and **Out Skerries** (£37 return). Also from Out Skerries to **Whalsay** (£21 return) and Sumburgh to **Fair Isle** (£76).
Bus There are daily buses to **Walls** from Lerwick, Mon-Sat, with **Shalder Coaches**, T01595-880217. A minibus runs to **Sandness** from **Walls** once a day (except Sun). Contact **Mr P Isbister**, T01595-809268. Ferries should be booked with **W Clark**, T01595-810460. See Lerwick transport section for details of flights and ferries to the area.

South Mainland *p343*

There are several daily buses (Mon-Sat; 2-3 on Sun) between **Lerwick**, **Sandwick** and **Sumburgh Airport**. Two buses daily (Mon-Sat) run to **Quendale** from **Lerwick**, with a change at **Channerwick junction**. There are regular daily buses from **Lerwick**, which stop at the **Sumburgh Hotel**, **Scatness** and **Grutness Pier** (for Fair Isle) en route to the airport. See the Lerwick transport section for details of flights and ferries to the area.

Fair Isle *p345*

For details of ferries and flights, see the Lerwick transport section. A day-return flight allows about 6 hrs on the island. You can also fly from **Kirkwall** on Orkney, which allows 2½ hrs on the island, T01856-872420. Ferries should be booked with J W Stout, T01595-760222.

North Mainland *p345*

Regular buses from **Lerwick** to **Brae** and **Hillswick** to the northwest, and **Toft** and **Mossbank** to the north, pass through **Voe** daily except Sun. Buses from **Lerwick** to **Hillswick** (see below) and to Toft/ Mossbank (see under Yell below) stop in **Brae**. There is a daily bus service from **Lerwick** to **Hillswick** (Mon-Sat), departing at 1710 and arriving at 1825. From there, a feeder service continues to **Eshaness** (20 mins). Contact Whites Coaches, T01806-809443.

Whalsay and Out Skerries *p346*

There are regular daily car and passenger ferries between **Laxo** and **Symbister**. To book, call T01806-566259. There are daily buses to **Laxo** and and **Vidlin** (see below) from Lerwick, run by Whites Coaches, T01595-809443.

There are ferries to the Skerries from Lerwick and also from Vidlin, about 3 miles northeast of Laxo. For bookings, call G W Henderson, T01806-515226. There are also flights from Tingwall Airport. See the Lerwick transport section for further details.

Yell, Fetlar and Unst *p347*

There are frequent car and passenger ferries from **Toft** on North Mainland to **Ulsta** on the south coast of **Yell**. It's not essential, but a good idea to book in advance, T01975-722259. Three buses daily (Mon-Fri; 2 on Sat, 1 on Sun) run between Lerwick and Toft (1 hr). There's a bus service on Yell which runs between Ulsta and Cullivoe and stops at villages in between, T01975-744214.

There are regular car and passenger ferries between **Oddsta** in the northwest of **Fetlar** and Gutcher on Yell and Belmont on Unst. There's a post car service which runs around the Fetlar from the ferry once a day on Mon, Wed and Fri, T01975-733227.

There are regular car and passenger ferries to **Belmont** on **Unst** from Gutcher on Yell. Booking is advised, T01975-722259. Also on Unst, there's an island bus service which runs a few times daily (except Sun) between **Baltasound**, **Belmont** and **Haroldswick**, T01975-711666.

For further details of ferries and flights see the Lerwick transport section above.

---

❶ Directory

Lerwick and around *p339, map p340*
Banks Bank of Scotland, **Clydesdale** and **Royal** are on Commercial St. **Lloyds TSB** is on the Esplanade. **Embassies and consulates** Denmark, Iceland, Netherlands and Sweden at Hay & Company, 66 Commercial Rd, T01595- 692533; **Finland, France, Germany** and **Norway** at Shearer Shipping Services, Garthspool, T01595-692556. **Laundry** Lerwick Laundry, 36 Market St, T01595-693043, closed Sun. Service washes only. **Medical Services** Gilbert Bain Hospital, Scalloway Rd, T01595-743000. Opposite is the **Lerwick Health Centre**, T01595-693201. **Post** Commercial St (Mon-Fri 0900-1700, Sat 0900-1200), also in Toll Clock Shopping Centre, 26 North Rd. **Travel agents** John Leask & Son, Esplanade, T01595-693162.

Background

History

Prehistory

Scotland's earliest known inhabitants are the hunter-gatherers of around 6000-5000 BC. By 2000-1500 BC these Mesolithic people had been joined by Beaker folk, so named from their distinctive pottery, and grain-cultivating Megalithic people, arriving by sea via Spain and Portugal, who were tempted to settle by a then prevailing near-Mediterranean climate. Several climate changes for the worse triggered much population movement and also, along with extensive deforestation, caused the formation of peaty soil, now characteristic of much of Scotland, by around 1000 BC.

The pottery and other artefacts of the Beaker people have been found in burial mounds or cairns, such as Maeshowe on Orkney Mainland (see page 319), and suggest a complex social structure and perhaps, more importantly, a belief in the afterlife, as do the prehistoric settlements and monuments in Caithness, Orkney, Shetland and the Outer Hebrides, notably at Skara Brae (see page 319), Stenness, and the Ring of Brodgar on Orkney Mainland, and Callanish on Lewis (see page 286). But throughout Scotland there are hundreds of standing stones and circles, a legacy of the megalithic peoples. In Aberdeenshire surveys reveal precise orientations indicating their use as observatories charting lunar cycles and eclipses. The layout of Clava Cairns, near Inverness (see page 170), bears similarities to the great temple at Newgrange in Ireland. And at Kilmartin in Argyll (see page 170), cup and ring marks, stone alignments and burial cairns, formed in a complete 'landscape temple', suggest a geomantic sophistication that has now been forgotten.

At the beginning of the first millennium BC, Bronze-Age traders from far afield were busy around the coasts. Celts arrived from Germany, bringing with them new agricultural technology and weaponry such as swords and shields, which in turn necessitated impressive earthwork defences in the form of hillforts and crannogs (see page 369) as competition for land increased. In about 200-100 BC more Celts arrived with superior iron-working skills, and consequently, more fortifications were also built. The brochs, or towers, the remains of many of which can still be seen dotted along the west coast and in the islands, date from this time (see also page 369).

The Picts and the Romans

Indigenous Iron-Age tribes inhabited most of the country and were identified by the Romans as 'Picts' – possibly meaning 'painted, or tattooed, people'. They thwarted Roman imperial ambition in Alba, the land north of the Forth and Clyde, in around AD 80, and a string of Roman military outposts along the Highland line remain from this abandoned campaign. At Fortingall near Aberfeldy, the ancient yew tree is said to mark the birthplace of Pontius Pilate, possibly the son of a Roman soldier who later found preferment in Rome. To add credence to this theory, a gravestone marked 'PP' was found.

Defensive walls built by Emperors Hadrian (circa AD 123 from the Solway Firth to the Tyne) and Antoninus (from the Clyde to the Forth circa AD 143) against the Picts inadvertently set a precedent for the eventual polarization of Scotland and England, beginning around the ninth century, out of the mass of tribal kingdoms. An endlessly disputed border led to centuries of retaliatory raids and devastation on either side.

Picts south of the Antonine wall became semi-Romanized and were known as Britons, kin to the Welsh. Their kingdom of Strathclyde, with a stronghold on Dumbarton Rock near Glasgow, once extended into Lancashire and retained a separate identity into the 11th century. The Lothians, territory of the British Gododdin, was overrun by Anglians from Northumbria. In the seventh century the Anglians challenged the Picts in Alba and were finally defeated at Dunnichen.

Meanwhile an Irish tribe, the Scots, who claimed descent from an Egyptian 357
Pharaoh's daughter, had been settling in Pictish territory in Argyll from around the
fourth century. Once in Argyll, the sons of the Scots' leader, Erc, established a
kingdom called Dalriada, sharing it between themselves under a high king at
Dunadd (see page 120). When their fellow countryman, Columba, arrived in the
sixth century on Iona, they were aided in their cause by his diplomatic skills at the
hostile Pictish court of King Brude, in Inverness. In the ninth century the Scots under
Kenneth MacAlpin took over the Picts. Although their written records were
destroyed, or falsified by the conquering Scots, they left a rich legacy of unique
sculptured stones denoting a civilized and artistic culture. When Kenneth set up at
Scone, and Alba became Scotland, the seven kingdoms of Pictland in the north and
east survived as great earldoms.

The early church
Some claim Joseph of Arimathea brought Christianity to Whithorn in Galloway, which
had been a religious centre since the first century. Around AD 397 Ninian founded a
Christian Mission in Whithorn, along eastern Mediterranean monastic lines vastly
different from the Roman model. From here he and countless missionaries such as
Kentigern, Moluag and Comgan went north to convert the Picts, as far as St Ninian's
Isle in Shetland. Their communities, oak churches and cells are remembered in
innumerable place names, wells and simple cross-marked stones, often established
on pre-Christian sacred sites.

In AD 563 Columba arrived on Iona (see page 143), where he went on to found the
Celtic Church, or the Church of the Culdees, with centres throughout Scotland, which
differed in many ways from the Church of Rome. Iona became known as the 'Cradle of
Christianity in Scotland', but the arrival of the Vikings inhibited sea travel and the
monks were driven from Iona. About this time, the Scots took over the Pictish nation
and the Columban church moved to Dunkeld, with Columba's relics transported in
the breacbannoch, or Monymusk reliquary. This was carried at Bannockburn and is
now in the Museum of Scotland in Edinburgh.

St Andrews later became the principal seat of the church, although Iona
retained special status. Communities of Culdees (one of which was at St Andrews)
survived into the 13th century, outwith the Columban and later Roman church.
These were thought to be adherents of Ninian's church, preserving elements of
pre-Christian druid religion.

A common origin for the cross symbol found on both the Pictish cross slabs and
the free standing crosses of Iona and Islay is the chi-ro, or wheeled cross, as found at
Whithorn. However, the enigmatic symbols, vivid hunting scenes and mythical beasts
of the Pictish stones found throughout Pictland are unique, and their function
remains a mystery. Another mystery is the brief flourishing in the early 13th century of an
accomplished school of sculptors around Loch Awe, in Argyll. In ancient burial grounds
throughout Knapdale are found grave slabs depicting swords, warriors, and foreign
ships, thought to mark the graves of the Knights Templar who fled here from France.

The Vikings
Pagan Norsemen in dragonships are first heard of in Argyll in AD 795, the first of
many such coastal raids of unimaginable savagery, which included ritual killings.
Colonies of monks were not spared; 68 suffered the 'red martyrdom' on Iona in 807,
and its library, 'a shop window crammed with the loot of centuries' was a magnet for
raiders. By the late ninth century Norsemen had colonized Orkney (see page 318),
and from Birsay Palace Earl Sigurd wielded power as far south as Moray. A renegade
bunch of mixed Norse and Gaelic ancestry, the Gall-Gaels, appeared in the Hebrides
and Galloway. Some of these, like chieftain Ketil Flatnose's family, became early
settlers of Iceland.

Once surrounded by aggressive Norse colonies, now also in Dublin and York, the newly formed 'Scotland' survived through a combination of fighting spirit and a network of shifting alliances with the various Norse powers. Some of these alliances were enduring. In the ninth century 'Torf' Einar, credited with introducing peat cutting, founded a dynasty from which sprang the Earls of Angus.

After the Dublin colony collapsed in 1014, a Viking kingdom of 'Man and the Sudreys' (Hebrides) filled the vacuum, and the isles continued to be ravaged by warring Norsemen. By around 1100 Norwegian king Magnus Barelegs' empire included the entire northern and western seaboard. Against this backdrop, pursuing his own interests, appears Somerled, Hebridean hero of Norse-Gaelic blood, progenitor of Clan Donald and the powerful Lordship of the Isles. In 1153 he supported a rebellion against the Scottish crown. Later, in the early 13th century, he built a series of castles around the coast, such as Sween, Tioram, Mingary and Dunstaffnage, which foiled the intermittent attempts made by the Scottish crown to assert control.

The last of the great Norse kings, Hakon, was defeated by the Scots in 1263 at Largs, with the aid of bad winter weather. Orkney and Shetland were only returned to Scotland in the 15th century. A Norse dialect was spoken there into the 18th century, and vestiges of Norwegian law still survive, as does the Viking St Magnus Cathedral in Kirkwall.

Macbeth and the battle for kingship

Macbeth, the earl-king of the vast land of Moray, rose to high kingship with popular support, reigning for a relatively long (1040-1057) and peaceful time with his queen Gruoch, grand-daughter of Kenneth III of Scots. The popular image of Macbeth as portrayed by Shakespeare is, in fact, a false one. The great bard vilified Macbeth in order to please his James VI, who claimed descent from Duncan, Macbeth's rival. But it was Duncan who was the nasty piece of work, and he was slain not at Glamis, as in the play, but on the battlefield, while invading Macbeth's territory. Duncan features in the *Orkneyinga saga*, a Viking history, as Karl Hundason, 'low-born son of the hound'.

Competition for the throne was a part of Pictish custom. A suitable 'tanist' or candidate was elected from anyone whose great-grandfather had been king, and the candidates would then fight it out: in practice survival of the fittest. This competition for the right to be king was complicated by the ancient dynastic rivalry among the Dalriadic Scots and perpetuated when they merged with the Picts under Kenneth MacAlpin. This later precipitated the Wars of Independence.

One part of Shakespeare's Macbeth which is historical fact is the Birnam Wood incident, when Malcolm, Duncan's son, and his Northumbrian allies used tree branches as camouflage to advance on Macbeth in his Dunsinnan stronghold near Perth. He was later hunted down and slain at Lumphanan by Malcolm's ally, MacDuff, Earl of Fife, and is buried on Iona.

Macbeth, the last truly Celtic king, was also one of the most able early kings. He was the first to establish and implement a fair legal system and, a firm supporter of the Celtic church, he went on pilgrimage to Rome where an Irish monk observed him liberally scattering money to the poor. Further evidence of the great disservice done to his memory by Shakespeare.

The Canmores and the Norman conquest

Macbeth's usurper, the uncouth Malcolm III, Canmore (meaning 'big head'), was an illegitimate son of Duncan and a miller's daughter. In 1067 Malcolm married Margaret, a Saxon princess born in Hungary and sister of Edgar Atheling, the English heir to the throne, who had fled north with his family to escape William the Conqueror and the Norman conquest. Margaret was a devout Catholic and was largely responsible for introducing the religious ideas of the Roman Catholic Church into Scotland, for which she was canonized in 1251. In 1072 she founded Dunfermline Abbey and introduced southern manners to the Scottish court.

Malcolm's belligerent instincts were not curbed by the influence of the saintly Margaret, however, and one of his many raids into Northumberland provoked a visit from William the Conqueror. The result was that Malcolm was forced to swear allegiance to William, an oath he didn't take too seriously, as he continued to raid England at whim, but one which would lead to a greater degree of southern interference in Scottish constitutional matters.

The Normans began to exert their influence over Scotland in many other ways. They were granted land as far as the Highland fringes, establishing a feudal system based on loyalty to the crown. The traditional patriarchal tribal culture was eroded, causing constant rebellions in the North and Galloway. The Norman successor to the Scottish throne, David I, like many of his Norman friends, had English estates, acquired through his wife. This wealth built the great Border abbeys and established the Roman church more fully. New parishes and dioceses revolutionized administration, and burghs were founded to develop international trade, attracting Flemish settlers. Society in medieval Scotland became more typically European than England or even France.

One of the depressingly familiar themes running through Scottish history has been the unwillingness of the Scots nobility to resist English ambitions towards Scotland. This has always been their Achilles heel and, in 1290, it provoked a crisis of succession, when the new child queen, Margaret, Maid of Norway, died en route from Norway. Margaret had been recognized as heiress of Scotland, the Hebrides and the Isle of Man, and the planned child marriage to the prince who would become Edward II, son of Edward I, was not to be. Following her death, no fewer than 13 rival contestants materialized. Two main factions emerged: the Balliols and Comyns against the Bruces. But instead of reverting to the traditional method of tanistry, or 'natural selection', the pusillanimous Scots nobles appealed to Edward I of England to adjudicate.

Wallace and Bruce: the Wars of Succession

Edward eventually chose John Balliol, and he was crowned king at Scone in June 1292. Balliol was anxious to prove to his fellow Scots that he was not as weak as they claimed him to be. He negotiated a defensive agreement with the French, the beginning of the Auld Alliance. He then invaded Cumberland in 1296, but in retaliation Edward attacked Berwick and slaughtered its inhabitants. The Scottish army was then defeated at Dunbar, and thereafter the castles of Edinburgh, Roxburgh, Perth and Stirling were captured.

In the same year, Balliol abdicated at Stracathro and went into exile. Edward then destroyed the great Seal of Scotland and, worse still, moved the Stone of Destiny, the traditional crowning throne for all Scottish kings, to Westminster Abbey, where it lay under the Coronation Chair for 700 years. Scotland, as a result, was left in disarray.

However, resistance found a leader in William Wallace, son of a Renfrew laird. He began a revolt against the English in 1297 and built up a substantial army. By September of that year he he had secured a small but strategic victory against English forces at Stirling Bridge. This galvanized support, and he was quickly declared 'Guardian of the Realm'. Following his defeat at Falkirk he was betrayed to Edward by one of the Scots noblemen, captured and taken south to be executed (disembowelled, then hung, drawn and quartered) in Smithfield, London, in 1305.

This stirred Robert the Bruce to take up the cause of independence. Encountering his treacherous rival, 'Red' Comyn, in a Dumfries church, he seized the initiative, stabbing him at the altar. With Comyn dead, and the support of patriotic church leaders, as well as Sir James, 'The Black Douglas', Bruce was able to consolidate his gains, and he was crowned king with full ceremony at Scone before the inevitable blow of Papal excommunication fell. But it was not only that Rome refused to recognize Bruce as king. Edward I, the self-proclaimed 'Hammer of the Scots', was not best pleased, and for the next seven years Bruce was a virtual outlaw fighting a guerrilla campaign against Edward from hiding in the west.

During this time the indomitable Edward died, and Bruce felt bold and confident enough to raid the northern counties of England as far south as Appleby and Richmond. Of his castles captured by the English, only Stirling remained to be wrested from Edward's successor, Edward II. So the scene was set for the most significant battle in Scottish history, at Bannockburn, near Stirling, in 1314, where Bruce confronted Edward II's vastly superior army. His incredible victory, aided by Angus Og of the Isles, and a number of Knights Templar recently arrived seeking sanctuary from persecution in France, has ensured him a place in the heart of every patriotic Scot.

Bannockburn brought the Scots a rare victory over their southern enemy, and led to the 'signing' of the Declaration of Arbroath, manifesto of Scotland's independence, in 1320. There followed a temporary peace with England, and Bruce was finally recognized as king by the Pope, before he died in 1329. His friend Douglas, as requested, took Bruce's heart on pilgrimage to the Holy Land, but when Douglas died en route it was returned to Melrose Abbey.

The Stewart Dynasty

From Robert the Bruce's title of 'High Steward' sprang the dynasty of Stewart kings. The early Jameses (of whom there were seven in all) all followed a tragic pattern: succeeding as infant kings, imprisoned throughout childhood, and suffering untimely deaths. James I and III were both murdered, and James II blew himself up accidentally with a cannon. Unscrupulous regents frequently took charge, and hugely powerful nobles like the house of Douglas competed both amongst themselves and against the king. James II hot-bloodedly murdered the Earl of Douglas over dinner at Stirling Castle by throwing him out of the window. The Lords of the Isles were put down by the Earl of Mar and his followers in one of the bloodiest battles of all, 'Red Harlaw' near Inverurie. Like the Douglases, they too were finally forfeited, in 1543.

However, the early Stewarts made progress towards rescuing the country from anarchy by laying the foundations for a modern state through a series of constitutional reforms. Mostly cultured and progressive, they found time to write poetry (James I wrote the King's Quair), to build Renaissance palaces, and to father sufficient illegitimate 'James Stewarts' to fill numerous ecclesiastical sinecures (James IV and V). James IV was a true Renaissance prince with a glittering court, but a self-destructive streak led to his early death – along with most of the nobility – at Flodden, in 1513, sacrificed for the long-standing 'Auld Alliance' with France.

Mary, Queen of Scots

There is no more tragic and romantic figure in Scottish history than Mary, Queen of Scots. Raised in France for safekeeping as a Catholic, her brief reign was dogged by bad luck, bad judgement and bad timing. She arrived back in Scotland in 1561, a young widow, at the height of Reformation turmoil in which both France and Catholicism were inimical. Something of a loose cannon, she was embroiled in a power struggle not helped by her disastrous choice of husbands. Implicated in the celebrated murder of the first one, her cousin, Henry Lord Darnley, she then swiftly married one of the chief suspects, the Earl of Bothwell, incurring the fury of everyone else. Imprisoned after the Battle of Carberry on the island fortress of Loch Leven, she escaped only to throw herself on the mercy of her cousin Queen Elizabeth I, who, mindful that in Catholic eyes Mary had the better claim to the English throne, locked her up at Fotheringhay for 19 years before deciding to do away with her altogether.

Reformation and the roots of Scottish education

The Reformation, converting the Catholic church to Protestant, came relatively late to Scotland and the motives were as much political as religious, though, of course, in 16th-century terms the two were inextricably linked. A pro-English Protestant faction had grown over decades, opposing the French Catholic Regent, Mary of Guise, and in

1560 a rebel parliament banned Catholic Mass, thus shattering for good the Auld Alliance with France, first formalized in 1295.

The casualties of the Reformation were countless, and included religious buildings, works of art and even whole libraries. It amounted to a complete obliteration of the past over which even today amnesia prevails, though, unlike in England, there were very few martyrs. So began 100 years of bitter struggle to establish the reformed church. Cue the Protestant exile, John Knox, a Calvinist rabble-rouser of dubious character and little diplomacy who was prone to blasting his trumpet off against the 'monstrous regiment of women,' namely Mary, Queen of Scots. Knox's skills as a colourful orator, and his self-appointed role as official historian of the Reformation, have allowed him to eclipse the real hero, Andrew Melville, who sacrificed his career of reforming university education to devote himself to the nuts and bolts of church reform.

Schooling for all as a passport to intellectual freedom and moral probity was a dream of the reformers. While grammar and song schools already existed, by the end of the 17th century most parishes had schools using the bible as textbook. The 'Dominie' (schoolmaster) was, until recently, a hugely influential community figure. Prior to the Reformation the Universities of St Andrews (1412), Glasgow (1451) and Aberdeen (1495) had been established, and Edinburgh University was added to the list in the 1580's.

James VI and the Union of Crowns

After Elizabeth's death, Mary's son became James VI of Scotland. Jacobean Scotland was vibrant and vigorously European. Religious extremists were checked by James VI, the 'Wisest fool in Christendom,' and unprecedented peace allowed Renaissance culture to blossom. But trouble was brewing. In 1603 James VI ascended to the English throne as James I, with the Union of Crowns. At this time the Scottish Parliament had so little power that James VI/I was able to write from his palace in London: "Here I sit and govern Scotland with my pen. I write and it is done." In contrast, the English parliament had begun to assume some genuine power.

Charles I and the Covenanters

James believed in the Divine Right of Kings – the God-given right of monarchs to rule their subjects. It was a belief that he passed on to his son Charles I, who succeeded in 1625 and quickly proved that he had little desire to consult parliament in either Scotland or England. Although he was born in Dunfermline, he showed little interest in Scotland and was essentially an absentee monarch. He did not even bother to come to Scotland to be crowned until 1633, calling a parliament at the same time – and then overseeing proceedings, making sure that the voting went his way.

Charles also showed little tact and diplomacy in matters ecclesiastical, and by reasserting the powers of the bishops he rode roughshod over the authority of the General Assembly of the Church of Scotland. Not surprisingly, the rumblings of revolution could soon be heard.

The struggle of the kirk (church) against the king erupted into full scale civil war, with hostility towards bishops the recurrent theme. A riot in St Giles in Edinburgh expressed public feeling and resulted in The National Covenant, signed in Edinburgh in 1638, pledging faith to 'the true religion' and affirming the authority of the powerful General Assembly of the Church of Scotland in all matters spiritual. Covenanters and king came to blows, followed by an extremist group of Presbyterians allying with the English parliament against the king, in the Solemn League and Covenant. Battle-hardened Scots flooded back from European campaigns to take up arms.

A supporter of the original Covenant, Montrose, led a spirited but doomed campaign for the king against the extremists. At Ardvreck in Assynt he was betrayed to his arch-enemy 'King Campbell', Duke of Argyll, who gave him a traitor's death in Edinburgh. After the Restoration Argyll found himself on the wrong side and met the same end on the same spot.

What's in a name?

Before Culloden and the Clearances, Highland tradition decreed that a person's loyalty lay first and foremost with their own particular clan, or family group. There were two classes of clan: clansmen of the clan who were related by blood and shared the same family name, and individuals and groups who sought and obtained the protection of the clan. This resulted in a clan having septs, or sub-groups, of different surnames. The first Scots to be organized into clans or kindreds were known in early Scots Gaelic as 'cenela', and there is documentation of three such clans in the 7th century kingdom of Dalriada, present-day Argyll. Certain features persisted from those early days until the demise of the clan system in the 18th century, in that chiefs could be elected or deposed, but there was no need for kilts or tartans. What held the clan together was a shared knowledge of history and genealogy, reinforced through the oral tradition of the bards and story-tellers. The great majority of 'clan' tartans are, in fact, a 19th century invention, inspired by the creative genious of Sir Walter Scott.

Civil War

Throughout the 17th century the dark side of religious idealism – fanaticism and paranoia – were epitomized by the 'kirk sessions': courts in which the church conducted an orgy of scapegoating and witch-hunts. Fundamental differences of ideology, constitution and culture between two countries only recently 'twinned', opened cracks in the alliance with the Parliamentarians. The following year Civil War broke out in England, with parliamentarians led by Oliver Cromwell fighting to wrest power from the king. In 1649 Charles was executed and England became a republic. The Scots, however, wanted to keep the monarchy and proclaimed his son, Charles II as their king, despite falling under Cromwell's military 'Protectorate'. Cromwell acted swiftly to bring the country under his control. In 1651 he forbade the Scots from holding their own parliament – forcing them to send representatives to Westminster instead.

Charles II and Restoration

The Commonwealth under Cromwell lasted until 1660, when Charles II was restored to the English throne. The Scottish Parliament was revived and met again in 1661. This time the Presbyterian Covenanters, who had gained such control of Parliament prior to the Commonwealth, were tamed. The Scottish Parliament was again largely run by nobles loyal to the king.

Although Charles II's was greeted with wild rejoicing, the reinstatement of the bishops once again proved problematic. Some unconsenting ministers of the church were outlawed and, finding a loyal following, especially in the southwest, they held illegal services, 'Conventicles', in the open air. Crippling fines and brutal persecution from officers of the crown, including Graham of Claverhouse, merely increased their resistance, and many died in the 'Killing Times' as martyrs to high principle.

Religion and the Monarchy

Scotland and England continued to disagree, both about the succession and about religion. Charles II's brother and successor, James VII/II, was a Roman Catholic, and in 1687 he tried to introduce more tolerant policies towards Catholics. His actions were seen as a threat to the privileged position held by the Church of England, which since the time of Henry VIII had been the official church in England, and also displeased Presbyterians in Scotland. At first the feeling was that this state of affairs wouldn't last:

James was ageing, and as both his daughters were Protestants, the Protestant
succession seemed safe. However, when his heir James Francis Edward was born and
brought up as a Catholic, a crisis was precipitated, James was ousted from the throne,
and fled ignominiously in 1689. His Protestant daughter, Mary, and her husband
William of Orange, were invited to take the throne of England, and were later reluctantly
accepted by the Scots under the terms of the Revolution Settlement.

The Darién Scheme

Although both countries shared a monarch, England was growing significantly
wealthier than Scotland. Like other European countries, it was thriving economically
through trade generated by its colonies. Scotland, however, had no colonies of its
own. To remedy this, a monopoly company was founded with the approval of the
King, modelled on the English East India Company. Wealthy Scots helped to fund it,
but much of the capital was raised in England. However, the English East India
Company exercised its considerable power to protect its monopoly. Strings were
pulled and the House of Commons soon threatened to prosecute the Scottish
company's English directors. The King, who had agreed to its establishment, now
came under pressure to oppose it. Not surprisingly, most of the English backers
withdrew and Scotland saw it as a matter of national pride to raise the starting capital
itself – a sum of £400,000, roughly half the nation's capital.

The intention of the scheme was to establish a permanent colony at Darién, on
the Panama Isthmus in Central America. Darién was a strategically important site, and
the plan was that goods sent to and from Europe would sail to Panama, be carried
overland across the isthmus, then reshipped – the new Scottish company carrying
out this lucrative work.

However, the project had not been thoroughly researched. For one thing, the land
was owned by Spain, a major world power who King William could not afford to
offend. Consequently, he ordered English colonists in the area not to help the
Scottish settlers defend their new home against the Spanish. In addition the terrain
was hostile (which was why the Spanish had not set up a similar scheme already),
and diseases like malaria and yellow fever were rife. Within months large numbers of
colonists had died. Another attempt was made and was also unsuccessful, and by
1700 the colony had been abandoned.

The consequences were far reaching. Scotland lost a vast proportion of her
wealth; national pride and confidence were dented; and the country lost faith in the
dual monarchy. The King had sided with his wealthiest subjects – and Scotland
felt betrayed.

Union of Parliaments

While Darién produced much anti-English feeling, a number of Scots began to feel that
greater co-operation with England could be economically advantageous. At around the
same time a further constitutional crisis was brewing. William of Orange had no
children and was to be succeeded by James VII/II's daughter, Anne, who was Protestant. However, Anne had no surviving children and English politicians began to search
for an heir – who had to be both Protestant and have Stuart blood. They decided on the
Hanoverians, who were descended from the daughter of James VI/I. In 1701 the English
parliament passed the Act of Settlement, ruling that on Anne's death the throne should
pass to the House of Hanover. In 1702 William died and the throne passed to Anne.

The assumption was that the Scots would follow England's lead and accept the
Hanoverian succession. But the nation was still smarting over Darién and, as Anne
turned out to have little interest in Scotland, relations were strained. The difficulties
over having two separate governments under one monarch would not go away. In 1703
the Scottish parliament passed the Act of Security which declared that on Anne's death
Scotland would take a different successor to England, unless some settlement could be

Death of the clans

Though events such as Culloden played a part in the demise of traditional clan society as central government sought to 'civilize' the lawless fringes of society, the repression of clanship had already been effected largely by the changing role of the clan elites.

By the time of Bonnie Prince Charlie's defeat at Culloden in 1746, the clan chief had virtually become a commercial landlord, no longer trustee of his people's territory but sole owner of the land, thanks to the new, legalistic definition of clanship agreed between the clan chiefs and central government.

Tensions between the state and the leading clans over authority and control of the Highlands and Islands of Scotland had grown in the wake of the Union of Crowns in 1603 and the government introduced a series of measures, known as the Statutes of Iona, in 1609 (revised 1615-16) to curb the most disruptive aspects of clanship and to educate the clan chiefs about their responsibilites as members of the Scottish landed classes.

These new laws defined the clan elite's superior position at the expense of their clansmen. Traditionally, all clansfolk considered themselves noble, due to their relationship with previous chiefs, but the Statutes limited the wearing and use of arms, lowered expectations of hospitality, restricted the deployment of military retinues and made the clan elite accountable to the Scottish legal establishment. This had particular impact in the Hebrides where further measures such as the promotion of English schooling and establishment of a Protestant Church ministry were designed to force the pace of change and assimilation.

During the course of the 17th century central government control was further extended. The notion of heritable trusteeship exercised by the clan chiefs over their clan territories gave way to the more legalistic alternative of heritable title, ending the notion of collective land rights and replacing it with sole ownership of the land by the clan elite.

The spread of agrarian capitalism further changed the nature of the clan system, as the clan elites took a more propietorial role in their dealings with their kinsfolk.Civil War, occupation by Oliver Cromwell's forces and the massive ideological and financial pressures generated by the Covenanting movement all had a devastating effect on the Scottish Gaeldom, leading to social dislocation and a polarisation of the clans.

The policies of the restored regime of Charles II only made things worse. The increased burden of high taxation and accountability for his clansmen consolidated the tendency of the clan chiefs to act in their own interests rather than as patrons and protectors. So clansmen became alienated from their elite and the role of the chief changed as head of the kindred was subordinated to his role as head of the elite.

The Jacobite Rebellions of 1715 and 1745 not only gave the British government the excuse to wipe out all traces of the clan system, and, in the process, the Gaelic language, in favour of commerce and "civility", but also provided clan leaders with an excuse to end their traditional responsibilities.

agreed upon that restored 'the honour and sovereignty of this Crown and Kingdom'. They wanted to guarantee the power of the Scottish parliament; the freedom of Scottish religion; and freedom of trade. In addition Parliament ordered people to arm themselves and prepare to fight. It was sabre rattling that the English could hardly ignore.

Although Anne signed the Act of Security, Scotland's triumph was shortlived.
England passed the Alien Act, which declared that all Scots except those resident in
England should be treated as aliens, and Scottish trade with England was to be
blocked. The Act was to remain in force until Scotland agreed to make moves towards
parliamentary union, or accepted Hanoverian succession.

There were obvious economic advantages to closer ties with England, and
Scotland was in a vulnerable position. Not only had the Darién venture weakened the
economy, the country was also suffering from several years of harvest failure which
had led to famine. Although public opinion was against union with England, it
counted for little. It certainly appealed to many in parliament. Financial inducements
were offered – and accepted, causing Robert Burns to comment later that Scotland
had been "bought and sold for English gold". The Church of Scotland, initially
suspicious of Union, withdrew its objections when it was assured that
Presbyterianism would be safeguarded. A propaganda campaign was carried out on
both sides of the border, many of the pamphlets being written by the author Daniel
Defoe. The English were assured that union would end the threat of invasion from
Scotland; the Scots assured of great economic benefits.

The people were not swayed. There were violent demonstrations in the streets,
and riots in Glasgow, Dumfries and Edinburgh. Opponents even went as far as
claiming that union would be sinful. The riots in Edinburgh were particularly violent,
causing Defoe, who was acting as a spy for the English government, to say: "A Scots
rabble is the worst of its kind. 'The Scots', he said, 'were a hardened and terrible
people'. Pro union MPs were attacked, and plans were made in Lanarkshire to raise
an army to march on Edinburgh. But public opinion was not of consequence. The
Duke of Argyll, for instance, stated that anti-union petitions were only fit to make
paper kites out of. Although some members, notably Andrew Fletcher of Saltoun,
were opposed to union, the treaty was comfortably passed by the Scottish
Parliament on 16 January 1707. It had to be signed in secret in Edinburgh to protect
politicians from the mob.

In April the act was passed in the English Parliament, and on 1 May 1707 the
Union came into effect. The Kingdoms of Scotland and England were united into
Great Britain, though Scotland preserved its separate legal system, educational
system and church. Despite the vigorous opposition, threats and bribery assured
that a bankrupt and exhausted Scotland was, in popular mythology, sold to
England for £398,085 – part compensation for Darién, part wages for the
Commissioners who closed the deal.

Jacobite rebellion and the Clearances

Rebellion against the imposition of William of Orange began in 1689, when William's
government redcoats clashed with supporters of James II (the Jacobites) at
Killiecrankie (see page 72). They were led by Graham of Claverhouse, 'Bonnie
Dundee', who was killed in the battle. In 1692 an expedition to weed out the Jacobites
in the Highlands resulted in the Glencoe massacre, which provoked unprecedented
public outcry (see page 196).

The Act of Settlement was not forgotten, and dwindling trade and increased
taxation fuelled dissatisfaction with the Union. A lively underground resistance,
aided by long-standing French connections, revolved around the Jacobite court in
exile at St Germain. Sympathy also came from English quarters.

Four attempts ensued to reinstate a Stewart monarchy, supported erratically by
France, and culminating at Culloden in 1746 (see page 170). Much support came from
north of the Tay, which was Catholic and Episcopalian country. The term 'Jacobite'
popularly denoted anti-establishment and Episcopalian. Also, pejoratively,
Highlander, and was evocative of a linguistic, social and cultural divide between
Lowlander and Highlander which had grown since the 15th century.

Highland culture and independence was not diminished after the demise of the
Lords of the Isles, hence the rise of the Campbells to enormous power as government
agents, dealing for instance with the troublesome MacGregors. Claiming descent
from Kenneth MacAlpin, the MacGregors were almost annihilated in 1603, and
outlawed until 1774. They played a significant part in the Jacobite rebellions.

Although traditionally indifferent to the monarchy, many clans came out in
support of Prince Charles (of 'Bonnie Prince Charlie' fame) in 1745. After defeat at
Culloden, savage reprisals were led by the 'Butcher' Cumberland. Rebels were
beheaded or hanged, estates confiscated, and the pipes and Highland dress
proscribed until 1782. Clansmen were enlisted into Highland regiments and 1,150
were exiled, swelling the ranks of emigrants to the colonies. Gaelic culture was
effectively expunged and Scotland as a whole suffered disgrace.

Rise and fall of Bonnie Prince Charlie

Charles Edward Stuart, the 'Young Pretender', grandson of James II, was born in Italy.
First setting foot on Scottish soil aged 23 with seven companions (the Seven Men of
Moidart), his forceful personality persuaded reluctant clan chiefs to join him in raising
the Standard for his father at Glenfinnan in 1745. Inadequately prepared government
troops under 'Johnny Cope' (of ballad fame) enabled his swift progress to Edinburgh,
where he held court at Holyrood, dazzling the populace with a grand ball. Edinburgh
was charmed but embarrassed.

With sights set on the English throne, he reached Derby. Encouraging
reports about panic in London were offset by news of advancing government troops
which prompted retreat. The pursuing redcoats were outwitted as far as Inverness,
and the ensuing bloodbath at Culloden, though Charles' only defeat, was decisive.
Fleeing to the Hebrides, he was given shelter by Flora MacDonald (see page 256)
and then spent a summer as a lone fugitive. Despite a £30,000 reward for his
capture, he managed to escape on a French frigate in 1746. Too late by just a
fortnight, 40,000 louis d'ors then arrived from France, enough to have revived the
whole campaign.

This failure has been ascribed to a fatal weakness of character and a collapse of
resolve at Derby. He ended his days a degenerate and broken man, ensuring
the complete collapse of the Jacobite cause. But Bonnie Prince Charlie is
remembered in numerous nostalgic songs, a toast to 'the King over the Water', and a
host of memorabilia.

The Enlightenment

Intellectual life flourished in late 18th-century Scotland. Embracing all the arts, its
roots lay in the philosophical nature, shaped by European thought, underlying Scots
law, education and the church. The sceptic David Hume (1711-1776) was the foremost
of a school of philosophers, best known for his *Treatise on Human Nature and Essays,
Moral and Political*. Kirkcaldy-born Adam Smith pioneered political economy in his
Wealth of Nations (1776), a powerful impetus to later political reform.

An emphasis on research and practicality in the sciences fostered inventiveness
in applied science, contributing much to industry and agriculture. James Watt
(1736-1819) developed the steam engine which powered the machinery of the
Industrial Revolution, medicine flourished at Edinburgh University, and further
generations spawned engineers and inventors like Alexander Graham Bell and John
Logie Baird, inventors of the telephone and television respectively.

Classicism was espoused in architecture and by painters like Allan Ramsay,
Raeburn and Naysmth, and gave way in literature to the Romanticism of Robert Burns
whose work profoundly influenced popular culture and notions of democracy.

Sir Walter Scott's best selling historical novels worked miracles for Scotland's
public image. It was he who stage-managed the visit of George IV, who sportingly

General Wade's Bridges

Most major roads in Scotland were planned in 1724 by George Wade. He was appointed Commander of His Majesty's forces in Scotland because of his far seeing plans for moving troops. The network began with 250 miles of roads in the Highlands, the first engineered since Roman days. Eventually Wade's roads covered over 1,000. Every summer, he deployed five hundred men to the task.

But he is best remembered for his substantial bridges, still sturdy and much used. The often painted bridge at Braemar is perhaps the best known. But his bridge at Aberfeldy spanning the Tay, Scotland's longest river, was his first. Designed by William Adam and built of local stone, it is nearly 400-miles long, with five arches. By present day prices it cost around £1 mn, which is good value over 250 years!

donned a kilt and, for modesty's sake, pink tights for the occasion. Later on, Queen Victoria was inspired to adopt a Highland home and, with the craze for 'Balmorality', the Highlands assumed a romantic glamour, becoming a fashionable resort for southern sportsmen.

Industrial revolution

Until around 1750 a large percentage of Scotland's population lived north of the Clyde and Tay. Emigration to the Lowlands or North America was already a problem, as a money economy threatened traditional ways of life. The decision of landlords to resettle their tenants on the coasts, replacing black cattle with sheep, was a disastrous economic and social experiment, with brutal evictions in some areas – although popular myth forgets that famine, disease and overpopulation were rife and many went willingly. Eventually, in 1886, crofters' rights were to some extent recognized (see also page 285).

The gap between Highland and Lowland life continued to widen as overgrazing, deforestation for industry, and deer 'forests', led to desolation in the Highlands, while improvements and drainage transformed Lowland agriculture.

At the same time industrialization was soon to bring a massive population shift. Wool, cloth and linen, long established as cottage industries, were undergoing mechanization. By 1820 mills were established in the coalfields of Lanark, Renfrew and Ayr. Linen declined in favour of cotton, spun and woven in Paisley and New Lanark, while tweed was first woven in Galashiels in 1830. Dundee substituted jute for linen and Kirkcaldy developed linoleum. Thriving on trade with America, Glasgow's population mushroomed, absorbing many from the Highlands, as well as thousands of Irish refugees from the potato famine of the 1840's. Poor housing, overcrowding and disease became chronic.

20th-century Scotland

By 1900 iron and later steel, mainly in the west, had become manufacturing mainstays, serviced by new canals, railways and roads. As well as emigrants, Scotland supplied goods to North America: locomotives, girders, bridges, textile machinery and tools. Shipyards flourished on the Clyde. The first iron steam ships were launched around 1800, although fast wooden clippers like the *Cutty Sark* were still competitive in the mid-19th century, when major shipping companies such as Cunard came to the fore. From 1880 skilled labour built steel ships for world markets as well as for the Royal Navy. Business boomed during the First World War, when political activity among skilled workers inspired by the Bolshevik revolution, led by Marxist and Scottish Nationalist John Maclean, gave rise to the myth of 'Red Clydeside'.

Post-war slump hit all industries in the 1920s, from which they never really recovered. A dangerous dependency on mining, metalworking and heavy engineering was a crucial factor in industrial decline, and the innovative spirit of the 19th century is only now re-emerging among pioneering computer software development companies in the central belt.

In a long Liberal tradition dedicated to political reform, the issue of Home Rule reared its head repeatedly after the 1880s. The first stirrings of nationalism were heard after the First World War and voiced by writers in the 1920's, such as Lewis Spence, Hugh MacDiarmid and Neil Gunn. These sentiments took political shape as the Scottish National Party (SNP) in 1934. Support grew through the 1950s and 1960s, and in 1967 the SNP was revealed as a potent political force when Winifred Ewing won the Hamilton by-election.

Nationalist fervour reached its height in the 1970s, roused by expectations that revenue from the oil and gas recently discovered in the North Sea would reverse economic decline. These hopes were dashed by oil revenues disappearing into the British Treasury at Westminster. In 1974, 11 SNP MPs were elected to Westminster – and, although many felt that this was a protest vote, Labour felt concerned. In 1979 it held a referendum on the establishment of a Scottish Assembly. Turnout was low and support was lukewarm, so no assembly was established.

Labour were soon ousted from office and the Thatcher government swept to power in 1979, bringing with them a disdain for Scotland that was to have far reaching consequences. The new Conservative government also introduced policies that did not sit easily with most Scots. When the unpopular Poll Tax, which notoriously taxed 'dukes the same as dustmen', was introduced in Scotland a year earlier than in the rest of Britain, the country felt that it was increasingly being governed by politicians who cared little for its people. Years of Tory rule served only to widen the gap between Scotland and Westminster, and it was almost inevitable that some form of devolution would follow.

The new parliament

Twenty years on, the Scots voted emphatically in favour of devolution, and the Scottish Parliament reconvened after 292 years on 12 May, 1999. The new Parliament has 129 MSPs (Members of the Scottish Parliament) who were elected by proportional representation. It has the power to pass legislation and to alter the rate of taxation. However, defence and foreign affairs are still handled by Westminster. The early years of the Parliament have not been without controversy, and its relationship with Westminster has at times proved frosty. The most pressing issue is the so-called 'West Lothian Question', the anomaly that allows Scottish MPs at Westminster to vote on issues solely affecting England, while English MPs cannot vote on solely Scottish issues. MSPs, for example, recently voted to fund personal care for the elderly in Scotland. Yet this went against the policy of the Labour government, leading to the possible scenario of Scottish Labour MPs at Westminster voting against such funding for the elderly in England. As one commentator said: "The English have been the silent and uninvited guests at the devolutionary feast". In addition, Scotland still benefits from higher spending per head than any other part of Britain – a situation which is almost certain to change in the near future.

The bold, stunning new parliamentary building, which finally opened in October, 2004, has more than its fair share of critics and was even subject to a public inquiry into why its costs increased tenfold (from an estimated £40 mn to over £400 mn), and why it opened three years later than planned. Blame was eventually apportioned to beaurocrats and politicians (so what's new?). But now, at least, it's there, fittingly overshadowing the queen's residence. Whether devolution is a step on the road to full independence, however, remains to be seen.

Culture

Architecture

Early structures: from brochs to towers

A thousand years before Stonehenge, a Neolithic architect was supervising the construction of Maes Howe (see page 319) in Orkney. Dramatically accompanied by two stone circles, its massive precision-cut stonework houses a tomb. Religious architecture evolved into the Bronze Age, and over 22 centuries of chambered tombs survive, notably at Camster and Kilmartin. Henges and stone circles, as at Cairnpapple, also abound. At Skara Brae (see page 319) is a 5,000 year-old village, a Neolithic Pompeii where stone furniture and utensils survive in rooms straight out of the 'Flintstones'.

Brochs, fortresses not dissimilar to diminutive industrial cooling towers such as at Mousa on Shetland (see page 344), appeared around 75 BC. A staircase ascended within double walls and a well often provided water for the besieged within. On duns and hilltops, timber laced forts, built from 700 BC into the Middle Ages, are sometimes found to have been fired to such an extent that stonework fused solid or vitrified. Whether this was intentional, or the result of attack, remains a mystery.

Ninth-century wheelhouses, with stone piers radiating from a central hearth, are visible at Jarlshof on Shetland, and appeared later in the Hebrides. Timber began to be used for Pictish hall houses, crannogs – lake dwellings on wooden rafts – and early churches (such as at Whithorn).

In the 11th century round towers, such as those at Brechin and Abernethy, were used for defence and as belfries by Culdee communities. Around this time the first cathedrals were built. The one at Birsay on Orkney, founded in 1050 by Earl Thorfinn, was soon replaced by another in Kirkwall commemorating the Norse St Magnus (see page 315). This was built by masons from Durham Cathedral after working at Dunfermline Abbey, also Romanesque, built for St Margaret. She also commissioned St Rule's in St Andrews, whose tall square tower suggests Northumbrian influence, echoed in those at Muthill, Dunning (in Strathearn) and Dunblane.

Abbeys and cathedrals

David I (1124-1153) granted land to Roman monastic orders and two centuries of abbey and cathedral building ensued, though mostly in the Lowlands. Years of neglect and depredations by English troops and iconoclastic reformers leave many as picturesque ruins, stripped of magnificent wood and stone carving, stained glass and wallpainting. The wallpaintings at Fowlis Easter, 15th-century collegiate churches, are a rare survivor. The ruins of Oronsay Priory and the Valerian clad cloisters of Iona's nunnery (see page 142) are the legacy of the Augustinians.

Medieval castles

Symbols of feudalism built by Norman settlers appear in the form of timber motte and bailey fortresses – timber towers with defensive earthworks – though they are found mostly south of the Forth and Clyde.

Square or oblong tower houses, with a defensive entry at first floor level, barrel vaulting and great hall, were to be an enduring form of dwelling, evolving from the 14th century into the 17th. More elaborate are L-plan and Z-plan versions, with one or two towers added at the corners to defend the entry.

Renaissance palaces

While ordinary folk lived in thatched turf and stone hovels (some into the 20th century), the cosmopolitan and cultured Stewart kings set about building new palaces and improving existing residences. The old castle at Linlithgow had emerged by 1540, a wholly residential Renaissance palace ranged around a quadrangle, which even impressed the French Mary of Guise. While the Great Hall at Stirling is a triumph of late Gothic, the later Palace block (1540-1542) reveals many Renaissance features, such as the recessed bays along the exterior with sculpted figures, and the famous carved wooden ceiling medallions, the 'Stirling Heads'.

The tower house

A minor building boom in the late 16th century was a result of church land being transferred over a long period into private hands. The old tower house formula found favour, preferred over earlier royal examples of Renaissance innovation. Everyone from nobility to minor gentry was afforded both defence against troublesome neighbours as well as gracious living. Claypotts in Dundee is a good example of 'the castle with a country house built on top', while at Craigievar (see page 93), finished as late as 1626, idiosyncratic inventiveness reaches its apogée where the roofline explodes in a flurry of fairytale turrets. Families of masons developed individual styles detectable in Aberdeenshire where many tower houses, great and small, are still inhabited or have been recently revived. Defensive features like gun loops (apertures for guns) survived less out of necessity than as status symbols, and interiors, especially timber ceilings, were vividly painted, with exuberant imagery, as at Crathes (see page 87).

16th- to 18th-century townhouses

'New towns' to promote trade were established by David I and settled with English and Flemish merchants, with a strict hierarchy of trading rights and privileges. Stone houses first replaced wood in the east coast burghs in the 16th century, setting a precedent for future urban design. Every burgh had its symbols of commerce and government at its centre: the Mercat (market) cross and the Tolbooth (town hall).

Two centuries later, the spirit of vernacular architecture had not changed dramatically. Nor had urban layout, many houses still being built gable end on to the street. The multi-storey tenement became a distinctive feature of urban living, pioneered in Edinburgh's Canongate, where buildings such as Gladstone's Land are still intact. Culross Palace and Argyll's Ludgings in Stirling are outstanding examples of grand town houses.

William Bruce and the 17th-century mansion

The country mansion was a concept pioneered by Alexander Seton, paragon of a new kind of architectural patron, at Pinkie House in Musselburgh, a daring essay in elegance and erudition. Post Restoration, William Bruce exemplifies a new concept: the architect. Introducing classical symmetry to existing buildings such as Holyrood and Thirlestane, he also designed Hopetoun in 1699-1703. The innovative oblong shape and hipped roof of Kinross are characteristic of his many other country house designs with their Anglo-Dutch interiors and plasterwork. He also revolutionized garden and landscape design. Bruce's protégé, James Smith, was a pioneer of British Palladianism. Rising from master mason to King's Master of Works and private architect, his own house, Newhailes (circa 1690), was the inspiration for countless lairds' houses, both grand and humble, built throughout Scotland in the 18th century.

Victorian Baronial

Not content with Classicism, architects raided the Gothic, Tudor, Jacobean and Scottish past, even Asia and Europe, for ideas. Late 18th-century country houses by

▪ Great Scots

For such a small country, Scotland has produced a remarkable number of intellectual geniuses who have been peculiarly influential. Many of them were great scientists, like James Clerk Maxwell, described by Einstein as the most important physicist after Newton, and who paved the way for Einstein's theory of relativity. There was also John Napier, the inventor of logarithms, Lord Kelvin, who devised the second law of thermodynamics, and James Hutton, Roderick Murchison and Charles Lyell, who together created modern geology.

In medicine, Scotland led the world. Robert Liston and James Young Simpson discovered the benefits of chloroform, and Alexander Fleming discovered penicillin, the most effective antibiotic ever devised. The number of technologists is incredible, and includes James Watt, who developed the steam engine, R W Thomson, who invented the fountain pen and pneumatic tyre, John Macadam, who gave us the metalled road, Charles Mackintosh, who invented waterproof fabric, Alexander Graham Bell, who invented the telephone, and not forgetting John Logie Baird, the father of television.

Scotland has also given the world the Bank of England, the decimal point, colour photographs, the fax machine, the photocopier, the bicycle, the bus, the thermos flask, the thermometer, the gas mask, the gravitating compass, the fridge, the grand piano, fingerprinting, Bovril, interferon, insulin, the gel-filled bra and Dolly, the cloned sheep.

Gillespie Graham were asymmetrical and castellated. Inspired by the picturesque movement, they are the harbingers of the High Victorian revival of Scottish baronial which reached its peak in the 1860s. New and unprecedented wealth found industrial tycoons and landowners beating a path to the doors of fashionable architects like Burn and Bryce, to build colossal and fantastic country seats with room for entertaining on a huge scale, and the latest in comforts – like plumbing. Some followed Queen Victoria's example at Balmoral, building extravagant Highland shooting lodges. Most eclectic of all is Mount Stuart on Bute (1870s) a neo-Gothic/Renaissance palace whose sumptuous interior even includes details from Charlemagne's tomb (see page 126).

Flamboyant design extended to monumental industrial buildings like textile mills and foundries, also railway stations, viaducts and bridges.

Glasgow's heyday: Thomson and Mackintosh

Glasgow grew phenomenally through the 19th century to become the 'Second City of the Empire'. While acres of tenements housed artisans and middle-class families, earlier Georgian suburbs were abandoned for commodious villas for the prosperous, designed by leading architects in areas like Kelvingrove. Many, especially on the south side, were designed by Alexander 'Greek' Thomson using Classical Greece and Egypt as inspiration. The best known of his public works is the Greek Revival church in St Vincent St (1858). The originality of his work is itself currently enjoying a long-overdue revival.

While Glasgow University (1870) by Gilbert Scott was inspired by medieval Flemish cloth halls, banks were modelled on Renaissance palazzos. Thomson designed Egyptian-style warehouses, and Burnet in the 1890s returned from New York to design tall, narrow-fronted buildings with steel frames. By 1896 and Charles Rennie Mackintosh's debut, Glasgow had the most exciting architecture in Europe.

The forward-looking Beaux-Arts rationalism of Burnet and company was challenged by Traditionalists reacting against aggressive modernity and advocating traditional building materials and craftsmanship, and referring back to 16th- and 17th-century vernacular architecture. Rennie Mackintosh was a leading, if independent exponent, as exemplified at Hill House in Helensburgh (see page 125), while a more mainstream Arts and Crafts aesthetic was adopted by Robert Lorimer who 'restored' many early houses, as well as designing anew.

In contrast, art deco was favoured by architects such as Glasgow's Jack Coia and, by the mid-century, Basil Spence was a champion of modernism. Traditionalism versus modernism was to become an enduring theme.

Economic depression and dramatic social change brought an urgent need for solutions to both rural depopulation, and urban overpopulation and decay. Already by the 1930s two contrasting visions of social progress were being proposed: restoration of organic unity versus modernist utopia.

Post-war to present day

A desperate need for housing resulted in massive building projects into the 1970's transforming cities. Many historic buildings were demolished and city centres gutted in an effort to remedy post-war dereliction. Edinburgh had the worst slums in Europe, where overpopulated tenements were literally collapsing. The first residential towerblocks, the epitome of the Modern Functionalist brave new world, appeared, most notoriously in Glasgow's Gorbals. Urban over-spill was re-housed in New Towns such as Cumbernauld which, although internationally acclaimed in the 1960s, was unpopular with its inhabitants.

Traditionalists meanwhile continued to advocate experiments in vernacular style, and a move was made to protect historic buildings. Most prominent of recent public buildings is the new wing of the Museum of Scotland in Edinburgh. Completed at a time of renewed national confidence and cultural awareness, historical references are foremost. The sandstone-clad exterior is reminiscent of a medieval fortress, and from within the view over the adjacent Greyfriar's church, scene of the signing of the National Covenant in 1638, has been emphasized.

With the building of the Scottish Parliament at Holyrood by Eric Miralles still under way, it is not inappropriate that its temporary home is in the Assembly Rooms of the Church of Scotland, that most democratic of institutions. The Parliament building, which was finally opened by HM The Queen on 9 October 2004, is the most important architectural structure in over 300 years in Scotland and will surely silence the critics when it opens (public inquiry notwithstanding). It is a project that has a reach far beyond this country. Like the Museum building, it reflects many aspects of Scottish history, but also, stunningly, was designed to appear to be growing organically from the surrounding landscape. It is a tragedy that its architect died, aged just 45, only a month after construction, and will never see the realisation of his ambition of creating a functioning work of art. The most extraordinary thing about the project is not the cost, nor the delay, but the fact that the Parliament looks set to prove just how much Miralles, and the team led by Benedetta Tagliabue and RMJM, the Edinburgh practice that took on the building after his death, have succeeded in achieving that ambition.

Literature

Any overview, no matter how brief, of Scotland's literary tradition must begin with a poet who has become inextricably linked with the image of Scotland and all things Scottish across the globe. **Robert Burns** was born on 25 January 1759 in Alloway, Ayrshire, in very humble surroundings, later referring to himself as 'a very poor man's but the emotions he described were so genuine that they appealed to all classes.

His poetry mainly concerned itself with life as he was living it. He was also keen to point out what he saw as a kinship between all living things, such as in his famous *To A Mouse*. The most frequently quoted lines of this poem; 'The best laid schemes o' mice an' men – Gang aft a-gley,' has entered the language, as have many sayings originated by Burns, and is a perfect summing up of his point of view. His most celebrated work, *Auld Lang Syne* expresses the joys of human companionship and is practically an anthem when friends gather to celebrate New Year around the world. His love of the companionship of friends is also a focus of *Tam O'Shanter*, which also serves as a cautionary warning against overindulgence and is a ghost story in the tradition of the mythic, while his irritation against the assumed superiority of some was put into words in *A Man's A Man For A' That*, which also returns to his theme of kinship.

The 'heav'n-taught' Ayrshire ploughman died on 21 July 1796, and was buried in St Michael's Churchyard, Dumfries. Such is his standing that his memory is celebrated every year on 25 January, his date of birth, now referred to as Burns Night.

Another writer forever associated with the Borders is **Sir Walter Scott**, who not only ruled the roost of his native Scotland but the world of literature in general. Born in 1771, the son of a wealthy Edinburgh lawyer, Scott spent much of his childhood in the Borders during which time he immersed himself in tales and ballads of Jacobites and Border heroes, giving him a passion for history which would infuse his later work. It was this material which would eventually become poems in his three volumes of *Minstrelsy Of The Scottish Border* which established his name as a literary figure. Other romantic poetic works followed, such as *The Lady Of The Lake*.

In 1811 Scott purchased Abbotsford, a farmhouse near Melrose, and during the following years developed the style which would remain his best-remembered contribution to literature, the historical novel. Collectively known as the Waverley novels, these included *Old Mortality*, *Rob Roy* and *The Heart Of Midlothian*. The original Waverley was a romantic tale of the Jacobite Rebellion of 1745 and the Highland society of the time. By 1819 Scott had moved beyond purely Scottish history and wrote Ivanhoe, set in 12th-century England. It remains his most enduring work, and he followed it with Kenilworth, Redgauntlet and The Talisman.

Scott died in ill health on 21 September 1832. His huge popularity was believed to have kept the spirit of Scotland alive and he is commemorated by the Scott Monument in Princes Street, Edinburgh.

A contemporary of Scott's, though far less well known, was **James Hogg**, the Ettrick Shepherd, born at Ettrickhall Farm in Selkirkshire in 1770. Like Burns before him, Hogg was of humble origins and did not receive a proper education he but inherited a vast store of balladry from his mother, Margaret, some of which Scott published in his *Minstrelsy Of The Scottish Border*. Like Burns, Hogg was lionised by the Edinburgh elite as another heaven-taught rustic with a flair for poetry, but that is to severely undermine his importance to the world of philosophy and psychology as well as literature. His writings dealt with the notion of a divided nature within a single individual, reflecting Hogg's own double life as rough Border shepherd and sophisticated urban intellectual. Hogg's thinking and writing reached their apotheosis is his extraordinary *The Private Memoirs and Confessions of a Justified Sinner*, published in 1824 and one of the true masterpieces of Scottish literature. There is nothing else like it and, prior to the Freudian era, nothing to match its insight into fractures of human nature.

This exploration of the dual nature of man received its quintessential expression in **Robert Louis Stevenson's** *The Strange Case of Doctor Jekyll and Mister Hyde*, published some 50 years after Hogg's death and one of the classics of horror literature. The tale was inspired by Edinburgh's notorious Deacon Brodie, a seemingly respectable pillar of the community by day and a criminal, gambler and womaniser by night.

Background Culture

Stevenson's fondness of the macabre is also stories like *The Bottle Imp* and *The Bodysnatcher*, but it is for his romantic historical adventures that he is best known. Born at 8 Howard Place, Edinburgh, on 13 November 1850, Stevenson was fond of travel which led to his employment as a writer of travel articles and essays. While staying in Braemar in 1881, Stevenson drew pirate maps of an island, and these became the basis of his tale, *Treasure Island*, published two years later. For Stevenson it was just the first of the many adventure tales, including *Kidnapped*, its sequel, *Catriona* and *The Master of Ballantrae*, he wrote before his death in Samoa on 3 December 1894. The tradition of the adventure story has continued throughout the 20th century in the works of Perth-born **John Buchan**, author of *The Thirty-Nine Steps*.

One of Stevenson's contemporaries at Edinburgh University was **Sir Arthur Conan Doyle**. Born at Picardy Place, Edinburgh, on 22 May 1859, Conan Doyle was schooled in Lancashire before returning to study medicine at Edinburgh University in 1876. It was while serving as an out-patient clerk at Edinburgh Royal Infirmary that Doyle met Doctor Joseph Bell, the man who was to influence most the creation of his famous character. "His strong point", Doyle later noted, "was diagnosis, not only of disease, but of occupation and character".

Doyle was living in London and had published several short stories and essays when memories of his former mentor, combined with a love of the detective fiction of Edgar Allan Poe, inspired him to write *A Study In Scarlet*, which first appeared in the 1887 edition of *Beeton's Christmas Annual*. Doctor Watson recounted Sherlock Holmes' unique detective skills in this, followed by a further three novels and 56 short stories, with all but *The Sign Of Four* making their initial appearance in *The Strand Magazine*.

Holmes became a phenomenon that not even Doyle could control. In fact, by 1893 he was so annoyed that his more serious literary endeavours were being neglected that he achieved what many criminals had failed to do. He killed Holmes. Following publication of *The Final Problem*, in which Holmes and his mortal foe, Professor Moriarty plunged over the Reichenbach Falls, there were public displays of grief and mourning. It was clear that the public were not going to let Holmes rest in peace, and eventually Doyle was forced to find an ingenious way of reviving the character. He penned his last Holmes story in 1927, a mere three years before his own death. Doyle's other famous character was Professor Challenger, who famously discovered the Lost World, which later inspired Steven Spielberg's *Jurassic Park*.

Another classic of literature was written by Doyle's 'older literary friend', **JM Barrie**. Born in Kirriemuir in 1860, James Matthew Barrie was the son of a weaver. Educated at Glasgow Academy and Edinburgh University, Barrie spent some years in Nottingham as a journalist before returning to Kirriemuir to write. He moved to London in 1885, and it was there that he wrote his first novel, *Better Dead*. More novels and plays followed, best known of which is *Peter Pan* and *The Lost Boys*. First published in 1904, it was written for the children of a friend, Llewelyn Davis. Barrie returned to Kirriemuir. Before his death in 1937, he bequeathed the copyright for Peter Pan to Great Ormond Street Hospital in London.

20th century

A common criticism of 19th and early 20th-century Scottish literature was the relative absence of novels dealing with the whole issue of industrialization, growing social division and immigration. Rather than explore the vexed issues of poverty, class division and the growing Celtic influence, most writers belonged to the 'Kailyard School', which presented a romantic, sentimental and completely unrealistic image of Scotland, perhaps reflecting the overwhelmingly middle-class background of novelists at that time.

The Kailyard came to be detested by a growing band of writers in the 20th century, and a new phase of realistic literature - known as the Scottish Renaissance - began in the 1920s, inspired by one of the greatest novels to emerge from Scotland,

George Douglas Brown's ground-breaking *House of the Green Shutters*. Published in 1901, the novel brings Greek tragedy to 19th-century rural Ayrshire and, more than any other, destroyed the bucolic escapism of the Kailyard School.

In the same year **James Leslie Mitchell** was born in rural Aberdeenshire. Better known by his pseudonym **Lewis Grassic Gibbon**, his novel, *Sunset song*, published in 1932 (only three years before his untimely death), has become one of the mainstays of modern Scottish literature, and taught as part of the national curriculum. It was written as the first book in the trilogy, *A Scots Quair*, which charts the life of Chris Guthrie, from late 19th century through to the 1920s. Written from the girl's perspective, it is remarkable not only for its strong evocation of this part of Scotland, but also for its uncanny emotional resonance.

Another renowned northeast writer is **Neil Gunn**, born in Dunbeath, Caithness, in 1891. His writings, which deal with the disintegration of the old Highland way of life in the wake of the Clearances and the struggle to adapt to new conditions, also convey a strong sense of place and are as important to Scottish literature and identity as Faulkner and Dostoevsky are to the USA and Russia. Amongst his best-known works is *Silver Darlings* (1939), the title of which refers to the booming herring industry. Gunn died in 1973.

For its size, Orkney has produced a disproportionate number of well-loved and much-read authors. The poet, novelist and playwright, **George Mackay Brown**, gained even more popularity after the posthumous publication of his autobiography, following his death in 1996. Like Gunn and Grassic Gibbon before him, Brown is inextricably linked to his homeland and evokes the spirit and landscapes of his beloved Orkney with a deft sensitivity, bringing a strong poetic impulse to bear on the social realism of his novels. Amongst his best is *Greenvoe*, published in 1972. **Eric Linklater** (1899-1974) is another Orcadian whose copious output of books and poems gained him international recognition. *The Dark of Summer* best represents his compelling style.

One of the most important 20th-century Scottish novelists is **Robin Jenkins**, referred to as "the Scottish Thomas Hardy". It was Jenkins who put his native city of Glasgow firmly on the literary map. His most Glaswegian of novels, *A Very Scotch Affair* (Gollancz, 1968), is still regarded as a highpoint in pre-1970s Glasgow fiction. Jenkins is also recognized as the founder of new Scottish fiction and a precursor to Kelman and Welsh as portraying an unsentimental view of Scottish life. Among his other novels are *The Cone Gatherers* (MacDonald 1955), *Fergus Lamont* (Edinburgh Canongate 1979) and *Childish Things* (Canongate 2001).

Another Glasgow literary talent of this time is **William McIlvanney**. Though he had already published two Glasgow novels in the 1960s, it was the following decade which saw him emerge as one of the city's greats. In *Laidlaw* (Hodder and Stoughton, 1977), McIlvanney explored Glasgow's seedy, criminal underbelly through the eyes of the eponymous police Detective-Inspector, who became as much a part of the city as Ian Rankin's Rebus has become a part of Edinburgh. Two subsequent crime thrillers featuring Laidlaw, *The Papers of Tony Veitch* (Hodder and Stoughton, 1983) and *Strange Loyalties* (Hodder and Stoughton, 1991) helped McIlvanney transcend the crime novel genre, in the same way that Ian Rankin has done today.

Writers, of course, are interested in people and as Ian Rankin says: "Edinburgh's dualism makes it perfect for tales of people who are not what they seem. It's a very secretive place, its residents reticent.". It was this characteristic that **Muriel Spark** captured in her classic novel *The Prime of Miss Jean Brodie* (1965). Spark was born and educated in Edinburgh, attending James Gillespie's School for Girls. The eponymous Jean Brodie teaches at a girls' school in the city in the 1930s and is the very model of respectability. She loves art and culture, and instils in her pupils the need to cultivate an air of 'composure'. She could be the stereotypical lady from the still genteel suburb of Morningside. A place where, as one writer recently said: "The nearest thing you'd find to a drugs war is two old ladies fighting over a bottle of Sanatogen in a chemist's shop." Yet Miss Jean Brodie also relishes the power she has over her pupils and has an alarming regard for the fascist teachings of Hitler and Mussolini.

If the 1970s were good for the image of Glasgow literature, then the 1980s were nothing short of earth-shattering. In 1981 **Alasdair Gray**'s totally original debut novel, *Lanark: A Life in Four Books* (Canongate, 1981), changed everything. It single-handedly raised the profile of Scottish fiction. Suddenly, the outside world stood up and took notice. Since then, Scottish writers have gone from strength to strength, most notably with **James Kelman**, a giant on the literary scene, whose brilliant fourth novel, *How Late It Was, How Late* (Secker and Warburg, 1994), won the Booker Prize. A one-time bus conductor, Kelman is a committed and uncompromising writer whose use of dialect has attracted as much criticism from the literary establishment as it has praise from fellow writers at home. When some reviewers accused him of insulting literature, he retorted that "a fine line can exist between elitism and racism. On matters concerning language and culture the distinction can sometimes cease altogether."

Kelman has revolutionized Scottish fiction by writing not just dialogue but his entire novels in his own accent, and the debt owed to him by young contemporaries is immense. Writers such as **Duncan Mclean, Alan Warner** and **Irvine Welsh** all cite Kelman as a major influence on their writing. Cairns Craig, who has written widely on the modern Scottish novel, states that Kelman's real importance lies in his original use of the English language. "He can be seen as a post-colonial writer who has displaced and reformed English in a regional mode". Among Kelman's finest is his first novel, *The Busconductor Hines* (Polygon Books, 1984) and *A Disaffection* (Secker and Warburg, 1989). Kelman's most recent work, *Translated Accounts* (Secker and Warburg, 2001) is his most 'difficult' to date. One literary critic claimed that, while it took Kelman three years to write, it might take the reader three years to understand it.

There are many other notable Glasgow novelists who began to make their name from the 1980s onwards. **Jeff Torrington**, the Linwood car-plant shop steward who was discovered by Kelman, won the Whitbread Prize for his debut novel *Swing Hammer Swing* (Secker and Warburg, 1992), which is set in the Gorbals of the late 1960s. **Janice Galloway** received much praise for her first novel, *The Trick is to Keep Breathing* (Vintage, 1990), which was on the short-list for Whitbread First Novel, and followed it up with an excellent collection of short stories, *Blood* (Secker and Warburg, 1991). Another brilliant collection of mostly Glasgow short stories is **AL Kennedy**'s *Night Geometry and the Garscadden Trains* (Edinburgh: Polygon, 1991), while *So I am Glad* (Jonathan Cape, 1995) is a Glaswegian take on Magic Realism.

The same year that Kelman's debut was published saw the death of one of Glasgow's forgotten literary sons, **Alexander Trocchi**. Born in 1925 to Italian immigrant parents, Trocchi moved to Paris where he rubbed shoulders with the likes of Samuel Beckett, William Burroughs and Alan Ginsberg and published his brilliant and influential debut novel, *Young Adam* (1954), which soon became a beat cult classic and which was recently made into a film starring Ewan MacGregor, Tilda Swinton and Peter Mullan. Trocchi's initial literary talents were soon diluted by his prodigious drug consumption and he became better known as a counter-culture icon than a literary figure. Nonetheless, he was an inspiration to a new generation of Scottish writers led by Irvine Welsh, who began publishing in magazines such as *Rebel Inc* in the early 1990s.

Scottish literature has long been known for its dark hue. Crime, poverty and social dysfunction have provided rich copy for writers in a world where detectives are never less than hardened and profanity is as prevalent as punctuation. **Irvine Welsh** whose 1994 cult novel, *Trainspotting* shone a spotlight on the city's drug-ridden underbelly and spawned an entire generation of gritty, realist writing. After a succession of hit and miss follow ups, Welsh is back to rude health with his latest, *Porno* (2002), a sequel to *Trainspotting*, which sees the return of Renton, Sick Boy, Spud and Begbie.

From the same stable is **Alan Warner**, whose bleakly humorous *Morvern Callar* not only put Oban on the literary map but also signalled the arrival of a major and serious new talent, and **Laura Hird**, whose debut novel, *Born Free* (Rebel Inc 1999), tells the tale of a dysfunctional family trying to cope with life in one of West Edinburgh's most notorious housing schemes.

One of the most successful and best-known Scottish authors is **Iain Banks**, whose shocking debut, *The Wasp Factory* (1984), heralded a new Scottish writer of considerable imagination and wit. Banks has gone on to become one of the most prolific writers around, penning his best-seller, *The Crow Road*, and many others, as well as science fiction novels written under the name **Iain M Banks**.

Perhaps the most successful current Scottish writer is Fife-born **Ian Rankin**, currently the finest exponent of so-called 'Tartan Noir'. Rankin's Inspector Rebus novels give a striking depiction of contemporary Edinburgh. Rankin lives in Edinburgh and walks around the city a lot while researching new titles. He uses real locations and gruesome historical events in his books. Rebus drinks in a real city pub, the Oxford Bar, and in one book *Set in Darkness*, Rankin uses the story of an act of cannibalism which took place in the 18th century Scottish Parliament. Like the rest of Rankin's Inspector Rebus novels, this paints a stark, honest picture of contemporary Edinburgh through the eyes of a cynical detective straight out of the Philip Marlowe school of hard cops. His other Rebus novels include *The Falls* (2001), *Black and Blue* (1998) and *A Question of Blood* (2003), his most recent. Rumour has it that, like Conan Doyle with Sherlock Holmes, Rankin is planning to get rid of Rebus.

Another fine exponent of the so-called 'tartan noir' genre is **Christopher Brookmyre**, hailed as the Scottish Carl Hiaasen and a satirist of considerable standing. His first novel, *Quite Ugly One Morning* (Little, Brown, 1996) received brickbats and blandishments in equal measure. His latest, *Be my Enemy* (Little, Brown, 2004), features the usual violence and scatological humour.

A recent addition to the Tartan Noir fold is **Louise Walsh**, whose much acclaimed debut novel, *The Cutting Room* (Canongate, 2002) explores the dark recesses of Glasgow through the eyes of a gay, middle-aged auctioneer.

Music

It could easily be argued that, in its music, Scotland produces the finest and clearest expression of its culture. All tastes are currently catered for within its music scene, reflecting the cosmopolitan nature of a country standing at the threshold of a new era with its own parliament and a deep sense of love of its history and traditions, while keeping a weather eye on the future. Although the words 'Scottish music' often conjure up images of a tartan-clad piper on a mist-covered moor, that same piper is just as likely to be found supplying stirring melodies to the decidedly nineties edge of 'drums and bass' styles heard in clubs around the country. And that's not all – the sheer number of options available to those seeking any style of music, ranging from folk to funk, from 'Tattoo' to 'T In The Park', is truly remarkable.

Yet, despite the fact a new millennium has come and gone, bringing with it so many changes in music and technology, Scotland as a nation still responds, virtually as one, to the skirl of a full set of **Highland bagpipes**. Little wonder the pipes have been a dominant instrument for centuries – in celebration, in battle, in mourning – and are never far from the traveller's notion of all things Scottish. The pipes' unique sound is enjoyed the world over, not just in Scotland – witness the large numbers of pipe bands in the USA, Canada, across Europe, Australia and New Zealand. However, perhaps the best way to enjoy the pipes is to visit the country in summer when, accompanied by a full complement of drummers, many pipe bands can be seen taking part in competitions or playing at Highland Games in the open air. It would also be totally remiss not to mention the **Edinburgh Military Tattoo**, which takes place annually during August at the world-renowned Edinburgh Festival on the esplanade of Edinburgh Castle.

Traditional Scottish music can be passionate or jocular, mournful or joyous. In the hands of a good player, few instruments compare to the violin, or **'fiddle'**. For confirmation, simply seek out the work of Ally Bain. With The Boys Of The Lough, Phil Cunningham or solo, his handling of all traditional Scottish styles is superb. The folk circuit is alive and well and, crucially, features many contemporary songwriters as well as tradionalists. As well as those already listed above, the players worth checking out include Dougie Maclean, Eric Bogle, Hamish Imlach, the Battlefield Band, Dick Gaughan and the Tannahill Weavers, all of whom have a worldwide following.

Delving a little deeper into traditional Scotland's music, you may come across Strathspey and Reel societies. These are groups of fiddlers, large or small, which are well attended across the length and breadth of Scotland. Most welcome visitors to their meetings to enjoy the music and, as most of these take place in pubs and hotels, to enjoy the local brew. On a more informal level, there are also ceilidhs which often employ the help of a 'caller' to call out the moves to beginners and experienced dancers alike. The emphasis here is on enjoyment rather than precision and it is well worth seeking out some of the finest ceilidh dance bands, such as Tayside's Benachally Ceilidh Band, featuring former members of Silly Wizard and Capercaillie, The Craigenroan Ceilidh Band, The Occasionals and Alisdair MacCuish and the Black Rose Ceilidh Band.

There are also numerous Scottish music festivals, which range from the massive **Celtic Connections** (see page 50) and the well-respected **Shetland Folk Festival**, to smaller events which feature ceilidhs and more informal jam sessions.

Folk fusion

Scottish folk music struggled hard to shake off its couthy image, no doubt fuelled by too many dreadful hogmanay TV shows and shameless shysters in kilts. Things then took a turn for the better in the 1970s with the emergence of bands such as North Uist's **Runrig**, who married Gaelic lyrics to rock stylings and even reached the UK Top 10, and **Capercaillie**, whose reworkings of traditional West Highland songs with Karen Mattheson's haunting vocals have brought them significant commercial success. These two in particular have managed to promote Gaelic language and culture as well as promoting the image of traditional music as an exciting, innovative and relevant medium. Another innovative folk fusion band are **Afrocelts**, formerly the Afro Celt Sound System, who have been at the cutting edge of Celtic/World Music for several years and strongly identified with the new age/rave scene.

Others worth checking out include **Silly Wizard** (featuring Phil Cunningham), **Salsa Celtica, The Easy Club, Mouth Music, Deaf Shepherd** and **Shooglenifty**, whose radical mixing of folk music with trance – 'acid croft' as they call it – has made a huge impact internationally. Also worth listening to are **The Peatbog Faeries**, from Skye, with their high octane fusion of Celtic folk with reggae, dub and soca, and newcomers **Pipedown**, from Edinburgh, who successfully marry the pipes with guitar, mandolin and percussion. Their debut album, The First Measure, has won many plaudits.

Scottish rock, pop and dance

The Scots may be stereotyped as a bunch of kilt-wearing, haggis-munching bagpipe players, but there's so much more to the country's musical heritage. This is the country that gave the world **Lonnie Donegan, Lulu, Donovan** and **The Incredible String Band**. Ex-Faces lead singer and sun-tanned bad-hair boy, **Rod Stewart**, though born in England, still remembers his roots and wraps himself in tartan every time Scotland (used to) qualify for a World Cup. And speaking of tartan, there's the market. The 1970s were also notable for the peerless white funk of **Average White Band**, whose singles *Pick up the Pieces* and *Let's Go round Again*, dented the charts. Glasgow-born **Sheena Easton** made it big stateside in the 1980s, while that decade was dominated by the **Eurythmics**, led by Aberdeen-born singer, **Annie Lennox** and **Dave Stewart**. Also big in the 1980s were **Simple Minds**, whose early post-punk sound and look gave no hint of their later stadium rock credentials.

One of the most influential bands of the 1980s were the **Jesus and Mary Chain**, whose distinctive feedback-drenched sound and notoriously shambolic live gigs brought them a huge cult following. Their drummer, **Bobby Gillespie** went on to form the equally influential **Primal Scream**, whose prodigious alcohol and drug consumption was only matched by the size of their egos.

The 1980s also saw the emergence of the innovative Postcard label, which launched the careers of **Orange Juice**, whose frontman **Edwyn Collins** went on to huge international solo success with A Girl Like You, Josef K, the Bluebells (featuring Lonnie Donegan's son) and the 16-year old **Roddy Frame** and his band, **Aztec Camera**. Also big in the 80s was the Celtic-influenced guitar sound of **Big Country**, fronted by former Skids man, **Stuart Adamson**, **Wet Wet Wet**, who still hold the record for the number of weeks at number one (15) with 'Love is all around', and who could forget **The Proclaimers** who released the unashamedly sentimental 'Letter from America'. Other notable Scots names from that decade include **The Cocteau Twins**, **Love & Money**, **Altered Images**, **Texas**, **Del Amitri**, **Blue Nile**, **Billy Mackenzie** and **The Associates**, **Waterboys**, **Danny Wilson**, **Goodbye Mr Mackenzie** (who featured Shirley Manson on vocals, later of Garbage). As dance began to take hold in the latter half of the decade, another Scottish band provided one of the key albums of the period, namely **Primal Scream**'s epic Screamadelica.

The 1990s were no less productive with **Bronski Beat**, **The Shamen**, **Soup Dragons**, the hugely important **Teenage Fanclub**, and the bizarre and enigmatic **KLF**, who produced one of the soundtracks of the time with their 1990 ambient classic, 'Chill Out'. The 90s also saw the arrival of **Travis**, whose 1999, 'The Man Who', brought them massive commercial success.

Behind the scenes, too, Scots have been influential, and none more so than **Alan McGee**, whose Creation label signed up the cream of talent north of the border in The Jesus and Mary Chain, Primal Scream and Teenage Fanclub (as well as a bunch of Mancunian upstarts by the name of Oasis). And Glasgow's fecund indie scene continues to produce a stream of contenders. There are established favourites like **Belle and Sebastian**, **Idlewild**, **Mogwai**, **Arab Strap**, **Idlewild**, **The Delgados**, **The Cosmic Roughrider** and **Uresei Yatsura**, and now the fabulous avant garde funk of **Franz Ferdinand**, who appear to be on the verge of world domination.

Language

Though the vast majority of Scots speak English, one ancient Scottish language which survives is Scottish Gaelic (*Gaidhlig*, pronounced 'Gallic'). Preceded by the speech of the Celts, it is now Scotland's oldest surviving language. Often referred to as the national language, it has been spoken the longest. Introduced to the country by Irish immigrants in the third and fourth centuries, its use soon spread and became well established. The language is spoken by about 60,000 people in Scotland (just over one per cent of the population). This is in the Gaidhealtachd, the Gaelic-speaking areas of the Outer Hebrides, parts of Skye and a few of the smaller Hebridean islands. Gaelic is one of the Celtic languages, which has included Irish Gaelic, Manx, Welsh, Cornish and Breton. Today only Scottish and Irish Gaelic, Welsh and Breton survive.

Argyll (which means 'coastland of the Gael') was the prime Gaelic- speaking area from the time Columba landed there in 563. Scottish Gaelic expanded greatly from the fifth century to around the 12th century and became the national language, spoken throughout most of the country with the exception of the Norse-speaking Orkney and Shetland isles. Galloway had a Gaelic community which was separated from the Highlands, but the language died out there about the 17th century.

From that point, Gaelic began a steady decline over the following centuries and, even before Union with England, was being usurped by English as more and more wealth and power passed into non-Gaelic hands. This transfer of power was given a major boost by the Reformation in the mid-16th century, as strong anti-Gaelic feeling was to the fore in the Church of Scotland.

Gaelic culture still flourished in the Highlands, but the failure of two successive Jacobite rebellions in the 18th century helped to seal its fate. In the wake of Culloden, all features of traditional Gaelic culture were proscribed and the clean sweep by government and landlords culminated in the Highland Clearances of the 19th century. The final nail in the coffin came in 1872, with the Education Act that gave no official recognition to Gaelic.

After two centuries of decline, Gaelic is now staging a comeback, thanks to financial help from government agencies and the EU which has enabled the introduction of bilingual primary and nursery schools and a massive increase in broadcasting time given to Gaelic language programmes. This renaissance can also be seen, and heard, in the fields of music and literature, and the recent return of the Scottish Parliament can surely only help to strengthen the position of Gaelic in Scottish society.

Arts and crafts

Many of the handicrafts you'll see during your visit to the highlands and Islands, such as pottery and jewellery, though undeniably beautiful, are produced by non-indigenous residents. Two traditional craft skills which have survived are weaving and knitting. Two areas where these skills reach their apotheosis are Harris and Orkney and Shetland and Fair Isle.

Knitting

Scottish sheep, particularly Orkney and Shetland, are characterized by their fine wool. The sheep of the original breed of Orkney and Shetlands, small bodied with low carcass weights, were probably a cross with Scandinavian animals. These Moorit sheep still thrive on North Ronaldsay, protected by the Rare Breeds Survival Trust. For most of the year they feed on seaweed but are moved on to grass in the lambing season. All the males and 20% of the females are horned.

Gossamer fine shawls made from Shetland wool are soft but hardwearing. Shetland wool is very loosely spun, which adds to the lightness of the finished garment. Knitted on fine needles the famed characteristic of the shawls is that they can be pulled effortlessly through a wedding ring.

Intricate patterns in bright colours characterise Fairisle knitting. When not being worked into the design, the wool in the spare colour is taken across the back of the work, caught at regular intervals in the stitches so that there are no long loops. It is important for the tension to be correct as too tight carrying of the spare wool would distort the finished garment. This double use of wool also means that Fairisle garments as well as being extremely colourful, are very warm, consisting as they do of two or more layers of wool.

Before the advent of mass produced fleece clothing and other warm store bought wear, a Scottish fisherman wore a sea jersey, sometimes known as a

Guernsey or a Gansey. Tradition says that each village had its own peculiar design. Thus, if a man were lost at sea, his jersey pattern might the only means of identification if he were not found very quickly. But in reality, every family and knitter in that family would have their own pattern. Cable stitch represented rope, hearts, anchors and waves could also be part of a design. The jerseys were made from five ply Yorkshire 'wheeling', still available from Richard Poppleton of Wakefield, Yorkshire. This is a pure wool worsted yarn, tightly spun which makes it warm and hardwearing. When unwashed, the wool would contain lanoline, the natural oil, which would make garments practically water proof too. Wool with the natural oils would be widely used for the knitting of seaboot stockings.

The jerseys are knitted in the round on four or five needles. There is no sewing together of the garment, all is done by knitting. Some jerseys have three little pearl buttons to close the neck. The sleeves are knitted from the armholes downwards and are never too long as they get wet as the seamen work with the nets. Also, when the wrist edges eventually become frayed, the knitter unravels the cuff and knits it up afresh.

The needles are long as more than 500 stitches are cast on. In order to make the work easier to handle, the right hand needle would be anchored at the waist by a 'shield', a pouch of straw or a bunch of feathers. Quite an intricate design might be woven into the shields and they fetch a good price in auctions today. Alternatively, a knitting stick or knitting goose would anchor a needle under the right arm.

It is said that Kaffe Fasset, who is now one the world's leading knitwear designers, began his career thanks to Scottish wools. He was in the north and saw for sale wools of every delicious colour. Knowing little about knitting at that point, he nevertheless bought wool of every shade and also two needles. Boarding the train from Inverness back to London, he was in a carriage with several women. Soon after they began the journey he said 'I'm sure that some of you ladies can knit?' Indeed they could. By the time that they reached London, they had shown Kaffe Fasset how to cast on and off and how to increase and decrease. This was all that was needed to start his amazingly successful career. To this day, his designs use no complicated stitches, their unique beauty derived from inspired use of vibrant or subtle colours.

Religion

The Highlands and Islands of Scotland are largely Protestant and religion, as in the rest of the country, plays a relatively small part in the lives of most people. This does not apply, however, in the Outer Hebrides, where religion plays a vitally important role in the islanders' lives, and priests and ministers still wield considerable power in the community, particularly in the Calvinist Protestant islands of North Uist, Harris and Lewis, which still strictly adhere to the creed of Sabbatariansim.

Here, Sunday is the Lord's Day and the whole community stops work. But despite the fact that the Outer Hebrides are sharply divided between the Protestant northern islands and the Roman Catholic southern islands of Benbecula, Barra and South Uist, there has been little confrontation.

The only conflict has arisen within the Presbyterian Church of Scotland (or Kirk) itself, which has split into various factions over the years. The main split had its roots in the 1712 Patronage act, which allowed a landlord the right to choose the parish minister, thus breaking the fundamental rule of the church ministers and elders. In 1843, in protest at the state's refusal to change the Patronage act, a third of Scottish ministers walked out of the established Church of Scotland to form the Free Church of Scotland – the so-called 1843 Disruption. In 1893 a second disruption occurred, this time within the Free Church of Scotland itself when a minority seceded and formed the Free Presbyterian Church. Now it becomes really confusing. In 1900 most congregations in the Free Church of Scotland and the United Presbyterian Church joined together to form the United Free Church of Scotland. However, a large proportion of people in Lewis were opposed to this union and the largest congregations decided to continue as the Free Church of Scotland, or 'Wee Frees' as they are popularly known. Later, in 1929, the United Free Church joined with the Established Church of Scotland. And it doesn't end there. As recently as 1988, the Wee Frees split over the threatened expulsion of a minister who attended a requiem mass during the Catholic funeral of a friend. He and his supporters have since formed the breakaway Associated Presbyterian Churches.

Now all this may seem pedantic in the extreme to many outsiders, but to the people of Lewis, Harris and North Uist (and also much of Skye and Raasay), the Free Church is of enormous social and cultural, as well as spiritual, importance. Not only did it organize resistance to the infamous Highland Clearances but it has also done the most to preserve the Gaelic language.

Land and environment

Geographically, Scotland can be divided into three areas: Southern Uplands, Central Lowlands and Highlands. The Southern Uplands is the area south from Edinburgh and Glasgow to the English border, and consists of a series of hill ranges sandwiched between fertile coastal plains. The Central Lowlands, the triangle formed by Edinburgh, Glasgow and Dundee to the north, contains most of the population, and is the country's industrial heartland. The Highland Boundary Fault is the geographical division running northeast from Helensburgh (west of Glasgow) to Stonehaven (south of Aberdeen). To the north of this line lie the Highlands and Islands, which comprise roughly two-thirds of the country. This is an area of high mountain ranges punctuated by steep-sided valleys, or glens, and deep lochs. The northwest coastline is indented by numerous steep, fjord-like sea lochs, and offshore are some 790 islands, 130 of which are inhabited. These are grouped into the Outer Hebrides, or Western Isles, the Inner Hebrides, and, to the north, the Orkney and Shetland Islands.

Much of Scotland was long ago covered by the Caledonian forest, which consisted mainly of the Scots pine, along with oak, birch and other hardwoods. Over the centuries, the trees were felled for timber and to accommodate livestock, and now only around one per cent of this ancient forest still remains. Small pockets of native Scots pine can be found scattered around the Highlands, at Rothiemurchus, near Aviemore, at Glen Tanar, near Ballater in Deeside, around Braemar, at Strathyre near Callander and Achray Forest near Aberfoyle, at Rowardennan on Loch Lomond, in Glen Affric and on the shores of Loch Maree.

Several decades ago the Forestry Commission, a government body, set about fencing off large areas of moorland for reforestation. Now much of the landscape is dominated by regimented rows of fast-growing sitka spruce, which are not particularly attractive. There are also serious concerns over the damage coniferization causes to the unique habitats in many areas, in particular to large areas of bogland in the 'Flow Country' of Caithness and Sutherland, a unique natural environment as precious as any tropical rainforest. This and other endangered habitats are registered as an SSSI – a Site of Special Scientific Interest – but this has proved less than adequate. The only real guarantee of protection is for such areas to be owned or managed by environmental organizations such as Scottish Natural Heritage, the Scottish Wildlife Trust, the Royal Society for the

Protection of Birds, the Woodland Trust and John Muir Trust (see page 60).

In recognition of this, the new Scottish Parliament produced a draft bill to establish a series of national parks, based on advice from Scottish National Heritage. This is aimed to reduce the conflict between social and economic development and long-term protection of the natural and cultural environment. The first new park to open, in April 2002, was Loch Lomond and Trossachs National Park, and the other was Cairngorms National Park, which opened in early 2003.

Wildlife

The Scottish countryside plays host to some of Europe's rarest and most celebrated wildlife, though much of it has disappeared over the centuries. The ancient Caledonian forests were once home to wildlife that we now identify with other far-flung countries: including the brown bear, lynx, wolf, reindeer and beaver to name but a few. Small numbers of beaver and reindeer have been reintroduced in recent years and there is the ongoing controversial debate regarding the reintroduction of the wolf.

Coastal wildlife

Scotland boasts over 13,000 km of the British coastline. As a result seabirds and some sea mammals abound and both the resident and visitor list is impressive. Some of the more notable avian 'stars' include the eider duck, most famous for its feather 'down' which the birds use to keep their eggs warm and we use in quilts to keep us cosy. Both sexes are about the size of a small goose yet are quite different in appearance. The male, for courting purposes, looks very regal, being predominantly black and white with lime green cheeks and a pastel pink breast, while the female, for the purposes of camouflage, is a dull brown colour. During the breeding season on the coast fringes and off-shore islands it is not unusual to encounter the females at very close quarters while she is on the nest. They are very confident about their camouflage and will stay perfectly still even when you are within a few feet.

During the winter the firths (large coastal inlets) and estuaries play host to large numbers of predominantly arctic seaduck including the beautiful jet black common and velvet scoter, the scaup (very similar to the common tufted duck) and the spectacular and rare king eider. Waders too are present in large numbers around the coast and again, especially in winter. Knot, dunlin and turnstones are also common along the beaches and mudflats. During the summer perhaps the most commonly seen coastal wader is the oystercatcher which is black and white with a conspicuous orange beak. While around estuaries keep your ears open for the high pitched call of the curlew.

These estuaries, along with many of the offshore islands also play host to Scotland's two resident seal species, the common seal and the grey seal. Although the two are at long range quite hard to distinguish, the common is generally lighter in colour and smaller with more delicate dog-like facial features. The common seal breeds in summer and generally tend to be independent of one another, while the grey breeds in mid-winter in rookeries predominantly on offshore islands. Both species can be seen throughout the year with the common most common on the west coast and the grey on the east.

Dolphins, porpoises, basking sharks and some species of whale can also been seen regularly around the Scottish coastline. The resident pod of bottlenose dolphins in the Moray Firth is best viewed between May and September, while minke whales, basking sharks and even orca (killer whales) are not entirely unusual off the west coast and Western Isles.

The many offshore islands scattered around the Scottish coast provide sanctuary to a wide variety of seabirds, often in huge numbers. These islands are important both nationally and internationally for many breeding species and as such are designated National Nature Reserves (NNRs) and Sites of Special Scientific Interest (SSSIs). The most noted are the islands around Orkney and Shetland and on the west coast Handa Island near Cape Wrath

To visit these islands and the massive seabird colonies that inhabit their towering cliffs in the breeding season (April to September) is an unforgettable experience. Classic residents include members of the auk family, including the guillemot, razorbill and the puffin, without doubt the most colourful and charming seabird in Britain. Unlike the hardy guillemots and razorbills that nest precariously on the cliff ledges, the puffin nests in burrows, which they excavate with razor-sharp claws. After the eggs are incubated and the eggs hatch the chicks are raised in the burrow and this is the best time to view the birds.

The best places to see puffin and the seabird colonies are in Orkney and Shetland, or Handa Island in the far north west of the country, near Cape Wrath. Several other species inhabit other neighbourhoods within these seabird cities including the Manx shearwater and fulmar, which are both specialist pelagic petrels. The fulmar is worth special mention because it has the admirable habit of vomiting all over you should you stray too close. One of the most famous seabirds around Scotland is the large and very stern looking gannet which is black and white in colour with a 2 m wing span and an ochre coloured head. Its most famous international breeding site is the Bass Rock in the Firth of Forth (see *Footprint Scotland* for more details) where over 50,000 pairs breed annually. So famous is the Bass that it lends its name to the Northern or Atlantic gannet's official scientific name, Morus bassanus.

Other more unusual rare and resident species you might be very lucky to see on the coast is the white-tailed sea eagle around the Western Isles or the beautiful snowy owl on Fetlar in Shetland. The sea eagle used to be fairly common but was wiped out in Scotland by early last century. Now, after a successful reintroduction on the Isle of Rùm on the west coast, several pairs breed. The specific nesting locations are understandably keep secret but you may still see one on a fishing foray over its huge territorial range. Like the golden eagle its sheer size is an instant give away while the tail of course distinguishes it from its more common relative. The snowy owl is rarely seen outside Shetland and of course is instantly recognizable.

Some islands around the coast of Scotland are also well known internationally as migratory stopovers for vagrant species. Fair Isle between Shetland and Orkney is particularly important and well known often providing life saving shelter in spring and autumn storms for such exotically named species as the jack snipe or black redstart.

Rivers, lochs and wetlands

Otters are more commonly found along riverbanks in Europe but in Scotland are best observed on the tidal fringes searching for seafood. The Isle of Skye and Shetland are the best venues. The otter was for decades almost hunted to extinction in Britain but is now fully protected. It is often confused with the feral mink or ferret, which is far more commonly seen in the countryside throughout Britain.

Loch Garten in Speyside near Aviemore is the home to the Osprey and the venue of one of Scotland's most successful avian conservation stories. After being absent for many years the Loch Garten breeding site became a catalyst for what is now the successful national comeback of the species. You can view the birds nesting in summer at Loch Garten but if you are really lucky you will see one catching fish in a spectacular display of aerial acrobatics on the lochs and rivers of the region. The rivers Tay and Spey are world famous for their salmon. Some of the hydroelectric dams in Scotland have fish ladders where you can observe this archetype of inherent motivation as the fish struggle relentlessly upstream to breed. Pitlochry is one such venue.

Although not endemic to Scotland one of the most beautiful bird species you may encounter on the more remote lochs are divers (or loons as they are called in North America) – most commonly the red throated diver, the rarer black throated diver and occasionally the largest, the great northern diver. All three can be seen on the coast in winter. The best time to see these birds is in their superb summer breeding attire but it is perhaps their call that is most memorable. The haunting cry of the great northern or black throat that carries for miles across the moors and wide-open spaces is quite simply unforgettable. Red throated divers breed on lochs throughout the highlands while black throated divers can be found in the far north, especially round Lochinver and in Caithness. Also both rare and beautiful is the delicate black neck grebe which supports a headpiece in the breeding season to beat any human fashion label at the annual Royal Ascot horse races. Loch Ruthven near Inverness is an excellent place to observe this particular avian fashion parade.

For any Scot who is in tune with the countryside the first calls of greylag and pink footed geese are a sure sign that summer has ended. Huge numbers winter in Scotland especially in the central lowlands and parts of the west coast. Similarly, barnacle geese invade the Solway Firth in the south in their thousands. The V-shaped flying formations and constant honking of course make the type of bird if not the actual species instantly identifiable. Of course no mention of Scotland's waterways and wildlife would be complete without mention of Scotland's most famous aquatic creature – the Loch Ness Monster. Nessie does of course exist but like the wild haggis is very very shy and elusive.

Forests and lowlands

As opposed to its introduced North American cousin the native red squirrel is a delicate and shy creature. Their beautiful rustic colours can often herald their occasional public appearance in the forests of the Central Highlands, especially Speyside. If it were not for the grey squirrel pushing them out of former habitats and man destroying the habitat itself they could once again be classed as common. Even rarer is the elusive and rarely seen wildcat and pine marten. The wildcat is larger than the domestic 'moggy' and has a much courser, thicker fur coat, piercing, wild eyes and untamed attitude. Over the years the feral cat and wild variety have interbred and now it is very unusual to see the species in its rawest form. The pine marten is about the size of a mink and is occasionally seen in forested areas of more remote and unpopulated areas of the country.

The forests and lowlands are also home to some familiar bird species. The quite bizarre and wonderfully named capercaille (pronounced 'capper-kay-lee') is a member of the grouse family and the largest of the three species found in Scotland. It is the handsome black male that is most often seen deep in the forests, most commonly crossing forest paths and fire breaks while guarding his extensive territory. This is necessary not so much as protection from predators, but invasion by other highly sexed males intent on one thing and one thing only. An encounter and subsequent dispute results in audible threats and much puffing up of the plumage. Even more spectacular are the fights between the capercaillie's smaller relative the black grouse. Their version of a 'boxing ring' is called a 'lek' and can be the sight of spectacular displays of male hormonal overload.

Other unusual birds of the forest includes the crossbill, which is about the size of a overweight canary and has a beak that intersects, which it uses to expertly extract pine seeds from the cone. Crossbills can regularly be seen in the central highlands with National Nature Reserves like Loch Garten being a good bet. While in the Loch Garten area you may also see the delicate little crested tit, which although not endemic, only breeds in this part of Scotland. In much of western Scotland the hooded crow, or 'hoodie' replaces the common crow found throughout Britain. The hooded crow can be distinguished by the diagnostic grey patches on its plumage.

Britain's only venomous snake the adder is relatively common throughout Scotland and is mainly found on open ground covered in bracken or heather. They are rarely seen and generally keep well out of your way, though you may be lucky enough to encounter one sunning itself on rocks early in the day.

Highlands

The red deer are as much an environmental problem as a feature of the Scottish landscape. They now number over 300,000 and in the absence of natural predators are essentially out of control in the central highlands. Extensive management through hunting and culling has so far failed to keep numbers in check. In summer they remain in herds on high ground and, despite their size, they are actually very hard to spot. In winter however you can often see them in large numbers on lower ground in the glens and beside the main roads. During the 'rut' in autumn the males (stags) become highly aggressive and use their impressive antlers in fierce combat to win the females (hinds). This fighting is often accompanied by a loud roar that carries for miles. Other deer species seen commonly in Scotland in the Highlands, Central Lowlands and Borders are the roe, sitka and fallow deer.

Another famous Highlands inhabitant is the golden eagle. After periods of decline they are now present in relatively healthy numbers especially in the central and western highlands but are not exactly widespread or commonly seen. To the uninitiated the eagle is very often confused with the common buzzard, though the latter is actually much smaller. The golden eagle also dwarfs the large and menacing raven that is also a regular sight in central and western Scotland-usually accompanied by a raucous, 'throaty' call. Another regal and masterful lord of the highland skies is the peregrine falcon. In both flight and appearance they are the epitome of power. To watch a peregrine hunting other birds in flight is to witness one of the most spectacular acts in nature.

Two quite common masters of camouflage on the mountain slopes are the mountain hare and the ptarmigan, a bird similar in size and appearance to a red grouse. Both go through an incredible phase of moult from dark browns in summer to pure white in winter. They do this of course in order to blend in with their surroundings and avoid predators like the peregrine. Any time spent around the ski-fields in summer or winter should reveal one or both species.

Other rarer birds found breeding on the inhospitable high tops, especially in the Cairngorms, are the dotterel, a small attractive wading bird and the sparrow sized snow bunting. The snow bunting, like the mountain hare and ptarmigan, assumes a predominantly white plumage in summer. Few breed in Scotland as it is predominantly a winter visitor to the coast. On the lower slopes the red grouse is a common sight. Vast tracks of land are maintained to provide the ideal breeding habitat for this 'game bird' which are then hunted for sport.

Books → *See also page 372.*

History, politics and culture

Daiches, D, *The New Companion to Scottish Culture* (Polygon, 1993). A comprehensive guide to Scottish culture.

Kennedy, L, *In Bed with an Elephant* (Corgi, 1996). An entertaining account of Scotland's often turbulent relationship with England.

Lynch, M, *Scotland A New History* (Pimlico, 1999). A worthy new contender.

Macdonald, M, *Scottish Art* (Thames & Hudson, 2000). Good overview.

Magnusson, M, *Scotland the Story of a Nation* (Harper Collins, 2000) is a mighty tome, and after reading it you're unlikely to pass on any questions on Scottish history.

Nairn, T, *The Break-up of Britain* (Common Ground pub, 2003)Gives a radical perspective of Scottish independence. *Scotland's Story* (Fontana) is also insightful.

Prebble, J. For a more emotive and subjective view of highland history, try *1,000 years of Scotland's History, The Lion in the North, Glen Coe, Culloden* and *The Highland Clearances* (Penguin).

Smout, T. C, *A History of the Scottish People* (1560-1830) (Fontana, 1998) and *A Century of the Scottish People* (1830-1950) (Fontana, 1997). The best general overview of Scottish social history.

Tranter, N, *The Story of Scotland* (Neil Wilson publishing, 1992).

Biographies, travelogues & memoirs

Bathurst, B, *The Lighthouse Stevensons* (HarperCollins, 1999). A well-documented account of the fascinating story of Robert Louis Stevenson's family, who built many of the lighthouses around Scotland's coast.

Boswell and Johnson, S, *A Journey to the Western Islands of Scotland* (UK Penguin). If you only read one travelogue, make it this.

Crumley, J, *A High and Lonely Place and Gulfs of Blue Air – A Highland Journey* (Mainstream). Decent travelogue.

Duff, D (ed), *Queen Victoria's Highland Journal* (UK Hamlyn). Another interesting read.

Elizabeth Grant of Rothiemurchus, *Memoirs of a Highland Lady* (Canongate).

Fraser, A, *Mary, Queen of Scots* (UK Mandarin). Excellent biography.

Maclean, F *Bonnie Prince Charlie* (Canongate). Excellent biography.

Maxwell, G, *The Ring of Bright Water* (Penguin). One of the best known Highland memoirs, a tale of otters and other wildlife set in Glenelg.

Miller, K, *Electric Shepherd: A Likeness of James Hogg* (Faber & Faber, 2003). For a fascinating study of the life and works of one of Scotland's most enigmatic literary figures look no further.

Morton, H.V, In Search of Scotland (Methuen). Another notable travelogue.

Skinner Sawyers, J (ed), *The Road North - 300 years of Classic Scottish Travel Writing*, (The Inn Pinn, 2000). A selection of the best, including **Daniel Defoe**, **Edwin Muir** and **Jan Morris**.

Tomkies, M, *A Last Wild Place* by naturalist Mike Tomkies is a fascinating account of life in a remote West Highland croft.

Outdoor activities

Walking

There are numerous walking guides available and this is only the briefest of selections. Two of the best are *Great Walks Scotland* by **Hamish Brown**, and *100 Best Routes on Scottish Mountains* by **Ralph Storer**.

Two helpful hillwalking guides published by the **Scottish Mountaineering Trust** are *The Munros* by **Donald Bennett** and *The Corbetts* by **Scott Johnstone et al**. The SMT also publishes a range of district guides listing mainly high level walks. Also useful are *The Munro Almanac* and *The Corbett Almanac* by **Cameron McNeish**.

Those wishing to attempt one of the long-distance walks should read *The West Highland Way* or *The Southern Upland Way*, both highly informative guides by **Roger Smith** (HM Stationery Office).

An excellent guide for both walkers and mountain bikers is **Ralph Storer's** *Exploring Scottish Hill Tracks*.

Other recommended cycling guides include: *The Scottish Cycling Guide* by **Brendan Walsh**; *101 Bike Routes in Scotland* by **Henry Henniker** (Mainstream); *Cycling in Scotland* by **John Hancox** (Collins Pocket Reference, Harper Collins); and *Cycling in Great Britain: Bicycle Touring Adventures in England, Scotland and Wales* by **Tim Hughes & Jo Cleary** (Bicycle Books, US).

Birdwatching

A good birdwatching guide is *Where to Watch Birds in Scotland* by **Michael Madders and Julia Welstead** (UK Christopher Helm).

Miscellaneous

Black, G, *The Surnames of Scotland: their origin, meaning and history* (New York, 1940). These books are available in most public libraries.

HM Stationary Office *Exploring Scotland's Heritage* is a beautifully- illustrated series of books on historic buildings and archaeological sites in different regions of Scotland.

Jackson, M, *The Malt Whisky Companion* (UK Dorling Kindersley). Those wishing to bone up on their malt whiskies should refer to this.

MacDonald, Lady C, *The Claire MacDonald Cookbook* (UK Bantam). An excellent Scottish recipe book by Lady Claire, who runs a hotel on Skye.

Sinclair, C, *Tracing your Ancestors* (HM Stationery Office). For more detailed genealogical study.

Stuart, M and Balfour Paul, J, *Scottish Family History* (Edinburgh, 1930). For a comprehensive history of Scottish clans and families. In most public libraries.

Poetry

Crawford, R and Imlah, M (eds) *The New Penguin Book of Scottish Verse*, (2000). An excellent overview.

Crichton-Smith, I *Collected Poems*. Bi-lingual (English and Gaelic) poet writing passionately about life in the Outer Hebrides.

McCaig, N *Selected Poems*. Challenging poet whose work is deeply rooted in the landscapes of the Highlands.

McDiarmid, H, *Selected Poems*. A huge figure on the Scottish literary landscape. His nationalist views and use of Scots have been as influential as they have been provocative.

Morgan, E, *New Selected Poems*. Scotland's new poet laureate is one of the country's foremost living writers and both entertaining and experimental.

Muir, E, *Collected Poems*. Recognized as one of the most distinguished poets of the last century, received an MBE in 1953 for his significant contribution to Scottish poetry.

Paterson, D, *Landing Light*. This is the latest work of a genuinely innovative new voice in Scottish poetry.

Footnotes

Glossary

Scottish terms

Ben	hill or mountain
Bothy	farm cottage/mountain hut
Brae	hill or slope
Brig	bridge
Burn	brook
Ceilidh	social gathering involving singing, dancing and drinking
Clan	tribe bearing same surname
Clearances	evictions of tenant crofters by landowners in the Highlands in late 18th and early 19th centuries in order to create space for more profitable sheep
Crannog	Celtic lake or bog dwelling
Croft	small plot of farmland and house
Dram	small measure of whisky
Elder	office bearer in Presbyterian church
Factor	manager of estate/landlord
Firth	estuary
Ghillie	personal hunting or fishing guide
Howff	traditional pub/haunt
Kirk	church
Lade	mill stream
Laird	landowner/squire
Mac/Mc	prefix in Scottish surnames denoting 'son of'
Machair	sandy, grassy coastal land used for grazing
Manse	vicarage
Merse	saltmarsh
Munro	mountain over 3,000 ft
Provost	mayor
Sassenach	literally 'Saxon', ie English
Sept	branch of clan
Wee Frees	Followers of the Free Church of Scotland
Wynd	lane
Yett	gate or door

Useful Gaelic

abhainn	river
aonach	ridge
aros	dwelling
ault, allt	stream
bagh	bay
bal, baile	town or village
ban, beinn	mountain
bealach	mountain pass
beg, beag	small
cairn	heap of stones marking a spot
camas	bay or harbour
cnoc, knock	hill
coll or coille	wood or forest
corran	point jutting into the sea
corrie, coire	hollow in mountainside or whirlpool
craig, from creag	rock, crag
drum	ridge
dubh	black
dun	fort
eas	waterfall
eilean	island
fin or fionn	white
gare, gear	short
garv, garbh	rough
geodha	cove
glen, glean	valley
inch, innis	meadow or island
inver, inbhir	river mouth
kyle, caolas	narrow strait
liath	grey
loch	lake
more, mór	great, large
rannoch	bracken
ross, rubha	promontory
sgeir	sea rock
sgurr	sharp point
strath	wide valley
tarbet, tairbeart	isthmus
tigh	house
tir, tyre	land
torr	hill, castle
tràigh	shore
uig	shelter
uige	water

Index

Footnotes Index

Map index

Map symbols

Administration

□ Capital city
○ Other city/town
⌇ International border
⌇ Regional border
⌇ Disputed border

Roads and travel

━━ Motorway
━━ Main road
━━ Minor road
- - - 4WD track
······ Footpath
✛▬ Railway with station
✈ Airport
🚌 Bus station
Ⓜ Metro station
- - - Cable car
┼┼┼┼ Funicular
⛴ Ferry

Water features

≋ River, canal
⬭ Lake, ocean
⌄⌄⌄ Seasonal marshland
▨ Beach, sand bank
💧 Waterfall

Topographical features

⬭ Contours (approx)
⛰ Mountain
⛰ Volcano
⇌ Mountain pass
⎍⎍⎍ Escarpment
⎍⎍⎍ Gorge
⎍⎍ Glacier
▨ Salt flat
🪨 Rocks

Cities and towns

═══ Main through route
═══ Main street
═══ Minor street
▭▭▭ Pedestrianized street
Σ ⊂ Tunnel
→ One way street

|||||||| Steps
⇌ Bridge
▬▬▬ Fortified wall
▨ Park, garden, stadium
● Sleeping
🍴 Eating
🍷 Bars & clubs
🎭 Entertainment
▢ Building
▪ Sight
⛪ Cathedral, church
🏯 Chinese temple
🏛 Hindu temple
🜊 Meru
🕌 Mosque
⛩ Stupa
✡ Synagogue
ℹ Tourist office
🏛 Museum
✉ Post office
🅟 Police
Ⓢ Bank
@ Internet
♪ Telephone
☎ Market
✚ Hospital
🅿 Parking
🛢 Petrol
⛳ Golf
Ⓐ Detail map
◀Ⓐ Related map

Other symbols

∴ Archaeological site
♦ National park, wildlife reserve
🌿 Viewing point
▲ Campsite
⌂ Refuge, lodge
🏰 Castle
🤿 Diving
🌳🌲🌴 Deciduous/coniferous/palm trees
⌂ Hide
🌿 Vineyard
⛺ Distillery
⚓ Shipwreck
✕ Historic battlefield

Acknowledgements

Alan would like to thank all those who helped in the research and writing of this guidebook. Norma Rowlerson, Rebecca Ford, Nigel Easton, Duncan Lindsay and Frank Nicholas all made valuable contributions. Thanks to Suzy Kennard for writing the History and Architecture sections and Darroch Donald for writing Wildlife.

Thanks also go to the staff of the many local and regional tourist offices for their invaluable advice and assistance, to Franciose Van Buuren at the National Trust for Scotland, Deborah Brown at Caledonian MacBrayne and to the staff at Historic Scotland.

Thanks also to the many travellers, and Scottish residents, who wrote in with their helpful comments, tips and suggestions. It's nice to be appreciated.

A special thank you to all at Footprint, especially Laura Dixon for all her hard work and for pushing me those extra few yards.

As always, this book is dedicated to Philippa, for her unstinting love and support and endless cups of coffee, and to Rosa and Ruben, two wonderful children who coped much better with the rough Hebridean seas than their dad.

Credits

Footprint credits
Editor: Laura Dixon
Map editor: Sarah Sorensen

Publisher: Patrick Dawson
Editorial: Sophie Blacksell, Sarah Thorowgood, Claire Boobbyer, Felicity Laughton, Nicola Jones, Angus Dawson.
Cartography: Robert Lunn, Claire Benison, Kevin Feeney, Thom Wickes, Esther Monzon.
Series development: Rachel Fielding
Design: Mytton Williams and Rosemary Dawson (brand)
Advertising: Debbie Wylde
Finance and administration:
Sharon Hughes, Elizabeth Taylor, Lindsay Dytham, Alice Cooke.

Photography credits
Front and back cover: Alamy
Inside colour section: Alamy

Print
Manufactured in Italy by LegoPrint
Pulp from sustainable forests

Footprint feedback
We try as hard as we can to make each Footprint guide as up to date as possible but, of course, things always change. If you want to let us know about your experiences – good, bad or ugly – then don't delay, go to **www.footprintbooks.com** and send in your comments.

Ordnance Survey®

This product includes mapping data licensed from Ordnance Survey® with the permission of the Controller of Her Majesty's Stationery Office. © Crown Copyright. All rights reserved. Licence No. 100027877.

Publishing information
Footprint Scotland Highlands and Islands
2nd edition
© Footprint Handbooks Ltd
January 2005

ISBN 1 904 777 279
CIP DATA: A catalogue record for this book is available from the British Library

® Footprint Handbooks and the Footprint mark are a registered trademark of Footprint Handbooks Ltd

Published by Footprint
6 Riverside Court
Lower Bristol Road
Bath BA2 3DZ, UK
T +44 (0)1225 469141
F +44 (0)1225 469461
discover@footprintbooks.com
www.footprintbooks.com

Distributed in the USA by
Publishers Group West

Scotland

Altitude in feet

	4,411
	1,820
	914
	457
	183
	0

Motorway

Primary Route,
A Road

B Road

Other Road

A1   Road Number

Rail

Border

N

0 km   40
0 miles   40

7

Shetland
Islands

Unst

Yell

Fetlar

Mainland

Lerwick ○

Orkney
Islands

1

Pentland Firth

2

North Sea

○ Wick

Lewis

Outer
Hebrides

Harris

The Minch

North Uist

Benbecula

The Little Minch

○ Ullapool

Skye

Moray Firth

Fraserburgh ○

Peterhead ○

○ Inverness

South Uist

Barra

Kyle of ○
Lochalsh

Rùm

○ Mallaig

Eigg

Inner
Hebrides

Fort William ○

Aviemore ○

Aberdeen ○

Coll

Tiree

Mull

○ Oban

Pitlochry ○

Crianlarich ○

Perth ○

Dundee ○

Atlantic
Ocean

Colonsay

St Andrews ○

3

Jura

Stirling ○

Firth of Forth

4

Greenock ○

Glasgow

EDINBURGH

Islay

Bute

Arran

Prestwick ○

Ayr ○

Jedburgh ○

Campbeltown ○

Dumfries ○

Stranraer ○

6

5

Solway Firth

ENGLAND

NORTHERN
IRELAND

Map 1

A

N

0 km   10
0 miles   10

Flannan
Islands or
Seven
Hunters

St Kilda
57° 50'   Boreray
Soay   Hirta
Dun   8° 30'

Outer Hebrides

Rubh
Robhanais   Po
Eoropaidh
Tabost
Dail Bho Dheas   Sgiogarstai
Gabhsann
Bho Dheas
A857
Siadar
Baile an Truiseil
Arnol   Barabhas   Muirneag
Siabost   Bragar   (814ft)   Tolastadh Ùr
Gearrannan   Leodhais   Tol
A858   Carlabhagh   (Lewis)   He
Bearnaraigh
Beag   Tolastadh   Beinn   A857   Griais   Loc
West Loch   a'Chaolais   Mholach   Tunga   a'Tua
Roag   Breascleit   (958ft)   Port nan Giùr   Rubha
Miabhig   Calanais   Newmarket   Siulaisiadar   t-Siump
Timsgearraidh   Cruiabhig   Steornabhagh   A866   An Rub
Gearraidh na   (Stornoway)
Bearnaraigh   h-Aibhne   A858
Meдlisval   Einacleit   Achadh   Crosbost
(1,884ft)   Loch   Mór
Breanais   Suainaval   Uig   Baile Ailein   Loch Erisort
Mealasta   Ceann a Tuath na   Loch   Cearsiadar   Grabhair
Island   Hearadh   Langavat   Airidh
Scarp   (North Harris)   a'Bhruaich   Leumrabhagh
Loch Reasort   Airidh   Beinn Mhór   Loch Shell
Gasker   a'Mhulaidh   (1,877ft)
Huisinis   Tirga Mòr   Loch
(2,228ft)   Clishham   Claidh
Abhainnsuidhe   (2,622ft)   A859   Loch   Loch Bhrollum
Bun Abhainn Eadarra   Seaforth
Aird Asaig   Urgha   Reinigeadal
Tarasaigh   Tarbert   A859   Shiant Islands
(An Tairbeart)   Caolas Scalpaigh
Toe Head   Ceann a Deas na   Scalpay
Hearadh   (Eilean Scalpaigh)
Shillay   (South Harris)
Taobh Tuath   A859
Pabbay   An t-Ob
Sound of Pabbay   Roghadal   Renish Point
Boreray   Bearnaraigh   Sound of Harris

Little Minch

Baile   Grimnis Point   Otternish
Mhartainn   Vallay   Rubha Hunish
Hogha Gearraidh   Solas   Duntulm   Kilmaluag
Cean a'Bhaigh   A865   Castle
Sound of Monach   Uibhist a'Tuath   Lochamaddy   Kilmuir   Staffin Bay
A865   (North Uist)   (Loch na Madadh)   Linicro   Staffir
A867   Vaternish   Culnaknoc
Heisker or   Claghan   Saighdinis   Point   Trotternish
Monach   na Luib   Loch Euphoirt   Uig   A855
Islands   Baile Seal   Ben Geary   A87   The Storr
Cairinis   Trumpan   (932ft)   (2,360ft)
Baile   Uachdar   Lusta   Loch Snizort   Edinbane   Kensaleyre
a'Mhanaich   A865   Dunvegan Head   Waternish   Bernisdale
Beinn na Faoghla   Boreraig   Dunvegan   Borve
(Benbecula)   Milovaig   Castle   A850   Carbost
Creag Ghoraidh   Dunvegan   Skye
Ardivachar   Loch   Bàgh nam Faoilean   Neist   Duirinish   Roskhill   Portree
Point   Bee   Wiay   Point   A87
Healabhal Bheag   Osk
Loch Sgioport   (1,602ft)   Bracadale   Clach
Stadhlaigearraidh   Peinchor
Uibhist a'Deas   Portnalóng   Sconser
(South Uist)   A863   Sligachan
Rubha Ardvuie   Talisker Carbost   A87
1   2   3   A

Map 2

Map 4

Map 4

A831 · Milton · Drumnadrochit · Urquhart Castle · Loch Ashie · Loch Duntelchaig · Dores · Farr · A9 · Moy · Findhorn · Lochindorb A939 · Marypa
Glen Affric · Loch Ness · Inverfarigaig · Errogie · Tormatin · Strath Dearn · Grantown-on-Spey · Dulnain Bridge · Strathspey · A939
A887 · Dundreggan · Invermoriston · Foyers · Loch Mhor · Carn Odhar (2,632ft) · Carrbridge · Nethy Bridge · Lynemore
Meal Fuarmhonaidh (2,284ft) · Stratherrick · A9 · Boat of Garten · Glenmore Forest Park ◆
A · Fort Augustus · Glen Morriston · Carn a'Chuilinn (2,678ft) · Monadhliath Mountains · Cnoc Fraing (2,445ft) · Aviemore · Loch Morlich · Inverdruie · Cairn Gorm (4,086ft)
A87 · Loch Garry · Invergarry · Loch Oich · Carn Dearg (3,101ft) · Kingussie · Feshiebridge · Lairig Ghru · Cairngorm Mountains · Ben Avon (3,843ft)
A82 · Laggan · Carn Dearg (2,678ft) · Garvamore · Spey · Laggan · A86 · Etteridge · Braeriach (4,250ft) · Ben Macdui (4,296ft)
Glen Roy · Roy · Glen Lochy · Loch Laggan · A889 · Dhalwhinnie · Cairn Toul (4,001ft) · Cairngorm National Park ◆ · Braemar
Roy Bridge · A86 · Tulloch · Geal Charn (3,443ft) · Carn na Caim (3,008ft) · Beinn Bhrotain (3,797ft) · Linn of Dee · Inverey · Auchallater
Glen Spean · Beinn a'Chlachair (3,571ft) · Loch Eric · A'Bhuidheanach Bheag (3,072ft) · An Sgarsoch (3,479ft) · Glenshee Ski Centre
Stob Choire Claurigh (3,863ft) · Aonach Beag (3,650ft) · Pass of Drumochter · Beinn Dearg (3,308ft) · Tilt · Glas Tulaichean (3,449ft)
Ben Alder (3,768ft) · Beinn Udlamain (3,069ft) · Loch Garry · Glen Gary · Carn nan Gabhar (3,679ft) · Spittal of Glenshee · A93
Blackwater Reservoir · Rannoch · Killichonan · Loch Errochty · Pitagowan · Falls of Bruar · Calvine · Blair Atholl · Straloch · Blackluna
B · Loch Laidon · Loch Rannoch · Kinloch Rannoch · Tummel Bridge · Tay Forest Park · Killiecrankie · Pass of Killiecrankie · Kirkmichael · A924
Glencoe Ski Centre · Rannoch Moor · Water of Tulla · Tay Forest Park · Schiehallion (3,547ft) · Loch Tummel · Tressait · Pitlochry · Ballintuim
A82 · Glen Lyon · Coshieville · Grandtully · Ballinluig · Bridge of Cally
Loch Lyon · Bridge of Balgie · Fortingall · Weem · Aberfeldy · Strath Tay · Dowally · Blairego
Beinn Heasgarnich (3,531ft) · Ben Lawers (3,984ft) · Kenmore · Dunkeld · A923 · Loch of the Lawes · Meikleo
Glen Lochy · Lochay · Morenish · Loch Tay · Milton · Trochry · Bankfoot · A9
A82 · Tyndrum · Killin · Amulree · Braan · Stanley · Guildtown
A85 · Crianlarich · Dochart · A85 · Lochearnhead · Glen Lednock · Ben Chonzie (3,056ft) · Harrietfield · Luncarty · Balbeg Scone Palace · New Scone · Per
C · Inverarnan · Ben More (3,853ft) · St Fillans · Loch Earn · A85 · Comrie · Gilmerton · A822 · A85 · Methven · Tibbermore · A9 · Glenc
Ardlui · Loch Voil · Kingshouse · Strathyre · Strathearn · Earn · Crieff · Muthill · Aberuthven · Dunning · Forgandenny · Bridge of Earn
Inversnaid · Ben Vorlich (3,233ft) · Glen Artney · Braco · Blackford · Gleneagles · A823 · Path of Condie · Glenfarg
Tarbet · Ben A'an (1,851ft) · Ben Ledi (2,882ft) · Loch Lubnaig · Callander · Greenloaning · A9 · Auchterarder · Ochil Hills · Milnathort · A91 · Kinr
Loch Long · Arrochar · Loch Katrine · Ben Venue (2,386ft) · Brig o'Turk · A84 · Doune · Braco · Dunblane · Carnbo · A977 · M90
Loch Lomond Regional Park · Ben Lomond (3,197ft) · Trossachs · Aberfoyle · A821 · Port of Menteith · A873 · Thornhill · Bridge of Allan · Yetts o'Muckhart · Dollar · Lochar Meadow Country Park · Cowdenbea
Rowardennan Forest ◆ · Queen Elizabeth Forest Park ◆ · Amprior · A811 · Kippen · Teith · M9 · Menstrie · Alva · Tillicoultry · Powmill · A823
Luss · Balmaha · Drymen · A875 · Gargunnock Hills · Bannockburn · Stirling · Fallin · Clackmannan · Alloa · A907 · Dunfermline
A817 · Arden · A811 · Craighat · Killearn · Fintry · Campsie Fells · Carron Valley Reservoir · Airth · Kincardine · A985 · Culross · Cairneyhill · Dalgety B
Rhu · Helensburgh · Balloch · Kilpatrick Hills · Strathblane · Milton of Campsie · Kilsyth Hills · Denny · Bonnybridge · Plean · Stenhousemuir · Grangemouth · Bo'ness · Limekilns · Inverkeithing · Abire
Craigendoran · Alexandria · A809 · Campsie · A891 · Kilsyth · A80 · Falkirk · Polmont · M9 · N Queensferry · S Queensferry

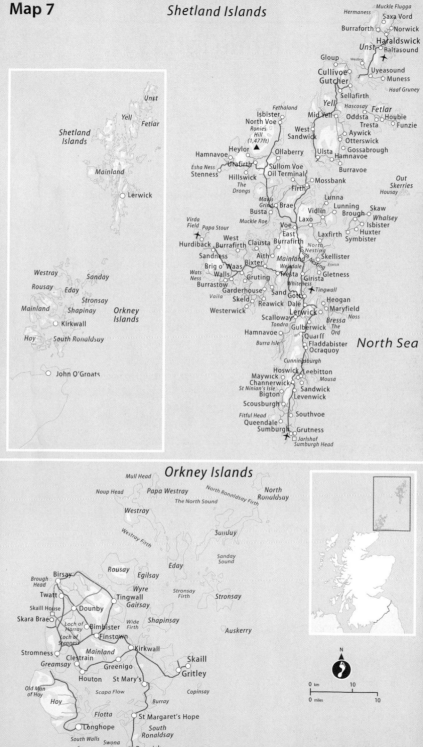

Map 7

Complete title listing

Footprint publishes
travel guides to over 150
destinations worldwide. Each
guide is packed with practical,
concise and colourful
information for everybody from
first-time travellers to travel
aficionados. The list is growing
fast and current titles are
noted below.
Available from all good
bookshops and online at
www.footprintbooks.com

(P) denotes pocket guide

For a different view of Europe, take a Footprint

❝❞ Superstylish travel guides – perfect for short break addicts.
Harvey Nichols magazine

Discover so much more...
Listings driven, forward looking and up to date. Focuses on what's going on right now. Contemporary, stylish, and innovative approach, providing quality travel information.